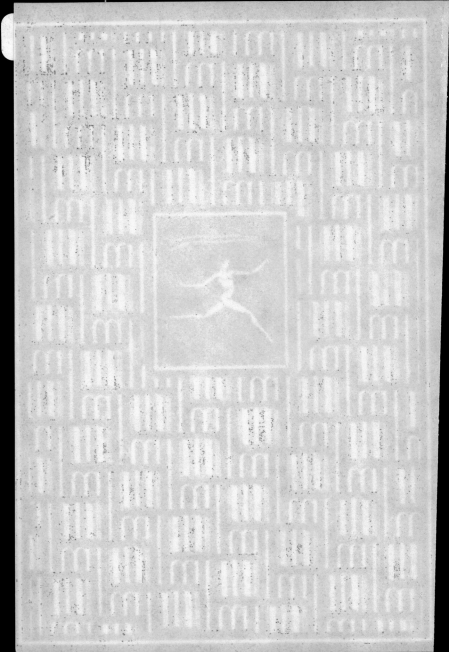

THE MODERN LIBRARY
OF THE WORLD'S BEST BOOKS

MONTAIGNE
SELECTED ESSAYS

The publishers will be pleased to send, upon request, an illustrated folder setting forth the purpose and scope of THE MODERN LIBRARY, *and listing each volume in the series. Every reader of books will find titles he has been looking for, handsomely printed, in definitive editions, and at an unusually low price.*

9th Sunday after Trinity —

Grant to us Lord the spirit to think and do
always such things as are right, that we who
cannot do anything good without thee may thus
be enabled to live according to thy will, through
Jesus Christ our Lord. Amen

A A remember

MONTAIGNE

SELECTED ESSAYS

The Charles Cotton—W. Hazlitt Translation,
Revised and Edited, with an Introduction by
BLANCHARD BATES
of Princeton University

THE MODERN LIBRARY : NEW YORK

Random House IS THE PUBLISHER OF

THE MODERN LIBRARY

BENNETT A. CERF · DONALD S. KLOPFER · ROBERT K. HAAS

Manufactured in the United States of America

By H. Wolff

CONTENTS

Book III (*continued*)

EDITOR'S NOTE

THE TRANSLATION used in this edition of essays from Montaigne is W. Hazlitt's revision of the translation made by Charles Cotton in the seventeenth century. The editor has revised the Hazlitt text, wherever he considered it necessary, in order to make it conform to the accepted French texts, to eliminate inaccurate translation, to modernize some of the English, and to make corrections in the translation of Latin quotations. His intent has been to let the English text stand unaltered whenever possible; considerable revision has, however, been necessary.

The French text used as a basis for the revision is the text presented by Pierre Villey in his editions of the *Essais* (Paris, Alcan: 1922-23, 3 v., and 1930-31, 3 v.)[1]

In the execution of the revision the editor has had the benefit of consulting the excellent work done by modern translators since Hazlitt's time; he is indebted, in particular, to the translations of Montaigne's *Essais* done by G. B. Ives (1925), E. J. Trechmann (1927), and Jacob Zeitlin (1934-36), and to Donald Frame's translation of selected essays from Montaigne (1943).

B.W.B.

[1] Standard text, derived from the monumental edition prepared by F. Strowski, F. Gebelin and Pierre Villey, *Les Essais . . . publiés d'après l'exemplaire de Bordeaux, avec les variantes manuscrites . . .* (Bordeaux, Pech, 1906-36, 5 Vol.)

INTRODUCTION
by Blanchard W. Bates

IT WOULD be difficult to discover in literature a more appropriate and descriptive title than the simple word *Essays* that Michel de Montaigne inscribed above his writings. It became at the same time the name of a particular masterpiece and of a specific literary form. Within itself it denoted a method applied, a truth attained, and even the formation of an author. This remarkable integration was succinctly stated by Montaigne when he observed that he and his Essays were "consubstantial." Containing the very essence of their author, the *Essays* necessarily reach far back into his life and are saturated with the complex of ideas, events, and persons about him.

In the years surrounding the birth of Montaigne (February 28, 1533) new movements and new convictions were stirring in France. Their general trend is revealed by a glance at a few of the pages that were being written at the time. In *Pantagruel* François Rabelais had just proclaimed the enthusiasm and confidence of men conscious of changing times. In his famous letter to his son, Gargantua rejoices that the "darkened" Gothic days are past, that light and dignity have now been restored to letters, and he exhorts his son to plunge into learning until "nothing is unknown to you." The revival of Greek and Roman letters and thought had become a fervent pursuit of all learning. In a report by a Venetian ambassador, we find that the courses, especially the humanities, offered to the 20,000 students at the University of Paris were well taught. The wretched living conditions which he noted were no deterrent to students avid to pursue these studies which presented not only intrinsic values

but a means of action. The social frame, as well as the intellectual, was changing, and education was the poor man's title to
enter a world in which his prospects were expanding. While the
bourgeois was enlarging his sphere, there was the beginning of
a rebirth of grace and elegance. In town and countryside could
be heard the sound of masons hammering on dwellings and
châteaux designed to be far more than mere fortresses for
security.

Opening up the pages of a "Bourgeois" of Paris, we feel another force that was impinging on the lives of men: "1534, the
10th of November, seven persons were condemned to confess
their sins publicly . . . and to be burned . . . The 18th November a mason burned alive . . . the next day a bookdealer
. . . who bound and sold books by Luther." The eager inquiry
into the civilization of Rome and Greece had been paralleled by
the study of the sources of Christianity, in which scholars
sought especially to regain the "purity" of the Christian faith
and to achieve greater directness and immediacy in its expression. But now the early evangelical stage of the Reformation
was passing. More and more emphasis was being placed on
questions involving the general doctrinal and institutional
framework of the Church. And with the growth of the Reformation the religious problem became part of the political moves of
state. Some reformists were burned to death, others, like Calvin,
departed from France to carry on the struggle, but the larger
part withdrew their opinions to the silence of their minds and
consciences.

The atmosphere was also alive with the challenge of action
abroad. The prospect of war in Italy or Provence still engrossed
many, but others felt the provocative mystery of the new lands
and peoples described by the explorers of the western and east-
ern seas. By 1533 interest in travel accounts had become so
widespread that Fabre collected and translated a French reader's digest of geographical literature.

Born at the moment when the two movements of Renaissance

and Reformation were becoming major forces in France, Montaigne constantly felt their influence. He was descended from very prosperous Bordeaux merchants who had risen in the changing social structure of the times. In 1477 his great-grandfather, Ramon Eyquem, purchased the noble property of Montaigne. Michel's father, Pierre Eyquem, turned from commerce to arms, campaigned in Italy, and then retired to the estate where he erected a château; Montaigne then became the family seat.

The formative years of Michel de Montaigne were profoundly influenced by his father, who was a highly accomplished man, constantly alert to new ideas and energetic in applying them. In his essay "Of the Education of Children," Montaigne relates the great attention that his father gave to his education. After sending Michel to be nursed in a poor family, he brought the child home and placed him in the charge of a German physician carefully selected to serve as a tutor. He planned a program of training for his son which had been derived from theories and practices current in Italian humanistic circles. First, in order that the boy should be thoroughly at home in Latin letters, he realistically decided that he should learn the language as his mother tongue. Montaigne relates that during these years his father permitted no other language but Latin to be used in his presence, and the family and even the servants were forced to acquire enough of it to be able to "jargonize" with him. Secondly, his father endeavored to foster in Michel a fondness for letters. His tutor was directed to substitute for the usual disciplinary approach to teaching a gentle and discreet guidance in order that the child might have as much freedom as possible in his activities.

This singularly individualized training produced the results that Pierre Eyquem had originally sought. At the age of six his son was using Latin as his natural tongue, and he had acquired an enduring taste for letters. Furthermore, the boy had been encouraged to be reflective, to exercise his judgment, and these qualities were to remain dominant elements in his intellectual equipment. Nevertheless Pierre Eyquem had begun to entertain some misgivings about the program; though Montaigne felt that his father might have been disappointed because the results were less than he had hoped, it seems more likely that he sensed the long, protective shadow that he was projecting along his son's path.

At any rate the experiment in education was at least partially abandoned, and Montaigne was sent off to Bordeaux to attend the Collège de Guienne, one of the finest schools in France. With the aid of his Latin he was able to finish his studies in seven years. His apparently satisfactory progress represented, in his opinion, time largely wasted. The only profit that he recognized in those years was the uncontrolled reading that one of his tutors discreetly allowed him to do. Again it was his father who by special permission had obtained such tutors for him. By nature Montaigne resisted compulsion; so, thrust into school discipline after his early years of unfettered training, he found it distasteful. In a negative way it might be said that this resistance on his part served to sharpen his judgment as well as to increase his fondness for reading. Positively it is fair to assume that the abilities he had shown in his childhood were further developed at school. Beyond his studies there were other sources of profit to him. He became an active participant in the plays put on at the school, and among his classmates he doubtless began to cultivate his flair for conversation and the give-and-take of social life. Such advantages were certainly corrective for one serious deficiency in his earliest training.

Montaigne speaks so freely of his own traits that it seems even more superfluous than uncharitable to dwell on them. It is well, however, to bear in mind certain elements that are significant to the man and his later work. Montaigne was, he tells us, of a gentle, tractable disposition. The inclination to take a receptive, tractable attitude which had been encouraged by his admiration for his father was accompanied by a capacity for independence and absolute resistance when essential principles were involved. This pairing, or balancing, of qualities was apparent in these early years and is a characteristic that permeates his personality. Montaigne tends to look at opposites while remaining, whenever feasible, in an intermediate positon; furthermore, one of the pair is quite often the superficial appearance and the other the real and essential. For example, he underlines his sluggish ways, his slowness in grasping things, and at the same time states, "What I perceived, I perceived well." By nature and by training he was inclined to be reflective; his slowness of wit was actually a false appearance about which he was indifferent, while the full grasp he obtained and the independent opinions he formed were the essential for him. Again in the case of his lack of memory which he so frequently underscores, we should note that an opposite may be tacitly understood. From the earliest moments of his life he was urged to acquire understanding and to exercise judgment rather than to learn by rote and to build up regurgitative memory. The latter was the scholastic procedure still in practice. In view of the numerous examples of the adequacy of his memory, we can feel that mentioning his lack of memory is a rather pleasant, gentlemanly gesture that clears him of any semblance of invidious scholastic erudition.

In these formative years, and later as well, we find scarcely any indication of the influence of his mother. However much she may have retired from the siege of Latin, her presence brought her children into close touch with one of the important problems of the day. The ancestors of Antoinette de Louppes were Jews who had fled from Spanish persecution. As the Reformation spread in Southwestern France, she joined the movement, and later two of her children became Huguenots. Thus his own family added its object lesson of both personal independence and tolerant understanding to the other training received by Michel.

The next twenty-two years of Montaigne's life followed the

pattern of a professional career. In 1554 when he finished his law studies, Montaigne became a counselor in the Cour des Aides of Périgueux and three years later, when the Périgueux functions were transferred to Bordeaux, he became a counselor of the Parlement of Bordeaux. Montaigne's participation was of the most routine sort. The real significance of this life to Montaigne lay in his rôle as spectator, not as counselor. The cases he observed afforded ample material for reflection on justice and the law's inadequacies, on the motivations of actions and the degree of responsibility to be assigned to them.

While pursuing his profession, Montaigne found time for other activities as well. In 1559 and again in 1561-62 he made extended trips to Paris and to the courts of Francis II and of Charles IX. It is possible that he had some hopes of a career at court; what is certain is that Montaigne was turning an inquiring mind in many directions. He shared his reflections with a fellow-counselor, Etienne de La Boétie, whom he had met in 1559. Joined by a profound bond of friendship and by an absorbing interest in ancient letters, the two men discussed contemporary problems in the light of the examples and wisdom offered by the Romans; as they debated the case histories of mankind, Montaigne felt that the moral fiber of Rome lived again in his friend. In 1563 this perfect friendship was abruptly ended by the death of La Boétie.

In the following years Montaigne began to assume more personal responsibilities. In 1565 he married Françoise de la Chassaigne. Three years later the death of his father left Montaigne in charge of the family property. In 1569 he published his first work, a translation of Raymond Sebond's *Theologia Naturalis* which he had undertaken at his father's request; and soon after, in 1570, he resigned his post and brought his professional life to a close. He proceeded at once to Paris to attend to the publication of writings which Etienne de La Boétie had left in his charge. While there he received the honor of being made a chevalier of the order of Saint Michel and a gentleman of the king's chamber. His affairs in order, Montaigne retired to his estate early in 1571.

In retiring to his estate, Montaigne was in reality entering upon the vitally active period of his life. This decision which he made at thirty-eight was prompted by considerations which were fairly common at the time. In part such a retirement was merely the assumption of the ordinary life of a gentleman engaged in the management of his estate. In part it was dictated by the desire, frequent among men of his training and profession, to gain freedom for reflection, time to organize their thoughts and find an understanding of life in an age harried by the strife of religious wars and by the conflict of ideas. In the inscription which he had placed on the beams of his tower library to mark his retirement Montaigne expressed both the hope of being able to improve "the sweet paternal" abode and the desire to find tranquillity and freedom among his books.

His spacious library, set apart from the rest of the dwelling, its walls lined with a thousand books, became his favorite room. In his early essay "Of Idleness," he tells us that as soon as he settled himself to his books, his mind set off with unaccustomed activity, throwing up one fancy after another. With his pen he noted down the oddity of these random thoughts; the essays were already starting. But he did not make his library an ivory tower. When he raised his eyes from the page, through the large tower windows he could oversee all the work on the estate, and he could easily step out when anything required his personal attention. His hours in the library were frequently broken off to engage in social life and military service. In 1574 he was called to the army in Poitou and then to a confidential mission to the Parlement of Bordeaux. Among the people he entertained at the château was Henry, King of Navarre, who was there on two occasions and who in 1577 made Montaigne a gentleman of his chamber. This full life of gentleman, man of letters, and man of action did not slacken greatly even when in 1578 he was undergoing the first attack of the stone from which he was

to suffer as his father had. In March, 1580, he had reached the
point of writing a foreword to the Reader on the manuscript of
the first two books of the *Essays* which were published in June
by Millanges at Bordeaux.

Gayer and more assured than he was nine years earlier, Montaigne tucked his books in his luggage and started off with some
friends on a long journey to Switzerland, Germany, and Italy.
The immediate purpose was to visit famous spas to see if their
waters might be effective against the stones which continued to
trouble him, but Montaigne turned the journey into a joyous
touring expedition that lasted a year and a half. The pages of
his *Travel Journal* make vividly clear to us Montaigne's absorption in all that he saw. He was constantly ready to turn his
mount into the by-ways in quest of more spectacles. His preeminent interest was mankind. Observing men's ways, sounding
out their ideas, verifying the relativity of customs, this, Montaigne felt, was the proper form of education to be placed beside
that of his early years. His observant eyes missed no detail, and
his keen mind found matter for thought in every event. He recorded with equal eagerness his audience with the Pope and his
experience as master of ceremonies at a beauty contest. In
Rome his journey was climaxed by the signal honor of receiving
Roman citizenship. From there he turned homeward in October
1581 to assume the office of mayor of Bordeaux to which he had
been elected in August.

As mayor of Bordeaux Montaigne enjoyed quiet success during his two-year term of office. He found time in 1582 to arrange
for the publication of the second edition of his *Essays*. The
success of his administration was marked by his being re-elected
in 1583. In this term he met the test of very serious problems,
for Bordeaux was caught in the contest for power that was
going on in France. Montaigne registered strong protests to
both the King of France and the King of Navarre about actions
detrimental to his people. They were so impressed by his forthright and wise conduct that they called upon him to serve as

an intermediary in their own dispute. It is to his great credit
that he kept the respect of both; and Henry of Navarre honored
him by spending two days at his château. During the second
year of his term he devised strategy and took direct leadership
in a successful defense of Bordeaux against the ultra-Catholic
forces of the Ligue. As his term of office was closing, the plague
struck the city. For his decision not to return to the city Montaigne was censured, not by his contemporaries but by later
critics; however, it has been amply demonstrated that, except
for the formality of handing over the keys, he had no responsi·
bility to assume at the time.

During the months immediately following, his estate suf·
fered the ravages of civil war and the plague. To escape the
contagion Montaigne took his household and moved through the
countryside for six months.

When he was again established in his château in 1586, he set
busily to work in his library. Two years later he had finished a
third book of essays, and he had made many additions and
corrections in the first two books. He took the manuscript to
Paris, where Langelier in June, 1588, published a new edition of
the *Essays*. During his sojourn at Paris he met his most devoted reader, Marie Le Jars de Gournay; both flattered and
sincerely touched by the interest of this intelligent, vigorous
young woman, Montaigne came to consider her his daughter
by spiritual alliance. Late in November, 1588, Montaigne was
again settled on his estate.

The remainder of his life was spent at Montaigne as a
gentleman and man of letters. Numerous attacks of his malady
forced him to withdraw into his shell like a tortoise, he tells us.
But within the shell of his library he remained very active in his
reading, and in the margins of a copy of the 1588 edition of the
Essays he was making numerous additions drawn from reflections on his experiences and readings. A severe attack of quinsy
finally stayed his hand on the 13th of September, 1592. Attended by a few friends he died a quiet, Christian death.

The narrative of Montaigne's actions has revealed that the years after his retirement were his most active years. When we consider the impressions he made on his contemporaries, we find that they were clearer and stronger during this period. He stopped off at Blois in 1588, after the publication of the last books of his *Essays,* to spend considerable time with Etienne Pasquier. This keen-witted attorney and man of letters observed that Montaigne bore himself boldly, with great assurance; and when he added that no man was ever less of a legal quibbler, he underscored the gentleman in Montaigne. De Thou, an equally talented observer, was impressed by the ingenuous, sincere ways of Montaigne and by his engaging personality. These impressions, supplementing one another, reveal a person who was both a lord and an ordinary man; nursed by the poor and raised as a landed gentleman, living in comfort and yet close to the soil, Montaigne had very natural recourse to the phrases, "We other little men," "we other naturalists." He is the first big "little man" of modern times. His bigness lay in recognizing his littleness; and this he achieved through the action of the other member of his life, the "consubstantial" book.

The twenty-five essays that have been chosen for this volume of selections are representative of the thought and movement of the whole work. In reading them we have to bear in mind not only that the work was built up over a considerable space of time, but also that many additions were made to the essays at later dates. Thus the stages of his thought are often leveled off by the additions. In these selections no indications are given to show what parts of an essay were written at a later date; they are presented as Montaigne last looked upon them, the living evolution of the past in the present.

The essays of the first two books represent writings spread out over nine years and thoughts that reach back into Montaigne's earliest memories. When he retired to his estate in 1571, the pattern of his thoughts was the outgrowth of the elements that had been his intellectual baptism in 1533 and that had entered into his prolonged discussions with Etienne de La Boétie. The Renaissance and the Reformation had poured forth vast streams of ideas and beliefs; the confidence and appetite of earlier years were beginning to give way to doubt and forebodings of indigestion. If it was hard to take in all the matter, it was far more defying to reconcile the conflicting thoughts. The religious issue had already flared into three wars in France; and it was more and more affected by the political interests. Men were raising critical questions on the most common matters. Were courts established for the benefit of the judge, or for the service of the man seeking judgment? Such questions and issues were often old ones, but now the circumstances were changing: they were not mere speculations; sanctions and authority were being questioned. History which had been such a strong cable to the anchor of the past had separated into so many strands that it was no longer the source of certainty. And from the explorations there came observed facts that were still more challenging. Montaigne missed very few of these.

When Montaigne set to work in his library his thoughts became more active, straying in all directions. The notes that he started to take down were primarily for amusement, he tells us; it is probable that they were similar to the little reading notes he was accustomed to write in his books. He knew that solitude itself had to be closely considered. In writing "Of Solitude," Montaigne refuses to renew the simple argument of the active life versus the life of contemplation; he expresses a long-felt conviction that the most vehement proponents of the active, public life are more interested in their own ends than in the public good. The essential point is neither activity nor solitude in itself, but rather to find the right way. To find it there is need of reflection and reasoning. He defends solitude as reflection, as contemplation, that may exist anywhere. Therefore it is necessary for a man to reserve for himself a "backshop" that is free and all his own. Secondly in this "backshop," which may exist in the midst of the most active life, a man must establish limits, know its extent and uses; otherwise it has no purpose. This principle of the "backshop" or of the independent judgment was fitted to Montaigne, but the question was how to delimit and make use of that shop.

The subject matter on which he was reflecting is underlined in the opening essay; it was that "marvelously vain, diverse, and fluctuating subject, man." At the beginning of the second book of the *Essays* and at the end of the two books, he gives full prominence to this fluctuating, inconstant nature of man. Beyond discerning that such a condition is due partly to Fortune and partly to inner instability, he is skeptical of man's competence to judge such a delicate matter; but man can endeavor by strength of mind to resist this condition. The flowing nature of man will remain the subject of the *Essays*. In stressing the power of the mind, Montaigne was assuming an attitude that was partly in keeping with the resurgence of Stoicism; it laid stress on reason and will. It was also the superior attitude of a man cultivating a way of life, feeling somewhat heroic. Yet since Montaigne's "backshop" was constantly open, there was always the action of skepticism.

Montaigne's first attitude toward his subject and also his early style are readily seen in the chapter, "That Men Must Not Judge of Our Happiness until after Our Death." Fortune, death, and the uncertainty of all things human are brought together; both stoically and skeptically he can state that only the last act will permit men to judge of our happiness. And he adds two significant remarks. He notes that there may be a "mask" in all parts of life except dying. Montaigne will constantly strive to lift that "mask," that false, surface appearance of life. Secondly, he observes that he puts off to death the "essay," the testing, of the profit derived from his studies. Montaigne introduces his central concern, the "essay" of life. But in this first approach to his subject, he leaves the "essay" to be made by death. Man's part is the bracing of himself against it. The style of this chapter is characteristic of the first essays. Starting with a quotation, he goes on to the story of Croesus and Cyrus, to which he attaches other anecdotes, finally stating, "And a thousand such examples." These first essays bring together examples of interesting situations and thoughts that for the most part came from his readings; to them he adds comments that serve to tie the fragments together in a loose, artificial way. He is following the common contemporary practice of compiling treasuries of sayings and singular tales in an effort to draw moral truths.

The banal manner in which Montaigne went about treating the continuing subject of his *Essays* may be attributed to his practice of making random notes in reading and to his assumption of an attitude, both in his thoughts and in their presentation, that would meet the literary challenge and the challenge of contemporary conditions. It was incomplete and temporary. Not long after the chapter just discussed, Montaigne wrote the essay, "Of Training." Its point of departure is still the question of training to brace against the blows of Fortune and death, but the discussion changes, and the presentation becomes quite different. The essay flows smoothly and dispenses with all the tissue of borrowed material; it is direct, immediate, and unusually unified. Here he is speaking from his own experience; here he is fully concerned with lifting the "mask" and trying to reach into the twilight zone of the human mind. As he ponders over the sensations experienced in slowly recovering his senses after the riding accident, as he compares this condition with the mental state in falling asleep, Montaigne comes to personal conclusions that he feels are fully justified. As he notes reflex action and conditioned response, and distinguishes them from conscious, willed action, Montaigne makes his "backshop" the scene of a full essay; there is implied a simple, but effective method: hypothesis, essay by experience, truth. The impressionism and preoccupation with sensations in this essay are remarkable for that period. This chapter introduces a second approach to his subject matter, an attitude of self-study. This attitude produces a radically different result—dying can be easy, with no pain involved—and an "essay" of the "backshop" from within; the manner of presentation is also altered.

His earliest attitude of lifting himself above problems by the bootstraps of his own reason was soon resisted on a general scale by Montaigne. His resistance was encouraged by reading Sextus Empiricus' account of Pyrrho's skepticism. The sentiments of Montaigne in 1576 were marked by a medal, on which he had engraved a pair of scales evenly balanced and the words, "What do I know?" At this time he composed the larger part of his longest essay, the "Apology for Raymond Sebond." Montaigne's declared intent is to reply to those who censured the fifteenth-century Spanish thinker for trying to establish the Christian religion on rational proofs and human experience, and to those who charged that Sebond's reasoning and proofs were inadequate. After briefly stating that we should use reason as much as we can in such matters, Montaigne refutes the second charge by stating that the critics' reasoning power is no better; from that point he devotes his whole attention to an exposition of the weakness of human knowledge and reason. Comparing men with animals, he brings in examples to demonstrate that despite his vaunted reason man is often surpassed by animals in mental and moral qualities. Man's knowledge, furthermore, is often seen to be detrimental to his happiness, to his integrity, to his whole way of living. Then Montaigne adds the stroke that had been formed in his mind during long reflections; it is a review of the conflicting opinions that great thinkers have had on fundamental issues of the cosmos, the soul, religion, God. Since the thinkers neutralize one another, it appears that human knowledge is verbal and devoid of real substance. This, he concludes, is natural; knowledge is obtained by means of reason which is uncertain and contradictory, since it is subject to the passions and is nourished by the senses, which are so defective.

In this attack on reason, Montaigne is following in the long line
of thinkers who as fideists in religion and as skeptics in philosophy had come to deny reason the power of attaining truth.
Within this chapter there is more than negation. In removing
the masks from the "hollow bones" of philosophy, Montaigne
supports those who with open mind seek truth rather than dog-
matically concluding about truth; this is his principle of sus-
pension of judgment, an attitude which Chauncey Wright considered one of the most difficult and one of the most vital for
man to maintain. Secondly, he firmly establishes in his mind a
belief in the relativity of human matters. Thirdly, he concludes
that man's error is in not looking closely at common things, in not
testing common impressions; his rule should be to inquire into
all and to turn to experience. In the fourth place, Montaigne
has obviously kept the use of rational analysis. Lastly, the chapter reveals that man's direct impressions, his self-experience,
should be his immediate subject. Sebond had made self-knowl-
edge gained through natural means the central doctrine of his
Natural Theology, and it was that which made Montaigne particularly interested in the work. During these reflections Montaigne's attitude of the early essays was, of course, rejected, and
he started forth with his reason chastened, but with his mind
provided with tools he could use.

He began writing, after 1577, the most significant and interesting essays of the first two books. These are, for the most part,
critical essays. In the first one, "Of the Education of Children,"
we notice that now he is making an "essay" of his natural faculties; it is no longer an external testing, but rather a self-testing
of his judgment in the face of varied problems. In this delightful
chapter on education, he makes a remarkably keen criticism of
the shortcomings of contemporary education and judicious sug-
gestions about desirable goals. At the heart of it is his belief that
education should have as its method and primary objective the
development of the child's judgment; there are too many people
with their pockets full of knowledge and too few who have really

assimilated knowledge and gained wisdom. Such an education should be rounded out with physical and social training, it should encourage public service in a sensible way, for it is educating a whole man, in whom body and soul should not be separated. Montaigne insists on the integration of life within the framework of education, and to activate it he urges that teaching let philosophy bear its proper air of gaiety which will give the students an incentive to virtue by "natural and palpable reasons." Montaigne was not interested simply in education, but in a way of living. His entire criticism may be embodied in a threefold concept that he was forming of the states of life: plain nature, art, artifice. Judgment and wisdom lie between ignorance and erudition; they represent an artistic, that is, a carefully cultivated realization of the natural capability of a man.

In writing "Of Cannibals" Montaigne broadened the area of his criticism by turning to the New World and to its impact on Europeans. There are several types of exoticism here. In the center there is the picturesque exoticism of evoking peoples and scenes that are quite unfamiliar. About the picturesque centerpiece Montaigne works in a critical exoticism, the comparison of ideas and practices. Lastly there is real primitivism involved in his exoticism. The movement of these elements, in and out, makes this essay particularly pleasant and provocative. At the outset he turns to the general impact of the new geographical knowledge on authority, on the suppositions of old that men had until recently regarded as "facts." Experience is, he sees, no respecter of persons; the beliefs of the most famous are often no more true than the notions of ordinary men. However, Montaigne's new critical attitude causes him to raise a warning finger to his contemporaries lest the confidence engendered by the discoveries produce for them a "fact," namely, the belief that there are no more lands to be found. The critical movement becomes pronounced when he takes up "barbary" which is, he notes, simply that another person uses things that differ from ours. With that he moves freely in the pleasant sport of the relativity of customs and tastes. At the same time, with lively interest, he considers these peoples not in the prioristic sense of the classical world looking back upon a golden age, but in the sense of true primitivism; he wants to observe men in their natural state, to describe their life. Again the critical thread reappears, for primitivism raises a full battery of questions concerning what is essential and desirable in civilization; for the thoughtful man it touches on everything, from religion to art to daily living. The essay with exotic subjects becomes a useful medium for flanking criticism, in which European customs and practices can be very tellingly satirized. If Montaigne's criticism suggests to us some of the strong eighteenth-century criticism on such subjects, we should not forget the little *boutade* at the end, "But they don't wear pants." The essay keeps its gracious touch, the savages, too, must submit to Montaigne's relativity.

In writing "Of Cannibals," as well as "Of Education," Montaigne sees a tripartite division in life—nature, art, and artifice—which he wishes to explore critically. Both essays are developed leisurely and pleasantly on the basis of personal experiences and reactions together with personal reflections on his reading. These essays, in contrast to the first ones, are not merely marked by personal elements; these personal elements are often far back in the life of Montaigne; they are elements that have finally taken on meaning. The "essay" of his natural faculties has been found, and at the same time the literary essay is taking form. Its basis is to be reflection for its own sake. What he achieves in the essay is apparent if we glance at Montaigne's sources for his chapter; Jean de Léry's account, good as it is, does not have the quality of expressing more than it actually says, but this quality is characteristic of Montaigne's essay. The detailed facts and ideas passed through the prism of Montaigne's mind emerge in the essay with their light enriched.

These same general traits are found in the other essays that Montaigne was then composing. The criticism in them is based in great part on personal experiences and impressions. The experiences and stories he introduces into them are generally effective and timely. Often the reflections that emerge are marked by keen psychological insight and suffused with a compassionate feeling for life. Another means by which he gains effect is an engaging sort of irony. Whether he is occupied with impressionistic literary criticism or with reflections on the art of living with one's own family, Montaigne is exploiting the possibilities of the essay; he manifests a strong inclination to draw upon his own sources. Realizing where he is proceeding, he wisely states that it is his method, and not his matter, that men should scrutinize.

In the chapter "Of the Affection of Fathers for Their Children" Montaigne states, in 1578, that his objective is to "portray himself to the life." The "essay of his natural faculties" passes readily into a portrayal of himself. This third stage of the *Essays* is found in the chapter "Of Presumption." Having found personal experience the most useful source material, Montaigne has one more step to take. In his readings, which were a laboratory to him, he had long reflected on the great usefulness of the personal forms of history to the study of man, and he had noted the rarity of memoirs that contained really intimate views of the writer. His self-portrayal was also encouraged by the contemporary cultivation of memoirs by the great figures of the Renaissance. While acknowledging his presumption, at least from the point of view of convention, Montaigne does not hesitate to draw in detail a frank self-portrait. As the details accumulate, we feel the earlier personal elements drawing together; we see that the essays themselves have begun to influence the course of his thoughts and writings. Their revelations have made him eager to seek more details; the early arabesques that Montaigne traced of his random thoughts have evolved into the portrait which is a climax to the two books. His purpose, he states in the following essay, is not to erect a public monument, but merely to leave to relatives and friends a little likeness of himself. This statement is sincere, but limited; in the portrait he had become engrossed in the discovery of himself. He writes in his simple foreword "To the Reader" that he is the subject matter of this book written only for "domestic and private" purposes; at the moment his only regret is that he cannot portray himself without any restrictions at all. The "backshop" has gradually become occupied with personal experiences and impressions.

The third book of the *Essays* is marked by a vast increase in depth and density and at the same time by a remarkable integration of life. The self-portrait, which had been gradually taking shape in the "backshop" of Montaigne's mind is the center of these last essays. As Montaigne turns again to his portrait, his attitude, however, has changed. Instead of stating that the sketch is intended for the corner of a friend's library, he declares that he has to give his portrait to the public. In the beginning of the essay "Of Repentance," he makes this attitude and its basis very apparent by remarking that he is setting forth a lowly life, devoid of splendor, but that the mediocrity of his life is really immaterial since all moral philosophy may be attached to an ordinary life as well as to one of richer stuff: "Every man bears the entire form of human nature." His depiction is not merely an accumulation of singularities. Other men have similar traits and problems. Because of this extended view of portraiture, Montaigne now speaks with greater confidence and fuller purpose. His inquiry also deepens, for he is uncovering underlying realities which permit him to find some unity within the apparent pluralism of life. In form these essays of the third book do not take the shape of set portraits; they remain essays which constantly enlarge the main portrait until the total effect of the book is that of a portrait-autobiography. The lines of this portrayal radiate directly from Montaigne as he reacts to three sets of relationships—self-association, society, and public life.

The man-to-man association that Montaigne had with himself was strengthened by two factors. The self-portrait had made him conscious of the range of his traits and had served to assemble them in his mind; since that time his experiences in traveling and in public service had provided him with more "essays," more insight and more certainty concerning the man he had sketched. Montaigne's principle was the old precept, "know yourself"; it was his attitude to it that was different. Hitherto this principle had been propounded for a purpose beyond itself: to make man realize that he was an earth-bound being, or to show him that he partook of the divine in his earthly frame. Initially Montaigne stopped at "know yourself" lest his glance focus more on the end than on the object at hand. His method was to avoid systems and to be content to "unmask" traits until they might of themselves offer proofs. But as he considered experiences from all periods of his life, Montaigne became more and more aware that, though the arabesques of his portrait changed, there was a certain pattern to the portrait that did not change. This new concept he records in the essay "Of Repentance." By means of it he ascertains that there is in him a "master-form" which resists efforts to change it. This "master-form," or personality, which self-portrayal had revealed to him, is tested throughout the new essays. He is enabled to see the response of his character to the situations confronting it. The recognition of his essential character is followed by a second step, the utilization of this inner form as a touchstone by which to try his actions. The book, which has become a tangible part of his being, serves as a guide and rule, permitting him to foresee his reactions to a situation and to adjust himself in advance. This was, as Ramon Fernandez demonstrated, a complete integration of Montaigne's personality. It was so complete that Montaigne could speak of acting as a whole, in one piece. Its effects were quite apparent to others; Etienne Pasquier stated that Montaigne's life was in complete agreement with the *Essays*.

In his social relations with other men, Montaigne's keen insight made him an equally effective participant and observer. In his essays "Of Three Kinds of Society" and "Of the Art of Conversing" he has left us the essential spirit of the company that he enjoyed: intelligent but without a trace of pedantry, lively, humorous and vigorous, seasoned with beauty and activated by hearty discussions. The full-bodied conversation of the Renaissance was to Montaigne one of life's greatest pleasures and a source of truth. He had observed that company and even the sound of his own voice drew more from his mind than he could ever obtain when alone; in matching wits with others sparks were struck, ideas were illuminated that the individuals would never have seen in solitary reflections. More than any other man of his age he knew the virtues of the Socratic dialogue. When he was alone, the *Essays* became his conversation, and books his friendly society. His fondness for society and conversation was most fully indulged during his travels. The minds and characters of strangers and foreigners offered a particularly rich source of new views of man; Montaigne rightly looked on such society as the best education. It offered him profit and enjoyment and training in understanding other men as well as himself. As a part of his consideration of society, he scanned the relationship of men and women with particular perspicacity. In his essay "On Some Verses of Virgil," he courageously, and with undisguised pleasure, expresses freely his views of marriage, its dignity and its weakness. Though he never showered adulation on women, Montaigne produces in this essay a notable commentary on man's stupidity and injustice in respect to them: the establishment of a double standard of morality, while at the same time training women for love. From observation he is ready to conclude that man and woman are mainly distinguished by training and usage, not by nature.

The relationship of man to public affairs received frequent attention in these chapters. In the essays "Of the Profitable and the Honorable" and "Of Husbanding Your Will," we find that Montaigne takes a realistic view of public life as a compound of good and evil. The man best fitted to engage in it is a man who is thoroughly at home with himself, who has learned the lesson of lending himself to others and of giving himself only to himself. Such a man is capable of taking charge of affairs without being possessed by them, without being blinded by passions; in his detachment he will calculate the risks and appraise his own capacity before acting. This man can perform, if necessary, the evil demanded by the public welfare and yet maintain a balanced self in his "backshop." As Montaigne explores the fact that governments are as good as the men who direct them, he pursues a conservative, but not a static, policy. His progressive view is fully implied in his desire to make the administrator more effective, rather than to espouse the easier course of discarding institutions with the hope of amelioration by change. This psychological bent of his political thinking is equally pronounced in his criticism of affairs in the New World in the essay "Of Coaches." He mingles in his vigorous denunciation of the motives and the methods of the Conquest an inquiry into the nature of these peoples of the New World and into the impact of European civilization upon them, and speculation on what might have been made of these peoples if a great leader of the past had conquered them. He still upholds his ideal of a state between nature and artifice. Indeed in the passing of time the idea of an art of living became a firm belief that he advocated for man in his private, social, and public relationships.

The central interest that runs through all these relationships is Montaigne's desire to gain some understanding of Nature, which he considered an organized whole, but incomprehensible because of man's limited grasp. His own preoccupation was with the nature of man. At this time he was constantly placing himself in the midst of his fellow men. In his reflections, religious views are seldom expressed. The interpretation of his religious beliefs has been subject to considerable difference of opinion. There is every indication that he was an orthodox Catholic in his life. In the *Essays* he takes the position of a fideist who believes that the primary causes rest in the inscrutable power of God and that faith and revelation, not reason, must be followed in such questions. Any investigation eventually will run into one insurmountable barrier, that life may be created in innumerable forms as God wills, and hence any observed facts cannot be taken as absolute truths. Accepting the religious doctrines, Montaigne devoted his attention to the limited knowledge that man could obtain from experience.

Following Cicero's words "We must penetrate into the nature of things and consider thoroughly what it demands," Montaigne found that Nature's trail was no longer clear. Men had blurred the trail of Nature with artificial tracks. Philosophers had drawn so many arbitrary lines that complete confusion existed. The first task was to reassemble Nature. In the case of man it was to reunite body and soul; their functions were interdependent and could be understood only if the two parts were joined. The passions were necessary elements in man, and the presence together of wisdom and pleasure, of reason and frivolity, of good and evil, was a normal condition. It was desirable that men should be conscious of their nature; by Montaigne's system it was the only way to proceed, since self-study through experience was his method. He criticized even Socrates for having recourse to his Daemon for explanations. Experience was Montaigne's main discipline. He used literature, especially poetry, as a laboratory, but it was his principle that "I prefer to understand myself in me rather than in Cicero." Montaigne observed the play of passions and his varied reactions; he was not concerned about errors in themselves. He sought the causes and related them to their signs in order to be forewarned in the future; above all he sought the processes involved, and he desired to depict not the static states of being, crystallized and nonhuman, but the ceaseless passage, the state of becoming. His efforts to treat the flow of consciousness were limited, but his comprehension of the problem was a notable achievement. An interesting case of this preoccupation is the attention he devotes to the rapid, irregular movement of fancies ("On Some Verses of Virgil"); they were especially active when he was musing freely on horseback, but by the time he was back at his paper, they had sped off into the dimness of dream impressions.

Montaigne's preoccupation with the elusive movement of man's fancy exerted its influence on the style and structure of the *Essays*. Montaigne's thought was expressed in very concrete images; he kept away from the abstract as far as possible in presenting his ideas. He wanted a soldierly, manly style. In the style of his sentences, as Morris Croll was able to show, Montaigne deliberately opposed the Ciceronian balanced style and became the leader in the cultivation of modern prose writing. In places the sentence structure often is loose and asymmetrical; connectives between clauses are frequently dropped or weakened. Elsewhere the sentence structure is put in relief by the curt style, by the introduction of summary sentences without verbs. Often a sentence rambles on, idea suggesting idea, and clause added to clause, and then suddenly returns to the original thought. These unordered chain reactions frequently occur. These and other devices were in keeping with Montaigne's natural inclinations, but he also consciously cultivated them, for he wanted the style of the essays to convey an impression of the movement of the writer's thought. Montaigne extended this concept to the structure of the essays, particularly in the third book. He wanted to make them more oblique; in the chapter "Of Vanity" he indicates that the titles often denote the subject matter only by some sign, and that the ideas look at each other only with a sidelong glance. With its meanderings and its abrupt sallies, the essay transmits some impression of Montaigne musing as he rides along.

By reaching into the hidden element of life Montaigne had gained insight not only into his own personality, but also into the consubstantialness of man and the general unity of his processes. Observation and self-study were the preliminary step. After recognizing traits, he wished to organize human conduct, to turn the passions from their straight course to a controlled circuit of action. The task of circumscribing the movement of our inner nature, which he presents so clearly in the chapter "Of Husbanding Your Will," is accomplished by "composing" our moral traits and our actions. By the full discovery of his personality he had been able, when desirable, to regulate and direct his actions intellectually until finally they were integrated to the point where wisdom was established. This composing of life was directed toward the golden mean, toward living and moving far from the extremes. Montaigne saw order, proportion, and harmony. His achievement in conduct had been to proceed from his early preoccupation with the Stoic notion of preparation and discipline to his method of self-study and of composing one's conduct, which was an organic process similar to methods practiced today. With it Montaigne attained the art of living.

The element of the golden mean that was probably most vital to Montaigne was the flexibility and independence that it preserved. Always opposed to dogmatic systems, Montaigne considered man's primary capacity to be adaptability. In this he had the humanist's sense of the principle of evolution and the little man's tenacious individualism.

In the society of the "consubstantial" book, Montaigne had developed a method, the "essay," by which life might be penetrated; he had attained a great truth, the comprehension of his own integrated self and its extensibility to man in general. With these he had come into the profound and joyous "possession of life," of "knowing how to enjoy rightfully his being."

Princeton, N. J.
April, 1949

TO THE READER

READER, this is an honest book. It warns you at the very outset that in it I have set for myself no other goal than a domestic and private one. I have given no consideration in it either to your service or to my glory. My powers are not capable of such an aim. I have dedicated it to the personal use of my relatives and friends, so that when they have lost me (which they must soon do), they may here find again some traits of my habits and humor and may by this means keep more intact and more alive the knowledge they have had of me. If I had intended to seek the favor of the world, I should have adorned myself better and should present myself in a studied bearing. I wish to be seen in my simple, natural, and ordinary fashion, without effort or artifice, for it is myself that I portray. My defects will here be read to the life, and my natural form, as far as respect for the public has permitted. Had I lived among those nations which are said to live still in the sweet liberty of the first laws of nature, I assure you I should very gladly have portrayed myself here at full length and entirely naked. Thus, reader, I am myself the matter of my book; there is no reason for you to spend your leisure on so frivolous and vain a subject. So farewell, from Montaigne, this first day of March, fifteen hundred and eighty.

BOOK 1

MEN BY VARIOUS WAYS ARRIVE
AT THE SAME END

THE MOST usual way of softening the hearts of those whom we have offended, when with vengeance in their grasp they hold us at their mercy, is by submission to move them to commiseration and pity. And yet daring and tenacity, quite contrary means, have sometimes served the same end.

Edward, Prince of Wales, the same who so long governed our Guienne, a person whose traits and fortune contain many notable aspects of grandeur, having been highly incensed by the Limousins, and taking their city by assault, could not be restrained by the outcries of the people and of the women and children abandoned to slaughter, crying to him for mercy and throwing themselves at his feet, until passing on farther into the city he saw three French gentlemen who with incredible boldness alone sustained the assault of his victorious army. Regard and respect for so remarkable a valor first turned the point of his fury; and he began with these three men to extend clemency to all the remaining inhabitants of the city.

Scanderbeg, Prince of Epirus, pursuing one of his soldiers with intent to kill him, and the soldier having tried by every sort of humility and supplication to appease him, resolved in the last extremity to await him sword in hand. This determination of his gave a sudden check to his captain's fury, who, seeing him make so manly a decision, took him into favor. This example might suffer another interpretation from those who have not read of the prodigious strength and valor of that prince.

The Emperor Conrad III, having besieged Guelph, Duke of Bavaria, would not condescend to milder terms, no matter what low and cowardly satisfactions were tendered to him, than to permit only the gentlewomen who were besieged with the Duke to go out without violation of their honor, on foot, with what they could carry away on them. With loftiness of heart, they hit upon the idea of loading on their shoulders their husbands, their children, and the Duke himself. The Emperor was so pleased to see their noble-heartedness that he wept for joy, and he suppressed all that bitterness of mortal, deadly hatred he had borne against this Duke and from that time on treated him and his with humanity.

Either one of these two ways would easily get the better of me. For I have an unusual propensity to mercy and mildness, so much so that I should be capable of surrendering more naturally to compassion than to esteem. Yet pity is for the Stoics a vicious passion; they want us to give aid to the afflicted but not to give way or sympathize with them.

Now these examples seem to me more to the point, inasmuch as we observe these souls, assailed and tested by these two ways, resisting the one without being shaken and bowing beneath the other. It may be said that to break your heart in commiseration is the result of an easygoing, kind, and soft disposition; whence it comes to pass that the weakest natures, such as those of women, children, and the common people, are the most subject to it. But after having disdained tears and prayers, to yield to the sole reverence of the sacred image of virtue, this can be no other than the effect of a strong and inflexible soul, cherishing and honoring a masculine and obstinate strength. Nevertheless astonishment and admiration may, in less lofty minds, beget a like effect. Witness the people of Thebes, who, having put their generals upon trial for their lives for having continued in arms beyond the time prescribed and designated for them in advance, with great difficulty pardoned Pelopidas, who, bowed under the weight of such an accusation and to defend himself, used only pleas and supplications; and in the contrary fashion Epaminondas, who related grandly the deeds performed by him and haughtily and arrogantly charged the people with ingratitude, they did not have the heart even to take the ballots in their hands, and the assembly departed, greatly praising the high courage of this man.

Having taken the city of Rhegium after extreme delays and difficulties and with it the captain Phyto, a very worthy man who had made so obstinate a defence, Dionysius the Elder wanted to make him a tragical example of vengeance. He first told him how he had the day before caused his son and all his kindred to be drowned. To which Phyto only replied that they were happier than he by one day. After that he had him stripped and seized by executioners and dragged through the town beneath a most ignominious and cruel whipping, and in addition heaping on him the most insulting terms. But he remained constantly steadfast of heart, without losing control of himself, and with undaunted countenance he even loudly reminded them of the honorable and glorious cause of his death—his refusal to deliver his country into the hands of a tyrant—and he threatened him with a speedy chastisement from the gods. Reading in his soldiers' looks that, instead of being incensed at the defiance of this conquered enemy, in contempt of their captain and his triumph they were giving way through astonishment at so rare a virtue and were leaning to mutiny, being on the verge of snatching Phyto from the hands of his sergeants, he had this martyrdom stopped and secretly sent him to be thrown into the sea.

Truly man is a marvelously vain, diverse, and fluctuating subject. It is hard to found a certain and uniform judgment on him. There is Pompey who pardoned the whole city of the Mamertines, though furiously incensed against it, in consideration of the virtue and magnanimity of the citizen Zeno,[1] who took the fault of the people solely upon himself and sought no other favor than to bear the pain of it alone. And Sulla's host, having

---

[1] Sthenon

in the city of Perusia² manifested the same virtue, obtained nothing by it, either for himself or his fellow-citizens.

And directly contrary to my first examples, Alexander, the boldest of all men and so gracious to the vanquished, having after many great difficulties forced the city of Gaza, met up with Betis, who commanded there and of whose valor during this siege he had experienced wonderful proofs, now alone, forsaken by his soldiers, his armor hacked and hewed to pieces, all covered with blood and wounds, still fighting in the midst of a great number of Macedonians who were flinging themselves at him from all sides. Nettled at so dearly bought a victory, for among other damages he had received two fresh wounds on his own person, he said to him, "You shall not die as you have wished, Betis; count on having to suffer all the torments that can be devised for a captive." The other with a countenance not only assured but arrogant and haughty stood firm without replying to these threats. Then Alexander, observing his proud and obstinate silence: "Has he bent a knee? Has any word of entreaty escaped him? Truly I will conquer this silence; and if I cannot wrench a word from it, I will at least wrench a groan from it." And converting his anger into fury, he commanded his heels to be bored through and had him thus dragged alive, mangled, and dismembered at a cart's tail.

Could it be that fearlessness was so familiar to him that he respected it less since he was not at all amazed by it? Or that he considered it so peculiarly his own that he could not without the vexation of envy bear to see it in so high a degree in another? Or that the natural impetuosity of his fury was incapable of standing opposition? In truth, if it would have let itself be bridled, it is likely that in the capture and sack of Thebes it would have done so at the sight of so many valiant men, lost and devoid of any further means of common defence, cruelly put to the sword. For fully six thousand were killed, of whom not one was seen to fly or heard to cry for quarter; on the con-

---

² Praeneste

trary, they sought, some here, some there, through the streets, to confront the victorious enemy, provoking them to put them to an honorable death. Not one was seen, no matter how beaten down with wounds, who did not still try in his last gasp to avenge himself and with the arms of despair to find consolation for his own death in the death of an enemy. Yet the distress of their valor found no pity, and the length of a day was not enough to satiate Alexander's revenge. This slaughter continued to the last drop of blood that was capable of being shed and stopped only at the unarmed old men, women, and children, in order to take thirty thousand of them as slaves.

OF IDLENESS

As WE SEE GROUND that lies fallow, if it is rich and fertile,
abound with innumerable sorts of wild and useless plants; and
that, to make it perform its true office, we must cultivate and
sow it with certain seeds for our service; and as we see that
women do entirely of themselves bring forth formless masses
and lumps of flesh, but that to produce a natural and perfect
generation they must be husbanded with another kind of seed;
even so it is with minds, if they are not applied to some certain
study that may check and restrain them, they will cast themselves in disorder hither and thither in the vague fields of the
imagination.

> As in a brazen bowl the water's shimmering light
> Reflects the radiant sun or Luna's glowing disk,
> And dances round on every side, and then aloft
> Springs up, and o'er the high and panelled ceiling strikes.[1]

There is no folly nor idle fancy that they do not bring forth
in this agitation:

> They form their idle fancies like
> A sick man's dreams.[2]

The mind that has no established aim loses itself; for as the
saying goes, to be everywhere is to be nowhere.

> He who dwells everywhere, Maximus, dwells nowhere.[3]

When I lately retired to my own house, determined as far as
possible to concern myself with nothing else than spending in

---
[1] Virgil, *Aeneid*   [2] Horace, *Ars Poetica*   [3] Martial

privacy and repose the little remainder of time I have to live, I fancied I could not more oblige my mind than to permit it a full leisure to entertain itself and come to rest in itself, which I hoped it might now the more easily do, having with time become more settled and mature; but I find,

Idleness produces ever-changing thoughts.[4]

tnat, quite the contrary, like a runaway horse it gives itself a hundred times more trouble than it used to take for others, and creates me so many chimeras and fantastic monsters, one upon another, without order or design, that, the better at leisure to contemplate their strangeness and absurdity, I have begun to record them, hoping in time to make it ashamed of them.

---

[4] Lucan

THAT MEN ARE NOT TO JUDGE OF OUR HAPPINESS
TILL AFTER DEATH

> Till man's last day is come, we should not dare
> Of happiness to say what was his share;
> Since of no man can it be truly said
> That he is happy till he first be dead.[1]

CHILDREN know the story of King Croesus, to this effect, that, having been taken prisoner by Cyrus and condemned to die, as he was about to be executed he cried out, "O Solon! Solon!" This being reported to Cyrus, and he inquiring what it meant, Croesus gave him to understand that he was now verifying at his own expense the warning Solon had once given him, namely, that men, however Fortune may smile upon them, cannot be called happy until they have been seen to pass the last day of their lives, because of the uncertainty and mutability of human things, which at a very slight impulse change from one state into another, entirely different. And for this reason Agesilaus replied to someone who was saying that the King of Persia was happy to have come so young to so mighty a kingdom: "True, but neither was Priam unhappy at that age." In a short space of time kings of Macedon, successors to the mighty Alexander, are turned into carpenters and clerks at Rome; tyrants of Sicily, into schoolmasters at Corinth. A conqueror of one half of the world and chief of so many armies is turned into a miserable suppliant to the rascally officers of a king of Egypt: such was the cost to the great Pompey of having his life prolonged five or six months. And in our fathers' days, Lodovico Sforza, the tenth duke of Milan, under whom all Italy had so long trem-

---

[1] Ovid, *Metamorphoses*

bled, was seen to die a prisoner at Loches, but not till he had lived ten years there, which was the worst part of his fortune. The fairest of queens,[2] widow of the greatest king in Christendom, has she not just died by the hand of an executioner? And a thousand such examples. For it seems that, as storms and tempests become angered at the pride and loftiness of our buildings, there are also spirits above that are envious of the grandeurs here below.

> So much so does some hidden force o'erwhelm
> Human affairs, and is seen trampling on
> The glorious rods and axes powerful,
> Making a mockery of those stately signs.[3]

And it seems that Fortune sometimes lies in wait for precisely the last day of our lives to show her power to overthrow in a moment what she had been so many years in building, and she makes us cry out with Laberius: *Certainly I have this day lived one day more than I ought to have done.*[4]

In this sense the good advice of Solon may reasonably be taken. But since he is a philosopher, men for whom the favors and disgraces of Fortune rank neither as happiness nor unhappiness, and with whom grandeurs and power are accidents of an almost indifferent nature, I find it likely that he had some further aim, and that his meaning was that this very felicity of our life, which depends upon the tranquillity and contentment of a wellborn spirit and upon the resolution and assurance of a well-ordered soul, ought never to be attributed to any man until he has been seen to play the last, and doubtless the hardest, act of his comedy. There may be disguise in all the rest: either these fine philosophical discourses are only for the sake of appearance, or circumstances, not testing us to the quick, give us leisure to keep our countenance always calm. But in this last scene between death and ourselves there is no more counterfeiting; we

---

[2] Mary Queen of Scots   [3] Lucretius   [4] Macrobius, *Saturnales*

must speak plain, we must show what there is good and clean
in the bottom of the pot,

> For then at last from deep within his breast
> True words are forced, the mask is wrenched away,
> Reality remains.[5]

That is why all the other actions of our life ought to be tried
and tested by this last act. It is the master-day, it is the day
that is judge of all the rest, "it is the day," says one of the ancients, "that must judge all my past years." To death do I refer
the test of the fruit of all my studies. We shall then see whether
my reasonings come only from my mouth or from my heart.

I have seen many by their death give a reputation for good
or evil to their whole life. Scipio, the father-in-law of Pompey
the Great, in dying well, wiped away the ill opinion that up to
then everyone had conceived of him. Epaminondas, being asked
which of the three he had in greatest esteem, Chabrias, Iphicra-
tes, or himself, "You must first see us die," said he, "before
being able to solve that." In truth, we should rob Epaminondas
of a great deal if we weighed him without the honor and grandeur of his end.

God has willed it as has pleased Him; but in my time the
three most execrable persons, and the most infamous that I
knew in all abomination of life, died a calm death and perfectly
composed in every way.

There are brave and fortunate deaths. In the case of a certain
man[6] I saw death cut the thread of a marvelously advancing
progress, in the flower of its growth, with an end so lofty that,
in my opinion, his ambitious and courageous designs contained
nothing so high as was their interruption. He reached the place
to which he aspired, without making his way to it, more grandly
and gloriously than he could have hoped or desired. And he sur-

---

[5] Lucretius   [6] Etienne de la Boétie; it has also been suggested that he
may have had the Duc de Guise in mind.

passed by his fall the power and name to which he aspired in his career.

In judging the life of another, I always observe how the end was borne; and one of the principal concerns of my own life is that the end be borne well, that is, calmly and insensibly.

OF THE EDUCATION OF CHILDREN
To Madame Diane de Foix, Comtesse de Gurson

I NEVER SAW a father who, however mangy or hunchbacked his son might be, failed to own him. Not that, unless he is totally besotted with his paternal affection, he does not discern his defects, but the fact remains that he is his own. Just so I see better than anyone else that these are but the reveries of a man that has tasted only the outer crust of the sciences in his childhood and retained only a general and formless image of them, a little of everything, and nothing thoroughly, in the French style. For I know, in short, that there is such a thing as medicine, jurisprudence, four parts in mathematics, and roughly what all these aim at. And, perhaps, I know, too, what the sciences in general aim at in the service of our life. But to dive deeper than that, and to have gnawed my nails over the study of Aristotle, the monarch of modern learning, or particularly addicted myself to any one science, I have never done it; nor is there any art of which I could draw even the first outlines. And there is not a boy in the middle grades of school that may not pretend to be wiser than I, who am not able to examine him on his first lesson, at least according to that lesson. And if I am forced to, I am constrained, rather ineptly, to draw from it some matter of universal interest on which I test his natural judgment: a lesson as strange to them as theirs is to me.

I never seriously settled myself to the reading of any book of solid learning, except Plutarch and Seneca, from whom I draw like the Danaïds, filling up and pouring out incessantly. Some of this I fix to this paper; to myself, little or nothing.

History is more my quarry, or poetry, which I love with a

particular affection. For, as Cleanthes said, just as sound compressed in the narrow passage of a trumpet comes out sharper and stronger, so, it seems to me, a thought compressed into the measured harmony of verse bounds forth much more briskly and strikes me with a livelier jolt. As to the natural faculties that are in me, of which this is the essay, I feel them bending under the burden. My ideas and judgment proceed only gropingly, faltering, tripping, and stumbling; and when I have gone as far as I can, I am still in no degree satisfied, for I see more land beyond, but with a troubled and clouded sight, so that I cannot make it out clearly. And taking upon me to write indifferently of whatever comes into my head, and therein making use of nothing but my own natural means, if I happened, as I often do, accidentally to meet in any good author the same subjects upon which I have attempted to write (as I have just done this moment in Plutarch's discourse on the power of imagination), seeing myself so weak and miserable, so heavy and sluggish, in comparison with those men, I at once pity and despise myself. Yet I am pleased with this, that my opinions have often the honor to tally with theirs, and that at least I follow the same path, though far behind them, saying, "That is so." Also that I have that faculty, which not everyone has, of knowing the vast difference between them and me. And notwithstanding all that, I let my ideas go their way, weak and lowly just as I produced them, without plastering up or mending the defects that this comparison has laid open to my own view. A man needs good strong loins to keep pace with these people. The indiscreet scribblers of our time, who among their laborious nothings insert whole sections out of ancient authors to do themselves honor, do quite the contrary. For the infinite difference in brilliance gives to the part that is their own so pale, dull, and ugly an aspect that they lose much more by it than they gain.

There were two opposite fancies. The philosopher Chrysippus mixed into his books not only passages but entire works of other authors and in one, the *Medea* of Euripides; and Apollodorus said that should you cut out of his writings all that was not his own, his paper would be left blank. Epicurus, on the contrary, in three hundred volumes that he left behind him, had not inserted so much as one quotation.

I happened the other day to strike such a passage. I was reading a French book, where, after I had a long time been dragging over a great many words, so bloodless, so fleshless, so void of all matter and sense that, indeed, they were nothing but French words; after a long and tedious travel I happened to come upon a piece that was lofty, rich, and elevated to the very clouds. Now had I found the slope gentle and the ascent a bit prolonged, there would have been some excuse; but it was so perpendicular a precipice and so abrupt that at the first six words I knew that I was flying into the other world. From there I saw the bog from which I had come, so deep and low that I have never since had the heart to descend into it again. If I should stuff one of my discourses with such rich spoils as these, it would too clearly light up the stupidity of the others.

To reprehend my own faults in others appears to me no more unreasonable than to reprehend, as I often do, those of others in myself. They should be everywhere denounced and ought to have no sanctuary allowed them. I know very well how audaciously I myself, at every turn, attempt to rise to the level of my thefts and to keep abreast of them, not without a daring hope of deceiving the eyes of the judges of my use of them as by virtue of my invention and my strength. Besides, I do not contend with the whole body of these old champions, hand to hand; it is only by sallies and little light skirmishes that I engage them. I do not stubbornly grapple with them, but try their strength only, and do not go so far as I sound out going. If I could hold them in play, I would be a good man, for I attack them only where they are strongest.

To cover a man's self, as I have seen some do, with another man's armor, so as not to show so much as their finger's ends, to carry out his design, as it is easy for the learned in an ordinary subject, under old inventions patched up here and there: in those who want to hide them and appropriate them, it is in the first place injustice and cowardice that, having nothing of their own by which to show their hand, they endeavor to present themselves in the trappings of others, and then a ridiculous folly that, contenting themselves with acquiring the ignorant approbation of the vulgar by such trickery, they discredit themselves in the eyes of men of understanding, the only persons whose praise has any weight, who will turn up their noses at our borrowed incrustation. For my own part there is nothing I want less to do. I utter the thoughts of others only to express my own thoughts better. That does not apply to the compilations that are published as compilations; and I have, in my time, seen some very ingenious ones, particularly one, under the name of Capilupus, besides the ancients. These are minds that attract attention both there and elsewhere, as, for example, Lipsius, in that learned and laborious compilation of his *Politics*.

However that may be, I mean to say; and whatever these absurdities may be, I have no intent to conceal them, any more than a bald, grizzled portrait of myself in which the painter had drawn not a perfect face, but mine. For these too, are my humors and opinions; I deliver them for only what I myself believe, and not what others are to believe. I aim here only at revealing myself, who shall, peradventure, be another thing tomorrow, if some new lesson of life should change me. I have no authority to be believed, neither do I desire it, feeling myself too ill instructed to instruct others.

Someone, then, having read the preceding chapter, told me the other day at my home that I should have enlarged a little more upon the education of children. Now, Madame, if I had any ability in this matter, I could not employ it better than to make a present of it to the little gentleman that threatens shortly to sally forth handsomely from within you (you are too noble of spirit to begin otherwise than with a male). For having had so great a part in the arranging of your marriage, I have a certain right and interest in the greatness and prosperity of all that shall proceed from it; besides that the ancient claim you have on my services suffices to oblige me to desire the honor, good, and advantage of everything that concerns you. But, in truth, I know nothing about it except this, that the greatest and most important difficulty in human knowledge seems to be in that part which deals with the nurture and education of children.

Just as in agriculture the work that precedes planting, as also planting itself, is certain and easy; but after that which is planted takes life, there is in raising it a great variety of methods and no little difficulty; so it is with men; to plant them requires little industry, but after they are born, we undertake the burden of a varied care, full of anxiety and fear, in training them and bringing them up.

The symptoms of their inclinations at that tender age are so slight and obscure, and the promises so uncertain and fallacious, that it is very hard to establish any solid judgment upon them. Look at Cimon, for example, and Themistocles, and a thousand others, how much they belied themselves. Bears' cubs and puppies reveal their natural inclination; but men, immediately casting themselves into certain habits, opinions, and laws, do easily change and disguise themselves. And yet it is hard to force the propensity of nature. Whence it comes to pass that, for not having chosen our course well, we often toil to no avail and spend a great deal of time in training up children to things in which they cannot gain a footing. In this difficulty, nevertheless, I believe that they ought to be always directed to the best and most advantageous things with little notice taken of those trivial conjectures and prognostications that we make from their childhood actions. Even Plato, in his *Republic,* gives them, I think, too much authority.

Madame, learning is a great ornament and a tool of marvelous use, especially to persons raised to that degree of fortune in which you are placed. In truth, it is not put to its true use in mean and lowborn hands. It is much prouder to lend its means to conducting a war, to governing a people, and to securing the friendship of a prince or a foreign nation, than to forming a dialectical argument, to pleading a process in law, or to prescribing a batch of pills. Wherefore, Madame, believing you will not omit this factor in the training of your children, yourself having tasted the delights of it, and being of a literary family (for we still have the writings of the ancient Counts of Foix, from whom my lord, your husband, and yourself are both descended, and François Monsieur de Candale, your uncle, does every day oblige the world with others, which will extend the knowledge of this quality in your family to many succeeding ages), I desire upon this subject to acquaint you with one particular fancy of my own that is contrary to the common usage; it is all I am able to contribute to your service in this matter.

The charge of the tutor you shall provide for your son, upon the choice of whom depends the whole success of his education, has many other important parts, but I do not touch upon them, being unable to add anything of moment; and also in this, wherein I take upon me to advise, he will follow it so far as it shall appear reasonable to him. For a boy of noble family who pretends to letters, not upon the account of profit (for so mean an object as that is unworthy of the grace and favor of the Muses; and, moreover, has reference to others and depends on them), nor so much for outward advantages as for his own advantages and to furnish and enrich himself within, having rather a desire to make of him an accomplished gentleman than a mere learned man, I would also desire that care be taken to select for him a tutor who had a well-made head rather than a well-filled one, and that both these qualities be required of him, but more particularly character and understanding than learning, and that he pursue the exercise of his charge after a new method.

It is the custom of schoolmasters to be eternally thundering in our ears as if they were pouring into a funnel, and our business is only to repeat what they have said to us. I would have a tutor correct this practice, and at the very outset, according to the capacity of the mind he has to deal with, begin to put it to the test, making it taste things and by itself choose and discern them, sometimes opening the way to him, and sometimes making him do it himself. I would not have him alone think and speak, I would have him hear his pupil speak in turn. Socrates and, since him, Arcesilaus, first made their scholars speak, and then they spoke to them. *The authority of those who teach is very often an impediment to those who desire to learn.*[1] It is good to make the pupil trot before him, that he may judge of his pace and how much he must lower his own speed to accommodate himself to his strength. For want of this proportion we spoil all; and to know how to strike it and to proceed in it within due measure is one of the hardest tasks I know, and it is the sign of a very strong and lofty mind to know how to condescend to his childish gait and direct it. I walk more firmly and surely uphill than down.

Such as, according to our common way of teaching, undertake, with one and the same lesson and the same measure of direction, to instruct many minds of such differing forms and capacities, need not wonder if in a multitude of scholars there are not found above two or three who bring away any good account of their instruction.

Let the master examine him not only about the words of his lesson, but also as to the sense and meaning of them, and let him judge of the profit he has made, not by the testimony of his memory, but by that of his life. Let him make him put what he has just learned into a hundred forms and apply it to as many different subjects, to see if he has yet rightly grasped it and has made it his own, taking account of his progress by the pedagogical method of Plato. It is a sign of crudity and indigestion to throw up what we have eaten in the same condition it was swallowed down. The stomach has not per-

---

[1] Cicero, *De Natura Deorum*

formed its office unless it has altered the form and condition of what was given to it to cook.

Our minds work only upon trust, being bound and constrained to the appetite of another's fancy, enslaved and captive under the authority of another's instruction. We have been so subjected to leading strings that we have no free pace of our own. Our vigor and liberty are extinct. *They never become their own guardians.*[2]

I saw privately at Pisa an intelligent man, but so great an Aristotelian that his main dogma was that the touchstone and rule of all solid speculation and of all truth is conformity to the teaching of Aristotle, and that all else is nothing but inanity and chimera; that he saw all and said all. That proposition, having been a little too broadly and maliciously interpreted, once brought him into and long kept him in great danger of the Inquisition at Rome.

Let the tutor make his pupil sift everything and lodge nothing in his head upon simple authority and trust. Let not Aristotle's principles be principles to him any more than those of the Epicureans and the Stoics. Let the diversity of opinions be laid before him, he will choose if he be able; if not, he will remain in doubt. Only fools are cocksure.

I love to doubt as well as know.[3]

For if he embrace the opinions of Xenophon and Plato by the exercise of his reason, they will no more be theirs, they will become his own. Who follows another, follows nothing. He finds nothing, nay, seeks nothing. *We are not under a king; let everyone dispose of himself.*[4] Let him, at least, know that he does know. It is for him to imbibe their ways to knowledge but not to adopt their precepts. And let him boldly forget, if he will, where he got them, but let him know how to apply them to his

---

[2] Seneca, *Epistles*   [3] Dante, *Inferno*   [4] Seneca, *Epistles*

own use. Truth and reason are common to everyone and are no more his who spoke them first than his who speaks them later. It is no more according to Plato than according to me since both he and I equally see and understand it in the same manner. Bees pillage the flowers here and there, but they then make honey of them which is all their own; it is no longer thyme and marjoram; so the fragments borrowed from others he will transform and blend together to make a work that shall be absolutely his own; that is to say, his judgment. His education, labor, and study aim only at forming that.

Let him conceal all the aid he has received and show only what he has made of it. Pillagers and borrowers parade their purchases and buildings, but not what they get from others. You do not see the fees and perquisites of a magistrate, you see the alliances he has gained and honors for his children. No man accounts to the public for his revenue; but everyone makes a show of his purchases.

The gain from our study is to have thereby become better and wiser.

It is, said Epicharmus, the understanding that sees and hears, the understanding that improves everything, that orders everything, and that acts, rules, and reigns; all other things are blind, deaf, and without soul. Certainly we render it cowardly and servile in not allowing it the liberty to do anything of itself. Who ever asked his pupil what he thought of grammar and rhetoric, or of such and such a remark of Cicero? Our pedagogues stick them full-feathered in our memories, like oracles, in which the letters and syllables are the substance of the thing. To know by rote is not to know; it is to retain what one has intrusted to his memory. That which a man rightly knows he is the free disposer of, without looking at the model or glancing at his book. Sorry proficiency, a purely bookish proficiency! I want it to serve as an ornament, not as a foundation, according to the opinion of Plato, who says that constancy, faith, and sincerity are the true philosophy, and the other sciences, that are directed to other ends, are but artifice.

I wish that Paluel or Pompey, those fine dancers of my time, could teach us to cut capers by only seeing them do it, without stirring from our places, as these men pretend to inform our understanding, without ever setting it to work; or that we could be taught to handle a horse or a pike, touch a lute, or sing, without practice, as these attempt to make us judge and speak well, without exercising us in judging or speaking. Now for this apprenticeship to learning, whatsoever presents itself before us is book enough: the arch trick of a page, a blunder of a servant, or a remark at a table are so many new subjects.

For this reason acquaintance with the world is of very great use and travel into foreign countries of singular advantage, not merely to bring back (in the manner of our French nobility) an account of how many paces Santa Rotonda[5] is in circuit, or of the richness of Signora Livia's drawers, or, like some others, how much Nero's face in a statue in some old ruin is longer and broader than that on some equally old medal; but chiefly to return with knowledge of the nature and customs of those nations, and to whet and sharpen our wits by rubbing them upon those of others. I would that a boy should be sent abroad very young and, in order to kill two birds with one stone, first into those neighboring nations whose language differs most from our own and to which, if it be not formed early, the tongue cannot be bent.

It is also the general opinion of all that a child should not be brought up in his parents' lap. The natural affection makes even the most discreet of them too tender and lax. They are capable neither of punishing his faults nor of seeing him brought up roughly, as he ought to be, and hazardously. They would not endure to see him return all dust and sweat from his exercise, to drink cold or hot, or see him mount an unruly horse,

---

[5] The Pantheon

or take a foil in hand against a rough fencer, or with his first harquebus. For there is no remedy; whoever wishes to make a man of him must by no means spare him when young and must very often transgress the rules of medicine:

> And let him live beneath the skies
> Among stirring alarms[6]

It is not enough to toughen his soul, you are also to make his sinews strong. The soul is too hard pressed if not assisted, and would have too hard a task to discharge two offices alone. I know very well how much mine struggles in the company of so tender and sensitive a body that leans so heavily upon it. And often in my reading I perceive that our masters, in their writings, make examples pass for magnanimity and fortitude of heart which really have more to do with toughness of skin and hardness of bones. I have seen men, women, and children born with such a constitution that a sound cudgeling is less to them than a flirt of a finger would be to me; and that neither cry out nor wince at a good swinging beating. When athletes imitate the philosophers in patience, it is rather strength of sinews than stoutness of heart. Now to be accustomed to endure work is to be accustomed to endure pain: *work produces callousness to pain.*[7] A boy must be broken in to the pain and hardship of severe exercise to train him to the pain and hardship of dislocations, colics, cauteries, and even of imprisonment and the rack. For he may even be reduced to the worst of these, which, in these times, befall the good as well as the bad. We are undergoing proof of it. Whoever draws his sword against the laws threatens the most honest men with the whip and the halter.

And, moreover, the authority of the tutor, which ought to be sovereign over the boy, is interrupted and hindered by the presence of parents; to which may also be added that the respect the whole household pay him and the knowledge he has

---

[6] Horace, *Odes*   [7] Cicero, *Tusculans*

of the estate and greatness of his family are, in my opinion, no small inconveniences at that age.

In one's converse with the world, I have often observed this vice: that instead of gathering observations from others, we make it our only business to give them our own and are more concerned how to peddle our own than how to acquire new. Silence and modesty are very advantageous qualities in that intercourse. This boy will be trained to be sparing and a good husband of what he knows, when once acquired; and to forbear taking exceptions to every idle saying or ridiculous story spoken or told in his presence, for it is a great rudeness to attack everything that is not agreeable to our own palate. Let him be satisfied with correcting himself, and not seem to condemn everything in another he would not do himself, nor oppose common customs. *A man may be wise without display and without offense.*[8] Let him avoid this pedagoguish and uncivil fashion, this childish ambition of wanting to appear cleverer by being different, and wishing to gain a reputation by carping and by assuming newfangled ways. For, as it becomes none but great poets to make use of the poetic license, so it is intolerable that any but men of great and illustrious souls should be privileged above the authority of custom. *If Socrates and Aristippus have done something contrary to the rules of conduct and custom, let him not think that he is entitled to do the same; for they have attained that privilege by great and divine merits.*[9] He will be instructed not to engage in argument or dispute but with a champion worthy of him, and even there, not to make use of all the subtleties that may serve his purpose, but only such as may best serve him. Let him be taught to be discerning in the choice of his arguments, fond of pertinence and, hence, of brevity. Above all, let him be taught to surrender to truth as soon as ever he shall discover it, whether in his opponent's argument, or upon better consideration of his own. For he will not be placed on the rostrum to give a set lecture. He is not bound to any

---

[8] Seneca, *Epistles* [9] Cicero, *De Officiis*

cause except by the fact that he approves of it. Nor will he follow the trade in which the liberty of being able to repent and admit one's mistakes is sold for ready money. *Nor is he compelled by any necessity to defend all that has been prescribed and ordered.*[10]

If his tutor be of my humor, he will form his will to be a very loyal servant of his prince, very devoted and very courageous in his service; but he will cool in him the desire of having any other tie to his service than public duty. Besides several other disadvantages which injure our liberty through these private obligations, the judgment of a man who is hired and bought is either less whole and less free or is blemished either with ingratitude or indiscretion. A courtier can neither have power nor will to speak or think otherwise than favorably of a master who, among so many thousands of other subjects, has picked out him to nourish and advance him with his own hand. This favor and the profit flowing from it must needs, and not without some show of reason, corrupt his freedom of speaking and dazzle him. Therefore we commonly see these people speak in another kind of phrase than is ordinarily spoken by the rest of the nation, and they are not much to be believed in such matters.

Let his conscience and his virtue be eminently manifest in his speech and have only reason for their guide. Make him understand that to acknowledge the error he shall discover in his own argument, though only perceived by himself, is an act of judgment and sincerity, which are the principal things he is to seek after; that obstinacy and contention are common qualities, most often seen in the meanest souls; that to change his mind and correct himself, and to forsake a bad argument in the height and heat of dispute, are rare, strong, and philosophical qualities.

Let him be warned, being in company, to have his eyes everywhere; for I find that the places of greatest honor are commonly seized by men that have least in them, and that the greatest fortunes are seldom accompanied with ability. I have been pres-

---

[10] Cicero, *Academica*

ent when, while they at the upper end of the table were discussing the beauty of a tapestry or the flavor of the wine, many
fine remarks have been lost or thrown away at the lower end of
the table. Let him examine every man's talent; a cowherd, a
bricklayer, a passer-by; he must put all to use and borrow from
each according to his goods, for everything is of use in a household; even the folly and weakness of others will contribute to
his instruction. By observing the graces and manners of all he
sees, he will create in himself an emulation of the good ones
and contempt of the bad.

Let an appropriate curiosity be planted in him to inquire after
everything; whatever there is singular around him, let him go
and see it; a house, a fountain, a man, the place where a battle
was anciently fought, the passage of Caesar or of Charlemagne:

> What lands are frozen, what are parched, explore,
> And what wind bears us to the Italian shore.[11]

Let him inquire into the habits, resources, and alliances of
this prince and that. These are things very pleasant to learn and
very useful to know. In this intercourse with men I mean to
include, and principally, those who only live in the memory of
books. Let him by means of histories converse with the great
souls of better ages. It is an idle study to those who choose to
make it so; but to those also who choose to make it so, it is a
study of inestimable fruit; and the only study, as Plato reports, the Lacedemonians reserved to themselves. What profit
shall he not reap there by reading the lives of Plutarch? But
let my tutor remember to what end his instructions are directed, and let him not so much imprint in his pupil's memory
the date of the ruin of Carthage as the characters of Hannibal
and Scipio, nor so much where Marcellus died as why it was
unworthy of his duty that he died there. Let him teach him not
so much the histories as how to judge them. It is this matter

---

[11] Propertius

to which, in my opinion, of all others, we apply our minds in the most differing measures. I have read a hundred things in Livy that another has not. Plutarch has read a hundred more than ever I could find or than, perhaps, the author had ever put there. To some it is merely a grammar-study; to others, the very anatomy of philosophy, into which the most abstruse parts of our nature penetrate. There are in Plutarch many long discourses very worthy of being observed, for he is, in my opinion, the master hand in that work; but there are a thousand others which he has only just touched upon; he only points with his finger to direct us which way we may go if we will, and contents himself sometimes with only giving one brisk hit in the very heart of the question. We must pull them out and put them on display. As for example his saying that the inhabitants of Asia served one single man for not having been able to pronounce one single syllable, which is "No," gave, perhaps, matter and occasion to La Boétie to write his *Voluntary Servitude*. Merely to see him pick out a light action in a man's life, or a word that does not seem to be of any importance, is in itself a whole discourse. It is a pity that men of understanding are so fond of brevity; no doubt but their reputation is the better for it; but we are the worse off by it. Plutarch had rather we should applaud his judgment than his knowledge, and had rather leave us with an appetite for more of him than glutted. He knew that a man may say too much even upon the best subjects and that Alexandridas justly reproached him who made good, but too long, remarks to the Ephors, when he said, "O stranger! you say what you should, but not in the way you should." Such as have lean and spare bodies stuff them out with padding, such as have meager substance blow it up with words.

Human judgment is marvelously enlightened by getting around in the world. We are all confined and banked up within ourselves and have our sight limited to the length of our nose. Someone asked Socrates of what country he was. He did not answer, "Of Athens," but, "Of the world." Having an imagination richer and more expansive, he embraced the whole world as his city and extended his society, his friendship, and his knowledge to all mankind; not as we do, who look no farther than our feet. When the vines of our village are nipped with the frost, my parish priest presently concludes that the indignation of God is gone out against all the human race, and that the cannibals have already got the pip. Who is it that, seeing these civil wars of ours, does not cry out that the machine of the whole world is upsetting and that the day of judgment has us by the throat, without considering that many worse things have been seen and that in the meantime ten thousand other parts of the earth do not fail to lead a joyous life? For my part, considering their licentiousness and impunity, I am amazed to see our wars so gentle and mild. To him that feels the hailstones patter about his ears, the whole hemisphere appears to be in storm and tempest. Like the Savoyard who said that if that simple king of France had managed well he might in time have come to be steward of the household to the duke his master. His imagination could not conceive any higher grandeur than that of his master. We are all of us insensibly in this error, an error of great consequence and harm. But whoever shall represent to his fancy, as in a picture, that great image of our mother Nature in her full majesty; whoever in her face shall read so general and so constant a variety; whoever shall observe himself in that figure, and not himself but a whole kingdom, as a point made with the least touch of a pencil, that man alone evaluates things according to their true proportion.

This great world, which some do yet multiply as a species under one genus, is the mirror wherein we are to behold ourselves in order to know ourselves from the right angle. In short, I would have this to be the book for my scholar. So many humors, so many sects, so many judgments, opinions, laws, and customs teach us to judge aright of our own and teach our judgment to recognize its imperfection and natural infirmity, which is no trivial lesson. So many mutations of states and so many changes of public fortune teach us to make no great won-der of our own. So many names, so many victories and con-quests buried in oblivion render our hopes ridiculous of eterniz-ing our names by the taking of half a score light horse or a henroost which is known only because of its fall. The pride and arrogance of so many foreign pomps, the inflated majesty of so many courts and grandeurs steady and fortify our sight to en-dure the luster of our own without blinking. So many millions of men buried before us encourage us not to fear to go seek such good company in the other world. And so of all the rest.

Pythagoras was wont to say that our life resembles the great and populous assembly of the Olympic Games. Some there exercise the body to acquire glory in the contests; others carry merchandise there to sell for profit. There are some, and those none of the worst sort, who pursue no other advantage than to see how and why everything is done and to be spectators of the lives of other men in order to judge and regulate their own.

To the examples may appropriately be added all the most profitable lessons of philosophy, to which human actions, for their standard, must be referred. He will be told,

> What rightly may be wished for, and what use
> Hard-earnèd coin has; how much should be given
> To country and to kin; what God has set
> For us to be, and in what station put;
> And what we are, and for what purpose made;[12]

what it is to know and what to be ignorant; what ought to be the end of study; what valor, temperance, and justice are; the difference between ambition and avarice, servitude and sub-mission, license and liberty; by what token a man may know true and solid contentment; how far death, pain, and shame are to be feared,

---

[12] Persius

How to avoid and how endure each strain;[13]

what springs move us, and the reason for so many different impulses in us. For, I think, the first lessons with which one should saturate his understanding ought to be those which regulate his habits and his common sense; that will teach him to know himself and how both to die well and to live well.

Among the liberal arts let us begin with that which makes us free. They all serve in some measure to the formation of our life and to the use made of life, as all other things in some sort do; but let us make choice of that which directly and professedly serves to that end. If we were able to restrain the functions of our life within their just and natural limits, we should find that most of the sciences in use are of no use to us, and, even in those that are, that there are very useless stretches and gulfs which we had better let alone, and, following Socrates' teaching, limit the extent of our studies in those subjects wherein utility is lacking.

> Dare to be wise! Begin! He who
> Defers the hour of uprightness awaits
> Like bumpkin for the drying of the stream;
> But on it flows and ever will flow on.[14]

It is very stupid to teach our children

> What influence Pisces and fierce Leo have,
> Or Capricorn bathed in Hesperian wave,[15]

the knowledge of the stars and the motion of the eighth sphere before their own movements:

> What are the Pleiades to me,
> And what to me Boötes' stars?[16]

---

[13] Virgil, *Aeneid*   [14] Horace, *Epistles*   [15] Propertius   [16] Anacreon

Anaximenes, writing to Pythagoras, "To what purpose," he said, "should I trouble myself in searching out the secrets of the stars, having death or slavery continually before my eyes?" (For the kings of Persia were at that time preparing to invade his country.) Everyone ought to say thus: "Being assailed by ambition, avarice, temerity, and superstition, and having within so many other enemies of life, shall I go cudgel my brains about the world's revolutions?"

After having taught our pupil what will make him wiser and better, you may then show him the elements of logic, natural philosophy, geometry, and rhetoric; and the science that he will choose, once his judgment is formed, he will quickly make his own. He will be taught, sometimes by conversation and sometimes by reading; sometimes his tutor shall put the author himself, which he shall think most proper for him, into his hands, and sometimes he will give him the marrow and substance well digested. And if he himself be not conversant enough in books to turn to all the fine passages that are in them, for the carrying out of his purpose, some man of letters may be joined to him, who upon every occasion shall supply him with the provisions he needs, to distribute them to his pupil. And who can doubt but that this way of teaching is much more easy and natural than that of Gaza? In the latter the precepts are so thorny and so harsh and the words so empty and meatless that there is no hold on them, nothing that stirs the mind. In the other the mind finds something to bite and feed on. This fruit is, without comparison, greater, and yet it will ripen sooner.

It is a strange thing that matters should be at such a pass in this age of ours that philosophy, even with men of understanding, should be looked upon as a vain and fantastic name, a thing of no use, no value, both in common opinion and in fact. I think that the snarled-up reasoning of these ergotists, by taking possession of the avenues unto it, is the cause. It is very wrong to represent it to children as a thing of such difficult access, and with a frowning, grim, and formidable aspect. Who is it that has disguised it thus with this false, pale, and hideous countenance? There is nothing more gay, more robust, more sprightly, I might almost say more wanton. She preaches nothing but merrymaking and jollity. A sad and dejected look shows that she does not inhabit there. Demetrius, the grammarian, finding in the Temple of Delphi a knot of philosophers seated together, said to them, "Either I am deceived or, judging by your cheerful and serene countenances, you are engaged in no very deep discussion." To which one of them, Heracleon, the Megarean, replied, "It is for those who are inquiring whether the future tense of the verb βάλλω be spelt with a double λ, or that hunt after the derivation of the comparatives χεῖρον, βέλτιον, and the superlatives χείριστον, βέλτιστον, to knit their brows while discoursing of their science. But as to philosophical discussions, they are wont to amuse and cheer up those that treat of them and never deject them or make them sad."

> For in a sickly body you may see
> The spirit's hidden torments and its joys;
> The face assumes the stamp of either one.[17]

The soul that entertains philosophy ought by its health to render the body healthful too. It ought to make its tranquillity and gladness shine so as to appear without; and it ought to fashion the outward behavior to its own mould, and consequently to fortify it with a graceful pride, an active and joyous carriage, and a good-natured and contented countenance. The most certain sign of Wisdom is a constant cheerfulness; her state is like that of things in the regions above the moon, always serene. It is *Baroco* and *Baralipton* that render their disciples so dirty and dingy, and not she; they know her only by hearsay. Why, she makes it her business to calm the tempests of the soul and to teach famine and fevers to laugh, not by certain imaginary epicycles, but by natural and palpable reasons. She has

---

[17] Juvenal

virtue for her end, which is not, as the schoolmen say, set upon
the summit of a steep, rugged, and inaccessible mountain. Such
as have approached her find her, quite on the contrary, to be
seated in a fair, fruitful, and flourishing plain, whence she easily
sees all things below her; but anyone may get there if he
know the way, through shady, green, and sweet-scented walks,
pleasantly, by an easy and smooth slope like that of the celestial
vaults. For not having frequented this supreme, this beautiful,
triumphant, and loving, this equally delicious and courageous
virtue, this professed and implacable enemy of sourness, displeasure, fear, and constraint, having Nature for her guide,
Fortune and Pleasure for her companions, they have gone, in
keeping with their weakness, and created this stupid image,
sorrowful, querulous, sullen, threatening, scowling, and placed it
upon a solitary rock among brambles, a hobgoblin to frighten
people.

My tutor, knowing it to be his duty to fill the spirit of his
pupil with as much or more affection than reverence for virtue,
will be able to inform him that the poets have evermore accommodated themselves to the common view, and make him
plainly feel that the gods have set more sweaty toil in the
approaches to the chambers of Venus than in those of Minerva.
And when he begins to take note of himself and Bradamante or
Angelica is offered to him as a mistress to be enjoyed—a
natural, active, spirited, not mannish, but manly beauty, in
comparison with a soft, affected, delicate, artificial beauty; the
one in the habit of a youth wearing a glittering helmet; the
other dressed like a girl, wearing a headdress of pearls—he will
then judge even his love to be manly if he chooses quite differently from that effeminate shepherd of Phrygia.

He will teach him this new lesson, that the height and value
of true virtue consists in the facility, utility, and pleasure of
its exercise, which is so far from being difficult that boys as well
as men, and the simple as well as the subtle, may make it their
own. Moderation is her tool, not force. Socrates, her first favor-

ite, deliberately abandons all forceful effort to slip into the naturalness and ease of her movements. She is the nursing-mother of human pleasures. In rendering them just, she renders them pure and permanent. In moderating them, she keeps them in breath and appetite. In curtailing those which she refuses, she whets our desire for those which she allows us; and, like a mother, she abundantly allows us all that nature requires, even to satiety, if not to lassitude; unless, perchance, we choose to say that the regimen that stops the drinker short of drunkenness, the glutton short of indigestion, and the wencher short of the scurf is an enemy to our pleasure. If the ordinary fortune fail her, she rises above it or does without it and forms another, wholly her own, not so fickle and unsteady. She can be rich, potent, and learned, and lie upon perfumed couches. She loves life, beauty, glory, and health. But her proper and peculiar function is to know how to make use of all these good things and how to part with them without concern: a function much more noble than troublesome, and without which the whole course of life is unnatural, turbulent, and deformed, and may fitly be associated with those reefs, thickets, and monsters. If this pupil shall happen to be of so strange a disposition that he had rather hear an idle tale than the true narrative of some noble expedition or some wise conversation when he chances to hear it; a fellow who, at the sound of the drum that excites the youthful ardor of his companions, leaves that to follow another that calls to the antics of the jugglers; a fellow who of his own taste does not find it more sweet and delightful to return all over dust victorious from a battle than from tennis or a ball, with the prize of that exercise; I see no other remedy but that his tutor in good time strangle him if there are no witnesses, or that he be apprenticed to a pastry-maker in some good town, though he were the son of a duke, according to Plato's precept that children are to be placed out in life not according to the resources of their father, but according to the resources of their minds.

Since philosophy is that which instructs us to live, and that childhood has therein its lessons, as do other ages, why is it not communicated to children?

> The clay is moist and soft; now, now make haste,
> And fashion him, as the sharp wheel turns on.[18]

They begin to teach us to live when we have almost done living. A hundred students have got the pox before they have come to read Aristotle on temperance. Cicero said that, though he should live two men's ages, he should never find leisure to study the lyric poets. And I find those quibbling ergotists yet more deplorably unprofitable. The boy we would train has a great deal less time to spare; he owes but the first fifteen or sixteen years of his life to schooling; the remainder belongs to action. Let us employ that short time in necessary instruction. Away with those thorny subtleties of dialectics; they are abuses, things by which our lives can never be amended. Take the plain teachings of philosophy, learn how to select them and handle them rightly; they are more easy to be understood than one of Boccaccio's tales. A child newly weaned is much more capable of them than of learning to read or to write. Philosophy has teachings equally proper for childhood as for old age.

I am of Plutarch's mind, that Aristotle did not so much trouble his great disciple with the trick of forming syllogisms, or with the elements of geometry, as with infusing into him good precepts concerning valor, prowess, magnanimity, temperance, and the contempt of fear; and with this provision he sent him, while yet a boy, with no more than 30,000 foot, 4,000 horse, and but 42,000 crowns, to subjugate the empire of the whole earth. As for the other arts and sciences, Alexander, he says, commended their excellence and charm and had them in very great honor; but, despite the pleasure that he took in them, he was not easily overcome by temptation to practice them.

---

[18] Persius

> Seek here, both young and old, a certain goal
> For your desires, and stores 'gainst old age's woes.[19]

Epicurus, in the beginning of his letter to Meniceus, says that neither the youngest should refuse to philosophize, nor the eldest grow weary of it. And who does otherwise seems tacitly to imply that either the time of living happily is not yet come or that it is already past.

For all these reasons, I would not have this pupil of ours imprisoned. Nor would I have him given up to the morose humor of a raging schoolmaster. I would not have his spirit cowed by keeping him to torture and toil, as the others are, fourteen or fifteen hours a day like a porter. Neither should I think it good, when by reason of a solitary and melancholy disposition he is discovered to be too inordinately addicted to his books, to nourish that inclination in him; that renders them unfit for social intercourse and diverts them from better activities. And how many have I seen in my time brutified by an immoderate thirst after knowledge! Carneades was so besotted with it that he no longer took time to do his hair and his nails. Neither would I have his noble manners spoiled by the incivility and barbarity of others. French wisdom was long ago proverbial for a wisdom that took hold early and that had scarcely any duration. In truth we yet see that nothing can be more charming than the little children in France; but they ordinarily deceive the hope that has been conceived of them, and, grown up to be men, they are without distinction. I have heard men of good understanding say these schools to which we send them (of which we have no lack) make them such animals as they are.

But for our pupil a study, a garden, the table and the bed, solitude, company, morning and evening, all hours shall be the same, and all places for him a study; for philosophy, which, as the moulder of judgment and character, shall be his principal

---

[19] Persius

lesson, has that privilege of having a hand in everything. The orator Isocrates being at a feast entreated to speak of his art, all the company considered that he was justified in replying: "It is not now a time to do what I can do; and that which it is now time to do I cannot do." For to deliver orations and rhetorical disputations in a company met together to laugh and make good cheer would produce an incongruous mixture. And as much might be said of all the other sciences. But as to philosophy, in that part of it that treats of man and of his functions and duties, it has been the joint opinion of all wise men that, because of the sweetness of her conversation, she is ever to be admitted in all sports and entertainments. And Plato having invited her to his feast, we see in how gentle a manner, suited both to time and place, she entertained the company, though it be one of his loftiest and most salutary discourses.

> It profits poor and rich alike, and when
> Neglected, harms alike both young and old.[20]

Thus, doubtless, he will idle less than the others. But as the steps we take in walking to and fro in a gallery, though three times as many, do not tire us so much as those we take in a set journey, so our lesson, occurring as it were accidentally, without any set obligation of time or place, and mingling with all our actions, will glide by without being felt. Our very exercises and games, running, wrestling, music, dancing, hunting, the handling of horses and arms, will be a good part of our study. I would have his outward behavior and social grace and the bearing of his body formed at the same time with his mind. It is not a mind, it is not a body, that we are training; it is a man, and we must not divide him into two parts; and, as Plato says, we must not train one without the other, but drive them abreast like two horses harnessed to the same pole. And to hear him, does he not seem to give more time and more care to exer-

[20] Horace, *Epistles*

cises of the body, and to believe that the mind gets its exercise at the same time and not the reverse.

As to the rest, this education ought to be carried on with a severe gentleness, not as it is being done. Instead of attracting children to letters they offer them, in truth, nothing but horror and cruelty. Away with violence and compulsion! In my opinion there is nothing that so dulls and degenerates a wellborn nature. If you would have him fear shame and chastisement, do not harden him to them. Inure him to sweat and cold, to wind and sun, and to dangers that he must despise. Wean him from all softness and delicacy in clothing and sleeping, eating and drinking: accustom him to everything. Let him not be a pretty, ladylike boy, but a hardy and vigorous young man. I have ever, as a child, a man, and an old man, thought and judged in the same way. But among other things, the discipline of most of our schools has always displeased me. Perhaps they might have erred less perniciously by leaning towards indulgence. They are veritable jails of imprisoned youths. They are taught to be disorderly by being punished for it before they are so. Do but come in when they are about their lesson, and you shall hear nothing but cries, both from tortured boys and from masters drunk with fury. What a way to arouse a desire for their lesson in these tender and timid souls, to lead them to it with a terrifying face and hands armed with rods! A wretched and pernicious way! Besides what Quintilian has very well observed, that this insolent authority is attended by very dangerous consequences, and particularly in our way of chastising. How much more fitting would it be to see their classes strewn with leaves and flowers than with bloody stumps of birch! I should paint the school with pictures of joy and gladness, Flora and the Graces, as the philosopher Speusippus did his. Where their profit is, let their frolic be too. Food that is wholesome for children should be seasoned with sugar and the harmful with gall.

It is wonderful to see how solicitous Plato is in his laws about

the gaiety and diversion of the youth of his city, and how he
dwells upon their races, games, songs, leaps, and dances, of
which he says that antiquity has given the conduct and patronage to the gods themselves, to Apollo, Minerva, and the Muses.
He extends that to a thousand precepts for his gymnasiums;
but as to the literary studies, he wastes very little time on them
and seems to recommend poetry particularly only for the sake
of the music.

All strangeness and singularity in our manners and conduct
is to be avoided as adverse to social intercourse and unnatural.
Who would not be astonished at the constitution of Demophon,
steward to Alexander, who sweated in the shade and shivered
in the sun? I have seen some run from the smell of an apple
more than from a harquebus shot, others take fright at a mouse,
others vomit at the sight of cream, others at seeing a feather bed
shaken; as Germanicus who could endure neither the sight nor
the crowing of a cock. There may, perhaps, be some occult
cause in these cases; but, in my opinion, a man might overcome
it if he set about it in time. Education has in this wrought so
effectually upon me (it was not without some endeavor on my
part, I confess) that, beer excepted, my appetite accommodates
itself indifferently to all sorts of diet.

While the body is still supple, one should, therefore, bend
it to all fashions and customs. And provided he can restrain
his appetite and will within limits, let a young man boldly be
rendered fit for all nations and all companies, even for debauchery and excess if need be. Let his training follow the customs. Let him be able to do everything but love to do nothing
but what is good. The philosophers themselves do not justify
Callisthenes for forfeiting the favor of his master, Alexander the
Great, by refusing to keep pace with him in drinking. Let him
laugh, carouse, and debauch with his prince. I would have him,
even in his debauches, excel his companions in endurance and
vigor, and I would not have him refrain from doing evil either
for want of power or knowledge, but for want of will. *There is*

<u>a great difference between not wishing to do evil and not know-
ing how.</u>[21] I thought I was complimenting a Lord, as free from
these excesses as any man in France, by asking him, in the
presence of good company, how many times in his life he had
got drunk in Germany in the interest of the king's affairs. He
took it as it was intended and replied that there had been three
occasions, which he related. I know some who, for want of this
faculty, have been put to great inconvenience in negotiating
with that nation. I have often with great admiration reflected
upon the wonderful constitution of Alcibiades, who could adjust himself so easily to such various fashions without harming
his health; now outdoing the Persian pomp and luxury, and
now the Lacedemonian austerity and frugality; as temperate
in Sparta as voluptuous in Ionia,

> To every form, state, and fortune Aristippus fitted himself.[22]

I would have my pupil be such a one,

> And him shall I admire whom endurance cloaks
> Within its double rags, if he can carry well
> An altered mode of life, and graceful play both parts.[23]

These are my lessons. He who puts them in practice has profited more by them than he who merely knows them. If you see
him, you hear him; if you hear him, you see him.

God forbid, says someone in Plato, that philosophizing be
merely learning a number of things and discussing the arts!
*They pursue this greatest of all arts, the art of living well, in
their lives rather than in their studies.*[24] Leon, prince of the
Phliasians, asking Heraclides Ponticus of what art or science
he made profession; "I know," said he, "neither art nor science,
but I am a philosopher." Someone reproached Diogenes that,
being ignorant, he should dabble in philosophy; "I dabble in

---

[21] Seneca, *Epistles*   [22] Horace, *Epistles*   [23] Horace, *Epistles*
[24] Cicero, *Tusculans*

it," he answered, "all the more appropriately." Hegesias begged him to read some book to him. "You are an amusing person," said he, "you who choose those figs that are true and natural, and not those that are painted, why do you not also choose activities which are natural and real, rather than written ones?"

He will not so much recite his lesson as do it. He will repeat it in his actions. We shall see if there is prudence in his undertakings, if there is goodness and justice in his conduct, if he manifests judgment and grace in his speaking, firmness in his sickness, moderation in his games, temperance in his pleasures, indifference in his tastes, whether flesh or fish, wine or water, order in his domestic economy: *Who considers his instruction not as a show of learning, but as the law of life; who obeys himself and complies with his own principles.*[25] The conduct of our lives is the true mirror of our doctrines.

Zeuxidamus, to one who asked him why the Lacedemonians did not draw up a written account of their rules of valor and give them to their young men to read, replied that it was because they wanted to accustom them to action, not to words. Compare this pupil of ours, after fifteen or sixteen years, with one of those school Latinists who has spent as much time in nothing but learning to speak. The world is nothing but babble; and I never saw that man who did not rather prate too much than speak too little; and yet half of our lives is lost this way. We are kept four or five years in making out the sense of words and tacking them together into clauses; as many more in shaping out of them a long discourse, elaborated in four or five parts; and another five years, at least, in learning succinctly to mix and interweave them after some subtle and intricate manner. Let us leave that to those who make it their trade.

Going one day to Orleans, I met in the plain on this side of Cléry two teachers traveling to Bordeaux, about fifty paces distant from one another. Farther off, behind them, I saw a company with a gentleman at the head of them, the late Mon-

---

[25] Cicero, *Tusculans*

sieur le Comte de la Rochefoucault. One of my men inquired of
the foremost of these teachers who that gentleman was that
came after him. He, not having seen the group that was following him and thinking that my man meant his companion, answered amusingly, "He is not a gentleman; he is a grammarian,
and I am a logician." Now we, on the contrary, do not here seek
to breed a grammarian or a logician, but a gentleman; let us allow them to throw away their time; our business lies elsewhere.
Only let our pupil be well furnished with things, words will
follow but too fast; he will pull them after him if they do not
come voluntarily. I hear some making excuses for being unable
to express themselves, and pretending to have their heads full
of many fine things, but, for want of eloquence, being unable
to produce them; that is a sham. Do you know what I think
they are? They are shadows which come to them of some formless conceptions which they cannot untangle and clarify within,
nor consequently produce outwardly; they do not yet understand themselves. And just observe how they stammer on the
point of giving birth, and you will conclude that their labor is
not in delivery, but in conception, and that they are only lick-
ing into shape this unfinished matter. For my part I hold, and
Socrates makes it a rule, that whoever has in his mind a vivid
and clear idea will express it, whether it be in Bergamask dialect, or by signs if he is dumb:

> The matter seen, the words freely follow.[26]

And as another, as poetically, said in his prose, *when things
have taken possession of the mind, words spread about.*[27] And
this other: *The things themselves carry the words along.*[28] He
knows nothing of ablative, conjunctive, substantive, or grammar, no more than does his lackey or a fishwife of the Petit
Pont; and these yet will give you your fill of talk if you will
hear them, and, perhaps, shall trip as little in the rules of their

---

[26] Horace, *Ars Poetica*   [27] Seneca, *Controversiae*   [28] Cicero, *De Finibus*

language as the best master of arts in France. He knows no rhetoric, nor how in a preface to catch the good will of the gentle reader; neither does he care to know it. Indeed all this fine painting is easily obscured by the luster of a simple and natural truth. These fine flourishes serve only to amuse the vulgar, of themselves incapable of more solid and stouter diet, as Aper does very evidently demonstrate in Tacitus. The ambassadors of Samos, prepared with a long, elegant oration, came to Cleomenes, King of Sparta, to incite him to the war against the tyrant Polycrates. After he had let them have their say, he replied, "As to your beginning and exordium, I remember it not, nor consequently the middle of your speech; and as to your conclusion, I will have nothing to do with it." A very pretty answer this, I think, and a pack of orators well squelched! And what about this other? The Athenians were to choose one of two architects to direct the construction of a large building. The first, more glib, offered his service in a fine prepared speech upon the subject of the job and swayed the judgment of the people in his favor. But the other had his say in three words, "Athenians, what this man has said, I will do."

When Cicero was at the height of his eloquence, many were struck with admiration; but Cato only laughed at it, saying, "We have an amusing Consul." Let it go before or come after, a useful thought, a thing well said, is always in season; if it neither suit well with what went before nor with what follows after, it is good in itself. I am not one of those who think that good rhythm makes a good poem. Let him make a short syllable long if he will, it is no great matter; if the inventions are attractive, if wit and judgment have well performed their functions, I will say: Here's a good poet but a bad versifier.

> Of keen taste, though harsh his verse.[20]

Let his work, says Horace, lose all its seams and measures,

---

[20] Horace, *Satires*

> Remove beat and measure, rearrange the words,
> The first of them put last, the last put first,
> There still you find a poet's scattered parts,[30]

he will not belie himself because of that; the fragments in themselves will be fine. This is what Menander replied when, as the day approached for which he had promised a comedy, he was reproved for not having yet set his hand to it: "It is put together and ready; the only thing left to do is to add the verses to it." Having the parts and the substance arranged in his head, he took little account of the rest. Since Ronsard and Du Bellay have brought recognition to our French poetry, every little dabbler swells his words as high and makes his cadences very nearly as harmonious as they. *More sound than sense.*[31] In the opinion of the common people, there were never so many poets as now; but though they find it no hard matter to reproduce their rhythms, they yet fall very short of the rich descriptions of the one and the delicate inventions of the other.

Yes, but what will our young gentleman do if he be attacked with the sophistic subtlety of some syllogism? "Ham makes a man drink, drink quenches thirst, therefore ham quenches thirst." Why, let him laugh at it, and it is subtler to laugh at it than to answer it. Let him borrow this amusing counter-finesse from Aristippus: "Why should I untie it since, tied as it is, it gives me so much trouble?" When someone was setting before Cleanthes some dialectic subtleties, Chrysippus said to him, "Play these tricks with the children and do not by such fooleries divert the serious thoughts of a man of years." If these ridiculous subtleties, *tortuous and thorny sophisms,*[32] are designed to make him believe an untruth, they are dangerous; but if they remain without effect and only make him laugh, I do not see why a man need be on his guard against them. There are some so foolish as to go a mile out of their way to run after a fine word, *or who do not fit words to things but seek out*

---

[30] Horace, *Satires*   [31] Seneca, *Epistles*   [32] Cicero, *Academica*

extraneous things to which their words may fit.[33] And another says: *There are some who are drawn by the charm of some pleasing word to something that they had not intended to write.*[34] I much more willingly twist a fine saying to sew it onto me than I twist the thread of my thought to go in quest of it. On the contrary, it is for words to serve and to follow; and let Gascon get there if French cannot make it. I would have the substance dominate and so fill the imagination of the listener that he will have no memory of the words. The speech that I love is a simple, natural speech, the same on paper as in the mouth; a succulent and sinewy speech, short and pithy, and not so much delicate and elegant as brisk and vehement:

The speech that strikes the mind will have real flavor,[35]

rather hard than tiresome, remote from affectation; irregular, disconnected, and bold; each bit forming there a body in itself; not like a pedant, a preacher, or a pleader, but rather a soldier-like style, as Suetonius calls that of Julius Caesar; and yet I do not fully see why he calls it so.

I have been ready enough to imitate that careless manner which our young men display in the wearing of their clothes: a cloak worn like a scarf, the hood over one shoulder, a stocking dangling, which seems to express a pride disdainful of those foreign adornments and careless of art; but I find that negligence still better used in the form of speaking. All affectation, particularly in the French gaiety and freedom, is ungraceful in a courtier. And in a monarchy every gentleman ought to be fashioned according to the court model; for which reason we do well to lean a bit towards the natural and the careless.

I do not like a fabric in which the knots and seams are to be seen, just as in a beautiful body one should not be able to count all the bones and veins. *Let the language that is dedicated to truth be artless and simple.*[36] *Who speaks precisely except him*

---

[33] Quintilian [34] Seneca, *Epistles* [35] Epitaph of Lucan [36] Seneca, *Epistles*

who wants to speak affectedly? [37] That eloquence does injustice to the subject matter. And as in our outward dress it is pettiness to wish to distinguish ourselves by some special and unusual fashion, so in language to seek new phrases and to affect words that are not of current use proceeds from a childish and pedantic ambition. Would that I might use only those that are used in the markets of Paris! Aristophanes, the grammarian, was quite wrong when he reprehended Epicurus for the simplicity of his words and the aim of his oratorical art, which was only perspicuity of speech. The imitation of words, by its facility, immediately disperses itself through a whole people; but the imitation of invention and judgment is of a slower progress. The generality of readers, because they have found a like robe, very mistakenly imagine they have a similar body. Strength and sinews are not to be borrowed, though the attire and the cloak may be. Most of those I converse with speak the same language as these Essays; but whether they think like them I cannot say.

The Athenians, says Plato, seek particularly fullness and elegance of speech; the Lacedemonians, brevity; and the Cretans, fertility of thought rather than of language; these last ones are the best. Zeno used to say that he had two sorts of disciples, one that he called φιλολόγους, curious to learn things, and these were his favorites; the other λογοφίλους, that cared only for the language. This is not to say that it is not a fine and good thing to speak well, but it is not so excellent as some would make it; and I am vexed that our whole life should be spent in that. I want first to know well my own language and that of my neighbors with whom I have the most regular dealings. No doubt but Greek and Latin are great and beautiful ornaments, but we buy them too dear. I will here mention a way which has been tried out on me by which they are to be had cheaper than usual. Whoever wants to may make use of it.

My late father, having made all the inquiries that any man

---

[37] Seneca, *Epistles*

can make among men of learning and judgment about a matchless method of education, was by them informed of the trouble with the method then in use; and he was told that the long time we applied to the learning of the languages of the ancients, who had them for nothing, was the sole cause of our inability to attain the grandeur of soul and perfection of knowledge of the ancient Greeks and Romans. I do not believe that to be the only cause. The expedient my father, however, found for this was that, in my infancy, and before I began to speak, he committed me to the care of a German (who since died a famous physician in France), totally ignorant of our language and very well versed in Latin. This man, whom he had sent for specially and whom he paid extremely well, had me continually with him. With him there were also two others, of less learning, to attend me and to relieve him. They conversed with me in no other language but Latin. As to the rest of his household, it was an inviolable rule that neither himself, nor my mother, nor any valet or maid should speak anything in my company but such Latin words as everyone had learned in order to gabble with me. It is wonderful how much profit everyone derived from this. My father and my mother by this means learned enough Latin to understand it and acquired enough proficiency to be able to speak it whenever necessary, as did also those of the servants who were most attached to my service. To be brief, we did *Latin* it at such a rate that it overflowed to all the neighboring villages, where there still remain, having taken root by usage, several Latin appellations of artisans and their tools. As for myself, I was over six years old before I understood either French or Perigordin any more than Arabic. And without art, book, grammar, or precept, without whip and without tears, I had learned to speak just as pure Latin as my master himself, for I could not have contaminated or corrupted it. If, as a test, they wanted to give me a theme after the college fashion, whereas they gave it to others in French, they had to give it to me in bad Latin, to turn it into good. And Nicholas Grouchy, who wrote a book *De*

Comitiis Romanorum, William Guerente, who wrote a commentary upon Aristotle, George Buchanan, that great Scotch Poet, and Marc Antoine Muret, whom both France and Italy acknowledge for the best orator of his time, my private tutors, have often told me that in my childhood I had that language so fluent and ready that they were afraid to accost me. Buchanan, whom I afterwards saw in the service of the late Maréchal de Brissac, told me that he was writing a treatise on education and that he was taking mine as a model, for he was then in charge of that Count de Brissac who afterwards proved so valiant and so brave a gentleman.

As to Greek, of which I have almost no knowledge at all, my father planned to have me taught it artificially, but in a new way, in the form of amusement and exercise. We volleyed our declensions to and fro in the manner of those who by certain table-games learn geometry and arithmetic. For he had been advised to make me relish science and duty by an unforced will and by my own desire, and to educate my mind in all liberty and gentleness without any severity or constraint. He did this so scrupulously that, because some maintain that it troubles the tender brains of children to wake them in the morning with a start and to snatch them suddenly and violently from sleep (wherein they are much more profoundly plunged than we), he caused me to be wakened by the sound of some musical instrument, and I was never without a man for that purpose. This example will suffice to permit you to judge the rest and also to commend both the prudence and affection of so good a father, who is not at all to be blamed if he did not reap any fruit answering to so excellent a cultivation. Of this two things were the cause: first, a sterile and improper soil; for though I was of a strong and healthy constitution and of a gentle and tractable disposition, yet I was withal so sluggish, limp, and drowsy that they could not rouse me from my sloth, not even to get me to play. What I saw, I saw clearly, and under that sluggishness nourished bold ideas and opinions above my age. I had a slow

mind that would go out only as far as it was led, a tardy understanding, a weak imagination, and, above all, an incredible lack
of memory; so that it is no wonder if from all that nothing considerable could be drawn out by him. Secondly, like those who
moved by a frantic desire for a cure submit to all sorts of advice,
that good man, being extremely afraid of failing in a thing he
had so much at heart, let himself finally be carried away by the
common opinion, which always follows the leader like a flight of
cranes, and fell in with custom, having no longer about him those
persons who had given him those first instructions which he had
brought from Italy. And he sent me, when I was about six, to
the Collège de Guienne, at that time very flourishing and the
best in France. And there he took all the care possible, both in
selecting for me capable tutors and in all the other details of my
education, reserving a number of special practices contrary to
school usage. But for all that, it was still school. My Latin immediately grew corrupt, and since then, by dropping the regular
practice of it, I have lost all use of it. And that new plan of
education of mine served me to no other end than to make me
jump at once to the upper classes; for at thirteen when I left
the school, I had completed my course (as they call it), and, in
truth, without any benefit that I can now take into account.

The first taste I had for books came from pleasure I took in
the fables of Ovid's *Metamorphoses*. For when I was about
seven or eight years old, I would steal away from all other pleasures to read them since this was my mother tongue and since
it was the easiest book that I knew and the best suited by its
content to my tender age. For as for the Lancelots of the Lake,
the Amadises, the Huons of Bordeaux, and such trashy books
on which children waste their time, I did not know even their
names, nor do I yet know their substance, so exact was my discipline. This made me more careless in the study of my other
prescribed lessons. Here I happened very opportunely to have
to do with an understanding tutor who knew enough to connive
cleverly at this escapade of mine and others of the same nature.

For by this means I ran straight through Virgil's *Aeneid*, and then Terence, and then Plautus, and some Italian comedies, allured always by the pleasantness of the subject. Had he been so foolish as to break up this activity, I believe I should have brought nothing away from school but a hatred of books, as almost all our noblemen do. He handled himself cleverly in that business. Pretending to see nothing, he whetted my appetite, allowing me to devour these books only on the sly and holding me gently at my job on the regular studies. For the chief qualities my father sought in those whom he put in charge of me were affability of manners and good humor. For my own character had no other vice but listlessness and laziness. The danger was not that I should do ill, but that I should do nothing. Nobody predicted that I should be wicked, but only useless; they foresaw idleness, but no viciousness. I see that it has turned out that way. The complaints that ring in my ears are these: "Idle, cold in the duties of friendship and kinship, and in public duties; too self-centered." The most insulting do not say, "Why has he taken?—why has he not paid?" but "Why does he not cancel (a debt)?—why does he not give?" And I should take it as a favor that men should find me wanting only in such acts of supererogation. But they are unjust to exact from me what I do not owe, far more rigorously than they exact from themselves what they do owe. And in condemning me to it they efface the pleasure of the action and the gratitude that would be due me for it; whereas the good that I do ought to have greater weight coming from me, in view of the fact that I have received none whatsoever. I may the more freely dispose of my fortune the more it is my own. However, if I were a great illustrator of my own actions, perhaps I could well thrust back these reproaches, and I could give some to understand that they are not so much offended that I do not do enough, as that I am able to do a great deal more than I do.

At the same time my mind did not, for all that, fail to have strong stirrings of its own and sure and open-minded judgments

about the objects it understood, and it digested them entirely
by itself. And, among other things, I do really believe that it
would have been totally incapable of submitting to violence and
force.

Shall I put in the account this faculty of my youth: great assurance of countenance and flexibility of voice and gesture in
adapting myself to any part I undertook to act. For before the
usual age,

My twelfth year had scarce laid hold on me,[38]

I played the leading parts in the Latin tragedies of Buchanan,
Guerente, and Muret, that were acted in our Collège de Guienne
with dignity. Here, as in all other parts of his undertaking, An-
dreas Goveanus, our principal, was, without comparison, the
best in France, and I was looked upon as a master-hand. It is
an exercise that I do not at all disapprove of for children of
good family; and I have since seen our princes, after the example of some of the ancients, take part in it in person, honorably
and commendably. It was even permissible for persons of quality to make a profession of it in Greece: *He disclosed the affair
to Aristo, a tragic actor. This man's family and fortune were
honorable; nor were they marred by his art since nothing of
that kind is considered a disgrace by the Greeks.*[39]

For I have always held guilty of injudiciousness those who
condemn these entertainments, and of injustice those who refuse
to admit into our good towns such comedians as are worthy of
it, and begrudge the people these public amusements. Good governments take care to assemble the citizens and bring them together not only for the solemn duties of devotion, but also for
sports and spectacles; sociability and friendship are augmented
by it. And besides, they could not be allowed more orderly pastimes than these performed in the presence of everyone and
right in the sight of the supreme magistrate himself. And I

---

[38] Virgil, *Eclogues*   [39] Livy

should think it reasonable that the magistrate and prince, at their own expense, should sometimes give such pleasure to the people, out of a sort of paternal kindness and affection, and that in populous cities there should be places assigned and arranged for these spectacles (some diversion from worse and more hidden actions).

To return to my subject, there is nothing like alluring the appetite and affection; otherwise you make nothing but asses laden with books. With strokes of the lash we give them their pocketful of learning to keep, which to do any good must not merely be lodged within, but must be espoused.

THAT IT IS FOLLY TO MEASURE TRUTH
AND ERROR BY OUR OWN CAPACITY

It is not perhaps without reason that we attribute facility of belief and of persuasion to simplicity and ignorance, for it seems to me I once learned that belief was like an impression made on our mind, and the softer and less resistant the mind, the easier it was to imprint something on it. *As the scale of the balance must necessarily be depressed when weights are put in it, so the mind must yield to clear demonstrations.*[1] The more a mind is empty and without counterpoise, the more easily it yields under the weight of the first persuasion. This is the reason that children, the common people, women, and sick people are most subject to being led by the ears. But then, on the other hand, it is a foolish presumption to disdain and condemn as false all things that do not seem to us likely; which is an ordinary vice of those who think they have more than ordinary competence. I used to do so once, and if I heard talk of returning spirits, prognostics of future events, enchantments, witchcrafts, or any other story that I could not swallow,

> Dreams and magic terrors, marvels, witches,
> Nocturnal spirits, and Thessalian spells,[2]

I presently pitied the poor people that were taken in by these follies. And I now find that I was at least as much to be pitied myself; not that experience has since shown me anything beyond my first beliefs; and it, moreover, has not resulted from a lack of curiosity; but reason has instructed me that thus reso-

---

[1] Cicero, *Academica*   [2] Horace, *Epistles*

lutely to condemn anything as false and impossible is to assume the privilege of knowing the bounds and limits of God's will and of the power of our mother Nature; and that there is no more notable folly in the world than to reduce these things to the measure of our capacity and competence. If we give the names of prodigy and miracle to everything our reason cannot reach, how many such are continually presented before our eyes! Let us but consider through what clouds, how gropingly, we are led to the knowledge of most of the things that are in our very hands; assuredly we shall find that it is rather familiarity than knowledge that takes away their strangeness,

> So very sated with the act of seeing, none
> Deigns now look on heaven's gleaming shrines,[3]

and that if those things were presented to us for the first time, we should think them as incredible, or more so, than any others,

> If mankind saw these things for the first time,
> Presented suddenly and unforeseen,
> They could not name a thing more wonderful,
> Or ancients would have less dared to believe.[4]

He that had never seen a river imagined the first he met with to be the sea. And the largest things that have fallen within our knowledge we judge to be the utmost that nature can do in that kind.

> And any river seems immense to him
> Who greater stream has never seen; just so
> A tree, a man seem huge. The biggest things
> Of each class he has seen, he fancies vast.[5]

The mind becomes accustomed to things by the habitual sight of them, so that it neither marvels at nor inquires into the reasons for the things that it constantly sees.[6] The novelty rather

[3] Lucretius　　[4] Lucretius　　[5] Lucretius　　[6] Cicero, *De Natura Deorum*

than the greatness of things incites us to inquire into their causes.

We must judge with more reverence, and with greater acknowledgment of our own ignorance and infirmity, the infinite power of nature. How many things of little likelihood there are, testified by trustworthy people, which if we cannot persuade ourselves to believe, we ought at least to leave in suspense! For to condemn them as impossible is by a rash presumption to pretend to know the utmost bounds of possibility. Did we rightly understand the difference between the impossible and the unusual, and between what is contrary to the order and course of nature and what is contrary to the common opinion of men, not believing rashly nor disbelieving easily, we should observe the rule of "Nothing too much," enjoined by Chilo. When we find in Froissart that the Count de Foix knew, in Béarn, the defeat of King John of Castile at Juberoth, the next day after it happened, and the means which he alleges for his knowledge of that, we can laugh at it; and also at what our annals report, that Pope Honorius, the same day that King Philip Augustus died at Mantes, performed his public obsequies and commanded them to be performed throughout Italy. For the authority of these witnesses has, perhaps, not enough standing to keep us in check. But what if Plutarch, besides several examples that he cites from antiquity, tells us he knows, with certain knowledge, that in the time of Domitian the news of the battle lost by Antony in Germany was published at Rome, many days' journey from there, and dispersed throughout the whole world the same day it was lost; and if Caesar holds that it has often happened that the report has preceded the event, shall we say that these simple people have let themselves be deceived like the common run of men for not being so clear-sighted as we? Is there anything more delicate, more clear, more alert than Pliny's judgment when he is pleased to set it to work, or anything more remote from inanity? Setting aside the excellence of his learning, of which I make less account, in which of these qualities do we excel him? Yet there is no schoolboy, however small, that does not convict him of lying and that does not want to give him a lesson on the progress of the works of nature.

When we read in Bouchet the miracles from Saint Hilary's relics, let it pass; his authority is not great enough to take away from us the liberty of contradicting him. But to condemn in one sweep all such stories seems to me a singular impudence. The great Saint Augustine testifies that he saw a blind child recover sight upon the relics of Saint Gervaise and Saint Protasius at Milan; a woman at Carthage cured of a cancer by the sign of the cross made upon her by a woman newly baptized; Hesperius, a familiar friend of his, drive away the spirits that infested his house with a little earth from the sepulchre of our Lord, and this earth being transported thence into the church, a paralytic suddenly cured by it; a woman in a procession, having touched Saint Stephen's shrine with a bouquet and rubbed her eyes with this bouquet, recover her sight lost long before; and several other miracles of which he professes himself to have been an eyewitness. Of what shall we accuse both him and the two holy bishops Aurelius and Maximinus whom he calls upon as his witnesses? Shall it be of ignorance, simplicity, and credulity, or of knavery and imposture? Is any man in our age so impudent as to think himself comparable to them either in virtue and piety, or in learning, judgment, and ability? *Who, though they brought forward no proof, would crush me by their very authority.*[7]

It is a presumption of great danger and consequence, besides the absurd temerity it implies, to scorn what we do not comprehend. For after, according to your fine understanding, you have established the limits of truth and error, and it turns out that by necessity you have to believe things even stranger than those you deny, you are from that moment on obliged to abandon them. Now what seems to me to bring so much disorder into our consciences, in the commotions we are now in concerning religion, is the partial giving up of their beliefs by

---

[7] Cicero, *Tusculans*

Catholics. They fancy they are acting like very moderate and prudent men when they yield to their adversaries some of the articles in question. But, besides the fact that they do not discern what advantage it is to the man charging you when you begin to give ground and to retire, and how much this encourages him to pursue his point, these articles which they select as the most trivial are sometimes of very great importance. We must either wholly submit to the authority of our ecclesiastical government or completely dispense with it. It is not for us to determine what position of obedience we owe to it. Moreover I can say this for having tried it, having in former times made use of this freedom of personal choice and selection, considering with negligence certain points in the observances of our Church which seemed in appearance very pointless or very strange; coming to mention them to learned men, I found that those things have a massive and very solid foundation and that nothing but stupidity and ignorance makes us receive them with less reverence than the rest. Why do we not recall how much contradiction we perceive even in our own judgment, how many things were yesterday articles of faith to us that today are fables to us? Vainglory and curiosity are the two scourges of our soul. The latter prompts us to thrust our noses into everything, and the former forbids us to leave anything unresolved and undecided.

✓ OF FRIENDSHIP

OBSERVING the way a painter I employ went about his work, I had a mind to imitate him. He chooses the best place, the middle of each wall, wherein to place a picture, elaborated with his utmost art, and the empty space all about it he fills with grotesques, which are fantastic paintings that have no other charm than their variety and strangeness. And, in truth, what are these things I scribble but grotesques and monstrous bodies pieced together of sundry members, without any definite shape, having no order, coherence, or proportion, except by accident?

> A lovely woman, up above, tails off into a fish.[1]

I go along all right with my painter to this second point, but I fall short of him in the first and better part; for my talent does not go far enough for me to dare to undertake a rich tableau, polished and formed according to art. I have taken it into my head to borrow one from Etienne de la Boétie which will do ~~Friend~~ honor to all the rest of this work. It is a discourse to which he gave the name *La Servitude Volontaire* (*Voluntary Servitude*); but those who did not know this have since very fitly rebaptized it *Le Contre Un* (*Against One Man*). He wrote it in his early youth by way of essay in honor of liberty against tyrants. It has been circulating for a long time in the hands of men of understanding, not without very great and well-merited commendation, for it is a noble thing and as full as can be. Yet it is far short of being the best he could do; and if in that more mature age wherein I knew him he had taken on a project, like

[1] Horace, *Ars Poetica*

this of mine, of putting his thoughts in writing, we should see a great many rare things such as would bring us very near to the glory of antiquity; for in natural gifts, especially, I know no man comparable to him. But he has left nothing behind him save this treatise (and that by chance, and I believe he never saw it after it went out of his hands), and some observations upon that Edict of January, made famous by our civil wars, which will, perhaps, yet find their place elsewhere. These were all I could recover of what he left (I, to whom, with such loving recommendation, with death upon his lips, he by his last will bequeathed his library and papers) except for the little volume of his works which I have had published. And the particular obligation I have to this treatise is that it was the means of our first becoming acquainted. For it was shown to me long before I had seen him and gave me the first knowledge of his name, thus getting under way that friendship which we nurtured together as long as God willed, so perfect and so entire that certainly the like is hardly to be found in story, and among the men of this age there is no trace of any such thing in practice. So many concurrents are needed to build it up that it is much if fortune bring it to pass once in three centuries.

There is nothing to which Nature seems so much to have inclined us as to society. And Aristotle says that good legislators have had more care for friendship than for justice. Now the supreme point in the perfection of society is this. For generally all relations that pleasure or profit, public or private interest create and nourish are so much the less beautiful and noble, and so much the less friendships, as they mix into friendship another cause and intent and product than friendship itself. Neither do the four ancient kinds—natural, social, hospitable, and amorous—either separately or jointly, conform to true friendship.

That of children for fathers is rather respect. Friendship is nourished by communication, which cannot exist between them because of their too great inequality, and would, perhaps, be detrimental to the duties of nature. For neither can all the secret thoughts of fathers be communicated to children, lest it beget an indecent familiarity between them, nor could the admonitions and corrections which are one of the principal offices of friendship be administered by children to fathers. There have been nations where it was the custom for children to kill their fathers, and others where the fathers killed their children, to prevent their being sometimes an impediment to one another; and by nature the expectation of the one depends upon the destruction of the other. There have been great philosophers who disdained this tie of nature, as Aristippus for one, who, being pressed about the affection he owed to his children for having come out of him, began to spit, saying that had come out of him just as much, and that we also bred worms and lice. And that other, whom Plutarch endeavored to reconcile with his brother, "I make no greater account of him," said he, "for having come out of the same hole." This name of brother is, indeed, a beautiful name and full of affection, and for that reason we formed our alliance on it. But the complication of property, the division of estates, and the fact that the wealth of the one may be the impoverishment of the other, wonderfully softens and loosens that solder of brotherhood. And brothers having to direct the progress of their advancement along the same path and at the same pace, they must of necessity often jostle and clash with one another. Besides why should the harmony and kinship which begets these true and perfect friendships be found in these relations? The father and the son may be of very different temperaments, and brothers also. He is my son, he is my relative, but he is a weird person, a rascal, or a fool. And, moreover, the more these are friendships that the law and natural obligation impose upon us, so much less is there in them of our own choice and free will. And our free will has no creation more properly its own than affection and friendship. Not that I have not experienced in that respect all that can be had in it, having had the best father that ever was, and the most indulgent, even in his extreme old age, and being of a family for many generations famous and exemplary in this matter of brotherly concord,

> And known myself
> For fatherly loving-kindness to my brothers.[2]

We cannot compare with it the love we bear to women, though this be an act of our own choice, nor can we put it in this class. Its fire, I confess,

> Nor is that goddess unaware of us,
> Who blends sweet bitterness with all her cares,[3]

is more active, more burning, and more intense. But it is a reckless and fickle flame, wavering and inconstant, a fever flame, subject to paroxysms and abatements, that has hold only on one corner of us. In friendship, it is a general and universal warmth, but temperate and even, a constant and steady heat, all gentleness and smoothness, without poignancy or roughness. What is more, in love there is nothing but a frantic desire for that which flies from us:

> Just as the hunter hard pursues the hare
> Through chill and heat, o'er mountain and o'er strand;
> Nor more esteems it once he sees it caught,
> And only hastens after that which flees.[4]

As soon as it enters into the terms of friendship, that is to say, into an agreement of wills, it grows faint and languid. Enjoyment destroys it, as having only a fleshly end subject to satiety. Friendship, on the contrary, is enjoyed proportionally as it is desired, and it is bred, nourished, and increased only by enjoyment, as being spiritual, and the soul growing refined by use. Under this perfect friendship those fleeting affections in bygone

---

[2] Horace, *Odes*   [3] Catullus   [4] Ariosto, *Orlando Furioso*

days found a place in me, to say nothing of him, who confesses it but too much in his verses. So these two passions came to know each other in me, but never to be compared with one another; the first maintaining its course in lofty and proud flight and disdainfully watching the other flying at a far humbler pitch below.

As to marriage, besides that it is a bargain to which only the entrance is free (the continuance in it being forced and compelled, having another dependence than that of our own will) and a bargain commonly made for other ends, there arise in it a thousand foreign snarls to unravel, enough to break the thread and to trouble the course of a lively affection; whereas friendship has no manner of business or traffic with anything but itself. Moreover, to say truth, the ordinary talent of women is not such as is sufficient to maintain that converse and fellowship which is the nurse of this sacred tie; nor do they appear to be endued with firmness of mind to endure the strain of so hard and durable a knot. And certainly, but for that, there could be such a free and voluntary familiarity formed where not only the souls might have this complete enjoyment, but the bodies also might share in the alliance, and the whole man be engaged in it, the friendship would certainly be more full and perfect. But this sex in no instance has ever yet been able to reach it, and by the common agreement of the ancient schools is excluded from it.

And that other Grecian license is justly abhorred by our morality. Moreover by there being, according to their practice, so necessary a disparity of age and difference of functions between the lovers, this answered as little to the perfect union and harmony that we here require: *For what is this love of friendship? Why does no one love either an ugly youth or a handsome old man?"* [5] For even the picture that the Academy presents of it will not, I believe, contradict me when I say this about it: that the first fury inspired by the son of Venus in the heart of

[5] Cicero, *Tusculans*

the lover at the sight of the bloom of tender youth, to which
they allow all the insolent and passionate efforts that an immoderate ardor can produce, was simply founded upon an external beauty, the false image of corporeal generation. For it
could not be grounded in the spirit, of which the indications, as
yet, lay concealed, which was only in its birth and before the
age of budding. If this fury seized upon a base heart, the means
of his courtship were rich presents, favor in advancement to dignities, and other such base stuff which they condemn. If it fell
on a more noble heart, the medium was likewise noble: philosophical instructions, precepts to revere religion, to obey the
laws, to die for the good of one's country; examples of valor,
wisdom, and justice; the lover studying to render himself acceptable by the grace and beauty of his soul, that of his body
being long since faded, and hoping by this mental society to
establish a more firm and lasting contract. When this courtship
came to its effect in due season (for that which they do not require in the lover, namely, leisure and discretion in his pursuit,
they strictly require in the person loved, inasmuch as he had to
judge of an internal beauty, difficult of knowledge and hidden
from discovery), there was born in the person loved the desire
of a spiritual conception by the mediation of a spiritual beauty.
This was here the principal part, corporeal beauty being an
accidental and secondary part, just the opposite of the lover.
For this reason they prefer the person beloved, maintaining that
the gods also prefer him, and very much blame the poet Aeschy-
lus for having in the love of Achilles and Patroclus given the
lover's part to Achilles, who was in the first beardless bloom of
his youth and the handsomest of all the Greeks. After this general community of interests is formed, the sovereign and most
worthy part of it exercising its functions and predominating,
they say that from it great utility was derived both personally
and to the public, that it formed the strength of countries which
took up the practice of it, and that it was the chief security of
liberty and justice: witness the salutary loves of Harmodius and

Aristogeiton. Therefore they call it sacred and divine. And they conceived that nothing but the violence of tyrants and the baseness of the common people were inimical to it. In short, all that can be said in favor of the Academy is that it was a love which ended in friendship; which well enough agrees with the Stoic definition of love: *Love is an effort to form a friendship inspired by beauty.*[6]

I return to my description of a more equitable and equal kind of friendship: *Only those are to be judged friendships in which the characters with age have been strengthened and matured.*[7]

For the rest, what we commonly call friends and friendships are nothing but acquaintances and familiarities, contracted either by some accident or convenience, by means of which our souls are held together. In the friendship I speak of, they mingle and merge together with so complete a blending that they efface and can no longer find the seam that joined them. If anyone should press me to say why I loved him, I feel that this cannot be expressed except by answering: "Because it was he, because it was I."

There is, beyond all my reasoning and beyond what I say of it in particular, I know not what inexplicable and fateful power that brought on this union. We sought one another before we met through reports we heard of one another, which had more effect upon our affections than in reason reports should do; I think it was by some decree of heaven. We embraced each other by our names. And at our first meeting, which was by chance at a great feast and gathering in the city, we found ourselves so taken with each other, so well acquainted, so bound together, that thenceforward nothing was so near to us as one another. He wrote an excellent Latin satire, which is published, wherein he excuses and explains the precipitance of our intimacy, so suddenly come to its perfection. Having so short a time to last, and having begun so late, for we were both full-grown men, and he some years the older, it could not lose time and conform to the

---

[6] Cicero, *Tusculans*   [7] Cicero, *De Amicitia*

example of those slow and regular friendships that require so many precautions of a long preliminary association. This has no other model than itself and can be compared only with itself. It is no one particular consideration, nor two, nor three, nor four, nor a thousand. It is I know not what quintessence of all this mixture which, having seized my whole will, led it to plunge and lose itself in his; which having seized his whole will, led it, with equal hunger and emulation, to plunge and lose itself in mine. I may truly say lose since we reserved for ourselves nothing that was our own, nor that was either his or mine.

When Laelius in the presence of the Roman consuls who, after they had condemned Tiberius Gracchus, prosecuted all those who had been in his confidence, came to ask Caius Blossius, who was his chief friend, how much he would have been willing to do for him, he answered, "Everything." "What, everything?" said Laelius. "And what if he had commanded you to fire our temples?" "He would never have commanded me to do that," replied Blossius. "But what if he had?" added Laelius. "I would have obeyed him," he replied. If he was so perfect a friend to Gracchus as the histories report him to have been, there was no need for him to offend the consuls by this last bold confession, and he should not have given up the assurance he had of Gracchus' disposition. Still, those who accuse this answer as seditious do not well understand the mystery, and they do not suppose, as was the fact, that he had Gracchus' will up his sleeve, both by power over him and by knowledge of him. They were friends more than citizens, and friends to one another more than either friends or enemies to their country, or than friends to ambition and disturbance. Having absolutely given up themselves to one another, each held absolutely the reins of the other's inclination, and assuming this team to be guided by the power and direction of reason (as, moreover, it is quite impossible to harness it without that), Blossius' answer is such as it ought to have been. If their actions pulled apart, they were neither, according to my measure, friends to one another nor friends to themselves. Besides this answer carries no better sound than mine would do to one that should question me in this fashion: "If your will should command you to kill your daughter, would you do it?" And I should answer that I would. For that bears no witness of any consent to do so because I have no doubt at all of my own will, and just as little of that of such a friend. It is not in the power of all the arguments in the world to dislodge me from the certainty I have of the intentions and judgments of my friend. No action of his, whatever face it might bear, could be presented to me of which I could not immediately find out the moving cause. Our souls pulled so unitedly together, they considered each other with so ardent an affection and with a like affection laid themselves open to each other to the very depths of our hearts, that I not only knew his as well as my own, but should certainly have trusted myself more willingly to him than to myself.

Let no one, therefore, rank those other common friendships with such a one as this. I have had as much knowledge of them as another, and of the most perfect of their kind; but I do not advise anyone to confuse the rules of the one and the other; for they would find themselves deceived. In those other friendships you must walk bridle in hand, with prudence and circumspection, the knot is not so well tied that a man may not have some reason to mistrust it. "Love him," said Chilo, "as if you were one day to hate him; and hate him as if you were to love him." This precept, which is so abominable in this sovereign and perfect friendship, is sound in the practice of common and customary ones, in regard to which we must employ the saying that Aristotle so frequently used: "O my friends, there is no friend."

In this noble relationship, services and benefits, by which other friendships are nurtured, do not deserve even to be taken into account; the reason for it is this full blending of our wills. For just as the friendship I have for myself receives no increase from the aid I give myself in time of need, whatever the Stoics say, and as I do not feel grateful to myself for any service I do myself, so the union of such friends, being really perfect, makes them lose the sense of such duties and makes them loathe and banish from between them these words implying separation and distinction: benefit, obligation, gratitude, entreaty, thanks, and the like. All things—wills, thoughts, opinions, goods, wives, children, honor, and life—being in effect common between them, and their fellowship being no other than that of one soul in two bodies according to the very apt definition of Aristotle, they can neither lend nor give anything to one another. This is the reason why the lawgivers, to honor marriage with some imaginary resemblance to this divine alliance, forbid all gifts between man and wife, wishing to imply by it that all should belong to each of them, and that they have nothing to divide and share between them. If, in the friendship of which I speak, one could give to the other, the receiver of the benefit would be the man that obliged his friend. For each of them above all things seeking to be useful to the other, he that provides the matter and the occasion is the generous man, in giving his friend the satisfaction of doing for him that which he most desires. When the philosopher Diogenes lacked money, he used to say that he asked it back of his friends, not that he asked for it. And to show how this is done in practice, I will relate an ancient and singular example.

Eudamidas, a Corinthian, had two friends, Charixenus, a Sycionian, and Aretheus, a Corinthian. When he approached death, being poor, and his two friends being rich, he made his will after this manner: "I bequeath to Aretheus the maintenance of my mother, to support and provide for her in her old age; to Charixenus I bequeath the care of marrying my daughter, and to give her the biggest dowry he can; and in case one of these should chance to die, I substitute the survivor in his place." They who first saw this will made fun of it; but his heirs, having been made acquainted with it, accepted it with very great satisfaction. And one of them, Charixenus, dying five days after, and the substitution falling to Aretheus, he sup-

ported the mother with very great care, and of five talents he
had he gave two and a half to his only daughter for her marriage and two and a half for the marriage of the daughter of
Eudamidas, and the same day solemnized both their nuptials.

This example is quite complete except for one objection,
namely, the number of friends. For this perfect friendship I
speak of is indivisible; each one gives himself so entirely to his
friend that he has nothing left to distribute to others; on the
contrary, he is sorry that he is not double, or quadruple, and
that he has not several souls and several wills to confer them
all upon this one object. Common friendships can be split up;
one may love beauty in this one, good humor in this other, liberality in another, paternal affection in that one, fraternal love
in this other, and so on; but this friendship that possesses the
soul and rules it with absolute sovereignty cannot possibly be
double. If two at the same time should call to you for succor,
to which of them would you run? Should they require of you
contrary services, how would you go about it? Should one commit to your silence a thing that would be useful for the other to
know, how would you disengage yourself? The friendship that
is single and dominant dissolves all other obligations. The secret I have sworn not to reveal to any other I may without
perjury communicate to him who is not another, he is myself.
It is miracle enough for a man to double himself, and those
that talk of tripling themselves do not know the height of it.
Nothing is superlative that has its like. And he who shall suppose that of two men I love one as much as the other, and that
they love one another and me as much as I love them, multiplies into a society that which is the most single and unified of
all things, of which even a single example is the rarest thing in
the world to find.

The remaining part of this story goes very well with what I
was saying, for Eudamidas, as a kindness and favor, makes the
donation to his friends of employing them for his needs. He
leaves them heirs to this liberality of his which consists in giv-

ing them the opportunity of conferring a benefit upon him. And, doubtless, the force of friendship is much more richly apparent in this act of his than in that of Aretheus. In short, these are actions beyond the imagination of anyone who had no experience of them, and which make me wonderfully honor the answer of that young soldier to Cyrus, who asked him how much he would take for a horse with which he had just won the prize in a race, and whether he would exchange him for a kingdom? "No, truly, Sire, but I would give him with all my heart to gain a friend, could I find a man worthy of such an alliance." He did not put it badly in saying, *could* I find; for it is easy to find men suitable for a superficial acquaintance. But in this, where a man deals from the very bottom of his heart, without any manner of reservation, certainly it is necessary that all the springs be perfectly clean and true.

In associations that hold but by one end, we have only to provide against the imperfections that particularly concern that end. It can be of no importance to me of what religion my physician or my lawyer is. This consideration has nothing in common with the functions of the friendship they owe me. And in the domestic relations which my servants have with me, I behave in a similar way. I scarcely inquire of a lackey whether he is chaste; I try to learn whether he is diligent. And I am not so much afraid of a gambling muleteer as of a stupid one, nor of a profane cook as of an incompetent one. I do not take upon me to say what should be done in the world—enough others do that—but what I do in it.

> Such is my practice: do as you deem best.[8]

With the familiarity of the table I associate pleasantries, not gravity; in bed, beauty before goodness; in discussion, competence, even without probity. Likewise in other things.

Just as he that was found astride upon a stick, playing with

St. Louis IX ?

---

[8] Terence, *Heautontimoroumenos*

his children, entreated the person who surprised him at it to say nothing of it till he himself came to be a father, supposing that the fondness that would then be born in his soul would render him a just judge of such an action, so I should like to speak to such as have had experience of what I say. But knowing how remote a thing such a friendship is from the common practice, and how rare it is, I do not expect to find any good judge of it. For even the discourses left us by antiquity upon this subject seem to me weak in comparison with the feeling I have of it. And in this particular the facts surpass even the precepts of philosophy:

> Nothing would I,
> While sound of mind, match with a joyous friend.[9]

Menander of old declared that man happy who had been able to meet with but the shadow of a friend. Certainly he had good reason to say so, especially if he spoke from experience. For, in truth, if I compare all the rest of my life,—though, thanks be to God, I have spent it pleasantly, comfortably, and, the loss of such a friend excepted, free from any grievous affliction, and in great tranquillity of mind, having been content with my natural and original advantages without seeking others—if I compare it all, I say, with the four years that were granted to me to enjoy the sweet company and society of that man, it is nothing but smoke, nothing but a dark and tedious night. From the day that I lost him,

> Which ever bitter will remain for me,
> And e'er revered, for so, Gods, did you will.[10]

I have only dragged on listlessly; and the very pleasures that present themselves to me, instead of consoling me, redouble my grief for his loss. We went halves in everything; it seems to me that I am robbing him of his part.

---

[9] Horace, *Satires*   [10] Virgil, *Aeneid*

> Nor right have I to pleasure here, I vowed,
> As long as he who shared my life is gone.[11]

I was already so shaped and accustomed to being double everywhere that it seems to me that now I no more than half exist.

> Since an untimely blow has borne away
> Part of my soul, why do I linger on,
> The other part, neither as dear, nor left
> Behind intact? That very day led both
> Of us to ruin.[12]

There is no action or thought wherein I do not miss him as, indeed, he would have missed me. For as he surpassed me infinitely in every other accomplishment and virtue, so he also did in the duty of friendship.

> Why should we stop the flowing tear?
> Why blush to weep for one so dear?[13]

> Oh, brother, wretched me deprived of you!
> With you our every joy has passed away
> Which, living, nourished was by your sweet love;
> You, brother, dying crushed my happiness.
> Our soul lies sepulchered as one with yours;
> And with your death I drove from all my mind
> My studies and my spirit's whole delight.
> Brother, more dear than life, shall I no more
> Behold you after this? Assuredly
> I'll love you, brother dear, eternally.[14]

But let us listen a bit to this lad of sixteen.

Because I have found that this work has since been brought out,[15] and with evil intent, by those who seek to disturb and change the state of our government, without minding whether they will improve it, and because they have mixed up this writ-

---

[11] Terence, *Heautontimoroumenos*   [12] Horace, *Odes*   [13] Horace, *Odes*
[14] Catullus   [15] Published by Huguenots

ing of his with some of their own grist, I have changed my mind about putting it in here. And in order that the memory of the author may not suffer with those who could not be closely acquainted with his opinions and actions, I here give them to understand that it was written by him in his boyhood, and by way of exercise only, as a common theme battered about in a thousand places in books. I have no doubt that he believed what he wrote, for he was so conscientious as not to lie even in jest. And I know, moreover, that, if he had had the choice, he would rather have been born at Venice than at Sarlac, and with reason. But he had another maxim sovereignly imprinted in his soul, very religiously to obey and submit to the laws under which he was born. There never was a better citizen, nor one more devoted to his country's peace, nor a greater enemy to all the commotions and innovations of his time. He would much rather have employed his talent in extinguishing them than in supplying them with matter that would stir them up more. He had a mind shaped to the pattern of other ages than this. Now in exchange for this serious work, I shall substitute another, gayer and livelier, produced in the same period of his life.[16]

---

[16] Montaigne placed at the end of the following essay (XXIX) twenty-nine sonnets by La Boétie.

OF CANNIBALS

When King Pyrrhus passed over into Italy, having observed the formation of the army the Romans sent out to meet him, he said, "I do not know what kind of barbarians these are" (for so the Greeks called all foreign nations), "but the disposition of this army that I see is not at all barbarous." As much said the Greeks of the army which Flaminius brought into their country, and likewise Philip, viewing from a knoll the order and distribution of the Roman camp in his kingdom under Publius Sulpicius Galba, spoke to the same effect. That is how we should take care not to cling to common opinions, and how we should judge by the way of reason, and not by common report.

I had with me for a long time a man that had lived ten or twelve years in that other world which has been discovered in our century, in the place where Villegaignon landed, which he called Antarctic France.[1] This discovery of so vast a country seems worthy of consideration. I do not know if I can be sure that in the future there may not be another such discovery made, so many greater men than we having been deceived in this. I am afraid our eyes are bigger than our bellies and that we have more curiosity than capacity. We grasp at all, but catch nothing but wind.

Plato brings in Solon, relating that he had heard from the priests of Saïs in Egypt that of old, before the Deluge, there was a great island called Atlantis, directly at the mouth of the Strait of Gibraltar, which contained more countries than Africa and Asia put together, and that the kings of that country, who not only possessed that isle, but extended their dominion so far

---

[1] Brazil, where he arrived in 1557

74

into the continent that they held the breadth of Africa as far as
Egypt and the length of Europe as far as Tuscany, attempted
to encroach upon Asia and to subjugate all the nations that bor-
der upon the Mediterranean Sea, as far as the gulf of the Black
Sea; and for this purpose overran all Spain, Gaul, Italy, as far
as Greece, where the Athenians stopped them; but that some
time after, both the Athenians, and they, and their island were
swallowed by the Flood.

It is very likely that this violent inundation of water made
amazing alterations in the habitations of the earth, as it is said
that the sea then cut off Sicily from Italy,

> These places, shaken once by a vast quake,
> Were split asunder, when they both had been
> Before one single land;[2]

Cyprus from Syria, the isle of Euboea from the mainland of
Boeotia; and elsewhere united lands that were separate by filling up the channel between them with sand and mud,

> A marsh long barren, only fit for boats,
> Feeds near-by towns, and feels the heavy plow.[3]

But there is not much likelihood that this isle was this new
world that we have just discovered; for it almost touched upon
Spain, and it would be an incredible effect of an inundation to
have thrust it far off as it is, more than twelve hundred leagues;
besides, our modern voyages have already almost discovered it
to be no island, but mainland joined to the East Indies on one
side and to the lands under the two poles elsewhere; or, if it
is separated from them, it is by so narrow a strait and interval
that it does not deserve the name of an island for that.

It seems that in these great bodies there are two sorts of
motions, the one natural, and the other feverish, as there are
in ours. When I consider the inroads that my river, the Dor-

---

[2] Virgil, *Aeneid*   [3] Horace, *Ars Poetica*

dogne, is making in my lifetime into the right bank in its descent, and that in twenty years it has gained so much and made away with the foundations of so many houses, I clearly see that it is an extraordinary disturbance; for, had it always gone on at this rate, or were hereafter to do it, the aspect of the world would be totally changed. But rivers are subject to changes, sometimes overflowing on one side and sometimes on the other, and sometimes keeping the channel. I do not speak of sudden inundations, the causes of which we understand. In Médoc, by the seashore, the Sieur d'Arsac, my brother, sees an estate of his buried before his eyes under the sands which the sea vomits before it; the tops of some houses are yet to be seen; his rents and domains have been converted into very thin pasturage. The inhabitants say that for some time the sea has been pushing so strongly towards them that they have lost four leagues of land. These sands are her harbingers; and we see great dunes of moving sand that march half a league before her and take possession of the land.

The other testimony from antiquity to which some would attach this discovery of the new world is in Aristotle; at least if that little book *Of Unheard-of Miracles* be his. He there relates that certain Carthaginians, having crossed the Atlantic sea outside of the Straits of Gibraltar and sailed a very long time, discovered at last a great and fruitful island, all covered over with woods and watered by broad and deep rivers, far remote from any continent, and that they, and others after them, allured by the goodness and fertility of the soil, went thither with their wives and children and began to dwell there. The lords of Carthage, perceiving their country little by little becoming depopulated, issued an express prohibition, that no one, upon pain of death, was any longer to travel there; and they drove out the new inhabitants, fearing, it is said, lest in the course of time they should so multiply as to supplant themselves and ruin their state. This relation of Aristotle does no more agree with our new-found lands than the other.

This man that I had was a plain ignorant fellow, which is a condition fit to bear true witness; for your sharp sort of men are much more curious in their observations and notice a great deal more, but they gloss them; and to give the greater weight to their interpretation and make it convincing, they cannot forbear to alter the story a little. They never represent things to you simply as they are, they slant them and mask them according to the aspect they saw in them; and to give authority to their judgment and to attract you to it, they are willing to contribute something there to the matter, lengthening it and amplifying it. We should have a man either of irreproachable veracity, or so simple that he has not wherewithal to contrive and to give a color of truth to false tales, and who has not espoused any cause. Mine was such a one; and, besides that, he has divers times brought me several seamen and merchants whom he had known on that voyage. I do, therefore, content myself with his information without inquiring what the cosmographers say about it.

We need topographers to make a detailed account for us of the places where they have been. But by having this advantage over us of having seen the Holy Land, they want to have the privilege of telling us stories of new things from all the rest of the world. I would have everyone write what he knows, and as much as he knows, not in this only, but in all other subjects; for such a person may have some particular knowledge and experience of the nature of a river or of a spring, who as to other things knows no more than what everybody does. Yet to make this little fragment circulate, he will undertake to write the whole body of physics. From this vice arise many great disadvantages.

Now to return to my subject, I find that there is nothing barbarous and savage in this nation according to what I have been told, except that everyone gives the title of barbarism to everything that is not according to his usage; as, indeed, we have no other criterion of truth and reason than the example and pat-

tern of the opinions and customs of the country wherein we
live. There is always the perfect religion, there the perfect government, there the perfect and accomplished usage in all things.
They are savages in the same way that we say fruits are wild,
which nature produces of herself and by her ordinary course;
whereas, in truth, we ought rather to call those wild whose natures we have changed by our artifice and diverted from the
common order. In the former, the genuine, most useful, and
natural virtues and properties are vigorous and active, which
we have degenerated in the latter, and we have only adapted
them to the pleasure of our corrupted palate. And yet, for all
this, the flavor and delicacy found in various uncultivated
fruits of those countries are excellent to our taste, worthy rivals
of ours. It is not reasonable that art should gain the point of
honor over our great and powerful mother, Nature. We have
so loaded the beauty and richness of her works with her inventions that we have entirely smothered her. Yet wherever
she shines in her own purity, she marvelously disgraces our
vain and frivolous undertakings,

> And ivy comes up better by itself;
> More fair in lonely caves, arbutus springs;
> More sweetly sing the birds from lack of art.[4]

Our utmost endeavors cannot succeed even in imitating the
nest of the smallest bird, its contexture, its beauty and its convenience: not so much as the web of a wretched spider. All
things, says Plato, are produced by nature, or by chance, or by
art; the greatest and most beautiful by one or the other of the
first two, the least and most imperfect by the last.

These nations then seem to me to be barbarous so far as having received very little fashioning from the human mind and as
being still very close to their original simplicity. The laws of
Nature govern them still, very little vitiated by ours; but they
are in such purity that I am sometimes troubled by the fact

---

[4] Propertius

that we were not acquainted with these people earlier when there were men who would have been better able to judge of them than we are. I am sorry that Lycurgus and Plato had no knowledge of them; for it seems to me that what we now see by experience in those nations does not only surpass all the images with which the poets have adorned the golden age and all their inventions in imagining a happy state of man, but also the conception and even the desire of philosophy. They were incapable of imagining so pure and so simple an innocence as we by experience see it; nor were they capable of believing that human society can be maintained with so little human artifice and solder. I should say to Plato that it is a nation wherein there is no manner of traffic, no knowledge of letters, no science of numbers, no name of magistrate or of political superiority; no use of servitude, riches or poverty; no contracts, no successions, no dividing of properties, no employments, except those of leisure; no respect of kindred, except for the common bond; no clothing, no agriculture, no metal, no use of wheat or wine. The very words that signify lying, treachery, dissimulation, avarice, envy, detraction, and pardon were never heard of. How far distant from this perfection would he find the republic he imagined: *Men fresh from the hands of the gods.* [5]

These were the manners nature first bestowed.[6]

For the rest, they live in a very pleasing and very temperate country, so that, according to what I have been told by my witnesses, it is rare to see a sick person there; and they assured me that they never saw any of the natives either palsied, blear-eyed, toothless, or crooked with age. They are located along the coast and are inclosed on the side towards the land with great and high mountains, having about a hundred leagues in breadth in between. They have great store of fish and flesh that have no resemblance to ours, and they eat with-

---

[5] Seneca, *Epistles*   [6] Virgil, *Georgics*

out any other artifice than that of cooking them. The first that rode a horse there, though in several voyages he had contracted an acquaintance with them, put them into so terrible a fright in that posture that they killed him with their arrows before being able to recognize him.

Their buildings are very long and capable of holding two or three hundred people, covered with the bark of tall trees, the sections fixed to the ground at one end and leaning against and supporting one another at the peak like some of our barns, of which the covering hangs way to the ground and serves for the side walls. They have wood so hard that they cut with it and make out of it their swords and grills to cook their meat. Their beds are of cotton weave, swung from the roof like those in our vessels, each one having his own; for the women lie apart from their husbands.

They rise with the sun, and as soon as they are up, eat for the whole day, for they have no other meal than that. They do not drink then, as Suidas reports of some other people of the East who never drank at their meals; they do drink several times a day, and a great deal. Their liquor is made of a certain root and is the color of our claret. They never drink it except lukewarm. This drink will keep only two or three days, has a somewhat sharp taste, is not at all heady, is wholesome to the stomach, laxative for those who are not used to it, and a very pleasant beverage to such as are accustomed to it. Instead of bread they make use of a certain white matter like preserved coriander. I have tasted of it; the taste is sweet and somewhat insipid.

The whole day is spent in dancing. The youngest go hunting after wild beasts with bows. Some of their women are employed in heating their drink meanwhile, which is their chief duty. Some one of the old men, in the morning before they fall to eating, preaches to the whole barnful in common, walking from one end to the other and several times repeating the same sentence until he has finished the round (for these buildings are a full hundred paces long). He recommends to them only two things: valor towards their enemies and love for their wives. And they never fail to note, as their refrain, this obligation, that it is their wives who keep their drink warm and seasoned.

The fashion of their beds, ropes, wooden swords, and the wooden bracelets with which they cover their wrists when they go to fight, and of their big canes, open at one end, by the sound of which they keep the cadence of their dances, is to be seen in several places, and among others at my house. They are close shaven all over, and much more closely than we, without any other razor than one of wood or of stone. They believe the immortality of the soul, and that those who have merited well of the gods are lodged in that part of heaven where the sun rises, and the accursed in the west.

They have some kind of priests and prophets that very rarely present themselves to the people, having their abode in the mountains. At their arrival there is a great feast and solemn assembly of many villages (each lodge, as I have described it, makes a village, and they are about a French league distant from one another). This prophet declaims to them in public, exhorting them to virtue and to their duty; but all their ethics consist in these two articles: resolution in war and affection for their wives. He also prophesies to them events to come and the results they are to expect from their enterprises; he prompts them to, or diverts them from, war. But it is on condition that, when he fails in his divination and anything happens otherwise than he has foretold, he is cut into a thousand pieces, if he is caught, and condemned for a false prophet. For that reason, the prophet who has once been mistaken is never seen again.

Divination is a gift of God, that is why it ought to be punishable to abuse it. Among the Scythians, when their diviners failed to strike it right, they were laid, bound hand and foot, upon carts laden with firewood and drawn by oxen, on which they were burned. Those who handle things subject to the conduct of human capacity are excusable in doing the best they can. But these others that come to delude us with assurances of an extraordinary faculty beyond our understanding, ought they not to be punished for the temerity of their imposture and for not making good their promise?

They have wars with the nations that live farther inland beyond their mountains, to which they go quite naked and without other arms than their bows and wooden swords pointed at one end like the points of our spears. The obstinacy of their battles is wonderful; they never end without slaughter and bloodshed; for as to running away and fear, they know not what it is. Everyone for a trophy brings home the head of an enemy he has killed and fixes it over the door of his house. After having a long time treated their prisoners well and with all the luxuries they can think of, he to whom the prisoner belongs forms a great assembly of his acquaintances. He ties a rope to one of the arms of the prisoner, by the end of which he holds him some paces away for fear of being struck, and gives to the friend he loves best the other arm to hold in the same manner; and they two, in the presence of all the assembly, dispatch him with their swords. After that they roast him and eat him among them and send some pieces to their absent friends. They do not do this, as some think, for nourishment, as the Scythians anciently did, but as a representation of an extreme revenge. And its proof is that having observed that the Portuguese, who were in league with their enemies, inflicted another sort of death on them when they captured them, which was to bury them up to the waist, shoot the rest of the body full of arrows, and then hang them; they thought that these people from the other world (as men who had sown the knowledge of a great many vices among their neighbors and were much greater masters in all kind of wickedness than they) did not exercise this sort of revenge without reason, and that it must needs be more painful than theirs, and they began to leave their old way and to follow this. I am not sorry that we should take notice of the barbarous horror of such acts, but I am sorry that, seeing so

clearly into their faults, we should be so blind to our own. I
conceive there is more barbarity in eating a man alive than in
eating him dead, in tearing by tortures and the rack a body
that is still full of feeling, in roasting him by degrees, causing
him to be bitten and torn by dogs and swine (as we have not
only read, but lately seen, not among inveterate enemies, but
among neighbors and fellow-citizens, and what is worse, under
color of piety and religion), than in roasting and eating him
after he is dead.

Chrysippus and Zeno, chiefs of the Stoic sect, were of opinion
that there was no harm in making use of our dead carcasses
in any way for our necessity, and in feeding upon them too;
just as our ancestors, being besieged by Caesar in the city of
Alésia, resolved to withstand the famine of this siege with the
bodies of their old men, women, and other persons who were
incapable of bearing arms.

> 'Tis well known that the Gascons once employed
> Such food in order to prolong their lives.[7]

And physicians are not afraid of employing it in all sorts of
ways for our health, applying it either inwardly or outwardly.
But there never was any opinion so irregular as to excuse
treachery, disloyalty, tyranny, and cruelty, which are our common vices.

We may, then, well call these people barbarians in respect
to the rules of reason, but not in respect to ourselves, who, in
all sorts of barbarity, exceed them. Their warfare is in every
way noble and generous and has as much excuse and beauty
as this human malady is capable of; it has with them no other
foundation than the sole jealousy of valor. Their disputes are
not for the conquests of new lands, for they still enjoy that
natural abundance that supplies them without labor and trouble
with all things necessary in such abundance that they have no

---

[7] Juvenal

need to enlarge their borders. And they are still in that happy stage of desiring only as much as their natural necessities demand; all beyond that is superfluous to them.

Men of the same age generally call one another brothers; those who are younger, children; and the old men are fathers to all. These leave to their heirs in common the full possession of their goods, without any manner of division, or any other title than that pure one which Nature bestows upon her creatures in bringing them into the world. If their neighbors pass over the mountains to come to attack them and obtain a victory, all the victors gain by it is only glory and the advantage of having proved themselves the better in valor and virtue; for otherwise they never meddle with the goods of the conquered, and they return to their own country, where they have no want of any necessity, nor of that great good, to know how to enjoy their condition happily and be content with it. These in their turn do the same. They demand of their prisoners no other ransom than the confession and acknowledgment that they are overcome. But there is not one found in a whole century that will not rather choose to die than either by word or look to recede one bit from the grandeur of an invincible courage. There is not a man among them who would not rather be killed and eaten than so much as request not to be. They treat them with all liberality in order that their lives may be so much the dearer to them; and they usually entertain them with menaces of their approaching death, of the torments they are to suffer, of the preparations that are being made for that purpose, of the cutting up of their limbs, and of the feast that will be made at their expense. All this is done for the sole purpose of extorting some weak or submissive word from them, or to make them want to run away, so that they may obtain the advantage of having terrified them and shaken their constancy. For indeed, if rightly taken, it is in this point only that a true victory consists:

No victory is complete,
But when the vanquished own their just defeat.[8]

The Hungarians, very bellicose fighters, did not of old pursue their advantage beyond reducing the enemy to their mercy. For, having wrenched this confession from them, they let them go without injury or ransom, except, at the most, to make them give their word never to bear arms against them again.

We get enough advantages over our enemies that are borrowed advantages, not truly our own. It is the quality of a porter, not of valor, to have sturdier arms and legs; agility is a dead and corporeal quality; it is a stroke of fortune to make our enemy stumble or to dazzle his eyes with the light of the sun; it is a trick of art and science, which may happen in any cowardly blockhead, to be a good fencer. The worth and value of a man consists in the heart and in the will; there his true honor dwells. Valor is strength, not of legs and arms, but of the heart and the soul; it does not lie in the goodness of our horse, or of our arms, but in our own. He that falls firm in his courage, *if he has fallen, he fights upon his knees.*[9] He who, despite the danger of death near at hand, abates nothing of his assurance; who in dying still looks at his enemy firmly and disdainfully; he is beaten, not by us, but by fortune; he is killed, not conquered. The most valiant are sometimes the most unfortunate.

So there are triumphant defeats rivaling victories. Those four sister-victories, the fairest the sun ever beheld, of Salamis, Plataea, Mycale, and Sicily, never dared oppose all their united glories to the single glory of the discomfiture of King Leonidas and his men at the Pass of Thermopylae.

Whoever ran with a more glorious and ambitious desire to the winning of a battle than Captain Ischolas to defeat? Whoever set about with more ingenuity and care to assure his safety

---

[8] Claudian, *De Sexto Consulatu Honorii*   [9] Seneca, *de Providentia*

than he did to assure his ruin? He was ordered to defend a certain pass in the Peloponnesus against the Arcadians. In order to do this, finding himself quite powerless in view of the nature of the place and the inequality of the forces, and concluding that all who presented themselves to the enemy must certainly be left upon the place; on the other hand, considering it unworthy of his own virtue and magnanimity and of the Lacedemonian name to fail in his charge, he chose a middle course between these two extremes, in this manner: the youngest and fittest of his men he preserved for the service and defense of their country and sent them back; and with the rest, whose loss would be of less consideration, he resolved to hold the pass, and by their death to make the enemy buy their entry as dearly as he could. And so it turned out. For being presently encompassed on all sides by the Arcadians, after having made a great slaughter of the enemy, he and his men were all put to the sword. Is there any trophy dedicated to conquerors which would not be more due to these vanquished? True victory has as its rôle the struggle, not the coming off safe; and the honor of valor consists in combating, not in beating.

To return to our story. These prisoners are so far from submitting in spite of all that is done to them that, on the contrary, during the two or three months that they are kept, they bear a cheerful countenance; they urge their masters to make haste to bring them to the test; they defy them, rail at them, and reproach them with cowardice and the number of battles they have lost against those of their country. I have a song composed by a prisoner in which there is this thrust, that they come boldly, all of them, and assemble to dine upon him, for they will be eating at the same time their own fathers and grandfathers, whose flesh has served to feed and nourish his body. "These muscles," says he, "this flesh and these veins are your own, poor fools that you are. You do not recognize that the substance of your ancestors' limbs is here yet; savor them well, and you will find in them taste of your own flesh."

An idea that does not smack at all of barbarity. Those that paint these people dying and reproduce the execution depict the prisoner spitting in the face of his executioners and making faces at them. In truth, to the very last gasp they never cease to brave and defy them both by word and gesture. In plain truth, here are men who are real savages in comparison with us; for either they must be absolutely so, or else we are savages; there is an amazing difference between their character and ours.

The men there have several wives, and the higher their reputation for valor, the more wives they have. It is a remarkably beautiful aspect of their marriages that the same jealousy our wives have to hinder us from the affection and good graces of other women theirs have to acquire them for them. Being more solicitous of their husband's honor than of anything else, they seek and are anxious to have as many companions as they can, inasmuch as it is a testimony of their husband's valor. Ours will cry out, "Miracle!" It is not so. It is a properly matrimonial virtue, but of the highest order. And in the Bible, Sarah, Leah, and Rachel, and the wives of Jacob gave their beautiful handmaids to their husbands; and Livia seconded the appetites of Augustus to her own disadvantage; and Stratonice, the wife of King Deiotarus, not only lent for her husband's use a very beautiful young chambermaid who was in her service, but carefully brought up the children he had by her, and assisted them in the succession to their father's estates.

And that it may not be supposed that all this is done through a simple and servile bondage to their common practice and under the weight of authority of their ancient custom, without reasoning or judgment, and from having minds so stupid as not to be able to take any other course, I must give some examples of their capacity. Besides the example that I have just quoted from one of their songs of war, I have another, a love song, that begins thus: "Adder, stay; stay, adder, that from the pattern of your markings my sister may draw the fashion and work of a rich girdle that I may present to my beloved; so may your beauty and the pattern of your scales be forever preferred to all other serpents." This first couplet is the refrain of the song. Now I am familiar enough with poetry to judge thus much: that not only there is nothing barbarous in this fancy, but that it is perfectly Anacreontic. Their language, moreover, is a soft language, agreeable in sound, resembling Greek in its endings.

Three of these people, not knowing how costly their knowledge of the corruptions of this part of the world will one day be to their happiness and repose, and that from this intercourse will spring their ruin, which, I suppose, is already advanced (miserable men to let themselves be deluded with desire of novelty and to have left the serenity of their own sky to come and gaze at ours!), were at Rouen at the time that the late King Charles the Ninth was there. The king talked to them a good while; and they were shown our fashions, our pomp, and the form of a fair city. After that someone asked their opinion and wanted to know what they had found most to be admired. They mentioned three things, of which I have forgotten the third, and I am very sorry for it, but two I still remember. They said that in the first place they thought it very strange that so many big men wearing beards, strong and well armed, who were about the king (it is likely they meant the Swiss of his guard) should submit to obey a child, and that they did not rather choose one from among them to command; secondly (they have a way in their language of calling men the halves of one another) that they had observed that there were among us men full and crammed with all kinds of good things, while their halves were begging at their doors, emaciated with hunger and poverty; and they thought it strange that these needy halves were able to suffer such an injustice, and that they did not take the others by the throat or set fire to their houses.

I talked to one of them a long while, but I had an interpreter who followed so badly and whose stupidity hindered him so from taking in my ideas that I could scarcely get any satisfaction out of him. When I asked him what advantage he received from the superiority he had among his own people (for he was a captain and our mariners called him king), he told me that it was to march foremost in war. How many men followed him? He showed me a space of ground to signify as many as could be contained in such a space, which might be four or five thousand men. Did all his authority expire with the war? He said this much remained, that when he visited the villages that depended on him, they cleared him paths through the underbrush by which he might pass at his ease.

All this is not too bad. But hold on! They don't wear breeches.

OF SOLITUDE

Let us leave aside that protracted comparison between the active and the solitary life; and as for the fine saying with which ambition and avarice cover themselves, "That we are not born for our private selves, but for the public," let us boldly appeal to those who are in the midst of the dance; and let them cudgel their conscience and say whether, on the contrary, the titles, the offices, and the hurly-burly of the world are not rather sought out to gain a private profit from the public. The corrupt ways by which men push themselves forward in our age show clearly that the end is not worth much. Let us reply to ambition that it is she herself that gives us a taste for solitude. For what does she avoid so much as society? What does she seek so much as elbow-room? There is opportunity everywhere for doing good or evil; yet if what Bias says is true, that the worst are in the majority, or what Ecclesiastes says, that there is not one man good in a thousand,

> For good men are so rare their numbers scarcely match
> The gates of Thebes or mouths of the fat Nile,[1]

contagion is very dangerous in the crowd. A man must either imitate the vicious or hate them. Both these things are dangerous: either to resemble them because they are many, or to hate many of them because they are unresembling.

And merchants that go to sea are in the right when they take care that those who embark in the same ship are not dissolute,

---

[1] Juvenal

blasphemous, wicked, looking upon such society as unlucky. And, therefore, it was that Bias humorously said to those who were undergoing with him the danger of a great tempest and calling upon the gods for help: "Be quiet, that they may not know you are here with me." And in a more pressing case, Albuquerque, viceroy in the Indies for Emanuel, King of Portugal, in an extreme peril of shipwreck took a young boy upon his shoulders for this sole end, that in their common danger his innocence might serve him as a guarantee and recommendation to the divine favor and bring him to safety.

It is not that a wise man may not live everywhere content, yes, and alone in the crowd of a palace; but if it be left to his own choice, he will fly, he says, the very sight of it. He will endure that, if need be; but if it is up to him, he will choose the other. He cannot think himself sufficiently rid of vice if he must still contend with those of other men. Charondas punished as evil men those who were convicted of keeping evil company.

There is nothing so unsociable and sociable as man; the one by his vice, the other by his nature. And Antisthenes, in my opinion, did not give him a satisfactory answer who reproached him with frequenting evil company when he said that physicians lived well enough among the sick; for if they contribute to the health of the sick, they impair their own by the contagion, continual sight, and treatment of diseases.

Now the aim of solitude, I take it, is all one: to live more at leisure and at one's ease. But men do not always choose the right way. They often think they have taken leave of all business when they have only exchanged one employment for another. There is scarcely less trouble in governing a family than a whole state. Whatever the mind is engaged in, it is all engaged in it, and domestic employments are not less importunate for being less important. Moreover, for having shaken off the court and market place, we have not shaken off the principal vexations of our life,

Reason and sense dispel our cares,
Not the bold site that wide commands the seas.[2]

Ambition, avarice, irresolution, fear, and inordinate desires do not leave us when we leave our country,

And there behind the horseman sits black care.[3]

They follow us often even to the cloisters and to the schools of philosophy. Neither deserts, nor rocky caves, nor hairshirts, nor fastings can disengage us from them:

The fatal shaft sticks in her wounded side.[4]

Someone said to Socrates that a certain man was not at all improved by his travels. "I very well believe it," he said, "he took himself along with him."

Why shift about in search of lands
Heated by other suns? Who, exile bound,
Escapes himself as well?[5]

If a man does not first discharge himself and his mind of the burden that oppresses it, motion will make it press the harder, as the cargo in a ship is less cumbersome when it is settled. You do a sick man more harm than good by removing him. You imbed the malady by disturbing it, as stakes go deeper and more fixedly into the earth by being moved and shaken. Therefore it is not enough to have gotten away from the people, it is not enough to change places, we must get away from the people's ways that are in us; we must sequester ourselves and regain possession of ourselves.

"Now," you may say, "I've burst my chains."
For after straining hard the dog may snap the rope,
Yet as he flies, a goodly part drags from his neck.[6]

---

[2] Horace, *Epistles*   [3] Horace, *Odes*   [4] Virgil, *Aeneid*   [5] Horace, *Odes*
[6] Persius

We carry our fetters along with us; it is not an absolute liberty; we still turn our eyes to what we have left behind; our
fancy is full of it.

> Unless the heart is purged, what struggles then,
> What perils, so unwanted, press on us!
> How great the bitter pangs of lust that rend
> The agitated man, and, too, what fears!
> What havoc pride and filth and wantonness
> Produce! What luxury and sloth! [7]

Our disease has us by the mind, and the mind cannot escape
from itself,

> The mind's to blame, which ne'er escapes itself. [8]

Therefore we must bring it back and withdraw it into itself:
that is the true solitude, which may be enjoyed in the midst
of cities and the courts of kings; but it is enjoyed more com-
modiously in private.

Now since we are undertaking to live alone and to do without company, let us so order it that our contentment may depend upon ourselves; let us cast off all the ties that bind us to
others; let us win from ourselves the power to live truly alone,
and there live at our ease.

Stilpo, having escaped from the fire that consumed his city,
in which he had lost his wife, children, and property, Demetrius Poliorcetes, seeing him unappalled amid the great ruin
of his country, asked him if he had received no loss. He answered, No; that, thanks to God, he had lost nothing of his.
That is what the philosopher Antisthenes humorously said: that
man should furnish himself with provisions that would float
on water and could swim ashore with him from a shipwreck.

Certainly a man of understanding has lost nothing if he has
himself. When the City of Nola was ruined by the barbarians,

---

[7] Lucretius   [8] Horace, *Epistles*

Paulinus, who was bishop of that place, having there lost all he had, and being their prisoner, prayed to God thus: "O Lord, keep me from being sensible of this loss, for Thou knowest they have yet touched nothing of that which is mine." The riches that made him rich and the goods that made him good were still entire. This is what it is to choose well the treasures that can secure themselves from harm and to hide them in a place into which no one may enter and which can be betrayed only by ourselves.

We should have wife, children, goods, and above all health if we can; but we must not so set our heart upon them that our happiness depends on them. We must reserve a back shop wholly our own, entirely free, wherein to establish our true liberty and our principal retreat and solitude. In this we must hold our ordinary conversation with ourselves, and so privately that no outside relationship or communication may find a place there; there to talk and to laugh as if without wife, without children, and without possessions, without followers and without servants; to the end that, when the occasion comes for us to lose them, it may be no new thing to be without them. We have a soul that can be turned upon itself; it can be its own company; it has the means to attack and to defend, to receive and to give: let us not fear that in this solitude we shall stagnate in tedious idleness,

> In solitude be to thyself a throng.[9]

Virtue, says Antisthenes, is content with itself, without rules, without words, without deeds.

In our ordinary actions there is not one in a thousand that concerns ourselves. He that you see scrambling up the ruins of that wall, frenzied and beside himself, a target for so many harquebus shots; and that other, all scarred, pale, and faint with hunger, resolved to die rather than open the gate to him,

---

[9] Tibullus

do you think that these men are there for their own sake? For the sake of a man whom, perhaps, they never saw and who is not at all concerned about their interests, plunged meanwhile in sloth and pleasure. This other sniveling, blear-eyed, dirty fellow whom you see coming out of his study after midnight, do you think he is seeking among his books how to become a better man, wiser and more content? No such thing. He will die at it, or he will teach posterity the measure of Plautus' verse and the true orthography of some Latin word. Who does not voluntarily exchange health, repose, and life for reputation and glory, the most useless, worthless, and false coin that passes current among us? Our own death did not frighten us enough; let us charge ourselves also with that of our wives, our children, and our servants. Our own affairs did not give us trouble enough; let us also torment and rack our brains with those of our neighbors and friends.

> What! Should a man desire or procure
> Something that's dearer to him than himself? [10]

Solitude seems to me to be more likely and more reasonable for those who have given to the world their most active and vigorous years, according to the example of Thales.

We have lived enough for others, let us at least live out this remnant of life for ourselves. Let us bring back our thoughts and interests to ourselves and our ease. It is no light matter to retire securely; it keeps us occupied enough without mixing other enterprises with it. Since God gives us leisure to arrange for our removal, let us make ready for it; let us pack up our baggage; let us take leave of the company in good season; and let us break loose from those violent holds that engage us elsewhere and remove us from ourselves. We must undo these bonds that are so powerful, and hereafter love this and that, but espouse nothing but ourselves. That is to say, let the other things

---

[10] Terence, *Adelphi*

be ours, but not so joined and glued that they cannot be taken away without skinning us and tearing away with them some part of our body. The greatest thing in the world is to know how to belong to ourselves.

It is time to untie ourselves from society since we cannot contribute anything to it. And he who cannot lend must forbid himself to borrow. Our powers begin to fail us; let us bring them in and concentrate them in us. He that can turn the offices of friendship and companionship back and make them become part of himself, let him do it. In this decline which renders him useless, burdensome, and troublesome to others, let him take care not to be troublesome to himself, and burdensome and useless to himself. Let him soothe and cherish himself, and above all things govern himself, respecting and fearing his reason and conscience to such a degree that he cannot without shame make a false step in their presence. *For it is rare for anyone to respect himself enough.*[11]

Socrates says that boys should have themselves instructed, men should exercise themselves in well-doing, old men should retire from all civil and military employments, living at their own discretion, without being bound to any fixed office.

There are some temperaments more fit for these precepts of retirement than others. Such as are of a soft and weak apprehension and of a sensitive affection and will which is not easily tied down or put to work, of whom I am one both by natural disposition and by reflection, will conform to this advice better than active and busy souls who embrace everything and engage themselves everywhere, who have a passion about everything, who offer, present, and give themselves up to every occasion. We should avail ourselves of these accidental and extraneous conveniences, so far as they are agreeable to us, but without making them our principal foundation; they are not; neither nature nor reason will have it so. Why should we, contrary to their laws, enslave our contentment by giving it into

---

[11] Quintilian

the power of another? Moreover, to anticipate the accidents of fortune, to deprive ourselves of the commodities that are in our hands, as many have done through piety and some philosophers through reason, to be our own servant, to sleep on the bare ground, to put out our eyes, to throw our wealth into the river, and to seek out pain (as some do, that by the torment of this life they may gain bliss in another; others, that by putting themselves on the lowest step they may make themselves safe from a new fall), these are acts of an excessive virtue. Let the sturdier and stronger natures render even their hiding place glorious and exemplary:

> When means run out, how firm amid
> The common things, I laud the safe and humble path;
> But when things better, richer come along, I then
> Assert that these alone live wisely and live well,
> Whose wealth, well-placed in gleaming villas, we behold.[12]

I have enough to do without going that far. It is enough for me, while in fortune's favor, to prepare myself for its disfavor, and while at my ease, to represent to myself, as far as my imagination can reach, the evil to come; just as we accustom ourselves to jousts and tournaments and imitate war in the midst of peace.

I do not think Arcesilaus, the philosopher, the less virtuous for knowing that he made use of gold and silver vessels in so far as the condition of his fortune allowed him to; and from the fact that he used them moderately and liberally, I have a better opinion of him than if he had given them up.

I see to what limits natural necessity goes; and seeing the poor beggar at my door often more jocund and more healthy than I myself am, I put myself into his place and attempt to fit my mind to his slant. And running in like manner over other examples, though I may think death, poverty, contempt, and sickness are at my heels, I easily resolve not to be frightened

---

[12] Horace, *Epistles*

at what a humbler man than I takes with so much patience. And I cannot believe that a weak understanding can do more than a strong one, or that the results of reason cannot be as great as those of custom. And knowing how uncertain these incidental conveniences are, I never fail, while in full enjoyment of them, to make it my sovereign request to God that he make me content with myself and the good things that spring from me. I see sturdy young men who never fail to carry a lot of pills in their trunks to take when they catch a cold, which they fear so much the less because they think they have the remedy at hand. So must we do; and, besides, if we feel ourselves subject to some more violent disease, we must provide ourselves with those medicines that numb and put to sleep the part affected.

The occupation we should choose for such a life ought to be neither laborious nor tedious, otherwise all the importance that we set on having come to it in quest of repose would be to no purpose. This depends upon each one's particular taste; mine is not at all adaptable to household management. Such as like it ought to apply themselves to it with moderation,

> Let them attempt to bend things to themselves,
> And not themselves to things.[13]

Besides the care of an estate is a servile job, as Sallust calls it. Some parts of it are more excusable, such as the care of gardens, which Xenophon attributes to Cyrus; and a mean may be found between that low and sordid application, tense and full of care, which is seen in men who plunge completely into it, and that profound and extreme negligence, letting all things go to ruin, which we see in others,

> The cattle of Democritus eat up his leas
> And crops, while swift his mind without his body roams.[14]

---

[13] Horace, *Epistles*   [14] Horace, *Epistles*

But let us hear the advice the younger Pliny gives his friend, Cornelius Rufus, upon this subject of solitude: "I advise you, in this full and prosperous retreat wherein you are, to leave to your servants the base and abject care of your household, and to give yourself to the study of letters in order to derive from them something that may be entirely your own." He means reputation; of the same inclination as Cicero, who says that he wishes to employ his solitude and repose from public affairs to acquire by his writings an immortal life:

> Is knowledge nothing worth, unless you show
> To others all that you pretend to know.[15]

It appears reasonable, when a man talks of retiring from the world, that he should look outside of himself. These men do it only by halves. They do, indeed, prepare their affairs for the time when they shall no longer be there; but by a ridiculous contradiction, they still aspire to reap the fruits of their plan from the world when absent from it.

The idea of those who seek solitude for religious motives, filling up their hearts with the certainty of the divine promises in the other life, is much more soundly founded. They place before their eyes God, an object infinite in goodness and power; the soul has there the wherewithal to satiate its desires in full liberty. Afflictions and sufferings come to them as profit, being used for the acquisition of eternal health and joy; death, as the fulfillment of their wishes, being the passage to so perfect a state. And the harshness of their rules is quickly smoothed by habits, and the carnal appetites are repulsed and put to sleep by denial, for nothing maintains them but use and exercise. This sole end of another life, happily immortal, rightly merits that we abandon the conveniences and pleasures of this life of ours. And he who can really and constantly inflame his soul with the ardor of this lively faith and hope erects for himself in

---

[15] Persius

solitude a life that is voluptuous and delightful beyond any other kind of life.

Neither the end, then, nor the means of that advice of Pliny satisfies me; for we are only falling out of the ague into a burning fever. This occupation with books is as laborious as any other and as great an enemy to health, which ought to be the first thing in our thoughts. And we should not let ourselves be deceived by the pleasure taken in it; it is the same pleasure that ruins the frugal man, the miser, the pleasure-lover, and the ambitious man. The sages teach us enough to beware of the treachery of our appetites and to distinguish true and entire pleasures from such as are mixed and spotted with more pain. For most pleasures, say they, tickle and embrace us only to strangle us like those thieves whom the Egyptians called Philistas. And if the headache came before drunkenness, we should take care not to drink too much. But pleasure, to deceive us, walks ahead and conceals from us her followers. Books are pleasant, but if by associating with them we finally lose our gaiety and health, the best things we have, let us give them over. I am one of those who think that the fruit derived from them cannot counterbalance the loss. As men who have long felt weakened by some indisposition give themselves up at last to the mercy of medicine and have certain rules of living prescribed for them by art, which they are nevermore to transgress; so he who retires, weary of and disgusted with the common way of living, must model this new one by the rules of reason and plan and arrange it by premeditation and reflection. He must have taken leave of every kind of labor, whatever aspect it may bear, and flee in general the passions which prevent tranquillity of body and soul, and choose the way that best suits his humor,

Let each one know the way that he should go.[16]

---

[16] Propertius

In domestic management, in study, in hunting, and in all other pursuits, we should go to the utmost limits of pleasure, but beware of engaging ourselves further where trouble begins to mingle with it. We must reserve only so much business and occupation as is necessary to keep us in breath and defend us from the inconveniences that the other extreme of a lax and indolent idleness brings with it. There are some sterile and thorny sciences, for the most part made for the busy crowd; we must leave them to those who are engaged in the service of the world. I, for my part, care only for books that are either pleasant and easy, which amuse me, or those that comfort and instruct me how to regulate my life and death.

> Strolling silent through the healthful wood,
> Tending thoughts fit for the wise and good.[17]

Wiser men, having a strong and vigorous soul, can make for themselves a wholly spiritual repose. But I, who have an ordinary soul, have to help support myself with bodily comfort; and age having of late robbed me of those pleasures that were more to my fancy, I train and sharpen my appetite for those that remain and are more suitable to this present season of my life. We must hold fast, tooth and nail, to the enjoyment of the pleasures of life that our years snatch, one after another, from our hands:

> Let's seize the sweets; life now is ours;
> Soon you'll be ashes, specters and a tale.[18]

Now, as to the end that Pliny and Cicero propose to us of glory, it is very far from my reckoning. Ambition is the humor most opposed to retirement. Glory and repose are things that cannot lodge in the same dwelling. As far as I can see, these men have only their arms and legs disengaged from the crowd; their soul, their intent, remain engaged more than ever:

---

[17] Horace, *Epistles*   [18] Persius

Old man, do you gather dainties for others' ears? [19]

They have only drawn back to take a better leap and with a greater impetus to thrust more deeply into the crowd. Do you wish to see how they shoot short by a grain's length? Let us put into the scales the advice of two philosophers, and of two very different sects, the one writing to Idomeneus, the other to Lucilius, their friends, to draw them out of worldly honors and the administration of affairs into solitude. "You have," say they, "hitherto lived swimming and floating; come away and die in the harbor. You have given the rest of your life to the light, give this portion to the shade. It is impossible to give up business if you do not also give up its fruits; therefore get rid of all care for name and glory. It is to be feared that the luster of your past actions may give you but too much light and follow you right into your lair. Quit, with the other pleasures, that which proceeds from the approbation of others. And as to your knowledge and ability, do not be concerned about them, they will not lose their effect if you yourself are the better for them. Remember the man who, being asked why he took so much pains in an art that could come to the knowledge of but few persons, replied, 'A few are enough for me, one is enough for me, none at all is enough for me.' He spoke truly: you and a companion are theater enough to one another, or you to yourself. Let the people be one to you, and let one be the whole people to you. It is a low ambition to want to get glory from our idleness and retreat. We must do like the animals that efface their tracks at the entrance to their den. What you must seek is no longer that the world should talk of you, but how you should talk to yourself. Retire into yourself, but first prepare to receive yourself there. It would be madness to trust yourself in your own hands if you do not know how to govern yourself. There are ways to fail in solitude as well as in company. Until you have made yourself one before whom you dare

---

[19] Persius

not trip, and until you are ashamed and respectful of yourself, *let true ideals be kept before the mind,*[20] keep continually in your mind Cato, Phocion, and Aristides, in whose presence even fools would hide their faults, and make them controllers of all your intentions; should these intentions get off the track, your reverence for those men will set them on the way again. They will keep you on the way of being contented with yourself, of borrowing nothing of any other but yourself, of restraining and fixing your mind on definite and limited thoughts in which it may take pleasure, and, having recognized the true blessings which men enjoy in proportion as they recognize them, of contenting yourself with them, without desire of prolonging life and name." That is the advice of true and natural philosophy, not of a showy and prating philosophy such as that of the first two.

---

[20] Cicero, *Tusculans*

BOOK II

BOOK II

OF THE INCONSISTENCY OF OUR ACTIONS

THOSE WHO MAKE it their business to compare human actions do not find themselves so much puzzled in anything as in putting them together and in setting them in the same light; for they commonly contradict each other so strangely that it seems impossible they have come from the same shop. One time the younger Marius is the son of Mars, another time the son of Venus. Pope Boniface the Eighth, it is said, entered into his charge like a fox, behaved in it like a lion, and died like a dog. And who would believe that it was Nero, that veritable image of cruelty, who, when according to the custom the sentence of a condemned criminal was brought to him to sign, cried out, "Would to God that I had never learned to write!" So much was his heart wrung to condemn a man to death! Everything is so full of such examples, and, indeed, every man is able to produce so many for himself, that I find it strange to see sometimes men of understanding give themselves the trouble of matching these pieces, seeing that irresolution appears to me the most common and manifest vice of our nature, witness the famous line of Publius, the writer of farces,

> The plan is bad that never can be changed.[1]

There seems some reason for forming a judgment of a man from the most common aspects of his life, but considering the natural instability of our habits and opinions, I have often thought even good authors are wrong in obstinately endeavor

[1] Publius Syrus, in Aulus Gellius, *Attic Nights*

ing to shape a consistent and solid contexture out of us. They choose one general trait, and following this idea, they arrange and interpret all the actions of a man, and if they cannot twist them enough, they impute them to dissimulation. Augustus has escaped them, for there is in this man so apparent, sudden, and continual a variety of actions throughout the whole course of his life that he has slipped away untouched and undefined from the boldest judges. Nothing is more difficult for me to believe in than men's consistency, and nothing easier than their inconsistency. He who would judge them in detail and distinctly, bit by bit, would more often strike on the truth.

Out of all antiquity it is difficult to pick out a dozen men who have directed their lives to one certain and fixed course, which is the principal aim of wisdom. For, says one of the ancients, to comprise it all in one word and to contract all the rules of human life into one, it is "to *will* and not to *will* always the same thing." I would not deign, says he, to add, "provided the *will* be just," for if it be not just, it is impossible it should be always one. I did, indeed, once learn that vice is nothing but lack of order and measure, and, therefore, it is impossible to attach consistency to it. It is said to be a maxim of Demosthenes that the beginning of all virtue is consultation and deliberation; and the end and perfection, consistency. If through reason we undertook a definite course, we should take the fairest; but nobody has thought of it,

> He scorns that which he sought; he seeks again what he just
>   scorned;
> He fluctuates, and his whole life a contradiction is.[2]

Our ordinary practice is to follow the inclinations of our appetite, to the left, to the right, upwards, downwards, according as the wind of chance bears us. We think of what we want only

---

[2] Horace, *Epistles*

at the moment we want it, and we change like that little creature which takes its color from what it is laid upon. What we
have just now proposed to ourselves, we immediately alter, and
presently retrace our steps again: it is nothing but wavering
and inconstancy,

> By outside strings like puppets we are led.[3]

We do not go, we are carried off like things that float, now
gently, now violently, according as the water is angry or calm:

> Do we not see each man
> In ignorance of what he wants, go seeking e'er
> From place to place, as if he might cast off his load?[4]

Every day a new whim, and our humors change with the
changes in the weather,

> Such are the minds of men, as is the fruitful light
> That father Jupiter himself shed o'er the earth.[5]

We float between different opinions. We desire nothing freely,
nothing absolutely, nothing constantly.

In anyone that had prescribed and laid down definite rules
and a definite regime in his own head, we should perceive an
evenness of conduct, an order, and an infallible relation of one
action with another shining through his whole life.

Empedocles observed this contradiction in the Agrigentines,
that they gave themselves up to pleasures as if they were to die
on the morrow, and built as if they were never to die. The
judgment of that man would be easy to make, as is seen from
the younger Cato; he who has touched one note of him has

[3] Horace, *Satires* [4] Lucretius [5] Homer, *Odyssey,* in Saint Augustine,
The City of God

touched all: he is a harmony of very concordant sounds that cannot clash. With us, on the contrary, every action requires a particular judgment. The surest way, in my opinion, would be to refer them to the nearest circumstances, without engaging in a longer quest or without drawing from them any other inferences.

I was told, during the disorders of our unhappy state, that a girl, living hard by the place where I then was, had thrown herself out of a high window to avoid being forced by a scoundrel of a soldier quartered in her house; she was not killed by the fall, and, redoubling her attempt, had sought to cut her own throat, but had been prevented, after having wounded herself seriously, however. She herself confessed that the soldier had as yet importuned her only by requests, solicitation, and presents, but that she had been afraid that in the end he would proceed to violence. And to top it all, her words, her expression, and this blood testifying to her virtue, in the true style of another Lucretia! Now I have learned as a fact that, both before and after, she had been a wench not so difficult to approach. As the story says: Be as handsome and as fine a gentleman as you will, when you have failed in your suit, do not immediately infer an inviolable chastity in your mistress; this does not mean that the muleteer will not find his chance there.

Antigonus, having taken a liking for one of his soldiers on account of his virtue and valor, ordered his physicians to treat him for a persistent internal malady which had long tormented him, and observing after his cure that he went much more coldly at his work than before, he asked him what had so altered and cowed him. "You, yourself, Sire," he answered him, "by having freed me of the ills because of which I did not value my life." One of Lucullus' soldiers, having been rifled by the enemy, performed a brave exploit against them by way of revenge. When he had recovered his loss, Lucullus, who had conceived a good opinion of him, sought to engage him in some hazardous exploit by all the finest persuasions he could think of,

With words that even might a coward's heart make bold.[6]

"Employ in it," he replied, "some wretched soldier who has been robbed,"

However much a bumpkin, he replied,
He'll go where'er you wish, will he who's lost his purse;[7]

and flatly refused to go.

When we read that Mahomet having outrageously berated Chasan, chief of his Janissaries, because he saw his troops broken by the Hungarians and himself behaving like a coward in the combat, Chasan, as his sole reply, went and hurled himself furiously, alone, just as he was, arms in hand, into the first body of the enemy that offered itself, by which he was promptly swallowed up; this was, perhaps, not so much self-vindication as a change of mood, nor so much his natural valor as sudden anger.

The man you saw so adventurous yesterday, do not think it strange to see him as great a poltroon the day after; either anger, or necessity, or company, or wine, or the sound of the trumpet had put heart into his belly. This was no courage formed by reason; those circumstances stiffened it. It is no wonder if by contrary circumstances he has now become different.

These so supple variations and contradictions that are seen in us have caused some people to imagine that we have two souls and others, two powers which accompany and move us, each one in its own way, one towards good, the other towards evil, since such sudden diversity cannot be well reconciled with a simple subject.

Not only does the wind of chance move me according to its bent, but also I move and trouble myself by the instability of

---

[6] Horace, *Epistles*   [7] Horace, *Epistles*

my position; and whoever observes very attentively will hardly find himself twice in the same state. I give my soul sometimes one face, sometimes another, according to the side to which I turn it. If I speak variously of myself, it is because I look at myself variously. All contradictions are to be found in me in some shape or manner. Bashful, insolent; chaste, lustful; talkative, taciturn; tough, delicate; ingenious, stupid; morose, affable; lying, truthful; learned, ignorant; and liberal, and miserly, and prodigal: I find all this in myself, more or less, according as I turn myself about; and whoever studies himself very attentively finds in himself, yes, even in his judgment, this mutability and discord. I have nothing to say about myself absolutely, simply, and solidly, without confusion and without mixture, or in one word. *Distinguo* is the most universal member of my logic.

Though I always intend to speak well of what is good, and rather to interpret in a good sense such things as can be so interpreted, yet such is the strangeness of our condition that we are often pushed on to do good by vice itself, if it were not that doing good is judged by the intention only. One gallant action, therefore, ought not to lead us to conclude that a man is valiant; a man who was truly valiant would be always so and upon all occasions. If it were a habit of virtue, and not a sally, it would make a man equally resolute in all accidents, the same alone as in company, the same in the lists as in a battle, for, whatever they say, there is not one valor for the pavement and another for the camp. He would bear a sickness in his bed as bravely as a wound in camp, and no more fear death in his own house than in an assault. We should not then see the same man charge into a breach with a brave assurance and afterwards torment himself like a woman over the loss of a lawsuit or of a son. When, though a coward in front of infamy, he is firm before poverty; when though yielding before the surgeons' knives, he is unyielding before the swords of the enemy, the action is commendable, not the man.

Many of the Greeks, says Cicero, cannot look at the enemy and are courageous in sickness; the Cimbrians and Celtiberians, quite the contrary: *for nothing can be uniform that does not proceed from a firm reason.*[8]

There is no valor more extreme in its kind than that of Alexander: but it is only of one kind and not full enough throughout, or universal. As incomparable as it was, it still has its blemishes; this is why we see him become so distracted at the slightest suspicions that he conceives of his men's plotting against his life, and behave in the investigations with such violent and undiscerning injustice and with a fear that subverted his natural reason. The superstition, also, with which he was so strongly tainted carries some impression of pusillanimity. And the excess of his penitence for the murder of Clytus is likewise evidence of the unevenness of his temper.

Our actions are only pieces patched together, *they despise pleasure, but are too cowardly in pain; they are indifferent to glory, but infamy breaks their spirit;* [9] and we would acquire honor by a false title. Virtue will not be followed but for her own sake; and if we sometimes borrow her mask for some other purpose, she promptly pulls it off our face. It is a strong and vivid dye when the soul is once steeped in it, it will not come out without taking the piece with it. That is why to judge a man we must follow his traces long and attentively. If consistency does not on its own maintain itself in him, *whose way of living has been well considered and looked after;* [10] if the variety of occurrences makes him alter his pace (his path, I mean, for the pace may be hastened or retarded), let him go: that man runs before the wind, as the motto of our Talbot has it.

It is no wonder, says one of the ancients, that chance has so great a dominion over us since it is by chance we live. It is not possible for a man who has not directed his life as a whole to a specific end to dispose his particular actions. It is not possible for a man to arrange the pieces who has not the form of the

---

[8] Cicero, *Tusculans*   [9] Cicero, *De Officiis*   [10] Cicero, *Paradoxes*

whole in his head. Of what use are colors to him who knows not what he is to paint? No one makes a definite plan of his life, and we reflect on it only piece by piece. The archer ought first to know at what he is to aim and then accommodate his arm, bow, string, shaft, and motion to it. Our plans go astray because they have no direction and no goal. No wind serves him who has no port of destination. I do not agree with the judgment that was given in favor of Sophocles by them who, from having seen one of his tragedies, concluded he was capable of managing his domestic affairs, contrary to the accusation of his son.

Nor do I think the conjecture of the Parians, sent to reform the Milesians, warranted the conclusion they drew. Coming to visit the island, they took notice of the grounds that were best cultivated and the country houses that were best governed, and having taken down the names of the owners, when they had assembled the citizens, they appointed these owners as the new governors and magistrates, judging that they, careful of their private affairs, would be careful of those of the public.

We are all made up of fragments, so shapelessly and strangely assembled that every moment, every piece plays its own game. And there is as much difference between us and ourselves as between us and others. *Deem it a great achievement to act consistently, like one and the same man.*[11] Since ambition can teach men valor, temperance, and liberality, and even justice; since avarice can plant in the heart of a shopboy, bred in obscurity and idleness, the boldness to cast himself forth so far from his fireside, at the mercy of the waves and angry Neptune, in a frail boat; since it also teaches discretion and wisdom; and since even Venus supplies resolution and boldness to boys still under the discipline of the rod, and emboldens the tender hearts of virgins in their mothers' arms with warlike courage,

> With Love as guide, by stealth across the sleeping guards,
> The maiden comes alone by night to her young man;[12]

---

[11] Seneca, *Epistles*   [12] Tibullus

it is not the rôle of a stable understanding to judge us simply by our outward action; we must sound the inner depths and see by what springs our motion is produced. But since that is a high and hazardous undertaking, I wish that fewer people would meddle with it.

OF TRAINING

It is difficult for reasoning and instruction, even though our belief be readily accorded to them, to be powerful enough to guide us as far as action if we do not, in addition, exercise and train our mind by experience to the course for which we wish to prepare it; otherwise, when it comes to the point of action, it will doubtless be at a loss. This is why those among the philosophers who were ambitious to attain to some greater excellence were not content to await the rigors of Fortune under shelter and in repose, lest she should surprise them inexperienced and new in the combat, but rather sallied out to meet her and purposely threw themselves into the trial of difficulties. Some of them have abandoned riches to exercise themselves in a voluntary poverty; others have sought labor and a painfully austere life to inure themselves to hardships and toil; others have deprived themselves of the most precious parts of the body, such as sight and the organs of generation, lest their too pleasant and too easy use should relax and soften the steadfastness of their souls. But as for dying, which is the greatest task we have to do, practice can give us no assistance. A man may by use and experience fortify himself against pain, shame, want, and other such accidents; but as for death, we can essay it but once: we are all apprentices when we come to it.

In ancient times there were men who were such excellent husbanders of their time that they tried even in death to taste and relish it and strained their minds to see what this passage was; but they have not returned to tell us news of it:

> No man wakes up
> On whom once falls the icy pause of life.[1]

_____
[1] Lucretius

116

Canius Julius, a noble Roman of singular virtue and firmness, having been condemned to die by that scoundrel Caligula, besides a number of other wonderful proofs that he gave of his fortitude, as he was about to receive the stroke of the executioner, he was asked by a philosopher, a friend of his: "Well, Canius, in what way is your soul now? What is it doing? What are your thoughts?" "I was thinking," he replied, "to keep myself ready and tensed with all my strength in order to see whether in this so short and quick instant of death I shall be able to perceive any sallying forth of the soul, and whether it will have any consciousness of its leave-taking, in order that, if I learn anything, I may hereafter return, if I can, to inform my friends." This man philosophizes not only up to the moment of death, but in death itself. What assurance was this, what intense courage, to desire his death to be a lesson to him, and to be free to turn his thoughts elsewhere in so great a pass!

> That mastery of mind he had in death.[2]

And yet I think there is some way of becoming familiarized with it and in some sort of making trial of it. We may have some experience of it, if not complete and perfect, at least such as may not be useless to us, and that may make us stronger and more assured. If we cannot come to grips with it, we can approach it, we can observe it; and if we do not advance as far as its fortress, we shall at least see and try its avenues of approach.

It is not without reason that we are taught to consider our sleep itself for the resemblance it bears to death. How easily we pass from waking to sleeping! With what little concern do we lose consciousness of the light and of ourselves!

Perhaps the faculty of sleep, which deprives us of all action and all feeling, might seem useless and contrary to nature were it not that by its means Nature instructs us that she has shaped

---

[2] Lucan

us to die as well as to live and presents to us, early in life, the eternal state she reserves for us after it, in order to accustom us to it and to take away our fear of it.

But they who by some violent accident have fallen into a swoon and lost all consciousness have, it seems to me, been very near to seeing its true and natural face. For as to the moment and the point of passing away, there need be no fear that it brings with it any pain or suffering, inasmuch as we can have no feeling without leisure. Our sufferings require time, which in death is so short and swift that it must necessarily be without feeling. It is the approaches that we have to fear, and these may fall within our experience.

Many things seem greater to us in imagination than they are in fact. I have passed a good part of my life in perfectly sound health; I may say not merely sound, but even sprightly and bubbling over. This state, full of fresh energy and jollity, made the thought of sickness so horrible to me that, when I came to experience it, I found its attacks weak and feeble compared with my fear.

Here is something that I experience daily: if I am warmly sheltered in a good room on a stormy and tempestuous night, I wonder at and feel distressed for those who are then in the open country; if I am there myself, I do not even desire to be anywhere else.

That thought alone, of being always shut up in a room, seemed to me unbearable. I was suddenly trained to be there for a week and a month, beset by agitation, disorder, and weakness; and I have found that when I was in good health I pitied the sick much more than I think myself to be pitied when I am one of them, and that the force of my imagination exaggerated by nearly a half the essence and reality of the thing. I hope that it will turn out the same way for me in the matter of death, and that it is not worth the pains that I take in making so many preparations and in calling in and assembling so many aids to sustain the shock. But at all events we cannot give ourselves too much advantage.

In the time of our third civil war, or the second (I do not well remember which), having gone one day to take the air about a league from my house, which is seated in the hub of all the trouble of the civil wars in France, thinking myself in all security and so near to my home that I stood in need of no better equipage, I had taken a horse of very easy gait, not very strong. On my way back, an occasion having suddenly arisen for me to use this horse in a kind of service that he was not quite used to, one of my men, big and strong, mounted upon a powerful work-horse that had a hopelessly hard mouth, fresh to boot and vigorous, to cut a bold figure and outstrip his fellows, forced his horse full tilt straight into my path, and bore down like a Colossus upon the little man and the little horse, and blasted us with his speed and weight, sending us both head over heels; so that there lay the horse prostrate and stunned and I ten or twelve paces beyond, stretched out on my back like a corpse, my face all bruised and skinned, my sword, which I had in my hand, more than ten paces farther on, my belt in pieces, having no more movement or feeling than a log. It was the only swoon I had experienced till that hour. Those who were with me, after having tried all the means they could to bring me to myself, thinking I was dead, took me up in their arms and carried me with much difficulty home to my house, which was about half a French league away. On the way, and after I had been for more than two good hours considered as being dead, I began to move and breathe, for so great an abundance of blood had fallen into my stomach that Nature had need to rouse her forces to discharge it. They put me up on my feet, whereupon I threw up a bucketful of clots of pure blood, and several times on the way I had to do it again. By this means I began to recover a little life, but it was by slow degrees and over so long a stretch of time that my first feelings were much nearer death than life,

> For still in doubt of its return to life,
> The stricken soul rests unsure of itself.[3]

This recollection, which is strongly imprinted on my mind, bringing the image and idea of death before me in so nearly natural an aspect, somewhat reconciles me to it. When I began to see, it was with so blurred, so weak, and so dead a sight that I could as yet distinguish nothing but the light,

> Like him who opens now, now shuts his eyes,
> Lying midway 'twixt sleep and wakefulness.[4]

As to the functions of the mind, they revived at the same rate as those of the body. I saw I was all bloody, for my doublet was stained all over with the blood I had vomited. The first thought that came to me was that I had been shot in the head by a harquebus; indeed at the same time as the accident several had been fired around us. It seemed to me that my life just hung upon the edge of my lips; I shut my eyes to help, so I thought, to thrust it out, and took a pleasure in languishing and letting myself go. It was an idea that only floated on the surface of my mind, as weak and feeble as all the rest, but, in truth, not only free from distress, but mixed with that pleasant tranquillity felt by us when we are gliding into slumber.

I believe it is the same condition those people are in whom we see faint with weakness in the agony of death, and I think that we pity them without cause, supposing that they are agitated with grievous suffering and their minds beset by painful thoughts. It has ever been my belief, contrary to the opinion of many, and even of Etienne de La Boétie, that those whom we see so overwhelmed and stupefied at the approach of their end, or crushed by the length of their sickness, or by an attack of apoplexy or the falling sickness,

---

[3] Tasso, *Jerusalem Delivered*   [4] Tasso, *Jerusalem Delivered*

> And oft before our eyes someone o'ercome
> By illness topples as by lightning struck,
> And spews forth foam; he twitches and he moans;
> His sinews tense, he drivels, writhes, and gasps,
> And wearies out his limbs with tossing wild,[5]

or hurt in the head, when we hear them moaning and at times uttering poignant sighs, although we gather from these signs and from some movements we see them make with the body that they still retain some consciousness, I have always believed, I say, that their mind and their body are shrouded and asleep:

> He lives, and is unconscious of his life.[6]

And I could not believe that in so great a stupefaction of the members and so great a failing of the senses the soul could maintain any force within to be conscious of itself, and that, therefore, they had no power of reflection to torment them and make them feel and measure the wretchedness of their condition, and that consequently they were not much to be pitied.

I can think of no state for me so unbearable and dreadful as to have the soul alive and afflicted without means of expressing itself. As I should say of those who are sent to execution with their tongues cut out, were it not that in this kind of death the most silent seems to me the most becoming if accompanied with a grave and firm countenance, and of those wretched prisoners who fall into the hands of the villainous, inhuman soldiers of this age, by whom they are tortured with every kind of cruelty to compel them to pay some excessive and impossible ransom, kept in the meantime in a condition and place where they have no means of expressing or signifying their thoughts and misery.

The poets have imagined some gods favorable to the deliverance of those who thus drag on a lingering death,

---

[5] Lucretius   [6] Ovid, *Tristia*

> This offering unto Dis I bear,
> As bid, and from thy body set thee free![7]

And the brief and disconnected words and replies which we extract from them by dint of shouting in their ears and storming at them, or the movements which seem to correspond somewhat to what is asked of them, are, however, no evidence that they are alive, at least fully alive. So it happens to us in the stammering beginnings of sleep, before it has fully seized us, that we perceive, as in a dream, what is done about us and follow the voices with a confused and uncertain hearing which seems but to touch upon the borders of the soul; and to the last words that were spoken to us we give answers that are made up more of chance than of sense.

Now that I have actually tried it, I make no doubt that my judgment of it hitherto has been correct. For in the first place, being fully unconscious, I was laboring with all the strength of my nails to open up my doublet (for I was not in armor), and yet I know that in my mind I was not aware of anything hurting me, for we make many motions that do not start forth from the direction of our will,

> Half-dead, the fingers move and clutch anew the sword.[8]

So falling people throw their arms out in front of them by a natural impulse which causes our limbs to lend each other their services and to be moved quite apart from our reason:

> They say that scythe-armed chariots lop off limbs
> So quickly that the part which is cut off
> Is seen to quiver on the earth below,
> While yet the mind and powers of the man
> Can through the rapid blow perceive no pain.[9]

My stomach was oppressed with the clotted blood, my hands hastened to it of their own accord, as they often do to the part

---

[7] Virgil, *Aeneid*   [8] Virgil, *Aeneid*   [9] Lucretius

that itches, against the direction of our will. There are many animals, and even men, whose muscles may be seen to contract and move after they are dead. Everyone knows by experience that there are parts which often stir, rise up, and lie down without his leave. Now these feelings which only touch the outward bark of us cannot be said to be ours. To make them ours the whole man must be involved in them; and the pains which are felt by the hand or the foot while we are sleeping are not ours.

As I drew near to my house, where the alarm of my fall had preceded me, and as the members of my family came out to meet me with the outcries usual in such cases, not only did I give some sort of reply to what was asked of me, but they even say that I had the sense to order them to give a horse to my wife, whom I saw stumbling and struggling on the road, which is hilly and rough. It seems that this thoughtfulness must have proceeded from a mind that was awake; yet I was not there at all: they were nothing but idle thoughts in the clouds, that were stirred up by the senses of sight and hearing; they did not come out of myself. I did not know, for all that, whence I was coming, or whither I was going, neither was I able to weigh and consider what was asked of me: those are slight effects that the senses produce by themselves, as if by habit; what the mind contributed was as in a dream, very lightly touched, only licked, as it were, and bedewed by the soft impression of the senses.

Meanwhile my condition was, in truth, very easy and peaceful. I was grieved neither for others, nor for myself; it was a languor and extreme weakness without any pain. I saw my house without recognizing it. When they had put me to bed, I found an inexpressible sweetness in that repose, for I had been wretchedly dragged about by those poor people who had taken the pains to carry me in their arms over a long and very bad road and in doing so had tired themselves out two or three times in relays. They offered me many remedies, none of which I took, holding it for certain that I was mortally wounded in the head. In all truth, it would have been a very happy death, for the weakness of my reason prevented me from having any opinions about it, and that of my body from feeling anything. I was letting myself glide away so gently, and in so soft and easy a manner, that I scarcely know any action less burdensome than that was. When I began to revive and to resume my faculties,

As my lost senses did at last return,[10]

which was two or three hours later, I felt myself suddenly involved again in pain, my limbs being all pounded and bruised by my fall, and I was so ill for two or three nights after that I thought I was dying once more, but by a more painful death; and I still feel the shock of that crash. I do not want to omit this, that the last thing I could recover was the recollection of this accident, and I had them tell me over and over again whither I was going, whence I was coming, and at what hour that had happened to me, before I could comprehend it. As to the manner of my fall, that was concealed from me for the sake of the man who had been the cause of it, and another story was invented. But a long time after, on the following day, when my memory began to return and picture to me the state I was in at the instant that I perceived this horse bearing down upon me (for I had seen him at my heels and thought I was a goner; but this thought had been so sudden that there was no time for fear to arise), it seemed to me that it was a flash of lightning that struck my mind with a jolt, and that I was returning from the other world.

This story of so unimportant an event is rather pointless were it not for the instruction I have derived from it for my own use; for, in truth, I find that to become familiar with death there is no way except to approach it. Now, as Pliny says, everyone is a very good subject of study to himself, provided he have the capacity to examine himself closely. This is not my

---
[10] Ovid, *Tristia*

teaching, it is my study; and it is not a lesson for others, but for me.

And yet one should not be displeased with me if I communicate it. That which is of use to me may also by chance be useful to another. Besides I spoil nothing, I make use of nothing but my own. And if I play the fool, it is at my own expense and without detriment to anyone. For it is a folly that dies with me and has no consequences. We hear of only two or three ancients who have trod this road, and yet we cannot say whether it was at all in this manner, knowing only their names. No one since has thrown himself on their trail. It is a thorny undertaking, and more so than it seems, to follow so roving a movement as that of our mind, to penetrate the opaque depths of its innermost folds, to choose and arrest so many little emanations of its stirrings. It is a new and extraordinary pastime which withdraws us from the ordinary occupations of the world, yes, and from those most recommended.

For many years my thoughts have had no other aim than myself; and if I study any other thing, it is to apply it at once to myself, or rather in myself. And I do not think it a fault if, as is done in other incomparably less useful sciences, I communicate what I have learned in this one, though I am not very well pleased with the progress I have made in it. There is no description equal in difficulty to the description of oneself, nor certainly in usefulness. Furthermore a man must have his hair well groomed, he must make himself trim and neat to appear in public. Now I am continually decking myself out, for I am continually describing myself. Custom has made it a vice to speak of oneself and obstinately forbids it in hatred of the boasting that seems always to be attached to men's testimony about themselves. Whereas a child's nose should be wiped, that is called pulling it off,

Fleeing a fault may lead into a vice.[11]

---

[11] Horace, *Ars Poetica*

I find more evil than good in this remedy. But even if it were true that to talk to people about ourselves is necessarily presumptuous, I ought not, following out my general plan, to forbear an action that publishes this infirmity, since it is in me; and I ought not to conceal this fault which I not only practise but profess. But to speak my mind freely, it is a wrong custom that condemns wine because some get drunk on it. Only things that are good can be abused. And I believe that this rule concerns only the weakness of the common people. Such rules are bridles for calves with which neither saints, whom we hear speak so highly of themselves, nor philosophers, nor theologians will curb themselves; nor will I, though I am as little the one as the other. If they do not expressly write about themselves, at all events, when the occasion arises, they do not hesitate to put themselves on parade. Of what does Socrates treat more largely than of himself? To what does he more often direct the conversation of his disciples than to speak of themselves, not of the lesson in their book, but of the essence and movement of their soul? We scrupulously confess ourselves to God and our confessor, as our neighbors do to the whole people. But, someone will answer me, we confess only our sins. Then we confess all, for our very virtue is faulty and repentable. My trade and my art is to live. He that forbids me to speak of it according to my own sense, experience, and practice, let him order an architect to speak of buildings not according to his own opinions, but according to his neighbor's, according to another's knowledge, not according to his own. If it is vainglory for a man to proclaim his own worthy traits, why does not Cicero push to the fore the eloquence of Hortensius, and Hortensius that of Cicero?

Perhaps they mean that I should give testimony of myself by works and deeds, not barely by words. I chiefly portray my thoughts, a shapeless subject which cannot be expressed in the productivity of deeds. It is all that I can do to couch it in this airy body of the voice. The wisest and devoutest men have lived shunning all visible actions. The actions would tell more about Fortune than about me. They testify to their rôle, not to mine, unless it be conjecturally and uncertainly: samples showing only certain particular details. I expose myself entire: it is a skeleton on which, at one view, the veins, muscles, and tendons are apparent, each part in its place. The effect of a cough brought into evidence one part of it; the effect of pallor or the beating of the heart another, and that dubiously. It is not my deeds that I write about; it is myself, it is my essence.

I maintain that we must be judicious in forming an estimate of ourselves and equally conscientious in giving an account of it impartially, be it high or low. If I thought myself good and wise, or nearly so, I should sing it forth at the top of my voice. To say less of ourselves than what we are is foolishness, not modesty. And to pay ourselves off with less than we are worth is cowardice and pusillanimity according to Aristotle. No virtue is helped by falsehood; and truth is never a matter of error. To say more of ourselves than is really true is not always presumption, it likewise is often foolishness. To be inordinately pleased with what one is, to fall into an undiscerning self-love, is, in my opinion, the substance of this vice. The supreme remedy for curing it is to do the very opposite of what is prescribed by those who in forbidding us to speak of ourselves consequently forbid us even more to think of ourselves. Pride lies in the thought. The tongue can have only a very slight share in it. It seems to them that to give attention to oneself is to be pleased with oneself, that to frequent and to converse with oneself is to hold oneself too dear. It may be so. But this excess arises only in those who try themselves only on the surface, who look to themselves only after their business, who call it dreaming and idleness to reflect upon themselves, and look upon the building up and the equipping of oneself as building castles in Spain, considering themselves as a third person and a stranger.

If anyone, looking at those beneath him, becomes intoxicated with his knowledge, let him but turn his eye upward towards past ages and he will lower his horns, finding there so many thousands of minds that trample him under foot. If he assume any flattering presumption of his own worth, let him recall the lives of the two Scipios, so many armies, so many nations that leave him so far behind them. No particular quality will make any man proud who will at the same time take account of the many other weak and imperfect qualities that are in him, and, in the end, the nothingness of the state of man.

Because Socrates alone had seriously bitten into that precept of his god, "to know himself," and by that study had come to scorn himself, he alone was considered worthy of the title of Sage. Whoever shall so know himself, let him boldly make himself known by his own mouth.

OF THE AFFECTION OF FATHERS
FOR THEIR CHILDREN
To Madame d'Estissac

MADAME, if strangeness and novelty, which generally give value to things, do not save me, I shall never come off with honor from this foolish undertaking; but it is so fantastic and has an aspect so far removed from the common practice that this may, perhaps, enable it to pass. It is a melancholy humor, and consequently a humor very much opposed to my natural disposition, engendered by the moodiness of the solitude into which some years ago I had thrown myself, that first put into my head this fancy of dabbling in writing. And then, finding myself totally devoid and empty of all other matter, I presented myself to myself for argument and subject. It is the only book in the world of its kind, of an outlandish and extravagant design. There is, moreover, in this affair nothing worthy of remark except this bizarreness; for to a subject so vain and frivolous the best workman in the world could not have given a form that merits any account being made of it.

Now, madame, having here to portray myself to the life, I should have omitted an important feature had I not represented in it the honor I have ever paid to your merits. And I wanted to express it particularly at the head of this chapter because, among your other fine qualities, that of the love you have shown to your children holds one of the chief places. Anyone who knows at what age Monsieur d'Estissac, your husband, left you a widow, the great and honorable matches that have been offered to you in as great number as to any lady of your rank in France, the steadiness and firmness with which you have sus-

tained for so many years, and through so many thorny difficulties, the charge and conduct of their affairs, which have
driven you into all corners of France and which still hold you
besieged, the happy direction you have given them by your
wisdom alone or good fortune, will readily say with me that we
have not in our time a more conspicuous example of maternal
affection than yours. I praise God, madame, that it has been so
well employed; for the good hopes that Monsieur d'Estissac,
your son, gives of himself, are sufficient assurances that when
he comes of age you will have from him the obedience and gratitude of a very good son. But inasmuch as because of his tender
years he has not been able to take notice of the supreme services which he has received from you in so great number, I desire, if these writings happen some day to fall into his hands,
when I shall have neither mouth nor speech left to express it,
that he receive from me this testimony in all good faith, which
will be even more keenly testified to him by their good results
which, if God so wills, he will perceive: that there is no gentleman in France who owes more to his mother than he does, and
that he cannot in the future give a more certain proof of his
goodness and his virtue than in acknowledging you for the excellent mother you are.

If there is any law truly natural, that is to say, any instinct
that is seen universally and everlastingly impressed in both
beasts and in us (which is not without controversy), I can say
that, in my opinion, after the care every animal has for its own
preservation and to avoid that which may hurt it, the affection
that the begetter has for his offspring holds the second place in
rank. And since Nature seems to have recommended it to us
with a view to extending and advancing the successive parts of
this machine of hers, it is no wonder if, turning backwards, that
of children for their parents is not so great.

To which we may add this other Aristotelian consideration,
that he who confers a benefit on anyone loves him better than
he is loved by him; and that he to whom it is owed loves better

than he who owes; and that every worker loves his work more than he would be loved by it if the work had feeling. For it is dear to us to be, and to be consists in movement and action. Therefore everyone in some sort exists in his work. He who confers a benefit practises a fine and honorable action; he who receives exercises only the useful; now the useful is much less lovable than the honorable. The honorable is stable and permanent, supplying him who has done it with a constant gratification. The useful loses itself, easily slides away, and the memory of it is neither so fresh nor so pleasing. Those things are dearest to us that have cost us most; and it is more difficult to give than to receive.

Since it has pleased God to endow us with some capacity for reasoning in order that we may not like brutes be slavishly subjected to the common laws, but rather that we should by judgment and free will adapt ourselves to them, we ought, indeed, to yield a little to the simple authority of Nature, but not let ourselves be tyrannically carried away by her; reason alone should have the guidance of our inclinations.

I, for my part, have a taste strangely dull to those inclinations that arise in us without the mediation and direction of our judgment. For example, on the subject I am speaking of, I cannot entertain that passion for fondling infants scarcely born, having neither motion of soul nor recognizable shape of body by which they can make themselves lovable. And I have not willingly suffered them to be reared near me. A true and well-regulated affection ought to spring up and increase with the knowledge they give us of themselves; and then, if they are worthy of it, the natural inclination going hand in hand with reason, we should cherish them with a truly paternal love; and we should likewise pass judgment on them if they be otherwise, ever submitting to reason notwithstanding the force of nature. It is often quite the reverse; and most commonly we feel ourselves more roused by the prancings, the games, and the infantile antics of our children than we do afterwards by their grown-up actions, as if we had loved them for our pastime, as monkeys, not as men. And some are very liberal in providing toys for their childhood, who become very closefisted for the smallest necessary expense when they grow up. Indeed it looks as if the jealousy we feel at seeing them appearing in and enjoying the world when we are about to leave it renders us more niggardly and stingy towards them; it vexes us that they tread upon our heels, as if to urge us to depart. And if we had to fear that, since the order of things provides that they cannot, to tell the truth, be or live but at the expense of our being and our life, we should never meddle with being fathers.

For my part, I think it cruelty and injustice not to receive them into a share and partnership of our goods, and not to make them partakers in the knowledge of our domestic affairs when they are capable, and not to cut down and restrict our comforts in order to provide for theirs, since we have begotten them to that end. It is unjust that an old father, broken-down and half dead, should enjoy alone in his chimney corner resources that would suffice for the advancement and maintenance of many children, and suffer them in the meantime to waste their best years for want of means to push themselves in public service and the knowledge of men. They are driven to the desperate plight of seeking by any means, however wrong, to provide for their needs; as I have seen in my time several young men of good family so addicted to stealing that no correction could turn them from it. I know one, well-connected, to whom at the request of a brother of his, a very honorable and brave gentleman, I once spoke on this account. He answered me and confessed very roundly that he had been led into this filthy practice by the severity and avarice of his father, but that he was now so accustomed to it he could not keep away from it. And at that very time he had just been caught stealing the rings of a lady at whose levee he had been present with many others. He put me in mind of a story I had heard of another gentleman so practised and accomplished in this fine trade in his youth that, coming later into his estate and resolved to give up this traffic, he could not refrain, nevertheless, if he were passing a shop where there was anything he needed, from stealing it, on pain of sending afterwards to pay for it. And I have seen several so schooled and hardened to this that even among their comrades they commonly stole things which they intended to restore.

I am a Gascon, yet there is no vice I so little understand as this. I hate it a little more by disposition than I condemn it by reason. I do not even in desire take anything away from another man. This region is, in truth, a little more decried than the others of France; yet we have in our age at various times seen men of good families of other regions in the hands of justice, convicted of many abominable robberies. I fear this corruption is in some sort to be blamed on that vice of the fathers.

And if a man should reply to me, as a lord of good understanding once did, that he hoarded up wealth not to extract any other fruit and use from it but to make himself honored and sought after by his own relations, and that age having deprived him of all other powers, it was the only remedy left to him for maintaining his authority in his family and for avoiding being scorned and despised by everybody (in truth, not only old age but all weakness, according to Aristotle, is the promoter of avarice), this is something, but it is medicine for a disease that we should prevent from being born. A father is very miserable that has no other hold on his children's affections than the need they have of his assistance, if that can be called affection. He must make himself worthy of respect by his virtue and by his ability, and worthy of love by his kindness and by the sweetness of his nature. The very ashes of a rich matter have their value, and we have been accustomed to hold the bones and relics of worthy men in respect and reverence. No old age can be so decrepit and offensive in a gentleman who has passed his life in honor but it must be venerable, especially to his children, whose souls he must have trained up to their duty by reason,

not by necessity and the need they have of him, nor by roughness and force,

> And he extremely differs from my sense,
> Who thinks the power obtained by violence
> Can ever prove more solid and secure,
> Than that which friendship's softer means procure.[1]

I condemn all violence in the education of a gentle soul that
is being trained for honor and liberty. There is an indescribable
element of servility in rigor and compulsion; and I hold that
what cannot be done by reason and by wisdom and tact is never
done by force. I was brought up that way. They say that in all
my childhood I never felt the rod but twice, and then very
softly. I have owed the same to my children; all of them died
at nurse; but Leonor, an only daughter who escaped that misfortune, has reached the age of six years and more without our
using in her guidance and for the punishment of her childish
faults (her mother's indulgence easily concurring) anything but
words, and very gentle ones. And even though my expectation
should be frustrated, there are other causes enough to lay the
fault on without blaming my educational system, which I know
to be right and natural. I should in this have been even more
scrupulous with boys, less born to serve and of a freer condition; I should have loved to swell their hearts with ingenuous-
ness and independence. I have never observed any other effects
from whipping than to make the soul more cowardly or more
maliciously obstinate.

Do we desire to be loved by our children? Do we remove
from them all occasion of desiring our death (though no occasion of so horrible a desire can be either right or excusable: *no
wicked deed is based on reason*[2])? Let us reasonably furnish
their lives with what is in our power. To do that we should not

---

[1] Terence, *Adelphi*   [2] Livy

marry so young that our age will be almost merged with theirs. For this inconvenience plunges us into many great difficulties. I am referring especially to the nobility, who are the leisure class and who live, as the saying is, only on their private income. For in other classes where life is given to earning money, the plurality and company of children is a means of fitting up the household; they are so many new tools and instruments wherewith to grow rich.

I married at thirty-three and commend the suggestion of thirty-five, which is said to be that of Aristotle. Plato will have nobody marry before thirty, but he rightly laughs at those who perform the works of marriage after fifty-five, and he condemns their offspring as unworthy of food and life.

Thales gave it the truest limits, who, when young and being urged by his mother to marry, answered that it was too soon, and when advanced in years, that it was too late. We must deny opportuneness to every inopportune action.

The ancient Gauls looked upon it as an extremely reproachable action to have had knowledge of a woman before the age of twenty and recommended particularly to the men who wanted to be trained for war to preserve their virginity until well on in years, since courage is softened and diverted by intercourse with women.

> But being married to a fair young bride,
> Then blessed with sons, his courage he had lost
> In the affection of a sire and spouse.[3]

Greek history observes of Iccus of Tarentum, of Chryson, of Astylus, of Diopompus, and others, that to keep their bodies trim for the races of the Olympic games, for wrestling and other exercises, they denied themselves as long as this training lasted any kind of sexual act.

---

[3] Tasso, *Jerusalem Delivered*

Muley-Hassan, King of Tunis, he whom the Emperor Charles the Fifth restored to his estates, censured the memory of his father for his frequentation of women and called him weakling, effeminate, and child-maker.

In a certain country of the Spanish Indies men were not permitted to marry until after they were forty years old, and yet the girls were allowed to do so at ten.

At the age of thirty-five it is not time for a gentleman to give way to his son who is twenty: he is himself in a condition to make a good showing both in military expeditions and at the court of his prince; he has need of his money, and he ought certainly to share it, but such a share that he does not neglect himself for others. And such a man may rightly use the reply that fathers commonly have in their mouths, "I do not want to strip myself before going to bed."

But a father, struck down by age and infirmities, deprived by his weakness and want of health of the ordinary society of men, wrongs himself and his family by uselessly brooding over a great pile of wealth. He is in the proper state, if he is wise, to want to strip himself for bed, not to his very shirt, but to a good warm nightgown. The remaining pomps, of which he has no further use, he ought willingly to bestow on those to whom by the order of Nature they belong. It is right that he should leave the enjoyment of those things to them, since Nature deprives him of it; otherwise there is doubtless malice and envy present.

The finest act of the Emperor Charles the Fifth was that, in imitation of some of the ancients of his own quality, he was able to recognize that reason sufficiently commands us to strip ourselves when our robes become a burden and encumbrance, and to go to bed when our legs begin to fail us. He resigned his possessions, his grandeur, and his power to his son when he felt fail in him the firmness and vigor necessary to conduct his affairs with the glory he had therein acquired.

Be wise, set free in time your aging steed,
Ere he mid jeers breaks down and bursts his wind.[4]

This fault of not being able to recognize oneself early and of not feeling the impotence and extreme changes that age naturally brings both to the body and to the soul, which, in my opinion, are evenly distributed to both (if the soul, indeed, does not get more than half), has ruined the reputation of most of the great men of the world. I have in my time seen and been intimately acquainted with personages of great authority who, it was very easy to see, had amazingly declined from that former capacity which I knew about through the reputation they had thereby acquired in their better years. I could heartily, for the sake of their honor, have wished them retired at home at their ease and freed from public and military tasks which were no longer suitable for their shoulders.

I was once on intimate terms in the house of a gentleman, a widower and very old, yet of a rather green old age. This man had several marriageable daughters and a son already old enough to come out into the world. That burdened his house with many expenses and visits of strangers, which little pleased him, not only out of concern for economy, but even more for having, because of his age, adopted a way of living far removed from ours. I told him one day a little boldly, as I am accustomed to do, that it would befit him better to make way for us younger folk and to leave his principal house (for that was the only one he had that was well situated and furnished) to his son and retire to an estate he had hard by where nobody would trouble his repose, since he could not otherwise avoid being troubled by us in view of the situation of his children. He took my advice afterwards and was the better for it.

I do not mean that we should make donations to them in such a binding way that we cannot retract. I, who am old

---

[4] Horace, *Epistles*

enough to play this part, would resign to them the enjoyment of my house and goods, but with the liberty to change my mind if they should give me occasion. I would leave to them the use of it because it would no longer be convenient for me; and of the authority over the affairs in general, I would reserve to myself as much as I thought good, having always considered that it must needs be a great satisfaction to an aged father to himself put his children in the way of managing his affairs and to be able during his own life to supervise their behavior, supplying them with instruction and advice according to the experience he has of them, and personally to set the ancient honor and good order of his house underway in the hands of his successors, and by that means to assure himself of the hopes he may conceive of their future conduct. And to achieve this I would not avoid their company; I would like to observe them near at hand and join, as far as my age permitted, in their fun and festivities. If I did not live in their midst (as I could not do without disturbing their gatherings because of the touchiness of my age and the troublesomeness of my infirmities, and without also cramping and doing violence to the rules and mode of living which I should then have), I should want at least to live near them in some part of my house, not the most showy, but the most comfortable. Not as I saw, some years ago, a Dean of Saint-Hilaire of Poitiers reduced by the molestation of his melancholy to such a solitude that at the time I came into his chamber he had not taken a step out of it for twenty-two years; and yet he was in full and easy possession of all his functions except for a cold that had attacked his stomach. Hardly once a week would he let anyone come to see him; he always kept himself shut up in his chamber, alone except for a servant who once a day brought him something to eat and who only came in and went out. His activity consisted of walking back and forth and of reading some book (for he was somewhat versed in letters), set, moreover, upon dying in this routine, as he soon did.

I would endeavor by gentle relations to foster in my children a lively and unfeigned affection and good will towards me, which in a wellborn nature is easily achieved; for if they are furious brutes, such as our age produces in profusion, we must hate and shun them as such.

I dislike the custom of forbidding children the word "father" and of ordering them to use a distant title as being more respectful, as if Nature had not herself sufficiently provided for our authority. We call Almighty God "Father" and disdain to have our children call us so. It is also wrong and foolish to deprive children when grown up of familiarity with their fathers, and to want to maintain an austere and disdainful attitude towards them, hoping by that to keep them in awe and obedience. For it is a most useless farce that renders fathers irksome and, what is worse, ridiculous to their own children. They have youth and vigor in possession, and consequently the breath and favor of the world; and they receive with mockery these fierce and tyrannical looks of a man who no longer has any blood in his heart or veins—veritable scarecrows in a hempfield! Even if I could make myself feared, I had yet much rather make myself loved.

There are so many sorts of failings in old age, so much impotency, it is so liable to contempt, that the best acquisition we can then make is the affection and love of our own family; command and fear are no longer our weapons. I have known one whose youth had been very imperious. Now that he is advanced in years, although he is getting along in the best health possible, he strikes, he bites, he swears, the most tempestuous master in France; he is gnawed by care and vigilance. And all is only a farce in which the family itself conspires: of his storeroom, of his cellar, nay, even of his purse, others have the greatest share of the enjoyment, while he keeps the keys in his pouch with fonder care than if they were his eyes. While he rejoices in the frugality and niggardliness of his table, everything is in disorder in various corners of his house: gaming, squandering, relating tales of his futile anger and foresight. Everyone is on guard against him. If by chance some wretched servant devotes himself to him, he immediately becomes suspicious to him, a feeling at which old age is very likely to bite of its own accord. How often has he boasted to me of the curb he kept on his family and of the strict obedience and reverence that he received from them. How clearly he saw into his own affairs!

He alone is ignorant of all.[5]

I do not know of any man who can master more parts, both natural and acquired, proper to maintain mastery than he; yet he is fallen from it like a child. For this reason I have picked him out from among a number of others I know in the same state as the best example.

It would be matter for a scholastic dispute whether he is better thus or otherwise. In his presence everything gives way to him. They let his authority run this futile course without ever resisting it: they believe him, they fear him, they respect him to his full. Does he dismiss a servant? He packs up his bundle, and there he is gone—but only out of his sight. The steps of old age are so slow, the senses so troubled, that he will live and do his old job in the same house for a year without being perceived. And when the time is ripe, they have letters sent from a long way off, pitiful, begging, and full of promise of amendment, by virtue of which he is received back into favor. Does Monsieur make some transaction or send some message that does not please? They suppress it, forging soon after reasons enough to excuse the lack of execution or of answer. Since no letters from outside are first brought to him, he sees only those that seem all right for him to know. If by accident he gets hold of them, being accustomed to rely on a certain person to read them to him, this fellow at once finds in them

---

[5] Terence, *Adelphi*

whatever he pleases and often manages to have a man asking his pardon who is insulting him in this very letter. In short, he sees his affairs only in an image prepared and arranged purposely, and as satisfactory to him as they can make it, in order not to rouse his ill humor and anger. I have seen under different forms enough of these household managements, long and constantly maintained, with a very similar result.

Women are always prone to disagree with their husbands. They lay hold with both hands on all pretexts to oppose them, and the first excuse serves for a plenary justification. I knew one who stole wholesale from her husband so that, as she told her confessor, she might distribute more liberal alms. Just trust in this pious charity! No authority seems to them of sufficient dignity if it comes as a concession from the husband. They must usurp it either by insolence or cunning, and always offensively, in order to give it grace and authority. When, as in the case I am speaking of, it is against a poor old man and for the sake of children, they seize this pretext and make it serve their passion as though it were a merit, and, as if in a common servitude, they readily conspire against his authority and rule. If there are grown-up and active sons, they also presently corrupt, either by force or favor, both steward and receivers and all the rest. Those who have neither wife nor son fall into this misfortune less easily, but at the same time more cruelly and shamefully. Cato the Elder said in his time, "So many servants, so many enemies." Consider whether, according to the difference in purity between his age and ours, he did not want to warn us that wife, son, and servant are so many enemies to us. It is well that decrepit age furnishes us with the sweet blessing of lack of perception and of ignorance and readiness to let ourselves be deceived. If we set our teeth to it, what would become of us, especially in such an age as this where the judges who have to decide our disputes are usually partisans of the young and interested ones?

In case the deception escapes my sight, at least it does not escape my sight that I am very deceivable. And can a man ever enough express the value of a friend, and how different it is from these civil ties? The very image of it which I see so pure in beasts, how religiously do I respect it!

If others deceive me, I do not, at least, deceive myself in thinking I am capable of defending myself against it or in eating out my brains to make myself capable. I escape from such treasons in my own bosom, not by a restless and agitated curiosity, but rather by diversion and resolution. When I hear talk of someone's condition, I do not dwell on him; I immediately turn my eyes upon myself to see how I am in this respect. All that concerns him relates to me. The chance that has befallen him warns me and rouses me on that side. Every day and every hour we say things of another that we might more properly say of ourselves if we could turn our observation inward as well as extend it outward. And many authors in this manner injure their own cause by running headlong upon the one which they attack and hurling against their enemies shafts capable of being hurled back at them.

The late Maréchal de Monluc, having lost his son, who died in the island of Madeira, in truth a brave gentleman and of great expectation, did to me, among his other regrets, very much insist upon the sorrow and heartbreak he felt at never having opened himself to him and at having lost by that humor of paternal gravity and stiffness the comfort of appreciating and understanding his son and also of letting him know the extreme affection he had for him and the well-merited opinion he had of his virtue. "And that poor boy," said he, "never saw in me other than a stern and disdainful countenance and has carried away the belief that I neither knew how to love or esteem him as he deserved. For whom did I reserve the revelation of that singular affection I had for him in my soul? Was it not he who ought to have had all the pleasure of it and all the gratitude? I forced and wracked myself to maintain this empty mask and have by this means lost the pleasure of his

company and along with it his affection, which could not but
be very cold towards me, having never received from me anything but harshness, nor perceived anything but tyrannical
bearing." I find this lament was well taken and reasonable;
for, as I know by too certain experience, there is no consolation so sweet in the loss of friends as that which is brought to
us by the knowledge of not having forgotten anything we
wanted to say to them and of having had with them perfect
and complete communion.

I open myself to my family as much as I can and very readily
let them know the state of my feelings and of my mind towards
them, as I do to everybody. I make haste to make myself known
and present myself to them; for I do not want them to be mistaken in me in any direction whatsoever.

Among other peculiar customs of our ancient Gauls, this,
as Caesar reports, was one: that the sons did not appear before their fathers, nor dared appear in their company in public, until they began to bear arms, as if they would intimate
by this that it was then also time for the fathers to receive
them into their familiarity and acquaintance.

I have observed still another sort of error of judgment in
some fathers of my time, who are not content to have deprived
their children during their own long lives of the share they naturally ought to have had in their fortunes, but afterwards
leave to their wives the same authority over all their estate and
the right to dispose of it according to their fancy. And I have
known a certain lord, one of the principal officers of the
crown, who, having in prospect by the right of succession
more than fifty thousand crowns of yearly revenue, died in
need and overwhelmed with debt when more than fifty years
old, his mother in her extreme decrepitude being still in the
enjoyment of all his estate by the will of his father, who had,
for his part, lived nearly eighty years. This does not seem at
all reasonable to me.

However, I think it of very little advantage to a man whose

affairs are well off to seek a wife who burdens him with a great dowry; there is no outside debt that brings more ruin to families. My ancestors have generally followed this counsel very profitably, and so have I. But those who dissuade us from rich wives, for fear they should be less tractable and grateful, err in making us lose a real advantage for so frivolous a conjecture. It costs an unreasonable woman no more to override one reason than another. The more wrong they are, the better they love themselves. Injustice allures them, just as the honor of their virtuous actions does good women; and the richer they are, the more kind-natured they are, just as women who are beautiful are more readily and proudly chaste.

It is right to leave the administration of affairs to mothers as long as the children are not old enough, according to the laws, to exercise the charge; but the father has brought them up very badly if he cannot expect that, when they have reached that age, they will have more wisdom and ability than his wife, considering the ordinary weakness of the sex. Yet it would, in truth, be much more contrary to nature to make the mothers dependent on the discretion of their children. They ought to be liberally provided with the means to maintain themselves according to the standing of their house and their age, since necessity and indigence are much more unbecoming and insupportable to them than to men; the burden should be laid on the children rather than on the mother.

In general the soundest distribution of our property when we come to die is, in my opinion, to let it be distributed according to the custom of the country. The laws have considered the matter better than we, and it is better to let them err in their choice than rashly to run the hazard of erring in ours. The estate is not properly ours since by a civil prescription and independent of us it is destined for certain successors. And although we have some liberty beyond that, I hold that there must be a great and very manifest cause for us to take away from one that which his fortune had allotted him and to which common justice gave him title, and that it is to abuse this liberty contrary to reason to make it serve our frivolous and private fancies. My destiny has been kind to me in not having offered me occasions to tempt me and to divert my affection from the common and legitimate order of things.

I know some with whom it is time lost to take long pains in doing them good services: a word taken amiss obliterates ten years' merit. Happy is he who is in a position to oil their good will at the last passage. The last action carries the day; not the best and most frequent services, but the most recent and present, do the trick. These are men who play with their wills, as with apples or rods, to reward or punish every action of those that pretend to an interest in them. It is a thing of too great weight and of too extensive consequence to be thus brought out every moment, and in which wise men take their stand once for all, having regard to reason and to public practices.

We take too much to heart these male substitutions. And we put before ourselves a ridiculous eternity for our names. We also give too much weight to the vain conjectures about the future which we derive from childish minds. Perhaps they might have done me an injustice in dispossessing me of my rank for having been the dullest and most leaden, the slowest and most unwilling at my lessons, not of all my brothers only, but of all the boys of my province, whether in mental or bodily exercises. It is folly to make extraordinary choices upon the credit of these divinations wherein we are so often deceived. If the rule may be violated and the destinies corrected in the choice they have made of our heirs, one may more plausibly do it in consideration of some remarkable and enormous physical deformity, a constant, incorrigible defect, and according to us, who are great admirers of beauty, very harmful.

The amusing dialogue between Plato's lawgiver and his citizens will do honor to this passage. "What," they said, feeling themselves about to die, "may we not dispose of our own to whom we please? Gods, what cruelty that it shall not be lawful for us, according as those near us have served us in our sickness, in our old age, in our affairs, to give them more or less according to our fancies!" To which the lawgiver answers thus: "My friends, you who are without question very soon to die, it is hard for you either to know yourselves or what is yours according to the Delphic inscription. I, who make the laws, hold that neither do you belong to yourselves nor does that belong to you which you enjoy. Both your goods and you belong to your families, the past as well as the future. But both your family and goods belong still more to the public. Wherefore, if some flatterer in your old age or in your sickness, or some passion, should unseasonably urge you to make an unjust will, I will guard you against it. But having regard to both the general interest of the city and that of your family, I shall establish laws and make it understood, as is reasonable, that individual interest must give way to the common interest. Go then, peacefully and cheerfully, where human necessity calls you. It belongs to me, who have no more respect for one thing than another, and who, as much as in me lies, am attentive to the public interest, to take care of what you leave behind you."

To return to my subject, it appears to me, I know not why, that by no means is mastery at all due to women over men, the maternal and natural excepted, unless it be for the punishment of those who by some feverish humor have voluntarily submitted themselves to them; but that does not concern the old ones, of whom we are here speaking. It is the reasonableness of this consideration which made us create and give force so readily to that law, which was never seen by anyone, by which women are excluded from the succession to our crown; and there is hardly a sovereignty in the world where it is not pleaded, as it is here, by the appearance of reason that gives it authority; but fortune has given it more credit in some places than in others. It is dangerous to leave the disposal of our succession to their judgment, according to the choice they shall make among the children, which is at all times unjust and fantastic. For that eccentric appetite and unhealthy taste they have during the time of their pregnancies they have at all times in their soul. We commonly see them attached to the weakest and most deformed children, or to those, if they have any, that are still hanging about their necks. For, not having sufficient force of reason to choose and embrace that which merits it, they are more apt to let themselves be carried away where the impressions of nature stand the most alone, like animals that know their young only as long as they give them suck.

Moreover it is easy to see by experience that this natural affection to which we give so great authority has very weak roots. For a very slight profit every day we tear their own children from the arms of mothers and make them take ours in charge. We make them abandon their own to some wretched nurse to whom we do not want to entrust ours, or to some goat, forbidding them not only to give them suck, whatever danger they may incur thereby, but even to take any manner of care of them, that they may devote themselves entirely to the care of ours. And we see in most of them a bastard affection begotten very soon by habit, more vehement than the natural, and a greater solicitude for the preservation of the foster children than of their own.

And I spoke about goats because it is usual all about where I live to see the women of the village, when they cannot suckle their children, call goats to their assistance. And I have at this hour two lackeys that never sucked woman's milk more than eight days. These goats are quickly taught to come to suckle the little children, recognize their voices when they cry and come running to them. If any other than their nursling is brought to them, they refuse it; and the child will do the same with any other goat. I saw one the other day from whom they had taken away his goat because his father had only borrowed it of a neighbor; he could never take to the other that was brought him and died, doubtless of hunger. Animals do as easily alter and corrupt their natural affection as we.

I believe that in the circumstances Herodotus relates of a certain district of Libya, where men mingle promiscuously with women, but the child, as soon as it can walk, takes as its father that man towards whom in the crowd natural inclination guides his first steps, there must often be mistakes.

Now, when we consider this simple reason for loving our children, namely for having begotten them, for which reason we call them our other selves, it appears that there is a very different kind of production proceeding from us that is not of less merit: for that which we engender by the soul, the offspring of our mind, of our heart and ability, is brought forth by a nobler part than that of the body and is more our own; we are both father and mother in this generation. These cost us much dearer and bring us more honor if there is any good in them. For the worth of our other children is much more theirs than ours; the share we have in them is very slight; but of these all the beauty, all the grace and value is ours. Thus it is that they represent and resemble us much more vividly than the rest. Plato adds that there are immortal children that immortalize their fathers, and even deify them, as in the case of Lycurgus, Solon, Minos.

Now history being full of examples of that common affection of fathers for their children, it seemed to me not altogether inappropriate to pick out some of this other kind.

Heliodorus, that good Bishop of Tricca, preferred to lose the honor, the profit, and the devout respect of so venerable a prelacy rather than lose his daughter, a daughter who lives on still very pretty, but perhaps a little too curiously and wantonly tricked out and of too amorous a fashion for an ecclesiastic and sacerdotal daughter.

There was one Labienus at Rome, a personage of great worth and authority and, among other qualities, eminent in all forms of literature. He was, I believe, the son of that great Labienus, the chief of the captains who served under Caesar in the wars in Gaul, and who afterwards, having thrown himself into the faction of the great Pompey, conducted himself so valiantly until Caesar defeated him in Spain. This Labienus of whom I am speaking was an object of envy to many because of his virtue, and, as it is likely, the courtiers and favorites of the emperors of his time were hostile because of his independence and his passion of opposition to tyranny, inherited from his father, with which we may believe he had colored his books and writings. His adversaries prosecuted him before the magistrate at Rome and succeeded in having a number of his published works condemned to the flames. It was with him that this new example of penalty was begun, which was afterwards continued against many others at Rome, of punishing with death even writings and studies. There was not enough occasion and matter for cruelty if we did not mix with them things that Nature has exempted from all feeling and suffering, such as reputation and the products of our mind, and if we did not extend corporal punishments to the teachings and monuments of the Muses. Now Labienus could not endure this loss nor survive that progeny so dear to him; he had himself conveyed and shut up alive in the tomb of his ancestors, where he managed to kill and bury himself at the same time. It is hard to show a more vehement paternal affection than that. Cassius Severus, a man of great eloquence and his intimate friend, seeing his books burning, cried out that by the same sentence they should have condemned him to be burned alive with them for he carried and preserved in his memory what they contained.

The like fate befell Greuntius Cordus, accused of having in his books praised Brutus and Cassius. That base, servile, and corrupt Senate, worthy of a worse master than Tiberius, condemned his writings to the flames. He was content to bear them company in death and killed himself by abstaining from food.

The good Lucan, having been condemned by that rascal of a Nero, at the last gasp of his life, when the most part of his blood had already flowed out through the veins of his arms, which he had caused his physician to open in order to bring on death, and when the cold had seized on all his extremities and began to approach his vital parts, the last thing he had in his memory was some of the verses from his work on the battle of Pharsalia, which he recited; and died with these last words on his lips. What was this but taking a tender and paternal leave of his children, resembling the farewells and close embraces that we give to ours when we come to die, and an effect of that natural inclination that recalls to our remembrance in this extremity those things which we held dearest during our life?

Do we think that Epicurus, who, while dying tormented, as he said, by acute pains of the colic, had all his consolation in the beauty of the teachings he left to the world, would have received as much satisfaction from a number of children, well-born and well brought up, if he had had any, as he did from the production of his rich writings; and that if he had had the choice of leaving behind him a deformed and ill-born child or a stupid and pointless book, he, and not he alone but any man of like ability, would not have chosen to incur the first misfortune rather than the other? It would have been, perhaps, an impiety in Saint Augustine (for example) if, on the one hand, it had been proposed to him to bury his writings, from which our religion receives such abundant fruit, or, on the other, to bury his children, had he had any, if he had not chosen rather to bury his children.

And I do not know whether I would not much rather have begotten a perfectly formed child through intercourse with the Muses than through intercourse with my wife.

To this child, such as it is, what I give I give purely and irrevocably, as men give to their bodily children. The little good I have done for it is no more at my own disposal. It may know many things that I no longer know and hold from me what I have not retained and what, just like a stranger, I should have to borrow from it if I had need of it. If I am wiser than it, it is richer than I.

There are few men devoted to poetry who would not be much prouder to be father of the *Aeneid* than of the handsomest youth in Rome, and who would not much better bear the loss of the one than the other. For, according to Aristotle, of all craftsmen, the poet in particular is the fondest of his work. It is hard to believe that Epaminondas, who boasted of leaving as his entire posterity daughters who would one day do their father honor (these were the two noble victories he had won over the Lacedemonians), would willingly have consented to exchange them for the most gorgeous creatures of all Greece, or that Alexander and Caesar ever wished to be deprived of the grandeur of their glorious exploits of war for the advantage of having children and heirs, however perfect and accomplished they might be. Indeed I greatly doubt whether Phidias, or any other excellent sculptor, would so lovingly desire the preservation and longevity of his natural children as he would of a rare statue which with long labor and study he had perfected according to art. And as to those vicious and frenzied passions that have sometimes inflamed fathers with love for their daughters or mothers with love for their sons, the like is also found in this other sort of parenthood: witness what is related of Pygmalion, who, having shaped the statue of a woman of singular beauty, became so violently smitten with an insane love for this work of his that the gods, in behalf of his passion, had to inspire it with life,

> The ivory softened at his touch, and giving way,
> It yielded to his hands.[6]

---

[6] Ovid, *Metamorphoses*

OF BOOKS

I HAVE NO DOUBT that I often happen to speak of things that are better and more truly handled by the masters of the trade. This work here is purely an essay of my natural faculties and not at all of my acquired ones; and whoever shall catch me in ignorance will not do so to my disadvantage, for I should hardly be answerable to another for my reflections, I who am not answerable to myself nor satisfied with them. Whoever goes in quest of knowledge, let him fish for it in its haunts; there is nothing I so little profess. These are fancies of my own, by which I do not try to give knowledge of things, but of myself; they will, perhaps, one day be known to me, or were once, according as chance may have borne me on the spots where they were made clear. But I remember them no more. And if I am a man of some reading, I am a man of no retention. So I promise no certainty, unless it be to make known how far the knowledge I now have reaches. Let no attention be given to the matter, but to the form that I give it.

Let them observe in what I borrow whether I have known how to choose what is proper to enhance my theme. For I make others say what, now for want of knowledge, now for want of understanding, I cannot so well myself express. I do not count my borrowings, I weigh them. And if I had wished to make them valued by their number, I should have laden myself with twice as many. They are all, or very nearly all, of such famous and ancient names that they seem to me to identify themselves sufficiently without my help. In the reasonings and ideas which I transplant into my soil and mingle with my own, I have sometimes purposely omitted the author in order to curb the temerity of those hasty judgments that are cast at all sorts of writings, particularly recent writings of men still living, and in the vulgar tongue, which welcomes everyone's discussing them and which seems to convict the thought and plan of being vulgar also. I would have them give Plutarch a fillip on my nose and be scorched in abusing Seneca through me. I must hide my weakness under these great reputations. I shall love anyone that can unplume me, I mean by clearness of judgment and by the sole distinction of the force and beauty of the words. For I, who, for want of memory, fall short at every stroke in picking them out according to their origin, can realize very well, by measuring my abilities, that my soil is quite incapable of producing any of the too rich flowers that I find planted there, and that all the fruits of my own growth could not compensate for them.

For this I am obliged to be responsible: if I get myself tangled up, if there is any triviality and faultiness in my writings, which I do not perceive at all, or which I am not capable of perceiving when pointed out to me, for faults often escape our eyes, but the infirmity of judgment consists in not being able to discern them when another uncovers them for us. Knowledge and truth can lodge in us without judgment, and judgment also without them; truly, the recognition of ignorance is one of the fairest and surest testimonies of judgment that I know. I have no other general officer but Fortune to draw up my pieces. As my fancies present themselves, I pile them up; sometimes they come crowding one another, sometimes they come dragging one by one. I want my natural and ordinary pace to be seen, irregular as it is. I let myself go as I am. Neither are these matters which a man is not permitted to be ignorant in or to speak of casually and lightly.

I should wish, indeed, to have a more perfect knowledge of things, but I do not wish to buy it as dear as it costs. My intent is to pass pleasantly, and not laboriously, the remainder of my life. There is nothing for which I wish to wrack my brains; not even knowledge, however valuable it may be.

I seek in books only to take pleasure through an honest diversion; or if I study, I seek in it only the science that treats of the knowledge of myself and instructs me how to die well and how to live well:

> And to this goal my steed must labor hard.[1]

I do not bite my nails over the difficulties if I meet any in my reading; after a charge or two on them I abandon them there. Should I dwell upon them, I should lose both myself and time, for I have an impulsive mind. What I do not see at the first charge, I see it less in persisting. I do nothing without gaiety; continuation and a too steady endeavor daze, deject, and tire my judgment. My sight becomes confused and blurred. I must withdraw it and apply it again spasmodically; just as, to judge the gloss of a scarlet fabric, we are told to cast our eye over it, glancing at it from different views, quickly renewed and repeated.

If this book bores me, I take another, and I indulge in it only at such times as the boredom of doing nothing begins to grip me. I do not take much to modern authors because the ancient seem to me fuller and more vigorous; nor to the Greeks, for my judgment cannot function satisfactorily on a puerile and elementary understanding.

Among the books that are simply amusing, I find, of the moderns, Boccaccio's *Decameron*, Rabelais, and *The Kisses* of Johannes Secundus, if they may be ranged under that title, worthy of being lingered over as a pastime. As to the *Amadis*, and such writings, they were unable to catch even my boyhood interest. And I will say even this, whether boldly or rashly, that this heavy old soul of mine no longer lets itself be tickled, not merely by Ariosto, but even by good Ovid; his facility and inventions which once charmed me scarcely amuse me at all now.

---

[1] Propertius

I speak my opinion freely of all things, even of those that, perhaps, exceed my capacity and that I do not conceive to be in any way under my jurisdiction. The opinion I express about them is, moreover, to show the measure of my own sight, not the measure of the things. When I find myself disliking Plato's *Axiochus,* as a work without power considering who the author was, my judgment does not trust itself; it is not so foolish as to oppose itself to the authority of so many other famous judgments of antiquity, which it considers as its mentors and masters and with whom it is rather content to err. It blames and condemns itself either for stopping at the outer bark, not being able to penetrate to the heart, or for looking at it by some false light. It is content with only securing itself from confusion and disorder; as to its own weakness, it frankly acknowledges and confesses it. It thinks it gives a just interpretation to the appearances that its apprehension presents to it; but they are weak and imperfect. Most of the fables of Aesop have several meanings and interpretations. Those who treat them as allegories choose some aspect that squares well with the fable, but for the most part it is only the first and superficial aspect; there remain others, more lively, more essential and profound, into which they have not been able to penetrate; just so do I.

But, to continue my way, I have always thought that in poetry Virgil, Lucretius, Catullus, and Horace hold first place by a long distance, and especially Virgil in his *Georgics,* which I look upon as the most finished work in poetry, in comparison with which a man may easily see that there are some passages in the *Aeneid* which the author would have still smoothed out a bit had he had the leisure. And the fifth book of the *Aeneid* seems to me the most perfect. I also love Lucan and readily turn to him, not so much for his style as for his own worth and the truth of his opinions and judgments. As for the good Terence, the embodiment of the delicacy and of the grace of the Latin tongue, I find him admirable in depicting to the life the movements of the soul and the nature of our characters; our actions throw me back upon him at every turn; and I cannot read him so often that I do not discover some new beauty and charm.

Those who lived near Virgil's time deplored that some compared him with Lucretius. I am of opinion that it is, in truth, an inexact comparison; but I have great difficulty in confirming myself in this belief when I find myself caught by some fine passage in Lucretius. If they were annoyed by this comparison, what would they say of the brutish and barbarous stupidity of those who now compare Ariosto with him. And what would Ariosto himself say?

> Oh, coarse and tasteless age! [5]

I think the ancients had more reason to complain of those who matched Plautus with Terence (the latter has much more the air of a gentleman) than of those who matched Lucretius with Virgil. It means much for the honor and preference of Terence that the father of Roman eloquence has him, and him alone of his class, so often in his mouth, as does the opinion that the first judge of Roman poets gives of his fellow-writer.

It has often come to my mind how those of our times who concern themselves with the writing of comedies (like the Italians who are rather happy in it) use three or four plots of those of Plautus or Terence to make one of theirs. They pile five or six of Boccaccio's tales into one single comedy. That which makes them so load themselves with matter is the distrust they have of being able to support themselves with their own charm; they must find a body to lean on; and not having enough matter of their own with which to hold us, they want the tale to amuse us. It is quite otherwise with my author, the perfections and beauties of his manner of expression make us lose our

---

[5] Catullus

appetite for his subject. His distinction and delicacy hold us throughout; he is so delightful everywhere,

> Clear, and like a crystal stream,[3]

and so fills our mind with his charms that we forget those of his plot.

This same consideration carries me further; I observe that the good ancient poets avoided the affectation and the pursuit not only of the fantastic flights of the Spanish and the Petrarchists, but even of the milder and more restrained conceits which form the adornment of all the poetical works of succeeding centuries. And yet there is no good judge who regrets their absence in the ancients and who does not incomparably more admire the even polish and the perpetual sweetness and flourishing beauty of Catullus' epigrams than all the barbs with which Martial sharpens the tails of his. This is for the same reason that I gave a moment ago, as Martial observed of himself: *He had less need for the exercise of talent, whose place had been taken by the subject matter.*[4] The first, without being moved or putting themselves out at all, make themselves sufficiently felt; they have matter enough for laughter everywhere, they need not tickle themselves. The others have need of foreign assistance; as they have less wit, they must have more body. They mount on horseback because they are not strong enough on their own legs. Just as at our balls those men of low station that teach dancing, not being able to imitate the port and dignity of our gentry, seek to gain commendation by dangerous cavorting and other strange acrobatic movements. And the ladies find it easier to display their appearance in dances where there are certain contortions and quick movements of the body than in some other formal dances where they have only to move with a natural step and to exhibit a natural bearing and their

---

[3] Horace, *Epistles*   [4] Martial

ordinary grace. As I have also seen excellent clowns in their everyday clothes and with their ordinary face give us all the pleasure which can be extracted from their art, while apprentices and those of less accomplishment have need of flouring their faces, of disguising themselves, and of aping wild movements and grimaces to get us to laugh. This conception of mine is nowhere more demonstrable than in comparing the *Aeneid* with the *Orlando Furioso*. We see the first on outspread wing, with lofty and sustained flight, always following his point; the latter, fluttering and hopping from tale to tale, as from branch to branch, trusting his wings only in very short flight, and perching at every turn lest his breath and force should fail,

He tries short flights.[5]

These, then, as to this sort of subjects, are the authors that best please me.

As to my other reading, which mixes a little more profit with pleasure, and through which I learn how to marshal my humors and opinions, the books that serve me to this purpose are Plutarch, since he has been translated into French, and Seneca. Both of them have this notable advantage for my humor, that the knowledge I seek is there treated in detached pieces that do not require the necessity of prolonged reading, of which I am incapable. Such are the minor works of Plutarch and the *Epistles* of Seneca, which are the finest and most profitable part of his writings. No great effort is needed for me to set myself to them, and I drop them whenever I please. For they have no continuity at all from one part to another. These authors concur in most opinions that are useful and true; just as Fortune also brought them into the world about the same period; they were both tutors to two Roman emperors; both came from foreign countries; both were rich and powerful. Their teaching is the cream of philosophy and presented in a plain and perti-

---

[5] Virgil, *Georgics*

nent manner. Plutarch is more uniform and constant; Seneca more mobile and diverse. The last toils, strains, and tenses himself to fortify virtue against frailty, fear, and vicious appetites. The other seems to heed less their power and to disdain to quicken his pace because of them or to stand upon his guard. Plutarch's opinions are Platonic, gentle, and accommodated to civil society; those of the other are Stoical and Epicurean, more remote from common use, but, in my opinion, more suitable for private life and more firm. Seneca would seem to lean a little to the tyranny of the emperors of his time, for I hold it certain that it is with a forced judgment that he condemns the cause of those noble-spirited assassins of Caesar; Plutarch is free throughout. Seneca abounds in points of wit and sallies, Plutarch in things. The former heats and moves you more, the latter contents you more and pays you better. He guides us, the other pushes us on.

As to Cicero, those of his works that are most useful to my purpose are those that treat of philosophy, especially moral. But boldly to confess the truth (for when one has cleared the barriers of impudence, there is no more curb), his way of writing, and all other similar styles, appears to me very tedious. For his prefaces, definitions, divisions, etymologies take up the greater part of his work; whatever there is of life and marrow is smothered in the long-windedness of the preparations. When I have spent an hour in reading him, which is a great deal for me, and try to recollect what juice and substance I have extracted, most of the time I find nothing but wind; for he has not yet come to the arguments that serve his purpose and to the reasons that properly touch on the crux which I am looking for. For me, who only ask to become wiser, not more learned or eloquent, these logical and Aristotelian arrangements of the parts are of no use; I would have a man begin with the conclusion. I understand well enough what death and pleasure are; let no time be wasted in anatomizing them. I look for good and solid reasons at the start to instruct me how to withstand their

action. Neither grammatical subtleties nor an ingenious contexture of words and argumentations are of any use for that
purpose. I want reasons that in the first charge drive into the
thick of the problem; his feebly beat about the bush. They are
good for school, for the bar, and for the pulpit, where we have
leisure to nap, and a quarter of an hour later we are in time
enough to pick up the thread of the discourse. It is necessary
to speak in this manner to judges whom we wish to prevail upon
by hook or by crook, to children, and to the common people, to
whom we must say everything and see what will carry home. I
do not want anyone to spend his time in making me attentive
and to shout at me fifty times "Or Oyez!" as our heralds do.
The Romans in their religious exercises used to say "Hoc age,"
as we in ours say "Sursum corda"; these are so many words lost
on me. I come fully prepared from the house. I need no allurement, no sauce; I can well eat the meat quite raw; and instead
of whetting my appetite by these preparatives and preliminaries, they tire and pall it.

Will the license of the times excuse the sacrilegious boldness
of my holding also that even the dialogues of Plato drag and
stifle too much his matter, and my lamenting the time spent by
a man, who had so many better things to say, in these long and
fruitless preliminary interlocutions? My ignorance will excuse
me better inasmuch as I have no perception of the beauty of
his language. I generally ask for books that make use of learning, not those that shape it. The first two and Pliny, and their
like, have nothing of this "Hoc age"; they want to deal with
men already instructed; or if they have it, it is a substantial
"Hoc age" and one that has a body of its own.

I also delight in reading the letters "To Atticus," not only
because they contain very ample information on the history and
the affairs of his time, but much more because I therein discover much of his personal nature. For I have a singular curiosity, as I have said elsewhere, to know the souls and the sincere judgments of my authors. A man should, indeed, judge

their ability, but not their characters nor themselves, by that
parade of their writings which they expose upon the stage of the
world. I have a thousand times regretted that we have lost the
treatise that Brutus wrote upon virtue; for it is a fine thing to
learn the theory from those who know well the practice. But
since the thing preached and the preacher are two different
things, I am as glad to see Brutus in Plutarch as in a book of
his own. I would rather choose to be truly informed of the conversation he had in his tent with some one of his particular
friends the night before a battle than of the harangue he made
the next day to his army; and of what he did in his study and
his chamber than what he did in the public square and in the
Senate.

As to Cicero, I am of the common opinion that, learning excepted, he did not have much distinction of mind. He was a
good citizen, of an affable nature, as all fat, jovial men, such as
he was, usually are; but, in truth, he had a goodly share of softness and ambitious vanity. Neither do I know how to excuse
him for thinking his poetry fit to be published. It is no great
imperfection to compose verses badly; but it is a lack of judgment in him not to have perceived how unworthy they were of
the glory of his name. As for his eloquence, that is completely
beyond comparison; I believe it will never be equalled. The
younger Cicero, who resembled his father in nothing but in
name, while commanding in Asia had several strangers one day
at his table, and among the rest Cestius, seated at the lower
end, as men often intrude on the open tables of the great. Cicero
asked one of his people who that man was, and was told his
name. But like one who had his thoughts turned elsewhere and
had forgotten the answer made him, he asked him the question
again later on two or three times; the servant, to be free of the
trouble of repeating so often the same thing and to make him
recognize him by some circumstance, said: "It is that Cestius
of whom it was told you that he makes no great account of your
father's eloquence in comparison with his own." Cicero, sud-

denly stung by this, commanded poor Cestius to be seized and caused him to be very well whipped in his own presence—a very discourteous host!

Even among those who, all things considered, esteemed his eloquence incomparable, there were some who did not fail to observe in it some faults; as for example that great Brutus, his friend, who said it was a *broken and enervated* [6] eloquence. The orators who lived near his time also reprehended in him his great care for a certain long cadence at the end of his periods and took notice of these words, *esse videatur,* which he there so often makes use of. For my part I prefer a cadence that falls more curtly, cut into iambics. Yet he sometimes shuffles his rhythms very roughly together, but it is very seldom. My ear took notice of this passage: *For my part, in truth, I should rather be old less long than to be old before my time.* [7]

The historians are the right ball for me. They are pleasant and easy; and at the same time man in general, whom I seek to know, appears in them more lively and entire than anywhere else—the diversity and truth of his inner qualities, in general and in detail, the variety of the means by which he is joined together, and the accidents that threaten him. Now those that write biographies, because they spend more time upon intentions than events, more upon what sallies from within than upon that which happens without, are the most suited to me. That is why in every way Plutarch is the man for me. I am very sorry we have not a dozen Laertiuses, or that he is not more extensive or more penetrating. For I am no less curious to know the lives and fortunes of these great instructors of the world than to know the diversities of their doctrines and opinions.

In this kind of historical study, a man must thumb over, without distinction, all sorts of authors, both ancient and modern, both gibberish and French, in order to learn in them the things of which they variously treat. But Caesar, in my opinion, particularly deserves to be studied, not for the knowledge of his-

---

[3] Tacitus. *Dialogue of Orators*   [7] Cicero, *De Senectute*

tory only, but for himself, so great an excellence and perfection he has above all the rest, though Sallust be one of the number. In truth, I read this author with a little more reverence and respect than is customary in reading human works, sometimes considering him in himself by his actions and miraculous greatness, sometimes the purity and inimitable polish of his language, wherein he excels not only all other historians, as Cicero says, but, perhaps, Cicero himself. He speaks of his enemies with so much sincerity in his judgment that, except for the false colors with which he strives to cover his evil cause and the pollution of his pestilent ambition, I think the only fault to be found with him is that he speaks too sparingly of himself. For so many great things could not have been performed by him without more of himself having gone into them than he puts down there.

I love historians who are either very simple or of the highest order. The simple, who have nothing of their own to mix with it and who bring to the task only the care and diligence of collecting all that comes to their knowledge and of faithfully recording all things without choice and selection, leave our judgment intact for discerning the truth. Such for example, among others, is the good Froissart, who has proceeded in his undertaking with such frank simplicity that, having committed an error, he is not at all afraid to confess it and to correct it in the place where he has been informed of it. He presents to us even the variety of rumors that were circulating and the different reports that were made to him. It is the naked and unformed matter of history; everyone may make his profit of it according to his understanding.

The truly outstanding historians have the capacity to pick out what is worth being known, they can select of two accounts the one that is the more likely to be true. From the character of princes and from their humors they infer their intentions and attribute to them suitable words. They are right to assume the authority of regulating our belief by their own; but certainly this privilege belongs to very few.

Those historians that are in between the two (which is the commonest sort) spoil all: they want to chew our morsels for us; they take upon themselves to judge and, consequently, to slant history to their own fancy; for as soon as the judgment leans to one side, a man cannot avoid wresting and twisting his narrative to the bias. They undertake to choose things worth being known and often conceal from us such a word, such a private action as would better instruct us; they omit as incredible the things that they do not understand, and also some things because they cannot express them in good Latin or French. Let them boldly display their eloquence and their reasonings, let them judge according to their fancy; but let them, however, leave us something to judge after them, let them not alter nor arrange by their abridgments and selections anything of the substance of the matter, but rather deliver it to us pure and entire in all its dimensions.

For the most part, and especially in these latter ages, persons are culled out for this work from among the common people upon the sole consideration of skill in the use of words, as if we were seeking to learn grammar there! And having been hired only for that, and having put on sale only their babble, they are right to be chiefly solicitous only of that element. And so, with a fine jingle of words, they go about cooking up for us a fine concoction of rumors they pick up on the street corners.

The only good histories are those that were written by the persons themselves who commanded in the affairs, or who participated in the conduct of them, or, at least, who had the fortune to conduct others of the same nature. Such are almost all the Greek and Roman histories. For several eyewitnesses having written of the same subject (as it happened in those times that greatness and learning usually met in the same person), if there is an error, it must be an extraordinarily slight one and upon a very doubtful incident. What can a man expect from a physician discussing war or from a scholar discussing the intentions of princes? If we want to note how scrupulous the Romans were in that, this example is enough: Asinius Pollio found in the histories even of Caesar some mistake into which he had fallen for not having been able to extend his vision to all parts of his army and for having believed individuals who often brought back to him insufficiently verified matters, or else for not having been carefully enough informed by his lieutenants of what they had done in his absence. By this example we can see how delicate is this pursuit of the truth when a man cannot believe the report of a battle from the knowledge of him who there commanded, nor trust the soldiers about what took place near them, unless, after the method of a judicial inquiry, the witnesses are confronted and the objections heard upon the evidence of the least details of every point. Truly, the knowledge we have of our own affairs is much looser. But this has been adequately handled by Bodin, and according to my own way of thinking.

To remedy a little the treachery and defect of my memory (so extreme that it has happened to me more than once to take books again into my hand as though new and unknown to me which I had carefully read a few years before and scribbled with my notes), I have taken a custom of late to put at the end of every book (I am speaking of those I do not intend to read again) the time when I finished reading it and the judgment I had formed of it on the whole, in order that this might at least reproduce for me the air and general idea I had conceived of the author in reading it. I will here transcribe some of these annotations.

Here is what I put some ten years ago in my Guicciardini (for whatever language my books speak, I speak to them in my own): "He is a diligent historiographer from whom, in my opinion, a man may learn the truth about the affairs of his time as exactly as from anyone else. Moreover, in the most of these he was himself also an actor and in an honorable position. There is no appearance that he disguised anything because of hatred, favor, or vanity; proof of this is found in the free judgments he passes upon great men and particularly those by whom he had been advanced and employed in important missions, such as Pope Clement the Seventh. As to the part which he seems to want to make the most of, namely his digressions and comments, there are some good ones and enriched with fine expressions, but he is too fond of them. For to wish to leave nothing unsaid, having a subject so full and ample and almost infinite, he becomes diffuse and smacks a little of the scholastic prattle. I have also observed this: that of so many persons and so many actions, so many motives and so many intentions that he judges, he never attributes any one of them to virtue, religion, or conscience, as if these qualities were utterly extinct in the world. And of all the actions, however fine in appearance they may be of themselves, he always traces the cause to some vicious motive or some prospect of profit. It is impossible to imagine that among the infinite number of actions which he judges there is none produced by the way of reason. No corruption can so universally have infected men that some one of them did not escape the contagion. That makes me fear that his own taste was therein a little faulty, and it may have happened that he judged other men by himself."

In my Philippe de Comines there is this: "You will here find the language soft and delightful, of a natural simplicity; the narration pure, in which the veracity of the author clearly shines, free from vanity when speaking of himself and from partiality or envy when speaking of others; his reflections and exhortations accompanied more with good zeal and truth than with any exquisite talent; and throughout authority and gravity, showing him to be a man of good extraction and bred up in great affairs."

Upon the memoirs of Monsieur du Bellay: "It is always pleasant to see things written by those that have experienced how they ought to be carried on; but it cannot be denied that there is clearly revealed in these two lords a great decline from the freedom and liberty of writing that shine in the older historians of their class, such as the Sire de Joinville, an intimate friend of Saint Louis, Eginhard, chancellor to Charlemagne, and of more recent memory, Philippe de Comines. We have here rather an apology for King Francis against the Emperor Charles the Fifth, than a history. I will not believe that they have altered anything in respect to the main facts, but they make a practice of turning the judgment of events to our advantage, often contrary to reason, and of omitting everything that is ticklish in the life of their master: witness the disgrace and dismissal of Messieurs de Montmorency and de Brion which are there overlooked; indeed, so much as the name of Madame d'Estampes is not found there. Secret actions may be covered up, but to pass over in silence what all the world knows, and matters that led to public actions of such consequence, is an inexcusable defect. In fine, whoever wants to have a full knowledge of King Francis and of the events of his time, let him turn elsewhere, if my advice is taken. The profit we can reap here is from the detailed narrative of battles and exploits of war wherein those gentlemen were engaged; from some words and private actions of certain princes of their time, and from the practices and negotiations carried on by the Seigneur de Langey, where there are many things worth knowing and comments above the ordinary."

OF CRUELTY

It seems to me that virtue is something other and more noble than the inclinations to goodness which are born in us. Well-regulated and wellborn souls pursue the same course and show in their actions the same face that the virtuous do. But virtue has a ring of something, I know not what, greater and more active than merely letting oneself by a happy disposition be gently and quietly led in the train of reason. He who, from a natural sweetness and easiness, should despise injuries received would do a very fine and a very laudable thing; but he who, provoked and nettled to the quick by an offence, should fortify himself with the arms of reason against the furious appetite of revenge and after a great conflict finally master it would doubtless do a great deal more. The first would do well; the latter virtuously. One action might be called goodness, the other virtue. For it seems that the name of Virtue presupposes difficulty and contention, and that it cannot be exercised without opposition. It is for this reason, perhaps, that we call God good, mighty, liberal, and just; but we do not call Him *virtuous,* all His operations are natural and without effort.

Of the philosophers, not only Stoics, but Epicureans (and this distinction of putting a higher value on one than on the other I borrow from the common opinion, which is wrong, notwithstanding that subtle rejoinder of Arcesilaus to him who reproached him with the fact that many people went from his school to the Epicurean, but never the reverse: "I can well believe it; of cocks capons are easily made, but of capons cocks are never made." For, in truth, in firmness and austerity of opinions and precepts the Epicurean sect yields in no degree to

the Stoic. And a Stoic, exhibiting better faith than those dis-
putants who, to combat Epicurus and give themselves an advantage, make him say things he never thought of, twisting his
words awry and deducing by the laws of grammar a sense different from the one he expressed and a belief different from the
one which they knew he had in his mind and in his conduct,
said that he gave up being an Epicurean for this consideration,
among others, that he thought their path too high and inaccessible; *and they who are called lovers of pleasure are actually
lovers of beauty and justice, and cultivate and maintain all the
virtues*[1]); of the Stoic and Epicurean philosophers, I say, there
are many who have judged that it was not enough to have the
soul well founded, well regulated and well disposed to virtue, it
was not enough to have our resolutions and our ideas above all
the efforts of Fortune, but we should also seek occasions for
putting them to the proof. They would go in quest of pain,
want, and contempt to contend with them and to keep the soul
in breath: *Through being challenged virtue becomes greatly
strengthened.*[2] That is one of the reasons why Epaminondas,
who was yet of a third sect, refuses the riches which Fortune
puts in his hand in a very legitimate way. In order, he says, to
have to contend with poverty; in this extremity he persisted to
the last. Socrates, it seems to me, put himself to a still harder
test, keeping for his exercise the spitefulness of his wife, which
is a bout with bare blades.

Metellus, having of all the Roman senators alone attempted
by the power of virtue to withstand the violence of Saturninus,
tribune of the people at Rome, who sought forcibly to have an
unjust law passed in favor of the plebeians, and by so doing
having incurred the capital penalities that Saturninus had established against those who refused, talked with those who
in this extremity were leading him in the public square, in these
terms: that it was too easy and too base a thing to do evil
and that to act well where there was no danger was a common

[1] Cicero, *Ad Familiares*   [2] Seneca, *Epistles*

thing; but to act well when there was danger was the proper
function of a man of virtue. These words of Metellus very
clearly show us what I wanted to prove, that Virtue refuses
Facility for a companion, and that the easy, gentle, and de-
scending way by which the regular steps of a good natural disposition are conducted is not that of true virtue. She requires
a rough and thorny path; she wishes to have either outward
difficulties to wrestle with, like that of Metellus, by means of
which Fortune delights to interrupt the intensity of her career,
or internal difficulties which our disordered appetites and the
imperfections of our nature bring before her.

I have come thus far much at my ease. But at the end of
this discussion it comes into my head that the soul of Socrates,
the most perfect that ever came to my knowledge, would by
my reckoning be worthy of very little commendation; for I
cannot conceive in that person any action of a vicious passion.
I cannot imagine there could be any difficulty or constraint
in the course of his virtue. I know his reason to be so powerful and sovereign in him that it would never have let a vicious
appetite even be engendered in him. For a virtue so elevated
as his I can imagine no rival. I seem to see her march with a
victorious and triumphant stride, in pomp and at her ease, without hindrance or obstacle. If Virtue cannot shine but by the
conflict of contrary appetites, shall we then say that she cannot
do without the assistance of vice, and that it is from vice that
she derives her reputation and honor? What, then, would become of that noble and generous Epicurean pleasure which
prides itself on nourishing Virtue tenderly in its bosom and
there making it frolic, giving it for toys disgrace, fevers, poverty, death, and torments? If I presuppose that a perfect virtue
is recognized in fighting and patiently enduring pain, in withstanding the attacks of the gout without being shaken from her
place; if I grant her austerity and difficulty as her necessary
objective, what will be the status of a virtue elevated to such

a degree as not only to despise pain, but to rejoice in it and to
feel tickled by the stabs of a sharp colic, such as is the virtue
that the Epicureans have established and of which many of
them by their actions have left us most evident proofs? As have
likewise many others, who I find have actually surpassed even
the rules of their discipline.

Witness the younger Cato. When I see him dying and tearing out his own bowels, I am not satisfied simply to believe
that his soul was then totally free from disturbance and terror; I cannot believe that he only maintained himself in the
attitude that the rules of the Stoics prescribed for him, composed, without emotion, and impassive. There was, I think, in
the virtue of this man too much sprightliness and vigor to stop
there. I fully believe that he felt satisfaction and sensual delight in so noble an action and was more pleased by it than by
any other of his life: *He departed from life as if rejoicing in
having found a reason for dying.*[3] I believe this so deeply that
I question whether he would have wished to be deprived of the
opportunity for so fine an exploit. And if the goodness that
made him embrace the public interest more than his own did
not restrain me, I should easily fall into the opinion that he
was grateful to Fortune for having put his virtue to so fine a
trial and for having favored that brigand in treading under
foot the ancient liberty of his country. I think I read in this
action an indescribable exultation in his soul and an emotion
of extraordinary pleasure and virile joy when she looked upon
the nobility and loftiness of his effort:

> Still bolder, once resolved to die,[4]

not stimulated by any hope of glory, as the vulgar and effeminate judgments of some men have concluded, for that consideration is too low to touch so generous, so lofty, and so inflexible

[3] Cicero, *Tusculans*   [4] Horace, *Odes*

a heart as his, but for the very beauty of the thing in itself, which he, who had the handling of its springs, discerned more clearly and in its perfection than we are able to do.

Philosophy has pleased me by deciding that so fine an action would have been improperly placed in any other life than that of Cato, and that it only belonged to his to end thus. Therefore it was according to reason that he commanded his son and the senators that accompanied him to provide otherwise for their concerns. *Since Nature had bestowed on Cato an incredible seriousness of character, and as he had strengthened it by unceasing consistency, and had always remained firm in the purpose he had set for himself, it was for him to die rather than to look on the face of a tyrant.*[5]

Every death ought to correspond to its life. We do not become different for dying. I always interpret the death by the life. And if anyone tells me of a death strong in appearance annexed to a feeble life, I hold it is produced by a feeble cause and in keeping with the life.

The easiness, then, of this death and the facility he had acquired by the vigor of his soul, shall we say that it ought to lessen somewhat the luster of his virtue? And who, out of all those whose brains are ever so little tinctured with the true philosophy, can be content to imagine Socrates merely free from fear and suffering upon the occasion of his prison, fetters, and condemnation? And who does not recognize in him not only firmness and stability (this was his ordinary state), but, moreover, I know not what new satisfaction and playful cheerfulness in his last words and actions? At the start he gave with the pleasure of scratching his leg after his irons were taken off, does he not make evident a like serenity and joy in his soul at being unfettered from past discomforts and ready to enter into the knowledge of things to come? Cato will pardon me if he please; his death is more tragical and more intense, but

---

[5] Cicero, *De Officiis*

this other is, I know not how, still finer. Aristippus said to those who were lamenting it, "The gods grant me such a death."

A man discerns in the souls of these two great men and their imitators (for I very much doubt whether there were ever their equals) so perfect a practice of virtue that it became part of their character. It is no more a laborious virtue nor so many precepts of the reason to maintain which the soul has to be tensed; it is the very essence of their soul, its natural and ordinary course. They have rendered it such by a long practice of philosophical precepts, having come upon a rich and fine nature. The vicious passions that spring in us can find no entrance into them. The strength and inflexibility of their soul stifles and extinguishes lusts as soon as they begin to stir.

Now I do not think it can be doubted that it is not more noble by a high and divine resolution to prevent the birth of temptations and to have so shaped ourselves to virtue that the very seeds of vice are rooted out, than to hinder by main force their progress and, having let ourselves be surprised by the first impulses of the passions, to arm and brace ourselves to stop their progress and to overcome them; and that this second state is not still more noble than to be simply endowed with a facile and affable nature, with a personal distaste for debauchery and vice. For this third and last sort seems, indeed, to render a man innocent, but not virtuous; free from doing ill, but not apt enough to do well. In addition this condition is so near a neighbor to imperfection and weakness that I know not very well how to separate the confines and distinguish them. The very names of goodness and innocence are for this reason to some extent names of scorn. I know that many virtues, such as chastity, sobriety, and temperance may come to us through a bodily defect. Firmness in front of danger (if firmness it must be called), contempt of death, patience in misfortunes may arise and often are found in men for want of judging well such matters and not apprehending them for such as they are. Want of understanding and stupidity thus sometimes counterfeit virtuous actions; as I have often observed it happen that men have been commended for what really deserved blame.

An Italian lord once said this in my presence, to the disadvantage of his own nation: that the subtlety of the Italians and the vivacity of their imaginations were so great that they foresaw the dangers and accidents that might befall them so far off that it must not be thought strange if they were often in war seen to provide for their safety, even before they had discovered the peril; that we French and the Spaniards, who were not so acute, went on further, and that we must be made to see the danger with our eye and touch it with our hand before we would take alarm; but that the Germans and Swiss, coarser and more sluggish, had scarcely the sense to look about them even at the moment when they were overwhelmed beneath blows. Perhaps it was only said jokingly. Yet it is most certain that in the business of war raw soldiers often rush into danger with more heedlessness than they do after they have felt fire:

> For well I know how potent is in arms
> Untasted glory and the first fight's gleam.[9]

That is why, when we judge a particular action, we must consider many circumstances and the whole of the man by whom it is performed before we give it a name.

To say a word about myself. I have sometimes seen my friends call prudence in me that which was merely fortune, and consider as a superiority due to courage and patience that which was a superiority due to judgment and thought, and attribute to me one title for another, now to my gain and now to my loss. As to the rest, I am so far from having arrived at that first and most perfect degree of excellence where virtue becomes

---

[9] Virgil, *Aeneid*

a habit, that even of the second I have made no great trial. I
have not made any great effort to curb the desires by which
I find myself harassed. My virtue is a virtue, or, to put it better, an innocence, casual and accidental. If I had been born
with a more disorderly nature, I am afraid it would have gone
sadly with me. For I have not experienced any great stability
in my soul to resist passions, however little violent they were.
I have not the knack of nourishing quarrels and disputes in
my own bosom. Consequently I can give myself no great thanks
that I am free from many vices:

> If by small faults and few my nature's marred,
> While otherwise quite sound, just as with moles
> Strewn o'er a lovely form you might find fault,[7]

I owe it rather to my fortune than my reason. To her it is
due that I am descended from a race famous for manliness and
from a very good father; I know not whether he has infused
into me part of his traits or whether, indeed, example at home
and the good training of my childhood have insensibly assisted
in it, or if I was otherwise born so,

> Whether I fell at birth 'neath Libra's sign
> Or dreaded Scorpio's more furious force
> Upon the natal hour, or Capricorn,
> The stormy tyrant of the western wave.[8]

But so it is that I have naturally a horror for most vices. The
answer of Antisthenes to him who asked him which was the
best apprenticeship, "To unlearn evil," seems to come to rest
on this idea. I have them in horror, I say, from an attitude so
natural and so much my own that the same instinct and impression I brought with me from my nurse I still retain, without any circumstances having had the power to make me alter

---

[7] Horace, *Satires*   [8] Horace, *Odes*

it; not even my own reasonings, which, in some things, having dashed out of the common road, might easily give me license for actions that my natural inclination makes me hate.

I will say a monstrous thing, but I will say it nonetheless. Because of that I find that in many things there is more restraint and order in my morals than in my thoughts, and my appetites are less wayward than my reason.

Aristippus set up such bold opinions in favor of pleasure and riches that he set all philosophy rumbling against him. But as to his morals, Dionysius, the tyrant, having presented three beautiful girls before him to take his choice, he made answer that he would choose all three, and that it had gone badly with Paris for preferring one over her companions; but having taken them home to his house, he sent them back untouched. His servant finding himself overloaded on the way with the money he was carrying after him, he ordered him to pour out and throw away that which troubled him. And Epicurus, whose doctrines are so irreligious and effeminate, was in the conduct of his life very devout and laborious. He writes to a friend of his that he is living only upon coarse bread and water, entreating him to send him a little cheese to have whenever he wanted to make a sumptuous meal. Could it be true that to be really good we must be so by an occult, natural, and universal property, without law, without reason, without example?

The excesses wherein I have been involved are not, I thank God, of the worst sort. I have thoroughly condemned them in myself according as they deserve it; for my judgment has not been infected by them. On the contrary, it censures them more severely in myself than in another. But that is all; for, as to the rest, I oppose too little resistance to them and let myself incline too easily to the other side of the balance, excepting that I moderate them and prevent them from mixing with other vices which, for the most part, cling together and become linked one to the other if a man is not on the lookout. I have cur-

tailed and confined mine to make them as single and as simple
as I could;

> Nor more than this do I indulge my faults.[9]

For, as to the opinion of the Stoics, who say that the wise
man, when he acts, acts by all the virtues together, though
one be more apparent according to the nature of the action
(and for this the comparison with the human body might serve
them somewhat; for the action of anger cannot operate without the assistance of all the humors, though anger may pre-
dominate), if thence they want to draw a like conclusion, that
when the wicked man does wickedly, he errs by all the vices
together, I do not believe it so simply, or else I do not understand them; for in effect I feel the contrary. These are fine,
unsubstantial subtleties on which philosophy sometimes pauses.

I am given to some vices, but I flee others as much as a saint
could do.

The Peripatetics, moreover, disown this indissoluble connection and seam; and Aristotle is of opinion that a wise and
just man may be intemperate and incontinent. Socrates confessed to those who discovered a certain inclination to vice in
his physiognomy that it was, in truth, his natural propensity, but
that he had by discipline corrected it. And the intimate friends
of the philosopher Stilpo said that, being born subject to wine
and women, he had by study become very abstinent in respect
to both.

What good I have in me, I have, on the contrary, by the
chance of my birth. I get it neither from law, nor from precept,
nor from any other apprenticeship. The innocence that is in
me is a natural innocence: little vigor and no art.

Among other vices I cruelly hate cruelty, both by nature and
judgment, as the extreme of all vices. But it is to such a de-

---

[9] Juvenal

gree of softness that I cannot see a chicken's neck slit without trouble, and I cannot bear to hear the cry of a hare beneath the teeth of my dogs, though the chase is a stirring pleasure.

Those who have to combat sensuality like to make use of this argument to show that it is altogether vicious and unreasonable: that when it is at its very height, it masters us so much that reason can have no access to it, and they allege our own experience of it in intercourse with women,

> When now the body senses the first joys,
> And Venus is about to sow the fields
> Of woman;[10]

wherein they conceive that the pleasure bears us so strongly beyond ourselves that our reason cannot then perform its office, being paralysed, ravished with delight. I know it may be otherwise and that we may sometimes, if we will, succeed in turning our mind away, even at this very moment, to other thoughts. But it must be tensed and braced carefully. I know that we can curb the violence of this pleasure; I have a good knowledge of it, and I have not found Venus so imperious a goddess as many men, and some more chaste than I, testify she is. I do not consider it as a miracle, as the Queen of Navarre does in one of the tales of her *Heptameron* (which is a pretty book for its matter), nor as a thing of extreme difficulty, to pass whole nights in all ease and freedom with a long-desired mistress, keeping the word one has pledged to her to content himself with kisses and simple embraces.

I believe that the example of the chase would be more appropriate (though in it the pleasure is less, the excitement and the surprise are greater, so that our upset reason loses all chance to prepare and brace itself for the encounter), when after a long quest the quarry starts up suddenly and appears in

---

[10] Lucretius

a place where, perhaps, we least expected it. This shock and the ardor of the hue and cry so strikes us that it would be hard for those who love this sort of chase to withdraw their thoughts elsewhere at this moment. And the poets make Diana triumph over the torch and shafts of Cupid:

> Amid these joys who does not drop
> From mind the cruel cares of love? [11]

To return to my subject, I am very tenderly compassionate of others' afflictions, and I should readily cry for company if, upon any occasion whatever, I could cry at all. Nothing tempts my tears but tears, and not only those that are real, but whatever they are, feigned or painted. I do not much pity the dead, and I should envy them rather; but I very much pity the dying. The savages do not so much shock me in roasting and eating the bodies of the dead as do those who torment and persecute the living. I cannot even look upon the executions of justice, however just, with a steady eye. Some one having to give testimony of Julius Caesar's clemency said: "He was mild in his vengeance. Having compelled the pirates to yield, by whom he had before been taken prisoner and put to ransom, inasmuch as he had threatened them with the cross, he condemned them to it, but it was after having had them strangled. He punished his secretary, Philemon, who had attempted to poison him, with no greater severity than simple death." Without saying who that Latin author is who dares allege as a testimony of clemency the merely killing of those by whom we have been injured, it is easy to guess that he was struck with the villainous and horrible examples of cruelty practised by the Roman tyrants.

For my part, even in justice itself, all that exceeds mere death appears to me pure cruelty, especially in us, who ought

---

[11] Horace, *Epodes*

to have care to dispatch the souls in a good state, which cannot be when we have agitated them and made them despairing by insufferable torments.

Not long ago a soldier who was a prisoner, having perceived from a tower where he was shut up that the people began to assemble in the public square and that the carpenters were busy erecting a scaffold, he concluded that it was for him, and becoming desperate, having nothing else with which to take his life, he seized an old rusty cart-nail that chance presented to him and with this he gave himself two great wounds in his throat; and seeing that he had not been able to make his life waver, he gave himself another in the belly, from which he fell unconscious. And the first of his keepers that came in to see him found him in this condition. He was revived, and to make use of the time before he should die, they at once read his sentence to him, which was to be beheaded, by which he was immeasurably overjoyed, and consented to take some wine which he had before refused; and thanking the judges for the unhoped-for mildness of their sentence, said that this resolution to kill himself had come from the terror of some cruel punishment, the fear of which had been increased in him by the preparations [he had seen being made in the public square. He thought that they intended to torment him with some horrible torture, and it seemed to him that he was saved from death by having changed its form].

I should advise that these examples of severity by which it is intended to retain the people in their duty might be exercised upon the dead bodies of criminals; for to see them deprived of burial, to see them boiled and torn to pieces, would affect the populace almost as much as the pain they make the living endure, though that, in reality, be little or nothing, as God says, *Who kill the body, and after that have no more that they can do.*[12] And the poets play singularly upon the horror of this picture, as something worse than death:

---

[12] St. Luke

Woe, that a sovereign's half-burned remains,
Besmeared with gore, and bones laid bare, should thus
Along the ground be foully pulled apart.[13]

I happened to be one day at Rome just as they were about
to execute Catena, a notorious robber. He was strangled without any emotion on the part of the spectators, but when they
came to quarter him, the hangman gave not a blow that was
not followed by a doleful cry from the people and an exclamation as if everyone had lent his feeling to that carcass.

Those inhuman excesses ought to be exercised upon the bark
and not upon the quick. In a somewhat similar case, Arta-
xerxes moderated thus the severity of the ancient laws of Persia, ordering that the nobility who had erred in their functions,
instead of being whipped, as they used to be, should be stripped
only, and their clothes whipped for them; and that, whereas
they formerly had their hair torn out, they should only take
off their high tiaras. The Egyptians, who are so devout, thought
they sufficiently satisfied the divine justice in sacrificing hogs
in effigy and pictures: a bold thought to want to pay God, so
essential a substance, in picture and in shadow.

I live in a time wherein we abound in incredible examples
of this vice through the license of our civil wars; and we see
nothing in ancient histories more extreme than what we experience every day. But that has not at all accustomed me to it.
I could hardly persuade myself, before I had seen it with my
eyes, that there could be found men so monstrous who would
wish to commit murder for the sole pleasure of it, would hack
and lop off the limbs of others, sharpen their wits to invent unusual torments and new kinds of deaths, without hatred, without profit, and for the sole end of enjoying the pleasant spectacle of the pitiful gestures and motions, the lamentable groans
and cries of a man dying in anguish. For that is the utmost

---

[13] Ennius. in Cicero, *Tusculans*

point to which cruelty can arrive. *That a man should kill a man not in anger, not in fear, but only for the spectacle.*[14]

For my own part I have not been able without pain to see even an innocent beast pursued and killed that has no defense and from whom we have received no harm at all. And as it frequently happens that the stag, finding himself out of breath and weak, having no other resource, turns back and surrenders to us who pursue him, imploring mercy by his tears,

> and with loud plaint, all stained with gore,
> And like a person begging aid,[15]

this has always seemed to me a very unpleasant sight.

I hardly ever take any beast or bird alive that I do not restore it to the fields. Pythagoras used to buy them of fishermen and fowlers to do the same:

> I think that first by killing beasts
> The blood-stained steel grew warm.[16]

Those natures that are bloodthirsty towards animals give evidence of a natural propensity to cruelty.

After they had accustomed themselves at Rome to the spectacle of the slaughter of animals, they proceeded to that of men and gladiators. Nature herself, I fear, fixes in man a kind of instinct to inhumanity. Nobody takes pleasure in seeing beasts play and caress one another, but no one fails to take pleasure in seeing them dismember and tear one another to pieces.

And that I may not be laughed at for the sympathy I have with them, theology itself bids us have some kindness in their behalf; and, considering that one and the same Master has lodged us in this palace for His service, and that they, as well as we, are of His family, it has reason to bid us have some regard and affection for them. Pythagoras borrowed metem-

---

[14] Seneca, *Epistles*   [15] Virgil, *Aeneid*   [16] Ovid, *Metamorphoses*

psychosis from the Egyptians, but it has since been accepted by several nations, and, particularly, by our Druids:

> Souls do not die; and leaving their old seat,
> They always go to live in new abodes,
> And well received they make their home therein.[17]

The religion of our ancient Gauls maintained that souls, being eternal, never ceased to move and shift their places from one body to another, mixing, moreover, with this notion some consideration of divine justice. For, according to the behavior of the soul while it had been in Alexander, they said that God ordered it another body to inhabit, more or less painful and proper for its condition:

> The yoke of speechless brutes he made them wear,
> Bloodthirsty souls he did inclose in bears;
> Those that rapacious were in wolves he shut;
> The sly and cunning he in foxes put;
> Where after having in a course of years,
> In numerous forms, quite finished their careers,
> In Lethe's flood he purged them, and at last
> In human bodies he the souls replaced.[18]

If it had been valiant, they lodged it in the body of a lion; if voluptuous in that of a pig; if timorous, in that of a stag or hare; if sly in that of a fox; and so of the rest, until, purified by this chastisement, it took again the body of some other man.

> And I myself, for I remember, in the days
> Of Troy's great war was then Euphorbus, Pantheus' son.[19]

As to the relation between us and the beasts, I do not take much account of it, nor also of the fact that a number of nations, and especially some of the most ancient and noble, have

---

[17] Ovid, *Metamorphoses*   [18] Claudian, *In Ruffinum*   [19] Ovid, *Metamorphoses*

not only received animals into their society and companionship, but have given them a rank very far above them, esteeming them sometimes familiars and favorites of their gods and
holding them in more than human reverence and respect, and
at other times knowing no other god or divinity but them:
*beasts deified by barbarians because of the benefits received
from them.*[20]

> This area adores the crocodile,
> That quakes before the Ibis gorged with snakes;
> The golden image of the sacred ape
> Shines here; and here whole cities venerate
> The river fish, and there the dog.[21]

And the very interpretation that Plutarch gives to this error,
which is very well put, is advantageous to them. For he says
that it was not the cat or the ox, for example, that the Egyptians adored; but that they, in those beasts, adored some image
of the divine faculties: in this patience and utility, in that
vivacity, or, like our neighbors the Burgundians with the whole
of Germany, intolerance of confinement; by which they represented the liberty they loved and adored above all other divine faculties, and so of the rest. But when, among the more
moderate opinions, I meet with arguments that endeavor to
demonstrate the near resemblance between us and animals and
how much they share in our greatest privileges, and with how
much probability they are compared to us, I certainly knock
down a great deal of our presumption and willingly resign that
imaginary sovereignty that some attribute to us over other creatures.

But even if all this were not so, there is, nevertheless, a certain regard and a general duty of humanity that ties us not
only to beasts that have life and feeling, but even to trees and
plants. We owe justice to men and graciousness and kindness
to other creatures that are capable of it. There is a certain re-

---

[20] Cicero, *De Natura Deorum* [21] Juvenal

lationship and mutual obligation between them and us. I am not afraid to confess the tenderness of my nature so childish that I cannot well refuse my dog the romp which he offers me at an inconvenient time, or which he begs of me.

The Turks have alms and hospitals for beasts. The Romans made a public duty of the feeding of geese, by whose vigilance their Capitol had been preserved. The Athenians made a decree that the mules and hinnies which served at the building of the temple, called Hecatompedon, should be free and allowed to pasture where they would without hindrance.

The Agrigentines had a common custom solemnly to bury the beasts they had cherished, such as horses of some extraordinary merit, dogs and birds that had been of use to them, or even had served to amuse their children. And the magnificence that was common with them in all other things was also remarkably apparent in the sumptuousness and number of the monuments erected to this end, which lasted in splendor many centuries after.

The Egyptians buried wolves, bears, crocodiles, dogs, and cats in sacred places, embalmed their bodies, and put on mourning at their death.

Cimon gave an honorable burial to the mares with which he had three times won the prize in racing at the Olympic games. The ancient Xantippus had his dog buried by the seacoast on a headland which has since retained that name. And Plutarch says that he scrupled at selling and sending to the slaughterhouse, for a slight profit, an ox that had been long in his service.

OF PRESUMPTION

THERE IS ANOTHER sort of glory, which is to have too good an opinion of our own worth. It is an unreasoning affection with which we cherish ourselves, and which represents us to ourselves other than we are; as the passion of love lends beauties and graces to the object it embraces and makes those who are smitten by it, with a disturbed and impaired judgment, consider the thing they love other and more perfect than it is.

Nevertheless I would not have a man, for fear of erring in that direction, not know himself or think himself less than he is. The judgment should in all things maintain its rights; it is right that it should see, in this matter as elsewhere, what truth sets before it. If he is Caesar, let him boldly think himself the greatest captain in the world. We are nothing but ceremony; ceremony carries us away, and we leave the substance of things; we hold on to the branches and abandon the trunk and the body. We have taught the ladies to blush at merely hearing named what they are not at all afraid to do; we dare not call our members by their right names, yet we are not afraid to employ them in all sorts of debauchery. Ceremony forbids us to express in words things that are permissible and natural, and we obey it; reason forbids us to do things illicit and wicked, and nobody obeys it. I find myself here entangled in the laws of ceremony, for she does not permit a man either to speak well of himself or to speak ill. We will leave her alone for the moment.

Those whom Fortune (call it good or bad as you wish) has caused to pass their lives in some eminent position can by their public actions manifest what they are. But those whom she has only employed in the crowd, and of whom nobody will speak unless they speak themselves, are to be excused if they take the boldness to speak of themselves to those who are interested in knowing them, after the example of Lucilius:

> His way was in his books to speak his mind,
> As freely as his secrets he would tell
> To his tried friends, and, take it ill or well,
> He held his custom, whence it came to pass
> That all the old man's life is there exposed
> As if upon a votive tablet drawn.[1]

That man committed to his paper his actions and thoughts, and there portrayed himself such as he felt himself to be. *Nor did Rutillius or Scaurus incur disbelief or disparagement for doing so.*[2]

So I remember that from my tenderest childhood there was observed in me a certain indefinable quality of bodily carriage and certain gestures giving evidence of some empty and stupid pride. I want to say this first, that it is not detrimental to have traits and propensities so personal and so incorporated into us that we have not the means to feel and recognize them. And of such natural inclinations the body is apt to retain a certain bent, without our knowledge or consent. It was a certain affectation suited to his beauty that made Alexander lean his head a little to one side and made the speech of Alcibiades soft and lisping. Julius Caesar used to scratch his head with one finger, which is the way of a man filled with troublesome thoughts; and Cicero, it seems to me, was wont to wrinkle up his nose, a sign of a mocking nature. Such gestures may arise in us unnoticed. There are other artificial ones of which I do not speak, such as bows and salutations, by which men, for the most part wrongfully, acquire the reputation of being very humble and courteous; one may be humble out of vainglory. I am prodigal enough of taking off my hat, especially in summer, and

[1] Horace, *Satires*   [2] Tacitus, *Agricola*

never receive such a salute without returning it, from whatever class of man it may be, unless he is in my pay. I should wish that some princes I know would be more sparing and discriminating in handing out these greetings; for being so indiscriminately scattered about, they no longer bear effect. If they are without respect of persons, they are without effect. Among the excessive bearings let us not forget the arrogance of the Emperor Constantius, who always in public held his head straight, without turning or bending it this way or that, not so much as to look upon those who saluted him from the side, keeping his body bolt upright, without letting it yield to the motion of his coach, without daring either to spit, or blow his nose, or wipe his face before people.

I do not know whether those gestures that were observed in me were of this first kind and whether I had really any secret propensity to this vice, as it may well be; and I cannot be responsible for the movements of the body; but as to the movements of the soul, I want to confess here what I think of them.

This vainglory consists of two parts; namely, to think too highly of ourselves, and not to think highly enough of others. As to the one, it seems to me that these considerations ought in the first place to be taken into account: that I feel myself oppressed by an error of the soul that displeases me, both as unjust and, even more, as troublesome. I attempt to correct it, but I cannot root it out. The reason is that I lessen the value of things that I possess because I possess them, and overvalue others because they are foreign, absent, and not mine. This humor spreads very far. As the prerogative of their authority makes husbands look upon their own wives with wicked disdain, and many fathers their children, so it is with me; and between two works of equal merit I should always weight the balance against my own. Not so much that zeal for my progress and improvement troubles my judgment and hinders my being satisfied with myself, as that dominion, of itself, begets a contempt of what we hold and control. Far off governments, manners, and languages delight me; and I am aware that Latin allures me by its dignity to value it above its due, as it does children and the common run of people. The domestic economy, the house, the horse of my neighbor, though no better than my own, I prize above my own because they are not mine—the more so since I am very ignorant of my affairs. I admire the assurance and confidence everyone has in himself, whereas there is hardly anything that I am sure I know or that I dare give my word that I can do. I have not my means of doing anything listed and arranged in advance, and I know about them only after they take place—as doubtful of myself as of anything else. Whence it comes to pass that, if I happen to perform some task commendably, I attribute it more to my luck than my ability, inasmuch as I plan all of them by chance and in fear.

Likewise I have this characteristic in general, that of all the opinions antiquity has held of man as a whole, I most willingly embrace and most adhere to those that most scorn, disparage, and nullify us. I think Philosophy has never so easy a game as when she assails our vanity and presumption; when she sincerely admits her uncertainty, weakness, and ignorance. It seems to me that the nursing mother of the falsest opinions, both public and private, is the excessively good opinion that man has of himself.

Those people who perch astride upon the epicycle of Mercury, who see so far into the heavens, give me a pain; for in the study I am making, the subject of which is man, finding so vast a variety of judgments, so deep a labyrinth of difficulties one on top of the other, so much diversity and uncertainty even in the school of wisdom, you can imagine (since those people have not been able to agree about the knowledge of themselves and their own state, which is continually before their eyes, which is within them; since they do not know how that moves which they themselves move, nor how to describe and explain to us the springs they themselves hold and manage) how much I should believe them about the cause of the ebb and flow of the

Nile. The curiosity of knowing things has been given to men for a scourge says the Holy Scripture.

But to come to what concerns myself, it would be very difficult, it seems to me, for any other man to have a lower opinion of himself, indeed, for any other to have a lower opinion of me than I have of myself. I look upon myself as one of the common sort, except in this, that I consider myself so; guilty of the meanest and most common defects, but not disowned or excused; and do not value myself upon any other account than because I know my own value.

If there is any vainglory in me, it is superficially infused into me by the treachery of my nature and has no body that is apparent to my judgment. I am sprinkled with it, but not dyed.

For in truth, as to any kind of mental accomplishment, nothing has ever come forth from me which satisfied me; and the approbation of others does not repay me. My taste is delicate and demanding, especially in things that concern myself. I disown myself constantly and feel myself, in every part, floating and wavering because of my weakness. I have nothing of my own that satisfies my judgment. My sight is clear and disciplined enough, but in working it becomes blurred, as I most manifestly find in poetry. I love it infinitely and am a rather good judge of other men's works; but, in truth, when I want to try my hand at it, I play the child; I cannot endure myself. A man may play the fool in everything else, but not in poetry,

> But neither gods, nor men, nor booksellers
> Have stood for poets' being mediocre.[3]

Would to God these words were written on the front of all our printers' shops to forbid the entrance of so many versifiers:

> None is more certain of himself
> Than a bad poet is.[4]

---

[3] Horace, *Ars Poetica*   [4] Martial

Why have not we such people as these? Dionysius the father valued nothing of his so much as his poetry. At the time of the Olympic games, with chariots surpassing all others in magnificence, he sent also poets and musicians to present his verses, with tents and pavilions royally gilt and hung with tapestry. When his verses came to be recited, the grace and excellence of the pronunciation at first attracted the attention of the people; but when they afterwards came to weigh the ineptitude of the work, they first became disdainful; becoming increasingly bitter in their criticism, they presently flew into a fury and ran to pull down and tear resentfully to pieces all his pavilions. And when his chariots no longer made any showing in the races, and the ship which brought back his people missed Sicily and was driven and wrecked by the tempest upon the coast of Tarentum, the people firmly believed that it was the wrath of the gods, incensed, as they themselves were, against that paltry poem. And even the mariners who escaped from the wreck seconded this opinion of the people.

The oracle that foretold his death also seemed to subscribe somewhat to that opinion. It brought forth that Dionysius would be near his end when he had overcome those who were better than himself; which he interpreted to be the Carthaginians, who surpassed him in power. And in war with them he often dodged the victory and tempered it so as not to incur the destiny of this prediction. But he understood it incorrectly; for the god was pointing to the time that by favor and injustice he triumphed at Athens over the tragic poets, better than himself, having caused his own play, called *The Leneians,* to be acted in the competition; suddenly after this victory he died, and partly of the excessive joy he felt at it.

What I find tolerable in my own work is not so really and in itself, but in comparison with other worse things that I see are well enough received. I envy the happiness of those that can rejoice and feel gratified in their work, for it is an easy way to give oneself pleasure because one extracts it from himself. Especially if there is a little firmness in their self-conceit. I know a poet against whom the strong and the weak, in public and in private, and heaven and earth cry out that he scarcely knows anything of his art. For all that he does not slash anything from the measure which he has cut himself out; he is always beginning anew, always reconsidering, and always persisting, so much the stronger and more unyielding in his opinion as it rests on him alone to maintain it. <u>My works are so far from pleasing me that as often as I try them,</u> so often am I irritated with them:

> When I reread I blush at what I wrote
> For even I, the author, can perceive
> So many things that ought to be struck out.[5]

I have always an idea in my mind and a certain confused image which offers me, as in a dream, a better form than that which I have put to use, but I cannot seize it and utilize it. And even that idea is only of a mediocre level. From that I conclude that the productions of those rich and great minds of the past are very far beyond the utmost stretch of my imagination and desire. Their writings do not only satisfy and fill me, but they astonish me and ravish me with admiration. I judge their beauty; I see it, if not to the utmost, at least so far that it is impossible for me to aspire to it. Whatever I undertake, I owe a sacrifice to the Graces, as Plutarch says of someone, to curry their favor:

> If anything is pleasing that I write,
> If it steals o'er men's senses with delight,
> It is unto the charming Graces due.[6]

They abandon me on all occasions. All I write is crude; it lacks refinement and beauty. I do not know how to set things off to

---

[5] Ovid, *Ex Ponto*   [6] Author unknown

greater advantage than they are worth; my handling adds nothing to the matter. That is why I need substantial matter that has plenty of grip and that shines with its own light. When I seize on popular and gayer subjects, it is to follow my own inclination, for I do not like a solemn and somber wisdom, as the world does, and to enliven myself, not my style, which is disposed rather to grave and austere subjects (at least if I should give the name of style to a formless and irregular way of speaking, a popular jargon, and a proceeding without definition, without division, without conclusion, confused, like that of Amafanius and Raberius). I do not know how to please, or delight, or tickle; the best story in the world dries up in my hands and becomes dull. I do not know how to speak except in earnest and I am totally lacking in that facility, which I observe in many of my acquaintances, of entertaining the first comers and keeping a whole company interested, or tirelessly amusing the ear of a prince with all sorts of talk, never lacking matter, because of the talent they have for being able to make use of the first thing that comes to hand and for accommodating it to the humor and capacity of those with whom they have to do. Princes do not much like earnest discussions, nor I to tell stories. The first and easiest arguments, which are commonly the best received, I do not know how to employ: poor preacher for the multitude; I am apt to say on everything the utmost that I know. Cicero is of the opinion that in treatises of philosophy the exordium is the hardest part. If it is so, I am sticking to the conclusion.

And yet we must tune the string to all kinds of notes, and the sharpest is that which comes most seldom into play. There is at least as much perfection in lifting up an empty subject as in sustaining a weighty one. One must sometimes handle things superficially, sometimes go deeply into them. I know very well that most men keep on that low level from conceiving things only by that outer bark; but I likewise know that the greatest masters, both Xenophon and Plato, are often seen relaxing into that humble and popular manner of speaking and treating of things, supporting it with graces which never fail them.

As to the rest, my language is not easy and polished; it is harsh and disdainful, free and unchecked in its disposition, and I like it thus, if not by judgment, then by inclination. But I very well perceive that I sometimes let myself go too far, and that by dint of trying to avoid art and affectation, I fall back into them in another direction:

I strive to be concise, and I become obscure.[7]

Plato says that length and brevity are not properties that either take away or give value to language.

Should I attempt to follow that other style that is even, smooth, and orderly, I should not attain to it; and though the concise periods and cadences of Sallust best suit my humor, yet I find Caesar much greater and much harder to imitate; and if my inclination leads me more to imitate Seneca's manner of expression, I, nevertheless, esteem more that of Plutarch. As in doing, so in speaking, I simply follow my natural bent; which, perhaps, is the reason that I am better at speaking than writing. Motion and action animate words, especially in those who move about briskly, as I do, and grow heated. The bearing, the countenance, the voice, the robe, and the posture may set off some things that of themselves are no more than prating. Messala complains, in Tacitus, of certain tight garments in his time and of the fashion of the benches where the orators had to speak, which weakened their eloquence.

My French tongue is corrupted, both in pronunciation and otherwise, by the barbarism of my region; I never saw a man from any of the provinces on this side of the kingdom who in his speech did not clearly reveal his native accent, offensive to ears purely French. Yet it is not because I am very expert in

---

[7] Horace, *Ars Poetica*

my Périgordian, for I have no more command of it than of German; and I do not much care. It is a language (as are the others around me on one side or the other, those of Poitou, Saintonge, Angoumois, Limoges, Auvergne) soft, drawling, prolix. There is, indeed, above us, towards the mountains, a Gascon dialect that I find unusually beautiful, blunt, brief, expressive, and, in truth, a more manly and soldierly language than any other I understand; as sinewy, powerful, and pertinent as the French is graceful, delicate, and copious.

As to the Latin, which was given me for my mother tongue, I have lost, through lack of practice, readiness in using it in speaking; yes, and in writing, wherein I used to be called a master hand. That is how little I am worth on that side.

Beauty is a thing of great recommendation in the relations of men; it is the primary means of bringing men together one with another, and no man is so barbarous and so morose that he does not feel himself in some sort struck by its charm. The body has a great share in our being, it has an eminent place there; therefore its structure and composition well merit consideration. Those who wish to disunite our two principal parts and separate them from one another are wrong. We must, on the contrary, reunite and rejoin them. We must command the soul not to draw aside and entertain herself apart, not to despise and abandon the body (neither can she do it but by some disguised apish trick), but to unite herself to it, to embrace it, cherish it, assist it, govern it, advise it, set it straight, and bring it back when it goes astray; in sum, to marry it and be a spouse to it, so that their acts do not appear to be different and contrary, but concurring and uniform.

Christians have a particular instruction concerning this bond; for they know that the divine justice embraces this relationship and union of body and soul, even to making the body capable of eternal rewards, and that God watches man act, as a whole, and wills that he, as a whole, receive chastisement or reward according to his merits.

The Peripatetic sect, of all the sects the most sociable, attributes to wisdom this sole care, to provide for and procure the common good of these two associated parts; and it shows that the other sects, in not having sufficiently devoted themselves to the consideration of this mixture, have become biased, one for the body, and another for the soul, with equal error, and have drawn apart from their subject, which is Man, and from their guide, which they in general confess to be Nature.

The first distinction that existed among men and the first consideration that gave some men pre-eminence over others was, it is likely, the advantage of beauty:

> they parcelled out the fields and gave to each
> According to his beauty, strength, and intellect;
> For beauty was much prized and strength well honored then.[a]

Now, I am a little under middle height. This defect is not only ugly but also disadvantageous, especially for those who are in command or in office; for the authority which a fine presence and bodily majesty give is wanting. C. Marius did not willingly accept any soldiers that were not six feet tall. The Courtier is, indeed, right to desire in the gentleman he is training an average stature rather than any other and to reject all strangeness that should cause him to be pointed at. But if he fails to be of this medium height, I would not choose in the case of a military man that he should fall below rather than exceed that height.

Little men, says Aristotle, are very pretty, but not handsome; and a lofty soul is recognized in greatness, as beauty is in a great, tall body. The Ethiopians and Indians, he says, in choosing their kings and magistrates, had a regard to the beauty and lofty stature of their persons. They were right; for it creates respect in those that follow them and terror in the enemy to see a leader of handsome and ample stature march at the head of a troop:

---

[a] Lucretius

> Turnus himself, with distinguished bearing, stands
> Holding arms amid the foremost, and o'er them
> Towers by a head.[9]

Our great, divine. and heavenly King, of Whom every circumstance should be carefully, religiously, and reverently observed, did not reject bodily recommendation, *thou art fairer than the children of men*.[10] And along with temperance and fortitude, Plato desires beauty in the conservators of his Republic.

It is a great annoyance to be addressed in the midst of your servants with the question: "Where is Monsieur?" and to receive only the last flourish of the salute that is made to your barber or your secretary. As it happened to poor Philopoemen. Having arrived the first of his company at a house where he was expected, his hostess, who did not know him and saw him to be of a rather poor appearance, put him to work in helping her maids draw water and make a fire to prepare for Philopoemen. The gentlemen of his suite, having arrived and surprised him busy in this fine occupation (for he had not failed to obey the order given him), asked him what he was doing there. "I am paying," he replied, "the penalty of my ugliness." The other kinds of beauty are for women; the beauty of stature is the only beauty of men. Where there is smallness of stature, neither the breadth and roundness of the forehead, nor the clearness and softness of the eyes, nor the moderate size of the nose, nor the littleness of the ears and mouth, nor the evenness and whiteness of the teeth, nor the even thickness of a beard brown as the husk of a chestnut, nor curly hair, nor the proper roundness of the head, nor a fresh complexion, nor a pleasant facial expression, nor a body without odor, nor the just proportion of limbs can make a handsome man.

I have, as to the rest, a strong and thickset body; a face, not fat, but full; a temperament between jovial and melancholy, moderately sanguine and hot,

---

[9] Virgil, *Aeneid*   [10] *Psalms*

> Whence 'tis my thighs so rough and bristled are,
> And that my breast is so thick set with hair;[11]

vigorous and lively health, rarely troubled by ailments until
well on in years. Such I was, for I am not considering myself
at this moment when I am moving along the avenues of old
age, having long since passed forty:

> By small degrees old age breaks down their strength
> And their full vigor, and dissolves into decay.[12]

What I shall be from this time forward will be but a half being, it will no longer be myself. I escape and steal away from
myself every day,

> The parting years steal all things from us one by one.[13]

Dexterity and agility I have never had, and yet I am the son
of a very nimble father whose sprightliness lasted until his extreme old age. He found hardly a man of his condition who
was his equal in bodily exercises; just as I have found hardly
any who have not excelled me, except in running, at which I was
fair. In music, either vocal, for which my voice is very unfit, or
instrumental, they could never teach me anything. In dancing,
tennis, or wrestling I have been able to acquire only very slight
and ordinary ability; in swimming, fencing, vaulting, and jumping, none at all. My hands are so clumsy that I cannot even
write legibly enough for myself; so that I had rather do over
what I have scribbled than give myself the trouble to untangle
it. And I do not read much better. I feel that I weigh on my
listeners. Otherwise, a good scholar. I cannot properly fold up
a letter, nor could I ever cut a pen, nor carve at table worth a
hang, nor saddle a horse, nor carry a bird correctly and let it
fly, nor talk to dogs, birds, or horses.

---

[11] Martial   [12] Lucretius   [13] Horace, *Epistles*

In fine, my bodily qualities agree very closely with those of my soul. There is no sprightliness; there is only a full and firm vigor. I hold out well under hard work, but it is only if I go voluntarily to it, and as much as my desire guides me to it,

> Excitement gently lightening the irksome toil.[14]

Otherwise, if I am not allured with some pleasure, and I have a different guide than my own pure free will, I am good for nothing. For I have reached the point where, except for health and life, there is nothing for which I would bite my nails and that I would purchase at the price of torment of mind and constraint,

> May all the sands of shady Tagus and the gold
> It rolls into the sea be not that dear to me:[15]

extremely idle, extremely independent, both by nature and by art. I would as willingly lend a man my blood as my pains.

I have a soul all its own, accustomed to guide itself in its own fashion. Having hitherto never had either master or governor imposed upon me, I have gone as far as I pleased and at my own pace. This has made me soft and useless for the service of others and of no use to anyone but myself. And for my sake there was no need of forcing this heavy, lazy, and do-nothing disposition. For having enjoyed from my birth such a degree of fortune that I had reason to be contented with it, and as much sense as I felt I had occasion for, I have sought nothing, and I have also acquired nothing:

> I am not wafted by the swelling gales
> Of winds propitious, with expanded sails,
> Nor do I guide my life 'mid adverse gales;
> In strength, wit, beauty, virtue, place, and wealth,
> I'm last among the first, and first among the last.[16]

---

[14] Horace, *Satires*   [15] Juvenal   [16] Horace, *Epistles*

I have had need only of sufficiency to content myself, which, nevertheless, is a well-ordered state of mind, to take it right, equally difficult in every sort of human lot, and that we see by experience even more easily found in want than in abundance; perhaps because, as with our other passions, the hunger for riches is sharpened more by their use than by the lack of them, and because the virtue of moderation is more rare than that of patience. And I have never had need of anything but pleasantly to enjoy the good things that God in His bounty had put into my hands. I have never tasted of any kind of tedious work. I have had hardly anything to handle except my own affairs; or, if I have, it has been on condition of handling them at my own times and in my own way, committed to my trust by people who trusted me, who knew me, and who did not press me. For experts get some service out of even a restive and broken-winded horse.

Even my childhood was guided in a free and gentle manner and exempt from any rigorous subjection. All this has shaped in me a delicate disposition, incapable of enduring cares; to such a degree that I like to have my losses and the disorders that concern me concealed from me. I put down to the account of my expenses what it costs me to nourish and maintain my nonchalance,

> Those things, of course, superfluous, which pass
> The master unperceived and profit thieves.[17]

I prefer not to know the count of what I have in order to feel my loss less exactly. I entreat those who live with me, when they lack affection for me and honest dealing, to deceive me and pay me with decent appearances. For want of firmness enough to support the annoyance of the adverse accidents to which we are subject, and from being unable to keep up the strain of regulating and managing my affairs, I foster all I can

---

[17] Horace. *Epistles*

in myself this idea, while abandoning myself to fortune, of expecting the worst in all things and resolving to bear that worst mildly and patiently. It is for that alone that I labor, and it is the goal to which I direct all my meditation.

In a danger I do not so much consider how I shall escape it as of how little importance it is whether I escape it. Even if I should be left on the spot, what would it matter? Not being able to govern events, I govern myself, and I adapt myself to them if they do not adapt themselves to me. I have hardly enough skill to be able to evade Fortune and to escape from her or to force her, and by prudence to direct and conduct things to my own purpose. I have still less patience to stand the harsh and painful care that it requires. And the most painful situation for me is to be in suspense about urgent matters and to be agitated between hope and fear. Deliberation, even in things of lightest moment, is very troublesome to me; and I find my mind more put to it to stand the varied agitation and shocks of doubt and deliberation than to settle down and acquiesce to any course whatever after the die is thrown. Few passions have troubled my sleep, but as for deliberations, the slightest one troubles it. Just as in roads I preferably avoid the sloping and slippery sides and take to the beaten track, however muddy and boggy, where I can fall no lower, and there seek my safety; so do I like pure misfortunes which do not torment and harass me any more, after the uncertainty about setting them right has passed, and which at the first leap plunge me directly into suffering:

Uncertain ills torment us most.[18]

When actions are taking place, I carry myself like a man; in their conduct, like a child. The fear of the fall gives me a greater fever than the fall. The game is not worth the candle. The covetous man suffers more from his passion than the poor

---

[18] Seneca, *Agamemnon*

man, and the jealous man than the cuckold. And often there is less harm in losing your vineyard than in going to law about it. The lowest step is the firmest. It is the seat of constancy. There you have need only of yourself. It is there founded and leans wholly upon itself. Has not this case of a well-known gentleman some air of philosophy? He married well advanced in years, having spent his youth in jolly company, a great talker and a gay blade. Calling to mind how much the subject of cuckoldry had given him occasion to talk and scoff at others, in order to get under cover, he married a woman whom he picked in a place where anyone finds them for a price and set up with her his plan: "Good-morning, whore," "Good-morning, cuckold." And there was not anything about which he more commonly and openly talked with those who came to see him than this plan of his by which he stopped the secret gossip of mockers and took off the edge of this reproach.

As to ambition, which is neighbor, or rather daughter, to presumption, Fortune to advance me would have had to come and take me by the hand. For to trouble myself for an uncertain hope and to submit to all the difficulties that accompany those who endeavor to thrust themselves into credit in the beginning of their career, I could never have done it;

> I do not purchase hope with ready cash.[19]

I cling to what I see and to what I hold, and go not very far from port;

> Let one oar skim the waves, the other touch the strand.[20]

And besides, a man very seldom arrives at these advancements except in first hazarding what he has of his own; and I am of opinion that if what a man has is enough to maintain the condition in which he was born and brought up, it is folly to let go

---

[19] Terence, *Adelphi*   [20] Propertius

of it on the chance of augmenting it. He to whom Fortune has denied a place to set his foot, and the means of establishing a tranquil and restful life, is to be excused if he does venture what he has because, happen what will, necessity sends him seeking his living.

> In evil we must take a headlong course.[21]

And I sooner excuse a younger brother for throwing his inheritance to the winds than him with whom the honor of his family is intrusted, who cannot be necessitous but by his own fault. I have certainly found the road shorter and easier, through the advice of the good friends of former days, by freeing myself from this desire and keeping still;

> Who would be certain of the prize without the dust;[22]

also judging very soundly that my strength was not capable of great things, and calling to mind the saying of the late Chancellor Olivier, that the French were like monkeys that clamber up a tree from branch to branch and never stop until they have reached the highest branch, and show their backsides when they get there.

> 'Tis shameful to put on your head
> A load you cannot bear, and then
> With knee bent 'neath its weight to quit.[23]

Even the qualities in me that are irreproachable I found useless in this age. My easy-going ways would have been called sloth and weakness; my faith and conscience would have been considered scrupulous and overnice; my frankness and independence, troublesome, inconsiderate, and rash. Ill luck is good for something. It is good to be born in a very depraved age, for

---

[21] Seneca, *Agamemnon*   [22] Horace, *Epistles*   [23] Propertius

by comparison with others you are considered virtuous without
its costing you much; he that in our days is but a parricide and
sacrilegious is a worthy man and a man of honor:

> Now if a friend does not deny a trust
> And gives back the old purse with all its rust,
> Prodigious faith, worthy to be inscribed
> In books of Tuscany and which should then
> Be celebrated by a lamb bedecked.[24]

And never was there time or place where there was set before
princes a surer or greater reward for goodness and justice. The
first who shall make it his business to get himself into favor
and esteem by that path, I am much mistaken if he does not
easily outstrip his fellows. Force and violence can do something, but not always everything.

We see merchants, country justices, and artisans moving
abreast of the nobility in valor and military knowledge. They
give an honorable account of themselves in both public and
private combats; they fight, they defend towns in our wars. A
prince's distinction is stifled in this crowd. Let him shine bright
in humanity, truth, loyalty, temperance, and especially in justice, marks rare, unknown, and exiled. It is solely by the will of
the people that he can carry on his affairs, and no other qualities can curry their will as much as those, being much more
useful to them than the others. *Nothing is so agreeable to the
people as goodness.*[25]

By this comparison I would have considered myself great and
rare, as I consider myself now pygmy and ordinary in comparison with some past ages, in which, if other better qualities did
not concur, it was common to see a man moderate in his re-
venges, gentle in resenting injuries, religious in observing his
word, neither two-faced nor supple, nor accommodating his
faith to the will of others or to the occasion. I would rather let

---

[24] Juvenal   [25] Cicero, *Pro Ligario*

affairs break their necks than twist my faith to serve them. For as to this new virtue of hypocrisy and dissimulation which is now in such great honor, I mortally hate it; and of all vices I find none that gives evidence of so much baseness and meanness of spirit. It is a cowardly and servile humor to hide and disguise ourselves under a mask and not to dare to show ourselves as we are. By it our men are trained for perfidy; being accustomed to utter false words, they make no conscience of breaking their word. A generous heart ought not to belie its own thoughts; it wants to make itself seen to its innermost. There all is good, or at least all is human.

Aristotle considers it the office of magnanimity to hate and love openly, to judge and to speak with all freedom, and not to value the approval or disapproval of others in comparison to truth. Apollonius said it was for slaves to lie and for freemen to speak truth.

It is the first and fundamental part of virtue. We must love it for itself. He who speaks truth because he is obliged to do so and because it serves him, and who is not afraid to lie when it does not matter to anybody, is not sufficiently truthful. My soul naturally shuns lying and hates even to think a lie. I have an inward shame and stinging remorse if sometimes a lie escapes me, as sometimes it does when occasions surprise and agitate me unexpectedly.

We must not always tell all, for that would be folly; but what we do say must be what we think, otherwise it is knavery. I do not know what advantage men expect from eternally dissembling and counterfeiting unless not to be believed even when they speak the truth; that may once or twice deceive men, but to make a profession of being covert and to brag, as some of our princes have done, that they would burn their shirt if it were privy to their true intentions (which is a saying of the ancient Metellus of Macedon), and that one who does not know how to dissemble knows not how to rule, is to give warning to all who have anything to do with them that all they say is nothing but deceit and lying. *The more subtle and cunning a man is, the more hated and suspected he is, once his reputation for probity is lost.*[26] It would be great naiveté in anyone to let himself be beguiled by the countenance or word of a man who prizes being always different on the outside than he is within, as Tiberius did; and I do not know what part such people can have in dealing with men since they offer nothing that is received as current coin. Whoever is disloyal to truth is also disloyal to falsehood.

Those who in our time have considered, in establishing the duty of a prince, only the good of his affairs, and have preferred that to the care of his faith and conscience, would have something to say to a prince whose affairs Fortune had so arranged that he might establish them once and for all by a single breaking and betrayal of his word. But it does not go that way. They often fall back on the same bargain; they make more than one peace, more than one treaty in their lives. The gain that tempts them to the first breach of faith (and almost always gain is present in it, as in all other evil acts: sacrilege, murder, rebellion, treason, are undertaken for some kind of advantage), this first gain brings on no end of subsequent harms, casting this prince out of all relations and means of negotiation because of the example of this infidelity.

When, during my childhood, Soliman, of the Ottoman race, a race careless about keeping promises and pacts, landed his army at Otranto, having learned that Mercurino de' Gratinare and the inhabitants of Castro were detained prisoners after having surrendered the place, contrary to the articles of the capitulation, he sent word that they should be released; and he said that, having other great enterprises in hand in those parts, such treachery, though it had some semblance of immediate utility, would in the future bring on him a disrepute and distrust of infinite prejudice.

Now, for my part, I had rather be troublesome and indis-

[26] Cicero, *De Officiis*

creet than a flatterer and a dissembler. I confess that some bit of pride and obstinacy may be mingled in keeping myself so upright and open, without consideration of others; and it seems to me that I am becoming a little freer where I ought to be less so, and that I grow heated through my opposition to the respect I should pay. It may be, also, that I let myself act according to my nature for want of artifice. Exhibiting to the great the same liberty of speech and countenance that I use at home, I am aware how much it leans towards indiscretion and incivility. But besides the fact that I am so made, I have not a wit supple enough to evade a sudden question and to escape it by some twist, or to invent a truth, or memory enough to retain it if thus invented, and certainly not enough assurance to maintain it; and I play the brave man out of weakness. And so it is that I abandon myself to candor and to saying always what I think, both by nature and by design, leaving it to Fortune to guide the outcome.

Aristippus used to say that the principal benefit he had extracted from philosophy was that he spoke freely and openly to all.

Memory is a tool of wonderful usefulness, and without it the judgment carries out with great difficulty its office; I lack it entirely. What anyone wants to put before me must be put before me piecemeal. For to answer a speech consisting of several topics is not in my power. I cannot receive a commission without my writing tablets. And when I have a speech of consequence to make, if it be long, I am reduced to the low and miserable necessity of learning by heart, word for word, what I have to say; I should otherwise have neither manner nor assurance, being in fear that my memory would play me a bad trick. But this way is no less difficult for me. I must have three hours to learn three verses; and then, in a work of my own, the liberty and authority of altering the order, of changing a word, incessantly varying the matter, makes it harder to keep in mind. Now, the more I distrust it, the more confused it gets; it serves me better by chance, I must solicit it nonchalantly. For if I press it, it is dazed; and after it has begun to stagger, the more I sound it, the more tangled up and embarrassed it becomes. It serves me at its own hour, not at mine.

This trait that I feel in my memory I feel in several other parts. I flee command, obligation, and constraint. That which I do easily and naturally, if I impose it upon myself by an express and strict order, I can no longer do it. Even in the case of my body, the members that have some particular freedom and jurisdiction over themselves sometimes refuse to obey me when I assign and set them to a certain time and place for obligatory service. This compulsory and tyrannical way of being ordered in advance repels them: they cower through fear or spite and become numb.

Being once in a place where it is a barbarous discourtesy not to pledge those who invite you to drink, though I was treated with full freedom, I tried to play the good fellow in honor of the ladies who were of the party according to the custom of the country. But then the fun began; for the threat and preparation of having to force myself beyond my custom and inclination so stopped up my gullet that I could not swallow one drop, and I was deprived of drinking even what I needed for my meal. I found myself gorged and my thirst quenched by the great quantity of drink that my imagination had anticipated.

This effect is more manifest in those who have a more lively and powerful imagination; but is natural, notwithstanding, and there is no one that does not in some measure feel it. An excellent archer, condemned to die, was offered his life if he would show some notable proof of his skill; he refused to try, fearing lest the excessive tension of his will should make him pull his hand off the mark and that instead of saving his life he should also lose the reputation he had got in shooting with the bow. A man whose thoughts are elsewhere will not fail, by an inch more or less, to repeat always the same number and length of steps in the place where he walks; but if he sets to it attentively

to measure and count them, he will find that what he did naturally and by chance he will not do so exactly by design.

My library, which is a fine one among country libraries, is
situated at one corner of my house; if anything comes into my
head that I want to look up or write down there, lest it escape
me while I am simply crossing my courtyard, I have to give
it in safekeeping to some other person. If I venture in speaking to digress ever so little from my thread, I never fail to lose
it, which is the reason why I keep myself constrained, dry, and
compressed in speech. I am forced to call the men who serve
me either by the names of their functions or of their province,
for it is very hard for me to remember names. I can tell, indeed,
that it has three syllables, that it has a harsh sound, and that
it begins or ends with such and such a letter. And if I should
live long, I do not doubt that I should forget my own name as
others have done. Messala Corvinus was two years without
any trace of memory, which is also said of George of Trebizond.
And in my own interest I often meditate what kind of a life
theirs was, and if without this faculty I shall have enough left
to support me with any ease; and looking at it closely, I fear
that this privation, if absolute, destroys all the functions of
the mind: *Certainly the memory alone contains not only philosophy, but also all the practice of life and all the arts.*[27]

I'm full of chinks, I leak out here and there.[28]

It has happened to me more than once to forget the watch-
word I had three hours before given or received from another,
and to forget where I had hidden my purse, whatever Cicero
may say of the matter. I help myself to lose what I carefully
lock up. Memory is the receptacle and container of knowledge;
mine being so defective, I cannot much complain if I do not
know much. I know in general the names of the arts and of
what they treat, but nothing more. I thumb through books,

---

[27] Cicero, *Academica*   [28] Terence, *Eunuchus*

I do not study them. What I retain of them is something that I no longer recognize as another's. It is only this from which my judgment has profited, the thoughts and ideas with which it has been imbued; the author, the place, the words, and other circumstances I immediately forget.

And I am so excellent at forgetting that I forget my own writings and compositions no less than the rest. I am very often quoted to myself without being aware of it. If anyone should want to know where the verses and examples that I have piled up here came from, I should be hard put to it to tell him; and yet I have begged them only at well-known and famous doors, not satisfied with their being rich unless they also came from rich and honorable hands; authority and reason concur in them. It is no great wonder if my book follows the fortune that other books do and if my memory lets go of what I write as well as what I read, and of what I give as well as what I receive.

Besides the defect of memory I have others which very much contribute to my ignorance. I have a slow and dull wit; the slightest cloud arrests its point so that, for example, I never set before it any riddle easy enough for it to untangle. No subtlety is so empty that it does not perplex me. Of games in which the mind has a part, such as chess, cards, draughts, and the like, I understand nothing but the most obvious elements. My apprehension is slow and confused; but what it once grasps, it grasps well and embraces very fully, closely, and deeply for as long as it does grasp it. My sight is long, sound, and whole, but it becomes easily tired in working and grows dim; for that reason I cannot have long communion with books except with the help of other persons. The younger Pliny can inform such as have not experienced it themselves how important an impediment this is to those who are given to this occupation.

There is no mind so wretched and brutish that some particular faculty is not seen to shine forth; there is none so buried but that it will break forth at some point. And how it comes to pass that a mind, blind and asleep to everything else, is found lively, clear, and excellent in some one particular accomplishment, we must inquire of the masters. But the fine minds are the universal minds, open, and ready for all things; if not instructed, at least capable of being instructed. I say this in condemnation of my own. For whether it is through weakness or indifference (and to be indifferent to what lies at our feet, what we have in our hands, what most concerns our use of life is something very remote from my doctrine), there is no mind so inept and so ignorant as mine of many such common things of which a man cannot without shame be ignorant. I must relate some examples.

I was born and bred in the country and in the midst of farming; I have had business and domestic management in my own hands ever since my predecessors in the possession of the estate I enjoy left me their place. Now I cannot reckon either with counters or with a pen. Most of our current money I do not know, nor do I know the difference between one grain and another, either in the ground or in the barn, if it is not too obvious; and scarcely the difference between the cabbage and lettuce in my garden. I do not so much as understand the names of the chief household implements, or the plainest principles of agriculture which children know. I know still less of the mechanical arts, of trade and merchandise, of the variety and nature of fruits, wines, and foods; nor do I know how to train a bird or doctor a horse or a dog. And since I must make my shame complete, it is not more than a month ago that I was surprised in ignorance of the fact that leaven was used to make bread and of what was meant by fermenting wine. They inferred of old at Athens an aptitude for mathematics in a man who was seen ingeniously arranging and binding a load of brushwood. Truly they would draw a quite contrary conclusion about me; for give me all the equipment of a kitchen, I shall starve.

From these lines of my confession men may imagine others

at my expense. But whatever I make myself known to be, provided I make myself known such as I am, I gain my end. And so I make no excuse for daring to commit to paper such mean and frivolous things as these. The meanness of the subject compels me to it. You may, if you please, condemn my project, but not my method. However that may be, without others telling me, I see well enough of how little weight and value all this is and the folly of my design. It is enough that my judgment is not disconcerted, of which these are the essays:

> Though you are nosy, even so large-nosed
> That Atlas to bear it would have refused,
> And though Latinus himself you can mock,
> Against my trifles you can say no more
> Than I have said myself. What good for tooth
> To gnaw on tooth? You must have flesh, my friend,
> If you'd be full. Waste not your efforts, keep
> Your sting for those who fancy most themselves;
> That these things nothing are, full well we know.[29]

I am not obliged not to utter absurdities, provided I am not deceived and know them to be such. And to trip knowingly is so common with me that I scarcely ever trip in any other way; I never trip by chance. It is no great matter to attribute my ridiculous actions to the temerity of my humor, since I cannot ordinarily help attributing my vicious ones to it.

I was present one day at Barleduc when there was presented to King Francis the Second, as a remembrance of René, King of Sicily, a portrait that he had drawn of himself. Why is it not, in like manner, allowable for everyone to portray himself with a pen as he did with a crayon? I do not desire, therefore, not to omit this further scar, very unfit to make public, namely irresolution, a defect very inconvenient in the negotiation of the affairs of the world. In doubtful enterprises I know not which side to choose:

[29] Martial

Nor yes, nor no, rings fully in my heart.[80]

I can maintain an opinion, but I cannot choose one.

Because in human things, to whatever side we incline, many probabilities present themselves to confirm us in it (and the philosopher Chrysippus said that he wished to learn from Zeno and Cleanthes, his masters, their doctrines alone; for as to proofs and reasons, he would furnish enough of his own); whichever way I turn, I always furnish myself with causes and probabilities enough to keep me there. So I detain within me doubt and the liberty of choosing until the occasion presses. And then, to confess the truth, I most often throw the feather into the wind, as the saying is, and abandon myself to the mercy of fortune: a very slight inclination and circumstance bears me off;

when the mind's in doubt,
The slightest matter moves it back and forth.[81]

The uncertainty of my judgment is so equally balanced in most occurrences that I would willingly refer it to be decided by the chance of the dice; and I remark, with deep consideration of our human weakness, the examples that even sacred history has left us of this custom of referring to fortune and chance the determination of choice in doubtful things: *The lot fell upon Matthias.*[32]

Human reason is a two-edged and a dangerous sword. And observe, even in the hand of Socrates, her most intimate and familiar friend, that it is a stick with many ends. Thus I am suited only to follow, and I let myself be easily carried away with the crowd. I have not confidence enough in my own strength to take upon me to command and lead; I am very glad to find my way marked out by others. If I must run the hazard of an uncertain choice, I prefer that it should be under some-

---

[80] Petrarch, *Sonnets*   [81] Terence, *Andria*   [32] *Acts*

one who is more confident in his opinions and is more wedded to them than I am to mine, whose foundation and ground I find slippery.

And yet I am not too easily changed since I discern a similar weakness in the contrary opinions. *The very habit of assenting seems to be dangerous and slippery.*[33] Especially in political affairs, there is a splendid field open for vacillation and dispute:

> As when just scales are pressed with equal weight,
> They neither dip, nor rise, but stay quite still.[34]

Machiavelli's arguments, for example, were solid enough for the subject, yet it was very easy to combat them, and they who did so made it no less easy to combat theirs. There would always be found in that kind of argument matter for answers, replies, rejoinders, rebuttals, counter-rebuttals, and that infinite fabric of debates which our wrangling lawyers have lengthened as far as possible in favor of lawsuits:

> The foe strikes us, and we deal out as much to him;[35]

the reasons having little other foundation than experience, and the variety of human events presenting us with infinite examples in all sorts of forms. A learned person of our times says that, if someone wants to say cold where they say hot in our almanacs, and wet where they say dry, and always put the contrary of what they foretell, if he were to lay a wager on one or the other taking place, he would not care which side he took, except in things where no uncertainty can occur, such as the promise of excessive heats at Christmas and the rigors of winter at midsummer. I have the same opinion of these political arguments; whatever rôle you are given to play, you have as good a chance as your adversary, provided you do not proceed so far as to jostle principles that are too plain and mani-

---

[33] Cicero, *Academica*   [34] Tibullus   [35] Horace, *Epistles*

fest. And yet, to my way of thinking, in public affairs there is no course so bad, provided it is old and stable, that is not better than change and agitation. Our morals are extremely corrupt and lean with extraordinary inclination towards the worse; of our laws and customs, there are many that are barbarous and monstrous; nevertheless, because of the difficulty of putting ourselves into a better state and the danger of everything crumbling, if I could put a spoke in our wheel and stop it at this point, I would do it with all my heart:

> At no time do we cite examples so debased,
> So shameful that there are not worse still left.[36]

The worst thing I find in our state is instability, and that our laws cannot, any more than our clothes, take any fixed form. It is very easy to accuse a government of imperfection, for all mortal things are full of it. It is very easy to beget in a people a contempt for their ancient observances; never did any man undertake it without succeeding. But to establish a better state in the place of the one which they have ruined, in this many of those who had attempted it wasted their efforts.

I grant my prudence a very small share in my conduct; I am willing to let myself be guided by the general movement of the world. Happy the people who do what they are commanded better than they who command, without tormenting themselves about the causes, who let themselves gently roll with the rolling of the heavens. Obedience is not pure or calm in him who reasons and argues.

In fine, to return to myself, the only thing for which I esteem myself somewhat is that in which never any man thought himself to be defective: my recommendation is vulgar, common, and popular, for who ever thought he lacked sense? It would be a proposition that would imply contradiction in itself. It is a disease that is never where it is seen; it is, indeed, tenacious

---

[36] Juvenal

and strong, but the first glance of the patient's sight, nevertheless, pierces through and disperses it, as the glance of the sun does a thick fog. To accuse oneself would be to excuse oneself in this case; and to condemn oneself would be to absolve oneself. There never was a porter or a silly woman who did not think they had sense enough to look out for themselves. We readily acknowledge in others an advantage of courage, bodily strength, experience, nimbleness, beauty; but an advantage in judgment we yield to none. And the arguments that issue from the simple, natural reasoning in others, we think that, if we had but turned our thoughts that way, we should have found them. As to knowledge, style, and such qualities that we see in the works of others, we are very readily aware if they excel our own; but for the simple products of the understanding, everyone thinks that he was capable of lighting upon the very same things and does not easily perceive their weight and difficulty, unless they are at an extreme and incomparable distance, and hardly even then. So it is a sort of exercise from which I must expect very little commendation and praise, and a kind of composition of small repute.

And then, for whom do you write? The learned, to whom the authority belongs of judging books, know no other value but that of learning and admit no other process in our minds but that of erudition and art. If you have mistaken one of the Scipios for the other, what have you left to say which is worth while? Whoever is ignorant of Aristotle, according to them, is by the same token ignorant of himself. Common and ordinary minds do not discern the grace and weight of a lofty and subtle style. Now these two sorts people the world. The third sort, into whose hands you fall, that of minds that are orderly and strong of themselves, is so rare that, therefore, it has neither name nor rank among us; it is time half lost to aspire and endeavor to please it.

It is commonly said that the fairest share Nature has given

us of her favors is that of sense; for there is no one that is not contented with the share of it she has apportioned to him. Is it not reasonable? Whoever should see beyond would see beyond his sight.

I think my opinions are good and sound; but who does not think the same of his? One of the best proofs I have of mine is the small esteem I have for myself; for if they had not been very assured, they would easily have let themselves be deceived by the singular affection I have for myself, being one who concentrates almost the whole of it upon himself and does not scatter much of it elsewhere. All the affection that others distribute to an infinite number of friends and acquaintances, to their glory, to their greatness, I dedicate entirely to the repose of my mind and to myself. That which escapes me in other ways is not properly by the direction of my reason,

> Trained to be strong and live for my own self.[37]

Now I find my opinions very bold and constant in condemning my own imperfection. Truly it is also a subject upon which I exercise my judgment as much as on any other. The world looks always outwards; as for me, I turn my sight inwards, I fix it there, I occupy it there. Everyone looks before him, I look within myself. I have no business but with myself. I constantly examine myself. I check on myself, I taste myself. Others are always going elsewhere if they really think about it; they are always going forward;

> No man attempts to plunge into himself;[38]

for my part, I revolve in myself.

This capacity for sifting truth, whatever it may amount to in me, and this independent inclination of not easily subjecting

---

[37] Lucretius   [38] Persius

my belief, I owe principally to myself. For the strongest and most general ideas I have are those which, so to speak, were born with me. They are natural and entirely my own. I produced them crude and simple, with a conception bold and strong, but a little confused and imperfect; I have since established and fortified them with the authority of others and the sound reflections of the ancients, with whom I have found myself conforming in judgment. These men have given me faster hold on my ideas and a more complete enjoyment and possession of them.

The commendation that everyone seeks for vivacity and promptness of wit I strive to obtain for orderliness; what everyone seeks for a brilliant and remarkable action or for some particular talent I strive to obtain for order, consistency, and tranquillity of opinions and habits. *Assuredly, if anything is becoming, it is uniformity in a man's whole life and also in the individual actions; which you cannot maintain if, imitating the nature of other men, you lay aside your own.*[39]

Here, then, you see to what degree I feel guilty of what I said was the first part of the vice of presumption. As to the second, which consists in not having a sufficient esteem for others, I do not know whether I can excuse myself so well; for whatever it costs me, I am resolved to speak the truth about it.

Whether, perhaps, it be that the continual association I have with the ancients' ways of thought and the idea I have formed of those richly endowed souls of past ages give me a distaste both for others and for myself; or whether, in truth, we live in an age which produces only very mediocre things; the fact remains that I know nothing worthy of great admiration. Furthermore I know scarcely any men with the intimacy that is needed to be able to judge them; and those with whom my situation throws me most commonly are, for the most part, men

[39] Cicero, *De Officiis*

who have little care for the culture of the soul and to whom honor alone may be proposed as the one and only blessing and valor as the one and only perfection.

Whatever I see that is fine in others I very readily praise and esteem. Indeed I often go beyond what I really think of it and permit myself to lie that far; for I cannot invent something false. I gladly testify for my friends about what I find praiseworthy in them; and of a foot of value I am inclined to make a foot and a half. But to attribute to them qualities that they do not have, I cannot do it, nor openly defend them for the imperfections they have.

Even to my enemies I frankly give the testimony of honor that is due. My feelings change, my judgment does not. And I never confound my accusation with other circumstances that are foreign to it; and I am so jealous of the liberty of my judgment that I can hardly part with it for any passion whatever. I do myself a greater injury in lying than I do him of whom I tell a lie. This commendable and generous custom is observed in the Persian nation, that they speak of their mortal enemies and make deadly war upon them as honorably and fairly as their valor deserves.

I know men enough that have various fine qualities; one wit, another courage, another skill, another conscience, another style; one, one science; another, another. But as for a man great in all respects, possessing all these fine parts together, or any one of them to such a degree of excellence as to cause us to be amazed or to compare him with those we honor of times past, my fortune has never shown me any such man. And the greatest I have known in person, I mean for the natural qualities of the soul, and the most gifted, was Etienne de la Boétie; his was a full soul revealing a lovely aspect on all sides, a soul of the old stamp that would have produced great results had his fortune so willed, for he had added much to those rich natural qualities by learning and study.

But I do not know how it happens (and yet it certainly does happen) that there is as much vanity and weakness of understanding in those who profess to have the greatest ability, who dabble in literary occupations and tasks that depend on books, as in any other sort of men; whether because more is required and expected of them and that common defects are not excusable in them, or because the opinion they have of their own learning makes them bolder to display and reveal themselves too far, by which they ruin and betray themselves. As an artisan much more clearly exhibits his stupidity on a rich material he has in hand if he arranges and blends it foolishly and contrary to the rules of his craft, than on a base material, and as men are more offended at a defect in a statue of gold than in one of plaster; so do these men when they exhibit things that in themselves, and in their place, would be good; for they make use of them without discretion, doing honor to their memory at the expense of their understanding. They do honor to Cicero, Galen, Ulpian, and Saint Jerome, and themselves they make ridiculous.

I willingly drop back into the subject of the ineptness of our education. Its objective has been to make us not good and wise, but learned; it has achieved it. It has not taught us to follow and embrace virtue and wisdom, but has imprinted in us their derivation and etymology. We know how to decline virtue if we do not know how to love it; if we do not know what wisdom is by practice and by experience, we know it by jargon and by rote. We are not content to know the extraction, kindred, and alliances of our neighbors; we want to have them as friends and establish some relationship and understanding with them. This education of ours has taught us the definitions, divisions, and partitions of virtue, like so many surnames and branches of a genealogy, without any further care of establishing any familiar association or intimate acquaintance between us and virtue. It has culled out for our instruction not such books as contain the soundest and truest opinions, but those that speak the best Greek and Latin; and among its fine words it has poured into our minds the emptiest fancies of antiquity.

A good education changes the judgment and way of living, as it happened to Polemon, that debauched young Greek, who, having gone by chance to hear one of Xenocrates' lectures, did not observe only the eloquence and knowledge of the teacher, and did not take home only the knowledge of some fine matter, but a more manifest and a more solid profit, which was the sudden change and reformation of his former life. Who has ever felt such an effect from our education?

> Will you do as converted Polemon
> Once did? Will you take off the signs
> Of your disease—the bindings, pads, and scarves—
> As he when drunk did furtively pull from
> His neck, they say, his crown of revelry
> When chided by his sober master's voice.[40]

That class of men seem to me to be the least contemptible who because of their simplicity hold the lowest rank; and they seem to exhibit to us a more orderly intercourse. I find the morals and the remarks of peasants commonly more disposed according to the dictates of true philosophy than are those of our philosophers. *The common people are wiser because they are only as wise as they need be.*[41]

The most remarkable men whom I have judged by outward appearances (for to judge them according to my own method it would be necessary to throw light more closely on them), in war and military ability, were the Duke of Guise, who died at Orleans, and the late Marshal Strozzi. For men of great ability and no common virtue, Olivier and L'Hôpital, Chancellors

---

[40] Horace, *Satires*   [41] Lactantius, *Divine Institutes*

of France. Poetry too, in my opinion, has flourished in our
century. We have an abundance of good craftsmen in the trade:
Daurat, Bèze, Buchanan, L'Hôpital, Montdoré, Turnebus. As
for those writing poetry in French, I believe they have raised
it to the highest point which it will ever attain; and in those
parts wherein Ronsard and Du Bellay excel, I find them but
little removed from the perfection of antiquity. Adrian Turnebus knew more, and knew better what he did know, than any
man of his time, or long before then.

The lives of the Duke of Alva, recently deceased, and of
our Constable de Montmorency were noble lives that had many
rare similarities in fortune; but the beauty and glory of the
death of the latter, in the sight of Paris and of his king, and
in their service against his nearest relations, at the head of an
army victorious through his leadership, and by a sudden stroke,
at such an extreme old age, merits, I think, to be placed among
the most remarkable events of my time. As also the constant
goodness, forbearing character, and conscientious affability of
Monsieur de la Noue amid that lawlessness of armed factions,
veritable school of treason, inhumanity, and brigandage, in
which he constantly lived—a great and very experienced war-
rior. Inserted by his —

[I have taken pleasure in making known in several places the
hopes I have for Marie de Gournay le Jars, my daughter by a
spiritual alliance, loved by me, indeed, even more than a father
loves his own child, and treasured in my retreat and solitude
as one of the best parts of my own being. I no longer consider
anyone but her in the world. If one may judge by youthful
promise, her soul will some day be capable of the finest things,
among others of perfection in that most sacred friendship,
to which we read her sex has not yet been able to rise. The
sincerity and firmness of her character are already sufficient
for it, her affection towards me more than superabundant, and
such, in short, that there is nothing to be desired unless it be

that the apprehension she feels about my end, because of the fact that I was fifty-five when she met me, might less cruelly afflict her. The judgment she made of the first Essays, being a woman, and in this age, and so young, and alone in her region, and the notable eagerness wherewith she loved me and for a long time desired my friendship, solely upon the esteem she took for me, before ever having seen me, is an unusual occurrence very worthy of consideration.]

Other virtues have little or no credit in this age; but valor has become common through our civil wars, and in this quality there are among us souls steadfast even to perfection, and in great number, so that a choice among them is impossible.

This is all the extraordinary and uncommon greatness that I have known up to now.

✓ OF GIVING THE LIE

YES, BUT SOMEONE will say to me that this design of making use of oneself as a subject to write about would be excusable in rare and famous men, who by their reputation had aroused some desire to know them. That is certain, I confess it, and know very well that an artisan will scarcely lift his eyes from his work to see a man of the common sort, whereas men forsake workshops and stores to see a great and prominent person arrive in a city. It ill becomes any other to make himself known except him who has qualities worthy of imitation and whose life and opinions may serve as a model. In the greatness of their deeds Caesar and Xenophon had something on which to found and fix their narrative as on a just and solid base. And so it were to be wished that we had the journals of Alexander the Great, the commentaries that Augustus, Cato, Sulla, Brutus, and others left about their deeds. Men love and study the figures of such persons even in bronze and stone.

This remonstrance is very true; but it concerns me very little:

> I ne'er recite except to friends, at their request,
> But not to everyone or everywhere. 'Tis sure
> That there are many men who read aloud their works
> While in the Forum's midst or even in the baths.[1]

I am not here shaping a statue to erect in the square of a city or in a church or public place:

---

[1] Horace, *Satires*

224

> I study not to make my pages swell
> With mighty trifles—private things I tell.[2]

It is for the corner of a library, and to entertain a neighbor, a kinsman, a friend, who may take pleasure in renewing his acquaintance and familiarity with me in this image. Others have been encouraged to speak of themselves because they found the subject worthy and rich; I, on the contrary, because I have found it so barren and meager that no suspicion of ostentation can fall upon my design.

I readily judge the actions of others; I give little of my own to be judged because they are nothing. I do not find so much good in myself that I cannot tell it without blushing.

What a satisfaction it would be to me to hear someone thus relate to me the habits, the face, the bearing, the everyday remarks, and the fortunes of my ancestors! How attentively I should listen to it! Truly it would arise from a bad nature to despise so much as the pictures of our friends and predecessors, the fashion of their clothes and their armor. I preserve their writing, their seal, the breviary, and a peculiar sword that they used, and I have not banished from my study some long staves my father generally carried in his hand. *A father's garment and his ring are the more dear to his children the more they loved him.*[3]

If my posterity, however, is of another mind, I shall have, indeed, the means of being revenged; for they could not care less for me than I shall then care for them. All the traffic that I have in this with the public is that I borrow their printing tools, which are faster and easier. In recompense I shall, perhaps, keep some pat of butter from melting in the market place:

> Lest tunny-fish and olives lack a coat;[4]

> And I shall often give loose shirts to mackerel.[5]

---

[2] Persius   [3] Saint Augustine, *City of God*   [4] Martial   [5] Catullus

And even if nobody reads me, have I wasted my time in entertaining myself so many idle hours with such useful and agreeable thoughts? In modeling this figure upon myself, I have been so often obliged to shape and compose myself in order to bring myself out that the model has thereby become firm and has to some extent formed itself. Painting myself for others, I have painted my inner self in clearer colors than were my first ones. I have no more made my book than my book has made me: a book consubstantial with its author, concerned only with me, a vital part of my life; not having an outside and alien concern and objective like all other books. Have I wasted my time by taking account of myself so continually, so carefully? For they who survey themselves only in their minds, and occasionally aloud, do not examine themselves so fundamentally nor penetrate so deeply as does he who makes it his study, his work, and his trade, who with all his faith, with all his strength, binds himself to make a lasting account.

The most delightful pleasures, indeed, are digested within; they avoid leaving any trace of themselves and avoid the sight not only of the public, but of any other person.

How often has this work diverted me from troublesome thoughts? And all that are frivolous should be counted as troublesome. Nature has bestowed on us the gift of an extensive faculty for entertaining ourselves apart, and often calls us to it to teach us that we owe ourselves in part to society, but in the best part to ourselves. For the purpose of disposing my fancy even to dream with some order and purpose, and to keep it from losing itself and roving with the wind, the best way is to give body to and record all the little thoughts that present themselves to it. I give ear to my reveries because I have to record them. How many times, being irked by some action that civility and reason prevented me from reproving openly, have I disgorged myself here, not without intent of instructing the public! And, indeed, these poetical lashes:

Wham on the eye, wham on the snout,
Wham on the back of the dirty lout![6]

imprint themselves even better upon paper than upon live
flesh. What if I lend ear a little more attentively to books,
since I have been on the lookout to purloin something from
them with which to adorn or support my own?

I have not at all studied to make a book; but I have studied
somewhat because I had made it, if it is studying somewhat
to skim over and pinch, by his head or feet, now one author
and then another, not at all in order to form my opinions, but
certainly to assist, second, and serve those long since formed.

But whom shall we believe when speaking of himself in so
corrupt an age, considering there are few, or none, whom we
can believe when speaking of others, where there is less advantage in lying. The first step in the corruption of morals is the
banishment of truth; for, as Pindar said, to be truthful is the
beginning of a great virtue, and it is the first article that Plato
requires in the governor of his republic. Our truth of today
is not what is, but what others can be persuaded to believe; as
we give the name of money not only to that which is legal, but
also to any false money that will pass. Our nation has long
been reproached with this vice; for Salvianus of Massilia,
who lived in the time of the emperor Valentinian, says that to
the French lying and perjury is not a vice but a way of speaking. If anyone desired to outstrip this testimony he could say
that it is now a virtue to them. Men form and mould themselves to it as to an honorable exercise; for dissimulation is
one of the most notable qualities of this age.

Thus I have often considered whence could have sprung
this custom we so religiously observe, of feeling more bitterly
offended at being reproached with this vice, which is so common with us, than with any other; and that it should be the

---

[6] Marot, epistle, *Fripelippes, valet de Marot, à Sagon*

strongest insult that can be offered us in words, to reproach us with falsehood. As to that, I find it is natural to defend ourselves most for the defects with which we are most stained. It seems that in resenting and being roused by the accusation we in some sort acquit ourselves of the fault; if we have it in fact, at least, we condemn it in appearance.

May it not also be that this reproach seems to imply cowardice and lack of courage? Is there a more manifest sign of cowardice than to deny our own word? What of this, to deny what we know?

Lying is a base vice that one of the ancients paints in its most shameful colors when he says that to lie is to give evidence of having contempt for God and at the same time of fearing men. It is not possible to represent more fully the horror, baseness, and madness of it. For what can we imagine more contemptible than to be a coward towards men and bold towards God? Since our understanding of one another is conveyed solely by means of the word, he who violates his word betrays society. It is the only tool by means of which our wills and thoughts communicate; it is the interpreter of our soul. If it fails us, we no longer have any hold upon one another, we no longer have any knowledge of one another. If it deceives us, it breaks up all our relations and dissolves all the ties of our government.

Certain nations of the new Indies (there is no point in mentioning their names, they are no more; for the desolation of that conquest has extended to the utter eradication of the names and the former knowledge of the places—an amazing and unheard-of example) offered to their gods human blood, but only such as was drawn from the tongue and ears, as expiation of the sin of lying, heard as well as uttered. That good fellow of Greece used to say that children amuse themselves with knuckle-bones, men with words.

As to the different usages in our giving the lie, and our laws of honor in that matter, and the changes they have undergone, I shall defer saying what I know of them to another time; and in the meantime I shall learn, if I can, at what time the custom began of so exactly weighing and measuring words, and of attaching our honor to them. For it is easy to conclude that it did not exist of old among the Greeks and Romans. And I have often thought it novel and strange to see them give one another the lie and insult one another without coming to blows. The laws of their duty steered some other course than ours. Caesar is sometimes called a thief, sometimes a drunkard, to his face. We see what freedom there was in the invectives they address to one another, I mean the greatest war chiefs of both nations, where words are revenged only with words and do not lead to any other consequence.

OF THE RESEMBLANCE OF CHILDREN
TO THEIR FATHERS

THIS BUNDLE OF SO MANY diverse pieces is composed under these conditions, namely, that I set my hand to it only when too listless an idleness weighs upon me, and nowhere but at home. So it has built itself up with several interruptions and intervals, circumstances keeping me sometimes many months away from home. Furthermore I do not correct my first thoughts by my second—certainly, perhaps a word or so, but only to vary and not to delete. I want to show the movement of my notions and to have each part be seen as it is born. I should like to have begun sooner and so examine clearly the course of my mutations. A servant who served me by writing them down at my dictation thought he had got a prize by stealing from me several pieces chosen to his taste. It consoles me that he will therein gain no more than I have lost.

I have grown older by seven or eight years since I began; it has not been without some new acquisition. I have in that time become acquainted with the stone by the liberality of the years. A long intercourse and acquaintance with them does not readily pass without some such fruit. I could have wished that of the many other gifts they have to bestow on those who are with them long they had chosen one that would have been more welcome to me, for they could not possibly have made me one of which I have had a greater horror since my childhood. And it was exactly, of all the happenings of old age, the one which I feared most. I had often thought to myself that I was going too far and that in making so long a voyage I should not fail finally to become involved in some unpleasant encounter. I felt, and often protested, that it was time to depart and that life should be cut off in the sound and living part according to the surgeons' rule when they have to amputate a limb; that Nature was accustomed to exact very stiff usury from him who did not pay on time. But these were idle propositions. I was then so far from being ready that in the eighteen months or thereabouts that I have been in this disagreeable condition I have already learned to adjust myself to it. I am already entering upon an understanding with this colicky existence. I am finding in it grounds for consolation and hope. So basely do men toady to their miserable being that there is no condition so harsh that they will not accept it in order to live! Listen to Maecenas:

> Make me be lame of hand
> And halt of foot and hip,
> Shake out my loosened teeth,
> While life remains, all's well.[1]

And Tamerlane cloaked with a foolish humanity the fantastic cruelty he exercised upon lepers by putting to death all he heard of to deliver them, as he said, from the painful life they were living. For there was not one of them who would not rather have been a leper three times over than not to live.

And Antisthenes the Stoic being very sick, and crying out, "Who will deliver me from these evils?" Diogenes, who had come to see him, offered him a knife, saying: "This will, very quickly, if you want to." "I do not mean from my life," he replied, "but from my evils."

The sufferings that strike us simply through the soul afflict me much less than they do most others: partly out of judgment (for the world looks upon many things as dreadful and to

---

[1] Seneca, *Epistles*

be avoided at the cost of life that to me are almost indifferent), partly from a dull insensibility I have to accidents which do not hit me point-blank, an insensibility that I look upon as one of the best parts of my natural condition. But the really essential and bodily sufferings I feel very acutely. And yet, in times past looking ahead to them with a feeble sight made tender and soft by the enjoyment of that long and happy health and repose that God granted to me for the best part of my life, I had in imagination conceived them as so insupportable that, in truth, my fear of them was greater than the suffering I have found in them. Through that I am ever more strengthened in this belief, that most of the faculties of our soul, as we employ them, trouble the repose of life more than they aid it.

I am at grips with the worst, the most sudden, the most painful, the most mortal, and the most irremediable of all diseases. I have already experienced five or six very long and painful attacks of it. And yet either I flatter myself, or there are even in this state means of standing fast for a man whose soul is free from the fear of death and unburdened of the menaces, conclusions, and consequences with which the doctors stuff our heads. But the actual pain itself is not such a harsh and piercing sharpness as to drive a well-balanced man to rage and despair. I have at least this advantage from my stone: that it will achieve what I had not hitherto been able to bring about in myself in order to become wholly reconciled and acquainted with death; for the more it oppresses and troubles me, the less fearful will death be to me. I had already attained the point of only being attached to life for the sake of life, but my pain will dissolve even this understanding; and God grant that in the end, if its sharpness happens to exceed my strength, it may not drive me to the other no less wicked extreme of longing and wishing to die!

Fear not the final day, nor long for it.[2]

---

[2] Martial

Those are two passions to be feared, but the one has its remedy much nearer at hand than the other.

Moreover I have always considered as affectation that precept which so strictly and precisely commands us to maintain a good countenance and a disdainful and indifferent bearing while enduring pain. Why should Philosophy, which is concerned only with the vital and effective, waste her time over these external appearances? Let her leave that care to actors and teachers of rhetoric that set so great a value upon our gestures. Let her boldly concede to pain this cowardice of the voice if it comes neither from the heart nor from the stomach, and let her put these voluntary complaints in the category of the sighs, sobs, palpitations, and pallors that Nature has put out of our control. Provided the heart is without fear, the words without despair, let her be content! What matter if we wring our hands, provided that we do not wring our thoughts! She trains us for ourselves, not for others, to be, not to seem. Let her confine herself to governing our understanding, which she has taken upon herself to instruct. In the attacks of the colic let her maintain the soul in a condition to know itself and to follow its accustomed way, combating pain and enduring it, not prostrating itself shamefully at its feet, stirred and heated by the combat, not cast down and overthrown; capable of conversation and distraction to a certain degree. In such extreme ills it is cruelty to require of us so composed a bearing. It is no great matter what wry faces we make if we are ahead in the game. If the body find itself relieved by complaining, let it complain; if agitation pleases it, let it tumble and toss at its pleasure; if it thinks that the pain evaporates somewhat (as some physicians hold that it helps women in delivery) by crying out with greater violence, or if that distracts its torment, let it give full vent. Let us not command this voice to issue forth, but let us allow it. Epicurus not only permits his sage to cry out in torment but advises it. *Even the pugilists groan when, flourishing the cestus, they strike their blows, because in throwing out the voice the whole body is extended, and the blow is driven home with greater force.*[3] We have enough to do to deal with the evil without troubling ourselves over these superfluous rules.

This I say in excuse of those whom we commonly see raging under the shocks and assaults of this disease, for, as to me, I have come through it up to now with a little better countenance. Not, however, that I put myself to any pains to maintain this exterior decorum, for I make little account of such an advantage. I allow herein to the pain as much as it requires; but either my pains are not so excessive, or I bring to them more than ordinary steadfastness. I complain and I fret when the sharp stabs assail me, but I do not let go of myself, like that fellow,

> Resounding wails, and plaints, and high pitched sighs,
> He answers back in very doleful tones.[4]

I examine myself in the midst of my suffering, and I have always found that I was capable of speaking, thinking, replying as sanely as at any other time, but not so steadily, being troubled and distracted by the pain. When I am considered the most stricken, and when those present refrain from disturbing me, I often try my strength, and I myself take up some subject of conversation as remote as possible from my condition. I can do anything by a sudden effort, but don't let it continue long.

Oh, why have I not the faculty of that dreamer in Cicero who, dreaming he was embracing a wench, found he had discharged his stone in the sheets! Mine strangely diswench me!

In the intervals of this excessive torment, when my ureters languish without stabbing me so sharply, I immediately recover my normal condition, inasmuch as my soul takes alarm only at that which comes through the senses and the body. I

---

[3] Cicero, *Tusculans*   [4] Attius, in Cicero, *Tusculans*

certainly owe this to the care I took to prepare myself by reason against such mishaps;

> No form of toil
> Before me rises unexpected and unknown.
> All things have I foreseen and in my mind lived through.[5]

I am, however, put to the test a little roughly for a beginner, having with a very sudden and very severe change fallen at once from a very easy and very happy condition of life into the most painful and uneasy that can be imagined. For, besides its being a disease very much to be feared in itself, its beginnings in me are much more sharp and severe than is customary. The attacks come so thick upon me that I now scarcely ever feel in perfect health. Yet I have hitherto kept my mind in such a state that, provided I can persist in it, I am in a rather better condition of life than a thousand others who have neither fever nor other ailment except that which they create for themselves from faulty reasoning.

There is a certain kind of subtle humility that springs from presumption, as, for example, when we confess our ignorance in many things and are so gracious as to acknowledge that there are in the works of nature some qualities and conditions that are imperceptible to us and of which our understanding cannot discover the means and causes. By this honest and conscientious declaration we hope to get people to believe us also in those that we say we do understand. We have no need to go and cull out miracles and remote difficulties; it seems to me that among the things we commonly see there are wonders so incomprehensible that they surpass all the perplexity of miracles. What a wonderful thing it is that this drop of seed from which we are produced bears in itself the impressions not only of the bodily form, but also of the thoughts and inclinations of

[5] Virgil, *Aeneid*

our fathers? Where can that drop of fluid contain that infinite number of forms?

And how do they convey those resemblances with so heedless and irregular a course that the great-grandson shall be like his great-grandfather, the nephew like his uncle? In the family of Lepidus at Rome there were three, not consecutive, but at intervals, who were born with the same eye covered with a cartilage. At Thebes there was a family that bore from their mother's womb the figure of a lance-head, and he who was not born so was looked upon as illegitimate. Aristotle says that in a certain nation, where the women were in common, they assigned the children to their fathers by their resemblance.

It is probable that I owe to my father this condition of being subject to stones for he died grievously tormented with a big stone in his bladder. He was not aware of his disease until his sixty-seventh year, and before that he had not had any threat or symptom of it, either in his back, sides, or any other part, and had lived till then in a happy state of health, very little subject to infirmities. And he lasted seven years more with this disease, dragging out a very painful end to his life. I was born twenty-five years or more before his disease came on, and in the time of his best health, his third child in order of birth. Where was the propensity to this defect incubating all that time? And when he was so far from the infirmity, how did that small part of his substance with which he made me carry away so great an impression for its share? And how did it remain so concealed that I have just begun to feel it forty-five years later, the only one to this hour among so many brothers and sisters, and all of one mother? If anyone will enlighten me on how this malady progresses, I will believe him in as many other miracles as he pleases; provided that he does not hand me out a theory, as they do, much more intricate and fantastic than the thing itself.

May the doctors excuse a little the liberty I take, for it is by this same fatal infusion and insinuation that I have received a hatred and contempt of their science. The antipathy I have against their art is hereditary. My father lived to be seventy-four, my grandfather sixty-nine, my great-grandfather nearly eighty, without ever tasting any sort of medicine; and with them whatever was not in ordinary use took the place of a drug. Medicine is formed from examples and experience; so is my opinion. And is not that a very positive and very useful experience? I do not know whether they can find me in their records three who were born and bred and who died at the same hearth, under the same roof, and lived so long according to their regimen. They must in this grant me that, if not reason, fortune, at least, is on my side; now with physicians fortune is much more effective than reason. Let them not take me now at a disadvantage, let them not threaten me, prostrate as I am; that would be abuse. Besides, to tell the truth, I have got enough the better of them by my family examples, though they stop there. Human affairs do not have so much constancy. It has been two hundred years, lacking only eighteen, that this experience of ours has lasted, for the first of them was born in the year 1402. It is, indeed, very reasonable that this experience should begin to fail us. Let them not reproach me with the infirmities which have me now by the throat. Is it not enough for me to have lived forty-seven years in good health? Though it should be the end of my career, it is of the longer sort.

My ancestors had an aversion to medicine by some mysterious and natural instinct; for the very sight of drugs horrified my father. The Seigneur de Gaviac, my paternal uncle, a churchman, and sickly from his birth, and who yet made that frail life hold out sixty-seven years, having once fallen into a very violent, prolonged fever, it was ordered by the physicians that he should be plainly told that, if he would not make use of help (they call help that which is more often hindrance), he would infallibly be a dead man. The good man, terrified as he was with this dreadful sentence, yet replied, "I am then a dead man." But God soon after made the prognostic false.

The youngest of the brothers—there were four—and by many years the youngest, the Sieur de Bussaguet, was the only one who submitted himself to this art, because, I suppose, of the contact he had with the other arts, for he was a counsellor in the court of Parliament; and it turned out so badly for him that, though appearing of a stronger constitution, yet he died long before any of the rest, except for one, Sieur de Saint Michel.

It is possible I have derived this natural antipathy to medicine from them; but had there been no other consideration, I should have tried to overcome it. For all those conditions that are born in us without reason are vicious; they are a kind of disease that we must combat. It may be I had this propensity, but I have supported and fortified it by arguments which have confirmed me in my opinion of it. For I also hate the idea of refusing medicine because of its bitter taste. That would hardly be like me since I hold health worth purchasing by all the most painful cauteries and incisions that can be applied.

And like Epicurus I think that pleasures are to be avoided if they bring after them greater pains, and that those pains are to be sought that bring after them greater pleasures.

Health is a precious thing and the only one truly meriting that we should lay out not only time, sweat, labor, worldly goods, but also life itself, in pursuit of it; inasmuch as without it life becomes painful and oppressive to us; without it pleasure, wisdom, learning, and virtue fade away and vanish; and to the strongest and most taut arguments that philosophy would impress on us to the contrary, we need only oppose the idea of Plato being stricken with an epilepsy or apoplexy, and in this supposition defy him to call the noble and rich faculties of his soul to his assistance. In my opinion any path that would lead us to health cannot be said to be either arduous or costly. But I have several other plausible ideas that make me strangely distrustful of all this merchandise. I do not deny

that there may be some art in it, that there are among the
many works of nature things proper for the preservation of our
health; that is certain.

I well know that there are some simples that have mois-
tening properties and others that have drying properties. I
know by experience that horse-radishes cause flatulence and
that senna leaves loosen the bowels. I know by experience many
other such facts, as I know that mutton nourishes and wine
warms me; and Solon said that eating was, like other drugs,
medicine against the disease of hunger. I do not deny the use
we derive from things the world produces, nor do I doubt the
power and fertility of Nature and its application to our needs.
I clearly see that pikes and swallows thrive under her. I mistrust the inventions of our minds, of our learning and art, in
favor of which we have abandoned Nature and her rules, and in
which we know not how to maintain moderation and bounds.

As we give the name Justice to the jumble of the first laws
that fall into our hands, and their application and practice,
which is often very inept and very unjust; and as those who
scoff at and condemn them do not intend thereby to malign that
noble virtue, but only condemn the abuse and profanation of
that sacred title; so in medicine I, indeed, honor that glorious
name, its goal, its promises so useful to mankind; but what it
denotes among us I neither honor nor esteem.

In the first place, experience makes me dread it; for, as far
as I know, there is no set of people so soon sick and so slowly
cured as those who are under the jurisdiction of medicine. Their
very health is impaired and corrupted by the constraint of their
regimen. Physicians are not content to have authority over
sickness; they make health sick to prevent men from being able
at any time to escape their authority. Do they not from a continual and perfect health derive an argument of some great
sickness to ensue? I have been sick often enough, and without
their help I have found my sicknesses as easy to bear (and I
have made trial of almost all sorts) and as short as those of

any other person; and yet I have not mixed with them the bitterness of their prescriptions. My health is full and free, without rule and without other discipline than my habits and pleasure. Any place serves me well enough to stay in for I need no other conveniences when sick than those which I need when I am well. I do not become upset at being without physician, or apothecary, or any assistance, by which I see most men more afflicted than by the disease. What! do the doctors themselves show us any happiness and longevity in their lives that may give evidence to us of some manifest effect of their skill?

There is not a nation that has not existed many centuries without medicine, and those the first ages, that is to say the best and most happy; and the tenth part of the world does not make use of it even now. No end of nations are ignorant of it, where men live in better health and longer than we do here, and among us the common people do without it happily. The Romans had existed six hundred years before they received it; but, after having made trial of it, they banished it from their city at the instance of Cato the Censor, who showed how easily he could do without it, having lived eighty-five years and kept his wife alive to an extreme old age, not without medicine, but certainly without a physician—for everything that is found healthful for us may be called medicine. He kept his family in health, Plutarch says, by the use, I believe, of hare; as the Arcadians, according to Pliny, cure all diseases with cows' milk. And the Libyans, Herodotus says, generally enjoy singularly good health because of a custom they have, after their children have arrived at four years of age, of burning and cauterizing the veins of the head and temples, by which means they cut off all catarrhal discharge for their whole lives. And the villagers of my region make use of nothing in all emergencies but the strongest wine they can get mixed with a great deal of saffron and spice, and all this with the same success.

And to tell the truth, of all this diversity and confusion of prescriptions what other end and effect is there after all but to purge the bowels, which a thousand household simples can do. And I do not know whether this is so useful as they say, and whether Nature does not require a residence of her excrements to a certain extent, as wine does of its lees for its preservation. You often see healthy men taken with vomiting and diarrhoea through some strange accident, and making a great evacuation of excrements without any preceding need or any following benefit, but rather with impairment and harm. It is from the great Plato that I lately learned that of the three sorts of motions which are natural to us the last and the worst is purging, which no man, unless he is a fool, ought to undergo except in the most extreme necessity. We disturb and irritate the disease by contrary oppositions. It must be the way of living that gently weakens it and brings it to its end. The violent struggle between the drugs and the disease are ever to our loss since the combat is fought within ourselves, and the drug is an assistant not to be trusted, being by its nature an enemy to our health and having access into our realm only through disturbance. Let it alone a little; the order of things that takes care of fleas and moles also takes care of those men who have the same patience in letting themselves be governed as fleas and moles have. It is useless for us to cry "Get on"; it serves to make us hoarse but not to hasten it. It is a proud and pitiless order. Our fear and our despair disgust and keep it from aiding us, instead of inviting it. It must let disease run its course as well as health. It will not let itself be corrupted in favor of the one to the prejudice of the other's right; it would fall into disorder. Let us follow, in God's name, let us follow! It leads those that follow, and those who do not follow it drags along, both their fury and medicine together. Order a purge for your brain; it will there be much better employed than in your stomach.

A Lacedemonian was asked what had made him live so long in good health. "Ignorance of medicine," he replied. And the Emperor Hadrian continually exclaimed as he was dying that the crowd of physicians had killed him. A bad wrestler turned physician. "Bravo," said Diogenes to him, "you are right; now you will throw those who have formerly thrown you."

But they have this good fortune according to Nicocles, that the sun shines on their successes and the earth hides their failures. And besides, they have a very advantageous way of making use of all sorts of events; for whatever Fortune, Nature, or any other extraneous cause (of which the number is infinite) produces that is good and healthful in us, it is the privilege of medicine to attribute to itself. All the happy results that befall the patient who is under its regime are due to it. The causes that have cured me, and that cure a thousand others who do not call the doctors to their aid, they usurp them in the case of their patients; and as to mishaps, either they absolutely disown them by laying the fault upon the patient with such frivolous reasons that they have no concern about failing to find a rather good number of them: he exposed his arm, he heard the rattling of a coach,

> the crossing of the carts
> Along the narrow winding of the streets;[2]

somebody opened his window, he has been lying upon his left side, or has had something disagreeable pass through his mind. In short, a word, a dream, a look seem to them sufficient excuse to clear themselves of error. Or, if they so please, they make use even of our growing worse and profit from it by this means which can never fail them, namely to pacify us, when the disease becomes aggravated by their medicaments, with the assurance they give us that it would have grown much worse without their remedies. He whom they have thrown from a chill into a quotidian fever would, without them, have had a continuous one. They are not concerned about doing their business badly since the damage turns to their profit. Truly they are right

---

[2] Juvenal

in requiring that the patient place confidence in them; it must be real confidence, in good earnest and very pliant, to adapt itself to ideas so hard to believe.

Plato said very appropriately that physicians were the only men that might lie without restraint since our health depends upon the emptiness and falsity of their promises. Aesop, an author of most rare excellence, of whom few men discover all the graces, amusingly depicts for us the tyrannical authority physicians usurp over poor creatures weakened and dejected by sickness and fear. He tells us that a sick person, asked by his physician what effect he felt from the medicament he had given him, replied, "I have sweated very much." "That's good," said the physician. Another time he also asked him how he had felt since then. "I have been very cold and have shivered a great deal," he said. "That is good," replied the physician. A third time he asked him again how he did. "Why, I find myself swelling and puffing up," he said, "as if I had the dropsy." "That is very well," said the physician. One of his friends coming soon after to inquire how he felt, "Truly, my friend," he said, "I am doing so well that I am about to die."

There was a more just law in Egypt, by which the physician for the three first days took charge of his patient at the patient's risk and fortune; but those three days being past, it was at his own. For why should their patron Aesculapius have been struck by a thunderbolt for having brought Helen back from death to life:

> Then the almighty father, angered that a man
> Should rise from the infernal shades to life's bright light,
> With thunderbolt hurled down into the Stygian waves
> The Phoebus-bred inventor of such cure and art;[7]

and his followers have been absolved, who send so many souls from life to death?

---

[7] Virgil, *Aeneid*

A physician was boasting to Nicocles that his art was of great authority. "It is so, indeed," said Nicocles, "since it can with impunity kill so many people."

For the rest, had I been in their place, I should have made my art more sacred and mysterious. They began well enough, but they have not ended so. It was a good beginning to make gods and demons the authors of their science, to adopt a language and writing of their own, notwithstanding that philosophy believes it is folly to advise a man for his own good in an unintelligible way: *Just as if a physician should order his patient to take*

> An earth-bred, grass-creeping, house-carrying,
> And bloodless thing.[8]

It was a good rule in their art, and one which accompanies all other fantastic, empty, and supernatural arts, that the patient's faith must, by good hope and confidence, imagine in advance the result and effect of their art. This rule they hold to such a degree as to consider that the most ignorant and inexpert physician is, in their opinion, more suitable for a patient that has confidence in him than the most experienced if he is a stranger. Even the choice of most of their drugs is in some sort mysterious and divine: the left foot of a tortoise, the urine of a lizard, the dung of an elephant, the liver of a mole, blood drawn from under the right wing of a white pigeon; and for us who have the stone (so scornfully do they take advantage of our misery), the excrement of rats beaten to powder, and other such apish tricks, which have the appearance of a magical enchantment rather than of solid science. I omit their pills prescribed in uneven numbers, the appointment of certain days and festivals of the year, the designation of certain hours for gathering the herbs of their ingredients, and that grim and solemn aspect affected in their bearing and mien, which even Pliny derides.

---

[8] Cicero, *De Divinatione*

But they have erred, I mean, in that they have not added to this fine beginning by making their meetings and consultations more religious and secret. No profane person ought to be admitted there, any more than to the secret ceremonies of Aesculapius. For the result of this error is that their irresolution, the weakness of their arguments, conjectures, and grounds, the sharpness of their disputes, full of hatred, jealousy, and self-interest, coming to be revealed to everyone, a man must be marvellously blind not to perceive that he runs a great hazard in their hands. Who ever saw a physician use a colleague's prescription without taking something away or adding something to it? By this they sufficiently betray their practice and make it manifest to us that they therein consider their reputation, and consequently their profit, more than their patients' interest. That doctor was wiser who of old gave them the rule that only one physician undertake to treat a sick person; for if he accomplishes nothing, one single man's failure can bring no great reproach upon the art of medicine. And, on the contrary, the glory will be great if he happens to strike it right; whereas, if they are many, they at every turn bring disrepute upon their calling, inasmuch as they more often do harm than good. They ought to be satisfied with the perpetual disagreement which is found in the opinions of the principal masters and ancient authors of this science, which is only known to men well read, without revealing, moreover, to the people the controversies and inconsistencies of judgment which they nourish and continue among themselves.

Will you have one example of the ancient controversy in medicine? Herophilus lodges the original cause of diseases in the humors; Erasistratus, in the blood of the arteries; Asclepiades, in the invisible atoms running through the pores; Alcmaeon, in the exuberance or deficiency of our bodily strength; Diocles, in the inequality of the elements of which the body is composed and in the quality of the air we breathe; Strato, in the abundance, crudity, and corruption of the nourishment we take; Hippocrates lodges it in the spirits. There is a friend of theirs, whom they know better than I, who exclaims upon this subject that the most important science in practice among us, as it is the one charged with our preservation and health, is by ill luck the most uncertain, the most confused, and agitated with the greatest number of changes. There is no great danger in miscalculating the height of the sun or the fraction of some astronomical computation; but here, where our whole being is concerned, it is not wise to abandon ourselves to the mercy of the agitation of so many conflicting winds.

Before the Peloponnesian War there was no great talk of this science. Hippocrates brought it into repute. All that he had established Chrysippus overthrew. After that Erasistratus, Aristotle's grandson, overthrew what Chrysippus had written. After them the Empirics started up, who took an entirely different way from that of their forerunners in the practice of this art. When the credit of these began to fail, Herophilus set another sort of practice on foot, which Asclepiades in turn arose to combat and annihilate. Then in their turn there came into authority the opinions of Themison, and then of Musa, and still later, those of Vectius Valens, a physician famous through the intimacy he had with Messalina. The empire of medicine in Nero's time fell to Thessalus, who abolished and condemned all that had been held until his time. His teaching was overthrown by Crinas of Marseilles, who again brought in the practice of regulating all medical operations by the Ephemerides and motions of the stars, and eating, sleeping, and drinking by the hours that were pleasing to Mercury and the moon. His authority was soon after supplanted by Charinus, a physician of the same city of Marseilles. The latter combated not only the earlier science of medicine, but also hot baths that had been generally and for so many ages before in common use. He made men bathe in cold water even in winter and plunged his patients in the natural waters of streams. No Roman until Pliny's time had ever deigned to practise medicine; that was practised by Greeks and foreigners, as among us Frenchmen it is practised by Latinizers. For as a very great physician says, we do not readily accept the medicine we understand, any more than we do the drugs we gather. If the countries from which we fetch our guaiacum, sarsaparilla, and china root have doctors, we may imagine how much they prize our cabbages and parsley through the same recommendation of strangeness, rarity, and costliness. For who would dare to scorn things fetched from so far at the hazard of so long and dangerous a voyage?

Since those ancient mutations in medicine, there have been infinite others down to our own times, and, for the most part, complete and universal mutations, such as those in our time produced by Paracelsus, Fioravanti, and Argenterius. For they, as I am told, alter not only a prescription, but the whole contexture and order of the body of medicine, accusing all others of ignorance and fraud that practised before them. I leave you to imagine where the poor patient is in this!

If only we were assured, when they mistake themselves, that it would do us no harm, even if it did us no good, it would be a reasonable bargain to risk acquiring some gain without running the danger of loss.

Aesop relates that a man who had bought a Moorish slave, believing that his color had been acquired through chance and the bad treatment of his former master, caused him to be carefully treated with many baths and potions. It turned out that the Moor did not improve at all in his tawny complexion, but he wholly lost his former health.

How often do we see physicians impute the death of their patients to one another? I remember an epidemic disease which, some years ago, was very dangerous and fatal in the towns of my neighborhood. When the storm, which had swept away an infinite number of men, had passed, one of the most famous physicians of all the region published a pamphlet upon that subject, in which he changes his mind about the blood-letting they had practised and confesses that it was one of the chief causes of the harm that had resulted. Moreover their authors hold that there is no medicine that has not something hurtful in it; and if even those which are useful to us do in some measure harm us, what must those do that are totally misapplied to us?

For my own part, even if there were no other factor, I am of opinion that to those that loathe the taste of medicine it is a dangerous effort, and harmful, to force it down at so inconvenient a time and with so much aversion; and I believe that that puts a tremendous test on a sick person at a time when he has so much need of repose. Besides, when we consider the grounds upon which they usually base the cause of our diseases, they are so slight and tenuous that I thence conclude that a very little error in administering their drugs may do us a great deal of harm.

Now if the mistake of a physician is dangerous, we are in a very bad way, for it is very difficult for him not to fall often into those mistakes. He has need of too many factors, considerations, and circumstances rightly to adjust his treatment; he must know the sick person's constitution, his temperament, his humors, inclinations, actions, his very thoughts and ideas. He must be assured of the external circumstances, of the nature of the place, of the condition of the air, of the weather, of the position of the planets and their influences. He must know in the disease the causes, the symptoms, the effects, and the critical days; in drugs, the weight, the strength, the region of its origin, the appearance, the age, and the administration; and he must know how to proportion all these elements and adapt them to one another in order to create a symmetry. Wherein if he makes the slightest error, if among so many springs there is a single one that goes awry, it is enough to destroy us. God knows how difficult it is to understand most of these things. For how, for example, will he find out the true symptom of the disease, every disease being capable of an infinite number of symptoms? How many controversies and doubts have they among themselves upon the interpretation of urines! Otherwise whence would come this continual altercation that we see among them about the knowledge of the disease? How would we excuse the error they so often fall into of taking marten for fox? In the maladies I have had, however little difficulty there was, I never found three of them in agreement. I more readily note examples that concern myself.

Recently at Paris, by the order of the physicians, an operation was performed on a gentleman in whose bladder there was found no more stone than in his hand. And in the same place, a bishop, who was my very good friend, had been earnestly urged by most of the physicians he consulted to have himself cut; I myself, on the faith of others, helped to persuade him. When he had died and was opened up, they found that he had trouble only in the kidneys. They are less excusable in this disease because it is in some sort palpable. Hence surgery seems to me much more certain because it sees and feels what it is doing. There is in it less conjecture and guesswork, whereas the physicians have no *speculum matricis* which permits them to see our brains, our lungs, and our liver.

The very promises of medicine are incredible. For having to provide against diverse and contrary accidents that often afflict us at one and the same time and that are almost necessarily related, such as heat in the liver and cold in the stomach, they set about persuading us that one of the ingredients of their medicine will warm the stomach and another cool the liver. One has its commission to go directly to the kidneys, and even to the bladder, without spreading its effects elsewhere, and retaining its power and virtue on that long course beset with obstacles until it reaches the place for the service of which it is destined by its occult property. One will dry the brain; another moisten the lungs. Having compounded a potion out of all that conglomeration, is it not a kind of madness to hope that these virtues may separate and sort themselves out of this mixture and confusion in order to hurry about such differing functions? I should very much fear that they would either lose or change their tags and confuse their destinations. And who could imagine that in this liquid confusion these faculties do not corrupt, confound, and spoil one another? What would one say of the fact that the compounding of this prescription depends upon another practitioner, to whose good faith and mercy we again abandon our lives?

As we have doublet-makers and breeches-makers to clothe us, and are so much the better fitted as each of them meddles only with his own business and has a skill more restricted and narrower than a tailor who undertakes all; and as in the matter of dining, great persons, for their comfort, have cooks with distinct functions, some for soups, others for roasts, which a cook who takes charge of everything cannot so perfectly perform; so in the matter of healing, the Egyptians were right to reject this general calling of physician and to split up the profession: to each disease, to each part of the body, its own workman, for it was much more properly and less confusedly treated because someone gave special attention only to it. Our doctors do not notice that he who sees to all sees to nothing; that the entire government of this microcosm is more than they can digest. While they were afraid of stopping the progress of a dysentery in order not to arouse a fever in him, they killed a friend [9] of mine who was worth more than the whole pack of them put together. They put their guesses in the scales against the present evils, and in order not to cure the brain to the prejudice of the stomach, they harm the stomach and make the brain worse with their seething and discordant drugs.

As to the variety and weakness of the reasonings of this art, they are more manifest than in any other. Aperitives are useful for a man subject to the stone because by opening and dilating the passages they start forward that sticky matter of which the gravel and the stone are formed and convey downward that

---

[9] Etienne de la Boétie.

which begins to harden and gather in the kidneys. Aperitives are dangerous for a man subject to the stone because by opening and dilating the passages they start forward the matter that forms the gravel towards the kidneys, and because it is difficult for the kidneys not to retain a great deal of what has been conveyed thither since they are apt to seize upon it owing to their natural inclination for it. Moreover, if by chance there is some body there a little too large to pass through all those narrow passages which still have to be cleared in order for it to be discharged, that body, being stirred by these aperitives and being thrown into these narrow passages, will block them and bring on a certain and most painful death.

They have a similar consistency in the advice they give us for our regimen. It is good to pass water often for by experience we see that in letting it lie long we give it time to discharge its excrements and lees, which will serve as matter to form a stone in the bladder. It is not good to pass water often for the heavy excrements it carries along with it will not be voided without violence, as we see by experience that a torrent that rolls with force sweeps the place it passes over much clearer than the course of a gentle and sluggish stream. Likewise it is good to have frequent intercourse with women for that opens the passages and pushes along the gravel and sand; it is also very bad because it heats, tires, and weakens the kidneys. It is good to bathe in hot waters inasmuch as that relaxes and softens the places where the sand and stone lie; and it is also bad because this application of external heat helps the kidneys to bake, harden, and petrify the matter deposited there. For those who are taking the baths it is more healthful to eat little at night so that the waters they are to drink the next morning may have more effect upon an empty and free stomach; on the contrary, it is better to eat little at dinner in order not to trouble the action of the water, which is not yet completed, and not to burden the stomach so soon after this other labor, and to leave the function of digestion to the night, which can do it better than the day, when the body and mind are in perpetual movement and action.

Thus do they juggle and trifle in all their reasonings at our expense. And they could not provide me with one proposition against which I could not erect a contrary one of equal force.

Let them, then, no longer exclaim against those who in this trouble let themselves be gently guided by their own appetite and the advice of Nature and commit themselves to the common fortune.

I have seen in the course of my travels almost all the famous baths of Christendom, and for some years past I have begun to make use of them; for I look upon bathing as generally healthful, and I believe that we suffer no slight inconveniences in our health through having left off the custom, which was generally observed in former times by almost all nations, and is still by many, of washing the body every day. And I cannot imagine but that we are much the worse for having our limbs so encrusted and our pores stopped up with dirt. And as to the drinking of the waters, Fortune has in the first place made it not at all opposed to my taste; in the second place, it is natural and simple and is at least not dangerous, even if it is without value. I take as testimony of this the vast number of people of every sort and constitution who gather there. And although I have not there observed any extraordinary and miraculous effects, but rather, after inquiring a little more carefully than is usually done, I have found ill grounded and false all the reports of such effects that are broadcast and believed in those places (as people are easily hoodwinked in what they desire), yet, at the same time, I have hardly known any that have been made worse by these waters, and a man cannot without malice deny that they rouse the appetite, help digestion, and give us a certain amount of new liveliness if we do not go there in too weak a condition, which I would dissuade anybody from doing. They are not capable of restoring a ponderous ruin, but they may prop up a slight cant or attend to some threatening deterioration. He who does not bring along with him enough cheerfulness to be able to enjoy the pleasure of the company he will meet there and the walks and exercises to which the beauty of the places in which these spas are generally situated invites us, will doubtless lose the best and surest part of their effect. For this reason I have hitherto chosen to stop at and make use of those which offered the most pleasant location and the most advantages in lodging, food, and company. Such are the baths of Bagnères in France; those of Plombières on the frontiers of Germany and Lorraine; those of Baden in Switzerland; those of Lucca in Tuscany; and especially those of Della Villa, which I have used most often and at various seasons.

Every nation has its own opinions concerning their use, and very different rules and methods in using them, and according to my experience the effect is almost the same. Drinking them is not at all accepted in Germany; for all diseases they bathe, and will stay in the water like frogs almost from sun to sun. In Italy, when they drink nine days, they bathe at least thirty, and usually drink the water mixed with other drugs to assist its action. Here we are ordered to walk to digest it; there they are kept in bed where they have taken it until they have voided it, the stomach and feet being constantly warmed. As the Germans have peculiar to them a general practice in the bath of having themselves cupped and bled with scarification, so the Italians have their *doccie,* which are certain little streams of hot water conducted through pipes, and they bathe an hour in the morning and as much in the afternoon, for a month together, either the head, or the stomach, or any other part of the body with which they are concerned. There are infinite other differences of customs in every country, or to put it better, there is almost no resemblance between one and another. Thus you see how this branch of medicine to which alone I have submitted, though it is the least artificial, has, nevertheless, its fair share of the confusion and uncertainty which is seen everywhere else in this art.

The poets say whatever they please with greater emphasis and grace, witness these two epigrams:

> Alcon touched yesterday the statue of great Jove.
> Though marble, he perceived the doctor's potent touch.
> Behold today, now ordered moved from his old shrine,
> He's carried to the grave, though he's a god and stone.[10]

And the other:

> Andragoras most merry bathed and dined with us,
>   And yet was found upon the morrow dead.
> You ask the cause, Faustinus, of such sudden death?
>   In dreams he'd seen Hermocrates the quack![11]

On this matter I want to tell two stories.

The Baron of Caupène in Chalosse and I have between us the patronage of a benefice of great extent at the foot of our mountains, called Lahontan. It is with the inhabitants of this corner as it is said to be with those of the vale of Angrougne. They lived a life apart, with their own manners, clothes, and habits, ruled and governed by certain particular laws and customs handed down from father to son, to which they submitted without other constraint than respect for their practices. This little state had continued from time immemorial in so happy a condition that no neighboring judge was ever put to the trouble of inquiring into their doings, no advocate ever retained to give them counsel, nor stranger ever called in to settle their quarrels, and no man in this region had ever been seen begging. They avoided all alliances and traffic with the outer world that they might not corrupt the purity of their government, until, as they say, one of them, in the memory of their fathers, having a soul spurred by noble ambition, took it into his head, in order to bring his name into credit and reputation, to make one of his sons a Maître Jean or a Maître Pierre, and having had

---

[10] Ausonius, *Epigrams*   [11] Martial

him taught to write in some neighboring town, finally made him into a fine village notary. This fellow, having become a personage, began to disdain their ancient customs and to put into their heads ideas about the pomp of the regions on this side of the mountains. He advised the first of his companions whose goat was dehorned by someone to seek justice from the royal judges of the area; and he went on from this one to another until he had corrupted the whole place. On the heels of this corruption they say that another immediately followed of worse consequence because of a physician who was seized with a desire to marry one of their daughters and to settle among them. This man began to teach them first the names of fevers, colds, and abscesses, the location of the heart, liver, and intestines, a science until then very far removed from their knowledge; and instead of garlic, with which they had learned to drive away all sorts of diseases, however severe or extreme, he accustomed them, for a cough or a cold, to take strange mixtures, and he began to make a trade not only of their health but of their death. They swear that only since then have they perceived that the night air made their heads heavy, that drinking when they were hot was harmful, and that the winds of autumn were more unwholesome than those of the spring; that since this use of medicine they find themselves overwhelmed by a legion of unaccustomed diseases, and that they perceive a general decline in their former vigor, and their lives cut short by half. This is the first of my stories.

The other is that before I was afflicted with the stone, hearing a number of people speak highly of the blood of a he-goat as a celestial manna sent down in these latter ages for the protection and preservation of the lives of men, and hearing it spoken of by men of understanding as an admirable drug and infallible in its effect, I, who have ever thought myself a target for all the accidents that can befall any other man, was pleased, though in perfect health, to provide myself with this miracle, and I gave orders to have a he-goat fed on my lands according to the recipe; for he must be withdrawn in the hottest months of summer and must be given only aperitive herbs to eat and only white wine to drink. I came home by chance the very day he was to be killed. They came and told me that the cook found two or three big balls in his paunch that rattled against one another among the stuff he had eaten. I was curious to have all his entrails brought before me, and I had that thick and large skin opened up. There came out three big lumps, light as sponges, so that they seemed to be hollow, yet hard and firm on the outside and spotted with several dull colors; one was perfectly round, the size of an ordinary ball, the other two a little smaller, not perfectly round, but apparently progressing towards it. I found through inquiring of those accustomed to open up these animals that it is a rare and unusual occurrence. It is likely these stones are cousins of ours; and if so, it is a very vain hope in those who have the stone to extract their cure from the blood of a beast who was himself about to die of the same disease. For as for saying that the blood does not partake of this infection and does not thereby alter its customary vigor, it is rather to be believed that nothing is engendered in a body but by the joint effort and participation of all the parts. The whole mass works together, though one part contributes more to it than another according to the diversity of operations. Wherefore it is very likely that there was some petrifying quality in all the parts of this goat. It was not so much for fear of the future and for myself that I was curious about this experiment, but because it happens in my house, as it does in many others, that the women store up such small drugs to aid the people, using the same recipe in fifty diseases, and such a recipe as they will not take themselves, and yet exult whenever these turn out well.

For the rest, I honor the physicians, not, according to the precept, out of necessity (for to this passage may be opposed another of the prophet reproving King Asa for having had recourse to a physician), but for love of themselves, having known many honest and lovable men among them. It is not against them that I have a grudge, but against their art, and I do not greatly blame them for taking advantage of our folly for most men do so. Many callings, both of greater and less dignity than theirs, have no other foundation or support than in the abuse of the public. When I am sick, I call them in for company if they happen to be near by, and I expect to be diverted by them, and I pay them as others do. I give them leave to command me to cover myself up warmly if I like it better that way than another; for my broth they may choose, as they please, between leeks and lettuce, and they may order me white wine or claret, and so with all other things that are indifferent to my palate and habit. I know very well that, for them, that is doing nothing because bitterness and strangeness are characteristics of the very essence of medicine. Lycurgus ordered wine for the sick Spartans. Why? Because they hated the use of it when well, just as a gentleman, a neighbor of mine, uses it as a very salutary drug for his fevers because by nature he mortally hates the taste of it.

How many doctors we see who are of my mind, disdaining medicine for their own use and adopting a free regimen, entirely contrary to that which they prescribe for others? What is this but baldly abusing our simplicity? For their life and health are no less dear to them than ours is to us, and consequently they would adjust their practice to their preaching if they did not themselves know its falsity.

It is the fear of death and pain, the inability to endure sickness, a violent and reckless thirst for a cure that so blinds us; it is pure cowardice that makes our belief so pliable and tractable. And yet most men do not so much believe as they acquiesce. For I hear them complain and talk about it as we do; but they decide at last, "What should I do then?" As if impatience were of itself a better remedy than patience. Is there any one of those who have submitted to this miserable servitude who does not equally yield to all sorts of impostures, who does not put himself at the mercy of whoever has the impudence to promise him a cure?

The Babylonians carried their sick into the public square. The physician was the people, everyone that passed by being in humanity and civility obliged to inquire about their condition and give them some salutary advice according to his experience. We hardly do any differently. We make use of the mumblings and incantations of even the simplest woman; and for my part, if I had to take some medicine, I would sooner take this than any other because at least there is no harm to be feared.

What Homer and Plato said of the Egyptians, that they were all physicians, should be said of all people. There is nobody who does not boast of some recipe and who does not venture it upon his neighbor if he is willing to believe him. The other day I was in a company where some one or other of my fellow-sufferers brought news of a kind of pill made up of a hundred-odd ingredients all told. There was great rejoicing and singular consolation for what rock could withstand the strength of so numerous a battery? Yet I understand from those who tried it that the least little particle of gravel did not deign to be moved by it.

I cannot take my hand from this paper without adding this remark about their offering us their experience as proof of the infallibility of their drugs. The greater part and, I believe, more than two thirds of the medicinal virtues consist in the quintessence or occult property of simples which we can learn only by use for quintessence is no other than a quality of which we cannot by our reason find out the cause. Among such proofs, those which they say they have acquired by the inspiration of some daemon I am content to accept (for as to miracles, I never touch upon them); and also the proofs which are drawn from things which are often used by us for a different purpose, as when in the wool which we are accustomed to wear there is found accidentally some occult desiccative property that cures

chilblains on our heels, or when in the radish we eat for food
there is discovered some aperitive action. Galen reports that a
leper happened to be cured by drinking wine out of a vessel
into which a viper had crept by chance. In this example we find
the means and a likely guide to this kind of experiment, as also
in those to which the physicians say they have been led by the
example of some animals. But in most of the other experiments
to which they say they have been led by fortune and have had
no other guide than chance, I find the development of their
inquiry impossible to believe. I imagine a man looking round
about him at the infinite number of things, plants, animals, and
metals. I do not know where to make him begin his experiment;
and even if his first fancy should light upon an elk's horn,
which would require a very pliant and easy faith, he will still
find himself equally perplexed in his second operation. He is
faced with so many maladies and so many circumstances that,
before he has arrived at certainty about the point which the
successful completion of his experiment should reach, human
reason will be at wit's end. And before he has found out, among
that infinite number of things, that it is this horn; among that
infinite number of diseases, that it is epilepsy; among so many
constitutions, the melancholic; among so many seasons, in win-
tertime; among so many nations, the French; among so many
periods of life, in old age; among so many celestial mutations,
at the conjunction of Venus and Saturn; among so many parts
of the body, in the finger; being in all this guided neither by
reasoning, nor by conjecture, nor by example, nor by divine inspiration, but by the sole movement of fortune, it would have
to be by a perfectly artificial, regular, and methodical fortune.
And then, even if the cure should be effected, how can he be
sure that it was not because the disease had reached its term,
or that it was not the result of chance, or the effect of some
other thing that he had eaten or drunk or touched that day,
or the efficacy of his grandmother's prayers? Moreover even
though this proof had been perfect, how many times was it re-

peated? How many times was this long bead-roll of chances and coincidences strung anew to deduce from it a rule?

When the rule is deduced, by whom? Among so many millions there will be but three men who take the trouble to record their experiences. Will chance have lighted exactly on one of these? What if another, and a hundred others, have had contrary experiences? We might, perhaps, see some light if all the reasonings and conclusions of men were known to us. But that three witnesses, and they three doctors, should lord it over mankind is against reason; they would have to be chosen and deputed and culled by human nature and declared our arbiters by express power of attorney.

To Madame de Duras[12]

Madame, when you recently came to see me, you found me at work on this chapter. Since these trifles may some time fall into your hands, I wish them also to bear witness that the author feels very highly honored by the favor you will show them. You will find in them the same bearing and the same air that you observed in his conversation. Even if I could have adopted some other than my ordinary manner and some better and more honorable shape, I would not have done it; for I wish to gain from these writings nothing except that they present me to your memory just as I naturally am. These same qualities and faculties that you have been familiar with and received with much more honor and courtesy than they deserve, I wish to lodge (but without alteration and change) in one compact body that may endure some years, or some days, after I am gone, where you will find them again when you are pleased to refresh your memory of them, without taking otherwise the trouble to recall them as, indeed, they are not worth it. I desire that you should continue the favor of your friendship for me

---

[12] Marguerite d'Aure de Gramont, widow of Jean de Durfort, Seigneur de Duras

for the same qualities by which it was acquired. I do not at all seek to be more loved and esteemed dead than living.

It was a ridiculous fancy in Tiberius, and yet a common one, to take more care to extend his renown to posterity than to win the esteem and favor of the men of his own time.

If I were one of those to whom the world can owe praise, I would acquit it and be paid in advance. Let the praise come quick and pile up all about me, more thick than drawn out, more full than lasting, and let it boldly vanish with my consciousness of it when its sweet sound will no longer reach my ears.

It would be a foolish fancy, now that I am about to leave the company of men, to show myself to them by a new recommendation. I make no account of the gifts I have not been able to employ in the service of my life. Whatever I may be, I wish to be elsewhere than on paper. My skill and industry have been employed to improve myself; my studies, to teach me to do, not to write. I have put all my efforts to shaping my life; this has been my trade and my work. I am less a maker of books than of anything else. I have desired capacity to serve my present and real conveniences and not to lay up a stock and reserve for my heirs.

If a man has any good in him, let him make it appear in his conduct, in his ordinary talk, in his love affairs and his quarrels, in play, in bed, at table, in the handling of his business and the management of his household. If those whom I see in poor breeches composing good books had been of my mind, they would have first tended to their breeches. Ask a Spartan whether he had rather be a good orator than a good soldier; as for me, not any better than being a good cook if I did not have one in my service.

Good Lord! Madame, how I should hate the reputation of being a clever fellow at writing and a good-for-nothing and a fool in other respects. I should even prefer to be a fool both here and there than to have made so bad a choice wherein to employ my talent. Moreover I am so far from expecting to gain any new honor by these follies that I shall do well not to lose in them the little I have acquired. For besides what this dead and mute painting will take away from my natural being, it does not resemble me at my best, but shows me greatly fallen off from my early vigor and liveliness; drawing on towards the withered and rancid. I am at the bottom of the cask, which begins to taste of the lees.

For the rest, Madame, I should not have dared to stir up the mysteries of medicine so boldly, considering the esteem that you and so many others have of it, if I had not been shown the way by its own authors. I believe they count among them only two ancient Latin writers, Pliny and Celsus. If you glance at them some day, you will find that they speak much more harshly of their art than I do. I only pinch it; they slaughter it. Pliny, among other things, twits them with this, that when they are at the end of their rope, they have hit upon this pretty device of sending off their patients whom they have teased and tormented with their drugs and diets to no purpose, some to seek aid from vows and miracles, others to the hot baths. (Be not angry, Madame, he does not speak of those on our side of the frontier which are under the protection of your house and are all attached to the Gramonts.) They have a third device for getting rid of us and clearing themselves of the reproaches we might make to them for the small improvement in our ills, which they had so long under their care that they can think of nothing else to put us off with: that is to send us to try the bracing air of some other country.

Enough, Madame. You will give me leave to resume the thread of my discourse from which I turned aside to talk with you.

It was, I think, Pericles, who being asked how he was, "You may judge by this," he replied, pointing to the amulets he had tied about his neck and arm. He wished to imply that he was in a very bad way since he was reduced even to having recourse to such vanities and to allowing himself to be rigged out that way. I do not say that I may not some day be carried away by the ridiculous notion of committing my life and health to the mercy and control of the physicians. I may fall into this frenzy. I cannot answer for my future firmness. But then, too, if anyone should ask me how I am, I shall be able to answer as Pericles did, "You may judge by this," showing my hand laden with six drachms of opiate. It will be a very evident sign of a violent sickness. My judgment will be marvellously unhinged. If fright and the inability to bear suffering get the upper hand over me, it may be concluded that there is a very violent fever in my soul.

I have taken the pains to plead this cause, of which I have but very slight understanding, in order to support and fortify a little the natural aversion to drugs and the practice of medicine among us that I have derived from my ancestors, so that it may not be merely a stupid and thoughtless inclination, but have a little more form, and also that they who see me so firm against the exhortations and menaces cast at me when sickness assails me may not think that it is mere obstinacy, or in case there may be anyone so ill-natured as to consider it the goad of vainglory. What a well-directed ambition it would be to seek to gain honor from a mode of action that I have in common with my gardener and my muleteer! Certainly my heart is not so puffed up and windy that I should set about exchanging so solid, meaty, and marrowy a pleasure as health for a pleasure that is imaginary, immaterial, and airy. Glory, even that of the four sons of Aymon, is too dearly bought by a man of my humor if it cost him three good attacks of the colic. Give me health, in God's name!

Those who are fond of our medicine may also have their good, great, and strong considerations; I do not hate opinions contrary to my own. I am so far from being provoked at seeing a disagreement between my opinions and those of other men, and from making myself unfit for the society of men because they are of a different sentiment and party from my own, that, on the contrary, as variety is the most general path that nature has followed—and more in minds than bodies since the former are of a more supple substance and susceptible of assuming more forms—I find it much rarer to see our humors and ideas agree. And there never were in the world two opinions alike, any more than two hairs or two grains. Their most universal quality is diversity.

BOOK III

BOOK III

OF THE USEFUL AND THE HONORABLE

No man is exempt from saying silly things. The misfortune is to say them painstakingly.

> Indeed this man with mighty toil will utter mighty trifles.[1]

This does not concern me. Mine escape me with as little care as they merit. So much the better for them. I would immediately part with them for very little. And I neither buy nor sell them but according to their weight. I speak to my paper as I speak to the first man whom I meet. That this is true, here is proof.

To whom ought not perfidy to be detestable when Tiberius refused it though it was so much to his interest? He received word from Germany that, if he thought fit, they would rid him of Arminius by poison (he was the most powerful enemy the Romans had, having so villainously treated them under Varus and alone prevented the enlargement of their dominions in those parts). Tiberius answered that the Roman people were accustomed to take vengeance on their enemies by open means, with their weapons in their hands, not deceitfully and covertly. He abandoned the profitable for the honorable. He was, you will tell me, an impudent deceiver. I believe so; it is no great miracle in men of his profession. But the acknowledgment of virtue is not the less valid in the mouth of him who hates it, inasmuch as truth tears it from him by force; and if he will not receive it wholeheartedly, he at least wears it as an ornament.

---

[1] Terence, *Heautontimoroumenos*

Our structure, both public and private, is full of imperfection. But there is nothing useless in Nature, not even uselessness itself. Nothing has made its way into this universe that does not have a proper place in it. Our being is cemented with sickly qualities; ambition, jealousy, envy, revenge, superstition, and despair dwell in us with so natural a possession that their image is discerned also in beasts. And even cruelty, too, so unnatural a vice; for in the midst of compassion we feel within I know not what bittersweet sting of malicious pleasure in seeing others suffer; and children feel it;

> Sweet, when the seas are heavy, tempestuous the winds,
> To watch from land another's great travail.[2]

Whoever should remove from man the seeds of these qualities would destroy the fundamental conditions of our life. Likewise in all governments there are necessary offices which are not only abject but vicious too; there vices find their place and are useful to the seaming together of our union, as poisons are useful for the preservation of our health. If they become excusable because they are needed by us, and because the common necessity effaces their true quality, we must let this part be played by the most robust and least fearful citizens, who sacrifice their honor and conscience as others of old sacrificed their lives for the good of their country. We others, who are weaker, let us take parts that are both easier and less hazardous. The public good requires that men should betray and lie and massacre; let us resign this commission to more obedient and more supple people.

Truly I have often been vexed to see judges by fraud and false hopes of favor or pardon induce a criminal to reveal his act, using therein deceit and shamelessness. It would become justice and Plato himself, who countenances this procedure,

---

[2] Lucretius

to furnish me with other means more to my taste. This is a malicious justice, and I look upon it as no less harmed by itself than by others. I replied not long ago that I should hardly betray my prince for a private individual, I who would be very distressed to betray any private individual for my prince; and I hate not only to deceive, but also to have anyone be deceived in me. I do not want even to furnish matter or occasion for it.

In the little I have had to negotiate between our princes, in the divisions and subdivisions by which we are today torn to pieces, I have been very careful that they should neither be deceived in me nor deceive others by me. People of that trade keep themselves the most covert, and they present and assume the most neutral and conformable ways that they can. For my part I present myself in my strongest opinions and in the form that is most my own. A tender negotiator and a novice, who would rather be found wanting in the affair than in myself! And yet up to now it has been with such good luck (for Fortune has doubtless the principal share in it) that few have passed from one side to the other with less suspicion or with more favor and privacy. I have an open way that easily insinuates itself and obtains credit upon first acquaintance. Sincerity and pure truth, in whatever age, still find their opportunity and their opening. And besides, the unfettered ways of those who treat without any interest of their own are little subject to suspicion or odium, and they may very well make use of the answer of Hyperides to the Athenians when they complained of his harsh way of speaking: "Gentlemen, do not consider whether I am freespoken, but whether I am so without a bribe and without improving thereby my affairs." My freedom of speech has also easily acquitted me from all suspicion of dissembling because of its vehemence (leaving nothing unsaid no matter how sharp and bitter, I could not have said worse behind their backs), and because it has a manifest show of simplicity and impartiality. I pretend to no other fruit by

acting than to act, and I attach to it no extensive consequences
and intentions. Every action plays its own game: let it hit the
mark if it can.

As to the rest, I am not moved by any passion either of love
or of hatred towards the great; nor is my will bound by personal injury or obligation. I look upon our kings with an affection simply loyal and respectful, neither stirred nor deterred
by any private interest. For this I am well pleased with myself.
The general and just cause attracts me no more than moderately and without passion. I am not subject to those intimate
and penetrating obligations and engagements. Anger and hatred
are beyond the duty of justice and are passions useful only
to those who do not keep themselves strictly to their duty by
simple reason. All lawful and equitable intentions are moderate
and equable of themselves; if otherwise, they degenerate into
the seditious and unlawful. This is it which makes me walk
everywhere with my head erect, my face and my heart open.

In truth, and I am not afraid to confess it, I should easily
in case of need carry one candle to Saint Michael and another
to his dragon, following the plan of the old woman. I will follow the good side even to the fire, but short of the fire if I
can. Let Montaigne be engulfed in the public ruin if need be;
but if there be no need, I shall be grateful to Fortune if it is
saved; and I will make use of all the length of line my duty
allows for its preservation. Was it not Atticus who, being on the
just but losing side, saved himself by his moderation in that
universal shipwreck of the world among so many changes and
variations? For private individuals such as he it is easier; and
in that kind of business I find a man may justly not be ambitious to insert himself at his own invitation. For a man, indeed, to be wavering and two-faced, to keep his affection un-
moved and without taking sides in the troubles of his country
and in civil divisions, I do not find it either handsome or honest.
That is not a middle way, but no way at all, just like that of

men awaiting the event so that they may adapt their plans to Fortune.[3]

That may be allowed in our neighbors' affairs; and Gelo, tyrant of Syracuse, suspended his inclination in this way in the war of the barbarians against the Greeks, keeping an ambassador with presents at Delphi to be on the lookout to see which way fortune would fall and to seize the right moment in order to conciliate the victor. It would be a kind of treason to proceed in this manner in our own internal affairs, wherein we must of necessity take sides by definite intent. But for a man not to engage in these affairs if he has no office or express command which presses him, I consider more excusable (and, nevertheless, I do not use this excuse for myself) than not to in foreign wars about which, however, according to our laws a man need not trouble himself unless he wishes. Nevertheless even those who fully engage in such a war may do so with such order and temperateness that the storm will be bound to pass over their heads without doing them any harm. Had we not reason to hope for such a result in the case of the late Bishop of Orleans, Sieur de Morvilliers? And among those who are toiling valorously in the present war, I know some whose ways are so even and gentle that they will remain firm however harmful a change and downfall heaven is preparing for us. I am of opinion that it properly belongs only to kings to quarrel with kings, and I laugh at those souls who out of gaiety of heart offer themselves to such disproportioned conflicts. For a man is not picking a personal quarrel with a prince when marching openly and boldly against him for his own honor and according to his duty; if he does not love such a person, he does better, he esteems him. And notably the cause of the laws and the defense of the established order have always this in their favor, that even those who for their own private interest disturb them excuse their defenders if they do not honor them.

---

[3] Livy

But we ought not to give the name of duty, as we do every day, to an inner bitterness and harshness which spring from private interest and passion, nor the name of courage to a treacherous and malicious conduct. They give the name of zeal to their propensity for mischief and violence: it is not the cause that inflames them but their interest; they kindle war, not because it is just, but because it is war.

Nothing prevents a man from conducting himself properly and loyally among men who are enemies. Bear yourself among them with an affection, if not completely equal (for it is capable of different degrees), yet at least moderate, and which does not bind you so much to one that he may demand everything of you; and be content also with a moderate proportion of their favor, and to swim in troubled waters without wishing to fish in them.

The other way, to offer yourself with all your strength to one side and to the other, has still less prudence in it than conscience. Does not he to whom you betray another, by whom you are equally well received, know that you will in turn do as much for him? He considers you a scoundrel, and in the meantime he listens to you, pumps you, and works his own ends out of your disloyalty; for double-dealing men are useful in bringing in, but we must have a care they carry away as little as possible.

I say nothing to one man which I may not at the right moment say to another with only a little alteration of the accent; and I report only the things that are either indifferent or known, or which are of common service to them. There is no personal consideration whatever for which I permit myself to tell them a lie. What has been entrusted to my silence I scrupulously conceal; but I take as little to conceal as I can. The secrets of princes are a troublesome charge to the man who has no part in them. I gladly present this bargain, that they trust little to me but that they trust confidently in what I bring them. I have always known more of these matters than I desired.

An open way of speaking opens another's speech and draws it out as do wine and love.

To King Lysimachus' remark, "Which of my possessions do you want me to transmit to you?", Philippides wisely replied, "What you will, provided it be none of your secrets." I see that everyone rebels if the bottom of the affair in which he is employed is concealed from him, or if some ulterior intent has been hidden from him. For my part, I am content to be told no more about it than what they desire me to carry out, and I do not want my knowledge to exceed or constrain my speech. If I must serve for an instrument of deceit, let my conscience at least be whole. I do not want to be considered so affectionate or so loyal a servant as to be found fit to betray any man. He who is unfaithful to himself is excusably so to his master.

But the princes I have in mind do not accept men by halves and despise limited and conditional services. There is no remedy. I tell them frankly my limits; for a slave I do not have to be except to Reason, and I can scarcely even manage that. And they also are wrong to require from a free man the same subjection and obligation to their service that they do from one whom they have made and bought, or whose fortune is particularly and expressly attached to theirs. The laws have delivered me from a great anxiety; they have chosen a side for me and given me a master; all other superiority and obligation ought to be relative to that and restricted. Yet this is not to say that, if my affection should otherwise move me, my hand would at once obey it. The will and the desires are a law to themselves; but actions must receive their law from public regulation.

All this procedure of mine is a little dissonant from ordinary forms; it would not be such as to bring forth great results or to be enduring. Innocence itself could neither negotiate among us without dissimulation nor deal without lying. And, furthermore, public affairs are by no means my quarry; what my profession requires I perform in the most private manner that

I can. When a boy, I was plunged into them to the ears, and succeeded; yet I disengaged myself in good time. I have often since avoided meddling in them, seldom accepted, and never sought them, keeping my back turned to ambition; but, if not like rowers who thus advance backward, yet in such a way that I am less obliged to my resolution than to my good fortune that I am not embarked in them. For there are ways less hostile to my taste and more suitable to my capacity by which, if she had formerly called me to public service and to my advancement towards worldly reputation, I know I should have passed over the arguments of my reason to follow her.

Those who commonly say, in opposition to what I profess, that what I call frankness, simplicity, and naturalness in my character is art and subtlety, and prudence rather than goodness, artifice rather than nature, good sense rather than good luck, do me more honor than they take away from me. But assuredly they make my subtlety too subtle; and whoever has followed me and observed me closely I will concede the victor if he does not confess that there is no rule in their school that could reproduce this natural movement and maintain an appearance of freedom and license so constant and inflexible amid such crooked and dangerous paths, and that all their effort and wit could not lead them to it. The way of truth is one and simple, that of private profit and the advantage of the affairs of which a man has charge is double, uneven, and fortuitous. I have often seen in use these counterfeit and artificial liberties, but for the most part without success. They fully take after Aesop's ass who, in emulation of the dog, threw himself very joyfully with his forefeet on his master's shoulders; but as many caresses as the dog received from such gaiety, the poor ass received twice as many cudgelings. *What best becomes any man is that which is peculiarly his own.*[4] I do not want to deprive deceit of its place; that would be to understand the world badly. I know it has often been of great use and that it

---

[4] Cicero, *De Officiis*

maintains and nourishes the majority of men's callings. There are lawful vices, just as many actions, either good or excusable, are unlawful.

Pure justice, natural and universal, is differently and more nobly regulated than is that other justice which is special, national, and restricted to the needs of our governments. *We have no solid and exact copy of true law and genuine justice; we have for our use only the shadow and reflection of it.*[5] So that the sage Dandamis, hearing the lives of Socrates, Pythagoras, and Diogenes related, judged them to be great men in every other thing except in being too subservient to reverence for the laws, for to sanction and support them true virtue must part with much of its original vigor; and many vicious actions take place not only with their permission, but by their advice: *Crimes are committed at the orders of the Senate and the popular assembly.*[6] I follow the common language that distinguishes between profitable and honorable things, so that some natural actions that are not only profitable but necessary are termed dishonorable and foul.

But let us continue our examples of treachery. Two pretenders to the kingdom of Thrace had fallen into dispute about their rights. The emperor prevented them from proceeding to arms; but one of them, under color of bringing about a friendly agreement by an interview, having invited his competitor to an entertainment in his own house, had him imprisoned and killed. Justice required that the Romans should have satisfaction for this crime; difficulty prevented the ordinary ways from being used. What they could not do lawfully without war and without danger they undertook to do by treachery. What they could not do honorably they did profitably. For that one Pomponius Flaccus was found fit; this man, by dissembled words and assurances having drawn the other into his snare, instead of the honor and favor he had promised him, sent him bound hand and foot to Rome. Here one traitor

---

[5] Cicero, *De Officiis*　　[6] Seneca, *Epistles*

betrays the other, contrary to common practice, for they are full of mistrust, and it is difficult to surprise them with their own art: witness the onerous experience we have just undergone.

Let who will be a Pomponius Flaccus, and there are enough who are willing; for my part both my word and my faith are, like the rest, parts of this common body. Their best action is public service; I consider that presupposed. But just as I should reply if I were ordered to take charge of the Palace of Justice and of its lawsuits: "I understand nothing about it;" or if charged with leadership of pioneers, I should say: "I am called to a more dignified rôle;" so likewise if anyone wanted to employ me to lie, betray, and forswear myself for some notable service, not assassination or poisoning, I should say: "If I have robbed or stolen anything from any man, send me rather to the galleys." For it is allowable for a man of honor to say as the Lacedemonians did when, having been defeated by Antipater, they were at the point of concluding terms: "You may impose as heavy and ruinous burdens upon us as you please, but to command us to do shameful and dishonest things will be a waste of time for you." Everyone ought to take the same oath to himself that the kings of Egypt made their judges solemnly swear, that they would not stray from the path of conscience no matter what command they might receive. In such commands there is an evident mark of ignominy and condemnation; and he who gives it to you accuses you, and he gives it to you, if you understand it well, for a burden and a punishment. As much as the public affairs are bettered by your action, so much are your own made worse; and the better you do at it, the more you lose. And it will be no new thing, nor, perhaps, without some color of justice, if the same person who set you at work punishes you for it. Perfidy may be excusable in some cases; it is so only when it is used to betray and punish perfidy.

There are examples enough of treachery not only refused, but punished by those in favor of whom it had been undertaken. Who is ignorant of Fabricius' denunciation of Pyrrhus' physician? But we also find this, that the very man who gave the order for a treacherous act avenged it severely upon him whom he had set to it, rejecting the reputation of such an unbridled authority and power and disowning such an aban- doned and such a base servitude and obedience.

Jarolpelc, Duke of Russia, tampered with a gentleman of Hungary to betray Boleslaus, king of Poland, either by kill- ing him, or by giving the Russians opportunity to do him some serious harm. This fellow set about it smartly, was more as- siduous in the service of that king than before, succeeded in becoming a member of his council and one of his most trusted men. With these advantages, and choosing opportunely the oc- casion of his master's absence, he betrayed to the Russians Vislicza, a great and rich city, which was entirely sacked and burned by them, with a total slaughter not only of its inhab- itants of both sexes, young and old, but also of a great number of the nobility of the vicinity that he had assembled there for that purpose. Jarolpelc, his vengeance and anger appeased, which, indeed, was not without some justification (for Boles- laus had greatly injured him, and in the same manner), and sated with the fruit of this treachery, coming to consider the naked ugliness of it all by itself, and to regard it with a sane view no longer troubled by his passion, felt for it such a horror and remorse that he had his agent's eyes put out and his tongue and privy parts cut off.

Antigonus persuaded the Argyraspidian soldiers to betray to him Eumenes, their general, his adversary; but after he had got hold of him through them, no sooner had he had him killed than he desired himself to be the agent of the divine Justice for the punishment of such a detestable crime, and put them in the hands of the governor of the province, giving him very express command to ruin them and bring them to an evil end by any means whatever. So that out of that great number of men not one ever saw again the skies of Macedonia. The better he

had been served by them, the more wicked he judged it to have
been, and the more deserving of punishment.

The slave that betrayed the hiding-place of his master P.
Sulpicius was set free according to the promise of Sulla's pro-
scription; but, according to the promise of the public justice,
he was, when completely free, thrown headlong from the Tar-
peian rock. They have them hanged with the purse of their
pay about their necks. Having satisfied their second and special obligation, they satisfy the general and primary one.

Mahomet the Second, wanting to rid himself of his brother
because of jealousy of supremacy, according to the fashion
of their race, set one of his officers to it, who choked him by
pouring a quantity of water too fast down his throat. That
done, to expiate this murder he delivered the murderer into
the hands of the dead man's mother (for they were brothers
only on the father's side); in his presence she opened up the
murderer's vitals, and immediately searching with her hands
for his heart, she tore it out and threw it to the dogs to eat.

And our King Clovis had the three servants of Cannacre
hanged after they had betrayed their master to him, an act
to which he had enticed them.

And even to those who are worthless it is very sweet, having
profited from a vicious action, to be able henceforth to fasten
to it with full assurance some mark of goodness and justice
by way of counterbalancing and adjusting the conscience. To
this may be added that they look upon the ministers of such
horrid crimes as people who reproach them with them; and
they seek by their death to stifle the knowledge and evidence
of such proceedings.

Now if by good fortune you are rewarded for it in order
that the public necessity for that extreme and desperate remedy
should not be defeated, the man who does it cannot fail to
consider you a cursed and execrable person unless he be so
himself; and he considers you more a traitor than does the

man whom you betray; for he tries the malignity of your heart by your own hands without disavowal or objection being possible. But he employs you just as abandoned men are employed to be executioners of high justice, an office as useful as it is dishonorable. Besides the baseness of such commissions there is in them a prostitution of conscience. As the daughter of Sejanus could not be punished with death in the established legal procedure at Rome because she was a virgin, in order to make way for the law, she was violated by the hangman before he strangled her: not only his hand, but his soul, is slave to the public convenience.

When the first Amurath, to sharpen the punishment of his subjects who had given support to the parricidal rebellion of his son against him, ordered that their nearest kindred should lend a hand to the execution, I find it very honorable in some of them to have rather chosen to be unjustly thought guilty of parricide than to serve justice by a parricide of their own. And when, at some ramshackle fortresses taken by assault in my time, I have seen rascals consenting, in order to save their own lives, to hang their friends and companions, I have looked upon them to be in a worse condition than the hanged. It is said that Vitold, Prince of Lithuania, once made this law, that the condemned criminals themselves would have to execute with their own hands the capital sentence pronounced against them, thinking it strange that a third person, innocent of the fault, should be employed in a homicide and burdened by it.

When some urgent circumstance or some sudden and unforeseen occurrence of state necessity makes a prince break his word and his faith, or otherwise forces him from his ordinary duty, he ought to attribute this necessity to a stroke of the divine rod. Vice it is not, for he has abandoned his own reason to a more universal and more powerful reason, but certainly it is a misfortune. So that to someone who asked me: "What remedy?" "No remedy," I replied, "if he was really racked between these two extremes (*but let him see to it that a pretext for perjury is not being sought* [7]), he had to do it; but if he did it without regret, if it did not grieve him to do it, it is a sign that his conscience is in a bad way."

Even if there should be a person of so tender a conscience as to think no cure whatever worthy of so burdensome a remedy, I should not esteem him the less for it. He could not perish more excusably or more decorously. We cannot do everything. In any case we must often commit the protection of our vessel to the conduct of Heaven as to a last anchorage. To what more just necessity does he reserve himself? What is less possible for him to do than what he cannot do but at the expense of his faith and honor, things that perhaps ought to be dearer to him than his own safety, even, and than the safety of his people? Even when with folded arms he simply calls God to his aid, may he not have reason to hope that the divine bounty will not refuse the extraordinary favor of its hand to a just and pure hand?

These are dangerous examples, rare and sickly exceptions to our natural rules. We must yield to them, but with great moderation and circumspection. No private advantage merits having our conscience put to that effort on its account; the public advantage, yes, when it is very apparent and very important.

Timoleon fitly secured himself against the strangeness of his deed by the tears he shed, calling to mind that it was with a brother's hand that he had slain the tyrant; and it justly pricked his conscience that he had been obliged to purchase the public welfare at such a price to the honor of his character. Even the Senate, released from slavery by his means, did not dare roundly to pass judgment on so great an action, split into two such grave and contrary aspects. But the Syracusans having very opportunely, just at that moment, sent to the Corinthians to seek their protection and a leader fit to restore their

---

[7] Cicero, *De Officiis*

city to its former dignity and to cleanse Sicily of a number
of tyrants who were oppressing it, they deputed Timoleon with
this novel evasion and declaration, that, according as he bore
himself well or ill in his charge, their verdict would be decided in favor of the liberator of his country or against the
murderer of his brother. This fantastic decision has, however,
some excuse on the grounds of the danger of the example and
the importance of so strange an action. And they did well to
discharge their own judgment of it and to make it rest upon
other and extraneous considerations. Now Timoleon's conduct
in this expedition soon made his cause clearer, so worthily and
virtuously did he bear himself in every way; and the good fortune that accompanied him in the difficulties he had to overcome in this noble task seemed to be sent to him by the gods
conspiring in favor of his justification.

This man's aim is excusable if any could be so. But the
advantage of increasing the public revenue, that served the
Roman Senate as a pretext for that foul decision which I am
about to relate, is not great enough to warrant any such injustice. By payment of money certain cities had redeemed
themselves and regained their liberty, by the order and consent of the Senate, from the hands of L. Sulla. The matter having come up again for decision, the Senate condemned them
to be taxable as they were before and that the money they
had put into redeeming themselves should be lost to them.
Civil wars often produce these villainous examples, namely
that we punish private individuals for having believed in us
when we were other than we are now; and the selfsame magistrate makes the penalty of his own change of judgment be
borne by a man who is not to blame for it; the master whips
his pupil for his docility, and the guide his blind man. Horrible image of justice!

There are rules in philosophy that are both false and lax.
The example that is proposed to us to make private advantage
prevail over the integrity of our word does not receive enough

weight because of the circumstance that they associate with it. Robbers seized you, they set you free after extracting from you an oath to pay them a certain sum; it is wrong to say that an honest man will be quit of his oath without paying, once out of their hands. It is no such thing. What fear has once made me willing to do, I am bound to be still willing to do when I am no longer afraid; and even if fear forced only my tongue without my will, I am still bound to make my word good to the last penny. For my part, when my tongue has sometimes heedlessly got ahead of my thoughts, I have scrupled at disowning it for that reason. Otherwise by degrees we shall come to overthrow all the rights that a third person acquires from our promises and oaths. *As if compulsion could be effectively employed on a brave man.*[8] In this alone is private interest justified, to excuse us for failing in our promise if we have promised something that is wicked and unjust in itself; for the right of virtue ought to prevail over the right of our obligation.

I once placed Epaminondas in the first rank of excellent men and do not retract it. To what height did he raise the consideration of his own personal duty, he who never killed a man whom he had overcome, who for the inestimable good of restoring liberty to his country scrupled at killing a tyrant or his accomplices without due form of justice, and who judged that man to be wicked, however good a citizen he might be, who among his enemies and in battle did not spare his friend and his host! There is a soul of rich composition. To the roughest and most violent human actions he united goodness and humanity, indeed the most refined that may be found in the school of philosophy. This heart, so large, so full, so resolute against pain, death, and poverty, was it nature or art that had softened it to the point of such an extreme sweetness and gentleness? Terrifying in arms and in gore, he goes shattering and crushing a nation invincible against all others but

---

[8] Cicero, *De Officiis*

him alone, and in the middle of such a fray he turns aside upon encountering his host and his friend. Truly this man exercised very fit command in war who could make it submit to the curb of benignity at the peak of its greatest heat, all inflamed as it was and foaming with fury and slaughter. It is a miracle to be able to mingle any image of justice with such actions, and it belongs only to the firmness of Epaminondas to be able to mingle with it the sweetness and ease of the gentlest manners and pure innocence. And whereas one said to the Mamertines that statutes had no application against armed men, and another said to the Tribune of the People that the time of justice and that of war were two different things, and a third said that the noise of arms kept him from hearing the voice of the laws, this man was not even kept from hearing the voices of civility and pure courtesy. Had he not borrowed from his enemies the custom of sacrificing to the Muses when he went to war in order to soften that martial fury and fierceness by their sweetness and gaiety?

Let us not fear, after so great a teacher, to believe that there is something not permitted even against an enemy, that the common interest ought not to require all things of all men against private interest, *the memory of private rights remaining even in the rupture of public ties:*[9]

No power can sanction treachery to a friend;[10]

and that all things are not allowable to a man of honor for the service of his king, or of the common cause, or of the laws. *For our country does not come before all other duties, and it serves its own interest to have citizens who are devoted to their parents.*[11] It is a lesson proper for the times. We do not need to harden our hearts with these plates of steel, it is enough for our shoulders to be so; it is enough to dip our pens in ink without dipping them in blood. If it is loftiness of heart and the

---

[9] Livy   [10] Ovid, *Ex Ponto*   [11] Cicero, *De Officiis*

effect of a singular and rare virtue to scorn friendship, private obligations, a man's word, and kinship for the sake of the common good and obedience to the magistrate, it is certainly sufficient to excuse us from it that it is a loftiness that cannot find lodging in the loftiness of Epaminondas' heart.

I abominate those mad exhortations of this other unbridled soul,

> While weapons gleam, let not the thoughts of love,
> Nor sight of kin in the opposing van
> Disturb your heart; disfigure with your sword
> These faces so revered.[12]

Let us take away from wicked, bloody, and treacherous natures this pretense of reason; let us abandon this monstrous and mad justice and stick to more humane forms. How much time and example can do! In an encounter in the civil war against Cinna one of Pompey's soldiers, having unknowingly killed his brother, who was of the opposite party, immediately killed himself out of shame and sorrow; and some years later in another civil war of the same people, a soldier demanded a reward from his leaders for having killed his brother.

We argue poorly the honor and beauty of an action from its utility, and we conclude badly in considering that everyone is obliged to act thus and that the action becomes everyone if it is useful:

> All things are not alike for all men fit.[13]

Let us take the most necessary and useful action of human society: it will, no doubt, be marriage. And yet the council of the saints finds the contrary way more honorable and excludes from it the most venerable calling of men, as we assign to stud those horses which are of least value.

---

[12] Lucan   [13] Propertius

OF REPENTANCE

OTHERS FORM MAN; I describe him and depict a particular one, ill formed enough and whom, if I had to shape him anew, I should certainly make very different from what he is. But now that's done. Now the lines of my painting do not go astray, though they change and vary. The world is but an eternal seesaw. All things therein are incessantly moving: the earth, the rocks of the Caucasus, and the pyramids of Egypt, both with the general motion and their own. Constancy itself is nothing but a more languid motion. I cannot fix my object; it goes muddled and reeling by a natural drunkenness. I take it just as it is at the instant I consider it. I do not paint its being. I paint its passage: not a passage from one age to another, or, as the people say, from seven to seven years, but from day to day, from minute to minute. I must accommodate my history to the hour. I may presently change not only by chance but also by intention. This is a record of various and changeable events and of ideas that are uncertain and, when it so happens, contradictory, whether it be that I am different myself or that I grasp subjects by other circumstances and considerations. So it is that I, indeed, contradict myself upon occasion, but truth, as Demades said, I do not contradict. Could my mind take footing, I would not make essays, I would offer positive opinions about myself. But it is always in apprenticeship and on trial.

I set forth a humble life, without luster; that makes no difference. All moral philosophy is applied as well to a common and private life as to one of richer stuff. Every man bears the entire form of human nature.

Authors communicate themselves to the people by some particular and external mark; I, the first of any, by my universal being; as Michel de Montaigne, not as a grammarian, or a poet, or a lawyer. If the world find fault that I speak too much of myself, I find fault that they do not so much as think of themselves.

But is it reasonable that, being so private in my way of life, I should seek to make myself publicly known? And is it reasonable, too, for me to offer to the world, where art and mode have so much credit and authority, crude and simple products of nature, and of a very weak nature to boot? Is it not to build a wall without stone, or some such thing, to write books without learning and without art? The fancies of music are directed by art, mine by chance. I have this, at least, according to the rules, that never any man treated a subject that he understood and knew better than I do that which I have undertaken, and that in this I am the most learned man alive; secondly, that never any man penetrated farther into his matter, nor more carefully picked over its parts and consequences, nor ever more exactly and fully arrived at the end he had set up for his work. To finish it, I need bring nothing but fidelity to the work; and that is there, the most sincere and pure fidelity that is anywhere to be found. I speak the truth, not to my fill, but as much as I dare; and I dare a little more as I grow older, for it seems that custom allows to age more liberty of prating and more indiscretion in talking of a man's self. There cannot happen here that which I often see happen, that the artisan and his product contradict one another: "Has a man of such distinguished conversation written so foolish a book?" or "Have such learned writings come from a man of such weak conversation?"

When a man's conversation is ordinary and his writings outstanding, this means that his capacity rests in the place from which he borrows it and not in himself. A learned man is not learned in all things; but an able man is able in all, even in ignorance.

Here my book and I go hand in hand and at the very same pace. Elsewhere men may recommend or condemn a work apart from the workman; here not so; who touches the one, touches the other. He that judges it without knowing it will more wrong himself than me; he who has known it will give me all the satisfaction I desire. Happy beyond my desert if I have only this share of the public approbation, that I make men of understanding perceive that I was capable of profiting from knowledge, had I had any, and that I deserved to be assisted better by my memory.

Let me excuse here what I often repeat, that I very seldom repent and that my conscience is satisfied with itself, not like the conscience of an angel, or that of a horse, but like the conscience of a man; always adding this refrain, not a refrain of ceremony, but of simple and real submission: that I speak as an inquiring and ignorant man, purely and simply referring myself to the common and authorized beliefs for the decision. I do not teach, I relate.

There is no vice truly a vice which does not offend and which a sound judgment does not censure; for it has such a manifest ugliness and troublesomeness that, perhaps, they are in the right who say that it is chiefly produced by stupidity and ignorance. So hard is it to imagine that a man may know it without abhorring it. Malice sucks up the greater part of her own venom and poisons herself with it. Vice leaves, like an ulcer in the flesh, repentance in the soul, which is always scratching itself and drawing blood. For reason effaces all other griefs and sorrows, but it begets that of repentance, which is so much the more grievous as it is born within, as the cold and heat of fevers are sharper than that which comes from without. I regard as vices (but each according to its measure) not only those which reason and nature condemn, but those also which the opinion of men has shaped, even false and erroneous opinion, if authorized by laws and custom.

There is likewise no good action which does not rejoice a

wellborn nature; there is, indeed, a kind of gratification in well-doing that gives us an inward rejoicing, and a noble pride that accompanies a good conscience. A soul daringly vicious may, perhaps, arm itself with security, but it cannot supply itself with this complacency and satisfaction. It is no slight satisfaction to a man to feel himself preserved from the contagion of so depraved an age and to say to himself, "If anyone should see way into my soul, he still would not find me guilty either of the affliction or of the ruin of anyone; or of revenge, or envy, or of any public offense against the laws, or of innovation and disturbance, or of failing in my word; and despite what the license of the times permits and teaches to everyone, yet I have not put my hand on the goods or into the purse of any Frenchman, and have lived in war, as well as in peace, upon what is my own; neither have I made use of the work of any man without paying him his hire." These testimonies of the conscience are pleasing; and this natural rejoicing is a great boon to us and the only reward that never fails us.

To ground the recompense of virtuous actions upon the approbation of others is to take too uncertain and shaky a foundation. Especially in so corrupt and ignorant an age as this, the good opinion of the people is no commendation; upon whom do you rely to see what is laudable? God defend me from being an estimable man according to the description I daily see everyone make in honor of himself. *What had been vices are now moral practices.*[1]

Some of my friends have sometimes undertaken to reprimand and lecture me with great frankness, either of their own accord, or by my entreaty, as a service which in a well-formed soul surpasses all other acts of friendship not only in utility, but also in kindness. I have always received it with wide-open arms of courtesy and gratitude. But now to speak of it in all conscience, I have often found so much false measure in their reproaches and praises that I would hardly have erred to err

---

[1] Seneca, *Epistles*

rather than to do good according to their style. Those of us in particular who live a private life, not exposed to any other view than our own, ought to have a pattern set up within ourselves by which to try our actions; and according to that, sometimes to caress, and sometimes to correct ourselves. I have my own laws and court to judge myself, and address myself more to these than anywhere else. I do, indeed, restrain my actions according to others, but I extend them only according to myself. There is only you who know if you are cowardly and cruel, or loyal and devout; others do not see you, they guess at you by uncertain conjectures; they see not so much your nature as your art. Do not hold fast, therefore, to their judgment, hold fast to yours. *You must use your own judgment. . . . In respect to virtues and vices your own conscience bears great weight: take that away, and everything collapses.*[2]

But the saying that repentance immediately follows sin seems not to consider sin in its high estate, which is lodged in us as in its own proper habitation; we may disown and retract the vices that surprise us and to which we are hurried by passions; but those which, by a long habit, are rooted and anchored in a strong and vigorous will are not subject to contradiction. Repentance is nothing but a recanting of our will and an opposition to our fancies, which leads us in all directions. It makes this person disown his former virtue and continence:

> Why did I lack in youth the mind I have today?
> Or why to now's desires do not smooth cheeks return?[3]

It is a rare life that stays orderly even in private. Everyone may take a part in the farce and assume the character of a worthy man upon the stage; but within, and in his own bosom, where all is permitted, where all is concealed—to be disciplined there, that is the point. The next degree is to be so in our own house, in our ordinary actions, for which we are accountable to

[2] Cicero, *Tusculans,* and *De Natura Deorum*   [3] Horace, *Odes*

no one; where there is no study or artifice. And, therefore, Bias, in depicting an excellent state of family life, says that it is one in which the master is the same within by his own will, as he is without for fear of the laws and the talk of men. And it was a worthy saying of Julius Drusus to the workmen who offered for three thousand crowns to arrange his house in such a way that his neighbors should no longer have the view into it that they had before: "I will give you," he said, "six thousand to make it so that everybody may see into it from all sides." It is honorably recorded of Agesilaus that he used in his journeys to take lodging in the temples in order that the people, and the gods themselves, might see into his private actions. Certain men have seemed miraculous to the world, in whom their wives and their servants have never seen anything even noteworthy. Few men have been admired by their own household.

No one has been a prophet, not merely in his own house, but in his own country, says the experience of history. It is the same in things of no consequence. And in this insignificant example the image of greater ones is seen. In my region of Gascony they look upon it as very droll to see me in print. The farther off knowledge of me moves from my den, the better I am esteemed. I buy the printers in Guienne, elsewhere they buy me. Upon this circumstance do those men base their expectations who conceal themselves while living and present in order to gain credit when dead and gone. I prefer to have less of it, and I throw myself upon the world only for the share that I am now getting. When I leave it, I'll hold it quit.

The people, with wonder, accompany that fellow from a public function back to his door; he puts off his rôle with his robe, and he drops back just so much the lower, the higher he had climbed; within, in his home, all is tumultuous and base. Even if order existed there, it requires a quick and choice judgment to perceive it in these humble and private actions. Besides order is a dull and somber virtue. To take a breach, conduct an embassy, govern a people, are brilliant actions. To reprehend, laugh, sell, pay, love, hate, and to have pleasant and just relations with our own family and with ourself, not to lose control, not to give ourself the lie, is a more rare and difficult thing and less remarked. So retired lives, whatever one may say, carry duties equally or more severe and strenuous than do the other lives. And private persons, says Aristotle, offer a more difficult and higher service to virtue than do those in authority. We prepare ourselves for eminent occasions more out of glory than conscience. The shortest way to arrive at glory should be to do for conscience what we do for glory. And the virtue of Alexander seems to me to exhibit much less vigor in his theater than that of Socrates in his lowly and obscure activity. I can easily conceive Socrates in the place of Alexander; but Alexander in that of Socrates, I cannot. If you ask the former what he can do, he will answer, "Subdue the world;" if you put the same question to the latter, he will say, "Carry on human life conformably to its natural condition;" a much more general, weighty, and legitimate knowledge than the other.

The worth of the soul does not consist in flying high, but in an orderly pace. Its greatness does not exercise itself in greatness, but in mediocrity. As they who judge and try us within make no great account of the luster of our public actions and see they are only slender threads and jets of clear water springing from an otherwise muddy and dense bottom; so likewise they who judge of us by this fine outward appearance in like manner conclude about our internal constitution, and cannot couple common faculties, such as their own, with these other faculties that astonish them and are so far beyond their aim. So we give outlandish forms to demons. And who does not give Tamerlane raised eyebrows, distended nostrils, a dreadful face, and a prodigious stature, just like the size of the image we have conceived of him from the fame of his name? If in other times anyone had brought me to see Erasmus, it would have been difficult for me not to take for adages and apophthegms all he said to his man and his hostess. We much more aptly imagine an artisan upon the toilet seat, or upon his wife, than a great president, venerable by his port and ability. It seems to us that from their lofty thrones they do not lower themselves even to live.

As vicious souls are often incited by some outside impulse to do good, so are virtuous souls to do evil. They are, therefore, to be judged by their settled state when they are at home, if they are ever there, or at least when they are nearest to repose and in their natural place. Natural inclinations are much assisted and fortified by education, but they can scarcely be changed and overcome. A thousand natures in my time have escaped towards virtue or vice through a contrary discipline:

> As when wild beasts, disused to woods, grow tame
> Closed in a cage, cast off their threatening looks,
> And learn to bear man's rule; but if blood touch
> Their thirsty mouths, their rage and fury's back,
> And goaded by the taste their throats swell out;
> With blazing ire their shaking keeper they scarce spare.[4]

We do not root out these original qualities, we cover them, we conceal them. The Latin language is like a native tongue to me; I understand it better than French, but I have not made use of it at all for speaking or writing for forty years. And yet, in extreme and sudden emotions, which I have fallen into twice or thrice in my life, and one of which was in seeing my father in perfect health fall upon me in a swoon, I have always cast forth from the depths of my vitals my first words in Latin; Nature welling up and forcibly expressing herself contrary to long habit. And this example is said of many others.

They who in my time have attempted to reform the morals of the world by new ideas reform surface vices, the essential vices they leave as they were if they do not increase them; and the increase is the thing to be feared there. We are inclined to desist from all other welldoing on account of these external, arbitrary reforms which are less costly and more rewarding, and

---

[4] Lucan

thereby we expiate at an easy rate for the other natural, consubstantial, and internal vices. Consider a little how our experience bears this out; there is no man, if he listens to himself, who does not discover in himself a form of his own, a master form that struggles against education and against the tempest of the emotions that are contrary to it. For my part, I seldom feel myself abruptly agitated; I am almost always in my place, as heavy and unwieldy bodies are; if I am not at home, I am always very close to it. My excesses do not carry me very far off. There is nothing strange or extreme in them; and, moreover, my feelings of reaction are vigorous and healthy.

The true condemnation, one which touches the common run of men nowadays, is that their very retirement is full of corruption and filth; their idea of reformation blurred; their penitence, sick and faulty, very nearly as much as their sin. Some, either from having been glued to vice by a natural attachment or by long addiction, no longer see the ugliness of it. Others (to which regiment I belong) do feel the weight of vice, but they counterbalance it with pleasure or some other pretext and suffer it and lend themselves to it for a certain price, but viciously, nonetheless, and basely. Yet there might, perhaps, be imagined so vast a disproportion of measure between them that, with justice, the pleasure might excuse the sin, as we say utility does; not only if it were incidental and apart from the sin, as in theft, but in the very exercise of the sin, as in the enjoyment of women, wherein the impulse is violent and, it is said, sometimes irresistible.

The other day when I was at Armagnac on the estate of a kinsman of mine, I saw a country fellow whom everyone nicknamed "The Thief." He told the story of his life in this way: Born a beggar, and finding that by earning his living by the toil of his hands he would never succeed in securing himself sufficiently against want, he decided to turn thief; and he had spent all his youth in safety at this trade because of his bodily strength; for he gathered his harvest and vintage upon other men's lands, but so far away and in such great quantities that it was inconceivable that one man could have carried away so much in one night upon his shoulders; and, besides, he was careful to equalize and distribute the damage he did so that the loss was less unbearable for each individual. He is now, in his old age, rich for a man of his position, thanks to this traffic, which he openly confesses. And to make his peace with God for his gains, he says he is daily by good services making restitution to the successors of those he robbed; and if he does not finish (for he is not able to do it all at once), he will leave it as a charge to his heirs in proportion to the knowledge he has of the wrong which he alone knows he has done to each one. According to this description, whether true or false, this man looks upon theft as a dishonorable action and hates it, but less so than poverty; he repents of it quite simply, but inasmuch as it was thus counterbalanced and compensated, he does not repent of it. This is not that habit that incorporates us with vice and makes even our understanding conform to it, nor is it that impetuous wind that by sudden gusts confuses and blinds our souls and for the moment hurls us, judgment and all, into the power of vice.

What I do, I customarily do with my whole being, and I move all in one piece; I have hardly any movement that hides and steals away from my reason, and that is not guided by the consent of nearly all parts of me, without division or internal sedition. My judgment has either all the blame or all the praise for it; and the blame it once has, it ever keeps for almost from its birth it has been the same: the same inclination, the same course, the same strength. And in the matter of general opinions, I fixed myself from my childhood in the position where I was to stick.

There are some sins that are impetuous, prompt, and sudden; let us set them aside. But in these other sins so often repeated, meditated, and contrived, or constitutional sins, even sins of profession and vocation, I cannot conceive that they may be so long implanted in one and the same heart unless the reason and conscience of him who has them constantly wishes and intends for it to be so; and the repentance he boasts comes to him at a given moment is a little hard for me to imagine and conceive.

I do not follow the opinion of the Pythagorean sect, that men take up a new soul when they approach the images of the gods to receive their oracles, unless he meant exactly this, that it must, indeed, be new and lent for the time being, their own showing so little sign of purification and cleanness fit for this office.

They act quite contrary to the precepts of the Stoics who, indeed, order us to correct the imperfections and vices which we recognize in us, but forbid us to be sorry and dejected about them. These men make us believe that they have great regret and remorse within, but of amendment, correction, or interruption they give us no indication. Yet it is no cure if a man does not rid himself of the disease. If repentance weighed in the scale of the balance, it would outweigh sin. I find no quality so easy to counterfeit as piety if conduct and life are not made to conform with it. The essence of it is abstruse and occult; its appearances, easy and showy.

For my own part, I may desire in general to be other than I am; I may condemn and dislike my whole nature and beg of God for my complete reformation and for pardon of my natural infirmity. But it seems to me that I ought not to call this repentance, any more than my displeasure that I am neither an angel nor Cato. My actions are regulated and conform with what I am and with my condition. I can do no better. And repentance does not properly concern things that are not in our power; but rather does regret. I imagine an infinite number of natures more elevated and better regulated than mine; I do not, for all that, improve my faculties, just as neither my arm nor my mind becomes more vigorous by imagining another that is so. If to imagine and desire a nobler way of acting than ours should produce a repentance of our own, we should have to repent of our most innocent actions, inasmuch as we may well suppose that in a more excellent nature they would have been carried on with greater perfection and dignity; and we should wish to do likewise. When I reflect upon the behavior of my youth in comparison with that of my old age, I find that I have generally conducted myself with order according to my opinion; this is all that my resistance can do. I do not flatter myself; in similar circumstances I should always be the same. It is not a spot, but rather a dye with which I am stained all over. I know no repentance that is superficial, lukewarm, put on for appearance. It must affect me in every part before I call it so, and it must seize my vitals and afflict them as deeply as God sees into me and as completely.

As to business, many good opportunities have escaped me for want of successful management. And yet my deliberations were sound enough according to the circumstances confronting them; it is their way to choose always the easiest and the safest course. I find that in my former deliberations I have, according to my rule, proceeded with discretion, considering the state of the matter proposed to me, and I should do the same for a thousand years to come in similar situations. I do not consider what it is now, but what it was then when I was deliberating on it.

The strength of any plan depends on the time; circumstances and things eternally shift and change. I have in my life stumbled into some serious and important errors, not for want of good counsel, but for want of good luck. There are secret and unforeseeable parts in the matters we handle, especially in the nature of men; mute conditions, that make no show, unknown sometimes to the possessors themselves, that are brought out and aroused by chance occasions. If my prudence could not penetrate into or foresee them, I bear it no grudge; its duty is confined within its own limits. It is the outcome that beats me, and if it favors the side I have refused, there is no remedy; I do not blame myself; I accuse my luck and not my work. That cannot be called repentance.

Phocion had given the Athenians some advice that was not followed. The affair, nevertheless, succeeding prosperously contrary to his opinion, someone said to him, "Well, Phocion, are you content that things are going so well?" "I am very well pleased," he replied, "that it has happened this way; but I do not repent of having counseled the other." When my friends address themselves to me for advice, I give it freely and clearly, without being deterred, as nearly everybody is, at the thought that, the affair being hazardous, it may come out contrary to my opinion, whereby they may have cause to reproach me for my counsel; I am quite indifferent about that. For they will be wrong, and I should not have refused them this service.

I can hardly blame anyone but myself for my mistakes and misfortunes. For, indeed, I seldom consult the advice of others, unless as a polite gesture, except when I stand in need of scientific information or knowledge of the facts. But in things where I have to use only my judgment, other men's reasons may serve to support me but hardly to turn me aside. I listen to them all with good will and civility; but, to the best of my memory, I have never up to this moment believed in any but my own. In my opinion they are but flies and atoms that distract my will. I value little my own opinions, but I value as little those of others. Fortune pays me properly. If I do not accept advice, I give even less. I am consulted very little, but I am believed even less; and I know no undertaking, either public or private, that has been straightened up and brought back on its course by my advice. Even they whom Fortune had in some sort tied to my advice have more readily let themselves be governed by any other brain. And like a man who is just as jealous of the rights of my repose as of the rights of my authority, I am better pleased that it should be so. Leaving me alone, they act according to the attitude I profess, which is to settle and wholly contain myself within myself. To me it is a pleasure not to be interested in other men's affairs and to be relieved of any responsibility for them.

In all affairs, once they are past, however it may be, I have little regret. For this idea relieves me of concern, that they had to happen thus; there they are in the great stream of the universe and in the chain of Stoical causes. Your fancy cannot by wish and imagination disturb one point without all the order of things being overturned, both the past and the future.

As to the rest, I abominate that accidental repentance which old age brings along with it. He who said of old that he was obliged to his age for having rid him of sensual pleasure was of an opinion different from mine; I shall never be thankful to impotence for any good it may do me. *Nor will Providence ever be seen so hostile to her own work that debility should be ranked among the best things.*[5] Our appetites are rare in old age; a profound satiety seizes us after the act. I see nothing of conscience in this; crabbedness and weakness imprint in us a sluggish and rheumatic virtue. We must not permit ourselves to be so wholly carried away by natural alterations as to let them corrupt our judgment. Youth and pleasure did not formerly cause me not to recognize the face of vice in sensual pleasure; neither does that distaste that years bring me cause me now not to recognize the face of sensual pleasure in vice. Now that I am no longer in it, I judge of it as if I were. I, who shake it up lively and attentively, find my reason is the very same that I had in my more licentious age, unless, perhaps, in so far as it has become weakened and impaired by growing old. And I find that though it refuses, out of consideration for the interests of my bodily health, to put me in the oven of this pleasure, it would not do so, any more than formerly, for the sake of my spiritual health. I do not esteem it more valiant in seeing it *hors de combat*. My temptations are so broken and mortified that they are not worth its opposition. Merely by holding out my hands, I exorcise them. Should anyone present again to it

---

[5] Quintilian

the former concupiscence, I fear it would have less power to resist than it used to have in other days. I do not see that reason in itself judges anything otherwise than it did then, nor that it has acquired any new light. Wherefore, if there is improvement, it is an impaired improvement.

Miserable kind of remedy, to owe our health to disease! It is not for our misfortune to perform this service, but it is for the good fortune of our judgment to do so. One does not make me do anything by evils and afflictions, except to curse them. That is for people who are roused only by lashes. My reason has a much freer course in prosperity. It is much more distracted and absorbed in digesting pains than pleasures. I see much more clearly in fair weather. Just as health admonishes me more cheerfully, so does it more usefully than sickness. I advanced as far as I could towards the reform and regulation of my life when I had health to enjoy. I should be ashamed and chagrined if the misery and misfortune of my old age were to be preferred before my good, healthy, sprightly, vigorous years, and if men were to esteem me, not for what I have been, but for what I have ceased to be.

In my opinion it is living happily and not, as Antisthenes said, dying happily in which human felicity consists. I have not striven to attach grotesquely a philosopher's tail to the head and body of a ruined man; or that this wretched remainder should disown and give the lie to the loveliest, soundest, and longest part of my life. I want to present myself and make myself seen uniformly throughout. If I had to live my life over again, I should live it just as I have lived it. I neither complain of the past, nor do I fear the future. And, if I do not deceive myself, things have gone on within me just about as they have without. It is one of the main obligations I have to fortune, that the course of my bodily state has been carried on with each thing in its season. I have seen its shoots, blossoms, and fruit, and now I see its withering. Happily, since it is naturally. I bear the infirmities I have much more easily because they come seasonably, and also because they make me with greater pleasure remember that long felicity of my past life. Likewise my wisdom may well be of the same stature in this age as in the other; but it was much more accomplished and graceful when fresh, gay, and natural than bowed down, peevish, and labored, as it is at present. I renounce, then, these casual and painful reformations.

God must touch our hearts. Our conscience must amend of itself, by the fortifying of our reason and not by the weakening of our appetites. Sensual pleasure is in itself neither pale nor discolored because of being discerned by dim and bleary eyes. We ought to love temperance for itself, and out of respect for God, Who has commanded it, and chastity; what is lent us by catarrhs and what I owe to the favor of my colic is neither chastity nor temperance. We cannot boast that we despise and resist sensual pleasure if we do not see it, if we do not know it, and its graces, its strength, its most alluring beauty. I know both, and it is proper for me to speak. But it seems to me our souls in old age are subject to more troublesome maladies and imperfections than in youth. I used to say the same when young; then they mocked me for my beardless chin. I still say so now that my gray hairs give me the authority to do so. We call the captiousness of our humors and the distaste for present things, wisdom. But, in truth, we do not so much forsake vices as we change them, and, in my opinion, for the worse. Besides a foolish and doddering pride, a tiresome prattle, crabbed and unsociable humors, superstition, and a ridiculous attention to riches when we have lost the use of them, I find therein more envy, injustice, and malice. Old age fixes more wrinkles in our minds than it does on our faces; and souls are never, or very rarely, seen that in growing old do not smell sour and musty. Man moves as a whole towards his growth and his decay.

In observing the wisdom of Socrates and many circumstances of his condemnation, I should dare to believe that he himself, by prevarication, in some measure purposely contributed to it, being, at seventy, so soon to suffer the benumbing of the rich movement of his mind and the dimming of its accustomed brightness.

What metamorphoses do I see age make every day in many of my acquaintances! It is a powerful malady which naturally and imperceptibly steals in upon us. A great provision of study and great precaution are needed to avoid the imperfections it loads us with, or at least to weaken their progress. Notwithstanding all my retrenchments, I feel age gaining on me foot by foot. I hold out as well as I can. But I do not know where it will bring even me at the last. At all events, I am content that the world may know whence I shall have fallen.

OF THREE KINDS OF SOCIETY

WE MUST NOT NAIL ourselves so fast to our humors and dispositions. Our principal talent is to know how to apply ourselves
to various practices. It is to exist, but not to live, to keep ourselves tied and bound by necessity to only one course. Those
are the fairest souls that have the most variety and the greatest
suppleness. Here is an honorable testimony to the elder Cato:
*His mind was so equally versatile in all things that whatever
he was doing you would say that he was born for that alone.*[1]
If it was for me to train myself in my own manner, there is no
fashion, however good, to which I should want to be so fixed as
to be unable to detach myself from it. Life is an uneven, irregular, and multiform movement. It is not to be friends to ourselves, even less our own masters, it is to be enslaved, to follow
ourselves incessantly and to be so seized by our inclinations
that we cannot turn aside from them or bend them. I say it now
because I cannot easily extricate myself from the importunity
of my soul, inasmuch as it cannot commonly linger except on
subjects in which it becomes involved or employ itself except
tensely and with all its being. However slight the subject that
is offered to it, it is inclined to enlarge it and stretch it to such
a point that it has to labor over it with all its strength. Its idleness is to me for that reason a very painful occupation and
harmful to my health. Most minds need foreign matter to
quicken and exercise them; mine needs it rather to quiet and
rest itself, *the vices of idleness must be shaken off by occupation,*[2] for its most laborious and chief study is to study itself.

---

[1] Livy   [2] Seneca, *Epistles*

Books are for it one of the types of occupation that distract it from its study. Upon the first thoughts that come to it, it stirs about and makes trial of its vigor in every direction, exercises its power of manipulation, now in respect to strength, and now in respect to order and grace, arranges, moderates and fortifies itself. It has the means to rouse its faculties by itself. Nature has given to it, as to all others, matter enough of its own for its own use, and subjects enough of its own upon which to invent and judge.

Meditation is a powerful and full study for anyone who knows how to test and exercise himself vigorously; I would rather fashion my mind than furnish it. There is no weaker or stronger occupation, according to the mind concerned, than that of entertaining one's own thoughts; the greatest minds make it their occupation, *for whom to live is to think*.[8] So Nature has favored it with this privilege, that there is nothing we can do so long, nor any action to which we can more commonly and easily apply ourselves. It is the employment of the gods, says Aristotle, from which arises both their happiness and ours.

Reading serves me particularly to arouse my reason by presenting various subjects to it, to put my judgment to work, not my memory. Few conversations, therefore, arrest my attention if devoid of vigor and effort. It is true that gracefulness and beauty fill and take possession of me as much, or more, than weight and depth. And inasmuch as I grow sleepy in all other conversation and give it only the husk of my attention, it often happens in such drooping and feeble sort of talk, superficial talk, that I either make nonsensical and stupid remarks and answers, ridiculous and unworthy of a child, or still more ineptly and rudely maintain an obstinate silence. I have a dreamy way of withdrawing into myself, and added to that a dull and childish ignorance of many ordinary things. By these two qualities I have merited that five or six stories can be truthfully

[8] Cicero, *Tusculans*

told about me, as ridiculous as can be told about anyone whatever.

Now proceeding with my subject, this exacting disposition of mine makes me particular in my relations with men (I have to cull them out on the sorting-tray) and makes me unfit for ordinary actions. We live and deal with ordinary people. If their society is troublesome to us, if we disdain to adapt ourselves to humble and vulgar souls, and the humble and vulgar are often as well regulated as the subtlest (all wisdom is foolish that does not adjust itself to the common folly), we should no longer meddle either with our own affairs or those of others: both public and private affairs have to be straightened out with these people. The least strained and most natural motions of the soul are the most beautiful; the best occupations are the least forced. Lord, how good a service does wisdom perform for those whose desires it accommodates to their power! There is no more useful knowledge. "According to one's ability" was the refrain and favorite saying of Socrates, a saying of great substance. We must direct and fix our desires on the easiest and nearest things. Is it not a foolish humor of mine to be out of harmony with a thousand to whom my fortune joins me and with whom I cannot dispense, in order to hold fast to one or two who are beyond the circle of my associations, or rather to a fantastic desire for a thing I cannot obtain? My mild habits, enemies of all bitterness and harshness, may very well have freed me from envy and animosities; to be loved I do not say, but never did any man give more occasion not to be hated. But the coldness of my society has rightly robbed me of the good will of many, who are to be excused if they interpret it in another and worse sense.

I am very capable of gaining and maintaining rare and select friendships. Inasmuch as I clutch so hungrily at acquaintances that suit my taste, I make myself known to them, I throw myself at them so eagerly that I hardly fail to attach myself and to make an impression where I strike. I have often made happy proof of this. In ordinary friendships I am somewhat barren and cold, for my movement is not natural if it is under full sail. Besides, my fortune, having shaped me from my youth to a sole and perfect friendship and given me a taste for it, it has in truth given me somewhat of a distaste for others and has too firmly imprinted on my fancy that it is an animal of company, not of the herd, as that ancient said. Moreover by nature I am loath to communicate myself by halves and moderately, and with that servile and suspicious prudence which is prescribed for us in the intercourse of these numerous and imperfect friendships; and it is particularly prescribed for us in these times when we cannot talk about the world except dangerously or falsely.

Yet I well see that whoever, like myself, has as his objective the conveniences of life (I mean the essential conveniences) ought to avoid like the plague these fastidious and over-nice humors. I should admire a soul having different levels, that can both extend itself and relax, that is well off wherever its fortune bears it, that can talk with a neighbor about his building, his hunting, and his lawsuit, and with pleasure converse with a carpenter and a gardener. I envy those who know how to be familiar with the humblest of their following and strike up a conversation with their own servants.

And I do not like the advice of Plato, that we should always talk to our servants, whether male or female, in lordly language, without playfulness and familiarity. For besides the reason I have mentioned, it is inhuman and unjust to turn this casual prerogative of fortune to such account. And the establishments wherein the least disparity exists between masters and servants seem to me the most equitable.

Others study how to elevate and hoist their minds to a high-flown pitch; I, how to humble mine and bring it to rest. It is faulty only in extending itself.

> Of Aeacus' line you tell
>> And wars waged 'neath the walls of sacred Troy.
> You do not say how much a jar
>> Of Chian wine will cost, who'll heat my bath,
> By what host's roof and at what time
>> I shall escape from the Pelignian cold.[4]

Thus, as the Lacedemonians' valor needed moderation and the sweet and pleasing sound of the playing of flutes to soothe it in battle lest it should hurl itself into temerity and fury, whereas all other nations commonly make use of shrill and strong voices and sounds that incite and heat the soldiers' courage to the last degree; so it seems to me, contrary to the usual view, that in the use of our minds we have for the most part more need of lead than wings, of coolness and repose than ardor and agitation. Above all it is, in my opinion, really playing the fool to act like a clever man among those who are not, to speak always affectedly, "to talk on the point of a fork." You must lower yourself to the level of those with whom you are and sometimes affect ignorance. Lay aside your strength and subtlety; in common usage it is enough to preserve order. As to the rest, drag along the ground if they desire it.

The learned are apt to stumble on this stone. They are always making a parade of their learning and are sowing their books everywhere. They have in these days so flooded the boudoirs and the ears of the ladies with it that if they have not retained its substance, they at least have the air of doing so. For every sort of subject and matter, however low and common, they make use of a new and learned way of speaking,

> In it they voice their fears, wrath, joys and cares,
> In it they vent each secret of the soul.
> What more? They copulate in learned style;[5]

and they quote Plato and Aquinas in things for which the first man met would serve as well as a witness. The learning that

---

[4] Horace, *Odes*   [5] Juvenal

could not penetrate to their mind is left on their tongue. If the wellborn ladies will believe me, they will content themselves with setting off their own natural riches; they conceal and cover their beauties beneath foreign beauties. It is a great folly to put out your own light in order to shine by a borrowed light. They are interred and buried under art. *All of them right out of a bandbox.*[6] It is because they do not sufficiently know themselves. The world has nothing fairer; it is for them to do honor to the arts and to beautify beautifiers. What do they need but to live beloved and honored? They have and know only too much for that. They need only rouse a little and rekindle the faculties that are in them. When I see them attached to rhetoric, astrology, logic, and similar drugs, so vain and useless for their purposes, I begin to fear that the men who recommend it to them do it in order to have means of governing them under this pretext, for what other excuse could I find for them? It is enough that they can, without our instruction, regulate the charm of their eyes to gaiety, severity, or sweetness, season a denial either with sternness, suspense, or favor, and that they need no interpreter for the speeches that we make in courting them. With this knowledge they wield the rod and rule the teachers and the school. If, nevertheless, it irritates them to give way to us in anything whatever, and if they want out of curiosity to have their share in books, poetry is a diversion suited to their needs; it is a wanton and subtle art, bedecked, verbal, all pleasure, all show, like themselves. They will also derive several advantages from history. In philosophy, from the part useful for living, they will select those teachings that will train them to judge our humors and traits, to defend themselves from our treacheries, to control the indiscretion of their own desires, to be careful of their liberty, to lengthen the pleasures of life, and to bear humanly the inconstancy of a lover, the rudeness of a husband, and the importunity of years and wrin-

---

[6] Seneca, *Epistles*

kles; and similar things. This is, at the most, the part that I should allot to them in learning.

There are some natures that are private, retiring, self-contained. My essential nature is suited to communicate and manifest itself; I am all in the open and in sight, born for society and friendship. The solitude that I love and preach is chiefly no other than to lead back my thoughts and feelings into myself, to restrain and check, not my steps, but my desires and cares, resigning all solicitude for outside things, and mortally avoiding servitude and obligation, and not so much the crush of men as the crush of business. Solitude of place, to say the truth, extends me rather and expands me; I throw myself into affairs of state and into the world more readily when I am alone. At the Louvre and in the crowd I retire and contract within my own skin; the crowd thrusts me back upon myself, and I never entertain myself so wantonly, so licentiously, or so personally as in places of respect and ceremonious prudence. Our follies do not make me laugh, it is our wisdom that does. By nature I am no enemy of the commotion of courts; I have therein passed part of my life, and I am constituted to bear myself cheerfully in great companies, provided it is at intervals and at my own time. But that sensitive discrimination of which I have been speaking ties me by force to solitude, even at home in the middle of a numerous family and in a house that is one of those most frequented by visitors. I see people enough there but rarely those with whom I like to converse; and I there reserve both for myself and others an unusual freedom. There is a truce on ceremony there, on waiting upon people and ushering them out, and such other painful prescriptions of our etiquette (Oh, servile and tiresome custom!); everyone there governs himself according to his own way; whoever wants to communes with his own thoughts; I remain mute, dreamy, and shut up in my thoughts without any offense to my guests.

The men whose society and intimate acquaintance I seek are

those they call well-bred, talented men; and the idea of these gives me a distaste for the rest. It is, if rightly taken, the rarest of our types, a type chiefly due to Nature. The purpose of this society is simply intimacy, association, and conversation; the exercise of minds, without any other fruit. In our talks all subjects are alike to me; it makes no difference to me if there is neither weight nor depth in them; charm and pertinency are always there. Everything there is tinctured with mature and constant good sense and mixed with goodness, frankness, gaiety, and friendship. It is not only on the subject of lineal substitutions and of the affairs of kings that our mind shows its beauty and strength; it shows it as much in private conversations. I know my men even by their silence and their smiles, and make them out better, perhaps, at table than in the council chamber. Hippomachus used to say acutely that he knew good wrestlers by seeing them merely walk in the street. If learning is pleased to join in our talk, she will not be turned away; even she being not magisterial, imperious, importunate, as she commonly is, but subordinate and docile. We seek only to pass the time; when it is time to be instructed and preached to, we will go seek her on her throne. Let her lower herself to us for once, if she so please; for, useful and desirable as she is, I imagine that even in need we could well do entirely without her, and carry out our business without her. A mind wellborn and practised in intercourse with men makes itself fully agreeable by its own efforts. Art is nothing else but the list and register of the productions of such minds.

The society of beautiful and well-bred women is also pleasant to me: *For we too have knowing eyes.*[7] If the soul has not so much to enjoy in this society as in the first, the bodily senses, which, moreover, participate to a greater extent in this one, bring it to a proportion near to the other, though, in my opinion, not equal. But it is a relationship in which a man must

---

[7] Cicero, *Paradoxes*

stand a little on his guard, especially those in whom the body exerts great influence, as in my case. I burned myself in it in my youth and suffered all the frenzies that poets say befall those who let themselves go in this relationship without order or judgment; it is true that this lash of the whip has since been a lesson to me,

> Whatever Greek escaped Capharean rocks
> Will always steer from the Euboean seas.[8]

It is madness to fix all our thoughts upon it and to engage in it with a furious and reckless passion. But, on the other hand, to engage in it without love and without obligating our will, to play, like actors, the common rôle of these times and customs, and not put anything into it of our own but words, is, indeed, to provide for our safety, but in a very cowardly manner like a man who would abandon his honor, profit, or pleasure for fear of danger. For it is certain that from such an association they who cultivate it can expect no fruit that will please and satisfy a noble soul. We must have genuinely desired that which we expect to take a genuine pleasure in enjoying; I say this even though those who assume the mask of passion may be unjustly favored by Fortune, which often happens, because there is no woman, however ill favored she may be, who does not think herself very attractive, and who does not find her recommendation either in her youth, her laugh, or her graceful movements; for there are no completely ugly women, any more than completely beautiful ones. And the Brahmin girls who have no other recommendation go into the market place, after the people have been assembled by the common crier for that purpose, and display their matrimonial parts to see if on account of these at least they are not worth enough to get a husband.

Consequently there is not one who does not easily let her-

---

[8] Ovid, *Tristia*

self be persuaded by the first vow of devoted service that a man makes to her. Now from this common and ordinary treachery of the men of today there has to happen that which experience already shows us, that they rally together and cast themselves back upon themselves or among each other to escape us; or else that they too range themselves on their side by the example we give them, play their part in the farce, and lend themselves to this affair, without passion, without care, and without love. *Not subject to passion, whether their own or another's,*[9] they think, according to the argument of Lysias in Plato, that they may the more profitably and conveniently give themselves up to us the less we love them. It will turn out as in plays; the public will have in it as much pleasure, or more, than the comedians.

For my part, I no more recognize Venus without Cupid than maternity without offspring; they are things that mutually lend and owe their essence to one another. Thus this cheat recoils on him who does it. It does not cost him much, but he also gets nothing worth having. They who made Venus a goddess considered that her principal beauty was incorporeal and spiritual; but the beauty that these people hunt after is not so much as human, or even brutish. The animals will not have it so gross and so earthy! We see that imagination and desire often heat and incite them before the body does; we see, in both sexes, that in the crowd they practise choice and selection in their affections, and that they have between them relationships of longstanding affection. Even those to whom old age denies bodily vigor still tremble, neigh, and quiver with love. We see them before the act full of hope and ardor, and when the body has played its game, still delighting in the sweetness of the memory; and we see some that swell with pride upon withdrawing from there and who, tired and sated, utter songs of joy and triumph over it. The man that has only to relieve his body of a natural necessity has no occasion to trouble others with such

---

[9] Tacitus, *Annals*

elaborate preparations; that is not meat for a gross and coarse hunger.

As one who does not ask that men should think me better than I am, I will say this of the errors of my youth. Not only on account of the danger to health (and yet I was not able to go about it well enough to avoid having two touches of it, slight, however, and incipient), but also out of disdain, I did not indulge much in venal and public intimacies. I wanted to sharpen this pleasure by difficulty, by desire, and by a certain glory. And I like the way of the Emperor Tiberius, who in his love affairs was as much taken with modesty and noble birth as by any other quality, and the caprice of the courtesan Flora, who never gave herself to less than a dictator, a consul, or a censor, and took her pleasure in the dignity of her lovers. Doubtless pearls and brocade, titles and attendants, add something to it.

Moreover I placed great value on the mind, only provided the body was not faulty; for, to answer in all conscience, if the one or the other of these two beauties necessarily had to be wanting, I should have chosen rather to renounce the mental. It has its use in better things; but in the matter of love, a matter chiefly related to seeing and touching, something may be done without the graces of the mind; without the graces of the body, nothing. Beauty is the true advantage of women. It is so entirely their own that ours, though it requires somewhat different features, is only at its peak when identified with theirs, boyish and beardless. It is said that at the Grand Turk's court those youths who because of their beauty are in his service, which are an infinite number, are at the latest dismissed at twenty-two years of age. Reason, wisdom, and the offices of friendship are found better among men, therefore they govern the affairs of the world.

These two kinds of society are fortuitous and dependent upon others. The one is annoying by its rarity, the other withers with age; so that they would not have provided sufficiently for the needs of my life. The society of books, which is the third, is much more certain and more our own. It yields the other advantages to the first two but has the constancy and facility of its service for its own share. It goes side by side with me throughout my course and accompanies me everywhere. It comforts me in old age and solitude. It eases me of the weight of a tiresome idleness and frees me at all hours from distasteful company. It blunts the stings of grief unless they are extreme and master me. To divert myself from a troublesome fancy I have only to resort to my books; they easily turn my thoughts to themselves and steal the other from me. And yet they do not revolt at seeing that I have recourse to them only for want of those other more real, lively, and natural pleasures; they always receive me with the same countenance.

He may well go on foot, it is said, who leads his horse by the bridle; and our James, King of Naples and Sicily, who, handsome, young, and healthy, had himself carried about the country on a stretcher, lying on a miserable feather pillow, clad in a robe of gray cloth, with a cap of the same, attended meanwhile by great royal pomp, litters, led horses of all sorts, gentlemen and officers, showed a still weak and faltering austerity. The sick man is not to be pitied who has his cure up his sleeve. In the experience and practice of this maxim, which is a very true one, all the benefit I reap from books consists. I use them, in fact, hardly any more than those who do not know them. I enjoy them as misers do treasures, through knowing that I may enjoy them when I please. My soul finds full satisfaction and contentment in this right of possession. I do not travel without books, either in peace or in war. Nevertheless many days, and sometimes months, will pass without my looking at them. It will be soon, say I to myself, or tomorrow, or when I please. Time runs on and passes away meanwhile without harming me. For it is impossible to express how much repose and rest I take in considering that they are beside me to give me pleasure whenever I wish, and in recognizing how much assistance they bring to my life. It is the best provision I have found for this human journey, and I thoroughly pity men of understanding who lack it. I more readily accept any other sort of amusement, however trivial, since this one cannot fail me.

When at home, I turn aside a little more frequently to my library, from which in one sweep I oversee my establishment. I am over the entrance, and I see below me my garden, my farmyard, my courtyard, and into most parts of my house. There I thumb through now one book and now another, without order and without plan, by disconnected fragments. Now I meditate; now I record and dictate, walking to and fro, these fancies of mine here.

It is on the third floor of a tower. The first is my chapel, the second a bedroom and a dressing room, where I often sleep in order to be alone. Above it is a great wardrobe. Formerly this was the most useless part of the house. There I pass most of the days of my life and most of the hours of the day. I am never there at night. Adjoining it there is a rather elegant study, where a fire may be laid in the winter, very pleasantly lighted by a window. And if I did not fear the trouble more than the expense, the trouble that drives me from all business, I could very easily join on each side a gallery a hundred paces long and twelve broad, on the same level, having found all the walls raised, for some other purpose, to the necessary height. Every place of retirement requires a place to walk. My thoughts go to sleep if I seat them. My mind does not move unless my legs stir it. Those who study without a book are all in the same fix.

The shape of my library is round with only sufficient flat wall for my table and chair; as it curves about, it offers me at a glance all my books arranged in five rows of shelves all around. It has three views of varied and wide prospect and sixteen paces of clear space in diameter. I am not so continually there in winter; for my house is perched upon a little hill, as its name implies, and it has no room more exposed to the winds than this one, which pleases me by being somewhat inaccessible and out of the way, both for the benefit of the exercise and for keeping back the crowd. There is my seat of authority. I endeavor to make my rule over it absolute and to sequester this one corner from all society, conjugal, filial, and civil. Elsewhere I have only verbal authority, in reality a divided one. Miserable, in my opinion, the man who has in his home no place wherein to be by himself, wherein to pay court privately to himself, wherein to hide. Ambition pays her followers well by keeping them always on show, like a statue in a market place: *A great fortune is a great bondage.*[10] They have not even their privy for privacy. I have thought nothing so harsh in the austere life that our monks practise as this which I observe in a certain one of their orders, to have as a rule perpetual society in any place and the presence of numbers of them in any action whatsoever. I find it somewhat more bearable to be always alone than never to be able to be alone.

If anyone tells me that it is to degrade the Muses to make use of them only as a plaything and pastime, he does not know, as I do, the value of pleasure, play, and pastime. I would very nearly say that any other aim is ridiculous. I live from day to day and, with reverence be it spoken, live only for myself; my plans end there. I studied when young for ostentation; later, a little, to acquire wisdom; now for recreation; never for gain. A vain and prodigal fancy that I had for this sort of furniture, not to supply merely my needs, but three steps beyond that, in order to cover and adorn myself with it, I have long ago abandoned.

Books have many charming qualities for those who know how to choose them; but there is no good without trouble; it is a pleasure that is no clearer and purer than the others;

---

[10] Seneca, *Consolation to Polybius*

it has its disadvantages, and very grave ones. The mind is exercised by them, but the body, the care of which I have not forgotten either, remains in the meantime without action, becomes heavy and downcast. I know of no excess more harmful to me nor more to be avoided in this decline of my life.

These are my three favorite and particular occupations. I do not speak of those which I owe to the world out of civic obligation.

ON SOME VERSES OF VIRGIL

IN PROPORTION as useful thoughts are fuller and more substantial, so are they also more absorbing and burdensome. Vice, death, poverty, disease are grave and grievous subjects. A man's mind should be provided with the means to sustain and combat evils and with the rules of right living and right thinking, and he should often be stirred up and exercised in this noble study. But by a mind of the ordinary sort it should be done with pauses and with moderation; it will becomes disordered if too continually strained.

When I was young, I had need of self-solicitations and admonitions to keep me to my duty; gaiety and health, it is said, do not go so well with those grave and serious meditations. I am at present in another situation. The conditions of old age are only too ready to give me admonitions, prudence, and preaching. From an excess of sprightliness I have fallen into that of gravity, which is more troublesome. For that reason I now purposely let myself go a bit to license and sometimes occupy my mind with youthful and wanton thoughts to give it a rest. I am now only too sober, too heavy, and too mature. The years read to me every day lectures of coldness and temperance. This body of mine avoids disorder and dreads it. It is now my body's time to guide the mind towards reformation. It dictates in its turn and more roughly and imperiously. It does not leave me an hour, sleeping or waking, at ease from the lessons of death, patience, and repentance. I defend myself from temperance, as I formerly did from sensual pleasure. It drags me back too much, even to insensibility. Now I want to be master of myself in every way. Wisdom has its excess and has no less need of moderation than folly. Therefore lest I should dry up, wither, and weigh myself down with prudence, in the intervals which my infirmities allow me,

> Lest that my mind should evermore be bent
> And fixed on subjects full of discontent,[1]

I very gently turn aside and avert my glance from the stormy and cloudy sky I have before me, which, thanks be to God, I can, indeed, regard without fear, but not without struggle and study, and I amuse myself in the remembrance of my past youth,

> The mind longs to regain what it has lost,
> And by things past is totally engrossed.[2]

Let childhood look forward and age backward; was not this the meaning of Janus' double face? Let the years haul me along, if they will, but backward! As long as my eyes can discern that lovely expired season, I shall now and then turn them that way. If it escapes from my blood and my veins, I shall not at least root the image of it out of my memory,

> The man lives twice, who can the gift retain
> Of memory, to enjoy past life again.[3]

Plato ordains that old men should be present at the exercises, dances, and games of young people, that they may enjoy in others the suppleness and beauty of body which they no longer possess and recall to memory the grace and charm of that flourishing age; and he desires that in these sports the honor of victory be accorded to the young man who has given the most recreation and joy to the greatest number of them.

---

[1] Ovid, *Tristia*   [2] Petronius, *Satyricon*   [3] Martial

I formerly used to mark the oppressive and gloomy days as extraordinary. These are now my ordinary ones; the extraordinary are the fine and bright ones. I shall soon reach such a point that I shall leap for joy at an unfamiliar favor when nothing pains me. Though I tickle myself, I can no longer force a smile from this wretched body of mine. I am merry only in fancy and in dreams, in order by artifice to divert the melancholy of age. But, indeed, it would require another remedy than a dream: feeble struggle of art against nature. It is great simplicity to lengthen and anticipate human discomforts, as everyone does. I prefer to be old a shorter time than to be old before my time. I seize on even the slightest occasions of pleasure I can meet. I know, indeed, by hearsay several kinds of pleasures that are discreet, strong, and showy; but common opinion has not power enough over me to give me an appetite for them. I do not so much desire them grand, magnificent, and ostentatious as soft, easy, and ready to hand. *We depart from nature; we surrender to the people, who are not a good guide in anything.*[4]

My philosophy is in action, in natural and present practice, little in fancy. Would that I could take pleasure in playing at cob-nut or in spinning a top!

For he put not the peoples' shouts before the commonweal.[5]

Pleasure is an unambitious quality; it thinks itself rich enough in itself without adding to it the reward of reputation and is best pleased in the shade. A young man who should spend his time in trying the flavors of wines and of sauces ought to be whipped. There is nothing that I have known less about and valued less. Now I am beginning to learn. I am greatly ashamed of it, but what can I do? I am even more ashamed and vexed at the occasions that impel me to it. It

---

[4] Seneca, *Epistles*   [5] Ennius, in Cicero, *De Officiis*

is for us to have our little fling and trifle away the time; it is
for the young to stand upon their reputation and to put their
best foot forward. They are going into the world and the
world's opinion; we are retiring from it. *Let them reserve to
themselves arms, horses, spears, clubs, tennis, swimming, and
races; and, of their numerous sports and exercises, leave to
us old men the dice and knuckle-bones.*[6] Even the laws send
us home. I can do no less to gratify this wretched condition
into which my age is forcing me than to furnish it with toys
and playthings, as we do children; after all we are dropping
back into childhood. Both wisdom and folly will have enough
to do to support and aid me by alternate services in this
calamity of old age:

> A dash of folly with your wisdom mix.[7]

I likewise avoid the lightest prickings; and those that formerly would not have made a scratch now pierce me through
and through; my habit of body begins to be so easily disposed to illness! *To a frail body every indisposition is painful.*[8]

> And a sick mind nothing that's hard endures.[9]

I have always been sensitive and susceptible to pain; I am
now more tender and exposed on all sides,

> The slightest blow will break a dish that's cracked.[10]

My judgment keeps me, indeed, from kicking and grum-
bling at the inconveniences that nature orders me to endure,
but it does not keep me from feeling them. I, who have no
other aim than to live and be merry, would run from one end
of the world to the other to seek out one good year of pleas-

---

[6] Cicero, *De Senectute*   [7] Horace, *Odes*   [8] Cicero, *De Senectute*
[9] Ovid, *Ex Ponto*   [10] Ovid, *Tristia*

ant and jocund tranquillity. A melancholy and dull tranquillity may be enough for me, but it benumbs and stupefies me; I am not contented with it. If there is any person, any good company, in country or city, in France or elsewhere, whether stay-at-home or traveling, who likes my humor and whose humors I like, they have only to whistle in their palms, and I will come and furnish them with essays in flesh and bone.

Seeing it is the privilege of the mind to rescue itself from old age, I advise mine to do so with all the power I have; let it keep green, let it flourish meanwhile, if it can, like mistletoe upon a dead tree. But I fear it is a traitor. It has formed such a close brotherly bond with the body that it abandons me at every turn to follow that in its need. I take it aside to flatter it, I make advances to it, but all for nothing. I try in vain to draw it away from this union, to offer it both Seneca and Catullus, both ladies and royal dances; if its companion has the colic, it seems to have it too. Even the activities that are peculiarly and properly its own cannot then be maintained; they give clear indications of a cold in the head. There is no sprightliness in its productions if at the same time there is not any in the body.

Our masters are wrong when, seeking the causes of the extraordinary soarings of our soul, besides attributing them to a divine ecstasy, to love, to martial fierceness, to poetry, to wine, they have not given its due share to health—bubbling, vigorous, full, lazy health, such as once the freshness of youth and freedom from care regularly supplied me with. That fire of gay spirits kindles in the mind vivid and bright flashes beyond our natural capacity and some of the most joyous, if not the most extravagant enthusiasms. It is then no wonder if a contrary state weighs down my spirits, nails them down, and produces a contrary effect.

> When body weakens, the work has no lift.[11]

---

[11] Maximianus

And yet my mind expects me to be grateful to it because, so it says, it gives itself much less to this union than is usual with most men. Let us at least, while we have truce, drive away the evils and difficulties of our relations:

> While yet we may,
> Let's chase old age with gloomy brow away;[12]

Severe things should be sweetened with pleasantries.[13]
I love a gay and sociable wisdom and fly from all sourness and austerity of manners, considering every surly countenance as suspect:

> The dismal arrogance of a gloomy face.[14]

> And the austere crowd have dissipations, too.[15]

I heartily agree with Plato when he says that an easy or a difficult humor greatly affects the goodness or wickedness of the soul. Socrates had a stable countenance, but serene and smiling, not stable like that of the elder Crassus, who was never seen to laugh.

Virtue is a pleasant and cheerful quality.

I know well that very few people will frown at the license of my writings who do not have more reason to frown at the license of their own thoughts. I conform well enough to their inclinations, but I offend their eyes. It is a finely adjusted taste that carps at the writings of Plato and glides over his supposed relations with Phaedo, Dion, Stella, and Archeanassa. *Let us not be ashamed to say what we are not ashamed to think.*[16]

I hate a surly and gloomy spirit that slides over all the pleasures of life and seizes and feeds upon its misfortunes: like flies that cannot stick to a very smooth and polished

---

[12] Horace, *Epodes*   [13] Sidonius Apollinaris, *Epistles*   [14] Buchanan, *Baptistes*   [15] Martial   [16] Author unknown

body, but fix and rest themselves upon rough and uneven
places, and like leeches that suck and crave only bad blood.

As to the rest, I have ordered myself to dare to say all that
I dare to do, and I dislike even unpublishable thoughts. The
worst of my actions and qualities does not appear to me so
ugly as it appears ugly and base not to dare to confess it.
Everyone is discreet in confession, they ought to be so in action. Boldness in doing wrong is somewhat balanced and
curbed by boldness in confessing it. If a man obliged himself
to tell all, he would oblige himself to do nothing about which
he is forced to keep quiet. God grant that this excessive
license of mine may draw our men the whole way to freedom,
up above those timorous and affected virtues born of our imperfections; that at the expense of my immodesty I may
draw them even to the point of reason! A man must see and
study his vice to correct it. They who conceal it from others
commonly conceal it from themselves. And they do not think
it hidden enough if they themselves see it; they withdraw
and disguise it from their own consciousness. *Why does no
man confess his vices? Because he is yet in them; it is for a
waking man to tell his dream.*[17]

The diseases of the body become clearer as they grow. We
find that to be the gout which we called a cold or a sprain.
The diseases of the mind become more obscure as they grow
stronger; the most sick are the least sensible of them. That
is why they must often be handled in the light of day, with a
pitiless hand, be opened up and torn from the hollow of our
bosom. As in good deeds, so also in evil deeds, the mere confession is sometimes a reparation. Is there any ugliness in doing wrong that can excuse us from the duty of confessing it?

It is so painful to me to dissemble that I avoid being entrusted with another's secrets, not having the boldness to
deny what I know. I can keep silent about it, but deny it I
cannot without effort and discomfort. To be really secretive a

[17] Seneca, *Epistles*

man must be so by nature, not by obligation. It is of little use to be secretive in the service of a prince if one is not a liar to boot. If the man who asked Thales the Milesian whether he ought solemnly to deny that he had committed adultery had applied to me, I should have told him that he ought not to do it for lying seems to me still worse than adultery. Thales advised him quite otherwise, bidding him to swear in order to shield greater fault by lesser. Yet this counsel was not so much a choice as a multiplication of vices.

Whereupon let us say this in passing, that we offer a fair deal to a man of conscience when we propose to him some difficulty as a counterpoise to a vice; but when we shut him up between two vices, we put him to a rough choice, as Origen was at the choice of either practising idolatry or letting himself be carnally enjoyed by a big Ethiopian villain who was brought before him. He submitted to the first condition, and sinfully, someone said. On this basis those women would not be in the wrong, according to their erroneous view, who protest to us these days that they would rather burden their consciences with ten men than one mass.

If it is an indiscretion thus to publish one's errors, there is no great danger of its becoming a precedent and custom; for Aristo said that the winds men fear most are those that uncover them. We must tuck up this ridiculous rag that covers our habits. They send their conscience to the brothel and keep their countenance in order. Even traitors and assassins espouse the laws of decorum and there fix their duty so that neither can injustice complain of incivility nor malice of indiscretion. It is a pity that a wicked man is not also a fool, and that outward decency should palliate his vice. These facings are only suitable to a good and sound wall that deserves to be preserved or whitewashed.

Favoring the view of the Huguenots, who condemn our private and auricular confession, I confess myself in public, scrupulously and purely. Saint Augustine, Origen, and Hip-

pocrates have published the errors of their opinions; I, besides, those of my morals. I am hungering to make myself
known, and I care not to how many provided it be done
truly; or to put it better, I hunger for nothing, but I have
a mortal fear of being taken for something other than I am
by those who come to know my name.

What can that man who does everything for honor and
glory think to gain by showing himself to the world in a
mask, concealing his true being from public knowledge?
Praise a hunchback for his fine figure, and he must take it
for an affront. If you are a coward and men honor you for
your valor, is it of you that they are speaking? They take
you for another. I should as soon honor the fellow who took
pleasure in the salutes that people gave him, thinking he was
master of the company, when he was one of the meanest of
the retinue. As Archelaus, King of Macedonia, was walking
along the street, somebody poured water upon him; those
who were with him said he ought to punish him: "Yes, but,"
he said, "he did not pour the water upon me, but upon the
man he took me for." Informed that the people were speaking ill of him, Socrates replied: "Not at all; there is nothing
in me of what they say." For my part, if anyone should commend me for being a good pilot, for being very modest or
very chaste, I should owe him no thanks. And similarly, if
anyone should call me a traitor, a robber, or a drunkard, I
should consider myself just as little offended. They who do
not rightly know themselves may feed upon false approba·
tions; not I, who see myself and search myself to my very
vitals and who know very well what belongs to me. I am
content to be less commended, provided I am better known.
I may be reputed a wise man in such a sort of wisdom as I
take to be folly.

I am annoyed that my Essays are of use to the ladies only
as a common piece of furniture, furniture for the parlor. This
chapter will put me in the boudoir. I love their society when

somewhat private; in public it is without favor or savor.

In farewells we stir up more than ordinarily our affection for the things we are giving up. I am taking my last leave of the pastimes of the world; these are our last embraces. But let us come to my theme.

What has the act of generation, an act so natural, so necessary, and so just, done to mankind, for us not to dare to speak of it without shame and for us to exclude it from all serious and orderly conversation? We boldly pronounce the words *kill, rob, betray,* and the other we would dare only to mutter between the teeth. Does it mean that the less of it we breathe out in words, the more right we have to swell our thoughts with it? For it is amusing that the words which are least used, least written, and most hushed are the best known and most generally familiar. No person, whatever his age or morals, is ignorant of them any more than of the word bread. They are impressed on everyone without being expressed, without voice, and without form. It is also amusing that it is action we have placed in the asylum of silence, from which it is a crime to tear it forth even for the purpose of accusing it and passing judgment on it. Nor do we dare to take the whip to it except in indirect and figurative terms. A great favor for a criminal to be so execrable that justice thinks it unjust to touch and see him: free and saved by the advantage of the severity of his condemnation. Is it not the same as with books that sell better and become more public through being suppressed? For my part I will take Aristotle at his word when he says that bashfulness is an ornament to youth, but a reproach to old age.

These verses are preached in the ancient school, a school to which I much more adhere than to the modern (its virtues appear to me to be greater, its vices less):

> They sin as much who Venus greatly flee
> As they who in her suite too frequent are.[18]

---

[18] Plutarch, *That a Philosopher should converse with Princes*

Thou, goddess, thou alone dost rule the world,
And nothing springs to heaven's shining shores
Without thee, nor does aught grow gay and lovable.[19]

I know not who could have set Pallas and the Muses at
variance with Venus and made them cold towards Love; but
I know of no deities that are better suited to each other or
more indebted to each other. Whoever deprives the Muses of
their amorous fancies robs them of the finest entertainment
they have and of the noblest matter of their work; and whoever makes Love lose the communication and service of poetry disarms him of his best weapons. In this way they
charge the god of intimacy and loving-kindness and the patron goddesses of humanity and justice with the vice of ingratitude and lack of appreciation.

I have not been so long cashiered from the rolls and retinue
of this god that my memory is not still aware of his power
and worth,

> I make out traces of my flame of old.[20]

There are yet some remains of heat and emotion after the
fever,

> In wintry years may this glow not fail me.[21]

Withered and drooping as I am, I still feel some tepid remains of that past ardor:

> As the deep Aegean, though abates the gust
> Of the North or South that rolled and tossed it first,
> Quiets not, but still retains the roar and swell
> Of tossing, towering waves.[22]

But from what I know about it, the power and worth of this
god are more lively and animated in the depiction of them
in poetry than in their own essence,

---

[19] Lucretius   [20] Virgil, *Aeneid*   [21] Joannes Secundus, *Elegies*
[22] Tasso, *Jerusalem Delivered*

And poetry has an exciting touch.[23]

It has an indescribable air more amorous than Amor itself.
Venus is not so beautiful all naked and alive and panting as
she is here in Virgil:

> The goddess ceased, and, with the soft embrace
> Of snowy arms about his body wound,
> Fondled him, as he faltered. Quick he caught
> The wonted fire: the old heat pierced his heart,
> Ran through his melting frame: as oftentimes
> A fiery rift, burst by the thunder-clap,
> Runs quivering down the cloud, with flash of light.
> . . . . So saying, he gave
> The embrace he longed for, on her bosom sank,
> And wooed calm slumber to o'erglide his limbs.[24]

What holds my attention is that he depicts her a little too
passionate for a married Venus. In this discreet pact the appetites are not usually so wanton; they are sober and more
blunted. Love hates people to be attached to one another by
any tie but himself, and he takes a very feeble hand in intimacies established and maintained under a different heading, as marriage is. Family standing and means therein rightly
have as much weight or more than charm and beauty. We
do not marry for ourselves, whatever they may say; we
marry as much or more for our posterity, for our family. The
custom and interest of marriage concern our race far beyond
our lives. Therefore I like the practice of having it arranged
by a third hand rather than by our own, and by the good
sense of others rather than that of our own. But how opposite
is all this to love pacts! Besides it is a kind of incest to employ in this venerable and sacred alliance the efforts and extravagance of amorous license, as I think I have said elsewhere. A man, says Aristotle, should approach his wife
discreetly and soberly, lest the pleasure of being fondled too

---

Juvenal   [24] Virgil, *Aeneid*

lasciviously should transport her beyond the bounds of reason. What he says upon the account of conscience, the physicians say upon the account of health: "that a pleasure excessively hot, voluptuous, and assiduous spoils the seed and hinders conception." They say, on the other hand, "that to a wearying encounter, as this is by its nature, one should offer himself rarely and at considerable intervals in order that a proper and fertile heat may be stored up,

> That thirstily may snatch up love
> And hoard it deep within.[25]

I know of no marriages that are sooner troubled and fail than those that progress by means of beauty and amorous desires. It needs more solid and more constant foundations, and we should go about it with circumspection; this fervent ardor is worth nothing to it.

They who think they honor marriage by joining love to it act, it seems to me, like those who, to do honor to virtue, hold that nobility is nothing else but virtue. They are, indeed, things that have some relation to one another, but there is a great deal of difference. There is no need to mix up their names and titles; we wrong both of them to confuse them. Nobility is a fine quality and introduced with good reason; but, inasmuch as it is a quality depending upon others and may come to rest on a vicious and worthless person, it is in esteem infinitely below virtue. It is a virtue, if it is one, that is artificial and apparent, depending upon time and fortune, varying in form according to countries, living and mortal, with no more source than the river Nile, genealogical and common to many, a thing of succession and resemblance, drawn by inference, and a very weak inference. Knowledge, strength, goodness, beauty, riches, all other qualities enter into the exchange and the relations between people; this is

---

[25] Virgil, *Georgics*

self-consuming and of no use in the service of others. There was proposed to one of our kings the choice of two competitors for the same office, one of whom was a nobleman, the other was not. He ordered that, without respect to that kind of quality, they should choose the man who had the most merit; but if the worth of the competitors should be entirely equal, that they should take nobility into consideration. This was to give it its proper place. Antigonus said to a young man, a stranger to him, who asked him for the post of his father, a valiant man who had just died: "My friend, in such preferments as these I do not consider so much the nobility of my soldiers as I do their prowess."

In truth it ought not to be as with the functionaries of the kings of Sparta, trumpeters, musicians, cooks, who were succeeded in their posts by their children, however ignorant they might be, in preference to the most experienced in the trade.

The people of Calicut make of their nobles a superhuman species. They are debarred from marriage and from every profession other than war. Of concubines they may have their fill, and the women as many lovers, without being jealous of one another. But it is a capital and unpardonable crime to mate with a person of a different class. And they think themselves polluted if they have been merely touched by them in passing, and as their nobility is marvelously injured and damaged by it, they kill those who have only approached a little too near them, so that the ignoble are obliged to cry out as they walk, like the gondoliers of Venice at the corners of streets to avoid colliding; and the nobles order them to jump aside in whichever direction they please. By this means the one avoids what they consider as a perpetual ignominy, and the other a certain death. No length of time, no princely favor, no office or virtue or wealth can ever make a plebeian become noble. To which this custom contributes, that marriages are forbidden between different trades; a girl of shoemaker stock cannot marry a carpenter, and the parents are obliged to train their sons exactly for the father's calling, and for no other, by which means the distinction and continuity of their fortune is maintained.

A good marriage, if there is such a thing, rejects the company and conditions of love. It tries to reproduce those of friendship. It is a sweet partnership in life, full of constancy, trust, and an infinite number of useful and substantial services and mutual obligations. No woman who appreciates its taste,

Whom the nuptial torch has joined with welcome light,[26]

would wish to serve her husband as a mistress or paramour. If she is lodged in his affection as a wife, she is much more honorably and securely lodged. Even if he is paying passionate attention elsewhere, let anyone even then ask him on whom he had rather a disgrace should fall, his wife or his mistress, whose misfortune would most afflict him, and for whom he wishes the most honor. These questions admit of no doubt in a sound marriage.

And that so few are observed to be happy is a sign of its price and value. If well arranged and rightly taken, there is no finer element in our society. We cannot do without it, and yet we go on belittling it. The outcome is that which is seen in cages: the birds outside despair of getting in, and those inside are equally anxious to get out. Socrates, when asked whether it was better to take or not to take a wife, replied, "Whichever a man does, he will repent it." It is a contract to which the saying may very fitly be applied, *man to man* is either *a god* or *a wolf*.[27] To build it up many qualities must come together. It is found nowadays better fitted to simple souls, souls of ordinary people, where luxury, curiosity, and

---

[26] Catullus   [27] Cecilius, in Symmachus, *Epistles;* Plautus, *Asinaria*

idleness do not disturb it so much. But unruly humors, such as mine, that hate any sort of restraint and obligation are not so suited to it,

> And it is pleasanter for me to live with neck unyoked.[28]

Of my own choice I would have fled from marrying Wisdom herself if she would have had me. But say what we will, the custom and practice of everyday life carry us along. Most of my actions are guided by example, not by choice. In any case I did not really urge myself to it, I was led and drawn to it by outside occasions. For not only inconvenient things, but nothing exists, however ugly, vicious, and abhorrent, that may not become acceptable through some condition or circumstance; so unsteady is human footing. And I certainly was brought to it more ill-prepared then and more reluctant than I am now that I have tried it. And, however licentious I am considered to be, I have in truth more strictly observed the laws of marriage than I had either promised or expected. It is too late for a man to kick once he has let himself be hobbled. A man must manage his liberty wisely; but having once submitted to obligation, he must confine himself within the laws of common duty, at least make an effort to do so. Those who enter into this pact with the intent of conducting themselves with hatred and contempt act unjustly and inappropriately; and this pretty rule that I notice passing from hand to hand among the women like a sacred oracle,

> Serve your husband as a master,
> And guard against him as a traitor,

which is to say, "Bear yourself towards him with a constrained, inimical, and distrustful reverence," a war cry and

---

[28] Maximianus

challenge, is equally unjust and harsh. I am too mild for such
thorny projects. To tell the truth, I have not yet arrived at
such perfection of cleverness and subtlety of wit as to confound reason with injustice and to laugh at all order and
rule that does not suit my taste. Because I hate superstition,
I do not immediately throw myself into irreligion. If a man
does not always perform his duty, he ought at least to love
and acknowledge it; it is treachery to marry without binding
oneself. Let us proceed.

Our poet sets forth a marriage that is fully harmonious
and very well matched in which, nevertheless, there is not
much loyalty. Did he mean that it is not impossible to yield
to the efforts of love and yet reserve some duty towards marriage, and that it may be injured without being completely
broken? A serving-man may connive against his master
whom, however, he does not hate. Beauty, opportunity, and
destiny (for destiny has also a hand in it),

> fate rules o'er those parts
> Which clothing hides; for if the stars become adverse,
> All semblance of virility will be of no avail,[29]

have attached her to a stranger; not so wholly, perhaps, but
that there remains some tie by which she is attached to her
husband. They are two plans which have routes that are distinct and not confused. A woman may yield to a certain man
whom she would by no means have married; I do not mean
because of the condition of his fortune, but even because of his
personal qualities. Few men have married their mistresses without repenting it. And even in the other world. What an unhappy life did Jupiter lead the wife whom he had first frequented and enjoyed freely in love affairs! It is as the proverb
goes, "to cack in the basket and then put it on your head."

---

[29] Juvenal

I have seen in my time, in a good family, love shamefully and dishonorably cured by marriage; the considerations are too different. Without being disturbed, we love two different and contrary things. Isocrates said that the city of Athens pleased after the fashion of ladies whom men serve for love. Everyone liked to come there to take a turn and pass the time; no one liked it so well as to espouse it, that is, to settle there and make it his residence. I have been vexed to see husbands hate their wives only because they themselves do them wrong. At least we should not love them less for our own fault; at least through our repentance and compassion they should become dearer to us.

They are different ends, he says, and yet in some sort compatible. Marriage has utility, justice, honor, and constancy for its share; a flat pleasure, but more general. Love is founded on pleasure alone and, indeed, its pleasure is more exciting, livelier, and sharper, a pleasure inflamed by difficulty. There must be in it a sting and a smart. It is no longer love if it is without darts and without fire. The bounty of ladies is too profuse in marriage and dulls the point of affection and desire. Observe what pains Lycurgus and Plato take in their laws to avoid this disadvantage.

Women are not at all in the wrong when they refuse the rules of life that have been introduced into the world, inasmuch as it is the men who made them without their consent. There is naturally bickering and dispute between them and us; the closest agreement we have with them is still turbulent and stormy. In the opinion of our author, we treat them without consideration in this: after we have discovered that they are incomparably more capable and ardent in the act of love than we, which was so affirmed by that priest of antiquity who was first a man and then a woman,

And in both forms was Venus known to him;[30]

---

[30] Ovid, *Metamorphoses*

and, moreover, after we have learned from their own mouths
the proof that was once given in different centuries by an
Emperor and an Empress of Rome, famous master workmen
in that pursuit (he, indeed, deflowered in one night ten Sarmatian virgins, his captives, but she actually gave herself in
one night to twenty-five bouts, changing company according
to her need and liking,

> Still raging with the fever of desire
> Her veins all turgid, and her blood all fire,
> Weary, but unsatisfied, she withdrew) ;[31]

and after the dispute which took place in Catalonia when a
woman complaining of her husband's too assiduous attentions, not so much, I believe, because she was inconvenienced
by them (for I believe miracles only in matters of faith) as,
under this pretext, to curtail and curb, in even that which is
the fundamental act of marriage, the authority of husbands
over their wives and to show that their churlishness and malice extend beyond the nuptial bed and tread under foot even
the graces and sweets of Venus; to this complaint the husband, a really brutish and perverted man, replying that even
on fasting days he could not do with less than ten, there in-
tervened that notable sentence of the Queen of Aragon, by
which, after mature deliberation with her council, this good
queen, to give for all time a rule and example of the moderation and modesty required in a just marriage, decreed the
number of six a day as a lawful and necessary limit, reducing
and giving up a great part of the needs and desires of her sex
in order to establish, she said, an easy and consequently a
permanent and immutable pattern. At this the doctors cry
out, "What must the female appetite and concupiscence be
when their reason, their reformation, and their virtue are
taxed at such a rate!" Considering these differing opinions
of our sexual needs, and that Solon, chief of the lawgiving

---

[31] Juvenal

school, fixes this conjugal intercourse, in order to keep it from failing, at only three times a month, and after having believed and preached all this, we have gone and given them continence as their particular share, and upon final and extreme penalties.

There is no passion more demanding than this which we expect them alone to resist, not simply as an ordinary vice, but as an abomination and execration, worse than irreligion or parricide; while we, at the same time, give way to it without blame or reproach. Even those of us who have tried to master it have sufficiently admitted how difficult, or rather how impossible, it was by using material remedies to subdue, weaken, and chill the body. On the other hand, we would have them healthy, vigorous, plump, well nourished, and chaste at the same time; that is to say, both hot and cold. For marriage, whose function we say it is to keep them from burning, brings them but little refreshment as we now live. If they take a husband in whom the vigor of youth is still seething, he will take pride in expending it elsewhere:

> Bassus, for shame! at length give o'er,
> Or I to justice must my cause resign;
> What I demand is yours no more:
> I bought it, and assert it mine.[32]

The philosopher Polemon was rightly haled before justice by his wife for sowing in a barren field the fruit that was due to the genital field. If they take one of those other broken down men, there they are in full wedlock worse off than virgins or widows. We think them well provided for because they have a man beside them, just as the Romans held Clodia Laeta, a Vestal virgin, to have been violated because Caligula had approached her, though it was averred that he did no more than approach her. But their need, on the contrary, is thereby augmented, since the contact and company

---

[32] Martial

of any man whatever rouses their heat, which in solitude would remain more quiet. And for the purpose, it is likely, of rendering their chastity more meritorious by this circumstance and consideration, Boleslaus and Kinge his wife, King and Queen of Poland, by mutual agreement consecrated it by a vow, while lying together on their very wedding night, and kept it even in the face of marital opportunities.

We train them from childhood in the affairs of love. Their charm, their attire, their knowledge, their language, and all their instruction have only this end in view. Their governesses imprint nothing in them but the idea of love, even if only in depicting it to them constantly in order to make them disgusted with it. My daughter (the only child I have) is now at the age at which the law allows the most forward girls to get married; she is of backward constitution, slight and tender, and has accordingly been brought up by her mother in a retired and particular manner, so that she is only now beginning to throw off her childish simplicity. She was one day reading a French book in my presence. She encountered the word "fouteau," the name of a familiar tree. The woman to whose care she is committed stopped her short somewhat severely and made her skip over that dangerous step. I let her alone in order not to disturb their rules for I never concern myself with that sort of government. Feminine polity has a mysterious procedure, we must leave it to them. But if I am not mistaken, the conversation of twenty lackeys could not in six months' time have so impressed in her imagination the meaning and use and all the consequences of the sound of those wicked syllables as this good old woman did by her reprimand and interdict.

> With pliant limbs the ripened maid
> Now joys to learn the wanton tread
> Of dance Ionic, and to prove
> Her childhood dreams of love forbid.[63]

---

[63] Horace, *Odes*

Just let them give up formality a little, let them talk freely, compared with them we are but children in the knowledge of these things. Listen to them describing our wooing and our conversation; they will make you clearly understand that we bring them nothing they have not known and digested without our help. Can it be, as Plato says, that they were once dissolute boys? My ear one day happened to be in a place where without being suspected it could snatch some of the remarks exchanged between them. Why can I not repeat it? By our Lady, I said, let us be off right now to study the phrases of Amadis and the books of Boccaccio and Aretino in order to look clever; we certainly are making fine use of our time! There is neither word, nor example, nor maneuver that they do not know better than our books; it is a discipline that is born in their veins,

> Venus herself inspired them,[34]

which those good schoolmasters, Nature, Youth, and Health, continually breathe into their souls. They have no need to learn it; they breed it.

> Not more delighted is the milk-white dove,
>   (Or if there be a thing more prone to love,)
> Still to be billing with her mate, than is
>   Woman with every man she meets to kiss.[35]

If this natural violence of their desire were not held a little in check by the fear and sense of honor with which they have been provided, we should be shamed. The whole movement of the world reduces itself and tends to this pairing; it is a matter infused throughout; it is a center to which all things turn. We still see some of the edicts of wise old Rome drawn up for the service of love and the precepts of Socrates for the instruction of courtesans:

---

[34] Virgil, *Georgics*   [35] Catullus

Besides, the Stoic's little books
Among silk cushions love to lie.³⁶

Zeno, among his laws, also set up rules for the spreading
apart and the attack in deflowering. What was the intent of
the philosopher Strato's book, "Of Carnal Conjunction"?
And of what did Theophrastus treat in those he entitled, one
"The Lover," the other "Of Love"? Of what Aristippus in
his work "Of Ancient Delights"? What is the aim of Plato's
so extended and lively descriptions of the boldest amours of
his time? And of the book on "The Lover" by Demetrius
Phalerius?" And "Clinias, or the Ravished Lover" by Heraclides Ponticus? And Antisthenes' "Of Begetting Children,"
or "Of Weddings," and the other "Of the Master or the
Lover"? And that of Aristo, "Of Amorous Exercises"? Those
of Cleanthes, one "Of Love," the other "Of the Art of Loving"? The "Amorous Dialogues" of Sphoerus and the fable
of Jupiter and Juno by Chrysippus, shameless beyond all tol-
eration, and his fifty very lascivious Epistles? For I must
pass by the writings of the philosophers who followed the
Epicurean sect. Fifty deities were in ancient times assigned
to this office, and there were nations where, to assuage the
lust of those who came to their devotions, they kept girls and
boys in the temples for their enjoyment, and it was an act of
ceremony to use them before going to service. *Doubtless in-
continence is necessary for the sake of continence; a confla-
gration is extinguished by fire.*³⁷

In most parts of the world that member of our body was
deified. In one and the same province some flayed off the skin
to offer and consecrate a piece of it; others offered and consecrated their seed. In another the young men publicly pierced
and opened it up in several places between the flesh and the
skin, and through the openings thrust skewers, the longest
and thickest that they could stand; and of these skewers they

---

³⁶ Horace, *Epodes*   ³⁷ Tertullian, *De Pudicitia*

afterwards made a fire as an offering to their gods. They were judged to be of little vigor and chastity if they were daunted by the violence of this cruel pain. Elsewhere the most sacred magistrate was revered and known by that member, and in many ceremonies an effigy of it was carried in pomp in honor of various divinities.

The Egyptian ladies, in the festival of the Bacchanals, carried about their necks a wooden one, exquisitely carved, big and heavy according to each one's capacity, besides which the statue of their god exhibited one which surpassed in size the rest of the body.

Around here the married women shape with their kerchiefs a figure of one on their foreheads to boast of the enjoyment they have from it; and coming to be widows, they put it in back and bury it beneath their coifs.

The most modest matrons of Rome thought it an honor to offer flowers and garlands to the god Priapus; and the virgins, at the time of their espousals, were made to sit upon his least seemly parts. And I know not but that I have in my time seen some semblance of a like devotion. What was the meaning of that ridiculous part of the breeches worn by our fathers and which is still seen on our Swiss? What is the purpose of the show we now make of the shape of our pieces under our galligaskins, and what is worse, often by falsehood and imposture above their natural size? I have half a mind to believe that this sort of garment was invented in the best and most conscientious ages that people might not be deceived and that every man might publicly and frankly give an account of his capacity. The most simple peoples still have it somewhat corresponding to the real size. In those days the workman was taught the art, just as is done in taking the measure of an arm or a foot.

That good man who, when I was young, castrated so many fine and antique statues in his great city that the eye might not be corrupted, following the advice of that other ancient worthy:

> To display nude bodies to the public view
> Is the start of shame;[38]

should have called to mind that, as in the mysteries of the Bona Dea[39] all semblance of masculinity was excluded, no progress would be made if he did not also have horses and asses castrated, and all nature in short.

> For all earthly creatures, both man and beast,
> Fishes of the deep, herds, gay-feathered birds,
> Dash on to passion's flames.[40]

The gods, says Plato, have furnished us with a disobedient and tyrannical member which, like a furious animal, attempts by the violence of its appetite to subject all things to itself. In like manner to women they have given a greedy and ravenous animal which, if denied its food in season, grows wild, impatient of delay, and breathing its rage into their bodies, stops up the passages and arrests breathing, causing a thousand kinds of ills, until, having imbibed the fruit of the common thirst, it has plentifully moistened and sown the ground of their matrix.

Now my legislator should also have considered that perhaps it is a more chaste and useful practice to let them know the living reality betimes than to let them guess it according to the freedom and heat of their imagination. Instead of the real parts, they substitute through hope and desire others that are three times greater. And a certain man of my acquaintance ruined himself by exposing his in a place where he was not yet in a position to put them to their more serious use.

---

[38] Ennius, in Cicero, *Tusculans*   [39] Roman goddess of chastity
[40] Virgil, *Georgics*

What mischief is not done by those enormous pictures that the boys scatter over the passages and staircases of royal houses? From them they acquire a cruel contempt for our natural capacity. And how do we know that Plato did not have this in mind when he prescribed, after the example of other well-established states, that men and women, young and old, should in gymnastics appear naked in view of one another? The Indian women, who see the men stark naked, have at least cooled their sense of sight. And, although the women of the great kingdom of Pegu, who have nothing to cover them below the waist but a cloth slit in front and so narrow that, whatever appearance of modesty they seek to have, you see the whole of them at each step, may tell us that it is a device to allure the men to them and to draw them away from the intercourse with men to which that nation is completely addicted, it could be said that they lose more by it than they gain, and that a complete hunger is sharper than one that has been satisfied at least by the eyes. Moreover Livia used to say that to a virtuous woman a naked man is no more than a statue. The Lacedemonian women, more virginal as wives than our maidens are, saw every day the young men of the city stripped naked in their exercises, little mindful themselves to cover their thighs in walking, considering themselves, as Plato says, sufficiently covered by their virtue without a hoop skirt. But a wonderful power of temptation has been attributed to nudity by those men, referred to by Saint Augustine, who questioned whether women at the universal judgment shall rise again in their own sex, and not rather in ours, for fear of still tempting us in that holy state.

In brief, we allure and flesh them by every means; we incessantly heat and stir up their imagination, and then we belly-ache. Let us confess the truth: there is scarcely one of us who is not more afraid of the shame that his wife's vices may bring upon him than his own, who does not give more attention (wonderful charity!) to the conscience of his good spouse than to his own, who would not rather commit theft and sacrilege and have his wife be a murderess and a heretic than that she should not be more chaste than her husband.

And they will gladly offer to go to the law courts to seek a living and to war to seek a reputation rather than in the midst of idleness and pleasure to have to keep so difficult a guard. Do not they see that there is neither merchant, nor lawyer, nor soldier who does not leave his business to run after this other, nor the porter and the cobbler, all weary and fagged out as they are with labor and hunger?

> Would you, for rich Achaemenes' hoard,
> Or wealth Mygdonian of fat Phrygia,
> Or for Arabia's full-stored palaces,
> Give up one lock of fair Licymnia
>
> While to your kisses sweet her neck so white
> She bends, or gently cruel she denies
> Those which, if snatched, would give her more delight,
> And which to pluck the fruit she sometimes tries?[41]

Iniquitous appraisal of vices! Both we and they are capable of a thousand corruptions more harmful and unnatural than lust. But we form and weigh vices not according to nature but according to our interest, whereby they assume such unequal shapes. The severity of our decrees makes the addiction of women to this vice more serious and evil than its nature admits of and involves it in consequences that are worse than their cause.

I do not know whether the exploits of Alexander and Caesar surpass in arduousness the determination of a beautiful young woman, brought up after our fashion in the open view and movement of the world, assailed by so many contrary examples, keeping herself entire in the midst of a thousand continual and powerful solicitations. There is no more thorny activity, nor more active, than this inactivity. I consider it

---

[41] Horace, *Odes*

easier to wear a suit of armor all one's life than a maiden-head; and the vow of chastity is the most noble of all vows, as being the hardest to keep: "The power of the devil is in the loins," says Saint Jerome.

Certainly we have resigned to the ladies the most arduous and most vigorous of human duties, and we leave to them the glory of it. That ought to serve as a singular spur to persist in it. It gives them a fine opportunity to confront us and to trample under foot that vain pre-eminence in valor and virtue that we claim over them. They will find, if they pay attention to it, that they will not only be very esteemed for it, but also better beloved. A gallant man does not give up his pursuit for being refused, provided it be a refusal of chastity, not of choice. It is useless for us to swear and complain; we lie, we love them the better for it. There is no allurement like a modesty that is not severe and forbidding. It is stupid and mean to persist in the face of hatred and disdain, but, against a virtuous and constant resolution mingled with a grateful disposition, it is the exercise of a noble and generous spirit. They may recognize our services to a certain degree and honorably make us feel that they do not disdain us.

For that law that commands them to abominate us because we adore them and to hate us because we love them is certainly cruel, if only for its difficulty. Why should they not give ear to our offers and requests, so long as they keep within the bounds of modesty? Why should they go about surmising that our words strike a more licentious note within? A queen of our time wittily said that to rebuff these advances was a testimony of weakness and an accusation of her own facility, and that a lady who had not been tempted could not boast of her chastity.

The bounds of honor are by no means cut so closely. There is room for it to relax; it can let itself go a bit without transgressing. On the edge of its frontiers there is some free space, indifferent and neuter. He who has been able to pursue and by force run it down even into its corner and stronghold is a very tactless fellow if he is not satisfied with his fortune. The value of the victory is estimated by its difficulty. Would you know what impression your service and merit have made on her heart? Judge of it by her character. Some may grant more who do not grant so much. The obligation of a benefit is entirely relative to the will of him who confers it. The other circumstances that enter into conferring a benefit are mute, dead, and fortuitous. This little may cost her more to grant than it does her companion to grant her all. If in anything rarity is a sign of value, it must be so in this; do not consider how little it is, but how few have it. The value of money changes according to the mould and stamp of the place.

Whatever the spite and indiscretion of some men may make them say in the excess of their discontent, virtue and truth will always recover their advantage. I have known some women whose reputation for a long time suffered under slander to re-establish themselves in the general esteem of everyone by their constancy alone, without any effort or artifice. Everybody is sorry and takes back what he has believed of them; from being a little under suspicion as girls, they advance to the first rank among ladies of virtue and honor. Somebody said to Plato, "The whole world is speaking ill of you." "Let them talk," he said, "I will live so as to make them change their note."

Besides the fear of God and the reward of so rare an honor which ought to incite them to keep themselves unsullied, the corruption of the age we live in compels them to it; and if I were in their place, there is nothing I would not rather do than intrust my reputation to such dangerous hands. In my time the pleasure of telling (a pleasure little inferior to that of doing) was only permitted to those who had some faithful and unique friend, but now the ordinary talk in gatherings and at the table is nothing but boasts of favors received and the secret liberality of ladies. Truly it is too abject and mean-spirited to allow those tender charms to be so cruelly persecuted, worked over, and ransacked by ungrateful, indiscreet fellows who are so fickle.

This immoderate and illegitimate exasperation of ours against that vice springs from the most vain and turbulent disease that afflicts human minds, which is Jealousy.

> Who will keep torch from kindling nearby torch?
> Though they do nought but give, nought's lost thereby.[42]

She and Envy, her sister, seem to me the most foolish of the troop. Of the latter I can scarcely speak; this passion, which is depicted so mighty and powerful, has of its own will no way in me. As to the other, I know her, at least by sight. Animals feel it: the shepherd Crastis having fallen in love with a goat, her ram out of jealousy came and butted his head as he lay asleep and crushed it. We have aggravated the excess of this fever, after the example of some barbarous nations; the best disciplined have been affected by it, which is reasonable, but not carried away by it:

> Ne'er did adulterer, by the husband slain,
> With purple blood the Stygian waters stain.[43]

Lucullus, Caesar, Pompey, Antony, Cato, and other brave men were cuckolds and knew it without stirring up a fracas over it. There was in those days only a fool of a Lepidus who died of grief on that account.

> Oh, miserable and ill-fated wretch
> Dragged by the heels through the wide open gate,
> Whom radishes and mullet play upon.[44]

And the god of our poet, when he surprised one of his companions with his wife, was satisfied with putting them to shame,

---

[42] Ovid, *De Arte Amandi*   [43] Joannes Secundus, *Elegies*   [44] Catullus

> And one of the gods, not of the dour sort,
> Wishes he might that way become disgraced;[45]

and, nevertheless, he is warmed by the sweet caresses she offers him, complaining that for such a thing she should distrust his affection:

> Why are, my goddess, all these reasons tried,
> Say why in me no longer you confide?[46]

Nay, she asks a favor of him for a bastard of hers,

> The mother for her son doth armor crave,[47]

which is generously granted to her; and Vulcan speaks honorably of Aeneas,

> Arms for a valiant hero must be made.[48]

A humanity truly more than human! And I am willing to leave this excess of kindness to the gods:

> Nor is it right to equal men with gods.[49]

As to the confusion of children, besides that the most serious legislators ordain and strive to have it in their republics, it does not concern the women in whom this passion of jealousy is somehow even more strongly fixed:

> And Juno with fierce jealousy inflamed,
> Her husband's daily slips has often blamed.[50]

When jealousy seizes these poor, weak, and unresisting souls, it is pitiful to see how cruelly it torments and tyrannizes over them. It insinuates itself into them under the title of friend-

---

[45] Ovid, *Metamorphoses*   [46] Virgil, *Aeneid*   [47] Virgil, *Aeneid*
[48] Virgil, *Aeneid*   [49] Catullus   [50] Catullus

ship, but once it possesses them, the same causes that served as the foundation of good will serve as the foundation of mortal hatred. Of all the diseases of the mind it is the one to which the greatest number of things serve as nourishment and the fewest as a remedy. The virtue, the health, the merit, the reputation of the husband are the firebrands of their ill will and fury:

> No enmities so keen as those of love.[51]

This fever defaces and corrupts all that is otherwise good and beautiful in them; and there is no action of a jealous woman, however chaste and however good a housewife she may be, that does not smack of bitterness and shrewishness. It is a furious agitation that casts them to an extreme completely opposite to its cause. This was prettily illustrated by one Octavius in Rome. Having lain with Pontia Posthumia, his affection was increased by the enjoyment, and he sought with urgent suit to marry her; not being able to persuade her, his extreme love threw him into the reactions of the most cruel and mortal hatred: he killed her. In like manner the ordinary symptoms of that other amorous disease are intestine hatreds, plots, conspiracies,

> 'Tis known what woman in her rage can do,[52]

and a rage which gnaws into itself the more it is compelled to shelter itself under the pretense of good will.

Now the duty of chastity has a vast range. Is it their will that we would have them curb? That is a very supple and active thing; it is too nimble to be stayed. What if dreams sometimes get such a hold on them that they cannot deny them. It is not in them, nor perhaps in Chastity herself, since she is a female, to ward off lust and desire. If their will alone

---

[51] Propertius   [52] Virgil. *Aeneid*

concerns us, where do we stand? Imagine the great rush if a man had the privilege of being borne at full flight, without eyes to see or tongue to tell, at the right moment to each woman who would receive him.

The Scythian women put out the eyes of all their slaves and prisoners of war to make use of them more freely and secretly.

Oh, what a terrific advantage is opportunity! Should anyone ask me what is the first essential in love, I should answer that it is the ability to seize the right moment; the second likewise and also the third: it is a factor that can achieve everything. I have often wanted luck, but I have also sometimes lacked enterprise. God keep him from harm who can laugh at this! It requires greater temerity in these days, which our young men excuse under the name of ardor; but if the women examined it closely, they would find that it rather proceeds from contempt. I used to be scrupulously afraid of giving offense and am inclined to respect the object of my love. Besides, in these affairs, if you take away respect for it, you do away with glamor. I like to have a man behave in this somewhat like a child: timid, devoted. If not altogether in this, I have in other situations some aspect of the foolish bashfulness of which Plutarch speaks, and the course of my life has been in various ways hurt and marred by it. It is a quality that is very ill suited to my general nature. Yet what are we made up of other than sedition and discord? My eyes are as tender to suffering a refusal as to refusing; and it troubles me so much to be troublesome to others that on occasions when duty compels me to call on the good will of someone in a matter that is doubtful and that may cost him some pains, I do so charily and reluctantly. But if it is for my personal benefit (although Homer truly says that bashfulness is a foolish virtue in a poor man), I usually commission a third person to blush for me. And I deny with just as much difficulty those who make requests of me, so that I have sometimes had the desire to refuse but not the strength to do so.

It is folly, therefore, to attempt to bridle in women a desire that is so ardent and so natural to them. And when I hear them brag of having so virginal and so cold a disposition, I laugh at them: they draw back too far. If it is a toothless and decrepit old woman or a dry and consumptive young one, though it is not altogether credible, at least they have some semblance of truth in saying it. But those who still move and breathe make their position worse by such remarks, inasmuch as ill-considered excuses serve for accusation. Like a gentleman, a neighbor of mine, who was suspected of impotence,

> Whose dagger hanging limper than a tender beet
> At no time raised itself to even middle height,[53]

who, three or four days after his wedding, to justify himself, went about boldly swearing that he had ridden twenty stages the night before, an oath that was afterwards used to convict him of pure ignorance and to nullify his marriage. Besides what those women say has no weight for there is neither continence nor virtue where there is no desire to oppose. "That is true, it must be admitted, but I am not ready to yield." The saints themselves talk that way. This refers to those who boast in good earnest of their coldness and insensibility and who expect to be believed with a serious countenance. For when it is said with an affected look, wherein their eyes belie their words, and when it is said with the jargon of their profession, which makes its point by a reverse approach, I find it amusing. I am very attached to naturalness and plainness, but there is no help for it: if it is not wholly simple and childlike, it is unbecoming in ladies and out of place in that intercourse; it very soon drops into impu-

---

[53] Catullus

dence. Their disguises and the faces they put on deceive only
fools. Lying is there in the seat of honor; it is a byway that
by a backdoor leads us to the truth. If we cannot curb their
imagination, what would we have of them? Deeds! There are
enough of them that escape all outside communication by
which chastity may be corrupted,

> He often does that which he does unseen.[54]

And those whom we fear least are perhaps most to be feared;
their silent sins are the worst:

> A simple prostitute offends me less.[55]

There are acts by which they may lose their virginity
without any immodesty on their part, and what is more,
without their knowledge: *A midwife, for instance, examining
the integrity of some virgin, by malice, unskilfulness, or accident, has destroyed it while inspecting it.*[56] Some have lost
their maidenhead in looking for it; others have destroyed it
in sport.

We cannot precisely circumscribe the actions that we forbid them. Our rules must be formulated in general and ambiguous terms. The very idea we form of their chastity is
ridiculous; for among the extreme examples known to me are
Fatua, the wife of Faunus, who never after her marriage let
herself be seen by any man whatever; and the wife of Hiero,
who never noticed her husband's bad breath, believing that
it was a characteristic of all men. They must become insensible
and invisible to satisfy us.

Now let us confess that the difficulty in judging this duty
lies principally in the will. There have been husbands who
have suffered this mishap not only without blaming their
wives or feeling injured by them, but with singular obligation

---

[54] Martial   [55] Martial   [56] Saint Augustine, *City of God*

to and commendation of their virtue. Some women, who prized their honor above their life, have prostituted it to the furious lust of a mortal enemy to save their husband's life, and have done for him what they would not have done for themselves. This is not the place to produce these examples; they are too lofty and too precious to be displayed in this light; let us reserve them for a nobler setting.

But for examples of more ordinary distinction, are there not every day women who surrender themselves solely for their husbands' advantage and by their express order and mediation? And, in ancient times, Phaulius of Argos offered his wife to King Philip out of ambition, just as was done out of civility by that Galba, who, having entertained Maecenas at supper and observing that his wife and he were beginning to conspire by oglings and signs, let himself sink down upon his cushion, like a man overcome by sleep, in order to forward their understanding. And he revealed it quite graciously; for at this point a servant having had the boldness to lay hands on the plate which was on the table, he shouted at him, "Don't you see, you rogue, that I am asleep only for Maecenas?"

This woman may be of loose conduct and yet be of a more moral will than that other whose conduct bears an orderly outward appearance. As we see some who complain of having vowed themselves to chastity before the age of discretion, I have also seen others sincerely complain of having been vowed to licentiousness before the age of discretion. The vice of the parents, or the force of necessity, which is a rude counsellor, may be the cause. In the East Indies, though chastity was unusually esteemed there, yet custom permitted a married woman to abandon herself to any man who presented her with an elephant, and that was accompanied with a certain glory of having been valued at so high a price.

Phaedo, the philosopher, a man of good birth, after the

taking of his country, Elis, made it his trade to prostitute
the beauty of his youth, as long as it lasted, to anyone that
would pay the price, thereby to gain his living. And Solon,
it is said, was the first in Greece who by his laws gave liberty
to women, at the expense of their chastity, to provide for the
necessities of life, a custom that Herodotus declares to have
been accepted in a number of governments before his time.

And then, what do we gain by this painful anxiety? For
whatever justification there may be for this passion,[57] we
should still have to consider whether it moves us usefully.
Is there anyone who thinks he can by his ingenuity shackle
them?

> Bar and bolt the door; keep her close confined.
> But who guards the guards? Crafty is the wife,
> And she'll begin with them.[58]

What occasion will not serve their turn in so knowing an age?

Curiosity is vicious in all things, but here it is deadly. It
is folly to wish to be enlightened about a disease for which
there is no medicine that does not aggravate it and make it
worse, of which the shame is increased and made public
chiefly by jealousy, and of which the revenge wounds our
children more than it heals us. You will wither and die in the
search for proofs of so obscure a thing.

How miserably have they fared who in my time have succeeded in this search! If the informer does not offer at one and
the same time the remedy and relief, it is injurious information and deserves a dagger-stab more than does the lie given.
We laugh at him who takes pains to prevent it no less than at
him who is unaware of it. The mark of cuckoldry is indelible;
once it is fixed to a man it is there forever; the punishment
brings it forth more than the fault. It is a fine thing to see
your private misfortunes dragged out of obscurity and doubt

---

[57] Jealousy   [58] Juvenal

to be trumpeted forth on the tragic stage, especially misfortunes that only pinch us by being told. For "a good wife" and "happy marriage" is said not of those that are so, but of those of which no man talks. We must be ingenious to avoid this troublesome and useless knowledge. And the Romans had a custom, when returning from a journey, of sending someone on ahead to the house to inform their wives of their coming so as not to surprise them. And for the same reason a certain nation introduced the practice that on the wedding day the priest take the first step with the bride, to free the husband from the doubt and curiosity of examining in the first trial whether she comes to him a virgin or damaged by another's love.

But the world will be talking. I know a hundred respectable men who are cuckolded respectably and not discreditably. A worthy man is pitied, not disesteemed, for it. Go about it so that your virtue may stifle your misfortune, that good men may curse the occasion of it, and that he who wrongs you may tremble at the very thought of it. And then, who escapes being talked of in this sense, from the little man even to the greatest?

> To whom so many legions once did bow,
> And who, poor wretch, was better far than thou.[59]

Do you notice how many decent men are entangled in this reproach in your presence. Bear in mind that neither are you spared in other places. But even the ladies will be laughing at it. And what are they more apt to laugh at in these days than at a peaceable and well-composed marriage? There is not one among you but has made somebody a cuckold; and nature fully runs in parallels, in compensation, and turn for turn. The frequency of this mishap ought by this time to have moderated its bitterness; we shall soon see it become a custom.

Miserable passion! which has this also, that it is incommunicable,

---

[59] Lucretius

And spiteful fortune too denies
To give an ear unto our cries.[60]

For to what friend dare you intrust your griefs, who, if he does not laugh at them, will not make use of them as an approach and an instruction to get a share in the quarry himself. The bitterness as well as the sweets of marriage are kept secret by the wise. And among the other troublesome conditions found in it, this, to a talkative fellow like myself, is one of the chief, that custom makes it improper and prejudicial to communicate to anybody all that we know and feel about it.

To give women the same advice in order to disgust them with jealousy would be time lost. There very being is so steeped in suspicion, vanity, and curiosity that to cure them by any legitimate way is not to be expected. They often recover from this trouble by a form of health much more to be feared than the disease itself. For as there are enchantments that cannot take away the evil but by throwing it upon another, so they are apt, when they lose this fever, to transfer it to their husbands. And yet I know not, to tell the truth, whether a man can suffer worse from them than their jealousy; it is the most dangerous of their conditions, as the head of their members. Pittacus used to say that everyone had his trouble, that his was the jealous temper of his wife, but for which he should think himself perfectly happy. It must be a very grievous misfortune if a man so just, so wise, so valiant felt his whole life poisoned by it; what are we other little fellows to do? The Senate of Marseilles was right to grant the request of the man who asked permission to kill himself so that he might be delivered from his squally wife; for it is a disease that is never removed but by removing the whole piece, and that has no effective remedy but flight or patience, both, however, very hard.

That was, to my mind, an understanding fellow who said

---

[60] Catullus

that a happy marriage was formed of a blind wife and a deaf husband.

Let us also look out that the great and violent severity of obligation we put upon them does not produce two results contrary to our intent: namely, that it may put the pursuers more on edge and make the women more ready to surrender. For as to the first point, by raising the value of the stronghold, we raise the value and desire of the conquest. Might not Venus herself have thus cunningly enhanced the price of her merchandise by making the laws her go-between, knowing how insipid a delight it would be if it was not heightened by fancy and dearness? In short, it is all swine's flesh to which the sauce gives variety, as Flaminius' host said. Cupid is a roguish god, he makes it his sport to wrestle with religion and justice. It is his glory that his power clashes with every other power and that all other rules give way to his.

> He seeks out matter for his sin.[61]

And as to the second point: should we not be less cuckolded if we were less afraid of being so, considering what the nature of women is, for prohibition incites and invites them?

> You would, they won't; you won't, they would.[62]
>
> They think it shame to follow the permitted path.[63]

What better interpretation could we find for Messalina's behavior? She at first made her husband a cuckold in secret, as is commonly done; but carrying on her affairs with too much ease, by reason of her husband's stupidity, she quickly disdained that practice. Behold her now making love openly, acknowledging her lovers, entertaining and favoring them in the sight of all. She wanted him to take notice of it. Since this animal could not be roused by all this, and since he made her

---

[61] Ovid, *Tristia*   [62] Terence, *Eunuchus*   [63] Lucan

pleasures dull and flat by this too lax facility with which he seemed to authorize and make them lawful, what did she do? Wife of a living and healthy emperor, and at Rome, the theatre of the world, at full noon, with public pomp and ceremony, and to Silius, whom she had long before enjoyed, she joins herself in marriage one day when her husband was out of the city. Does it not seem as if she were on the way to becoming chaste through her husband's indifference, or that she sought another husband who might sharpen her appetite by his jealousy and who by opposition might rouse her? But the first difficulty she met with was also the last. The beast woke up with a start. We often have the worst time of it with these insensitive, sluggish men. I have found by experience that this extreme tolerance, when it comes to dissolve, produces the harshest acts of revenge; for anger and fury, being heaped up together and taking fire all of a sudden, discharge all their energy at the first charge,

> And gives full rein to wrath.[64]

He put her to death and a great number of those who were intimate with her, even some who could not help it, having been invited to her bed with scourges.

What Virgil says of Venus and Vulcan, Lucretius had more fitly said of a stolen enjoyment between her and Mars:

> All-powerful Mars,
> He who commands the furious works of war,
> O'ercome by the eternal wound of love,
> Oft throws himself down prone upon your breast.
> Gazing with open mouth, goddess, at you,
> On love he feasts full well his greedy sight,
> And his breath hangs upon your upturned lips.
> Round him, reclining in your arms divine,
> Oh! goddess, shed your charms, and pour forth words
> Of sweetness from your lips.[65]

---

[64] Virgil, *Aeneid*   [65] Lucretius

When I reflect upon this *rejicit, pascit, inhians, molli, fovet, medullas, labefacta, pendet, percurit,* and that noble *circumfusa* mother of the gentle *infusus,* I despise those little conceits and verbal triflings that have since sprung up. Those worthy hands had no need of clever and subtle playing upon words; their language is quite full and rounded-out with a natural and constant vigor. They are all epigram; not the tail alone, but the head, stomach, and feet. There is nothing forced, nothing dragging; it all moves at the same pace. *There whole contexture is manly; they are not concerned about pretty little flowers.*[66] It is not a mild and merely inoffensive eloquence. It is sinewy and solid and does not so much please as it fills and ravishes most the strongest minds. When I see these brave forms of expression, so lively, so profound, I do not say, "This is well said;" I say, "This is well thought." It is the sprightliness of the imagination that elevates and swells the words. *It is the heart that creates eloquence.*[67] Our people call judgment language and fine words full conceptions.

This painting is executed not so much by dexterity of hand as by having the object more vividly imprinted in the soul. Gallus speaks simply because he conceives simply. Horace is not content with a superficial expression; it would betray him. He sees more clearly and farther into the matter. His mind delves into and ransacks the whole storehouse of words and figures wherewith to express itself; and he must have them beyond the commonplace because his conceptions are beyond the commonplace. Plutarch says that he sees the Latin tongue through things. It is the same here; the sense illuminates and brings out the words, no longer words of air, but of flesh and bone. They mean more than they say. Even the feeble-minded show some signs of this; for when I was in Italy I said whatever I pleased in ordinary talk, but in intense discussion I should not have dared to trust myself with an idiom that I

[66] Seneca, *Epistles*   [67] Quintillian

could not bend and turn out of its ordinary course. I want to be able to introduce something of my own.

A language is enriched by the handling and use that talented minds make of it, not so much by innovation as by putting it to more vigorous and various services, by stretching and bending it. They do not bring in new words, but they enrich their own, give more weight and depth to their meaning and use, teach them unaccustomed movements, but discreetly and skilfully. And how little this talent is given to all is seen in the numerous French writings of our time. They are bold and disdainful enough not to follow the common road, but want of invention and of judgment ruins them. There is nothing to be seen in them but a wretched affectation of singularity, of cold and absurd disguises which, instead of elevating, depress the matter. Provided they can be rigged out in newfangled ways, they do not care about the effect. In order to grab a new word they drop the usual which is often more vigorous and sinewy than the other.

In our language I find plenty of stuff but a little lack of style. For there is nothing that might not be made out of our hunting and military jargon, which is a fruitful soil to borrow from; and forms of speech like plants improve and grow stronger by being transplanted. I find it sufficiently abundant but not sufficiently pliable and vigorous. It usually succumbs under a powerful conception. If you strain at it, you often feel it flagging and giving way under you, and that when it fails you, Latin comes to your aid, as Greek does to others. Of some of those words which I have just picked out we find it harder to perceive the energy because the frequent use of them has somewhat debased and vulgarized their beauty for us; as in our vernacular there are found excellent phrases and metaphors whose beauty has withered with age and whose color has become dulled by too common handling. But that takes nothing from their relish for a man who has a good nose, nor does it detract from the glory of those old authors who, it is probable, first brought these words into that luster.

Learning treats of things too subtly, in a manner too artificial and different from the common and natural way. My page makes love and understands it. Read to him Leo Hebreo and Ficino: they speak of him, his thoughts and actions, and yet he does not understand anything in it. I do not recognize in Aristotle most of my ordinary notions; they have been covered and clad in another robe for the use of the school. God grant they may be right! If I were of the trade, I should naturalize art as much as they artify nature. Let us leave Bembo and Equicola alone.

When I am writing, I can very well do without the company and remembrance of books lest they should break into my style. Also, in truth, because good authors humble me too much and dishearten me. I am inclined to do like the painter who, having made a wretched picture of some cocks, ordered his boys not to let any real cock come into his shop. To give myself a little luster I should rather need the device of the musician Antinonides, who, when he had to perform, took care that, either before or after him, the audience should be doused by some other bad singers.

But it is more difficult for me to do without Plutarch. He is so universal and so full that, on all occasions, and however extravagant the subject you have taken up, he will thrust himself into your business and hold out to you a generous hand, inexhaustible in riches and embellishments. It vexes me that he is so greatly exposed to plunder by those who constantly turn to him. I cannot be with him the least bit without purloining a leg or a wing.

For this design of mine, it also suits me to write at home, in an uncivilized region, where I have nobody to assist or correct me, where I usually am not in contact with any man who understands the Latin of his Paternoster, and of French a little less. I might have made it better elsewhere, but the work would have been less my own; and its principal end and perfection is to be precisely my own. I would, indeed, correct an accidental error, which errors I am full of as I run heedlessly on; but the imperfections which are usual and constant with me it would be treachery to remove. When another tells me or I say to myself, "You are too thick in figures of speech. Here is a word of Gascon growth. This is a dangerous phrase." (I do not avoid any of those that are used in the streets of France, those who would fight usage with grammar make fools of themselves.) "This is ignorant reasoning. This is paradoxical reasoning. This one is too extravagant. You often jest. People will think you are telling straight what you are actually saying in make-believe." "Yes," I reply, "but I correct the faults of inadvertence, not those of habit. Do I not speak that way throughout? Do I not represent myself to the life? Enough! I have done what I wanted to do: all the world recognizes me in my book and my book in me."

Now I have an aping and imitative bent. When I used to dabble in writing verses (and I never wrote any but Latin), they clearly disclosed the poet I had last been reading; and some of my first Essays smell a bit of foreign origins. At Paris I speak a somewhat different language than I do at Montaigne. Whatever man I look at attentively easily leaves upon me some impression of himself. Whatever I consider, I usurp: a foolish countenance, a disagreeable grimace, a ridiculous way of speaking. Vices, most of all, as soon as they prick me, they stick to me and will not leave without a shaking. I have more often been known to swear by imitation than naturally.

It is a murderous imitation, like that of the terribly big and strong apes that King Alexander encountered in a certain region of the Indies. Except for that it would have been very difficult for him to master them. But they furnished him the means by that inclination of theirs to imitate everything they saw done. For thus the hunters hit upon the idea of putting on shoes in their sight with many knots tied in the laces, of rigging themselves up in headgear provided with running nooses, and of seeming to anoint their eyes with glue. So those poor beasts were imprudently brought by their apish nature to their own ruin. They glued up their own eyes, put on their own hobbles, and garroted themselves.

That other talent of cleverly mimicking the words and gestures of another on purpose, which often gives occasion to amusement and amazement, is not in me any more than in a stump. When I swear in my own way, it is only, "by God," which is the most straightforward of all oaths. They say Socrates swore by a dog, Zeno by the same interjection which is now in use among Italians, *cappari*, and Pythagoras by water and air.

I am so facile at receiving these superficial impressions without thinking of them that if I have had "Sire" or "Highness" in my mouth for three days in a row, a week after they will slip from me instead of "Excellency" or "Lordship." And what I may have started to say in sport and jest I shall say seriously the next day. Wherefore in writing I am more unwilling to take up well-trod subjects, lest I treat of them at another's expense. Every subject is equally fertile for me. A fly will serve my purpose; and God grant that this I have here in hand has not been taken up at the bidding of as flighty an intent! Let me begin with the subject I please for all subjects are linked to one another.

But I am displeased with my mind in that it ordinarily brings forth its deepest ideas, its wildest, and those which I like the best, unexpectedly and when I am seeking them the least; and then they suddenly vanish, having at the moment nothing to which to attach themselves: on horseback, at table, in bed, but mostly on horseback where my thoughts range most widely. When speaking I am somewhat sensitively jealous of attention and silence; if I am speaking vigorously, whoever interrupts, stops me. In traveling the very demands of the roads cut up conversation; besides that I most frequently travel without company fit for these protracted discussions, whereby I take every occasion to converse with myself. It turns out as in my dreams; while dreaming I recommend them to my memory (for I am apt to dream that I dream), but the next morning I may, indeed, call to mind their color just as it was, whether gay, or sad, or strange, but as to what they were besides, the more I strain to recover them, the more deeply I plunge them into oblivion. Similarly of those fortuitous thoughts that drop into my mind there remains in my memory only a vague image, only as much as I need to make me fret and chafe in pursuit of them futilely.

Well then, laying books aside, and speaking more materially and simply, I find after all that love is nothing else than the thirst for this enjoyment of a desired object, and that Venus is not any other thing than the pleasure of discharging one's vessels, which becomes vicious either by immoderation or indiscretion. For Socrates love is the appetite of generation by the mediation of beauty. And reflecting time and again on the ridiculous titillation of this pleasure, on the absurd, crack-brained, and giddy motions with which it stirs Zeno and Cratippus, the blind rage and the countenance inflamed with fury and cruelty in the sweetest act of love, and then that grave, severe, and ecstatic air in so extravagant an action; and considering that our joys and our excrements have been lodged together pell-mell, and that the supreme sensual pleasure is accompanied, like pain, by faintness and moaning, I believe what Plato says is true, that man is the plaything of the gods,

What a strange sporting cruelty is this? [68]

and that it was in mockery that Nature left to us the most disturbing and the most common of our actions, to make us thereby all alike and to put on the same level fools and wise men, beasts and us. The most contemplative and wisest of men,

[68] Claudian, *in Eutropium*

when I imagine him in that situation, seems to me an impostor to pretend to be wise and contemplative; it is the peacock's feet that humble his pride:

Why may not truth in laughing guise be dressed? [69]

Those who refuse to consider serious ideas in the midst of play act, as someone says, like the man who is afraid to worship the statue of a saint if it is undraped.

We eat and drink, indeed, as beasts do, but these are not actions that hinder the activities of our mind. In these we maintain our advantage over them. That other puts every other thought under its yoke and by its imperious authority brutifies and bestializes all the theology and philosophy that is in Plato; and yet he complains not of it. In everything else you may maintain some decorum. All other activities come under rules of decency; this one cannot even be imagined other than vicious or ridiculous. Find, if you can, some moderate and prudent way of doing it. Alexander used to say that he knew himself to be mortal chiefly by this action and by sleeping. Sleep stifles and suppresses the faculties of our mind; the sexual act likewise absorbs and dissipates them. Truly it is a mark not only of our original corruption but also of our inanity and deformity.

On the one hand Nature pushes us on in it, having joined to this desire the most noble, useful, and pleasant of all her operations; and on the other hand she lets us condemn and shun it as immoderate and indecent, blush at it, and recommend abstinence.

Are we not, indeed, brutes to call that operation brutish which begets us? In their religions peoples have come together in a number of conventions, such as sacrifices, lamps, burning incense, fasts, offerings, and among other things, in the condemnation of this action. All opinions come to that stand, as

---

[69] Horace, *Satires*

well as to the widespread custom of circumcision, which is a punishment of it. We are, perhaps, right in blaming ourselves for producing so foolish a thing as man, in calling the action shameful and shameful the parts that are employed in it (at the present time mine are really shameful and miserable).

The Essenians, of whom Pliny speaks, kept up their numbers for several centuries without nurses or baby-clothes, by the influx of foreigners who, following this pretty humor, continually joined them—a whole nation having risked being exterminated rather than be entangled in a woman's embrace, and forfeiting the continuity of men rather than create one. It is said that Zeno never had to do with a woman but once in his life, and that then it was out of civility, that he might not seem too obstinately to disdain the sex. Everyone avoids seeing a man born; everyone runs to see him die. To destroy him a spacious field is sought out in the full light of day; but to make him they creep into a dark little corner. It is a duty to hide and blush in making him, but it is a glory and a source of many virtues to be able to unmake him. One is offense, the other is grace; for Aristotle says that to do someone a kindness, in a certain phrase of his country, is to kill him. The Athenians, to put on the same level the disgrace of these two actions, having to purify the island of Delos and to justify themselves to Apollo, forbade both all burials and all births within its territory. *We are ashamed of ourselves.*[70] We regard our being as a vice.

There are countries where they cover themselves in eating. I know a lady, and one of the greatest, who holds the same opinion, that chewing causes a disagreeable appearance which takes a great deal away from the grace and beauty of women; and she does not like to appear in public with an appetite. And I know a man who cannot bear to see another eat, nor be seen himself, and who is more shy of company when he is filling than when he is emptying himself.

---

[70] Terence, *Phormio*

In the empire of the Turk there are a great number of men who to excel others never let themselves be seen when they are having their meals; who have only one a week; who cut and mangle their faces and limbs; who never speak to any one: all of them people who honor their nature by disnaturing themselves, who value themselves by their contempt and grow better by growing worse! What a monstrous animal it is that becomes a horror to himself, to whom his pleasures are a burden, and who clutches to unhappiness!

There are some who conceal their lives,

They change for exile their sweet hearths and homes,[71]

and withdraw them from the sight of other men; who avoid health and cheerfulness as hostile and injurious qualities. Not only many sects but many nations curse their birth and bless their death. There are some among whom the sun is abominated and the darkness adored.

We are ingenious only in treating ourselves ill; that is the real quarry of the power of our intellect—a dangerous tool when misapplied!

O wretched men, whose pleasures are a crime![72]

Alas, poor man! you have enough inevitable ills without increasing them by your own invention, and you are miserable enough by nature without being so by art. You have real and essential deformities enough without forging imaginary ones. Do you feel that you are too much at your ease if your ease does not come to you as displeasure? Do you think that you have performed all the necessary duties to which Nature binds you, and that she is failing and idle in you if you do not bind yourself to new duties? You are not afraid of violating her universal and undoubted laws, and you are madly set on your

---

[71] Virgil, *Georgics*   [72] Maximianus

own, which are partial and fantastic; and the more partial, uncertain, and disputed they are, the more do you devote your efforts to them. You are held and bound by the positive rules of your invention and by the rules of your parish; those of God and of the world do not touch you at all. Just run a bit over the examples of this kind; in them is your whole life.

The verses of these two poets, treating so reservedly and discreetly of wantonness as they do, seem to me to reveal it and illuminate it more clearly. Ladies cover their bosoms with lacework, priests veil many sacred things, painters shade their work to make it more luminous, and it is said that the sun and wind strike more oppressively by reflection than in a direct line. When he was asked "What are you carrying there hidden under your cloak?" the Egyptian answered discreetly, "It is hidden under my cloak in order that you may not know what it is." But there are certain other things that people hide only to show them. Listen to this fellow who is more open,

And pressed her naked body close to mine;[73]

I feel he is caponizing me. Let Martial turn up Venus' skirts as high as he pleases, he will not succeed in making her appear so completely. He who says all satiates and disgusts us. He who is afraid to express himself draws us on to guess at more than is meant. There is treachery in this sort of modesty and especially in half opening, as these do, so fair a path to imagination. Both the action and the depiction should smack of theft.

I like the love-making of the Spaniards and Italians, which is more respectful and timid, more mannered and discreet. Somebody in ancient times, I don't know who, wished for a gullet as long as a crane's neck that he might relish longer what he was swallowing. This wish is more appropriate to this quick and impetuous pleasure, especially in such natures as mine that have the fault of being too sudden. To restrain its flight and

---

[73] Ovid, *Amores*

prolong it with preliminaries, everything serves as a favor and recompense between them: a glance, a bow, a word, a sign. If a man could dine off the steam of a roast, would he not make a handsome saving? It is a passion that with very little solid substance mixes much more vanity and feverish fancy; it should be paid and served accordingly. Let us teach the ladies to make the most of themselves, to respect themselves, to beguile us and fool us. We make our final attack at the first onset; the French impetuosity is ever present. By spinning out their favors and spreading them out in small amounts, every man, even miserable old age, may find there some little shred according to his worth and merit.

He who has no enjoyment except in enjoyment, who wins nothing unless he sweeps the stakes, who loves the chase only for the capture, has no business to mix in our school. The more steps and degrees there are, so much higher and more honorable is the uppermost seat. We should take pleasure in being conducted to it, as in magnificent palaces, by divers porticoes and passages, long and pleasant galleries, and many windings. This disposition of things would turn to our advantage; we should stay there longer and love longer. Without hope and without desire we cease to make any real effort at progress. Our mastery and entire possession is what they ought infinitely to dread. Once they have wholly surrendered to the mercy of our fidelity and constancy, they run a very considerable hazard. Those are rare and difficult virtues. As soon as they are ours, we are no longer theirs:

> When our desires and lusts once sated are,
> For oaths and promises we little care.[74]

And Thrasonides, a young Greek, was so in love with his love that, having won his mistress' heart, he refused to enjoy her that he might not by enjoyment deaden, satiate, and make

---
[74] Catullus

listless that restless ardor on which he prided and nourished himself.

Dearness gives relish to the meat. See how much the form of salutation which is peculiar to our nation debases by its facility the charm of kisses, which Socrates says are so powerful and dangerous at stealing our hearts. It is a disagreeable custom and unjust to the ladies to have to lend their lips to any man who has three footmen at his heels, however unpleasant he may be,

> Down from whose dog-like muzzle hang
> Livid icicles and the stiffened beard . . .
> A hundred lechers I would rather meet.[75]

And we ourselves do not gain much by it; for as the world is divided, for three beautiful women we must kiss fifty ugly ones. And for a tender stomach, such as men of my age have, a bad kiss buys too dearly a good one.

In Italy they play the part of suitors, and of stricken suitors, even with the women who are for sale, and they justify themselves in this manner: that there are degrees in enjoyment, and that by their attentions they desire to procure for themselves that which is the most complete. These women sell nothing but their bodies; the will cannot be put on sale, it is too free and too much its own master. Therefore these men say that it is the will that they seek to gain; and they are right. It is the will which we must devote our attentions to and seek to win. I abhor the thought of a body void of affection being mine. And this madness is, it seems to me, close to that of the youth who defiled with his love the beautiful statue of Venus that Praxiteles had made, or that of the frenzied Egyptian whose lust was stirred by the corpse of a dead woman he was embalming and shrouding, which was the occasion of the law later made in Egypt that the bodies of beautiful young women

---

[75] Martial

and of those of good family should be kept three days before being placed in the hands of those who were charged with attending to their interment. Periander behaved more monstrously in carrying his conjugal affection (more regular and legitimate) to the point of enjoying his wife Melissa after she was dead.

Does it not seem a lunatic humor in Luna, seeing she could not otherwise enjoy her darling Endymion, to put him to sleep for several months and gratify herself with the enjoyment of a youth who stirred only in his dreams?

So I say that we love a body without a soul or without feeling when we love a body without its consent and without its desire. All enjoyments are not alike. Some are thin and languid. A thousand other causes besides good will may procure us this favor from the ladies; it is not sufficient evidence of affection. Treachery may lurk there, as elsewhere; they sometimes go to it with only one buttock,

> As if preparing wine and incense offering;
> You'd think her absent or of marble formed.[76]

I know some who had rather lend that than their coach and who impart themselves only that way. You must observe whether they like your company on any other account or on that alone, like that of some husky stable boy; in what rank and at what rating you are lodged there,

> Whether she gives herself to thee alone,
> And marks thy day out with the whiter stone.[77]

What if she eats your bread with the sauce of a more pleasing image?

> Embracing thee, she sighs for other loves.[78]

[76] Martial   [77] Catullus   [78] Tibullus

What! Have we not seen somebody in our own time who made use of this action for the purpose of a horrible revenge, to poison and kill, as he did, an honorable woman?

Those who know Italy will never think it strange if, for this subject, I do not look elsewhere for examples; for that nation may be called the instructress of the rest of the world in this matter. Among them there are commonly more beautiful women and fewer ugly ones than among us, but in rare and surpassing beauties I think we are on a par. And I judge as much of their intellects: of the ordinary sort they have many more, and brutish stupidity clearly is incomparably rarer; in unusual minds of the loftiest standing we do not fall short of them at all. If I had to extend this comparison further, I should think I could say of valor on the other hand that, as compared with them, it is common and natural with us; but sometimes we see it among them so full and so forceful that it surpasses the stoutest examples we can produce.

The marriages of that country are lame in this: their custom commonly imposes so harsh and so slavish a law upon the women that the most distant acquaintance with a stranger is for them as capital an offense as the most intimate. This law brings it about that every approach is necessarily of a substantial nature; and since, for them, all comes to the same, they have a very easy choice to make. And once they have broken through these partitions, you may well believe that they take fire: *Lust, like a wild beast, provoked by its shackles and then let loose.*[79] They should be given a little more rein:

> Of late I saw a horse, fighting his curb,
> Rush on, hard-mouthed, just like a thunderbolt.[80]

The desire for company is allayed by giving it a little liberty.

We run pretty nearly the same fortune. They are too extreme in constraint; we in license. It is a fine custom we have in our

---

[79] Livy   [80] Ovid, *Amores*

nation that our sons are received into good families to be brought up and trained as pages, as in a school of nobility. And it is looked upon as a discourtesy and an affront to refuse this to a gentleman. I have perceived (for so many houses, so many different styles and forms) that the ladies who have sought to place the strictest rules on the maidens of their retinue have not the best luck. There is need of moderation in it; a good part of their conduct must be left to their own discretion, for in any case there is no discipline that can curb them at all points. But it is very true that the girl who has come forth safe, bag and baggage, from an unfettered schooling inspires much more confidence than the one who comes forth sound from a severe, prison-like school.

Our fathers trained their daughters to look bashful and timid (hearts and desires were the same); we train ours to look self-assured. We understand nothing of the matter. That is all right for the Sarmatian women who may not lie with a man until with their own hands they have killed another in war.

For me, who have no rights therein except through the ears, it is enough if they retain me for their counsel according to the privilege of my age. I advise them, then, as well as us, to abstinence; but if this generation is too hostile to it, at least to discretion and modesty. For as the story says of Aristippus, speaking to some young men who blushed to see him enter the house of a courtesan, "The vice is in not coming out, not in going in." If she has no care for her conscience, let her have some regard to her reputation; if the substance is not worth much, let the appearance hold good.

I commend gradation and delay in the distribution of their favors. Plato shows that in every kind of love an easy and prompt yielding is forbidden to the defenders. It is a sign of greediness, which they should disguise with all their art, to surrender so rashly, fully, and impetuously. By conducting themselves with order and measure in granting their favors, they allure our desires much better and hide their own. Let them ever fly before us, I mean even those who intend to let themselves be caught; they conquer us better by flight, like the Scythians. Indeed according to the law that Nature has imposed upon them, it is not properly for them either to will or to desire; their part is to suffer, obey, and consent. That is why Nature has given them a perpetual capacity; to us a rare and uncertain one. They always have their hour that they may always be ready for ours: *born to be passive*.[81] And whereas she has ordered that our appetites should have a prominent showing and declaration, she has brought it about that theirs should be hidden and internal and has furnished them with parts suitable simply for the defensive and not for show.

Such proceedings as this that follows should be left to Amazonian license. When Alexander was marching through Hyrcania, Thalestris, Queen of the Amazons, came to see him with three hundred troopers of her own sex, well mounted and well armed, having left the remainder of a large army that was following her beyond the neighboring mountains; and she said to him aloud and publicly that the fame of his valor and victories had brought her thither to see him and to offer him her resources and her power to help him in his enterprises, and that, finding him so handsome, young, and vigorous, she, who was perfect in all his qualities, suggested to him that they should lie together so that from the most valiant woman of the world and the bravest man then living there might spring some great and wonderful issue for the time to come. Alexander thanked her for the rest; but to allow time for the accomplishment of her last request he stayed thirteen days in that place, which he celebrated as joyously as possible in honor of so courageous a princess.

We are in almost everything unjust judges of their actions as they are of ours. I confess the truth when it goes against me as when it is on my side. It is a wretched aberration that pushes them on so often to change and keeps them from fixing

[81] Seneca, *Epistles*

their affection on any object whatever, as is evident in that goddess to whom are attributed so many changes and so many lovers. But it is true that it is contrary to the nature of love if it is not violent, and contrary to the nature of violence if it is constant. And they who are astonished by it exclaim against it and seek the causes of this frailty in them as if it were something unnatural and incredible. Why do they not see how often they lodge it in themselves without horror and without miracle? It would, perhaps, be more strange to see any stability in it. It is not simply a physical passion. If there is no end to avarice and ambition, neither is there to lechery. It still lives after satiety, and it is impossible to prescribe either constant satisfaction or limit to it; it ever goes beyond its possession. And yet inconstancy, perhaps, is somewhat more pardonable in them than in us. They may plead, as well as we, the inclination to variety and novelty common to us both; and secondly, they may plead, as we cannot, that they buy a cat in a poke. (Joan, Queen of Naples, caused her first husband, Andreasso, to be hanged at the bars of her window with a cord of gold and silk woven with her own hands because in matrimonial services she found that neither his parts nor efforts answered the expectation she had formed of them upon seeing his stature, beauty, youth, and liveliness, by which she had been caught and deceived.) They may plead that action involves more effort than submission, so that on their part necessity is always taken care of, whereas on our part it may turn out otherwise. For this reason it was that Plato wisely held in his laws that, in order to determine the suitableness of marriages, the judges should see the young men who were seeking it stark naked and the girls naked down to the girdle only. When they come to try us, they do not, perhaps, find us worthy of their choice,

> All efforts vain to excite his vigor dead,
> The married virgin flies the injoyous bed.[82]

---

[82] Martial

It is not enough that a man's will bear straight. Weakness and incapacity lawfully break a marriage:

> And somewhere else a stronger lover must be sought
> Who has the power to undo her virgin zone,[83]

why not? and, according to her standard, a more licentious and more active capacity for love,

> If he be unequal to the enticing toil.[84]

But is it not a great impudence to bring our imperfections and weaknesses where we desire to please and leave a good opinion and recommendation of ourselves? For the little that I now need,

> Good for only one encounter,[85]

I would not trouble a person whom I have to reverence and fear:

> Suspect not him
> Whose life, alas, has sped beyond
> The fifty mark.[86]

Nature should be satisfied with having made this time of life miserable without also making it ridiculous. I hate to see it for one inch of pitiful vigor which heats it up three times a week strut and swagger with such fierceness as if it had some great and lawful day's work in its belly: a veritable flash in the pan. And I am amazed in seeing so lively and frisky a flame so heavily chilled and spent in a moment. This appetite ought to be found only in the flower of youth and beauty. Rely on it, if you wish to see, to second that indefatigable, full, constant, and high-spirited ardor that is in you; it will certainly leave you in the lurch at your greatest need. Boldly send it off rather

---

[83] Catullus   [84] Virgil, *Georgics*   [85] Horace, *Epodes*
[86] Horace, *Odes*

to some tender, dazed, and ignorant boy who still trembles under the rod and blushes at it,

> And as if Indian ivory should be stained
> With blood-red purple, or as lilies white
> When mixed with roses color up.[87]

He who can await the morning after, without dying of shame, the disdain of those fair eyes that will know his limpness and impertinence,

> And despite silence, her glance throws reproof,[88]

has never felt the satisfaction and the pride of having wearied them and dulled them by the vigorous exercise of a busy and active night. When I have seen one of them become tired of me, I did not immediately accuse her of fickleness; I questioned whether there were not good reason rather for me to complain of Nature. She has certainly treated me very unfairly and unkindly,

> If not long enough, if not stout of parts:
> No doubt they are wise, and matrons, also, view
> Without joy a man of scanty parts,[89]

and with enormous injury. Each part of me makes me what I am as much as any other; and no other does more properly make me a man than this.

I owe a full portrait of myself to the public. The wisdom of my instruction rests wholly in truth, in frankness, in reality, disdaining to include in the list of its real duties those little, feigned, customary, and provincial rules—an entirely natural wisdom, constant, universal, of which civility and ceremony are daughters, but illegitimate daughters. We are sure to get the better of the vices of appearance when we have mastered

---

[87] Virgil, *Aeneid*   [88] Ovid, *Amores*   [89] *Priapea*

those of our inner essence. When we have done with the latter, we may rush upon the others if we find it necessary to rush at them. For there is danger of our imagining new duties to excuse our negligence towards the natural ones and to obscure them. As good proof of this we see that in places where faults are crimes, crimes are only faults; that in nations where the laws of propriety are more infrequent and looser, the primitive and common laws are better observed since the innumerable multitude of so many duties stifles, weakens, and dissipates our attention. Application to trivial things takes us away from urgent ones. Oh, what an easy and pleasant path do these superficial men take in comparison with ours! These are shadows wherewith we plaster ourselves and pay one another off; but we do not thereby pay, but rather add to our debt to that great judge who tucks up our rags and tatters from around our shameful parts and does not hesitate to look us all over, even to our inmost and most secret filth. Our virginal modesty would be a useful propriety if it could keep him from making this discovery.

In short, whoever could rid man of the stupidity of so scrupulous a verbal superstition would do the world no great harm. Our life consists partly in folly, partly in wisdom. He who writes of it only reverently and canonically leaves more than half of it unsaid. I make no excuses to myself; and if I did, it would rather be for my excuses that I should excuse myself than for any other fault. I excuse myself to people of a certain temper, whom I take to be more numerous than those who are on my side. In consideration of them, I will also say this (for I desire to please everyone, though it is a very difficult thing, *for one man to adapt himself to so great a variety of manners, discourses, and wills*[90]), that they ought not strictly to take me to task for what I bring out of the mouths of authorities accepted and approved by many centuries, and that it is not right that, simply because I do not write in verse, they should

[90] Cicero, *De Petitione Consulatus*

refuse me the liberty that even some of our churchmen, and the most highly crested, enjoy in this present age. Here are two specimens:

> May I die if your crack is not a faint line.[91]

> A friendly yard contents and satisfies her.[92]

And what about so many others? I love modesty, and it is not out of judgment that I have chosen this scandalous way of speaking; it is Nature that has chosen it for me. I do not commend it, any more than I do all forms that are contrary to the accepted practice; but I excuse it and, by particular and general circumstances, lighten the accusation.

But to proceed. Likewise whence can come that usurpation of sovereign authority that you assume over the women who grant you favors at their own expense?

> If in the darkness of the night
> She has granted furtive delight,[93]

why do you immediately assume the self-interest, coldness, and authority of a husband? It is a free compact: why do you not stick to it as you would have them hold to it? There is no prescribed form for voluntary things.

It is contrary to form, but it is true, however, that in my time I have carried out such an affair, as far as the nature of it would permit, as conscientiously as any other bargain and with some air of justice, and that I displayed to them no more affection than I felt, and I openly revealed to them its decline, its vigor and birth, its outbursts, and its abatements. A man does not always go at the same pace. I have been so sparing of my promises that I think I have done more than I promised or owed. They have found me faithful even to the point of serving their inconstancy—I mean an avowed and sometimes multi-

---

ple inconstancy. I never broke with them as long as I was attached to them by so much as a thread; and whatever cause they may have given me, I never broke with them to the point of feeling scorn or hatred. For such intimacies, even when obtained upon the most shameful terms, still oblige me to have some kindly feeling for them. Upon the occasion of their tricks and evasions and of our quarrels, I have at times shown anger to them and somewhat rash impatience for I am naturally subject to sudden outbursts which, though slight and brief, are often harmful to my affairs. If they desired to test the freedom of my judgment, I did not shirk giving them sharp and paternal advice and pinching them where they smarted. If I have given them any cause to complain of me, it is rather for having found in me a love that was foolishly conscientious as compared with modern practices. I have kept my word in things wherein I might easily have been excused. Then sometimes they would surrender with honor and on conditions that they were willing enough should be broken by the conqueror. I have more than once made pleasure in its greatest stress yield to the interest of their honor; and when reason urged me, I have armed them against myself, so that they conducted themselves more securely and more decorously by my rules, when they freely relied upon them, than they would have done by their own.

I took solely upon myself, so far as I could, the hazard of our rendezvous to free them of the responsibility, and I have always arranged for our meetings to be by the hardest and most unexpected way, as being less suspected, and, moreover, as being, in my opinion, more accessible. Places are chiefly open in the spots where they are considered to be closed. Things least feared are least guarded and watched. You can more easily dare what nobody thinks you will dare, which by its difficulty becomes easy.

Never did any man make his approaches with less sexual reference. This way of loving is more in keeping with the rules, but who knows better than I how ridiculous it seems to people nowadays, and how ineffectual? Yet I shall not repent of it; I have nothing more to lose there:

> For me my votive tablet shows
> That I have hung my dripping clothes
> At Neptune's shrine.[94]

It is now time to speak openly about it. But just as I might, perhaps, say to another, "My friend, you are dreaming; the love of your time has little to do with faith and uprightness,"—

> if this you seek
> With reason to make sure, you do no more
> Than if you strove with reason to grow mad:[95]

so, on the contrary, if I were to begin over again, it would certainly be the same path and the same procedure, however fruitless it might be for me. Incapacity and folly are commendable in an incommendable action. The further I depart from their attitude in this, the nearer I draw to my own.

For the rest, in this traffic, I did not let myself go entirely; I took pleasure in it, but I did not forget myself. I kept intact the little sense and discretion that Nature has given me for their service and for my own; a little excitement, but no mad passion. My conscience was also involved in it to the point of licentiousness and dissoluteness, but to the point of ingratitude, treachery, malice, and cruelty, never. I did not purchase the pleasure of this vice at any price, but contented myself with its own proper and simple cost: *No vice is self-contained*.[96]

I hate a stagnant and slothful idleness almost as much as a thorny and toilsome activity. The latter pinches me, the other makes me drowsy. I like wounds as much as bruises, and cuts as much as dry blows. I found in this traffic, when I was fitter for it, a just moderation between those two extremes. Love is a sprightly, lively, and gay agitation; I was neither troubled

---

[94] Horace, *Odes*   [95] Terence, *Eunuchus*   [96] Seneca, *Epistles*

nor afflicted with it, but I was heated by it and, furthermore, made thirsty. A man should stop there; it is harmful only to fools.

A young man asked the philosopher Panaetius whether it was becoming in a wise man to be in love? "Let us leave the wise man aside," he answered, "but let not you and me, who are not wise men, get entangled in so excited and violent an affair, which enslaves us to others and makes us contemptible to ourselves." He put it truly, that we should not intrust a thing so impetuous in itself to a soul that has not the means to withstand its assaults and to disprove in practice the saying of Agesilaus, that prudence and love cannot keep together. It is a vain activity, it is true, unbecoming, shameful, and illegitimate; but if carried on in this manner, I look upon it as healthy, proper to enliven a dull body and soul; and, as a physician, I would prescribe it to a man of my temperament and condition, as readily as any other recipe, to rouse and keep him in vigor till well on in years and to defer the clutches of old age. While we are but in the outskirts and the pulse still beats,

> While hair is freshly grey, and age still straight and trim,
> While yet Lachesis has some threads to twist and spin,
> And on my feet I move without a helping staff,[97]

we need to be urged and tickled by some such biting incitation as this. Observe what youth, vigor, and gaiety it gave back to the wise Anacreon. And Socrates, when older than I am, said, in speaking of an object of his love: "My shoulder touching his, and my head close to his, as we were looking together into a book, I suddenly felt, I assure you, a stinging in my shoulder like some insect bite, and for more than five days it prickled, and a continual itching crept into my heart." A touch, and merely by chance, and by a shoulder, kindle and change a soul cooled and weakened by age, and the most chastened of all

---

[97] Juvenal

human souls! And why not, indeed? Socrates was a man, and he wanted neither to be nor to seem anything else.

Philosophy does not contend against natural pleasures provided that measure be included, and it preaches moderation in them, not flight. The power of its resistance is employed against outlandish and bastard pleasures. She says that the appetites of the body ought not to be augmented by the mind, and she wisely warns us not to try to stir up hunger by satiety, not to stuff instead of merely filling the belly, to avoid all enjoyment that brings us to want and all food and drink that make us thirsty and hungry. So in the service of love she directs us to take an object that simply satisfies the body's need, that does not stir the soul, which must not make that its concern, but rather simply follow and assist the body.

But am I not right in considering that these precepts, which by the way are, in my opinion, somewhat rigorous, apply to a body that is functioning properly, and that for a rundown body, as for an upset stomach, it is excusable to warm and support it by art and by means of the imagination to restore to it appetite and cheerfulness since on its own it lost them?

May we not say that there is nothing in us during this earthly imprisonment that is purely either corporeal or spiritual, and that we unjustly tear a living man apart, and that it seems but reasonable that we should have to the use of pleasure at least as favorable an attitude as we do to that of pain? The latter was (for example) vehement even to perfection in the souls of the saints through penitence; the body naturally had a share in it by virtue of their union, and yet it could have little share in the cause. And yet they were not content that it should simply follow and assist the afflicted soul; they afflicted the body itself with atrocious and appropriate torments in order that vying with each other the soul and body might plunge man into misery, the harsher, the more salutary.

In like manner, is it not wrong in the cause of bodily pleasures to make the soul cool to them and to say that she must be dragged to them as to some servile and enforced obligation and necessity? It is rather her part to bring them forth and nourish them, to invite and offer herself to them, since the authority of ruling belongs to her; as it is also her part, in my opinion, in pleasures that are her own, to inspire and infuse into the body all the feeling they are capable of, and to try to make them be sweet and wholesome to it. For it is, indeed, reasonable, as they say, that the body should not pursue its appetites to the prejudice of the mind; but why is it not also reasonable that the mind should not pursue hers to the prejudice of the body?

I have no other passion to keep me in breath. What avarice, ambition, quarrels, lawsuits do for others, who, like me, have no definite occupation, <u>love would do more conveniently. It would restore to me vigilance, sobriety, grace</u>, care of my person; it would reassure my countenance so that the grimaces of old age, those deformed and pitiable grimaces, might not come to disfigure it. It would take me back to sound and wise studies by which I might make myself more loved and esteemed, removing from my mind its despair of itself and its use, and reintegrating it in itself. It would divert me from a thousand troublesome thoughts, from a thousand melancholy humors that idleness and the poor state of our health load us with at such an age. It would warm again, at least in dreams, this blood that Nature is abandoning; it would hold up the chin and stretch out a little the nerves and the vigor and gaiety of the soul for this poor man who is going full speed towards his ruin.

But I well understand that it is an advantage very hard to recover. Through weakness and long experience our taste has become more delicate and more exacting. <u>We demand more when we bring less</u>; and we most want to choose when we least deserve to be accepted. Knowing ourselves for what we are, we are less confident and more distrustful; nothing can assure

us of being loved, knowing our condition and theirs. I am
ashamed of being found in the midst of these bright and ardent
young folks,

> Whose sinew rests in their unsubdued flesh
> More firm than does the sapling on the slope.[98]

Why should we go and intrude our misery into the midst of
their gaiety?

> That glowing youths may come to see,
>   With laughter on their lips,
> The waning torch that crumbles into ash?[99]

They have strength and reason on their side; let us give way
to them, we have no hold left.

And this shoot of budding beauty does not let itself be held
by such stiff hands nor be won by mere material means. For, as
the old philosopher answered the man who jeered at him because he could not gain the favor of a youth he was pursuing:
"My friend, the hook will not bite into such fresh cheese."

This is an intercourse that requires mutual understanding
and reciprocity. The other pleasures that we receive may be
acknowledged by recompenses of a different nature; but this
one can be paid only in the same kind of coin. In truth, in this
pastime, the pleasure I give tickles my imagination more than
that which I feel. Now there is no nobility of soul in a man
who can receive pleasure where he confers none; it is a mean
soul that is willing to be indebted for everything and is pleased
to maintain relations with persons to whom he is a charge.
There is no beauty, no favor, no intimacy so exquisite that a
gentleman ought to desire at that price. If they can be kind to
us only out of pity, I had much rather not live at all than live
on charity. I should like to have the right to ask it of them in

---

[98] Horace, *Epodes*   [99] Horace, *Odes*

the way that I saw begging done in Italy: "Do good for your own good;" or in the manner of Cyrus exhorting his soldiers: "Who loves himself, let him follow me."

Keep company, someone will say to me, with women of your own situation, who, being of the same fortune, will be more easy of access to you. Oh, ridiculous and stupid compromise!

> I will not tug on the dead lion's beard.[100]

Xenophon uses it as an objection and an accusation against Meno that in his amours he worked over faded flowers. I take more pleasure in merely seeing the proper and sweet union of two fair young people, or in merely considering it in my fancy, than in becoming myself the second in a sorrowful, ill-formed union. I leave that fantastic appetite to the Emperor Galba that was only fond of meat that was tough and old and to this poor wretch,

> Oh! would to heav'n I such might you behold,
> To place fond kisses on your altered locks,
> And your thin body in my arms enfold![101]

And among the foremost forms of ugliness I count artificial and forced beauty. Hemon, a young boy of Chios, thinking by finery to acquire the beauty that Nature had denied him, went to the philosopher Arcesilaus and asked him if it was possible for a wise man to fall in love. "Yes, indeed," he replied, "provided it be not with a bedecked and sophisticated beauty like yours." An ugliness and an old age that is confessed is, in my opinion, less old and less ugly than another that is painted and polished.

Shall I say it, provided that you do not throttle me for it? Love, in my opinion, is not properly and naturally in its season except in the age next to childhood,

---

[100] Martial   [101] Ovid, *Ex Ponto*

> Should you put him amid a troop of maids,
> With his loose-hanging locks and downy cheeks,
> His difference from the other ones would pass
> Unnoticed by the sharpest stranger's glance.[102]

Nor beauty either. For while Homer extends it up to the time when the chin begins to be shaded, Plato himself remarked that that was rare. And it is well known why the sophist Dion so amusingly called the downy hairs of adolescence Aristogeitons and Harmodiuses. I find it in manhood already out of place; not to speak of old age:

> For scornful Love flies past the withered oaks.[103]

And Margaret, Queen of Navarre, like a woman, greatly extends the advantage of women, ordaining that at thirty it is the season for them to change the title of "beautiful" for that of "good."

The shorter the hold we give him over our lives, the better it is for us. Look at his port; he is a beardless boy. Who knows not how, in his school, they proceed contrary to all order? Study, exercise, use are the ways leading to inefficiency; there the novices teach the lessons: *Love knows no rule.*[104] Certainly his conduct is much smarter when mingled with heedlessness and disorder; mistakes and miscarriages point it up and give it grace. Provided it be eager and hungry, it matters little whether it be prudent. See how he goes reeling, tripping, and wantonly romping; you put him in the stocks when you guide him by art and prudence, and you restrain his divine freedom when you put him into those hairy and callous hands.

For the rest, I often hear women describing this relationship as entirely spiritual and disdaining to take into consideration the part the senses play in it. Everything contributes to it. But I can say that I have often seen us excuse their intellectual

---

[102] Horace, *Odes*   [103] Horace, *Odes*   [104] Saint Jerome, *Letter to Chromatius, Jovinus, and Eusebius*

weakness in favor of their bodily beauty; but I have not yet seen any of them willing, in favor of intellectual beauty in us, however wise and mature, to be well disposed to a body that is slipping the least little bit into decline. Why is not some one of them seized with the desire for that noble Socratic exchange of body for soul, purchasing a philosophical and spiritual intelligence and generation at the price of her thighs, the highest price at which she can set them? Plato ordains in his *Laws* that he who has performed any signal and useful exploit in war shall not during its duration be refused, however old and ugly he may be, a kiss or any other amorous favor from any woman he may choose. Can what he finds so proper in recommendation of military worth not also be so in recommendation of some other kind of worth? And why is not one of them seized with the desire to gain before her sisters the glory of this chaste love? I may well say chaste,

> For if to join love's battle they engage,
> Like fire in straw they weakly spend their rage.[105]

The vices that are restricted to thought are not the worst.

To conclude this notable commentary, which has escaped from me in a torrent of babble, a torrent sometimes impetuous and hurtful,

> For as an apple, lover's secret gift,
> Falls out from the chaste bosom of the maid,
> Which, 'neath the poor girl's flowing robe forgot,
> Shakes loose as at her mother's step she starts;
> As swift it rolls on downward and away,
> A conscious blush steals o'er her downcast face.[106]

I say that male and female are cast in the same mould; education and habits excepted, the difference is not great. Plato calls upon both sexes, without distinction, to share all studies, exer-

---

[105] Virgil, *Georgics*   [106] *Catullus*

cises, charges, and occupations of war and peace in his commonwealth; and the philosopher Antisthenes eliminated all distinction between their virtue and ours. It is much easier to accuse one sex than to excuse the other. It is, as the old saying goes, the pot calling the kettle black.

OF COACHES

It is easy to prove that great authors, when they write of causes, make use not only of those they think to be the true causes, but also of those they do not believe, provided there is some originality and beauty in them. They speak truly and usefully enough if they speak ingeniously. We cannot make sure of the master-cause; we pile up a number of them to see if it may not accidentally be found among them,

> for it is not enough to state one cause
> But many, one of which, however, is correct.[1]

Do you ask me whence comes that custom of blessing those who sneeze? We produce three sorts of wind: that which issues from below is too foul; that which issues from the mouth carries with it some reproach of gluttony; the third is sneezing, and because it comes from the head and is without offense, we give it that civil greeting. Do not laugh at this subtle reasoning; they say it is from Aristotle.

I think I have read in Plutarch (who, of all the authors I know, is the one who has best blended art with nature, and judgment with knowledge) his giving as a reason for the heaving of the stomach in those who travel by sea, that it is occasioned by fear; having found out some reason by which he proves that fear may produce such an effect. I, who am very subject to it, know well that that cause does not affect me, and I know it, not by reasoning, but by necessary experience. Without alleging what I have been told, that the same thing often

---

[1] Lucretius

happens to animals, and especially to pigs, that have no idea of danger; and what an acquaintance of mine vouched to me about himself, that, though very subject to it, the desire to vomit left him two or three times when beset by fright in a heavy storm, as it did that ancient: *I was too upset to think of the danger.*[2] I have never been afraid on the water, nor, indeed, anywhere else (and I have often had just occasion to be afraid, if death be one), at least to the point of being upset or bewildered by it.

Fear springs sometimes from want of judgment as well as from want of courage. All the dangers I have seen, I have seen with open eyes, with free, sound, and whole sight; besides, a man must have courage to be afraid. It once served me in good stead, compared with others, to conduct and control my flight so that it was done, if not without fear, at any rate without terror and without dismay; I was excited in the flight, but not dazed or bewildered.

Great souls go yet much further and set before us examples of flights not merely orderly and steady, but proud. Let us tell what Alcibiades relates of Socrates, his comrade in arms: "I found him," he says, "after the rout of our army, him and Laches, last among the fugitives; and I observed him at my leisure and in safety, for I was mounted on a good horse, and he on foot, and we had fought that way in the battle. I noted first how much presence of mind and resolution he showed in comparison with Laches; and then the boldness of his step, not at all different from his ordinary gait, his firm and steady gaze, observing and judging what was going on around him, looking now at one, now at another, friends and enemies, in such a way as to encourage the former and signify to the latter that he intended to sell his blood and life very dearly if anyone should try to take them from him. And thus they made their escape, for people do not readily attack men like these; they pursue the frightened." There is the testimony of this great captain, which teaches us what we experience every day, that there is

---

[2] Seneca, *Epistles*

nothing throws us into dangers so much as a heedless eagerness to get ourselves clear of them. *Where there is less fear, there is generally less danger.*[3] Our common people are wrong to say that such-and-such a man is afraid of death when they mean to say that he thinks about it and that he foresees it. Foresight is equally proper in whatever concerns us, whether for good or evil. To consider and judge the danger is in some sort the reverse of being scared by it.

I do not feel myself strong enough to sustain the force and impetuosity of this passion of fear, or of any other vehement passion. If I were once conquered and beaten down by it, I should never get completely on my feet again. If anyone should make my soul lose her footing, he would never set her upright again in her place. She probes and searches herself too keenly and deeply and, therefore, would never let the wound that has pierced her close up and heal. It has been well for me that no sickness has yet overcome her. To every charge made upon me I come forth and resist completely armed; hence the first that should rout me would leave me without resources. I have no secondary defense; at whatever spot the torrent should break my dike, there I am exposed drowned beyond remedy.

Epicurus says that the wise man can never pass into the opposite state. I have an opinion which is the converse of that saying: that he who has once been very foolish will never after be very wise.

God tempers the cold according to the coat and gives me passions in proportion to my means of withstanding them. Nature, having laid me open on one side, has covered me on the other; having disarmed me of strength, she has armed me with insensibility and a controlled or dull apprehensiveness.

Now I cannot bear for long (and I could bear them much less in my youth) either coach, or litter, or boat, and I hate any other form of transportation except on horseback, both in town and country. But I can bear a litter less than a coach, and for

---

[3] Livy

the same reason I can more easily bear a rough tossing upon the water, whence fear is produced, than the motion felt in calm weather. By the slight jolt given by the oars, stealing the vessel from under us, I feel somehow both my head and my stomach disturbed, as I cannot bear a shaky seat under me. When the sail or the current carries us along smoothly, or when we are towed, this even movement does not disturb me at all. It is an interrupted motion that troubles me, and most of all when it is slow. I cannot otherwise describe the form it takes. The doctors have ordered me to bind and gird my abdomen with a towel in order to remedy this trouble; I have not tried this, being accustomed to wrestle with my own defects and to overcome them by myself.

If my memory were sufficiently stocked with them, I should not think my time ill spent in relating here the infinite variety that histories offer us of the use of coaches in the service of war, varying according to the nations, according to the ages, and, in my opinion, very effective and necessary, so that it is a wonder that we have lost all knowledge of them. I will only say this, that quite recently, in our fathers' time, the Hungarians put them very usefully to work against the Turks, having in each of them a targeteer and a musketeer and a number of harquebuses lined up, loaded and ready, and with the whole vehicle covered with a girdle of shields like a galliot. They formed their battle-front with three thousand such coaches, and after the cannon had played, they had them advance and make the enemy swallow that volley before tasting of the rest, which was no slight advantage. Or they sped the coaches into their squadrons to break them and open them up; besides the use they could make of them to flank in ticklish spots the troops marching in the open country, or to protect a camp in haste and to fortify it.

In my time a gentleman on one of our frontiers, unwieldy of body and not finding a horse able to bear his weight, whenever he had a feud on his hands, used to ride through the country in a coach like those described here and found it worked very well. But let us leave these war coaches. The kings of our first dynasty traveled about in a chariot drawn by four oxen.

Mark Antony was the first who had himself drawn in Rome by lions harnessed to a chariot, with a minstrel girl beside him. Heliogabalus later did the same thing, calling himself Cybele, the mother of the gods; and he was also drawn by tigers, in imitation of the god Bacchus; he also sometimes harnessed two stags to his coach, another time four dogs, and still another four naked girls, having himself dragged by them in pomp, he being stark naked too. The Emperor Firmus had his chariot drawn by ostriches of prodigious size, so that it seemed to fly rather than roll.

The strangeness of these inventions puts this other idea into my head, that it is a kind of pettiness of spirit in monarchs and evidence of their not perceiving sufficiently what they are, when they strive to take on an air of importance and pomp by excessive expense. It would be excusable in a foreign country, but among their own subjects, where they are all-powerful, they derive from their dignity the highest degree of honor that they are able to reach. Just so, in my opinion, it is superfluous in a gentleman to be meticulous in his dress at home; his house, his retinue, and his table sufficiently vouch for his rank.

The advice given by Isocrates to his king seems to me to be grounded upon reason: that he should be sumptuous in furniture and plate, inasmuch as it is an outlay on lasting things that pass on to his successors, and that he should avoid all magnificences that pass immediately out of use and memory.

When I was a young fellow, for want of other adornments I was fond of decking myself out in fine clothes, and it was becoming to me. There are some on whom fine clothes weep. We have extraordinary stories of the frugality of our kings about their own persons and in their gifts—kings great in reputation, in valor, and in fortune. Demosthenes bitterly fought the law of his city that allotted public money to the lavish display of their games and feasts; he wanted their greatness to show itself in the number of well equipped ships and good, well supplied armies.

And Theophrastus was rightly taken to task for having set up a contrary opinion in his book on Riches and for maintaining that an expense of that sort was the true fruit of opulence. These are pleasures, says Aristotle, that affect only the lowest of the people and that vanish from the memory as soon as they are sated with them; no serious and judicious man can value them. The expenditure would, in my opinion, be much more royal as well as more useful, just, and durable if made on ports, harbors, fortifications, and walls, on sumptuous buildings, churches, hospitals, colleges, the improvement of streets and highways, for which Pope Gregory the Thirteenth has left a commendable reputation in my time, and in which our Queen Catherine would leave to posterity evidence of her natural liberality and munificence if her means were equal to her desire. Fortune has greatly vexed me in interrupting the noble structure of the new bridge of our great city and taking from me the hope of seeing it in full use before I die.

Moreover it seems to the subjects, spectators of these triumphs, that their own riches are displayed before them and that they are entertained at their own expense. For the people are apt to assume about kings, as we do about our servants, that they should take care to make ready for us in abundance all we need, but that they should by no means lay hand on it for themselves. And, therefore, the Emperor Galba, having during his supper taken pleasure in a musician's performance, called for his money-box and gave him a handful of crowns that he fished out of it, with these words: "This is not the public money, but my own." Nonetheless it most often happens that the people are right and that their eyes are feasted with what should go to feed their bellies.

Liberality itself does not appear in its really proper light in the hands of a sovereign; private individuals have more right to exercise it. For, to consider it exactly, a king has nothing that is properly his own; he owes even himself to others.

The authority to judge is not given in behalf of the judge, but in behalf of the man being judged. A superior is never appointed for his own benefit, but rather for the benefit of the inferior; and a physician for the sick person, and not for himself. All authority, like all art, has its end outside of itself: *no art is enclosed within itself*.[4]

Wherefore the tutors of young princes who strive to imprint in them this virtue of liberality and preach to them that they should be unable to refuse anything, and to think nothing so well spent as what they give away (a teaching that I have seen in great favor in my time) either look more to their own profit than to their master's or do not really understand to whom they are speaking. It is too easy a thing to imprint liberality in him who has the means to practice it as much as he wishes at the expense of others. And as the value set on it is proportioned not to the measure of the gift, but to the measure of the means of him who practises it, it comes to be empty in such mighty hands. They become prodigal before they are liberal. Therefore it is but little commendable in comparison with other royal virtues, and the only one, as the tyrant Dionysius said, that goes well with tyranny itself. I should rather teach him this verse of the ancient plowman:[5] *that whoever wants to reap a good crop must sow with the hand, not pour out of the sack* (he must scatter the seed, not spill it); and as he has to give, or, to put it better, to pay and compensate so many people according as they have deserved, he ought to be a fair and wise distributor. If the liberality of a prince is without discretion and without measure, I would rather he were a miser.

Royal virtue seems to consist most of all in justice; and of

[4] Cicero, *De Finibus*   [5] Montaigne translates the Greek verse quoted. Corinna, in Plutarch, *Whether the Athenians were more excellent in Arms than in Learning*

all the parts of justice, that best denotes a king which is accompanied by liberality; for they have particularly reserved it as their function, whereas they are disposed to exercise every other kind of justice through the intermediary of others. An immoderate bounty is a feeble means of acquiring good will, for it repulses more people than it attracts: *The more you have already favored by it, the fewer you will be able to favor. What greater folly is there than to take pains to render yourself unable to do any longer that which you enjoy doing?* [6] And if it is exercised without regard to merit, it puts him to shame who receives it, and it is received ungraciously. Tyrants have been sacrificed to the hatred of the people by the hands of the very men they have unjustly advanced; such men think they will make secure their possession of goods unduly received by making a show of contempt and hatred for the man from whom they hold them, and by rallying to the judgment and opinion of the public in that matter.

The subjects of a prince excessive in gifts become excessive in requests; they trim their requests not to reason but to example. Certainly there is often reason for us to blush at our impudence; by rights we are overpaid when the recompense equals our service; for do we not owe some natural obligation to our princes? If he bears our expenses, he does too much; it is enough for him to contribute to them. The surplus is called benefit, and it cannot be exacted, for the very name of liberality has the ring of liberty. In our way of doing there is no end to it; what has been received is no longer taken into account, we care only for future liberality. Therefore the more a prince exhausts himself in giving, the poorer he grows in friends. How could he satisfy desires that increase as they are fulfilled? He who has his thoughts on taking no longer has them on what he has taken. Nothing is so characteristic of covetousness as ingratitude.

The example of Cyrus will not be amiss in this place, to

---

[6] Cicero, *De Officiis*

serve the kings of our time as a touchstone to know whether their gifts are well or ill bestowed and to make them see how much more happily that Emperor dealt them out than they do. Thereby they are reduced to borrowing from unknown subjects, and rather from those they have wronged than from those they have helped, and thereby receive aid in which there is nothing gratuitous but the name. Croesus reproached him for his bounty and calculated how much his treasure would amount to if he had been more closefisted. Cyrus wanted to justify his liberality; and sending dispatches on all sides to the grandees of his state whom he had particularly advanced, he begged each one to aid him with as much money as he could for a great need of his, and to send him a declaration of the amount. When all these statements were brought to him, since each one of his friends had thought it not enough to offer him only as much as he had received from his munificence and had added to it much more of his own, it was found that the sum amounted to much more than the savings estimated by Croesus. Whereupon Cyrus said to him: "I am not less in love with riches than other princes, and I am a rather better manager of them. You see at how small an outlay I have acquired the inestimable treasure of so many friends, and how much more faithful treasurers they are to me than mercenary men without obligation, without affection would be; and my wealth is better placed than in chests, where it would call down upon me the hatred, envy, and contempt of other princes."

The emperors found an excuse for the superfluity of their public games and spectacles in the fact that their authority depended somewhat (at least in appearance) on the will of the Roman people, who time out of mind had been accustomed to be flattered by that sort of spectacle and extravagance. But it was private individuals who had nourished this custom of gratifying their fellow-citizens and friends, chiefly out of their own purse, by such profusion and magnificence; it had a very different flavor when it was the masters who came to imitate it. *The transference of property from its rightful owners to strangers should not be regarded as liberality.*[7] Because his son was trying by presents to gain the good will of the Macedonians, in a letter Philip took him to task for it in this manner: "What! do you want your subjects to look upon you as their purse-bearer and not as their king? Do you want to win them over? Win them over with the favors of your virtue and not with the favors of your money-chest."

It was, however, a fine thing to bring and plant within the amphitheater a great number of big trees, all branched out and all green, representing a large, shady forest, arranged in lovely symmetry, and on the first day to turn loose into it a thousand ostriches, a thousand stags, a thousand wild boars, and a thousand fallow-deer, leaving them to be run down by the people; on the next day to have a hundred big lions, a hundred leopards, and three hundred bears slaughtered in their presence; and for the third day, to make three hundred pairs of gladiators fight it out to the death, as the Emperor Probus did.

It was also a fine thing to see those great amphitheaters, faced with marble on the outside, embellished with ornaments and statues, the inside sparkling with many rare decorations,

Behold a jeweled band, behold a gold-incrusted portico;[8]

all the sides of this vast space filled and surrounded from top to bottom with three or four score tiers of seats, also of marble, covered with cushions,

"Begone," says he,
"For shame, let him who does not pay the lawful tax
Rise from the cushioned seat of rank;"[9]

where a hundred thousand men can be placed, seated at their ease. And the area at the bottom where the games were played

---

[7] Cicero, *De Officiis*   [8] Calpurnius, *Eclogues*   [9] Juvenal

would first be artificially opened and split into chasms representing caverns that vomited forth the beasts intended for the
spectacle; and then, secondly, it would be flooded with a deep
sea that bore many sea-monsters, and was laden with ships of
war to represent a naval battle; and, thirdly, it would be dried
out again and levelled off for the combat of the gladiators; and
for the fourth scene, it would be strewn with vermilion and
storax instead of sand, in order to set up there a stately banquet for all that infinite number of people—the last act of a
single day—

> How often have we seen
> The sandy floor sink down in parts, and, from the chasm
> Forced open in the earth, wild beasts emerge, and oft
> From these same caves rose golden groves with yellow bark.
> Not only did we chance to see the woodland beasts,
> But I observed sea-calves along with fighting bears,
> And the misshapen beast well named the water-horse.[10]

Sometimes they made a high mountain spring up full of fruit
trees and trees in leaf, spouting a rivulet from its summit as from
the mouth of a living spring. Sometimes a big ship was sailed
about, which parted and opened up of itself and, after having
vomited from its belly four or five hundred combat beasts, closed
up again and vanished without assistance. At other times, from
the bottom of the place they made spouts and thin streams of
water burst forth which shot upwards and from that tremendous height sprinkled and perfumed the great multitude. To
shield themselves from the weather they had that immense
space canopied sometimes with purple curtains of needlework,
sometimes with silk of one color or another, and they pulled
them forward or back in a moment as they had a mind:

> Though the amphitheater glows beneath a torrid sun,
> As Hermogenes appears the awnings are drawn back.[11]

---

[10] Calpurnius, *Eclogues*   [11] Martial

The nets also that were put in front of the people to protect them from the violence of the animals turned loose were woven of gold:

> The woven nets refulgent are with gold.[12]

If there is anything excusable in such extravagances, it is those parts in which the inventiveness and the novelty, not the expense, provide amazement.

Even in these vanities we discover how fertile those ages were in wits different from ours. It is with this sort of fertility as with all other productions of Nature. That is not to say that she then put into it her utmost resources. We do not go straight ahead; we rather rove about and turn this way and that. We retrace our steps. I am afraid our knowledge is weak in every direction; we see neither very far ahead nor very far behind us. It embraces little and lives but a little while, short both in extent of time and extent of matter:

> Ere Agamemnon many heroes lived,
> But all of them unwept, unknown are plunged
> Into unending night.[13]

> Before the Trojan war and Troy's downfall,
> Sang many other bards of other things.[14]

And Solon's account of what he had learned from the Egyptian priests about the long life of their state and their manner of learning and preserving the histories of other lands is not, it seems to me, a testimony to be slighted in this connection. *Could we view that expanse of lands and ages, boundless in every direction, into which the mind, plunging itself and spreading forth, travels so far and wide that it can find no final extremity at which it can come to a full stop, we should discover in that immensity an infinite power of producing an endless*

---

[12] Calpurnius, *Eclogues*   [13] Horace, *Odes*   [14] Lucretius

number of forms.[15] Even though all that has come by report from the past to our times should be true and known by some-one, it would be less than nothing in comparison with what is unknown. And of this very image of the world, which glides along while we live upon it, how puny and limited is the knowl-edge of the most curious! Not only of particular events, which chance often renders exemplary and weighty, but of the state of great governments and nations, a hundred times as many escape us as ever come to our knowledge. We exclaim over the miracle of the invention of our artillery, of our printing; other men, another corner of the world, in China, enjoyed their use a thousand years earlier. If we saw as much of the world as we do not see, we should perceive, it seems likely, a perpetual mul-tiplication and vicissitude of forms.

There is nothing single and rare as regards Nature but cer-tainly there is as regards our knowledge, which is a wretched foundation for our rules and is apt to set before us a very false image of things. As vainly as we infer nowadays the decline and decrepitude of the world from the arguments we draw from our own weakness and decay,

> Right now the age is breaking down,
> The earth is giving out;[16]

so vainly did this poet infer its birth and youth from the vigor he observed in the minds of his time, abounding in novelties and inventions in various arts:

> Indeed, I think the universe is new,
> The world is young, of recent origin,
> Hence certain arts are being even now
> Refined, and others are still growing now,
> There now is much improvement in our ships.[17]

Our world has lately discovered another (and who will as-sure us that it is the last of its brothers, since the Daemons,

---

[15] Cicero, *De Natura Deorum*   [16] Lucretius   [17] Lucretius

the Sibyls, and we ourselves have been up to now ignorant of this one?) no less big, complete, and well-limbed than himself, yet so new and so young that he is still being taught his A B C; it is not fifty years since he knew neither letters, nor weights, nor measures, nor clothes, nor wheat, nor vines. He was still a naked babe-in-arms and lived only on what his nursing mother provided. If we are right in our inference about the end of the world, and this poet about the youth of that age of his, this other world will only be coming into the light when ours is departing from it. The universe will fall into paralysis; one member will be helplessly crippled, the other in full vigor.

But I fear, indeed, that we shall have very greatly hastened its decline and ruin by our contagion, and that we shall have sold it our ideas and our arts at a very dear price. It was an infant world, and yet we have not whipped and subjected it to our discipline by the advantage of our natural valor and strength; nor have we won it over by our justice and goodness, nor subdued it by our magnanimity. Most of their replies in our dealings with them witness that they were by no means behind us in natural clearness of understanding and in pertinency.

The astonishing magnificence of the cities of Cuzco and Mexico, and among many similar things, the garden of that King, in which all the trees, fruits, and all the herbs were superbly formed in gold, conforming to the arrangement and size they have in a garden, as in his cabinet were all the animals native to his lands and seas; and the beauty of their handicraft in jewels, feathers, cotton, and painting show that neither were they inferior to us in industry. But as to devotion, observance of the laws, goodness, liberality, loyalty, and plain dealing, it served us well that we had not as much as they; by this advantage they lost, sold, and betrayed themselves.

As to boldness and courage, as to firmness, constancy, and fortitude in bearing pain, hunger, and death, I should not fear to oppose the examples I could find among them to the most famous examples of ancient times that we possess in the records of our world over here. For, as to the men who subjugated them, take away the tricks and artifices they practised to deceive them, and the natural astonishment that those nations experienced on seeing the so-unexpected arrival of bearded men, differing in language, religion, shape, and countenance, from so remote a part of the world, where they had never imagined there was any human habitation, mounted upon big, unfamiliar monsters, opposed to men who had not only never seen a horse, but never seen any animal whatever trained to carry and support a man or any other burden; outfitted with a hard and shining skin and with a sharp and glittering weapon against men who for the wonder of a shining looking glass or a knife would exchange a great treasure in gold and pearls, and who had neither the knowledge nor the material with which, even with plenty of time, they could pierce our steel; add the lightning and thunder of our cannon and harquebuses—enough to throw even Caesar into confusion if he had been surprised with as little experience and at that time—against people who were naked, except where they had arrived at the invention of some cotton fabric, without other arms, at the most, but bows, stones, clubs, and bucklers of wood; people caught off their guard, under color of friendship and good faith, by the curiosity of seeing strange and unknown things. Put, I say, to the account of the conquerors all this advantage and you take from them the whole source of so many victories. When I look upon that invincible ardor with which so many thousands of men, women, and children so often stepped forth and hurled themselves into inevitable dangers for the defense of their gods and their liberty, that noble obstinacy in suffering all extremities and hardships, and death itself, rather than submit to the domination of those by whom they had been so shamefully deceived; and some of them, after being captured, choosing to let themselves die of hunger and fasting rather than to accept food from the hands of such basely victorious enemies; I foresee that if anyone had attacked them on equal terms in respect to arms, experience, and numbers it would have been as dangerous, or more so, in this war than in any other we know about.

Why did not so noble a conquest fall to Alexander or to the ancient Greeks and Romans; and why did not such a great change and alteration of so many empires and nations fall into hands that would have gently smoothed off and cleared away all that was barbarous in them and that would have strengthened and developed the good seeds that Nature had there produced, not only mingling with the cultivation of their lands and the adornment of their cities the arts of our side of the ocean, in so far as they might have been necessary, but also mingling the Greek and Roman virtues with those indigenous to that land! What a restoration it would have been and what an improvement for the whole world if the first examples of our conduct exhibited over there had called those people to the admiration and imitation of virtue and had set up between them and us a brotherly fellowship and understanding! How easy it would have been to turn to good account minds so fresh and so hungry to learn, which had for the most part such fine natural beginnings! On the contrary, we have taken advantage of their ignorance and inexperience to bend them more easily towards treachery, luxury, avarice, and towards every sort of inhumanity and cruelty by the example and pattern of our conduct. Who ever set such a price on the utility of commerce and trading? So many cities razed to the ground, so many nations exterminated, so many millions of people put to the sword, and the richest and most beautiful part of the world turned upside down for the traffic in pearls and pepper! Base mechanized victories! Never did ambition, never did public enmities impel men one against another to such horrible hostilities and such wretched calamities.

Certain Spaniards, coasting the sea in quest of their mines, landed in a fertile and pleasant and very well-peopled region and made their usual declarations to the inhabitants: "That they were peaceable men, come from distant voyages, sent on behalf of the King of Castile, the greatest prince of the habitable world, to whom the Pope, representing God on earth, had given the principality of all the Indies; that if they would become tributaries to him, they would be treated very kindly." They demanded of them provisions for their sustenance and gold for the needs of a certain medicine. They, moreover, expounded to them the belief in one God and the truth of our religion, which they advised them to embrace, adding to this a few threats.

The reply was as follows: "That as to being peaceable, they did not look like it if they really were. As to their king, since he was begging, he must be indigent and needy, and that he who had made that allotment must be a man fond of dissension to go and give to another something which was not his own and set him at strife with its ancient possessors. As to provisions, they would supply them; of gold they had little, and it was a thing they did not value at all, since it was of no use to the service of their life, whereas their entire care aimed solely at passing life happily and pleasantly; however, they might freely take all they could find, except what was employed in the service of their gods. As to a single God, the account given had pleased them, but they did not want to change their religion, having followed it so profitably for so long a time, and they were not accustomed to take counsel but of their friends and acquaintances. As to their threats, it was a sign of want of judgment to go threatening those whose nature and means were unknown to them. Therefore they had better make haste to quit their land quickly, for they were not accustomed to take in good part the civilities and declarations of armed strangers; otherwise they would do to them as they had done to those others," showing them the heads of some executed men around their city. There is an example of the babbling of these children. At all events, neither in this place nor in several other places where they did not find the merchandise they were seeking, did the Spanish make any stay or any assault, whatever other advantages there were there; witness my Cannibals.

Of the two most powerful monarchs of that world, and, perhaps, of this, kings of so many kings, the last they drove out, the King of Peru, having been taken in a battle and put to so excessive a ransom that it surpasses all belief, and this having been faithfully paid, and he having in the dealings with him given signs of a frank, liberal, and steadfast spirit and of a clear and well-ordered understanding, the conquerers were seized with the desire, after having exacted one million three hundred and twenty-five thousand five hundred weight of gold, besides silver and other things that amounted to no less, so that their horses went henceforth shod only with solid gold, to see also, at the price of any treachery, what the remainder of this King's treasure might be and to take possession freely of what he had put in reserve. They trumped up against him a false accusation and false evidence, that he was planning to rouse his provinces to revolt in order to set himself free. Whereupon, by the lovely sentence of the very men who had set up this treachery against him, he was condemned to be publicly hanged and strangled, after having been made to buy off the torment of being burned alive by the baptism they gave him at the moment of execution. Horrible and unheard-of calamity, which, nevertheless, he bore without belying himself either by look or word, with a truly royal bearing and gravity. And then, to lull the people, stunned and overcome by such a strange thing, they counterfeited great sorrow at his death and arranged a sumptuous funeral for him.

The other, King of Mexico, having long defended his beleaguered city and having shown in this siege all that endurance and perseverance are capable of, if ever prince and people did, had the misfortune of falling alive into his enemies' hands, with the stipulation of being treated as a king (nor did he in his captivity let them see anything unworthy of that title); after this victory not finding all the gold that they had promised themselves, once they had moved and ransacked everything, they set about seeking information by inflicting on the prisoners they held the most cruel tortures they could think up. But having accomplished nothing by this, encountering hearts stronger than their torments, they became at last so furious that, contrary to their word and all the laws of nations, they condemned the King himself and one of the principal lords of his court to be put to the torture in the presence of each other. This lord, finding himself overcome with pain, surrounded with burning braziers, finally turned his glance piteously towards his master as if to ask his pardon for not being able to stand it any longer. The King, fixing his eyes on him proudly and severely as a reproach for his weakness and pusillanimity, said only these words to him, with a stern and firm voice: "And I, am I in a bath? Am I more at my ease than you?" Immediately after this the other succumbed to the pain and died on the spot. The King, half roasted, was carried away from there, not so much out of pity (for what pity ever touched souls that, for dubious information about some gold vessel to be pillaged, had a man broiled before their eyes, and even more, a king so great in fortune and merit?), as because his fortitude made their cruelty more and more shameful. They hanged him afterwards for having courageously attempted to deliver himself by arms from such a long captivity and subjection, and he died in a manner worthy of a noble-spirited prince.

On another occasion they burned alive at one time, and in the same fire, four hundred and sixty men—the four hundred being of the common people, the sixty being the principal lords of a province, merely prisoners of war.

We have these narratives from themselves, for they do not only admit these actions, but boast of them and broadcast them. Can it be for a testimony of their justice or their zeal for religion? Truly, those are ways too contrary and hostile to so holy an end. If their intent had been to extend our faith, they should have considered that it does not spread by taking possession of territories, but by taking possession of men, and they should have been more than satisfied with the murders that the necessity of war brings with it, without indiscriminately adding to it a butchery, as of so many wild beasts, as universal as fire and sword could make it, having purposely spared only as many as they wanted to make miserable slaves for the working and service of their mines. So it was that many of the captains were punished with death on the scene of their conquests by order of the Kings of Castile, rightly shocked by the horror of the men's conduct, and almost all of them were despised and hated. God deservedly allowed this great plunder to be swallowed up by the sea while transporting it, or by the intestine wars in which they devoured one another, and most of the men were buried on the spot of their actions without enjoying any fruit of their victory.

As to the fact that the revenue from these lands, even in the hands of a thrifty and prudent prince,[18] corresponds so little to the expectation given of it to his predecessors and to that first abundance of riches encountered in setting foot on those new lands (for, though a great deal is collected from there, we see it is nothing in comparison with what should be expected), the reason is that the use of money was utterly unknown, and that consequently their gold was found all massed together since it was used only for show and parade, like a piece of furniture preserved from father to son by many powerful kings who were constantly draining their mines to make this vast heap of vessels and statues for the adornment of their palaces and temples; whereas our gold is all in currency and trade. We cut it up into small pieces and change it into a thousand forms, scatter and disperse it. Imagine our kings heaping up thus all the gold they could get during many centuries and keeping it idle.

The people of the kingdom of Mexico were somewhat more

---

[18] Philip II, King of Spain

civilized and more accomplished in arts than the other nations were over there. They, too, thought as we do, that the world was near its end, and they took as a sign of it the desolation we brought upon them. They believed that the existence of the world was divided into five ages and into the life of five successive suns, of which four had already run their time, and that the one which gave them light was the fifth. The first perished with all other creatures by a universal inundation of water; the second, by the heavens falling upon us, which suffocated every living thing: to which age they assigned the giants and showed the Spaniards some of their bones according to the proportion of which the stature of these men amounted to twenty hands high; the third by fire, which burned and consumed all; the fourth by a tempest of air and wind which leveled even many mountains: the men did not die in it, but were turned into baboons (what notions will not the weakness of human belief accept!); after the death of this fourth sun, the world was twenty-five years in perpetual darkness, in the fifteenth of which a man and a woman were created, who restored the human race; ten years after, upon a certain one of their days, the sun appeared newly created, and ever since the reckoning of their years begins with that day. The third day after its creation the ancient gods died; the new ones have been born since, one at a time. Their idea of how they think this last sun will perish my author did not learn. But their computation of this fourth change coincides with that great conjunction of stars which produced, some eight hundred years ago, according to the reckoning of astrologers, many great alterations and innovations in the world.

As to pomp and magnificence, whereby I entered upon this subject, neither Greece nor Rome nor Egypt can compare any of its works, either in utility or difficulty or magnificence, with the road which is seen in Peru, laid out by the kings of the country, from the city of Quito as far as that of Cuzco (a distance of three hundred leagues), straight, even, twenty-five paces wide, paved, lined on both sides with high and beautiful walls, and along these, on the inside, two everflowing streams, bordered by beautiful trees which they call *molly*. When they met with rocks and mountains, they cut through them and leveled them and filled the gullies with stone and chalk. At the end of each day's journey there are beautiful palaces furnished with provisions, clothes, and arms, both for travelers and for the armies that have to pass that way. In my estimate of this work I have reckoned the difficulty, which is particularly great in that place. They did not build with any stones less than ten feet square; they had no other means of transport than by strength of arm, dragging their loads along; and they did not even have the art of scaffolding, knowing no other artifice than to pile up so much earth against the building as it rose, and to remove it afterwards.

Let us return to our coaches. Instead of these or any other sort of carriage, they had themselves carried by men and on their shoulders. This last King of Peru, the day that he was taken, was thus carried upon shafts of gold, seated in a chair of gold in the middle of his battle-array. As many of his carriers as they killed to make him fall to the ground (for they wanted to take him alive), so many others vied with each other to take the place of the dead so that they could never bring him down, however great a slaughter they made of those people, until a horseman seized him by the body and threw him to the ground.

OF THE ART OF CONVERSING

IT IS a practice of our justice to condemn some as a warning to others. To condemn them because they have done wrong would be stupidity, as Plato says. For what is done cannot be undone; but it is done in order that they may not err again in the same way, or that others may avoid the example of their wrongdoing.

We do not correct the man we hang; we correct others through him. I do the same. My errors will soon be a part of my nature and incorrigible; but the good which eminent men do the public in making themselves imitated, I shall, perhaps, do in making them avoid my example:

> Behold the wretched life of Albius' son
> And Barrus' poverty. Fine warning lest
> Someone be led to squander his estate.[1]

By my publishing and criticising my imperfections, somebody will learn to be afraid of them. The parts that I most esteem in myself derive more honor from self-criticism than from self-commendation. That is the reason why I more often drop back into it and pause upon it. But, when all is summed up, a man never speaks of himself without loss. His condemnation of himself is always credited, his praise of himself discredited.

There may be some people of my temperament who learn more by opposition to bad examples than by imitation of good ones and more by fleeing than by following. The elder Cato had this sort of teaching in mind when he said that the wise

---

[1] Horace, *Satires*

have more to learn of fools than fools of the wise; and so did that ancient lyre player who, Pausanias says, used to make his scholars go listen to a bad musician who lived opposite him, where they might learn to hate his discords and false measures. The horror of cruelty repels me more towards clemency than any model of clemency could attract me to it. A good rider does not improve my seat so much as an attorney or a Venetian on horseback; and a bad style of speech does more to reform mine than a good one. Every day the stupid bearing of another warns and prompts me. That which pricks touches and arouses more than that which pleases. These times are not fit to improve us, except backwards, by disagreement more than by agreement, by difference more than by similarity. Having learned little by good examples, I make use of the bad ones, whose lessons are commonly at hand. I have endeavored to render myself as agreeable as I saw others offensive, as firm as I saw others lax, as mild as I saw others harsh. But I set before myself unattainable standards.

The most fruitful and natural exercise of our mind, in my opinion, is conversation. I find the practice of it more pleasant than that of any other action of our life; and that is the reason why, if I were right now compelled to choose, I should sooner, I believe, consent to lose my sight than my hearing or speech. The Athenians, and also the Romans, kept this exercise in great honor in their academies. In our times the Italians retain some traces of it to their great advantage, as is manifest in a comparison of our intelligence with theirs. The study of books is a languishing and feeble activity that produces no heat, whereas conversation teaches and exercises at the same time. If I converse with a man of strong mind and a stiff jouster, he presses hard upon me and digs at me right and left, his ideas spur on mine. Rivalry, glory, and contention thrust and lift me up above myself. And agreement is a very tiresome quality in conversation.

As our mind becomes strengthened by communication with

vigorous and orderly minds, so it is impossible to state how much it loses and degenerates by the continual association and company we have with inferior and sickly minds. There is no contagion that spreads like that. I know sufficiently by experience what it is worth a yard. I love to dispute and discuss, but with a small number of men and for my own interest. For to serve as a spectacle for great personages and to vie in parading our wit and chatter is, in my opinion, a very unbecoming occupation for a man of honor.

Folly is a wretched quality; but not to be able to endure it, to be irritated and gnawed by it, as I am, is another sort of disease which is scarcely less annoying than folly; and this is what I would now criticize in myself.

I enter into conversation and argument with great freedom and ease, inasmuch as opinion finds in me a soil into which it cannot readily penetrate and take deep root. No propositions astonish me, no belief offends me, however contrary it may be to my own. There is no fancy so frivolous and extravagant that it does not seem to me quite in keeping with the capacity of the human mind. Those of us who deprive our judgment of the right of making decisions look calmly at differing opinions; and if we do not lend our opinion to them, we readily lend our ears. When one scalepan is totally empty, I let the other waver under old wives' dreams. And it seems to me excusable if I rather take the odd number, Thursday rather than Friday; if I had rather be twelfth or fourteenth than thirteenth at table; if I had rather on a journey see a hare run alongside my path than cross it, and rather give first my left foot than my right to be shod. All such idle fancies which enjoy credit about us deserve at least to be listened to. For me they only outweigh emptiness, but they do outweigh that. Moreover popular and chance opinions are in weight something else than nothing in nature. And he who does not let himself go so far as that, perhaps, falls into the vice of obstinacy to avoid that of superstition.

Contradictions of opinions, then, neither offend nor trouble me; they only arouse me and exercise me. We fly from being corrected; we ought to face it and go to meet it, especially when it comes in the form of conversation, not of lecturing. At every opposition we do not consider whether it be just, but, right or wrong, how to get rid of it. Instead of stretching out our arms to it, we stretch out our claws. I could let myself be roughly jolted by my friends: "You are a fool; you are dreaming!" I like to see gentlemen together express themselves in a forthright manner, letting their words go wherever their thought does. We must fortify and harden our hearing against this tenderness about the ceremonious sound of words. I like a strong and manly familiarity and association, a friendship that takes delight in the sharpness and vigor of its intercourse, like love in its bites and scratches that draw blood. It is not vigorous and spirited enough if it is not quarrelsome, if it is mannered and artificial, if it fears the clash and moves with constraint. *For there can be no discussion without contradiction.*[2]

When anyone contradicts me, he arouses my attention, not my anger; I advance towards the man who contradicts me, who instructs me. The cause of truth ought to be the common cause of both. What will be his answer? The passion of anger has already struck his judgment. Confusion has seized it before reason. It would be useful if we should lay wagers on the outcome of our arguments, if there were a material mark of our losses, so that we might take some account of them, and so that my valet might be able to say to me: "Your ignorance and obstinacy cost you last year a hundred crowns twenty different times."

I greet and welcome truth in whatever hand I find it, and cheerfully surrender and extend to her my conquered arms as soon as I see her approach in the distance. And I lend a hand to the criticisms made of my writings, provided that a person does not go about it with too imperious and dogmatic a mien;

---

[2] Cicero, *De Finibus*

I have often altered them more from civility than for the sake of improvement, liking to gratify and nourish the freedom of admonishing me by the readiness with which I yield, even at my own expense. And yet it is certainly hard to bring the men of my time to it. They have not the courage to correct because they have not the courage to let themselves be corrected, and speak always with dissimulation in the presence of one another. I take such great pleasure in being judged and known that it is almost indifferent to me in which of the two forms I am so. My thought so often contradicts and condemns itself that it is all one to me if another does it, especially considering that I give to his criticism only as much authority as I wish. But I break off relations with him who bears himself so high-handedly, like someone I know who regrets having given advice if not believed, and takes it as an affront if someone resists following it.

That Socrates always received smilingly the objections made to his arguments might be said to be due to his strength and to the fact that, the advantage being certain to fall on his side, he accepted them as grounds of new glory. But we see, on the contrary, that there is nothing which makes our feelings so sensitive to contradiction as the idea of our superiority and disdain for our adversary; and that in reason it is rather for the weaker to take in good part the opposition that corrects him and sets him right. In truth I seek the company of those who handle me roughly rather than of those who fear me. It is a flat and harmful pleasure to have to do with people who admire and give way to us. Antisthenes commanded his children never to thank or be grateful to a man who praised them. I feel much prouder of the victory I obtain over myself when, in the very heat of the combat, I make myself bow beneath the force of my adversary's reason, than I feel pleased by the victory I obtain over him through his weakness.

In short, I accept and admit any kind of blow that is straightforward, however weak it may be, but I am extremely intolerant of those that are made irregularly. I care little about the matter, all opinions are the same to me, and which view wins is almost indifferent to me. I will peaceably argue a whole day long if the debate is carried on with order. It is not so much force and subtlety that I demand, as order: the order which is seen every day in the altercations of shepherds and shop-boys, never among us. If they get off the track, it is by way of incivility; and we do the same. But their turbulence and impatience never put them off their theme; their argument follows its course. If they jump ahead of one another, if they do not wait for their turn, they at least understand one another. In my opinion a man answers only too well if he answers to the point. But when the argument is confused and disorderly, I leave the subject and cling to the form angrily and injudiciously, and throw myself into a headstrong, malicious, and imperious manner of arguing, which I have to blush at afterwards.

It is impossible to discuss matters rightly with a fool. Not only is my judgment corrupted at the hands of so impetuous a master, but my conscience also.

Our arguments ought to be forbidden and punished like other verbal crimes. What evil do they not rouse and heap up, being always governed and commanded by anger? We quarrel first with the reasons, then with the men. We learn to argue only that we may contradict; and with everyone contradicting and being contradicted, it turns out that the fruit of arguing is to destroy and nullify truth. So Plato, in his Republic, prohibits this exercise to inept and ill-bred minds.

What use is there for you to start in quest of truth with a man whose stride and pace are inadequate? We do no harm to the subject when we leave it to seek some way of handling it; I do not mean an artificial and scholastic way, I mean a natural way, with a sound understanding. What will it be in the end? One goes to the east, the other to the west; they lose track of the main issue and push it aside in the pack of incidental points. After an hour of tempest they don't know what they are looking for; one is low, the other high, and another wide of the mark. One catches at a word and a simile; another is no longer aware of what is said in opposition to him, so involved is he in his own course; and he is thinking of following himself, not you. Another, finding himself weak-backed, fears all, refuses all, and from the very outset mixes up and confuses the issue; or at the height of the debate balks to the point of becoming quite contemptible, through spiteful ignorance affecting a haughty disdain or a stupidly modest avoidance of contention. Provided that he strikes home, this man here does not care how much he lays himself open. Another counts his words and weighs them as so many reasons. That man there makes use only of the advantage of his voice and lungs. Here is one who concludes against himself, and another who deafens you with useless preambles and digressions. This other arms himself with out-and-out insults and seeks a groundless quarrel to get rid of the company and conversation of a wit that crowds his own. This last man sees nothing in reason but holds you besieged with the dialectic encompassment of his clauses and with the formulas of his art.

Now who does not begin to distrust the sciences and to doubt whether he can derive from them any solid benefit for the service of life, considering the use we put them to? *Studies that cure nothing.*[3] Who has acquired understanding from logic? Where are her fair promises? *Neither for living better nor for reasoning more fitly.*[4] Is there any more of a muddle in the cackle of fishwives than in the public debates of men whose profession is logic? I had rather my son should learn to speak in the taverns than in the schools of speech.

Take a Master of Arts, converse with him; why does he not make us aware of the excelling nature of those arts, why does he not captivate the women and ignoramuses such as we are with admiration for the strength of his reasons and the beauty

---

[3] Seneca, *Epistles*   [4] Cicero, *De Finibus*

of his orderly exposition? Why does he not sway and persuade us at his will? Why does a man with such advantages in matter and method mix insults, unrestraint, and fury with his fencing? Let him strip off his hood, his robe, and his Latin, let him not batter our ears with plain, undigested Aristotle, and you will take him for one of us, or worse. It seems to me that with this involvement and interlacing of words, with which they beset us, it is as with performers of sleight of hand: their dexterity attacks our senses, but does not at all shake our belief. Aside from this legerdemain, they do nothing that is not common and base. For being more learned they are none the less fools.

I love and honor learning as much as those who have it; and in its true use it is the most noble and the most powerful acquisition of men. But in those (and there is an infinite number of that kind) who base their fundamental capacity and value on it, who appeal from their understanding to their memory, *hiding in the shadow of others,*[5] and who can do nothing but by book, I hate it, if I may dare to say so, a little more than I do stupidity. In my country and in my time, learning often enough mends purses, rarely minds. If it meets with dull ones, like a crude and undigested mass it weighs them down and suffocates them; if with shrewd ones, it is likely to purify, clarify, and subtilize them even to exhaustion. It is a thing of almost indifferent quality: a very useful accessory to a well-endowed mind, but pernicious and harmful to others. Or rather it is a thing of very precious use that will not let itself be had at a low price; in some hands it is a scepter, in others a fool's bauble. But let us proceed.

What greater victory can you expect than to teach your enemy that he is not able to stand up to you? When you gain the advantage by the substance of your proposition, it is truth that wins; when you gain the advantage by your arrangement and presentation, it is you who win. I am of the opinion that in Plato and Xenophon Socrates argues more for the sake of

---

[5] Seneca, *Epistles*

the arguers than for the sake of the argument, and to instruct Euthydemus and Protagoras in the knowledge of their own impertinence more than of the impertinence of their art. He takes hold of the first subject like one who has a more useful purpose than to clear it up, namely, to clear up the minds that he undertakes to direct and exercise.

Agitation and the chase is properly our quarry; we are not to be excused if we carry it on badly and inappropriately; to fail to seize the prey is another thing. For we are born to quest after truth; to possess it belongs to a greater power. It is not, as Democritus said, hidden in the bottom of abysses, but rather elevated to an infinite height in the divine knowledge. The world is but a school of seeking. The point is not who shall hit the ring but who shall run the best courses. He who speaks true can play the fool as much as he who speaks false; for we are concerned with the manner, not the matter, of speaking. I am disposed to consider the form as much as the substance, the advocate as much as the cause, as Alcibiades prescribed for us to do.

And every day I while away my time reading in authors without any care about their learning, looking for their style, not their matter. Just as I seek out the company of some man well known for his intelligence, not that he may teach me, but that I may know him.

Any man may speak truly, but to speak methodically, wisely, and competently is within the capacity of few men. Thus the falsity that proceeds from ignorance does not offend me; it is the ineptitude that does. I have broken off several affairs that were useful to me because of the irrelevant wrangling of those with whom I was dealing. I am not excited once in a year at the faults of those over whom I have authority, but over the stupidity and obstinacy of their brutish and asinine assertions, excuses, and defenses, we are every day ready to seize each other by the throat. They neither understand what is said nor why, and answer accordingly; it is enough to drive a man to despair. I never feel my head roughly jarred except by another head, and I sooner put up with the vices of my servants than their heedlessness, their troublesomeness, and their stupidity. Let them do less, provided they are capable of doing something. You live in hopes of heating up their will; but there is nothing worth while to be had or to be hoped for from a log.

But what if I take things otherwise than they are? It may be so; and, therefore, I blame my impatience and hold in the first place that it is equally a fault in one who is right and in one who is wrong, for it is always a tyrannical harshness not to be able to endure a way of thinking differing from your own; and besides, there is not in truth a greater and more constant, or stranger absurdity than to be stirred up and stung by the absurdities of the world. For it irritates us chiefly with ourselves, and that philosopher of olden times would never have lacked an occasion for his tears as long as he had himself to contemplate. Miso, one of the Seven Sages, who was of a Timonian and Democritic humor, being asked what he was laughing at all to himself, replied: "At the fact that I laugh all to myself."

How many ridiculous things, in my opinion, do I say and reply every day; and surely then how much more numerous they must seem to the opinion of others! If I bite my own lips over them, what must the others do? In fine, we must live among the living and let the river run under the bridge without our troubling ourselves, or at least without our being upset. True, but why can we meet someone with a crooked and misshapen body without being moved, and cannot endure to meet with an ill-ordered mind without getting angry? This improper severity is more closely connected to the judge than to the fault. Let us always have this saying of Plato in our mouths: "If I find a thing unsound, is it not because I myself am unsound? Am I not myself at fault? May not my censure be turned against me?" A wise and divine refrain which lashes the most common and universal error of mankind. Not only the reproaches that we throw at one another, but our reasons also and our arguments in controversial matters can ordinarily be turned against us, and we wound ourselves with our own weapons. Of that antiquity has left me weighty examples enough. This was very cleverly put, and much to the point, by the man who originated it:

> Each man prefers the smell of his own dung.[6]

Our eyes can see nothing behind us. A hundred times a day we laugh at ourselves in the person of our neighbor and detest in others the defects which are more clearly in us and wonder at them with extraordinary impudence and heedlessness.

Only yesterday I had occasion to hear an intelligent man, a personage of good birth, scoffing with as much humor as aptness at the foolish habit of another who splits everyone's head with his genealogies and alliances, more than half of them false (those men are most apt to jump upon such ridiculous subjects whose quality is most doubtful and least certain); and he, if he had drawn back upon himself, he would have found himself to be hardly less intemperate and tiresome in broadcasting and extolling the prerogatives of his wife's family. Oh! importunate presumption with which the wife sees herself armed by the hands of her husband himself! If they understood Latin, we ought to say to them:

> If of herself she be not mad enough,
> Come, goad her on.[7]

I do not mean that no man may criticize another unless he is clean himself, for then no one would criticize another; no, nor do I even mean clean from the same sort of fault. But I mean that our judgment, placing upon another the blame which is then in question, should not spare us from an inner judg-

---

Erasmus, *Adages*   [7] Terence, *Andria*

ment. It is a charitable service for him who cannot eradicate
a vice in himself to endeavor, nevertheless, to remove it from
another in whom it may not have so malignant and stubborn
a root. Nor do I think it is an appropriate reply to one who
warns me of a fault, to say that he also has it. What of that?
The warning is still true and useful. If we had a good nose,
our ordure ought to stink worse to us, inasmuch as it is our
own. And Socrates is of opinion that if a man should find himself and his son and a stranger guilty of some violence and
wrong, he ought to begin with himself, submitting himself to
the sentence of justice and, to purge himself, imploring the
help of the hangman's hand; secondly, he should proceed to
his son, and lastly to the stranger. If this precept takes a little
too lofty a tone, he ought at least to present himself the first
for the punishment by his own conscience.

The senses are our first and proper judges, which perceive
things only by external accidents; and it is no wonder if in all
the parts in the functioning of our society there is such a perpetual and universal mixture of ceremonies and superficial appearances, so much so that the best and most effective part of
our regulations consists therein. It is still man we are dealing
with, whose condition is wonderfully corporeal. Let those who
these late years have tried to construct for us such a contemplative and immaterial practice of religion not be astounded if
there are some who think it would have melted and slipped
through their fingers if it had not held fast among us as a mark,
title, and instrument of division and faction more than by its
own power. As in conversation, the gravity, the gown, and the
fortune of the speaker often give authority to vain and absurd
remarks. It is not to be presumed that a personage so formidable and with such a following may not have within him more
than ordinary capability, and that such a disdainful and super-
cilious man who is given so many missions and offices may not
be more capable than this other man who bows to him at such
a great distance and whom no one employs. Not only the words

but also the grimaces of these people are considered and taken into account, everyone striving to give some fine and substantial interpretation to them. If they stoop to common conversation, and if you offer them anything but approbation and reverence, they will knock you senseless with the authority of their experience: they have heard, they have seen, they have done; you are overwhelmed with examples. I should like to tell them that the fruit of a surgeon's experience is not the history of his practice and his remembering that he has cured four people of the plague and three of the gout, unless he is able from that experience to derive means of forming his judgment and makes us aware that he has become wiser in the practice of his art. So in a concert of instruments we do not hear a lute, a spinet, and the flute, we hear a general harmony, the effect of the fusion of that whole mass. If travel and offices have improved them, it is up to the action of their understanding to make it appear. It is not enough to count experiences, we must weigh and sort them, we must have digested and distilled them in order to extract from them the reasons and conclusions they contain. There were never so many historians. It is always good and of use to listen to them for they furnish us fully with excellent and laudable instructions from the storehouse of their memory, a great contribution, certainly, to the aid of life. But we are not seeking that right now; we are seeking to know whether these narrators and collectors are themselves commendable.

I hate any kind of tyranny, whether of words or acts. I commonly brace myself against these vain circumstances that delude our judgment through the senses; and keeping a wary eye on those extraordinary grandees, I have found that for the most part they are but men like the rest,

For common sense is rare in that estate.[8]

---

[8] Juvenal

Perhaps we esteem and look upon them as less than they are because they undertake more and reveal themselves more: they are not equal to the load they have taken up. There must be more vigor and power in the bearer than in the burden. He who has not used his full strength leaves you to guess whether he has still some strength beyond that and whether he has been tested to the utmost; he who sinks under his load reveals his measure and the weakness of his shoulders. That is why we see so many inept souls among the learned, and more than of the other kind. They would have made good husbandmen, good merchants, good artisans; their natural strength was cut out to that proportion. Learning is a thing of great weight; they collapse beneath it. Their natural capacity has neither vigor nor skill enough to spread out and distribute that noble and powerful matter, to put it to use and to be helped by it. It can be effective only in a strong nature, and such natures are very rare. And the weak ones, says Socrates, debase the dignity of philosophy in handling it. It appears both useless and harmful when it is badly incased. This is how they harm themselves and make fools of themselves,

> Just like the monkey, mimic of man's face,
> That laughingly a boy dressed up in silks
> And left the buttocks and the back all bare,
> The butt of all the dinner guests.[9]

Likewise it is not enough for those who rule and command us, who hold the world in their hands, to have an ordinary understanding, to be able to do what we can do. They are very far below us if they are not very far above us. As they promise more, so do they owe more; and, therefore, silence is for them not only the restrained air of formality and gravity, but it is also often profitable and economical. For Megabysus, having come to see Apelles in his workshop, stood a long time without saying a word and then began to discuss the painter's

---

Claudian, *Against Eutropius*

works, for which he received this rude reprimand: "As long as you kept silent, you seemed to be something great because of your chains and pomp; but now that we have heard you speak, there is not a boy in my shop who does not despise you." That magnificent attire, that lofty state, did not permit him to be ignorant with a common ignorance and to speak impertinently of painting. He ought to have maintained, by staying silent, that external and presumptive look of competence. To how many stupid souls in my time has a cold and taciturn mien served as a mark of wisdom and capacity!

Honors, offices, are of necessity conferred more by fortune than through merit; and we are often wrong in blaming kings for it. On the contrary, it is a wonder they should have such good luck, having so few ways of being informed in these matters:

To know his people is the greatest virtue of a prince; [10]

for Nature has not given them a vision that can reach out to so many people to discern pre-eminence, and pierce our bosoms, where lies the knowledge of our wills and of our greatest worth. They must pick us out by conjecture and gropingly, by family, wealth, learning, the voice of the people: very feeble evidence. If anyone could find a way by which to judge men justly and choose them rationally, he would by that single stroke establish a perfect form of government.

"Yes, but he directed this great affair successfully." That is saying something, but it is not saying enough; for this maxim is justly accepted, that we must not judge the plans by the results. The Carthaginians punished the bad decisions of their commanders, even though they were set right by a happy outcome. And the people of Rome often refused a triumph for great and very advantageous victories because the conduct of the leader did not correspond to his good fortune. We com-

---

[10] Martial

monly see in the actions of the world that Fortune, to teach us how powerful she is in all things, and because she delights in humbling our presumption, having been unable to make the incompetent wise, makes them fortunate, as if to vie with virtue. And she likes to take a hand in favoring those actions in which the web is most purely her own. Whence we see every day that the simplest among us bring to success great tasks, both public and private. And as Siramnes the Persian replied to those who were astonished that his affairs were turning out so badly, in view of the fact that his plans were so wise, that he was sole master of his plans, but that of the success of his affairs Fortune was mistress; these may answer the same, but with a contrary bias. Most things in the world are performed by themselves,

> The fates find out a way.[11]

The outcome often justifies a very foolish conduct. Our intervention is little more than a routine, and more commonly the result of considering usage and example than reason. Astonished at the greatness of an affair, I once learned from those who had carried it out their motives and their management of it; I found nothing in them but very commonplace ideas. And the most commonplace and most used are also, perhaps, the surest and best adapted to practice, if not to show.

What if the shallowest reasons are the most firmly seated, if the lowest, loosest, and most battered are the best adapted to affairs? To maintain the authority of the King's Council there is no need that outsiders should participate in it or peer into it nearer than from the outermost barrier. It must be revered on trust and as a whole if its reputation is to be maintained.

In my deliberations I outline the matter a little and consider it lightly in its first aspects; the very essence of the matter I am accustomed to entrust to heaven:

---

[11] Virgil, *Aeneid*

Leave to the gods the rest.[12]

Good and ill fortune are, in my opinion, two sovereign powers. It is unwise to think that human wisdom can fill the rôle
of Fortune. And vain is his attempt who presumes to embrace
both causes and consequences and to lead by the hand the
progress of his affair—especially vain in the deliberations of
war. There was never greater circumspection and prudence in
military matters than is sometimes seen among us. Can it possibly be that they are afraid of losing themselves on the way,
reserving themselves for the catastrophe of that drama?

I will add that even our wisdom and deliberation follow for
the most part the lead of chance. My will and my reasoning
are moved now by one breath, now by another, and there are
many of these movements that are carried on without my direction. My reason is subject to accidental impulses and agitations that change from day to day:

> Their moods now change and in their hearts they feel
> Emotions other than those stirring them
> When winds were driving on the clouds.[13]

Just see who are the most powerful in the cities and who are
most successful in their business: you will usually find that
they are the least capable. It has happened that women, children, and madmen have ruled great states equally well with
the most able princes. And Thucydides says that the thick-
witted more commonly succeed in it than the sharp-witted. We
attribute to their wisdom the results of their good fortune.

> Each man excels according to the use
> He makes of luck, and then we call him wise.[14]

Wherefore I aver that, in every way, events are meager evidence of our worth and capacity.

---

[12] Horace, *Odes*   [13] Virgil, *Georgics*   [14] Plautus, *Pseudolus*

Now I was about to say that we need only look at a man who has been elevated to dignity: even if we had known him three days before as a man of little account, there slips imperceptibly into our minds an image of greatness and ability, and we are persuaded that, growing in state and reputation, he has grown in merit. We judge him not according to his value, but, after the manner of counters, according to the prerogative of his place. Let chance turn again, let him fall again and mix again with the crowd, everyone will inquire with wonder into the cause that had hoisted him so high. "Is this he?" they will say; "Did he know no more about it when he was there? Are princes satisfied with so little? We were certainly in good hands!" This is a thing that I have often seen in my time. And even the mask of grandeur put on in our plays affects and deceives us somewhat. What I myself adore in kings is the crowd of their adorers. All deference and submission is due to them, except that of the understanding. My reason is not trained to bow and bend, it is my knees.

Melanthius, being asked what he thought of the tragedy of Dionysius, said: "I did not see it, it was so obscured by words." So the most of those who judge the speeches of the great ought to say: "I did not understand his meaning, it was so obscured by gravity, greatness, and majesty."

Antisthenes one day was trying to persuade the Athenians to order their asses to be put to tilling the fields, as the horses were; whereupon he received the answer that that animal was not born for such a service. "That doesn't matter," he replied, "it is only a question of your giving the order; for the most ignorant and incapable men that you place in command in your wars do not fail to become at once very worthy of their posts since you place them there."

To that is related the custom of so many peoples who canonize the king they have created from among them and are not content to honor him if they do not adore him. Those of Mexico, after the ceremonies of his coronation are finished,

dare no more look him in the face; but, as if they had deified
him by his royalty, among the oaths they make him swear to
maintain their religion, their laws, their liberties, to be valiant,
just, and mild, he, moreover, swears to make the sun move in
its customary light, the clouds sprinkle rain at a fit season, the
rivers run in their beds, and to make the earth bear all things
necessary for his people.

I differ from this common fashion and am more suspicious
of capacity when I see it accompanied with grandeur of fortune and public esteem. We have to consider how advantageous it is to a man to speak when he pleases, to choose his
point, to interrupt or change the discussion with a magisterial
authority, to defend himself against the opposition of others by
a nod, a smile, or silence, in the presence of an assembly that
trembles with reverence and respect.

A man of prodigious fortune, adding his opinion to a certain
light discussion which was being quite loosely bandied about
at his table, began just this way: "It can be only a liar or a
fool that will say otherwise than so and so." Pursue this philosophical point with a dagger in your hand.

Here is another observation from which I derive great use:
it is that in arguments and conversations every remark that
seems good to us should not immediately be accepted. Most
men are rich in borrowed talent. It may happen that a man
makes a witty remark, a good reply and maxim, and advances
it without realizing its force. That we do not possess all we
borrow may, perhaps, be verified in myself. We must not always
yield to it, whatever truth or beauty it may have. We must
either stoutly oppose it or draw back, under color of not understanding it, to feel out on all sides how it is lodged in its author.
We may happen to impale ourselves on his point and aid his
thrust to carry beyond its reach. I have sometimes, in the necessity and press of the combat, employed counter-thrusts that
have penetrated beyond my intent and hope: I only gave them
for their number; they were received for their weight. Just as

when I debate against a vigorous man I delight in anticipating his conclusions, I ease him of the trouble of explaining himself, I strive to forestall his thought while it is yet nascent and imperfect (the order and pertinency of his understanding warn and threaten me from afar), so with these others I do just the contrary: we must understand nothing except what they say and we must assume nothing. If they express their opinion in general terms: "This is good, that is not," and if they hit it right, see if it is not Fortune that hits it for them. Let them circumscribe and limit their judgments a little: why it is so, how it is so.

These universal judgments, that I see so common, signify nothing. They are like men who salute a multitude of people as a crowd and en masse. Those who have real acquaintance with them greet and take notice of them by name and individually. Wherefore I have more often than every day seen it happen that minds of weak foundation, wanting to appear ingenious in pointing out, as a work is being read, the passage of beauty, bring their admiration to rest with so poor a choice that, instead of making us aware of the excellence of the author, they make us aware of their own ignorance. This exclamation is safe enough: "This is lovely!" after having heard a whole page of Virgil. In that way the cunning ones save themselves. But to undertake to follow him step by step and with exact and discriminating judgment to want to indicate where a good author excels himself, where he rises to heights, weighing the words, phrases, inventions, one after another, keep away from that. *We must consider not only what each one says, but also what he thinks, and even on what grounds he thinks it.*[15] Every day I hear fools say things that are not foolish. They make a good remark; let us examine how far they understand it, let us see where they got it. We help them to make use of this fine expression and that fine reason which they do not possess; they only have it in keeping. They quite likely brought it

---

[15] Cicero, *De Officiis*

forth by chance and gropingly; we put it to their credit and give it its value. You lend them a hand. To what purpose? They are not grateful to you for it and become more foolish by it. Do not give them your collaboration, let them go; they will handle this matter like people who are afraid of burning their fingers. They do not dare to change its setting or its light, nor enter into it. Shake it ever so little, it slips from them. They give it up to you, however strong and fine it may be. These are fine blades, but they are ill-mounted. How many times have I seen the proof of this? Now, if you chance to enlighten and support them, they snatch and steal at once from you the advantage of your interpretation: "That is what I meant to say; that is exactly my idea; and if I did not express it so, it was only for lack of words." Blow hard! Malice itself must be employed to correct this arrogant stupidity. Hegesias' doctrine, that we are neither to hate nor condemn, but instruct, is right elsewhere, but here it is injustice and inhumanity to aid and set right a man who stands in no need of it and is the worse for it. I like to let them sink and get mired even more than they are, and so deep that, if it is possible, they may at last recognize themselves.

Stupidity and muddleheadedness are not something curable by a bit of admonition. And we can properly say of this kind of correction what Cyrus answered to him who urged him to harangue his army upon the verge of battle: "That men are not made valiant and warlike all of a sudden by a fine oration, any more than a man becomes at once a good musician by hearing a fine song." These are apprenticeships that have to be served beforehand by a long and continued education. We owe this care and this assiduity of correction and instruction to our own; but to go preach to the first passer-by and to give lessons to the ignorance and stupidity of the first man we meet is a practice that I abhor. I rarely do it, even in my private discussions, and rather abandon all than bring myself to these pedantic lessons that are out of place. My nature is unfit either to speak or write for beginners. But as for things that are said in company or before other people, I never oppose them, either by word or sign, however false or absurd I may consider them.

Moreover nothing vexes me so much in foolishness as that it is more pleased with itself than any reason can reasonably be. It is unlucky that wisdom forbids you to be satisfied with and trust in yourself and always dismisses you discontented and timorous, whereas opinionativeness and foolhardiness fill their hosts with joy and assurance. It is for the most incompetent to look at other men over their shoulders, always returning from the combat full of vainglory and joy. And, moreover, this arrogance of speech and gaiety of countenance often gives them the better of it in the opinion of the audience, which is commonly weak and incapable of judging well and discerning the real advantages. Obstinacy and heat of opinion are the surest proofs of stupidity. Is there anything so assured, resolute, disdainful, contemplative, grave, and serious as an ass?

May we not put under the heading of conversation and intercourse the quick and sharp repartees which mirth and familiarity introduce among friends, in a witty and lively fashion jesting and having fun with one another? An exercise for which my natural gaiety makes me fit enough; and if it is not so tense and serious as that other exercise I just spoke of, it is no less keen and ingenious, nor of less utility, as Lycurgus thought. For my part I contribute to it more liberty than wit and have therein more luck than inventiveness. But I am perfect in forebearance for I put up with retaliation that is not only sharp, but indiscreet to boot, without being moved at all. And when attack is made on me, if I have not a brisk rebuttal immediately ready, I do not go wasting my time in pursuing the point with tedious and weak contention bordering upon obstinacy; I let it pass, and, gaily lowering my colors for the time, put off getting my revenge until a better moment. There is no merchant who always gains. Most men change their countenance and their voice when strength fails them and by an unseasonable fit of anger, instead of revenging themselves, set in relief their weakness together with their impatience. In this gay mood we sometimes pluck secret strings of our imperfections, which, when tranquil, we cannot touch without offense, and we profitably give one another a hint of our defects.

There are other games, played by hand, rash and violent, after the French manner, that I mortally hate: I have a tender and sensitive skin. In my life I have seen two princes of our royal blood brought to their graves as a result of them. It is ugly to fight in play.

As to the rest, when I want to judge someone, I ask him how far he is satisfied with himself, to what extent he is pleased with his words or his work. I want to get away from those fine excuses: "I did it in play;

> This work unfinished from the anvil came.[16]

I was not an hour at it; I have not looked at it since." Well, then, I say, let us put these pieces aside, give me one that expresses you fully, by which you would like to be measured. And then, what do you consider the finest element in your work? Is it this part or that? Is it the graceful expression, or the matter, or the invention, or the judgment, or the learning? For I notice generally that men are as wide of the mark in judging their own work as that of others, not only because of the affection mingled in it, but because of not having the capacity to perceive and distinguish its value. The work, by its own strength and fortune, may second the workman beyond his inventiveness and knowledge and outstrip him. For my part, I do not judge the value of any other work less clearly than my own, and very changeably and uncertainly I place the Essays now low, now high.

There are many books that are useful because of their subjects, from which the author derives no praise; and there are

---

[16] Ovid, *Tristia*

good books, as well as good works, which shame the workman. I may write of the fashion of our banquets and of our clothes, and write reluctantly; I may publish the edicts of my time and the letters of princes that pass into the hands of the public; I may make an abridgment of a good book (and every abridgment of a good book is a stupid abridgment), which book will eventually be lost, and similar things. Posterity will derive remarkable benefit from such compositions; but what honor shall I get, unless it is from my good fortune? A goodly part of the famous books are of this nature.

When, some years ago, I read Philip de Comines, certainly a very good author, I took notice of this remark as an uncommon one: "That a man must take good care not to do his master such great service that he hinders him from finding a just reward for it." I ought to have praised the idea, not him; I came across it in Tacitus not long ago: *Benefits are agreeable so long as they seem capable of being returned; but when they go much beyond that, they are repaid with hatred instead of thanks;*[17] and Seneca vigorously says: *For the man who thinks it is shameful not to repay would not have that man live to whom he is indebted.*[18] Q. Cicero, with a weaker approach: *The man who thinks he cannot pay you back can by no means be your friend.*[19]

The subject matter, according to its nature, may give a man a reputation for learning and a good memory; but to judge in the book the qualities which are most his own and most distinguished, the strength and beauty of his mind, we must know what is his own and what is not; and in that which is not his, how much we are indebted to him in consideration of the choice, the arrangement, the embellishment, and the style that he has contributed to it. What if he has borrowed the matter and made the form worse, as it often happens? We others who have little contact with books are in this strait, that when we

---

[17] Tacitus, *Annals*   [18] Seneca, *Epistles.*   [19] Q. Cicero, *De Petitione Consulatus*

come upon some fine fancy in a new poet, some strong argument in a preacher, we do not dare to praise them for it until we have been informed by some learned man whether that element is their own or whether it is from another man. Until then I always stand on my guard.

I have just run straight through Tacitus' History (which seldom happens with me; it is twenty years since I have put a whole hour at one time on a book), and I did it at the persuasion of a gentleman for whom France has great esteem, both for his own worth and for a consistent kind of excellence and goodness which is also seen in his several brothers. I do not know of any author who introduces into a record of public affairs so many reflections on the conduct and dispositions of individuals. And quite contrary to his opinion, it seems to me that, having as his special intent to trace the lives of the emperors of his time, so strange and extreme in every way and shape, so many notable actions which their cruelty in particular brought forth in their subjects, he had a more powerful and more attractive matter to treat of and to narrate than if he had had to relate battles and general commotions. So that I often find him sterile, hastening over those noble deaths as if he feared to tire us with their great number and length.

This form of history is by far the most useful. Public movements depend more upon the guidance of Fortune, private ones upon our own. It is rather a judging than a narrating of history; there are in it more precepts than stories. It is not a book to read, it is a book to study and learn. It is so full of maxims that they are found right and left. It is a nursery of ethical and political reflections for the outfitting and adornment of those who hold a place in the managing of the world. He always pleads by solid and vigorous reasons, in a pointed and subtle manner, according to the affected style of that age. They were so fond of a blown-up style that when they did not find any point and subtlety in things, they borrowed them from words. He rather takes after Seneca's way of writing: he seems to me more sinewy, and Seneca more pointed. His service is more suited to a troubled and sick state, as ours is at present; you would often say that he is depicting us and criticizing us. Those who doubt his sincerity clearly reveal themselves to be ill disposed to him on some other account. His opinions are sound, and he leans to the right side in Roman affairs. Yet I find fault with him a bit for having judged Pompey more harshly than is consistent with the opinion of the trustworthy men that lived and had dealings with him, and for rating him quite on a par with Marius and Sulla, excepting that he was more covert. His intent in the government of affairs has not been acquitted of ambition or vengeance, and even his friends were afraid that victory would have transported him beyond the bounds of reason, but not to so unbridled a degree as in the other two. There is nothing in his life to have threatened us with such manifest cruelty and tyranny. Besides we ought not to balance suspicion against evidence; therefore I do not believe Tacitus in that matter.

That his narratives are sincere and straightforward might, perhaps, be argued even from this, that they are not always exactly applicable to the conclusions drawn by his judgment, which he follows according to the bias he has taken, often beyond the matter he is presenting to us, which he has not deigned to slant in the least respect. He needs no excuse for having approved the religion of his time, in accordance with the laws that ordered him to do so, and for having been ignorant of the true religion. That was his misfortune, not his fault.

I have chiefly considered his judgment, and I am not very clear about it in every instance. For example, these words in the letter that Tiberius, when old and sick, sent to the senate: "What shall I write to you, sirs, or how shall I write to you, or what shall I not write to you at this time? May the gods and the goddesses destroy me in a worse manner than that in which I feel myself perishing every day if I know." I do not see why he ascribes them so positively to a poignant remorse, tormenting the conscience of Tiberius; at least, when I was reading the passage, I did not see it.

This also seemed to me a little mean spirited, that having had to say that he had held a certain honorable office in Rome, he goes on to offer the excuse that it is not out of ostentation that he said it. This comment seems shabby to me for such a mind as his. For not to dare to speak roundly of a man's self reveals some want of spirit. A firm and lofty judgment, which judges soundly and surely, makes ready use of its own examples on all occasions just as if it were foreign matter and gives testimony about itself as frankly as about anything else. We have to override those common rules of politeness in favor of truth and liberty. I dare not only speak of myself, but to speak only of myself; I go astray when I write of anything else and take myself away from my subject. I am not so excessively enamoured of myself and I am not so attached and wedded to myself that I cannot distinguish and consider myself apart, as I do a neighbor or a tree. It is equally a fault not to see how far our worth extends, or to say more of it than we see. We owe more love to God than to ourselves, and we know Him less; and yet we speak of Him to our fill.

If Tacitus' writings express at all his qualities, he was a great man, upright and courageous, not of a superstitious but of a philosophical and noble-spirited virtue. We may think him bold in his testimony, as when he maintains that the hands of a soldier, carrying a load of wood, froze stiff and stuck to his load so that they remained there attached and dead, having parted from his arms. I am accustomed in such things to bow to the authority of such great witnesses.

When he says also that Vespasian, by the favor of the god Serapis, cured a blind woman in Alexandria by anointing her eyes with his spittle, and I know not what other miracle, he does so through the example and duty of all good historians. They keep a record of important events; among public happenings are to be included popular rumors and opinions. It is their part to relate common beliefs, not to regulate them. That part concerns divines and philosophers, directors of consciences. Therefore it was that his fellow-historian, a great man like himself, very wisely said: *For my part, I set down more things than I believe, for I cannot bear to give assurance of things about which I am in doubt, nor to suppress what I have heard.*[20] And this other: *These are things that it is not worth while either to affirm or to refute; we must adhere to report.*[21] And writing in an age when the belief in prodigies was beginning to decline, he says he will not on that account fail to insert in his *Annals* and to give a footing to things accepted by so many worthy men and with such great reverence for antiquity. That is very well said. Let them deliver history to us more as they receive it than as they believe it. I who am monarch of the matter whereof I treat and who am accountable for it to nobody do not, however, believe myself in all of it. I often hazard sallies of my wit which I distrust, and certain verbal subtleties at which I shake my ears; but I let them run at a venture. I see that some are honored for such things. It is not for me alone to judge them. I present myself standing and lying, front and rear, on the right and on the left, and in all my natural habits. Minds, even if alike in strength, are not always alike in their manner of applying themselves and in taste.

This is what my memory of Tacitus sets before me in the gross, and with uncertainty enough. All generalizations are loose and imperfect.

---

[20] Quintus Curtius   [21] Livy

OF VANITY

THERE IS NOT, perhaps, any more manifest vanity than to write of it so vainly. That which the Deity has so divinely expressed to us about it ought to be carefully and continually meditated by intelligent people.

Who does not see that I have taken a road along which I shall go without cease and without effort, so long as there is ink and paper in the world? I cannot keep a record of my life by my actions; Fortune places them too low. I keep it by my thoughts. So I knew a gentleman who made his life known only by the workings of his belly; at his house you saw on display a row of chamber pots for the last seven or eight days. That was his study, his conversation; all other talk stank to him. Here you have, a little more decently, the excrements of an old mind, sometimes hard, sometimes loose, and always indigested. And when shall I have done depicting the continual agitation and change of my thoughts, whatever matter they tumble on, since Diomedes[1] filled six thousand books with the sole subject of grammar? What must prattle produce, since the stammering and untying of the tongue smothered the world with such a horrible load of volumes? So many words for the sake of words alone. Oh, Pythagoras, why did you not conjure away this tempest? [2]

A certain Galba of olden times was blamed for living idly; he replied that everyone ought to give account of his actions,

---

[1] Didymus, rather than Diomedes, was reported by Seneca to have produced four thousand such works.   [2] A silence of two to five years was imposed by Pythagoras on his disciples.

not of his leisure. He was mistaken, for justice has cognizance and corrective power even over those who are taking a holiday.

But there should be some restraint of law against foolish and useless scribblers, as there is against vagabonds and idlers. Both I and a hundred others would be banished from the hands of our people. This is no jest. Scribbling seems some symptom of an unchecked age. When did we write so much as since our civil wars began? When did the Romans write so much as at the time of their downfall? Besides the fact that the refining of the mind does not thereby mean wiser conduct in a state, that idle business springs from this, that everyone sets laxly about the duties of his office and turns aside from them.

The corruption of the age is formed by the individual contribution of each one of us: some contribute treachery, others injustice, irreligion, tyranny, avarice, cruelty, according as they are more powerful; the weaker ones bring to it folly, vanity, and idleness, and of these I am one. It seems as if it were the season for vain things when the hurtful weigh upon us. In a time when doing ill is so common, to do what is only useless is, as it were, praiseworthy. I take consolation in the thought that I shall be one of the last on whom they will have to lay hands. While they are attending to the more pressing cases, I shall have leisure to reform. For it seems to me that it would be contrary to reason to prosecute petty disturbances while we are infested with the great ones. And the physician Philotimus said to a man who presented him his finger to dress, and by whose complexion and breath he recognized an ulcer of the lungs: "My friend, this is not the time to busy yourself with your fingernails."

And yet, on this subject, I saw some years ago that a person whose memory I hold in unusual esteem, in the midst of our great disorders, when there was neither law, nor justice, nor any magistrate who did his duty, any more than there is now, proposed to the public some reforms or others in clothes, cookery, and law practice. These are amusements with which they feed a people that are ill used, to tell them that they are not totally forgotten. Those others do the same who fix their attention upon forbidding insistently certain forms of speech, dancing, and games to a people ruined by all sorts of execrable vices. It is no time to wash and clean up when we are seized by a violent fever. It is for the Spartans alone to fall to combing and fixing their hair when they are on the point of running headlong into some extreme danger to their lives.

For my part, I have this other worse habit, that if my shoe is on askew, I also leave my shirt and my cloak on askew; I scorn to mend my ways by halves. When I am in a bad way, I doggedly pursue misfortune; I abandon myself through despair, and let myself go towards the precipice, and, as the saying is, throw the helve after the hatchet. I am obstinate in growing worse and think myself no longer worth my care; either entirely well or entirely ill.

It is a boon to me that the desolation of this realm coincides with the desolation of my age; I more willingly suffer that my ills be increased than I would have if my well-being had been disturbed by it. The words I utter in misfortune are words of anger; my courage bristles up instead of lying down. And, contrary to others, I am more devout in good than in evil fortune, following the precept of Xenophon, if not his reason for it, and I am more ready to turn loving eyes to Heaven to give thanks than to ask favors. I am more solicitous to improve my health when it smiles on me than I am to restore it when I have parted from it. Prosperity is discipline and instruction to me as adversity and rods are to others. As if good fortune were incompatible with good conscience, men never grow good but in evil fortune. Good fortune is to me a singular spur to moderation and modesty. Prayer wins me, threats repel me; favor makes me bend, fear stiffens me.

Among human traits this one is rather common: to be better

pleased with the things of others than with our own, and to
love stir and change.

> The light of day itself doth chiefly please,
> Because the hours those steeds have changed for these.[3]

I have my share of it. Those who follow the other extreme, of
being pleased with themselves, of valuing what they have above
other things, and of recognizing nothing as more beautiful than
what they see, if they are not wiser than we, are really happier. I do not envy their wisdom, but their good fortune.

This greedy desire for new and unknown things greatly helps
to nourish in me the desire to travel, but enough other circumstances contribute to it. I am glad to turn away from the government of my house. There is a kind of pleasure in commanding, though it were but in a barn, and in being obeyed by one's
people; but it is too uniform and languid a pleasure. And then
it is necessarily mixed with many vexatious thoughts: now the
poverty and oppression of your tenants, now a quarrel among
your neighbors, now the trespasses they make upon you afflict you;

> Whether the vines be smit with hail,
> Whether the promised harvests fail,
>   Perfidious to your toil;
> Whether the drooping trees complain
> Of angry winter's chilling rain,
>   Or stars that burn the soil;[4]

and that God hardly once in six months will send a season with
which your steward is fully satisfied, and which if it is good for
the vines, does not harm the meadows:

> The sun on high burns with too great a heat,
> Or sudden rains and icy frosts destroy,
> And windy blasts with mighty swirls harass.[5]

Petronius　　　　[4] Horace, *Odes*　　　[5] Lucretius

Add to that the new and well-shaped shoe of the man of old which hurts your foot;[6] and that a stranger does not understand how much it costs you and how much you sacrifice to maintain that show of order that is seen in your family, and that, perhaps, you buy it too dear.

I was late in setting myself to the charge of a household. Those whom Nature had sent into the world before me eased me for a long time of the trouble. I had already taken another bent more suitable to my nature. Yet, from what I have seen of it, it is an occupation more troublesome than hard; whoever is capable of anything else will very easily be capable of this. If I sought to become rich, that way would seem to me too long; I would have served kings, a more fruitful traffic than any other. Since I aspire to acquire only the reputation of having acquired nothing, just as I have wasted nothing, conformably to the rest of my life, not suited either to do good or to do evil, and since I seek only to pass along, I can do it, thank God, without any great attention.

If it comes to the worst, always go out to meet poverty by retrenching your expenses. That is what I am aiming at, and at mending my ways before poverty forces me to. Moreover I have set up in my soul enough levels so that I can live upon less than I have; contentedly, I mean. *Not by the evaluation of your income, but by your mode of living and by your cultivation is the extent of your wealth determined.*[7] My real need does not so wholly take up all I have that Fortune has not something of mine on which to bite without piercing to the quick.

---

[6] Allusion to Plutarch's account of the Roman who after divorcing his wife was censured by his friends. To their query, *"Was she not chaste? was she not fair? was she not fruitful?"*, he held out his shoe and asked them, *Whether it was not new? and well made? "Yet,"* added he, *"none of you can tell where it pinches me."* Certain it is that great and open faults have often led to no separation; while mere petty repeated annoyances, arising from unpleasantness or incongruity of character, have been the occasion of such estrangement as to make it impossible for man and wife to live together with any content. Life of Aemilius Paulus

[7] Cicero, *Paradoxes*

My presence, ignorant and indifferent as I am, is a great help in my domestic affairs. I engage in them, but grudgingly. Furthermore in my household I have this situation, that while in private I burn the candle at my end, the other end is not spared at all.

Journeys do me no harm except by their expense, which is great and beyond my means; being accustomed to travel with not only a necessary, but an elegant, retinue, I have to make my journeys so much the shorter and less frequent, and I spend in them only the skimmings and reserves, delaying and deferring according as these come in.

I do not want the pleasure of traveling about to spoil the pleasure of my repose; on the contrary, I intend for them to nourish and favor one another. Fortune has assisted me in this, that since my principal profession in this life was to live at ease, and rather idly than busily, she took from me the need of multiplying my riches to provide for a multitude of heirs. As for the one I have, if she has not enough with what I have had so plentifully enough, so much the worse for her; improvidence on her part will not merit my wishing her any more. And every man, according to the example of Phocion, provides sufficiently for his children who provides for them in so far as they are not unlike him. I should by no means agree with Crates' action. He left his money in the hands of a banker, with this condition: that if these children were fools, he should then give it to them; if they were clever, he should then distribute it to the simple-minded of the people. As if fools, for being less capable of doing without riches, were more capable of using them!

Be that as it may, the damage which is occasioned by my absence seems not to deserve, so long as I am able to support it, that I should waive the occasions that come up of diverting myself from that troublesome task of attendance.

There is always something that goes wrong. The affairs now of one house and now of another tug at you. You pry into everything too closely; your perspicacity hurts you here as it does often enough elsewhere. I steal away from occasions of becoming vexed and turn away from the knowledge of things that go amiss, and yet I cannot so order it but that every hour at home I bump into something that displeases me. And the knaveries that they most conceal from me are those that I know best. There are some we must ourselves help to conceal in order that they will do less harm. Trifling pinpricks, trifling sometimes, but always pinpricks. The smallest and slightest impediments are the most piercing; and as small print most hurts and tires the eyes, so do little affairs the most disturb us. The pack of petty troubles hurts us more than the violence of a single big one, no matter how big. In proportion as these domestic thorns are crowded and sharp, they prick us more sharply and without warning, easily catching us unawares.

I am no philosopher; evils crush me according to their weight, and they weigh as much by their form as their matter, and very often more. If I have therein more experience than the common people, I have also more patience. In short, if they do not wound me, they do hurt me.

Life is a tender thing and easily disturbed. As soon as I turn towards bad humor—*for nobody holds himself back when he begins to be impelled on*[8]—however foolish the cause that moved me to it, I stir my humor in that direction, and it then nourishes and exasperates itself by its own movement; attracting and heaping up matter upon matter whereon to feed.

> The fall of dripping water hollows out the stone.[9]

These day-by-day drippings eat away at me. Everyday vexations are never light. They are continual and irreparable, especially when they spring from the details of household management that are continual and unavoidable.

When I consider my affairs from a distance and as a whole, I find, perhaps because my memory of them is hardly exact,

[8] Seneca, *Epistles* [9] Lucretius

that they have gone on up to now prospering beyond my expectations and calculations. It seems to me that I get more out of them than there is in them; their success fools me. But if I am in the midst of the work and see all these parts in operation,

> Then is our soul divided among endless cares,[10]

a thousand things give me over to desire and fear. To give them up completely is very easy for me to do; to become engaged in them without fretting over them, very difficult. It is a pitiful thing to be in a place where everything you see involves and concerns you. And it seems to me I enjoy more gaily the pleasures of another man's house and go to them with a purer relish. Diogenes answered according to my humor the man who asked him what sort of wine he liked best: "Another man's," said he.

My father took a delight in building up Montaigne where he was born; and in all this administration of domestic affairs I love to follow his example and his rules, and I shall attach my successors to the same procedure as much as I can. If I could do better for him, I would. I am proud that his will still functions and acts through me. God forbid that I should permit to fail in my hands any semblance of life that I could restore to so good a father. And the fact that I have taken in hand to finish some old piece of wall and to fix up some poorly made building has certainly been more out of regard to his intentions than to my own satisfaction. And I blame my indolence that I have not proceeded further towards completing the things he so handsomely began in his house; so much the more so because I am very likely to be of my race its last possessor and to give the last hand to it. For, as to my own personal inclination, neither the pleasure of building, which is said to be so engaging, nor hunting, nor gardens, nor the other pleas-

---

[10] Virgil, *Aeneid*

ures of a retired life are able to amuse me very much. That is a thing for which I am displeased with myself, as for all other notions that are troublesome to me. I do not care so much to have them vigorous and learned as I care to have them easy and fitted for life; they are sure and sound enough if they are useful and pleasing.

They are the death of me, those people who, hearing me declare my incompetence in household matters, whisper in my ear that it is disdain and that I neglect to learn the implements of farming, its seasons, its order, how they make my wines, how they graft, the names and shapes of herbs and fruits, the manner of preparing the food on which I live, and the names and prices of the materials I wear, because I have set my heart upon some higher knowledge. That would be folly and rather stupidity than vainglory. I had rather be a good horseman than a good logician:

> Why not at least prepare something that is of use,
> By weaving withes and supple reeds? [11]

We snarl our thoughts in generalities and in the causes and operation of the universe, which carry on very well without us, and we leave in the lurch our own affairs and Michel, who concerns us even more closely than man in general.

Now I do, indeed, for the most part stay at home, but I should like to enjoy myself there more than elsewhere.

> Oh, that it may a haven be for my old age,
> Oh, may it set the bound for me, tired of voyages
>   And campaigns. [12]

I do not know whether I shall bring it about. I could wish that instead of some other portion of his estate my father had passed on to me that passionate love he had in his old age for his household. He was very happy in being able to subject his de-

---

[11] Virgil, *Eclogues* [12] Horace, *Odes*

sires to his fortune and to be satisfied with what he had. Political philosophy may condemn, for all I care, the meanness and sterility of my occupation, if I can only get a taste for it, as he did. I am of the opinion that the most honorable calling is to serve the public and to be useful to many. *For the fruit of genius and virtue, and of all excellence, is most fully obtained when bestowed on some neighbor.*[13] For my part, I keep out of it; partly out of conscience (for just as I see the weight connected to such employments, I see also the little capacity I have to bring to them; and Plato, a master workman in all political government, nevertheless abstained from it), partly out of indolence. I am content to enjoy the world without pressing after it, to live a merely excusable life, one that may merely be no burden to myself or to others.

Never did any man more fully and relaxedly hand himself over to the care and rule of another than I should do if I had someone. One of my wishes at this moment would be to find a son-in-law who could spoon-feed my old age comfortably and put it to sleep, in whose hands I might deposit in full sovereignty the management and use of my property, that he might do with it as I do and make on me what profit I make therein, provided he brought to it a truly grateful and friendly heart. But what is the use, we live in a world where loyalty in our own children is unknown.

He that has the charge of my purse in my travels, has it completely and without control. He could cheat me as well even if I kept accounts; and, if he is not a devil, I oblige him to act honestly by such complete trust. *Many, afraid of being cheated, have taught how to cheat, and by being suspicious have given others a right to do wrong.*[14] The commonest security I take from my people is ignorance. I assume the presence of vices only after having seen them, and I put more trust in the younger ones, whom I consider less corrupted by bad examples.

---

[13] Cicero, *De Amicitia*　　　[14] Seneca, *Epistles*

I had rather be told at the end of two months that I have spent four hundred crowns than to have my ears battered every evening with three, five, seven. Yet I have been robbed as little as any other man by this sort of larceny. It is true that I lend a helping hand to my ignorance; I purposely keep my knowledge of my money somewhat hazy and uncertain; to a certain point I am content to be in doubt about it. A little leeway must be left for the dishonesty or improvidence of your servant. If we have enough left in all for our purposes, let the surplus of Fortune's liberality run a little more at her will: it is the gleaner's portion. After all, I do not so much value the fidelity of my people as I despise the harm they do me. Oh! what a low and stupid study, to study your money, to take pleasure in handling, weighing and counting it over and over. It is by such ways that avarice makes its approaches!

In the eighteen years that I have been directing the estate, I have been unable to bring myself to look over either the title deeds or my principal affairs, which necessarily have to be submitted to my knowledge and attention. This is not a philosophical disdain of worldly and transitory things. My taste is not as purified as that, and I value them at least as much as they are worth; but it is, indeed, an inexcusable and puerile laziness and negligence. What would I not rather do than read a contract or than go turning over dusty old documents, a slave to my affairs, or, still worse, to those of others, as so many do for the sake of money? Only care and trouble cost me dearly, and I seek only to become unconcerned and relaxed.

I was, I believe, more suited to live on another man's fortune if it could be done without obligation and servitude. And yet I do not know, when I examine it closely, whether, considering my temperament and my lot, what I have to suffer from business and servants and household is not more abject, troublesome, and bitter than it would be to serve a man born to higher rank than myself who would rule me somewhat to my comfort. *Servitude is the obedience of a crushed and abject mind lacking free will.*[15] Crates did worse in throwing himself into the liberty of poverty in order to rid himself of the base concerns and cares of a household. I would not do that (I hate poverty as much as pain), but I would, indeed, change this kind of life for another one less brilliant and less busy.

When absent from home, I strip myself of all such thoughts, and I should feel less keenly the ruin of a tower than I do, when present, the fall of a tile. My mind very easily straightens itself out when standing apart, but on the spot it suffers like that of a vine-grower. A bridle rein on the wrong way on my mount, the end of a stirrup-leather striking on my leg, will keep me out of sorts a whole day. Faced with inconveniences I lift up well enough my spirit, my eyes I cannot.

> The senses, Oh ye gods, the senses.

At home I am responsible for all that goes amiss. Few masters—I speak of those of medium condition, such as mine—if there be any such they are the happier, can rely so much upon another that a good part of their burden does not still rest on them. This is apt to detract somewhat from my grace in entertaining visitors (and I have, perhaps, been able to keep some, as tiresome people do, more by the table I set than by my graciousness), and it takes away much of the pleasure I ought to take at my own house from the visits and gatherings of my friends. The most ridiculous appearance for a gentleman to have in his own house is for him to be seen bustling about the business of the house, whispering to one servant, threatening another with a glance; it ought to flow along imperceptibly and have the appearance of an ordinary course. And I think it unseemly to talk much to one's guests of the entertainment extended to them, whether to excuse it or to laud it.

I love order and cleanliness,

---

[15] Cicero, *Paradoxes*

and plate and cup
Display myself to me,[16]

as much as abundance; and in my house I give close heed to necessities, little to show.

If a servant starts a fight at another man's house, if a dish is upset, you only laugh at it; you sleep while the master of the house is arranging with his steward for your next day's entertainment.

I speak of these matters according to my own taste, not failing in general to appreciate how pleasant an occupation it is for certain natures to have a peaceful, prosperous household directed with regular discipline; and not wishing to attach my own errors and shortcomings to the matter, nor to give the lie to Plato, who considers the happiest occupation for each man is to carry on his own affairs without injustice.

When I travel, I have only myself and the use of my money to think about; that is disposed of by a single precept. In order to amass it too many qualities are required; about that I know nothing. About spending I know a little, and about making a show of expenditure, which is really its principal use. But I set myself to it too ambitiously, which makes it uneven and out of shape, and, moreover, immoderate in both aspects. If it makes a show, if it is useful, I let myself go without discretion, and I draw in my purse-strings with just as much lack of discretion if it does not shine and does not please me. Whatever it may be, whether art or nature, that imprints in us this disposition to live with reference to others, it does us much more harm than good. We cheat ourselves out of our own advantages to make appearances conform to the common opinion. We care not so much what our being is within us and in reality, as what it is to public knowledge. Even the goods of the mind and wisdom seem fruitless to us if enjoyed by only ourselves, and if they do not display themselves to the view and approbation of others.

[16] Horace, *Epistles*

There are some men whose gold flows in great streams through underground places, imperceptibly; others beat all of it out into sheets and leaf; so that to some farthings are worth crowns, and to others the reverse, the world esteeming its use and value according to the show. All attentive care about riches smells of avarice, even as does the spending of it and liberality that is too systematic and artificial. They are not worth a painful supervision and care. He who tries to make his spending exact makes it pinched and constrained. Saving or spending are in themselves indifferent things and take on the color of good or ill only according to the application of our will.

The other thing that invites me to these excursions is that the present moral state of our country does not suit me. I could easily console myself for this corruption as regards the public interest,

> More evil than the Iron Age,
> These times for whose depravity Nature herself can find
> No name, nor with a metal places them,[17]

but with regard to my own, no. I, in particular, suffer too much from it. For in my neighborhood we have now, by the long license of these civil wars, grown old in so riotous a form of government,

> Where right and wrong are turned about,[18]

that, in truth, it is a wonder that it can subsist.

> In arms they work the soil, and ever are they pleased
> To heap up booty fresh, and live by plundering.[19]

In fine I see by our example that human society is held and knit together at any cost whatever. In whatever position they are placed they pile up and arrange themselves by moving and crowding together, just as unmatched objects that are put into

---

[17] Juvenal   [18] Virgil, *Georgics*   [19] Virgil, *Aeneid*

a bag without order find of themselves a way to unite and put themselves together, often better than they could have been arranged by art. King Philip rounded up a rabble of the most wicked and incorrigible men he could find and put them all together in a city he had built for them which bore their name. I believe that from their very vices they formed a political structure among themselves and a serviceable and regular society.

I see not one action, or three, or a hundred, but morals in common and accepted usage, so monstrous, especially in inhumanity and treachery, which are to me the worst kinds of vices, that I have not the heart to think of them without horror; and I marvel at them almost as much as I detest them. The practice of these signal villainies bears the mark of vigor and strength of soul as much as of error and disorder.

Necessity reconciles and brings men together. This accidental bond afterwards takes the form of laws; for there have been some as savage as any human opinion can produce, which, nevertheless, have maintained their body with as much health and length of life as those of Plato or Aristotle could do.

And certainly all those imaginary, artificial descriptions of a government are found to be ridiculous and unfit to put into practice. These great lengthy altercations about the best form of society and the rules most suitable to bind us are altercations proper only for the exercise of our wits; as in the liberal arts there are several subjects which have their being in discussion and controversy and have no life apart from that. Such a description of a government would be applicable in a new world, but we take men already bound and formed to certain customs; we do not create them, like Pyrrha or Cadmus. By whatever means we may have power to correct and reform them, we can hardly wrench them from their accustomed bent without breaking all. Solon was asked whether he had established the best laws he could for the Athenians. "Yes, indeed," he replied, "the best they would have accepted."

Varro excuses himself in the same manner, stating that if he had to write of religion as though new, he would say what he thinks of it; but since it is already formed and accepted, he will speak of it more according to custom than according to nature.

Not in opinion, but in truth, the best and most excellent government for each nation is that under which it has maintained itself. Its form and essential fitness depends upon custom. We are apt to be displeased with the present state of things. But I maintain that to go wishing for the government of a few in a democratic state, or another sort of government in a monarchy, is both foolish and wrong.

> Hold dear the state, and be it what it will:
> If it is royal, love then royalty;
> If of the few, or of the many, love
> It still, for God put you in it.[20]

Good Monsieur de Pibrac, whom we have just lost, such a noble mind, such sound opinions, and such a gentle character. This loss and that of Monsieur de Foix, which we suffered at the same time, are important losses to our crown. I do not know whether France has left another couple, comparable to these two Gascons in sincerity and ability, to substitute for them in the councils of our kings. They were souls beautiful in different ways, and certainly, according to the standards of this age, rare and beautiful, each in his own way. But who placed them in these times, men so out of keeping and so out of proportion with our corruption and tempests?

Nothing overwhelms a state except innovation; change alone gives form to injustice and tyranny. When any piece gets out of place, it may be propped up; we can resist being carried too far from our beginnings and principles by the alteration and corruption natural to all things. But to undertake to recast so great a mass and to change the foundations of so great a structure is for them to do who, to clean a picture, wipe it out, who

---

[20] Pibrac, *Quatrains*

want to reform particular defects by universal confusion and cure diseases by death, *desirous not so much of changing as of overthrowing everything.*[21] The world is not fitted to cure itself; it is so impatient of anything that oppresses it that it aims only at getting rid of it without considering the cost. We see by a thousand examples that it usually cures itself to its own loss. Being rid of a present evil is no cure if there is not a general improvement in conditions.

The surgeon's aim is not to kill the diseased flesh; that is only the way to his cure. He looks beyond, to make the natural flesh take life there again and restore the member to its proper state. Whoever proposes only to remove what is eating into him falls short, for good does not necessarily succeed evil; another evil may succeed it, and a worse one, as happened to Caesar's killers, who brought the Republic into such a state that they had reason to repent of having meddled with it. The same thing has since happened to many others right down to our own times. The French, my contemporaries, can certainly say something on that subject. All great mutations shake the state and cast it into disorder.

Whoever would aim straight at a cure and would reflect on it before taking any action would be likely to cool off about setting his hand to it. Pacuvius Calavius corrected the defect of this procedure by a notable example. His fellow-citizens were in mutiny against their magistrates. He, a man of great authority in the city of Capua, found means one day to shut up the senate in the palace, and, calling the people together in the market place, told them that the day had come when at full liberty they might revenge themselves on the tyrants by whom they had been so long oppressed, and whom he held alone and disarmed at his mercy. He advised that these men should be brought forth one by one, by lot, and that each man's fate should be determined individually, with their sentence to be executed on the spot; with this proviso also, that they

---

[21] Cicero, *De Officiis*

should at the same time see to appointing some honorable man in the place of the condemned man, so that the office might not remain vacant. They had no sooner heard the name of one senator than there arose a cry of universal dissatisfaction against him. "I see very well," says Pacuvius, "that we must dismiss this one; he is a wicked fellow; let us have a good one in exchange." There was a prompt silence, everyone being much at a loss whom to choose. In reply to the first bolder man who named his choice there was a still greater agreement of voices to refuse him, a hundred defects and just causes for rejecting him. These contradictory humors having become heated, it fared still worse with the second senator, and the third: as much disagreement about election as agreement about dismissal. Having uselessly tired themselves out in this confusion, they began, some one way, some another, to steal away from the assembly bit by bit, each one carrying away this conclusion in his mind, that the oldest and best-known evil is always more bearable than an evil that is new and untried.

Because I see us pitifully agitated (for what have we not done?),

> Our scars, and crimes, and brothers' blood,
> Alas, our shame. What have we shunned,
> Hard age? What evil have we left
> Untouched? What has our youth in dread
> Of heaven kept hands off? Where are
> The altars spared by them? [22]

I do not at once conclude:

> Though Safety may herself so wish,
> Indeed she cannot save this family. [23]

For all that we are not, perhaps, at our last term. The preservation of states is a thing that probably surpasses our understanding. A civil government is, as Plato says, a powerful thing

---

[22] Horace, *Odes*   [23] Terence, *Adelphi*

and hard to dissolve. It often holds out against mortal internal diseases, against the mischief of unjust laws, against tyranny, against the excesses and the ignorance of the magistrates, and the license and sedition of the people.

In all our fortunes we compare ourselves with what is above us and look towards those who are better off; let us measure ourselves with what is below us: there is no one so ill-starred that he may not find a thousand examples with which to console himself. It is our failing that we are more unhappy in seeing men ahead of us than happy in seeing men behind us. Yet Solon used to say that, if all the ills were heaped up together, there is no one who would not choose rather to take back with him the ills he has than to come to a legitimate division of the heap with all other men and take his exact share. Our government is in a bad way; yet some have been sicker without dying. The gods play handball with us and toss us in every way:

Assuredly the Gods use us like balls.[24]

The stars fatally destined the state of Rome for an example of what they could do in this way. In it are comprised all the forms and vicissitudes that affect a state: all that order can do, and disorder, and good and evil fortune. What state ought to despair of its condition, seeing the shocks and commotions by which Rome was agitated and which it withstood? If extent of dominion is the health of a state (which I by no means believe; and Isocrates pleases me when he instructs Nicocles not to envy princes who have broad dominions, but rather those who know how to preserve those that have been handed down to them), that of Rome was never so healthy as when it was most sick. The worst of its forms was the most fortunate.

One can hardly discern the form of any kind of government under the first emperors; it was the thickest and most horrible confusion that can be imagined. Nevertheless Rome endured it

[24] Plautus, *Captivi*

and continued in it, preserving not a monarchy confined within its own bounds, but a great number of nations, so unlike, so remote, so ill-disposed, so confusedly ruled and unjustly conquered;

> And Fortune grants
> No nation its ill will against the state
> That rules o'er land and sea.[25]

Everything that totters does not fall. The structure of so great a body holds together by more than one nail. It holds together even by its antiquity, like old buildings whose foundations have been worn away by age, without cement and mortar, which yet live and support themselves by their own weight,

> No longer holding fast by robust roots,
> It stands secure in its own weight.[26]

Moreover it is not a good procedure to reconnoitre only the flank and the moat; to judge the security of a place we must see from which way it can be approached and in what condition the assailant is. Few vessels sink of their own weight and without some external violence. Now let us turn our eyes in every direction: all is crumbling about us; in all the great states known to us, whether in Christendom or elsewhere, just look into them, you will find an evident threat of change and ruin;

> They have their own misfortunes, and for all alike
> The storm.[27]

The astrologers have an easy game when they warn us, as they do, of great and imminent changes and revolutions. Their prophecies are present and palpable, there is no need to go to the heavens for that.

There is for us not only consolation to be extracted from this universal fellowship of evils and menaces, but even some hope

---

[25] Lucan   [26] Lucan   [27] Virgil, *Aeneid*

for the duration of our state, inasmuch as naturally nothing
falls where all falls. Universal sickness is individual health;
conformity is a quality opposed to dissolution. For my part, I
do not at all despair about it, and I think I see in it ways of
saving ourselves;

> A god, perhaps, with happy change,
> May soon restore these things to place.[28]

Who knows but that God will have it happen as with bodies
that purge themselves and are restored to better condition by
long and grievous maladies which give them back a clearer
and more complete health than they took from them?

What troubles me most is that in reckoning up the symptoms
of our trouble I see as many that are natural and that Heaven
sends us from its very own as of those that our disorder and
human imprudence contribute to it. It seems as if the very stars
ordain that we have endured long enough beyond the ordinary
term. And this, too, troubles me, that the evil which most
closely threatens us is not an alteration in the entire and solid
mass, but its dissipation and disintegration, the worst of our
fears.

Moreover in these ramblings of mine, I fear the treachery of
my memory, lest by inadvertence it should have made me record a thing twice. I hate to re-examine myself and never re-
read, if I can help it, what has once escaped me. Now I am
bringing in here nothing I have newly learned. These are common ideas; having, perhaps, conceived them a hundred times, I
am afraid I have already set them down. Repetition is tiresome
everywhere, though it were in Homer; but it is ruinous in
things that have only a superficial and transitory appearance.
I dislike inculcation, even of useful things, as in Seneca; and I
dislike the practice of his Stoical school of repeating, upon
every subject, at full length and breadth, the principles and

---

[28] Horace, *Epodes*

presuppositions that are of general use, and of always restating anew their common and universal reasons and arguments.

My memory grows cruelly worse every day,

> As if with dried up throat I'd quaffed
> The cups inducing Lethean sleep.[29]

Whereas others seek time and opportunity to think over what they have to say, I must henceforth (for hitherto, thank God, nothing has happened much amiss) avoid any preparation, for fear of tying myself to some obligation on which I might have to depend. To be held and bound puts me off my track, and it does also to depend upon so weak an instrument as my memory.

I never read the following story without being struck by it with a natural and personal resentment. Lyncestes, accused of conspiracy against Alexander, on the day that he was brought before the army, according to the custom, to be heard in his defense, had in his head a studied speech, of which, very hesitant and stammering, he pronounced a few words. As he was growing more and more confused, struggling with his memory and groping in it, the soldiers nearest him charged him and killed him with their pikes, considering him as convicted. His confusion and his silence was to them as good as a confession. Having had so much leisure to prepare himself in prison, it was not, in their opinion, his memory that failed him; it was his conscience that tied his tongue and took away his strength. That was a well put conclusion, indeed! The place, the audience, their expectation, stun a man even when there is nothing at stake but the ambition to speak well. What can a man do when it is a speech on which his life depends?

For my part, the very fact of being tied to what I have to say serves to shake me loose from it. When I have wholly committed and entrusted myself to my memory, I lean so heavily

---

[29] Horace, *Epodes*

on it that I overwhelm it; it becomes frightened at its burden. As long as I trust to it I put myself outside of myself, to the point of running the risk of being put out of countenance; and I have sometimes been very much put to it to conceal the slavery in which I was bound, whereas my intention in speaking is to display extreme carelessness and casual and unpremeditated gestures, as though arising from the immediate occasion. I would as soon say nothing worth while as show that I had come prepared to be eloquent, an unbecoming thing, especially to men of my profession, and a matter of too great obligation on him who cannot live up to much. The preparation gives more to hope for than it actually brings. A man often stupidly strips to his doublet to leap no further than he would have done in a coat.

There is nothing so unfavorable to those who wish to please as the expectation they raise.[30] It is recorded of the orator Curio that when he set forth the division of his oration into three or four parts, or the number of his arguments and reasons, it often happened that he either forgot one or added one or two more. I have always carefully guarded against falling into this predicament, having always hated these promises and declarations, not only out of distrust of my memory, but also because this method relishes too much of artifice. *The simpler ways become a soldier.*[31] Enough that I have promised myself never again to take it upon me to speak on formal occasions. For as to reading one's speech, besides being very unnatural, it is very disadvantageous to those who could naturally achieve some effect by direct delivery. And as for throwing myself on the mercy of my ability to improvise on the spot, still less should I do it; my ability at that is dull and uncertain and would not be able to fulfill sudden and important needs.

Reader let this essay of myself run on, and this third extension of the other parts of my portrait. I add, but I do not correct. First of all because it appears to me that the man who

[30] Cicero, *Academica*   [31] Quintillian

has given his work in pledge to the world has no further right to it. Let him speak better elsewhere if he can, but let him not adulterate the work he has sold. Nothing should be bought from such people until after they are dead. Let them give good thought to the matter before bringing themselves forth to the public. Who hurries them?

My book is always the same. Except that as new editions are prepared, in order that the buyer may not go away quite empty-handed, I take the liberty to add (as it is only an ill-joined patchwork) a few extra embellishments. These are but over-weights that do not damage the original form, but, by a little ambitious subtlety, give some special value to each of the sub-sequent forms. Because of that, however, it will easily happen that some transposition of chronology will be introduced, my stories taking their place according to their aptness and not always according to their age.

Secondly, because, so far as I am concerned, I am afraid of losing by the change. My understanding does not always go forward, it goes backward too. I scarcely distrust my fancies any less for being second or third than for being first, or my present ones less than my past ones. We often correct ourselves as foolishly as we do others. My first edition was in the year 1580. Since then I have grown older by a long stretch of time, but I certainly have not grown one inch wiser. The present I and I of a while ago are, indeed, two different persons; but at which moment better, I cannot say. It would be a fine thing to be old if we moved only towards improvement. It is a drunk-ard's movement, lurching, reeling, unsteady, or like that of reeds which the wind moves about haphazardly at its will.

Antiochus had written vigorously in favor of the Academy; in his old age he took a different side. Whichever of the two I should follow, should I not still be following Antiochus? After having affirmed the doubtfulness of human opinions, to want to affirm their certainty, was not that to establish doubt rather than certainty and to promise that, if he had been granted another span of life, he would still be in a period of new agitation, not better so much as different?

The favor of the public has given me a little more boldness than I expected; but what I most fear is cloying the public. I had rather goad than tire the public, as a learned man of my time has done. Praise is always pleasing, from whomever or for whatever reason it may come; yet, to enjoy it properly a man ought to be posted about the source of it. Even faults have a way of recommending themselves. The vulgar and common esteem seldom hits it happily; and I am much mistaken if in my time the worst writings are not those which have won the popular acclaim. I certainly thank those discerning men who deign to take my feeble efforts in good part. There is no place where the faults of workmanship are so apparent as in a substance which of itself has nothing to commend it. Do not blame me, reader, for those that slip in here by the whim or inadvertency of others; every hand, every workman adds his share to it. I do not concern myself with orthography—merely requesting them to follow the old style—or with punctuation; I am little expert in either one. When they wholly break the sense, I am very little concerned, for at least they relieve me of responsibility; but when they substitute a false meaning, as they so often do, and turn me aside to their views, they ruin me. However when the thought is weaker than my capacity, an intelligent man ought to reject it as not mine. Anyone who knows how little laborious I am and how much I am shaped to my own humor will easily believe that I had rather write as many more essays again than subject myself to going over these again for so childish a correction.

So I was saying a while ago that, being planted in the deepest mine of this new metal, I am not only deprived of any great familiarity with people of different ways and opinions from mine, by which they hold together by a tie that shuns all other ties, but also I do not live without danger among people to whom all things are equally permissible, and most of whom cannot henceforth make their situation in respect to the law worse, whence arises the extreme degree of licentiousness. Reckoning up all the particular circumstances concerning myself, I do not find one man of my country who pays more dearly for the defense of our laws, both in gains ceasing and in damages ensuing, as the lawyers say, than myself. And some there are who play up their zeal and keenness who, if things were justly weighed, do much less than I.

As a house that has ever been free, very accessible, and at the service of all (for I have never let myself be induced to make it an instrument of war, in which I most readily participate when it is farthest removed from my neighborhood), my house has merited considerable popular affection, and it would be very difficult to take me to task on my own dunghill. And I look upon it as a wonderful and exemplary masterpiece that it is still virgin of blood and plunder beneath so long a storm with so many changes and disturbances round about. For, to tell the truth, it was possible for a man of my makeup to escape from any one constant and continued form of danger, whatever it might be; but the conflicting invasions and incursions and the alternations and vicissitudes of fortune around me have up to now more exasperated than mollified the temper of the country and laden me time and again with insuperable dangers and difficulties. I escape, but it displeases me that it is more by chance, and even of my own prudence, than through justice, and it displeases me to be outside the protection of the laws and under any other safeguard than theirs. As matters stand, I live more than half by the favor of others, which is a harsh obligation. I do not want to owe my safety either to the kindness and benevolence of great persons who are pleased with my respect for the law and my independence, or to the affable manners of my predecessors and myself: for what if I were different? If my conduct and the frankness of my dealings put my neighbors or my kindred under obligation, it is cruel that they can acquit themselves of that obligation by letting me live, and that they can say: "We grant him the liberty of holding divine service freely in the chapel of his house, all the churches round about having been emptied and ruined by us, and we grant him the use of his goods and his life since he shelters our wives and our cattle in time of need." For a long time we of my house have shared in the praise of Lycurgus the Athenian who was the general depositary and guardian of the purses of his fellow-citizens.

Now I hold that a man should live by right and by authority and not by reward or favor. How many gallant men have chosen rather to lose their lives than to owe them? I shun subjecting myself to any sort of obligation, but above all to that which binds me by the duty of honor. I find nothing so costly as that which is given to me and for which my will remains mortgaged under the title of gratitude, and I more willingly accept services that are for sale. This is, indeed, my belief: for the latter I give only money, for the others I give myself. The knot that binds me by the laws of honor seems to me much tighter and more burdensome than that of legal constraint. A notary binds me more gently than I do myself. Is it not reasonable that my conscience should be much more firmly bound when men rely on it alone? In other cases my fidelity owes nothing because nothing has been lent it; let them use the trust and security they have taken outside of me. I had much rather break the imprisonment of a wall and of the laws than my word. I am scrupulous to the point of superstition in keeping my promises, and in all matters I am inclined to make them uncertain and conditional. To those of no weight I give weight by jealous regard for my rule: it plagues and burdens me with its own interest. Yes, even in actions wholly my own and free from others, if I state the plan, it seems to me that I prescribe it for myself, and that to give it to the knowledge of another is to impose it upon myself; it seems to me that I promise it when I mention it. Therefore I seldom air my plans.

The sentence that I pass upon myself is sharper and stiffer

than that of the judges who only consider me from the point of view of common obligation; the grip of my conscience is tighter and more severe. I follow laxly the duties to which I should be dragged if I did not go to them. *Even that which is done rightly is just only in so far as it is voluntary.*[32] If the action has not some gleam of liberty, it has neither grace nor honor.

What law exacts from me is from my will scarce gained.[33]

When necessity draws me, I like to relax my will because, *whatever is exacted by power is ascribed to him who commands rather than to him who performs.*[34] I know some who follow this procedure even to injustice, who will sooner give than give back, sooner lend than pay, and do good most sparingly to the one to whom they are obliged. I do not go that far, but I come close to it.

I like so much to rid myself of burdens and obligations that I have sometimes counted as profit the ingratitude, affronts, and indignities which I have received from those to whom, either by nature or accident, I owed some duty of friendship, taking this occasion of their offense for that much acquittance and discharge of my debt. Although I continue to pay them the outward civilities required by society, nevertheless, I find a great saving in doing for the sake of justice what I used to do for the sake of affection and in relieving myself a little of the inner tension and solicitude of my will (*it is the part of a wise man to check, as he would a chariot, the impulsive rush of a good will*)[35] which in me is a little too urgent and pressing when I give myself over to a friendship, at least for a man who does not want to be at all under pressure. And this husbanding of my friendship serves me as some consolation for the imperfections of those in whom I am concerned. I am, indeed, sorry that they are worth less for it, but the fact remains that there-

---

[32] Cicero, *De Officiis*   [33] Terence, *Adelphi*   [34] Valerius Maximus
[35] Cicero, *De Amicitia*

by I am also spared some of my attentiveness and obligation towards them.

I approve of a man who loves his son less for being mangy or hunchbacked, and not only when he is malicious, but also when he is ill-favored and ill-born (God himself has abated that much from his natural value and estimation), provided he carry himself in this coolness towards him with moderation and exact justice. With me nearness of kin does not alleviate defects, it rather aggravates them.

After all, as far as I understand the science of benefaction and gratitude, which is a subtle science and of great utility, I see nobody freer and less indebted than I am up to this moment. What I do owe, I owe to the common and natural obligations. There is no one who is more absolutely clear of any others,

The gifts of mighty men are to me unknown.[36]

Princes give me much if they take nothing from me, and do me enough good when they do me no harm; that's all I ask of them. Oh, how much I am obliged to God that it was His pleasure I should receive directly from His bounty all that I have, and that He has reserved all my indebtedness quite to Himself! How earnestly do I beseech His holy mercy that I may never owe thanks to anyone for the essentials of life! Blessed liberty which has led me so far! May it continue to the end!

I try to have no express need of anyone. *All my hope is in myself.*[37] It is a thing that everyone can do for himself, but more easily those whom God has sheltered from natural and urgent necessities. It is very pitiful and hazardous to depend on another. We ourselves, who are our truest and most certain support, have not sufficiently assured ourselves. I have nothing of my own but myself, and even the possession of this is partly defective and borrowed. I fortify myself both in courage, which is the stronger, and also in fortune, to find therein the means to satisfy me even if everything else should forsake me.

---

[36] Virgil, *Aeneid* [37] Terence, *Adelphi*

Hippias of Elis furnished himself not merely with learning, that in the lap of the Muses he might, at need, cheerfully withdraw from all other company, not merely with knowledge of philosophy, to teach his soul to be contented with itself and manfully to dispense with the comforts which come to it from outside when Fate so orders it; he was so careful as to learn also to cook, to shave himself, to make his clothes, his shoes, his rings in order to become as self-sufficient as he could and to get himself away from outside help.

We enjoy borrowed goods much more freely and gaily when the enjoyment is not forced and constrained by need, and when we have, both in our will and fortune, the force and means to do without them.

I know myself well; but it is hard for me to imagine any such pure liberality from anyone, any such frank and free hospitality that it would not appear to me ill-starred, tyrannical, and tainted with reproach if necessity had entangled me in it. As giving is an ambitious quality, mark of prerogative, so is accepting a quality of submission. Witness the insulting and quarrelsome refusal that Bajazet made of the presents that Tamerlane sent him. And those that were offered on behalf of the Emperor Solyman to the Emperor of Calicut threw him into such great anger that he not only refused them rudely, saying that neither he nor his predecessors were accustomed to take and that it was their rôle to give, but in addition he had the ambassadors sent for that purpose thrown into a dungeon.

When Thetis, says Aristotle, flatters Jupiter, when the Lacedemonians flatter the Athenians, they do not keep refreshing their memory of the good they have done them, which is always odious, but their memory of the benefits they have received from them. Those whom I see so freely making use of one and all and putting themselves under obligation to them would never do so if they weighed as fully as a wise man should the bond of an obligation: it is sometimes, perhaps, paid, but it is never dissolved. Cruel bondage for a man who likes to make elbowroom on all sides for his freedom.

My acquaintances, both those above and those below me, know whether they have ever seen a man less demanding of others. And if I surpass all modern examples in this respect, it is no great wonder since so many parts of my character contribute to it: a little natural pride, inability to put up with refusal, limitation of my desires and plans, inaptitude for any kind of business, and my most favored qualities, idleness and freedom. Through all these I have conceived a mortal hatred of being bound to any other or by any other than myself. I very vigorously use all my power to do without before I make use of the kindness of another, however slight or important the occasion may be. My friends annoy me strangely when they ask me to ask a favor of a third person. And it seems hardly less costly to me to free a man who is indebted to me by making use of him, than to bind myself for them to a man that owes me nothing. Apart from that condition and this other, that they desire of me nothing involving trouble and care, for I have declared open war against all care, I am readily accessible to the need of any man.

But I have avoided receiving still more than I have sought occasions for giving, and that is much easier, according to Aristotle. My fortune has allowed me but little to do good to others, and the little it has allowed me it has placed in rather lean surroundings. If it had brought me into the world to hold some high rank among men, I should have been ambitious to make myself loved, not to make myself feared or admired. Shall I express it more baldly? I should have given as much attention to pleasing as to profiting. Cyrus very wisely, and by the mouth of a very good captain and a still better philosopher, esteems his kindness and good deeds way beyond his valor and his warlike conquests. And the elder Scipio, whenever he wants to put himself to good vantage, gives greater weight to his affability and humanity than to his hardihood and victories; and he has always this proud saying in his mouth: that he has given his enemies as much reason to love him as his friends.

I mean to say, then, that if we must thus owe something, it ought to be by a more legitimate title than that of which I am speaking, to which the necessity of this miserable war binds me, and not with so great a debt as that of my total preservation: that overwhelms me. I have gone to bed a thousand times in my own house imagining that I should be betrayed and murdered that very night, contriving with Fortune that it might be without terror and not lingering. And after my Paternoster I have cried out:

> Shall impious soldiers have these well-tilled fields? [38]

What remedy is there? It is my birthplace and that of most of my ancestors: on it they put their affection and their name. We become hardened to whatever we are accustomed to. And for a miserable condition such as ours habit has been a very kind gift of Nature since it benumbs our senses to the suffering of many evils. Civil wars are worse than other wars in this, that they make each of us stand sentinel in our own house.

> How wretched to defend our life with gate and wall,
> And in the strength of our own house be scarcely safe. [39]

It is great extremity to be beset even in our household and domestic repose. The region where I live is always the first and the last in the conflicts of our troubled times, and the place where peace never shows her full face,

> E'en when at peace, they quake with fear of war. [40]

> Whenever Fortune challenges the peace.
> The path of war is here. Oh, Fortune, better far
> If you had given me a place way to the East,
> Or in the frozen North, a nomad's tent. [41]

---

[38] Virgil, *Eclogues*   [39] Ovid, *Tristia*   [40] Ovid, *Tristia*   [41] Lucan

I sometimes get from nonchalance and unconcern the means of strengthening myself against these considerations; they too lead us a bit towards fortitude. It often happens to me to imagine and await mortal dangers with some pleasure: I stupidly plunge head down into death, without looking closely at it and examining it, as into a silent and dark abyss which swallows me up at one leap and involves me in an instant with a profound sleep, devoid of feeling and of pain. And in these quick and violent deaths, the comfort received from the consequence that I foresee is greater than the fear aroused by the occurrence. They say that as life is not better for being long, so death is better for not being long. I do not so much keep myself apart from being dead as I enter into familiar terms with dying. I wrap and enclose myself in this storm which is to blind me and then snatch me away furiously with a sudden and insensible attack.

Still if it happened, as some gardeners say, that roses and violets spring up with more fragrance near garlic and onions because these draw to themselves and suck up whatever bad odor there is in the ground, similarly if these depraved natures should draw in all the poison of my air and climate and make me so much better and purer by their vicinity, I should not be wholly a loser! That is not so; but there may be something in this, that goodness is more beautiful and attractive when it is rare, and that contrariety and diversity strengthen and compress well-doing within itself and enflame it by the jealousy of opposition and love of glory.

Robbers by inclination have no particular grudge against me. Have I any against them? I should have my hands too full. Like consciences under different kinds of fortune harbor like cruelty, disloyalty, and rapine, and so much the worse as it is more cowardly, more secure and dark beneath the shadow of the laws. I hate an open injury less than a treacherous one, a warlike one less than a peaceful one. Our fever has seized upon a body that is not much the worse for it; the fire was there, it has burst into flames; the noise is greater, the evil but little greater.

I generally reply to those who ask me the reason for my travels that I know well what I am fleeing from but not what I am looking for. If they tell me that among foreigners there may be as little health, and that their ways are no better than ours, I reply, first of all, that that is hardly likely,

So many are the shapes of crime! [42]

secondly, that it is always a gain to change a bad state for an uncertain one, and that the troubles of others ought not to pain us so much as our own.

I do not want to forget this, that I never rebel so much against France that I do not look at Paris with a friendly eye; she has had my heart since my childhood. And there has happened to me in this as with excellent things: the more other beautiful cities I have seen since, the more the beauty of this one sways and gains my affection. I love her for herself, and more in her very own being than overloaded with foreign pomp. I love her tenderly, even to her warts and blemishes. I am a Frenchman only by this great city: great in population, great in the felicity of her situation, but above all great and incomparable in variety and diversity of the good things of life, the glory of France, and one of the most noble ornaments of the world. May God drive our discords far from her! Entire and united I consider her secure from all other violence. I warn her that of all parties the worst will be the one that puts her into discord. And for her I fear only herself. And certainly I feel as much fear for her as for any other part of this state. As long as she endures, I shall not lack a retreat in which to give up the ghost, sufficient to make me lose my regret for any other retreat.

Not because Socrates said it, but because it is really my

---

[2] Virgil, *Georgics*

feeling, and, perhaps, a little too much so, I look upon all men as my compatriots and I embrace a Pole as I do a Frenchman, placing this national bond after the universal and common one. I am not greatly infatuated with the sweetness of my native air. Acquaintances wholly new and wholly my own seem to me fully as good as those other common chance acquaintances of the neighborhood. Friendships that are purely of our own acquiring usually prevail over those to which community of climate or of blood attach us. Nature has placed us in the world free and unbound; we imprison ourselves in certain narrow districts, like the kings of Persia, who bound themselves never to drink any other water than that of the river Choaspes, foolishly renouncing their right of using any other waters, and dried up, so far as they were concerned, all the rest of the world.

What Socrates did towards the end of his life, in considering a sentence of banishment against him as worse than a sentence of death, I shall never, I think, be so broken or so strictly habituated to my own country as to do. These divine lives have enough aspects that I embrace more by esteem than by affection. And they also have some so elevated and extraordinary that I cannot embrace them even by esteem, inasmuch as I cannot comprehend them. That was a very soft feeling in a man who considered the whole world his city. It is true that he disdained travel and had hardly set foot outside the territory of Attica. What are we to say of his grudging the money offered by his friends to save his life, and of his refusing to get out of prison by the mediation of others so as not to disobey the laws, and that at a time when they were so very corrupt? These examples are of the first kind for me. Of the second kind there are others that I could find in this same person. Many of these rare examples exceed my power of action, but some of them even exceed my power of judgment.

Besides these reasons, travel seems to me a profitable exercise. By it the mind is continually exercised in observing new and unknown things; and I know no better school, as I have often said, for forming one's life than to set before it constantly the diversity of so many other lives, ideas, and customs, and to make it taste so perpetual a variety of forms of our nature. The body is therein neither idle nor overworked, and this moderate movement puts it in good condition.

I stay on horseback, tormented with the stone as I am, without dismounting and without weariness for eight or ten hours,

Beyond the strength and lot of age.[48]

No season is hostile to me except the fierce heat of a scorching sun; for umbrellas, which Italy has used ever since the time of the ancient Romans, burden a man's arm more than they relieve his head. I should like to know what device the Persians had so long ago in the infancy of luxury to produce for themselves a fresh breeze and shade at their pleasure, as Xenophon reports. I love rain and mud like a duck. Change of air and climate does not affect me; all skies are alike to me. I am beaten down only by the inward troubles that I produce in myself, and these come upon me less when I am traveling.

I am hard to get moving, but once underway I go as far as one wants. I hold out as much against little undertakings as against great ones, and against outfitting myself for a day's trip and a visit to a neighbor as for a real journey. I have learned to make my day's journey in the Spanish fashion in a single stage: long and reasonable stages; and in extreme heat I make them by night, from sunset to sunrise. The other way, of having your dinner on the way in haste and confusion, is inconvenient, especially on short days. My horses are the better for it. Never has a horse failed me that was able to hold out the first day's journey with me. I water them everywhere and only see to it that they have enough road left between to work off their water. My laziness in rising gives my attendants time to dine at their ease before setting out. As for me, it is never too late

---
[48] Virgil, *Aeneid*

for me to eat; appetite comes to me in eating, and not otherwise; I am never hungry but at table.

Some people find fault with my taking pleasure in continuing this exercise now I am married and old. They are wrong.
It is a better time to leave your family when you have put it
on the way to continue without you, when you have left it in
an order that may not belie its old form. It is a much greater
imprudence to go off leaving in your household a less faithful
guardian who will be less solicitous to provide for your needs.

The most useful and honorable knowledge and occupation
for a woman is the science of housekeeping. I know some who
are miserly but very few who are good managers. It is her
chief quality, one which a man ought to seek before any other,
as the only dowry that serves to ruin or save our houses. Don't
tell me! Following what experience has taught me, I require of
a married woman, above all other virtues, the virtue of being
a good housewife. I put my wife on her own, leaving the entire
direction of affairs in her hands by my absence. I am vexed to
see in many households Monsieur coming home about midday,
harassed and dirty from the hurly-burly of business, when
Madame is doing her hair and decking herself out in her boudoir. That is for queens to do; and I don't even know about
that. It is ridiculous and unfair that the idleness of our wives
should be supported by our sweat and labor. No one, if I can
help it, shall have a more ready, calm, and free enjoyment of
my property than I. If the husband provides the matter, Nature
herself wills that the wife provide the form.

As to the duties of conjugal love that some consider injured
by absence, I do not believe it. On the contrary, it is a relationship that is likely to grow cool by a too continual presence
and that is hurt by assiduity. Every strange woman appears to
us an attractive woman. And everyone feels by experience that
seeing one another continually cannot equal the pleasure of
parting and coming together at intervals. These interruptions
fill me with a fresh love for my family and make the restored

enjoyment of my home sweeter to me. Alternation warms my appetite for leaving home and then for returning.

I know that friendship has arms long enough to hold and join from one end of the world to the other, and especially this kind in which there is a continual exchange of services that keep awake the bond and memory of it. The Stoics say, indeed, that there is so close a bond and relationship between sages that he who dines in France nourishes his companion in Egypt; and that if one of them merely holds out his finger, wherever he may be, all the sages on the habitable earth feel help from it.

Enjoyment and possession are principally a matter of imagination. It embraces more warmly what it is in quest of than what we hold, and more continually. Count up your daily musings, and you will find that you are most absent from your friend when he is in your company; his presence relaxes your attention and gives your thoughts liberty to absent themselves at any moment and for any reason. From the distance of Rome I keep and govern my house and the goods I have left there; I see my walls, my trees, and my revenue rise and decrease, within a couple of inches or so, as when I am there:

Before my eyes there flits my home and forms of places dear.[44]

If we enjoy nothing but what we touch, we may say farewell to our crowns when they are in our coffers and to our children when they are gone hunting. We want them nearer. In the garden, is that far? Half a day's journey away? What about ten leagues, is that far or near? If it is near, what about eleven, twelve, thirteen, and so on, step by step? Truly, if there is a woman who will prescribe to her husband at just how many steps the near ends, and at just what number of steps the far begins, I would advise her to stop him in between the two:

Let then a limit fixed cut off dispute. . . .
I take what is allowed, and bit by bit,

---

[44] Ovid, *Tristia*

Like hairs pulled from a horse's tail, I pluck
And take away your numbers one by one
Till you fall baffled by this old sophism.[45]

and let them boldly call philosophy to their assistance, to which someone might address the criticism that, since it sees neither one end nor the other of the joint between the too much and the little, the long and the short, the light and the heavy, the near and the far, since it recognizes neither the beginning nor the end of it, it is a very uncertain judge of the middle. *Nature has given us no knowledge of the limits of things.*[46] Are they not still wives and mistresses of the dead, who are not at the end of this world but in the other world? We embrace both those who have been and those who are not yet, not merely the absent. We have not made a bargain in getting married to stay continually tied to each other by the tail like some little animals or other that we see, or like the bewitched people of Karenty, in dog-like manner. And a wife ought not to have her eyes so greedily fixed on the front of her husband that she cannot see the back of him if need be.

But would not this saying of that most excellent painter of their humors be appropriate here to show the cause of their complaints?

Your wife, if you are late, thinks you are making love,
Or someone's loving you, or you are on a spree,
And having all the fun, while things are hard for her.[47]

Or could it not be that opposition and contradiction pleases them and nourishes them, and that they are comfortable enough provided they make you uncomfortable?

In true friendship, in which I am an expert, I give myself to my friend more than I draw him to me. I prefer not only to do good to him rather than for him to do good to me, but also for him to do good to himself rather than to me; he does

---

[45] Horace, *Epistles*   [46] Cicero, *Academica*   [47] Terence, *Adelphi*

the most for me when he does good to himself. And if absence is either pleasant or useful to him, it is sweeter to me than his presence; and it is not really absence when there are means of communicating with each other. In former times I have made good use of our separation and derived advantage. We filled and extended our possession of life better in being parted: he lived, he enjoyed, he saw for me, and I for him, as fully as if he had been there. One part of us remained idle when we were together: we were fused into one. The separation of place made the conjunction of our wills richer. This insatiable hunger for bodily presence reveals a little a certain weakness in the enjoyment of souls.

As to old age, which is brought up against me, it is, on the contrary, for youth to subject itself to public opinion and to curb itself for the sake of others. It has the means to satisfy both the public and itself; we have only too much to do to satisfy ourselves alone. As natural advantages fail us, let us sustain ourselves with artificial ones. It is unjust to excuse youth for pursuing its pleasures and to forbid old age to seek any. When young, I covered up my gay passions with prudence; now old, I rout my gloomy ones by dissipation. Besides, the Platonic laws forbid traveling before the age of forty or fifty in order to make travel more useful and instructive. I should sooner subscribe to the second article of the same laws, which forbids it after sixty.

"But at such an age you will never return from so long a journey." What do I care? I undertake it neither for the purpose of returning from it, nor for the purpose of completing it; I undertake it only to keep on the move while moving pleases me. And I walk for the sake of walking. They who run after a benefice or a hare do not run; they only run who run at prisoner's base and to practice running.

My plan is divisible throughout; it is not based on great hopes; each day's journey forms an end. And the journey of

my life is carried on in the same manner. And yet I have seen
enough distant places where I should have liked to be detained.
Why not, if Chrysippus, Cleanthes, Diogenes, Zeno, Antipater,
so many sages of the surliest sect, left, indeed, their country
without reason for complaint about it and only for the enjoyment of a different atmosphere? Truly, the most unpleasant
aspect of my travels is that I cannot bring to them the firm
intent to set up my abode wherever I please, and that I must
always think about returning in order to conform to the common inclinations.

If I were afraid to die in any other place than that of my
birth, if I thought I should die less comfortably away from
my own family, I should hardly go out of France; I should
not without terror go out of my parish. I feel death continually
clutching me by the throat or by the back. But I am made
differently: death is the same to me everywhere. Yet, if I had
the choice, it would be, I think, rather on horseback than in a
bed, out of my own house, and far from my people. There is
more heartbreak than consolation in taking leave of our friends.
I am willing to forget that duty of our social intercourse for
of all the duties of friendship that is the only unpleasant one,
and I would as willingly forget to bid that great and eternal
farewell. If some advantage is derived from the attendance of
acquaintances, there are a hundred disadvantages. I have seen
many dying men piteously besieged by all this throng: the
crowd stifles them. It is contrary to duty and testimony of little
affection and little care to let you die in peace: one torments
your eyes, another your ears, another your tongue; there is
not a sense or a member that they do not shatter. Your heart
is wrung with pity to hear the laments of your friends, and,
perhaps, with anger to hear other laments that are feigned and
put on. A man who has always been of sensitive tastes is
even more so when in a weakened state. In such great necessity he needs a gentle hand, suited to his feelings, to scratch

him just where he itches; otherwise let him not be touched at all. If we need a wise woman[48] to bring us into the world, we do, indeed, need a still wiser man to help us out of it. Such a man, and a friend to boot, should be purchased at any cost to aid on such an occasion.

I have not attained that disdainful vigor which finds fortitude in itself, which nothing can aid or disturb; I am a point lower. I try to take to my heels and slip away from this passage, not through fear, but through desiring. It is not my idea, in this act of dying, to give proof or make a show of my fortitude. For whom? Then will cease all my right to reputation and my interest in it. I am content with a collected, calm, and solitary death, all my own, in keeping with my retired and private life. Quite contrary to the Roman superstition, in which a man was looked upon as unfortunate if he died without speaking and did not have his nearest relatives to close his eyes, I have enough to do to console myself without having to console others, enough thoughts in my head without circumstances bringing me new ones, and matter enough to keep me busy without borrowing. Dying is not a social rôle; it is an act for a single character. Let us live and laugh among our friends; let us go die and be crabbed among strangers. You will find by paying money someone who will turn your head and rub your feet, who will trouble you no more than you wish, turning to you an indifferent countenance, letting you meditate and lament as you please.

By reflection I rid myself every day of that childish and inhuman humor that makes us want by our misfortunes to arouse compassion and mourning in our friends. We make our troubles appear greater than they are in order to draw their tears. And the firmness in supporting adverse fortune which we commend in all men we censure and reproach in our friends when the misfortune is our own. We are not content that they should be conscious of our woes unless they are also afflicted

---

[48] literal sense of *sage-femme,* a midwife

by them. We should extend joy but curtail sadness as much as
we can. He who makes himself pitied without reason is a man
not to be pitied when there is reason. To be always complaining
is the way never to be pitied, putting on a piteous appearance
so often as to be pitiable to no one. He who acts dead when
living is subject to be thought alive when dying. I have seen
it get some people's goat to be told that their color was good
and their pulse steady; I have seen them check their laughter
because it betrayed their recovery and hate health because it
was not pitiable. What is more they were not women.

I describe my ailments, at most, just as they are and avoid
words of foreboding and made-up exclamations. If not cheerfulness, at least a composed countenance is appropriate on the
part of people attending on a sick sage. He does not pick a
quarrel with health because he sees himself in the opposite
condition; he likes to contemplate it sound and entire in others
and to enjoy it at least by association. Because he feels himself slipping, he does not completely reject the thoughts of life,
nor avoid ordinary conversation. I want to study sickness when
I am well; when it is present, it makes its impression real
enough without the help of my imagination. We prepare ourselves beforehand for the journeys we undertake and are
resolved on them; the hour when we are to take horse we leave
to our companions, and we defer it in their favor.

I notice this unexpected profit from the publication of my
way of life, that in some sort it serves me as a rule. Occasionally some thought comes over me about not betraying the
history of my life. This public declaration obliges me to keep
on my course and not to give the lie to the picture of my qualities, which are usually less disfigured and contradicted than
might be expected from the malice and infirmity of the judgments of this age. The uniformity and simplicity of my behavior produces, indeed, an appearance easy to interpret, but
because its manner is a little new and unusual, it gives too fine
an opportunity to slander. Yet so it is that to anyone who

wants to abuse me fairly I think I offer a great play to bite on in my known and avowed imperfections, and enough to gorge on without skirmishing with the wind. If it seems to him that by anticipating the accusation and revelation I am drawing the teeth of his censure, it is reasonable for him to make use of his right of amplification and extension (attack has rights beyond justice), and that he should enlarge into trees the vices whose roots I show him in myself, that he make use of not only those that possess me but also those that merely threaten me. Harmful vices, both in quality and number; let him beat me with them.

I would frankly follow the example of the philosopher Bion. Antigonus wanted to taunt him on the subject of his origin; he cut him short. "I am," said he, "the son of a slave, a butcher, branded, and of a whore whom my father married because of the baseness of his fortune. Both of them were punished for some misdeed. An orator bought me when I was a child, finding me attractive, and on dying left me all his goods; having transported them to this city of Athens, I devoted myself to the study of philosophy. Let the historians not be at a loss in seeking information about me. I'll tell them what's what about it." Free and generous confession weakens reproach and disarms slander.

Yet the fact is that, everything considered, it seems to me that I am as often praised as dispraised beyond reason. As it also seems to me that from my childhood, in rank and degree of honor, I have been given a place rather above than below what belongs to me.

I should find myself more at ease in a country where these orders of precedence were either regulated or scorned. Among men, as soon as an altercation about precedence in walking or in sitting exceeds three replies, it is uncivil. I have no fear of yielding or taking precedence unfairly to avoid such a troublesome dispute; and never did any man have a desire to go before me but that I yielded it to him.

Besides this profit I derive from writing of myself, I hope for this other advantage, that if my humors happen to please and suit some worthy man before I die, he will seek to bring us together. I give him a big start; for all that a long acquaintance and familiarity could have gained for him in many years he can see in three days in this record, and more surely and exactly. Amusing fancy: many things that I would not want to tell to anybody I tell to the public; and concerning my most secret knowledge and thoughts I send my most faithful friends to a bookseller's shop.

Our hearts we offer to the scrutiny of men.[49]

If by such good signs I knew of someone who was suited to me, I would certainly go very far to find him; for the sweetness of suitable and agreeable company cannot, in my opinion, be bought too dearly. Oh! a friend! How true is that old saying that the use of a friend is sweeter and more necessary than that of the elements of water and fire!

To return to my story, there is then no great evil in dying far off and alone. Indeed we consider it a duty to retire for natural actions less unseemly and less hideous than this. But besides, those who are reduced to dragging out a long, lingering life ought not, perhaps, to wish to trouble a large family with their misery. Therefore the Indians in a certain province thought it just to kill a man who had fallen into such straits; in another province they abandoned him alone to survive in any way he could. To whom do they not at last become tedious and insupportable? Ordinary duties do not go that far. You teach your best friends to be cruel perforce, hardening both wife and children by long habit not to feel and pity your troubles any more. The groans of my colic no longer agitate anyone. And though we should extract some pleasure from their company (which does not always happen because

---

[49] Persius

of the disparity of conditions, which easily begets contempt or envy of anyone whatever) is it not too much to abuse it over a long space of time? The more I should see them gladly restraining themselves for me, the more I should be sorry for their pains. We have a right to lean, but not to lie down so heavily upon others, nor to get our support out of their ruin. Like the man who caused little children's throats to be cut to make use of their blood to cure a disease of his own. Or that other who was supplied with tender young girls to keep his old limbs warm at night and mix the sweetness of their breath with the sourness and oppressiveness of his own. I should be inclined to suggest Venice to myself for a retreat in such a feeble state of life.

Decrepitude is a solitary quality. I am sociable even to excess. Yet I think it reasonable that henceforth I should withdraw my troublesome person from the sight of the world and brood on it by myself, that I should shrink and withdraw into my shell like a tortoise. I am learning to see men without clinging to them: that would be an outrage in so steep a pass. It is time to turn my back on company.

"But on so long a journey you will be detained miserably in some hovel where you will lack everything." Most of the necessary things I carry around with me. And besides, we cannot evade Fortune if she undertakes to attack us. I need nothing extraordinary when I am sick; what Nature cannot bring about in me, I do not want to have a pill do. At the very beginning of my fevers and of the sicknesses that lay me low, while still whole and close to health, I reconcile myself with God by the last Christian offices and find myself thereby freer and more unburdened, seeming thus to be so much the more victorious over my malady. Of notary and counsel I have less need than of physicians. What I have not settled in my affairs when in full health, let no one expect me to settle when sick. What I mean to do for the service of death is always done; I should not dare to delay it a single day. And if there is nothing done, it means either that doubt has held up my choice (for sometimes not to choose is to choose well) or that I have absolutely decided to do nothing.

I write my book for few men and for few years. Had it been matter likely to endure, it would have had to be submitted to a more stable language. In view of the continual variation that ours has been subject to up to now, who can expect that its present form will be in use fifty years from now? It slips every day from our hands, and during my life it has changed by one half. We say that at this moment it is perfect. Every century says as much of its own. I am far from considering it at that point so long as it flees and changes form as it does. It is for the good and useful writings to nail it to themselves, and its credit will proceed according to the fortunes of our state.

For that reason I am not afraid to insert in it a number of personal items, the usefulness of which will be exhausted among the men who are now living, and which bear on things particularly known to some who will see further into them than does the common understanding. After all I do not want people to go on debating, as I often see the memory of the dead tossed about: "He thought, he lived thus; he wanted this; if he had spoken when he was dying, he would have said, he would have given; I knew him better than anyone else." Now as far as decency permits, I here make known my inclinations and feelings; but I do it more willingly and freely by word of mouth to anyone who desires to be informed of them. The fact is that in these memoirs, if you look into them, you will find that I have told everything, or indicated everything. What I cannot express I point at with my finger:

> For a sagacious mind these little tracks
> Suffice; by them you may find out the rest.[50]

---
[50] Lucretius

I leave nothing concerning me to be desired or guessed at. If people have to talk about me, I want it to be truly and justly. I would willingly come back from the other world to give the lie to anyone who portrayed me other than I was, even though it were to honor me. Even of the living I notice that people always talk of them quite otherwise than they are. And if with all my strength I had not upheld a friend whom I have lost, they would have torn him into a thousand contradictory aspects.

To finish relating my frail humors, I confess that in my travels I hardly ever arrive at my lodgings but that the idea passes through my mind whether I could be sick and die there in comfort. I want to be lodged in a place that is very much to myself, free from noise, not dirty, or smoky, or stuffy. I endeavor to soothe death by these frivolous circumstances, or rather to unburden myself of all other encumbrances that I may give my attention only to it, which very likely lie heavy enough upon me without any other load. I would have my death share in the ease and comfort of my life. It is a great and important part of it, and I hope that from this day on it will not belie the past.

Death has some shapes that are easier than others and takes on different qualities according to each man's fancy. Among natural deaths, that which comes from weakness and stupor seems to me gentle and pleasant. Among violent ones, I can less comfortably fancy falling from a precipice than being crushed by a falling building, and a piercing sword blow than a harquebus shot; and I would rather have drunk Socrates' potion than stabbed myself like Cato. And though it is all one, yet my imagination feels as great a difference between throwing myself into a burning furnace and into the channel of a shallow river, as between life and death. So foolishly does our fear look more at the means than the result. It is only an instant; but it is of such gravity that I would willingly give many days of my life to pass through it in my own fashion.

Since everyone's imagination finds degrees of more and less in its bitterness, since everyone has some choice between the forms of dying, let us try a little further to find one that is free from all unpleasantness. Might we not make it even voluptuous, as did the "Partners in Death" of Antony and Cleopatra? I leave aside the harsh and exemplary results achieved by philosophy and religion. But among men of little note there have been found some such as a Petronius and a Tigillinus at Rome, who, pledged to kill themselves, lulled death as it were to sleep by the gentleness of their preparations. They made it slip and glide away amid the indolence of their accustomed diversions, among wenches and gay companions: no talk of consolation, no mention of a will, no ambitious affectation of constancy, no talk of their future state, but amidst games, feastings, jests, common and ordinary conversation, music, and amorous verses. Could we not imitate this resolution with more decent bearing? Since there are deaths good for fools, deaths good for the wise, let us find some that are good for those in between the two.

My imagination offers to me of death a certain easy and, since we must die, desirable aspect. The Roman tyrants thought they were giving a criminal his life when they gave him the choice of his death. But was not Theophrastus, so delicate, modest, and wise a philosopher, forced by reason to dare to say this line, put into Latin by Cicero:

Fortune, not wisdom, rules the life of man.[51]

How much Fortune aids in easing the bargain of my life, having so placed it that for the future it can be neither a necessity nor a hindrance to anyone! It is a condition that I would

---

[51] Cicero, *Tusculans*

have accepted at any time in my life, but on this occasion of bundling up my left-overs and packing up I am particularly pleased that in dying I shall hardly please or displease anyone. She has so fixed it by an artful compensation that they who can lay claim to any material gain from my death will also receive along with it a material loss. Death often is more grievous to us in that it is grievous to others and concerns us out of concern for them almost as much as for ourselves, and much more sometimes.

Among the comforts that I seek in lodgings I do not include pomp and elegance—I hate them rather—but a certain simple neatness which is often found in places where there is less art and which Nature honors with some grace that is all her own. *A repast not lavish but neat.* [52] *More wit than expense.* [53]

And besides it is for those whom business drags in full winter through the Grisons to be surprised on the way by this extremity. I, who most often travel for my pleasure, do not guide myself so badly. If it looks ugly on the right, I take to the left; if I find myself unfit to ride my mount, I stop. And so doing I really see nothing that is not as pleasant and comfortable as my own house. It is true that I find superfluity always superfluous and experience uneasiness even in refinement itself and in abundance. Have I left something behind me unseen? I go back to see it; it is still my route. I trace no definite line, either straight or crooked. In the places to which I go, do I fail to find what I had been told about? As if often happens that the judgments of others do not agree with mine, and I have oftener found them false, I do not regret my bother; I have learned that what I was told about is not there.

I have an adaptable constitution and tastes as common to mankind as anyone's. The diversity of fashions from one

---

[52] Lipsius, *Saturnalium Sermonum libri*   [53] Nepos, *Life of Atticus*

nation to another strikes me only by the pleasure of variety. Every custom has its reason. Let there be plates of pewter, wood, or earthenware, boiled meat or roasted, butter or nut oil or olive oil, hot food or cold, it is all one to me and so much one that, as I grow old, I find fault with this liberal bent and have need that discrimination and choice should correct the immoderateness of my appetite and sometimes relieve my stomach.

When I have been outside of France and the people out of courtesy have asked me if I wanted to be served in the French style, I have laughed at the question, and I have always hustled to the tables thickest with foreigners. I am ashamed to see my countrymen besotted with that foolish humor of being shocked by ways contrary to their own; they think they are out of their element when they are out of their village. Wherever they go, they stick to their own ways and abominate foreign ones. Do they encounter a compatriot in Hungary, they celebrate this adventure: see them rally about and join forces and condemn all the barbarous manners they see. Why not barbarous, since they are not French? Yet these are the shrewdest ones who have noticed them enough to speak ill of them. Most of them go only for the sake of returning. They travel covered and enclosed in a taciturn and incommunicative prudence, preserving themselves from the contagion of an unknown atmosphere.

What I am saying about these men reminds me, in a similar case, of what I have sometimes observed in some of our young courtiers. They associate only with men of their own sort and look upon us as people from the other world, with disdain or pity. Take away from them their talk of the mysteries of the court, and they are out of their range, as raw and clumsy to us as we are to them. It is very truly said that a well-bred man is an all-round man.

I, on the contrary, travel very much fed up with our

own ways, not to look for Gascons in Sicily (I have left enough of them at home); I rather look for Greeks and Persians; I strike up an acquaintance with these men, I study them; that is where I bestow and employ myself. And what is more I believe that I have met hardly any customs that are not as good as ours. I am not wagering much, for I have scarcely been out of sight of my weathervanes.

For the rest, most of the chance company you encounter on the road provides more nuisance than pleasure. I do not attach myself to it, even less now that old age singles me out and sequesters me somewhat from the common formalities. You suffer for others, or others for you; both inconveniences are painful, but the latter seems to me even harsher. It is rare good fortune, but of inestimable comfort, to have a well-bred man, of sound judgment and of ways conforming with yours, who likes to bear you company. I have felt an extreme lack of such a man on all my travels. But such company must have been chosen and acquired before you set out. No pleasure has any savor for me if I cannot communicate it. Not even a sprightly thought comes into my mind without my being annoyed at having produced it alone, having no one to offer it to. *If wisdom were given me on this condition, that I keep it confined and not disclose it, I should reject it.*[54] This other had strained it one tone higher. *If such a life should befall a wise man that, with an abundance of everything pouring in, he might in full leisure consider and contemplate everything worth knowing, still, if his solitude were such that he could never see a human being, he would forsake life.*[55] I like Archytas' idea, that it would be unpleasant even in heaven, and to wander among those great and divine celestial bodies, without a companion. But yet it is better to be alone than in foolish and boring company. Aristippus liked to live as a stranger in all places.

---

[54] Seneca, *Epistles*   [55] Cicero, *De Officiis*

> If fate would let me at my own free will
> Direct my life,[56]

I should choose to spend it with my seat in the saddle:

> Desirous to behold
> Those parts where blazing suns are riotous,
> And those where clouds and dripping rains hold forth.[57]

"Have you no easier pastimes? What do you lack? Is not your house situated in fine, healthful air, sufficiently furnished, and more than sufficiently large? Royal majesty has with all its pomp been put up there more than once. Does not your family leave more below it in orderliness than it has above it in eminence? Is there some local thought, extraordinary, indigestible thought that festers in you?

> That fixed within your breast now burns and harries you?[58]

Where do you think you can live without interference and without disturbance? *Fortune never bestows unmixed blessings.*[59] Then notice that it is only you that interferes with yourself, and that you will follow yourself everywhere and be sorry for yourself everywhere. For there is no satisfaction here below except for either brutish or divine souls. If a man has no contentment with such just occasion for it, where does he think he will find it? For how many thousands of men does such a condition as yours fix the limits of their desires? Reform yourself alone, for that is wholly in your power, whereas towards Fortune you have the right only of patience. *There is no really tranquil repose except that which reason has prepared.*"[60]

I see the reasonableness of this admonition, and see it perfectly well; but it would have been quicker and more pertinent to say to me in a word: "Be wise." This resolution is

---

[56] Virgil, *Aeneid*   [57] Horace, *Odes*   [58] Ennius, in Cicero, *De Senectute*
[59] Quintus Curtius   [60] Seneca, *Epistles*

beyond wisdom; it is her work and her product. Thus does the physician who keeps shouting at a poor languishing patient to be cheerful; he would be advising him a little less inanely if he said to him: "Be well." For my part, I am but a man of the lower sort. It is a salutary precept, certainly, and easily understood: "Be content with what you have; that is to say, with reason." And yet the execution of it is no more in the power of the wisest men than in mine. It is a common saying, but terribly far-reaching. What does it not comprehend? All things are subject to distinction and qualification.

I know well that, if taken literally, this pleasure in traveling is a testimony of restlessness and irresolution. And, indeed, these are our governing and predominant qualities. Yes, I confess it, I see nothing, even in a dream or in a wish, to which I may hold myself; variety alone satisfies me, and the enjoyment of diversity, at least if anything satisfies me. In traveling I am sustained by the very thought that I can stop without any loss and that I have a place where I can turn aside from it comfortably.

I love a private life because it is by my own choice that I love it, not because of unfitness for public life, which is, perhaps, as much in accord with my nature. I serve my prince the more cheerfully because it is by the free choice of my judgment and my reason, without personal obligation, and because I am not driven back on it and forced to it through being unacceptable and unwelcome to every other party. So of the rest. I hate the morsels that necessity carves for me. Any advantage on which I had to depend solely would have me by the throat:

Let this oar sweep the water, that the shore.[61]

A single cord never holds me down. "There is vanity," you say, "in this amusement." But where is there not? And these fine precepts are vanity, and all wisdom is vanity. *The Lord*

---

[61] Propertius

knoweth the thoughts of the wise, that they are vain.[62] These exquisite subtleties are only fit for sermons; they are arguments that would send us all saddled into the other world. Life is a material and corporeal movement, an action that is imperfect by its very essence, and irregular; I engage myself in serving it in its own way.

> We suffer each the fate of his own self.[63]

We must so act as not to contend against the universal laws of nature; but yet these being safeguarded, let us follow our own nature.[64]

What is the use of these lofty points of philosophy on which no human being can be seated and those rules that exceed our use and our strength? I often observe that we have patterns of life set before us which neither the proposer nor his listeners have any hope of following, or, what is more, any desire to follow. From this same sheet of paper whereon he has just written the sentence against an adulterer, the judge steals a piece to write a love-note to his colleague's wife. She whom you have just now illicitly embraced will presently, in your very presence, cry out more violently against the same fault in her companion than would Portia. And some condemn men to die for crimes that they do not consider so much as faults. In my youth I have seen a gentleman present to the public with one hand verses that excelled both in beauty and in licentiousness, and with the other at the same moment the most querulous treatise on theological reform that the world has feasted on for a long time.

This is the way men behave. We let laws and precepts go their way, we keep to another; not only through unbridled habits, but often through a contrary opinion and judgment. Listen to a philosophical lecture; the invention, the eloquence, the pertinence immediately strike your mind and stir you;

---

[62] Corinthians; Psalms   [63] Virgil, *Aeneid*   [64] Cicero, *De Officiis*

there is nothing that tickles or pricks your conscience; she is not the one to whom they are talking, is she? So Aristo used to say that neither a bath nor a lesson is of any good unless it cleans and scours. You may dally about the bark, but only after you have drawn out the pith; just as after swallowing the wine out of a beautiful cup, we examine its engraving and workmanship.

In all the ranks of ancient philosophy this will be found, that the same workman there publishes rules of temperance and publishes at the same time amorous and licentious writings. And Xenophon, in the bosom of Clinias, wrote against the Aristippic sensuality. It is not that there is any miraculous conversion stirring them fitfully. But the reason is that Solon represents himself now as himself, now in the form of a lawgiver; now he speaks for the crowd, now for himself; and he takes for himself the free and natural rules, feeling sure of firm and complete health.

And let the greatest doctors care for the severely ill.[65]

Antisthenes allows the sage to love and to do in his own way whatever he finds opportune, without regard to the laws, inasmuch as he is better advised than they and has more knowledge of virtue. His disciple Diogenes said to oppose reason to perturbations, confidence to fortune, nature to laws.

For tender stomachs strict and artificial diets are needed. Good stomachs simply follow the prescriptions of their natural appetite. So do our physicians who eat melons and drink new wine while they confine their patient to syrups and sops.

"I do not know what their books are," said the courtesan Laïs, "or their wisdom or their philosophy, but those men knock at my door as often as any others." Since licentiousness always carries us beyond what is lawful and allowed, men have

---

[65] Juvenal

often narrowed beyond universal reason the precepts and laws of our life.

> No one believes it is enough to sin
> Only as much as you permit.[66]

It would be desirable that there were more proportion between the command and the obedience; and a goal that cannot be reached seems unjust. There is no man so good who, if he submitted all his actions and thoughts to the consideration of the laws, would not deserve hanging ten times in his life, even such a man that it would be a great loss and very unjust to punish and destroy him.

> Olus, what is it to thee
> What he does with his skin, or she?[67]

And a certain man might not offend the laws in any way, who would, nonetheless, not deserve the praise of being a virtuous man, and whom philosophy would very justly cause to be whipped. So confused and uneven is this relationship. We are far from being good men according to God; we cannot be so according to ourselves. Human wisdom never yet came up to the duties that it had itself prescribed for itself, and if it had come up to them, it would prescribe itself others beyond to which it would ever aspire and pretend, so hostile to consistency is our human condition. Man decrees that he himself shall be necessarily at fault. He is not very shrewd to cut out his own duty by the measure of another being than his own. To whom does he prescribe what he does not expect anyone to do? Is he culpable in not doing what it is impossible for him to do? The laws which condemn us not to be able themselves accuse us for not being able.

At the worst this deformed liberty of presenting ourselves in two facets, the actions in one fashion and the words in

---

[66] Juvenal   [67] Martial

another, may be allowed to those who speak of things, but it cannot be so for those who speak of themselves, as I do; I must proceed with my pen as I do with my feet. The life lived in society ought to have some relation to other lives. The virtue of Cato was vigorous beyond the measure of the age he lived in; and for a man who had a hand in governing others, a man dedicated to the public service, it might be said that it was a justice, if not unjust, at least futile and out of season. Even my own conduct, which hardly differs an inch from that which is current, makes me, nevertheless, somewhat forbidding and unsociable to my contemporaries. I do not know whether I am disgusted without reason with the world I frequent, but I know well that it would be without reason if I complained of its being more disgusted with me than I am with it.

The virtue that is assigned to the affairs of the world is a virtue with many windings, angles, and elbows, in order to join and adapt itself to human frailty, mixed and artificial, not straight, clean, constant, nor purely innocent. Our annals to this very day reproach one of our kings for having too simply let himself be carried away by the conscientious persuasions of his confessor. Affairs of state have bolder precepts:

> Let him who would be good from court retire.[68]

I once tried to employ in the service of public affairs ideas and rules of living as crude, raw, unpolished, or unpolluted as they were born in me or acquired from my education, and of which I make use, if not conveniently, at least surely, in personal matters—a scholastic and novice virtue. I found them ill-adapted and dangerous. He who walks in the crowd must swerve, keep his elbows in, retire or advance, and quit the straight way according to what he encounters. He must live

---

[8] Lucan

not so much according to himself as according to others, not according to what he proposes to himself but according to what is proposed to him, according to the time, according to the men, according to the business.

Plato says that whoever escapes with clean breeches from handling the affairs of the world escapes by a miracle. And he also says that when he appoints his philosopher as the head of a government, he does not mean a corrupt government like that of Athens, and still much less one like ours, in which wisdom itself would be at a loss. Just as an herb transplanted to a soil very unsuited to its own nature much sooner adapts itself to the soil than it reforms the soil to itself.

I feel that if I had to train myself thoroughly for such occupations, it would require a great deal of change and remodeling in me. And even if I could prevail upon myself to do it (and why could I not with time and pains?) I should not want to. From the little experience I have had in that profession, I am by that much disgusted with it. I sometimes feel rising in my soul the fumes of certain temptations towards ambition, but I stiffen and obstinately hold out against them:

But thou, Catullus, carry on steadfast.[69]

I am seldom called to it and as seldom offer myself to it. Liberty and laziness, which are my ruling qualities, are qualities diametrically opposite to that trade.

We cannot distinguish the faculties of men; they have divisions and boundaries that are delicate and hard to determine. To conclude from the competence of a person's private life some competence for public affairs is to conclude badly. A certain person governs himself well who does not govern others well, and produces Essays who could not produce results; another directs a siege well who would direct a battle

---

[69] Catullus

badly, and talks well in private who would be poor at addressing the populace or a prince. Indeed to him who can do one it is, perhaps, rather evidence of not being able to do the other, than otherwise. I find that lofty souls are scarcely less adaptable to low things than low souls are to lofty things. Was it believable that Socrates should have given the Athenians occasion to laugh at his expense for having never been able to count up the votes of his tribe and make a report on them to the council? Truly the veneration I have for the perfections of that great man deserves that his fortune should furnish such a magnificent example as excuse for my principal imperfections.

Our ability is cut up into small pieces. Mine has no breadth and is, besides, pitiful in number. Saturninus said to those who had conferred upon him full command: "Comrades, you have lost a good captain to make a bad general."

Whoever boasts, in a sick age like this, of employing a pure and sincere virtue in the world's service either does not know what such virtue is, since ideas grow corrupt with our habits (indeed, hear them depict it, hear most of them glorying in their behavior and laying down their rules; instead of depicting virtue, they depict injustice pure and simple, and vice, and present it thus falsified for the education of princes), or, if he does know it, he boasts wrongly and, let him say what he will, does a thousand things of which his conscience accuses him. I should willingly take Seneca's word about the experience he had in such circumstances, provided he was willing to speak frankly about it to me. The most honorable mark of goodness in such a pass is to acknowledge freely our fault and that of others, to push against and hold back with all our power the inclination towards evil, to go down that slope unwillingly, to hope for the better and to desire the better.

I perceive that in these dismemberments of France and divisions into which we have fallen everyone labors to defend his cause, but, even the best of them, with dissimulation and lying. Whoever would write about them roundly would write about them rashly and harmfully. The juster party is still a member of a worm-eaten and rotten body. But in such a body the member that is least diseased is called sound; and with good reason, since our qualities have no title except by comparison. Civic innocence is measured according to the places and the times. I should like to see in Xenophon a eulogy of Agesilaus for an action like this: being asked by a neighboring prince, with whom he had once been at war, to let him pass through his lands, he granted it, giving him passage across the Peloponnesus, and not only did he not imprison or poison him when he had him at his mercy, but he received him courteously, without doing him any harm. To such natures as his, that would not be saying anything; elsewhere and in other times the honesty and magnanimity of such an action will become noteworthy. These begowned baboons in our schools would have laughed at it, so little does Spartan innocence resemble that of France.

We are not without virtuous men, but it is according to our standard. Whoever has morals established as a discipline above his times, either let him twist or blunt his rules, or, what I rather advise him, let him draw aside and not mix with us at all. What would he gain by it?

> If I perceive an excellent and upright man,
> I rank this marvel with a double-headed child,
> Or with the fish found with surprise beneath the plow,
> Or with a pregnant mule.[70]

We may regret better times, but we cannot escape from the present; we may wish for different magistrates, but we must, nevertheless, obey those we have. And, perhaps, there is more merit in obeying the bad than the good. So long as the image of the ancient and accepted laws of this monarchy shall shine

---

[70] Juvenal

in any corner, there will I be planted. If by bad fortune they happen to contradict and thwart one another and to produce two factions presenting a doubtful and difficult choice, my choice will be in favor of stealing away and escaping from that tempest; in the meantime Nature, or the hazards of war, may lend me a hand. Between Caesar and Pompey I should have declared myself openly, but among those three robbers who came after I should have had either to hide or to go along with the wind; which I consider permissible when Reason no longer guides.

> Whither dost thou wandering go? [71]

This stuffing is a little out of my subject. I go out of my way, but rather by license than carelessness. My ideas follow one another, but sometimes it is at a distance, and they look at one another, but with a sidelong glance. I have run my eyes over a certain dialogue of Plato divided into two parts in a fantastic motley, the front part about love, and all the lower part about rhetoric. They are not afraid of these changes and have a marvelous grace in letting themselves roll along in the wind, or seem to. The titles of my chapters do not always embrace their matter; often they denote it only by some sign, like those other titles, *Andria, Eunuchus*,[72] or those other names, Sulla, Cicero, Torquatus. I love the poetic gait, by leaps and gambols. It is an art, as Plato says, light, flighty, and daemonic. There are works in Plutarch where he forgets his theme, where the exposition of his subject is found only incidentally, completely smothered in foreign matter. See his movements in *The Daemon of Socrates*. Lord! What beauty there is in these spirited sallies and this variation, and more so as they seem the more unstudied and fortuitous. It is the inattentive reader that loses my subject, not I; there will always be found in a corner some word of it, which will not fail to

---

[71] Virgil, *Aeneid*   [72] The names of two of Terence's comedies.

suffice, though it be compressed. I seek after change undiscern-
ingly and tumultuously. My style and my mind go roving
in the same way. "A man must have a dash of madness if he
does not want to have still more stupidity," say both the
precepts of our masters, and even more their examples.

A thousand poets drag and languish prosaically; but the
best ancient prose (and I strew it here indifferently as verse)
shines throughout with the vigor and boldness of poetry and
bears an air of its frenzy. We must certainly grant it mastery
and pre-eminence in speech. The poet, says Plato, seated on
the tripod of the Muses, pours out with fury whatever comes
into his mouth, like the spout of a fountain, without ruminat-
ing and pondering it, and there escape from him things of
varied colors, of contradictory substance, and with an irregular flow. He himself is entirely poetic, and the old theology
is poetry, scholars say, and the first philosophy. It is the
original language of the Gods.

I intend for the matter itself to establish its parts. It shows
sufficiently where it changes, where it concludes, where it begins, and where it resumes, without interlacing it with words,
with joints and seams introduced for the benefit of weak or
negligent ears, and without writing commentaries on myself.
Who is there that does not prefer not to be read than to be
read in a drowsy or cursory manner? *Nothing is so useful that
it can be profitable when taken in passing.*[73] If to take up books
were to take them in, if to look at them were to consider them,
and to run through them were to grasp them, I should be
wrong to make myself quite as ignorant as I say I am.

Since I cannot arrest the attention of the reader by weight,
it is that much to the good if I chance to arrest it by my in-
tricacy. "True, but he will afterwards repent of having mused
over it." That is so, but he will still have mused over it. And
then there are natures like that in whom understanding produced disdain, who will think better of me because they will

---

[73] Seneca, *Epistles*

not know what I say; they will conclude that there is depth to my meaning because of the obscurity, which, to speak in good earnest, I hate very greatly, and I would avoid it if I could avoid myself. Aristotle boasts somewhere of affecting it; vicious affectation!

Since such frequent cutting up into chapters, which I used at the beginning, seemed to me to break and dissolve the attention before it was stirred, making it disdain to settle and collect itself for so little, I have started to make them longer, thus requiring a definite purpose and assigned leisure. In such an occupation, if you will not give a man a single hour, you will not give him anything. And you do nothing for a man for whom you do something only while you are doing something else. In addition perhaps I have some personal obligation to speak only by halves, to speak confusedly, to speak discordantly.

I was about to say that I hold a grudge against that killjoy reason; and that those extravagant projects that harass our lives, and those very subtle ideas, if they have any truth in them, I find it too costly and inconvenient. On the contrary, I make it my business to turn even vanity and asininity to account if it bring me any pleasure, and let myself follow my natural inclinations without keeping too close a check on them.

I have seen elsewhere ruined houses, and statues, and sky and earth: they are men after all. All that is true; and yet I cannot so often revisit the tomb of that great and mighty city[74] that I do not marvel at it and revere it. The care of the dead is recommended to us. Now I have been brought up from childhood with these dead. I had knowledge of the affairs of Rome long before I had any of those of my own house. I knew the Capitol and its location before I knew the Louvre, and the Tiber before the Seine. I have had the qualities and fortunes of Lucullus, Metellus, and Scipio more in my mind than those

---

[74] Rome

of any of our people. They are dead. So, indeed, is my father, as completely as they, and he has drawn as far away from me and from life in eighteen years as they have in sixteen hundred. Nevertheless I do not cease to embrace and cultivate his memory, friendship, and society in a perfect and very living union.

Indeed by my own inclination I give greater service to the dead. They can no longer help themselves; it seems to me that they, therefore, require my help all the more. It is here that gratitude appears in its right luster. A benefit is less richly bestowed where there is reciprocity and return. Arcesilaus, visiting Ctesibius, who was sick, and finding him poorly off, very quietly tucked under his pillow some money he was giving him; and in concealing it from him, he also gave him acquittal of being grateful for it. Those who have merited friendship and gratitude from me have never lost it through being no longer there; I have paid them better and more carefully when they were absent and ignorant of it. I speak more affectionately of my friends when there is no longer any way for them to know it.

Now I have undertaken a hundred quarrels in defense of Pompey and for the cause of Brutus. This friendship still endures between us; even present things we hold only by the imagination. Finding myself of no use for this age, I throw myself back upon that other and am so enticed by it that the state of that ancient Rome, free, just, and flourishing (for I love neither her birth nor her old age), interests me passionately. Therefore I cannot so often revisit the site of their streets and of their houses, and those ruins as deep as the Antipodes, that I do not muse over them. Is it by nature or by an error of the imagination that the sight of the places which we know were frequented and inhabited by persons whose memory is held in esteem somehow stirs us more than hearing the account of their deeds or reading their writings? *Such power do places have to call up memories! And truly in this city that is certainly infinite; for wherever we go we set our foot on history.*[75] I like to reflect on their faces, their bearing, and their clothes. I chew those great names over between my teeth and make them resound in my ears. *I venerate them and always rise in honor of such great names.*[76] Of things that are in some part great and admirable, I admire even the common parts. I would enjoy seeing them talk, walk, and sup. It would be ingratitude to despise the remains and images of so many worthy and very valiant men whom I have seen live and die, and who give us so many good instructions by their example if we only knew how to follow them.

And then, this very Rome that we behold deserves to be beloved, allied for so long and by so many titles to our crown: the only common and universal city. The sovereign magistrate who commands there is acknowledged equally elsewhere. It is the metropolitan city of all the Christian nations; the Spaniard and the Frenchman, every man is at home there. To be one of the princes of that state one has only to be a member of Christendom, wherever it may be. There is no place here below that heaven has embraced with such favorable influence and with such constancy. Her very ruin is glorious and majestic,

More precious for her glorious ruins.[77]

Even in the tomb she retains some marks and likeness of empire. *That it may be manifest that in one place Nature rejoiced in her work.*[78]

Some might blame themselves and rebel within at feeling themselves tickled by so vain a pleasure. Our humors are not too vain if they are pleasant; whatever they may be, if they constantly content a man capable of common sense, I would not have the heart to pity him.

I am much indebted to Fortune for having up to this mo-

---

[75] Cicero, *De Finibus*   [76] Seneca, *Epistles*   [77] Sidonius Apollinaris, *Carmina*   [78] Pliny, *Natural History*

ment done nothing hostile to me, at least nothing beyond my endurance. Might it not be her way to leave in peace those who do not trouble her?

> The more a man himself denies,
> The more to him does Heaven supply.
> Stark destitute I seek to join
> The ranks of those who nothing crave . . .
> They lack a lot who seek a lot.[79]

If she continues, she will send me off well contented and satisfied,

> For nothing more do I disturb the gods.[80]

But beware the crash! There are thousands who are wrecked in port.

I easily console myself for what will happen here when I am here no longer; present things keep me busy enough,

> To Fortune I leave all the rest.[81]

Besides I do not have that strong connection that they say attaches men to the future by the children who bear their name and their honor;[82] and, perhaps, I ought to desire them all the less if they are so much to be desired. I am only too much attached to the world and to this life by myself. I am content to be in Fortune's grasp by the circumstances really necessary to my existence, without extending her jurisdiction over me in other directions; and I have never thought that to be without children was a want that should make life less complete and less contented. The sterile state has its advantages too. Children are among the things that have no great reason to be desired, especially now when it would be so hard to make them

---

[79] Horace, *Odes* [80] Horace, *Odes* [81] Ovid, *Metamorphoses*
[82] Montaigne had a daughter, no sons.

good. *Good things cannot be produced now, so corrupted are the seeds;*[83] and yet they rightly have reason to be regretted by whoever loses them after having had them.

He who left me the charge of my house predicted that I was due to ruin it, considering my very slight inclination to domesticity. He was mistaken: here I am as when I first came into it, if not a little better off; and yet without office and without benefice.

For the rest, if Fortune has done me no violent or extraordinary injury, neither has she done me any favor. All that my house has in the way of gifts from her was there more than a hundred years before me. Personally I possess no essential and solid good that I owe to her liberality. She has done me some windy favors, honorary and titular, without substance; and, moreover, in truth she did not grant them, but offered them to me, Lord knows, to me who am completely material, who am satisfied only with reality, and a very massive reality, and who, if I dared confess it, should not consider avarice much less excusable than ambition, nor pain less to be avoided than shame, nor health less desirable than learning, nor riches less than nobility.

Among her empty favors there is none that so much pleases that silly humor in me which feeds upon it as an authentic bull of Roman citizenship, which was granted to me lately when I was there, pompous in seals and gilded letters, and granted with all gracious liberality. And because these bulls are granted in various styles, more or less favorable, and because before I had seen one I should have been very glad to have been shown their formula, I will, to satisfy someone, if there is anyone sick with the same curiosity as mine, transcribe it here in due form:

ON THE REPORT MADE TO THE SENATE BY ORA-ZIO MASSIMI, MARZO CECIO, ALESSANDRO MUTI, CONSERVATORS OF THE CITY OF ROME, CONCERN-

---

[83] Tertullian, *De Pudicitia*

ING THE RIGHT OF ROMAN CITIZENSHIP TO BE GRANTED TO THE MOST ILLUSTRIOUS MICHEL DE MONTAIGNE, KNIGHT OF THE ORDER OF ST. MICHAEL, AND GENTLEMAN OF THE CHAMBER IN ORDINARY TO THE MOST CHRISTIAN KING, THE SENATE AND PEOPLE OF ROME HAVE DECREED:

Considering that, by ancient custom and practice, those men have ever been adopted among us with ardor and eagerness, who, distinguished in virtue and nobility, have been of great service and distinction to our Republic, or might be so in the future; We, deeply moved by the example and authority of our ancestors, resolve that we should imitate and follow this glorious custom. Wherefore, since the most illustrious Michel de Montaigne, Knight of the Order of St. Michael, and Gentleman of the Chamber in ordinary to the Most Christian King, is most zealous for the Roman name, and, by the honor and distinction of his family and his own excellent merits, most worthy to be admitted to Roman citizenship by the supreme judgment and will of the Senate and People of Rome: it has pleased the Senate and People of Rome that the most illustrious Michel de Montaigne, highly adorned with all qualities and very dear to this noble people, should be inscribed as a Roman citizen, himself and his posterity, and furnished with all the privileges and honors enjoyed by those who were born Citizens and Patricians of Rome, or who have very justly been made such. Herein the Senate and People of Rome consider that they do not so much confer the Rights of Citizenship on him as a favor, as pay them as a debt, nor do him more service than they receive from him, who, in accepting this Citizenship, singularly honors and distinguishes the City itself. Which Senatus-Consultus these Conservators have caused to be transcribed by the secretaries of the Roman Senate and People and deposited in the archives of the Capitol, and have had this act drawn up and sealed with the common seal of the City. In the year 2331 since the foundation of Rome, A.D. 1581, 13th of March.

ORAZIO FOSCO,
Secretary of the Sacred Senate and of the People of Rome.
VINCENTE MARTOLI,
Secretary of the Sacred Senate and of the People of Rome.

Being a burgess of no city at all, I am very glad to be one of the noblest city that ever was or ever shall be. If other men observed themselves attentively, as I do, they would find themselves, as I do, full of inanity and nonsense. Get rid of it I cannot without getting rid of myself. We are all steeped in it, one as much as another; but those who are aware of it have a little the better of it—still I don't know.

This common attitude and practice of looking elsewhere than at ourselves has been very useful for our business. We are a very depressing spectacle; we see there nothing but misery and vanity. In order not to dismay us, Nature has very appropriately cast the action of our vision outwards. We go forward with the current, but to turn our course back towards ourselves is a painful movement: thus the sea becomes stirred up and troubled when it is thrust back on itself. Look, says everyone, at the movement of the heavens, look at the public, at that man's quarrel, at this one's pulse, at this other's last will and testament; in short, be always looking high or low, or to one side, or in front of or behind you. It was a paradoxical command that was of old given us by that god at Delphi: "Look into yourself, know yourself, keep to yourself; bring back your mind and will, which are spending themselves elsewhere, into themselves; you are running out, you are scattering yourself; concentrate yourself, hold yourself in; you are being betrayed, you are being dispersed, you are being stolen away from yourself. Do you not see that this world keeps its full sight fixed within and its eyes open to contemplate itself? It is always vanity for you, within and without, but it is less vanity when it is less extended. Except for you, Oh man," said that god, "each thing studies itself first and has limits to its labors and desires according to its need. There is not a single thing so empty and needy as you who embrace the universe: you are the investigator without knowledge, the magistrate without jurisdiction, and, after all, the fool of the farce."

OF HUSBANDING YOUR WILL

In comparison with most men few things touch me, or, to put it better, hold me fast; for it is right that they touch, provided they do not possess us. I take great care to increase by study and by reasoning this privilege of insensibility, which is naturally well advanced in me. I espouse, and consequently become passionate about, very few things. My sight is clear, but I fix it on few objects; my sensitivity, delicate and tender. But my apprehension and application is hard and unreceptive: I do not easily engage myself. As much as I can, I employ myself wholly upon myself; and even in this subject I should still willingly bridle and hold my affection back from plunging too fully into it since it is a subject that I possess at the mercy of others and over which Fortune has more right than I. So that even in respect to health which I value so much, I ought not to desire it and devote myself to it so frantically as to find illnesses therefore insupportable. A man ought to moderate himself between hatred of pain and love of pleasure, and Plato prescribes a middle course of life between the two.

But the passions which distract me from myself and attach me elsewhere, those certainly I oppose with all my strength. My opinion is that we should lend ourselves to others and give ourselves only to ourselves. If my will happened to be easily mortgaged and engaged, I should not last: I am too tender, both by nature and by practice,

Fleeing affairs and born to leisure free from care.[1]

Contested and obstinate disputes that would in the end give the advantage to my adversary, the outcome that would make my

[1] Ovid, *Tristia*

hot pursuit shameful, would, perhaps, eat at me cruelly. If I bit in just as others do, my soul would never have the strength to bear the alarms and emotions that pursue those who embrace so much; it would be immediately dislocated by this inner agitation. If sometimes I have been pushed into the management of other men's affairs, I have promised to take them in hand, not into my lungs and liver; to take them upon me, not to incorporate them into me; to take care of them, yes, to become impassioned about them, not at all. I keep an eye on them, but I do not brood over them. I have enough to do to order and arrange the pressure of domestic matters that I have in my entrails and veins without lodging there an outside pressure and being crushed by it; and I am sufficiently concerned about my essential, personal, and natural affairs without inviting in other foreign ones. Those who know how much they owe to themselves, and for how many duties they are obligated to themselves, find that Nature has given them a commission that is full enough and not at all idle. You have plenty to do at home, don't go off.

Men let themselves out to hire. Their faculties are not for themselves, they are for those to whom they enslave themselves; their tenants are at home, not they. I do not like this common humor. We must husband the freedom of our soul and mortgage it only on fit occasions, which are very few, if we judge soundly. See the people who have been taught to let themselves be seized and carried away; they do so everywhere, in small things as in big, in what does not concern them as in what does concern them; they throw themselves in indiscriminately wherever there is business and duties to assume, and they are without life when they are without tumultuous agitation. *They are in business for business' sake.*[2] They seek business only for the sake of being busy. It is not so much that they want to be on the go, as that they cannot keep still; no more nor less than a stone started on its fall, which does not stop

[2] Seneca, *Epistles*

until it comes to rest. Being busy is to a certain sort of people a mark of ability and dignity. Their mind seeks its repose in movement like children in the cradle. They may be said to be as serviceable to their friends as they are troublesome to themselves. No one distributes his money to others, but everyone distributes his time and his life. There is nothing of which we are so prodigal as of those things in which alone avarice would be for us useful and commendable.

I take an altogether different attitude. I keep myself to myself, and commonly desire mildly what I desire, and desire little; I occupy and busy myself in the same way: rarely and tranquilly. All that they want and direct they do with all their will and vehemence. There are so many bad spots that for the greatest safety we must glide over this world a little lightly and on the surface. We must slide over it, not plunge into it. Even pleasure is painful in its depth:

> You walk through fires
> 'Neath treacherous ashes set.[3]

The Messieurs[4] of Bordeaux elected me mayor of their city while I was far from France and still farther from such a thought. I asked to be excused, but I was informed that I was wrong, the king's command also being interposed. It is a charge that must seem so much the handsomer as it has no remuneration or gain other than the honor of its execution. Its term is two years, but it may be extended by a second election, which very rarely happens. It was so extended in my case, and it had been done only twice before: some years earlier to Monsieur de Lanssac, and recently to Monsieur de Biron, Marshal of France, to whose place I succeeded; and I left mine to Monsieur de Matignon, also Marshal of France. Proud of such noble company,

> Each a good minister in peace and war![5]

---

[3] Horace, *Odes*　　　[4] "Jurats," city fathers　　　[5] Virgil, *Aeneid*

Fortune wished to have a hand in my promotion by this particular circumstance which she put in of her own. Not altogether vain: for Alexander disdained the ambassadors of Corinth who were offering him citizenship in their city; but when they went on to tell him that Bacchus and Hercules were also on that list, he graciously thanked them for it.

On my arrival I faithfully and conscientiously deciphered myself to them, just exactly as I feel myself to be: without memory, without vigilance, without experience, and without vigor; also without hate, without ambition, without avarice, and without violence; so that they might be informed and instructed about what they were to expect of my service. And because their knowledge of my late father had alone incited them to that, and their honor for his memory, I added very clearly that I should be very sorry if anything at all pressed as heavily upon my will as their affairs and their city had formerly done on his while he had the administration of them in this same post to which they had called me.

I remembered in my childhood having seen him old, his soul cruelly stirred up by this public turmoil, forgetting the sweet air of his home, to which the weakness of age had attached him a long time before, and his household and his health, and truly despising his life, which he almost lost in this, engaged in long and painful journeys on their behalf. Such was he; and this attitude came in him from a great goodness of nature: there was never a more kindly and public-spirited soul. This course, which I commend in others, I do not like to follow, and I am not without excuse. He had heard it said that we must forget ourselves for our neighbor, that the individual was not to be considered at all in comparison with the general.

Most of the rules and precepts of the world take this course of pushing us out of ourselves and chasing us into the market place for the benefit of public society. They thought they would produce a fine result by diverting and distracting us from ourselves, assuming we were but too much attached to ourselves, and by too natural a bond; and they have spared no words to that end. For it is no new thing for sages to preach things as they serve, not as they are. Truth has its drawbacks, inconveniences, and incompatibilities with us. We must be often deceived that we may not deceive ourselves, and our eyes sealed, our understanding stunned in order to redress and amend them. *For it is the ignorant who judge, and they must frequently be deceived, lest they err.*[6] When they order us to love three, four, fifty degrees of things before ourselves, they imitate the art of the archers who, to hit the mark, go and take their aim a great deal above the target. To straighten a bent stick we bend it back the other way.

I believe that in the temple of Pallas, as we see in all other religions, there were apparent mysteries to be shown to the people and other mysteries, more secret and high, to be shown only to those who were initiated. It is likely that in the latter is to be found the true point of the friendship that every man owes to himself. Not a false friendship that makes us embrace glory, learning, riches, and such things, with principal and immoderate affection, as members of our being, nor over-indulgent and undiscerning friendship, in which it happens as we see with ivy, that it decays and ruins the walls to which it clings; but a salutary and well-ordered friendship, useful and pleasant alike. He who knows its duties and practises them, he is truly of the cabinet of the Muses; he has attained the summit of human wisdom and of our happiness. This man, knowing exactly what he owes to himself, finds in the part he has to play that he must apply to himself the practices of other men and of the world and, in order to do this, contribute to public society the duties and services that pertain to him. He who lives not at all for others hardly lives for himself. *He who is a friend to himself, be assured that this man is a friend to all.*[7] The principal charge that we have is every man his own conduct; and that is what we are here for. Just as he who should forget to live a good and

---

[6] Quintilian   [7] Seneca, *Epistles*

holy life and should think he was quit of his duty by guiding and training others to do so would be a fool; even so he who abandons his own healthy and gay living to serve others thereby takes, in my opinion, a bad and unnatural course.

I do not want a man to refuse to the charges that he assumes attention, efforts, eloquence, and sweat and blood if need be:

> For cherished friends
> Or fatherland I do not fear to die.[8]

But it is by way of loan and accidentally, the mind keeping itself always in repose and in health, not without action, but without vexation, without passion. Simply to act costs it so little that it acts even in sleep. But it must be set in motion with discretion. For the body receives the loads that are put on it exactly according as they are; the mind often extends them and makes them heavier at its own expense, giving them what measure it pleases. We perform like things with different degrees of effort and a different amount of tension of the will. The one gets on well without the other.[9] For how many people hazard themselves every day in the wars, which are no concern to them, and press on into the dangers of battles, the loss of which will not trouble their next night's sleep! This other man in his house apart from this danger which he would not have dared to face is more passionate about the outcome of this war and is more worked up in his soul about it than is the soldier who is putting his blood and his life into it. I have been able to engage in public service without departing a nail's breadth from myself, and to give myself to others without taking myself from myself.

This fierceness and violence of desires hinders more than it serves the execution of what we undertake, fills us with impatience towards matters that come out contrary or late, and with bitterness and suspicion towards those with whom we are

---

[8] Horace, *Odes*   [9] Action, without passion

dealing. We never conduct well the thing by which we are possessed and conducted;

> For passion handles badly everything.[10]

He who puts therein only his judgment and his address proceeds more gayly. He feints, he gives way, he puts everything off at his convenience according to the need of the occasions; he misses his target without vexation and without distress, intact and ready for a new undertaking; he always goes bridle in hand. In the man who is drunk with that violent and dominating drive, we see of necessity a great lack of sagacity and of justice; the impetuosity of his desire carries him away. They are reckless movements and, unless Fortune assists them a great deal, of very little fruit.

Philosophy would have us, in the punishing of injuries received, keep anger out of it, not that the vengeance may be less, but, on the contrary, that it may be the better dealt out and heavier; it seems to her that this impetuosity brings hindrance to doing that. Not only does anger cause confusion, but by itself it also tires the arms of those who chastise. This fire benumbs and consumes their strength. As in precipitation, *More haste, less speed*,[11] haste trips itself up, gets tangled up in itself, and brings itself to a stop. *Speed gets entangled in itself.*[12] For example, according to what I see in common experience, avarice has no greater impediment than itself: the more strained and vigorous it is, the less it produces. Generally avarice catches wealth more readily when disguised in a mask of liberality.

A gentleman, a very honest man and my friend, very nearly muddled his wits by a too passionate application and attachment to the affairs of a prince, his master. That master portrayed himself to me in this manner: that he perceives the gravity of mishaps as well as another, but that in those for which

---

[10] Statius, *Thebaid*, in Lipsius' *Politics*   [11] Quintus Curtius   [12] Seneca, *Epistles*

there is no remedy he at once makes up his mind to bear them; in other cases, after making the necessary provisions, which he can do quickly because of the liveliness of his mind, he tranquilly awaits what may ensue. In truth, I have seen him at work, keeping up a great nonchalance and freedom in his actions and countenance in the midst of very great and thorny affairs. I find him greater and more capable in misfortune than in good; his losses are more glorious to him than his victories, and his sorrow than his triumph.

Consider that, even in actions that are idle and frivolous, in the game of chess, tennis, and the like, this fierce and ardent attachment of a driving desire immediately throws the mind and members into bewilderment and disorder: we are dazed and confused by ourselves. He who bears himself more moderately towards gain and loss always has his wits about him; the less excited and passionate he becomes about the game, the more surely and successfully he handles it.

As to the rest, we hinder the mind's grasp and hold by giving it so many things to seize. Some things we must only hold out before it, others attach to it, still others incorporate in it. It can see and feel all things, but it ought to feed only on itself, and it ought to be instructed in what peculiarly concerns it and what is peculiarly of its own possession and substance. The laws of Nature teach us exactly what we need. After the sages have told us that according to Nature no one is needy, and that everyone is so according to opinion, they distinguish subtly between the desires that come from her and those that come from the disorder of our imagination in this manner: those of which we can see the end are hers, those that flee before us and whose end we cannot overtake are ours. Poverty of material goods is easy to cure; poverty of soul, impossible.

> If what's for man enough, enough could be,
> It were enough; but as we plainly see
> That won't suffice, how can I e'er believe
> That any wealth my mind content can give? [13]

---

[13] Lucilius, in Nonius Marcellus

Seeing a great quantity of riches, jewels, and costly furniture carried in pomp through his city, Socrates said: "How many things I do not desire!" Metrodorus lived on twelve ounces a day, Epicurus upon less. Metrocles slept in winter with the sheep, in summer in the cloisters of churches. *Nature provides for its own demands.*[14] Cleanthes lived by the labor of his hands and boasted that Cleanthes, if he would, could maintain yet another Cleanthes.

If that which Nature exactly and originally requires of us for the preservation of our being is too little (as, in truth, how little this is and how cheaply our life can be maintained cannot be expressed better than by this consideration, that it is so little that it escapes the grasp and shock of Fortune by its littleness), let us grant ourselves something further: let us call the habits and condition of each one of us Nature; let us appraise and treat ourselves by this measure, let us stretch our appurtenances and accounts that far. For that far it seems to me, indeed, that we have some excuse. Custom is a second Nature and no less powerful. What is lacking to my customary way of living I hold to be lacking to me. And I should almost as soon have my life taken from me as to have it reduced and cut down very far from the state in which I have so long lived.

I am past the age for any great change and for throwing myself into a new and unaccustomed way of living. Even towards improvement. It is no longer time to become other than I am. And just as I should complain of any remarkable experience that might now fall within my grasp because it had not come in a time when I could enjoy it,

> For what are Fortune's gifts, if I'm denied
> Their use?[15]

so likewise should I complain of any inward acquisition. It is almost better never to become an intelligent man and well

---

[14] Seneca, *Epistles*   [15] Horace, *Epistles*

versed in living than to become one so late when one has no more life. I, who am leaving, would readily resign to anyone who might come along what wisdom I am acquiring for dealing with the world. Mustard after dinner! I have no use for goods of which I can make no use. For what good is knowledge to a man who no longer has a head? It is an insult and unkindness for Fortune to offer us presents that fill us with a just resentment at their having failed us in their season. Guide me no more, I can walk no more. Of the many parts that excellence possesses, patience is enough for us. Give the capacity of an excellent treble to a singer who has rotten lungs, and eloquence to a hermit relegated to the deserts of Arabia. No art is needed for a fall: the end comes of itself at the conclusion of every task. My world has waned, my form is emptied; I belong wholly to the past, and I am bound to hold it supreme and to make my departure be in keeping with it. This is what I mean: that the recent effacement of ten days by the Pope[16] has so taken me aback that I cannot well get used to it. I belong to the years in which we reckoned differently. Such an ancient and long practice claims me and calls me back to it. I am constrained to be a little heretical on this point, incapable of innovation, even for the better. My imagination, in spite of my teeth, keeps throwing me ten days forward or backward and mutters in my ears: "This rule concerns those who are to come." If health itself, sweet as it is, happens to revisit me by spells, it is to give me regret rather than possession of it; I no longer have any place to harbor it. Time abandons me; without it nothing can be possessed. Oh, what little account I should make of those great elective dignities I see in the world that are given only to men ready to leave it; in these offices consideration is given not so much to how properly they will discharge them as to how briefly they will do so: from their very entry others were sighting their exit.

In short I am in the act of finishing this man and not of mak-

---

[16] Calendar reform of 1582 by Gregory XIII

ing another out of him. By long usage this form of mine has turned into substance, and Fortune into Nature.

I say, then, that every one of us feeble creatures may be excused for considering as his own that which is comprised under this measure. But also beyond these limits there is nothing but confusion. It is the broadest scope that we can grant to our claims. The more we enlarge our needs and our possessions the more we involve ourselves in the blows of fortune and adversity. The range of our desires ought to be circumscribed and restricted to the narrow limit of the closest and most contiguous things that are to our interest; and their course ought, moreover, to be directed not in a straight line that ends elsewhere, but in a circle whose two points by a brief sweep meet and terminate in ourselves. Actions which are performed without this reflexive movement, I mean a close and real reflection, like the actions of the avaricious, the ambitious, and so many others who run straight ahead, whose course always carries them forward, are erroneous and sickly actions.

Most of our occupations smack of comedy. *The whole world plays a part.*[17] We must play our part properly, but as the part of a borrowed character. Of the mask and the appearance we must not make a real essence, nor of something foreign something that is our own. We cannot distinguish the skin from the shirt. It is enough to make up the face without making up the heart. I see some who transform and transubstantiate themselves into as many new shapes and new beings as the offices they undertake, and who become prelates to their very liver and entrails and drag their position along with them even into their water closet. I cannot teach them to distinguish the bonnetings that are addressed to them from those addressed to their office, or their retinue, or their mule. *They give themselves up so much to fortune that they even unlearn their nature.*[18] They swell and puff up their soul and their natural speech to the height of their magisterial seat.

[17] Petronius   [18] Quintus Curtius

The Mayor and Montaigne have always been two, with a very clear separation. Because we are lawyers or financiers, we must not ignore the knavery there is in such callings. An honest man is not accountable for the vice or stupidity of his trade, and should not, therefore, refuse to practice it: it is the custom of his country, and there is usefulness in it. We must live in the world and make the best of it such as we find it. But the judgment of an emperor ought to be above his imperial authority and ought to view and consider it as an extraneous circumstance; and he himself ought to know how to enjoy his own self apart and to make himself known like James or Peter, at least to himself.

I cannot involve myself so deeply and so completely. When my will commits me to a party, it is not with so violent an attachment that my understanding is infected by it. In the present broils of this kingdom my own interest has not made me blind to the laudable qualities in our adversaries, nor to the reprehensible qualities in those men whom I have followed. Men adore everything which is on their own side; for my part I do not even excuse most of the things that I see on mine. A good work does not lose its grace for pleading against my cause. Except for the knot of the controversy I have kept myself in a state of equanimity and pure indifference. *And beyond the necessities of war I bear no special hatred.*[19] For which I am pleased with myself, and the more because I commonly see men fail in the opposite direction. *Let him make use of passion who cannot make use of reason.*[20] Those who prolong their anger and hatred beyond the affairs in question, as most men do, show that their passion issues from another source, from a personal cause; just as to a man whose fever still remains after he has been cured of an ulcer, it is evident that it had another more hidden cause. The fact is that they have nothing against the cause in general, and in so far as it injures the interest of all and of the state, but they resent it only so far as it grinds

[19] Livy   [20] Cicero, *Tusculans*

upon their private interests. That is why they are nettled by it with a personal passion beyond justice and common reason. *They did not collectively so much censure the terms as a whole as they did individually those articles that concerned each of them personally.*[21]

I want the advantage to be on our side, but I do not become frenzied if it is not. I adhere firmly to the soundest of the parties, but I do not seek to be specially noted as an enemy to the others and beyond the bounds of common reason. I condemn very vigorously this vicious form of reasoning; "He is of the League for he admires the charm of Monsieur de Guise. The activity of the King of Navarre astonishes him: he is a Huguenot. He finds some fault with the king's morals; he is seditious in his heart." I did not even concede the magistrate to be right in condemning a book for having placed a heretic[22] among the best poets of this century. Should we not dare to say of a thief that he has a fine leg? If she is a prostitute, must she necessarily have a stinking breath? Did they, in the wisest ages, revoke the proud title of Capitolinus, which they had previously given to Marcus Manlius, as the preserver of religion and public liberty? Did they suppress the memory of his liberality and his feats of arms and the military rewards granted to his valor because he afterwards aspired to kingship, to the prejudice of the laws of his country?

If they have taken a strong dislike for an advocate, the next day in their opinion he becomes ineloquent. I have elsewhere touched upon the zeal that impelled good men to similar faults. For my part I can well say: "He does this wickedly and that virtuously." So also, in the matter of the predictions or the adverse outcome of affairs, they desire that everyone, in his cause, be blind and dull witted, and that our belief and judgment serve, not the truth, but the purpose of our desires. I should rather err towards the other extreme, so much do I fear being

---

[1] Livy   [22] Théodore de Bèze

suborned by my desire. Besides I am somewhat tenderly distrustful of things that I wish.

I have in my time seen wonders in the undiscerning and
prodigious ease with which men have let their belief and hope
be led and directed wherever it has pleased and served the purpose of their leaders, in spite of a hundred mistakes one on the
top of another, in spite of dreams and phantasms. I am no
longer astonished at those who were hoodwinked by the mon-
key tricks of Apollonius and Mahomet. Their sense and understanding are completely smothered by their passion. Their judgment leaves them no other choice than that which smiles upon
them and supports their cause. I had observed this to a supreme degree in the first of our feverish factions.[23] The other
which has since been born[24] in imitating it surpasses it. Because of which I believe that this is an inseparable characteristic of popular errors. In the wake of the first that sets out,
opinions drive on one another, following the wind like waves.
One is not part of the body if one can renounce it, if one does
not wander along with the general movement. But truly we
wrong the just side when we wish to assist it with fraud. I have
ever been against that practice. This means has effect only on
sickly heads; for sound ones there are not only more honest
but surer ways for keeping up their courage and explaining
away adverse happenings.

The heavens have not seen, nor will they see again in the
future, such a grave discord as that between Caesar and Pompey. Yet I seem to discern in those noble souls a great moderation towards one another. It was a rivalry of honor and authority, which did not transport them to a furious and blind
hatred, and was without malignity and detraction. In their
sharpest encounters I discover some vestige of respect and good
will; and so I conclude that, if it had been possible, each of
them would have liked to attain his ends without the ruin of

---

[23] Protestants   [24] The League

his rival in arms rather than with his ruin. How different it is with Marius and Sulla! Take note of it.

We must not cast ourselves so madly after our passions and interest. Just as, when I was young, I used to resist the progress of love which I felt advancing too fast upon me and took pains that it should not become so pleasing as to end up by storming me and completely subjecting me to its mercy. So I do likewise in all other cases when my will is seized with too warm an appetite. I lean in the direction opposite to its inclination as I see it plunging in and getting drunk on its own wine. I avoid feeding its pleasure so far that I can no longer recover it without painful loss.

The souls that through their stupidity only half see things enjoy this good fortune, that harmful things hurt them less. It is a spiritual leprosy that has some appearance of health, and such health as Philosophy does not at all scorn. But yet it is not right to call it wisdom as we often do. And in this manner somebody in antiquity made fun of Diogenes, who in the depth of winter, stark naked, was hugging a snow figure as a test of his patience. Meeting him in this posture, that man said to him: "Are you very cold now?" "Not a bit," Diogenes answered. "Then," continued the other, "why do you think you are doing something difficult and exemplary in remaining there?" To measure fortitude we must necessarily know suffering.

But as for the souls that will have to meet with adversities and the injuries of Fortune in all their depth and sharpness, that will have to bear their full weight and taste their natural bitterness, let them employ their skill to keep from involving themselves in the causes, and let them turn aside from the paths that lead to them. What did King Cotys do? He paid liberally for the beautiful and costly vessel that had been brought to him; but, because it was singularly fragile, he immediately broke it himself to remove in good season so easy an occasion for anger against his servants. In like manner I have by choice avoided having my affairs mixed up with others, and I have not sought to have my estate contiguous to those of my relations and of the people with whom I am to be joined by close friendship: whence grounds for estrangement and discord commonly arise.

I used to be fond of games of chance with cards and dice. I have long since given them up for this sole reason, that, however good a face I put on my losses, I did not fail to be stung inwardly by them. A man of honor, who must be touched to the quick by a contradiction or an affront, who is not able to take a silly excuse as payment and consolation for his loss, should avoid the complications of dubious affairs and contentious disputes. I flee from gloomy dispositions and from surly men as I would from men with plague, and I do not meddle with subjects that I cannot discuss disinterestedly and unexcitedly unless duty forces me to. *It is better not to begin than to desist.*[25] The safest way, then, is to be prepared before the occasions.

I know well that some wise men have taken another way and have not feared to grapple and fully contend with many subjects. Those men feel sure of their strength, under which they take shelter in all kinds of adverse occurrences, making their power of endurance wrestle with misfortunes:

> Just as a rock that juts into the far-flung waves
> Athwart the raging winds, exposed to the full sea,
> Bears all the vigor and the threats of sky and deep,
> And stays itself unmoved.[26]

Let us not tackle these examples; we should not come up to them. They are tenaciously intent on viewing resolutely and without agitation the ruin of their country which once possessed and commanded all their affection. There is too much effort and too much harshness in that for common souls like ours. Cato gave up to it the noblest life that ever was. We other little men must fly the storm from a greater distance; we must have

---

[25] Seneca, *Epistles*   [26] Virgil, *Aeneid*

a care for our feelings and not for our endurance, and dodge the blows we cannot parry. Zeno seeing Chremonides, a young man whom he loved, approaching to sit beside him, quickly stood up. And when Cleanthes asked him the reason, he said: "I understand that the doctors especially prescribe repose and forbid excitement in all cases of swellings." Socrates does not say: "Do not surrender to the charms of beauty, resist it, strive to oppose it." "Fly from it," says he, "run from the sight of it and from meeting it as from a powerful poison that darts and strikes from afar." And his good disciple, either imagining or recounting, but in my opinion recounting rather than imagining, the rare perfections of the great Cyrus, makes him distrustful of his power to resist the charms of the divine beauty of that illustrious Panthea, his captive, and has him commit the charge of visiting and guarding her to another who had less liberty than he. And the Holy Ghost in like manner: "Lead us not into temptation." We do not pray that our reason may not be combated and overcome by concupiscence, but that it may not even be put to the test, that we may not be brought into a state in which we may even have to suffer the approaches, solicitations, and temptations of sin; and we entreat our Lord to keep our conscience tranquil, fully and perfectly delivered from all association with evil.

Those who say that they are justified in their passion for revenge, or in some other kind of vexatious passion, often tell the truth as things are, but not as they were. They speak to us when the causes of their error have been fostered and advanced by themselves. But go further back, bring these causes back to their beginning; there you will take them unawares. Do you mean to say that their fault is less for being older, and that of an unjust beginning the sequel can be just?

Whoever desires the good of his country, as I do, without fretting or pining, will be grieved, but not dazed, to see it threatened either with ruin or with a no less ruinous continuance. Poor vessel that the waves, the winds, and the pilot yaw about with such conflicting purposes:

> So diversely winds,
> And waves, and pilot pull.[27]

He who does not gape after the favor of princes as after a thing he could not do without is not much annoyed by the coolness of their reception and countenance, nor at the inconstancy of their inclination. He who does not brood over his children and his honors with a slavish fondness does not fail to live comfortably after their loss. He who does good principally for his own satisfaction is not much troubled at seeing men judge his action contrary to his merit. A quarter of an ounce of patience provides against such vexations. I find myself well off with this rule, buying my freedom from the beginnings as cheaply as I can, and I feel that by its means I have escaped much trouble and many difficulties. With very little effort I arrest the first impulse of my emotions and abandon the subject that begins to weigh on me, and before it carries me away. He who does not arrest the start is unable to arrest the course. He who cannot close the door to them will not drive them out once they are in. He who cannot master the beginning will not master the end. Nor will he resist the fall who has not been able to resist the shaping. *For once separated from reason, the passions drive forward; and weakness yields to itself and is carried out into the sea without knowing it, and finds no place to come to rest.*[28] I feel betimes the little breezes that come groping and murmuring within me, the forerunners of the storm: *the mind is shaken long before it is overpowered.*[29]

> As when the rising winds, caught in the woods,
> Murmur and roll along with a dull hum,
> Forewarning sailors of the gales to come.[30]

---

[27] Buchanan, *Franciscanus*   [28] Cicero, *Tusculans*   [29] Seneca, *Epistles*
[30] Virgil, *Aeneid*

How often have I done myself a very manifest injustice in order to avoid the hazard of having yet a worse done me by the judges after an age of vexations, of vile and dirty practices, more enemies to my nature than the rack or fire? *It is right for a man to shrink back from lawsuits as much as is permissible, and, perhaps, even more than is permissible. For it is not only generous, but sometimes even advantageous, to give way a little from one's right.*[31] If we were really wise, we ought to rejoice and boast like a young gentleman of a noble family whom I heard one day in a very natural way greet everyone with the statement that his mother had just lost her lawsuit, as though it were a cough, a fever, or some other thing troublesome to keep. Even the favors that Fortune might have given me through kinship or friendship with those who have sovereign authority in such things I have very conscientiously and earnestly avoided employing to the prejudice of others and for elevating my rights above their real value. In short, I have managed so well by my daily efforts (happy am I to be able to say it) that I am to this day virgin of lawsuits, though many times they have offered themselves to my service with very just claim if I had wanted to listen to them, and virgin of quarrels. I shall soon have spent a long life without having undergone or inflicted any grave offense, and without having heard anything worse than my own name: a rare favor of Heaven.

Our greatest agitations have ridiculous springs and causes. What a calamity did our last Duke of Burgundy incur because of a quarrel about a cart-load of sheepskins! And was not the engraving of a seal the first and principal cause of the most terrible upheaval that this machine ever suffered? For Pompey and Caesar are only the offshoots and the sequel of the other two, and I have in my time seen the wisest heads in this kingdom assembled, with great ceremony and public expense, for

---

[31] Cicero, *De Officiis*

deliberations on treaties and agreements of which the real decision in the meantime depended absolutely upon the chatter of the ladies' boudoir and the inclination of some little woman. The poets very well understood this when they put Greece and Asia to fire and sword for an apple. See why this man hazards his honor and life on his sword and dagger; let him tell you where the source of this quarrel comes from; he cannot do so without blushing, so frivolous is its cause.

To get a thing underway takes only a little reflection; but once you are embarked all the rigging starts pulling. There is then need of great precautions that are more difficult and more important. How much easier it is not to enter in than it is to get out! Now we must proceed in a way opposite to that of the reed, which in its first growth produces a long and straight stem, but afterwards, as if it had become weary and out of breath, it starts forming thick and frequent knots, like so many pauses, which show that it no longer has its first vigor and firmness. We must rather begin gently and coolly and save our breath and our vigorous efforts for the height and culmination of the task. We govern affairs at their outset and hold them at our mercy; but afterwards, when they are put in motion, it is they that govern us and carry us off, and we have to follow them.

Yet I do not mean to say that this plan has relieved me of all difficulty, and that I have not often been at pains to curb and bridle my passions. They are not always governed according to the importance of the causes, and even their beginnings are often sharp and violent. However, a fine saving and profit may be gained from it, except by those who in doing good are not satisfied with any profit if there is no reputation in it. For, in truth, such an act is only valued by each man in himself. You are happier for it, but not more esteemed by having reformed before joining in the dance and before the matter was in sight. Yet not in this only, but in all other duties of life, the path of those who aim at honor is very different from that which is followed by those who set order and reason as their goal.

I see some who rashly and furiously enter the lists and slow down in the charge. Just as Plutarch says that those who through the defect of false shame are soft and ready to grant whatever is asked of them are afterwards ready to break their word and recant; so he who enters lightly into a quarrel is apt to get out of it just as lightly. This same difficulty which keeps me from entering into it would spur me on when I was once set in motion and heated. It is a bad affair: once you are in it, you must go through with it or die. "Undertake weakly," said Bias, "but pursue hotly." For want of prudence men fall into want of courage, which is still less tolerable.

Most of the settlements of our quarrels nowadays are shameful and deceitful; we only seek to save appearances, and at the same time we betray and disavow our true intentions. We plaster over the fact: we know how we said it and in what sense, and those present know it, and our friends whom we wanted to make aware of our advantage. It is at the expense of our sincerity and the honor of our courage that we disown our thoughts and seek rabbit-holes in falsehood in order to come to an agreement. We give ourselves the lie to save the lie we have given another. You must not consider whether your action or your word may have another interpretation; it is your true and sincere interpretation that you must henceforth maintain, whatever it cost you. Your virtue and your conscience are addressed; they are not things to be put in a mask. Let us leave these base means and expedients to the chicanery of the Palace of Justice. The excuses and reparations that I see made every day to purge away imprudence seem to me more odious than the imprudence itself. It would be better to offend your adversary a second time than to offend yourself by giving him such reparation. You defied him when you were stirred by anger, and you are about to appease and flatter him in your cooler and better mood; thus you lower yourself more than you had elevated yourself. I do not find anything a gentleman can say is so depraved and vicious in him as the unsaying of it seems to me to be shameful in him when it is recantation that is wrenched from him by authority, inasmuch as obstinacy is more excusable in him than pusillanimity.

Passions are as easy for me to avoid as they are hard for me to moderate. *They are more easily torn from the mind than restrained.*[32] He who cannot attain that noble impassibility of of the Stoics, let him take refuge in the bosom of this insensibility which I share with the populace. What those men did through virtue I train myself to do by temperament. The middle region harbors the storms; the two extremes, those of the philosophers and the rustics, concur in tranquillity and happiness:

> Happy he who could learn the cause of things,
> And trampled on all fears, and on harsh Fate,
> And on the howls of greedy Acheron!
> And happy he who knows the rustic gods,
> Pan, old Sylvanus, and the sister nymphs![33]

All things are weak and tender at their birth. Therefore we must have our eyes open to the beginnings; for as, when it is little, we do not discover its danger, so, when it is grown, we no longer discover the remedy for it. In the course of ambition I should have encountered every day a million hindrances more difficult to tolerate than it has been for me to check the natural inclination that bore me towards it:

> I quaked with rightful dread
> Of raising to full view my head.[34]

All public actions are subject to uncertain and diverse interpretations for too many heads judge them. Some say of this

---

[32] Seneca, *Epistles*   [33] Virgil, *Georgics*   [34] Horace, *Odes*

civic occupation of mine (and I am glad to say a word about it, not that it is worth it, but to serve as an example of my conduct in such things) that I bore myself in it like a man stirred too feebly and with a listless zeal; and they are not at all far wrong. I endeavor to keep my soul and my thoughts in repose. *Always calm by nature and even more so now with age.*[35] And if they sometimes turn aside towards some harsh and piercing attack, it is, in truth, without my intent. Yet from this natural sluggishness one ought not to infer any proof of incapacity (for lack of assiduity and lack of sense are two different things) and still less any want of appreciation or any ingratitude towards the people of that city, who employed the utmost means available to them to extend their favor to me, both before they knew me and after, and did much more for me in renewing my term of office[36] than in bestowing it on me the first time. I wish them all possible good, and certainly, if there had been occasion for it, there is nothing that I should have spared in order to serve them. I have swung into action for them as I do for myself. They are a good people, warlike and noble-spirited, capable, therefore, of obedience and discipline and of serving some good purpose if well guided. They also say that my administration passed without leaving any mark or trace. That's good! I am accused of inaction at a time when almost everybody was convicted of doing too much.

My action is sprightly when my will bears me on. But this eagerness is an enemy to perseverance. If anyone wants to make use of me according to my character, let him give me tasks in which there is need of vigor and freedom, whose management is direct, brief, and even hazardous; I might be able to do something in them. If it must be long, subtle, laborious, artful, and tortuous, they would do better to address themselves to some other person.

[35] Cicero, *De Petitione Consulatus*　　　[36] Re-elected Mayor of Bordeaux, 1583

Not all important offices are hard. I was prepared to throw myself into the work a little more vigorously if there had been great need of it. For it is in my power to do something more than I do or than I like to do. I did not, so far as I know, neglect any action that duty really required of me. I readily overlooked those which ambition mixes up with duty and covers with its name. These are the ones that most often fill the eyes and ears and satisfy men. Not the thing, but the appearance pays them. If they hear no noise, they think we are asleep.

My humor is the opposite of noisy humors. I would, indeed, check a disturbance without being disturbed and punish a disorder without any change in me. Have I need of anger and of flaring up? I borrow it and put it on as a mask. My ways are mild, rather listless than violent. I do not condemn a magistrate who sleeps, provided that those who are under his care sleep with him; the laws sleep too. For my part I commend a life that glides along, obscure and quiet, *neither groveling and abject, nor overbearing.*[37] My fortune will have it so. I was born of a family that flowed along without brilliance and without commotion, and that was from far in the past particularly ambitious of a character for manliness.

Men nowadays are so bred up to bustle and ostentation that goodness, moderation, equability, steadiness, and such quiet and obscure qualities are no more appreciated. Rough bodies make themselves felt; the smooth are handled imperceptibly. Sickness is felt; health little, or not at all, nor the things that soothe us in comparison with those which sting us. It is acting for our own reputation and personal profit, not the public good, to reserve for performance in the public square what we can do in the council chamber, and in the full light of noon what we might have done the night before, and to be jealous to do ourselves what our colleague can do as well. So some surgeons of Greece used to perform the operations of

---

[37] Cicero, *De Officiis*

their art on platforms in the sight of the passers-by in order to draw more practice and clientele. They think that good rules can be heard only with the sound of trumpets.

Ambition is not a vice for little fellows and for such efforts as ours. Someone said to Alexander: "Your father will leave you a great dominion, at ease and peaceful." That youth was envious of his father's victories and of the justice of his rule. He would not have wanted to enjoy the dominion of the world in soft peace. Alcibiades, in Plato, prefers to die young, handsome, rich, noble, supremely learned rather than stop in the state of his present condition. This malady is, perhaps, excusable in so strong and so full a soul. When these puny and dwarfish little souls become as self-satisfied as baboons and think to spread their name for having given a correct judgment in some affair or continued the posting of the guard at a city gate, the more they hope to raise their heads, the more they show their tails. These petty accomplishments have neither body nor life: they vanish in the first telling and are only paraded from one street corner to another. Tell it boldly to your son or your valet, like that ancient who, having no other auditor of his praises or witness of his valor, boasted to his chambermaid, exclaiming: "O, Perrette, what a brave and accomplished man your master is!" Tell it to yourself, if worse comes to worst, like a councillor of my acquaintance who, having disgorged a boatload of paragraphs with extreme effort and with equal inappropriateness, and having retired from the council chamber to the Palace urinal, was heard muttering very conscientiously between his teeth: *Not unto us, Oh Lord, not unto us, but unto Thy name give glory.*[38] If he cannot get it from another, let him pay himself out of his own purse.

Fame does not prostitute herself at so cheap a rate. The rare and exemplary actions to which it is due would not endure the company of that innumerable crowd of petty every-day actions. Marble will exalt your titles as much as you please

---

[38] Psalms

for having had a piece of wall patched up or a public gutter cleaned out; but men who have any sense will not. Renown does not follow every good deed if unusualness and difficulty are not associated with it. Indeed, according to the Stoics, not even esteem is due to every action that springs from virtue, and they do not want even so much as merit accorded to a man who out of temperance abstains from a blear-eyed old woman. Those familiar with the admirable qualities of Scipio Africanus deny him the glory that Panaetius gives him of having abstained from taking gifts, as a glory not so much his own as characteristic of all his age.

We have the pleasures suitable to our lot; let us not usurp those of greatness. Our own are more natural, and the more solid and sure as they are more humble. Since we do not do as much through conscience, let us at least through ambition reject ambition. Let us disdain that low and beggarly hunger for honor and renown that makes us toady to all sorts of people. *What praise is that which may be obtained in the market place*,[39] by abject means and at no matter how low a price? It is dishonor to be so honored. Let us learn to have our greed for glory not exceed our capacity. To be puffed up at every useful and harmless action is well enough for people with whom they are extraordinary and rare; they want to put them at the price they cost them. In proportion as a good act is more dazzling, I discount its goodness by my growing suspicion that it was performed more to be dazzling than to do good: put on display, it is half sold. Those actions are much more graceful which slip from the hands of the workman unconcernedly and quietly and which some discerning man later picks out and raises up out of obscurity to push them into the light for their own sake. *To me all things certainly seem more praiseworthy that are done without display and without public witness*,[40] says the most vainglorious man in the world:

I had nothing to do but to conserve and endure, which are

[39] Cicero, *De Finibus* [40] Cicero, *Tusculans*

noiseless and imperceptible acts. Innovation has great luster, but it is forbidden in these times when we are hard pressed and have to defend ourselves chiefly against innovations. Abstention from doing is often as noble as doing, but it is less conspicuous; and the little that I am worth is almost all on that side.

In short, the occasions in my term of office were in keeping with my disposition, for which I am very grateful to them. Is there anyone who wants to be sick in order to see his physician at work, and shouldn't the physician be whipped who would wish the plague on us in order to put his art into practice? I have not had that wicked and rather common bent of wanting the trouble and sickness of this city's affairs to enhance and honor my government; I heartily lent a shoulder to easing and lightening them. He who will not be thankful to me for the order, the gentle and silent tranquillity that accompanied my administration at least cannot deprive me of the share that belongs to me by the right of my good fortune. And I am so made that I like as much to be lucky as wise and to owe my successes purely to the grace of God as to the intervention of my own action. I had made known clearly enough to the world my inadequacy in such public administration. I have something still worse than inadequacy, which is that it hardly displeases me and that I hardly try to cure it, in view of the course of life that I have marked out for myself. In this service I did not satisfy myself either, but I achieved very nearly what I had promised them with whom I had to deal; for I am apt to promise a little less than what I am able to do and than what I hope to make good. I am sure that I left no cause for offense or hatred. As for leaving regret and desire of me, at the very least I know this well, that I did not greatly aspire to it:

> Me, in this monster put my trust?
> Me, be deceived by the appearance of the placid sea,
> And by the quiet waves? [41]

---

[41] Virgil, *Aeneid*

OF EXPERIENCE

THERE IS NO DESIRE more natural than the desire for knowledge. We try all the ways that can lead us to it. When reason fails us, we make use of experience,

> Experience, by diverse trials, art has made,
> Example pointing out the way,[1]

which is a weaker and less dignified means. But truth is so great a thing that we ought not to disdain any medium that will lead us to it. Reason has so many shapes that we do not know which one to take hold of; experience has no fewer. The inference which we try to draw from the resemblance of events is uncertain because they are always dissimilar. There is no quality so universal in this aspect of things as diversity and variety. Both the Greeks and the Latins, and ourselves, use eggs as the most express example of similarity. Yet there have been men, and notably one at Delphi, who recognized marks of difference between eggs, so that he never took one for another; and although there were many hens, he could tell from which one the egg came. Dissimilarity intrudes by itself into our works; no art can attain similarity. Neither Perrozet nor any other can so carefully smooth and whiten the backs of his cards that some gamesters will not distinguish them simply by seeing them slip through another's hands. Resemblance does not make things so much alike as difference makes them unlike. Nature has committed herself to make nothing other that was not different.

[1] Manilius

Therefore I do not much like the opinion of the man who thought by the multitude of laws to curb the authority of judges by cutting up their meat for them. He was not aware that there is as much liberty and latitude in the interpretation of laws as in the making of them. And those people fool themselves who think they can lessen and stop our disputes by recalling us to the express words of the Bible. For our mind finds the field no less spacious in examining the meaning of others than in putting forth its own, as if there were less animosity and tartness in commenting than in inventing. We see how much he was mistaken. For we have in France more laws than all the rest of the world together, and more than would be necessary to rule all the worlds of Epicurus, *as formerly we suffered from crimes, so now we suffer from laws;*[2] and yet we have left so much to the opinions and decisions of our judges that there never was such a powerful and licentious freedom. What have our legislators gained by selecting a hundred thousand particular cases and acts and applying to them a hundred thousand laws? This number bears no proportion to the infinite diversity of human actions. The multiplication of our invented cases will never equal the variety of the real cases. Add to them a hundred times as many more: it still will not happen that out of future events there will be found any which will encounter one, in the many thousands of selected and recorded events, that will fit and match it so exactly that there will not remain some circumstances and difference which will require a different consideration in judgment. There is little relation between our actions, which are in perpetual mutation, and fixed and immutable laws. The most desirable laws are those that are most rare, most simple and general; and I even believe that it would be better to have none at all than to have them in such numbers as we have.

Nature always gives us better laws than those we give

ᵛ Tacitus, *Annals*

ourselves. Witness the picture of the Golden Age of the poets and the state in which we see nations live who have no other laws. Here are some who for the sole judges of their quarrels take the first passer-by who is traveling through their mountains. And these others on market-day elect one from among themselves who decides all their suits on the spot. What danger would there be if the wisest should settle ours in this way, according to the circumstances and at sight, without being bound by past case and future precedent? For every foot its own shoe. King Ferdinand, when he sent colonists to the Indies, wisely provided that no students of law should be taken there, for fear that lawsuits might abound in that new world, since it is by nature a science generating altercation and division, judging, with Plato, that lawyers and doctors are a bad provision for a country.

Why is it that our common language, so easy for all other uses, becomes obscure and unintelligible in contracts and wills, and that a man who expresses himself so clearly, whatever he says or writes, finds in this subject no way of stating himself that does not fall into doubt and contradiction? Unless it be that the princes of this art, applying themselves with a particular attention to picking out solemn words and contriving artificial phrases, have so weighed every syllable and so closely examined every sort of combination that there they are at last entangled and embroiled in the endless number of figures and in such minute partitions that they can no longer fall within any rule or prescription or any sure understanding. *Whatever is split up into dust becomes confused.*[3] Who has seen children trying to divide a mass of quicksilver into a certain number of parts? The more they press and knead it and try to constrain it to their will, the more they stir up the independence of this spirited metal; it escapes their skill and keeps breaking up and scattering in little particles beyond all reckoning. This is the same, by subdividing these subtleties

---

[3] Seneca, *Epistles*

they teach men to increase their doubts; they put us into a way of stretching and diversifying the difficulties, they lengthen them, they spread them. By sowing questions and cutting them up they make the world to fructify and abound in uncertainty and quarrels, as the earth is made more fertile the more deeply it is plowed and crumbled. *Learning makes difficulties.*[4] We were perplexed over Ulpian, we are still perplexed over Bartolus and Baldus. We should have effaced the traces of this innumerable diversity of opinions, not bedeck ourselves with them and swell the heads of posterity with them.

I do not know what to say of it, but it is evident from experience that so many interpretations disperse the truth and break it up. Aristotle wrote to be understood; if he did not succeed, still less will another man who is less skillful and is not treating his own ideas. We open the matter and spread it out by watering it; of one subject we make a thousand, and, in multiplying and subdividing, fall back into Epicurus' infinity of atoms. Never did two men judge alike about the same thing; and it is impossible to find two opinions exactly alike, not only in different men, but in the same man at different times. Ordinarily I find matter for doubt in what the commentary has not deigned to touch on. I am most apt to stumble on flat ground, like certain horses that I know that stumble more often on a smooth road.

Who would not say that glosses augment doubts and ignorance since there is no book to be found, whether human or divine, about which the world busies itself, the difficulties of which are cleared up by interpretation? The hundredth commentator passes it on to his successor, thornier and rougher than the first one had found it. When is it agreed upon among us: "This book has enough commentary; henceforth there is nothing more to say about it?" This is best seen in the practice of law. We give the authority of law to innumerable doctors, innumerable decisions, and as many interpretations. Do

---

[4] Quintilian

we, therefore, find any end to the need of interpreting? Do we see any progress and advance towards tranquillity? Do we need fewer lawyers and judges than when this great mass of law was yet in its very infancy? On the contrary we obscure and bury the meaning; we no longer find it except at the mercy of so many enclosures and barriers.

Men do not know the natural infirmity of their mind: it does nothing but ferret and quest, and keeps incessantly spinning about, constructing and getting entangled in its own work, like our silkworms, and is suffocated in it. *A mouse in a pitch barrel.*[5] It thinks it observes in the distance some sort of gleam of imaginary light and truth; but while it is running to it, so many difficulties, obstacles, and new quests cross its path that they lead it astray and intoxicate it. Not much different from what happened to Aesop's dogs, who, discovering something like a dead body floating in the sea, and not being able to approach it, attempted to drink up this water and dry up the passage, and so choked themselves. To this may appropriately be added what a certain Crates said of the writings of Heraclitus, that they required a reader who was a good swimmer so that the depth and weight of his learning should not engulf him and drown him.

It is nothing but our personal weakness that makes us content ourselves with what others or ourselves have found out in this chase after knowledge. A more able man will not rest content with it. There is always room for a successor, yes, and for ourselves, and a route in another direction. There is no end to our researches; our end is in the other world. It is a sign of contraction of the mind when it is content, or of weariness. No spirited mind stops within itself; it is ever aspiring and going beyond its strength; it has impulses beyond its effective capacity. If it does not advance and press forward and turn at bay and contend, it is only half alive. Its pursuits are without bound and without form; its food is wonder, the chase,

---

[5] Erasmus, *Adages*

ambiguity. Apollo brought this out sufficiently, always speaking
to us in a double, obscure, and oblique sense, not satisfying
us, but keeping our minds absorbed and busy. It is an irregular, perpetual motion, without model and without aim. Its inventions excite, pursue, and produce one another.

> So in a running stream one wave we see
> After another roll incessantly;
> And, as they glide, each does successively
> Pursue the other, each the other flee;
> By this one that one e'er is pushed, and this
> By that one constantly preceded is;
> The water still does into water go—
> Still the same brook, but different waters flow.[6]

It is more of a job to interpret the interpretations than to
interpret the things, and there are more books upon books than
upon any other subject: we do nothing but write glosses upon
one another. The whole world swarms with commentaries; of
authors there is a great scarcity.

Is it not the principal and most reputed learning of our
times to understand the learned? Is it not the common and
ultimate end of all studies?

Our opinions are grafted upon one another. The first serves
as a stock to the second, the second to the third. Thus step
by step we scale the ladder. Thence it happens that he who
has mounted highest has often more honor than merit for he
has only mounted a grain higher on the shoulders of the next
last man.

How often and, perhaps, how foolishly have I extended
my book to make it speak of itself! Foolishly, if for no other
reason than this, that I ought to remember what I say of others
who do the same: that these frequent loving glances at their
own work are evidence that their heart thrills with love for it,
and that even the disdainful rough treatment which they mete
out to it is only the fondlings and mannerisms of maternal af-

---

[6] La Boétie, "To Marguerite de Carle"

fection, according to Aristotle, for whom self-appreciation and self-depreciation often spring from the same trait of arrogance. For as for my excuse, that I ought to have more liberty in this than others, precisely because I write of myself and of my writings as of my other actions, because my theme turns about into itself, I do not know whether everyone will accept it.

I have observed in Germany that Luther has left as many divisions and disputes about the uncertainty of his opinions, and more, as he himself has raised about the Holy Scriptures. Our disputes are verbal. I ask what is nature, pleasure, circle, and substitution? The question is one of words and is answered in the same coin. A stone is a body. But if you should press on: "And what is a body?"—"Substance."—"And what is substance?" and so on, you would finally drive the respondent to the end of his lexicon. We exchange one word for another, and often for one less understood. I know better what man is than I know what animal is, or mortal, or rational. To satisfy one doubt, they give me three; it is the Hydra's head. Socrates asked Meno what virtue was. "There is," said Meno, "the virtue of a man and of a woman, of a magistrate and of a private individual, of a child and of an old man." "This is fine," exclaimed Socrates, "we were in quest of one virtue, and here is a whole swarm of them." We put one question, they give us back a hive of them. As no event and no shape entirely resembles another, so none entirely differs from another—an ingenious mixture on the part of Nature. If our faces were not similar, we could not distinguish man from beast; if they were not dissimilar, we could not distinguish man from man. All things hold together by some similarity, every example is lame, and the comparsion which is drawn from experience is always faulty and imperfect; and yet we connect our comparisons by some corner. Thus the laws serve and adapt themselves to each of our affairs by some indirect, forced, and biased interpretation.

Since the ethical laws, which concern the individual duty of each man in himself, are so hard to draw up, as we see they are, it is no wonder if those that govern so many individuals are more so. Consider the form of this justice that governs us: it is a true testimony of human imbecility, so full is it of contradiction and error. What we find to be leniency and severity in justice—and we find so much of them that I do not know whether the mean between them is as often met with—are sickly parts and faulty members of the very body and essence of justice.

Some peasants have just informed me in great haste that a moment ago they left in a wood that belongs to me a man stabbed in a hundred places, who is still breathing and who begged them in the name of pity for some water and some help to get him up. They say that they did not dare go near him and ran for fear that the officers of the law might catch them there, and, as is done with those who are found near a murdered person, they might be held to account for this accident to their total ruin, having neither ability nor money to defend their innocence. What could I say to them? It is certain that that act of humanity would have got them into trouble.

How many innocent people have we discovered to have been punished, I mean without the fault of the judges; and how many have there been which we have not discovered? This happened in my time. Certain men are condemned to death for a murder; their sentence, if not pronounced, at least decided and determined. At this point the judges are informed by the officers of an inferior court near by that they have some prisoners who clearly confess this murder and throw a conclusive light on the whole business. They deliberate whether because of this they ought to interrupt and defer the execution of the sentence passed upon the first accused. They consider the novelty of the case and its consequence for suspending judgments; that the sentence has been passed by law and that the judges have no right to change their minds. In short these poor devils are sacrificed to the forms of justice.

Philip, or some other, settled a similar problem In this manner. By a definitive judgment he had condemned a man to pay a heavy fine to another. The truth coming to light some time after, it turned out that he had made an unfair judgment. On one side were the just interests of the case, on the other side the just interests of the judicial forms. He in some sort satisfied both, letting the sentence stand and out of his own purse compensating the loss of the condemned man. But he had to do with a reparable accident; my men were irreparably hanged. How many condemnations have I seen more criminal than the crime!

All this calls to my mind these ancient opinions: That a man is forced to do wrong in detail if he wants to do right in gross, and injustice in little things if he wants to achieve justice in great things; that human justice is formed after the model of medicine, according to which all that is useful is also just and proper; and what the Stoics hold, that Nature herself proceeds contrary to justice in most of her works; and what the Cyrenaics hold, that there is nothing just in itself, that customs and laws shape justice; and the Theodorians, who believe that theft, sacrilege, and every kind of lechery are just for a wise man if he knows that it is profitable to him.

There is no remedy. I stand in this matter as Alcibiades did, namely, I will never, if I can help it, hand myself over to a man who can dispose of my head, where my honor and my life depend on the skill and diligence of my attorney more than on my innocence. I would risk a kind of justice that would recognize my good deeds as well as my bad, from which I would have as much to hope as to fear. To be unpunished is not sufficient pay to a man who does better than not to do amiss. Our justice offers us only one of her hands, and the left at that. Whoever he is, he comes out of it with loss.

In China, a kingdom whose government and arts, without

intercourse with or knowledge of ours, surpass our counter-
parts in many aspects of excellence, and whose history teaches
me how much greater and more varied the world is than either
the ancients or we discern, the officers deputed by the prince
to inspect the state of his provinces, even as they punish those
who are corrupt in their office, also reward, from pure liberality,
those who have borne themselves well above the common level
and beyond the requirements of their duty. Men report to them
not merely to defend themselves, but to gain by it, not simply
to be paid, but also to receive gifts.

No judge has yet, thank God, spoken to me as a judge in any
cause whatever, whether my own or that of another, whether
criminal or civil. No prison has received me, not even as a
visitor. Imagination makes the sight of one, even from the outside, displeasing to me. I am so impassioned about freedom
that if I were forbidden access to some corner of the Indies, I
should live somewhat less at ease. And as long as I can find
earth or air open elsewhere, I will never lurk in any place where
I must hide. Lord! how ill should I endure the condition in
which I see so many people, nailed down to one area of the
kingdom, deprived of the right of entrance to the principal
cities and courts and the use of the public roads for having
quarreled with our laws! If those that I serve threatened even
the tip of my finger, I should immediately be off to find others,
wherever it might be. All my little prudence in the civil wars
in which we are now engaged is employed to keep them from
interrupting my liberty of coming and going.

Now laws maintain their credit not because they are just,
but because they are laws. That is the mystic foundation of
their authority; they have no other. That serves them well.
They are often made by fools, more often by men who, in their
hatred of equality, are wanting in equity; but always by men,
vain and irresolute authors.

There is nothing so grossly and widely and ordinarily faulty
as laws. Whoever obeys them because they are just does not

obey them for just the reason he should. Our French laws, by their irregularity and lack of form, lend somewhat of a helping hand to the disorder and corruption that is manifest in their application and execution. Their bidding is so confused and inconsistent that it excuses somewhat both disobedience and faultiness in their interpretation, administration, and observance. Whatever, then, may be the fruit we can get from experience, that which we derive from foreign examples will hardly be of much service for our education if we make such little profit from that which we have of ourselves, which is more familiar to us and certainly sufficient to inform us of what we need.

I study myself more than any other subject. It is my metaphysics, it is my physics.

> By what art God controls the structure of the world;
> Whence comes the rising moon, where she withdraws, how she
> With joined horns returns to full each month; whence come
> The winds that rule the sea; what Eurus with his blast
> Does seek; and whence the water that ne'er fails the clouds;
> Whether some day these citadels will be thrown down.[7]

Inquire, you whose ideas the world's exertions goad.[8]

In this universe of things I let myself be ignorantly and negligently guided by the general law of the world. I shall know it well enough when I feel it. My learning could not make it alter its course; it will not modify itself for me. It is folly to hope it, and greater folly to be troubled about it since it is necessarily uniform, public, and common. The goodness and capacity of the governor ought to free us absolutely and fully from concern about his government.

Philosophical inquiries and meditations serve only as food for our curiosity. Philosophers very rightly refer us to the rules of Nature, but these have nothing to do with such sublime knowledge. The philosophers falsify them and show us her face

[7] Propertius   [8] Lucan

If know self + had experiences,
better than learning about it.

painted too high in color and too sophisticated, whence spring so many different portraits of so uniform a subject. As she has supplied us with feet to walk with, so has she given us wisdom to guide us in life: a wisdom not so ingenious, robust, and pompous as that of their invention, but correspondingly easy and salutary, that performs very well what the other talks about, in him who has the good fortune to know how to employ himself simply and in an orderly fashion, that is to say, naturally. To trust to Nature most simply is to trust her most wisely. Oh, what a sweet and soft and healthy pillow is ignorance and incuriosity to rest a well-made head!

I would rather be well versed about myself than about Cicero. In the experience I have of myself I find enough to make me wise if I were a good scholar. He who calls to mind the excess of his past anger and how far that fever carried him away sees the ugliness of this passion better than in Aristotle and conceives a juster hatred of it. He who remembers the evils he has passed through, and those that have threatened him, and the slight causes that have changed him about from one state to another, prepares himself thereby for future changes and for the comprehension of his condition. The life of Caesar has no more of a lesson for us than our own; and whether an emperor's or an ordinary man's, it is still a life that is subject to all human accidents. Let us just listen to it: we tell ourselves all that we chiefly need. He who remembers having so many, many times been mistaken in his own judgment, is he not a fool if he does not ever after distrust it? When by another man's reasoning I find myself convicted of a false opinion, I do not so much learn the new thing he has told me and this particular instance of ignorance—that would be small gain—as I learn my weakness in general and the treachery of my understanding, whence I derive the reformation of the whole mass. With all my errors I do the same, and I find this rule very useful to my life. I do not regard the species and the individual as I should a stone that I have stumbled on; I learn to distrust my gait throughout, and I strive to regulate it. To learn that we have said or done a foolish thing, that is nothing; we must learn that we are nothing but fools, a much more extensive and important lesson.

The slips that my memory has so often made, even when it reassures me the most about itself, are not idly wasted on me; it is useless for her to swear to me now and assure me, I shake my ears. The first opposition that is raised to her testimony puts me in suspense, and I would not dare to rely on her in any weighty matter, nor guarantee her in another's concerns. And were it not that what I do for want of memory others do still more often for want of good faith, I should always accept the truth in matters of fact from another's mouth rather than from my own.

If everyone watched closely the effects and circumstances of the passions that sway him, as I have done with the one into whose hands I had fallen, he would see them coming and would check a little their impetuosity and course. They do not always leap at our throats at the first bound; there are threats and degrees.

> As when the wave begins to foam 'neath rising wind
> The sea heaves slowly, and its billows higher lifts,
> Then from the lowest depths it rears up to the skies.[9]

Judgment holds in me a magisterial seat; at least it carefully endeavors to make it so. It lets my feelings go their own way, both hatred and friendship, even the friendship that I bear myself, without being changed and corrupted by them. If it cannot reform the other parts according to its own model, at least it does not let itself be deformed by them: it plays its game apart.

The advice to everyone to know himself must have an important effect since the god of learning and light had it en-

---

[9] Virgil, *Aeneid*

graved on the front of his temple as comprising all the counsel he had to give us. Plato also says that wisdom is nothing else than the execution of this command, and Socrates, in Xenophon, verifies it in detail. The difficulties and obscurity in any science are perceived only by those who have access to it. For at least some degree of intelligence is needed for a man to be able to notice that he does not know; and we must push against a door to know that it is closed to us. Whence arises this Platonic subtlety, that neither those who know need to inquire, since they know, nor those who do not know, since in order to inquire they must know what they are inquiring about. So in this matter of knowing oneself, the fact that every man is seen to be so decided and self-satisfied that everyone thinks he understands enough about himself signifies that everyone understands nothing about it, as Socrates teaches Euthydemus in Xenophon.

I, who make no other profession, find in me such infinite depth and variety that my apprenticeship in learning produces no other fruit than to make me perceive how much I still have to learn. To my weakness, so often recognized, I owe the inclination I have to modesty, to obedience to the beliefs that are prescribed me, to a constant coolness and moderation in my opinions, and my hatred of that troublesome and wrangling arrogance that believes and trusts wholly in itself, the mortal enemy of discipline and truth. Hear them laying down the law: the first stupidities that they put forth are in the style with which men establish religion and laws. *Nothing is more discreditable than that assertion and conviction should precede knowledge and perception.*[10] Aristarchus used to say that in former times there were scarcely seven wise men in the world, and that in his time there were scarcely seven ignorant men. Would we not have more reason than he to say that in this age of ours? Affirmation and opinionatedness are express signs of stupidity. This fellow has fallen on his nose probably a hun-

---

[10] Cicero, *Academica*

dred times in one day; there he is up on his "ergos" as positive and unshaken as before. You would think he had since had some new soul and vigor of understanding infused into him, and that he had the lot of that ancient son of the earth who renewed his strength and courage by his fall,

> Whose limbs, though now worn out,
> Whene'er he touches Mother Earth, gain strength anew.[11]

Does not this stubborn, incorrigible man think that he picks up a new mind by picking up a new argument. It is by my experience that I point out human ignorance, which is in my opinion the surest part of the world's school. Those who will not conclude their own ignorance from so vain an example as mine, or as theirs, let them recognize it through Socrates, the master of masters. For the philosopher Antisthenes used to say to his pupils: "Let us go, you and I, to hear Socrates; there I shall be a pupil with you." And maintaining this doctrine of the Stoic sect, that virtue was sufficient to make a life fully happy and with no need of anything whatever, he added, "excepting the strength of Socrates."

This long attention that I put into studying myself trains me also to judge passably of others, and there are few things on which I speak more felicitously and pardonably. It often happens that I see and distinguish the characters of my friends more exactly than they do themselves. I have astonished one or two with the pertinency of my description and have informed them about themselves. By having trained myself from my childhood to see my own life mirrored in that of others, I have acquired a studious bent in that matter, and when I am thinking about it, I let few things about me escape which may be useful for that purpose: countenances, humors, talk. I study everything: what I must avoid, what I must follow. So to my friends I reveal by their outward manifestations their inward

---

[11] Lucan

inclinations; not in order to arrange this infinite variety of actions, so diverse and so disconnected, into certain types and categories, and to distribute my lots and divisions clearly into recognized classes and sections,

> But what the number of their kinds may be, and names,
> Cannot be told.[12]

The learned divide and mark out their ideas more specifically and in detail. I, who see no farther into things than practice informs me, without any system, present my ideas in a general way and tentatively. As in this: I express my thought in disjointed parts, as something that cannot be said all at once and as a whole. Relationship and conformity are not found in low and common minds such as ours. Wisdom is a solid and whole structure, each part of which keeps its place and bears its mark. *Wisdom only is wholly turned into itself.*[13] I leave it to artists, and I don't know whether they will succeed in so complex, minute, and fortuitous a thing, to draw up into bands this infinite diversity of forms, to make our inconsistency stand fast, and set it down in order. Not only do I find it hard to attach our actions to one another, but I find it hard to designate properly each one separately by some principal characteristic, so ambiguous and motley do they appear in different lights.

What is remarked as rare in Perseus, King of Macedonia, that his mind, fixing itself to no one condition, kept wandering through every kind of life and manifesting a character so flighty and erratic that neither he nor anyone else knew what kind of man he was, seems to me to fit nearly everybody. And above all men, I have known another of his stature to whom this conclusion would still more properly apply, I believe: no middle position, always being carried away from one extreme to the other by causes not to be guessed at; no sort of course without traverse and amazing changing of direction; no simple, unmixed

---

[12] Virgil, *Georgics*   [13] Cicero, *De Finibus*

quality; so that the most likely idea that men will be able to form of him some day will be that he affected and studied to make himself known by being unknowable.

Very strong ears are needed to hear yourself judged frankly; and since there are few who can endure it without being nettled, those who venture to undertake this for us exhibit a remarkable act of friendship; for to undertake to wound and offend a man for his own good is evidence of having a healthy love. I find it a harsh job to judge a man in whom the bad qualities outnumber the good. Plato requires three qualities in a man who wants to examine another man's soul: knowledge, good will, and boldness.

Sometimes I have been asked what I should have thought myself fit for if anyone had thought of making use of me while I was young enough,

> While better blood gave strength, nor grudging age
> Had scattered yet its snows o'er both my brows.[14]

"For nothing," I said. And I readily excuse myself for not knowing how to do anything that would enslave me to others. But I would have told home truths to my master, and I would have watched over his conduct if he had so wished. Not in the gross by schoolmasterly lessons, which I do not know (and I do not see them engender any true information in those who know them), but by observing his conduct step by step, at every opportunity, and judging it by direct observation, piece by piece, simply and naturally, making him see what the public opinion is of him and opposing his flatterers. There is not one of us who would not be worse than kings if he were as continually spoiled as they are by that riffraff. How otherwise, if Alexander, that great man both as king and philosopher, could not hold out against them! I should have had fidelity, judgment, and independence enough for that. It would be a name-

---

[14] Virgil, *Aeneid*

less office; otherwise it would lose its grace and its effect. And it is a part that cannot be taken indiscriminately by all. For truth itself does not have the privilege to be employed at all times and in all ways; its use, noble as it is, has its circumscriptions and limits. It often happens, as the world goes, that it is blurted into a prince's ear not only fruitlessly, but harmfully, and even unjustly. And no one shall make me believe that a virtuous remonstrance cannot be wrongly applied, and that the interest of the substance must not often give way to the interest of the form.

For this business I should want a man that is content with his fortune,

> Who likes that present state of his,
> And would not be but what he is,[15]

and of middle rank by birth; because on the one hand he would not be afraid to touch his master's heart deeply and to the quick lest he lose thereby his preferment, and on the other, being of middle station, he would have easier communication with all sorts of people. I would have this office for one man alone, for to extend the privilege of this freedom and intimacy to several would beget a harmful irreverence. And certainly I would require of that man above all things the fidelity of silence.

A king is not to be believed when he brags of his constancy in awaiting the shock of the enemy for the sake of his glory if, for his own good and improvement, he cannot stand the freedom of a friend's words, which have no other power than to sting his ear, the rest of their effect being in his own hands. Now there is no class of men that stands in such great need as they of true and frank admonitions. They bear the weight of a public life and have to satisfy the opinions of so many spectators that, as men have taken the habit of concealing from them everything that disturbs their plans, they insensibly find themselves involved in the hatred and detestation of their peo-

---

[15] Martial

ple, often for reasons that they could have avoided without any sacrifice even of their pleasures had they been advised of it and set right in time. Their favorites commonly look out for themselves more than for their master; and it is well for them that they do since, in truth, most of the duties of true friendship when turned towards the sovereign are put to a hard and dangerous test; so that there is need not only of great affection and frankness, but also of great courage.

In fine all this fricassee that I am scribbling here is nothing but a record of the essays of my life, which for spiritual health is exemplary enough if its instruction is taken in reverse. But as to bodily health, no one can furnish more useful experience than I, who present it pure, not at all corrupted or changed by art or theorizing. Experience is really on its own dunghill in the subject of medicine, where reason wholly gives way to it. Tiberius used to say that whoever had lived twenty years ought to be responsible to himself for all things that were harmful or wholesome for him and know how to take care of himself without medicine. And he might have learned it of Socrates, who, recommending to his disciples, carefully and as a principal study, the study of their health, used to add that it was difficult for an intelligent man who was careful about his exercise, his drinking, and his eating not to know better than any doctor what was good or bad for him. And, indeed, medicine professes always to have experience as the touchstone of its procedure. So Plato was right in saying that to be a true doctor it would be necessary for the man who would practice it to have passed through all the diseases he wants to cure and through all the accidents and circumstances on which he is to give an opinion. It is reasonable that he should catch the pox if he wants to know how to treat it. Truly I should trust such a man. For the others guide us like the man who paints seas, reefs, and ports while seated at his table and sails the model of a ship there in all safety. Toss him into the reality, and he does not know at which end to begin. They describe our illnesses like a town crier proclaiming a lost horse or dog: such and such a color, such and such a height, such and such ears; but present it to him, and he does not know it for all that.

By heavens, let medicine some day give me some good and visible relief, and you will see how I shall cry out in good earnest:

> To an effective science I yield at last.[16]

The arts that promise to keep our bodies in health and our souls in health promise us a great deal; but at the same time there are none that keep their promise less. And in our time those who profess these arts among us show the results of them less than any other men. The most that can be said for them is that they sell medicinal drugs; but it cannot be said that they are doctors.

I have lived long enough to be able to give an account of the practice that has guided me so far. For anyone who wants to try it, I have already tasted it, like his cupbearer. Here are a few parts of it, as my memory supplies me with them. (I have no habit that has not varied according to circumstances, but I record only those that I have seen most frequently in action and that have had the most hold on me up to the present moment.)

My way of life is the same in sickness as in health; the same bed, the same hours, the same food served me, and the same drink. I make no changes at all except for controlling the amount according to my strength and appetite. For me health means maintaining my accustomed state without disturbance. Do I see that sickness dislodges me in one direction? If I trust the doctors, they will turn me off in another. So, either by fortune or by art, here I am off my way. I believe nothing more certainly than this: that I cannot be hurt by the use of things to which I have been so long accustomed.

---

[16] Horace, *Epodes*

It is for habit to give form to our life just as it pleases; it is all-powerful in that; it is the draught of Circe, which varies our nature as it sees fit. How many nations, and but three steps from us, consider ridiculous the fear of the night dew that appears so hurtful to us; and our boatmen and peasants laugh at it. You make a German sick if you put him to bed upon a mattress, as an Italian will be on a feather bed, and a Frenchman without curtains and a fire. A Spanish stomach cannot stand our way of eating, nor ours to drink like the Swiss.

A German amused me at Augsburg by assailing the disadvantages of our fireplaces by the same arguments which we ordinarily use in condemning their stoves. For, in truth, that oppressive heat along with the smell of that heated material of which they are made gives most of those who are not used to them a headache; not me. But after all, this heat being even, constant, and general, without flame, without smoke, and without the wind that the opening of our chimneys brings us, it has in other respects very good reasons to be compared with ours.

Why do we not imitate the Roman architecture? For they say that in ancient times the fire was not made inside their houses but outside, and at the foot of them; whence the heat was drawn into the whole dwelling by pipes contrived in the thickness of the walls and embracing the rooms that were to be warmed. This I have seen clearly pointed out somewhere in Seneca.

This German, hearing me praise the advantages and beauties of his city, which certainly deserves it, began to pity me because I had to leave it; and one of the first disadvantages he mentioned to me was the heaviness of head that the fireplaces elsewhere would give me. He had heard someone make this complaint and connected it with us, being prevented by habit from noticing it at home.

All heat that comes from a fire makes me feel weak and heavy. Yet Evenus said that fire was the best condiment of life. I prefer any other way of escaping from the cold.

We are afraid of the wine at the bottom of the cask; in Portugal its flavor is thought delicious, and it is the drink of princes.

In short every nation has many customs and practices that are not only unknown but barbarous and miraculous to some other nation.

What shall we do with this people that admits of no evidence that is not in print, that does not believe men unless they are in a book, nor truth unless it is of competent age? We dignify our stupidities when we put them in print. With this people it carries very different weight to say, "I have read it," than if you only say, "I have heard it." But I, who do not disbelieve men's mouths any more than their hands, and who know that men write with as little judgment as they speak, and who esteem this age as much as another that is past, I quote a friend as willingly as Aulus Gellius or Macrobius, and what I have seen as what they have written. And as they hold of virtue that it is no greater for being of long stand, so do I hold of truth that it is no wiser for being older. I often say that it is pure stupidity that makes us run after foreign and bookish examples. Their abundance is the same at the present moment as in the time of Homer and Plato. But is it not true that we seek more the honor of quoting than the truth of the statement? As if it were more effective to borrow our proofs from the shop of Vascosan or of Plantin than from what may be seen in our own village. Or rather, indeed, that we have not the wit to pick out and turn to account what takes place before our eyes and to judge of it keenly enough to bring it out as an example? For if we say that we lack authority to gain credence for our testimony, we say so without reason. For, in my opinion, from the most ordinary, common, and familiar things, if we could but find the proper light for them, can be formed the greatest miracles of nature and the most wonderful examples, especially in the matter of human actions.

Now, in my subject, setting aside the examples that I know through books and what Aristotle says about Andro of Argos, that he crossed the arid sands of Libya without drinking, a gentleman who has given a worthy account of himself in several charges said in my presence that he had ridden from Madrid to Lisbon in midsummer without drinking. He is in vigorous health for his age and has nothing extraordinary in his way of living except this, of going sometimes two or three months, even a year, so he told me, without drinking. He feels some thirst, but he lets it pass, and he holds that it is an appetite which easily weakens by itself; and he drinks more out of caprice than for need or pleasure.

Here is another. Not long ago I found one of the most learned men in France, and a man of no mean fortune, studying in the corner of a hall which had been partitioned off for him with hangings; and around him an unrestrained hubbub of servants. He told me, and Seneca said almost the same of himself, that he turned this uproar to his profit, as if, pounded by this noise, he thus retired and gathered more within himself for contemplation, and that this tempest of voices drove back his thoughts inward. While a scholar at Padua he had for so long a time a study exposed to the rattle of coaches and the tumult of the square that he trained himself not only to disregard the noise, but to make use of it for the benefit of his studies. Socrates replied to Alcibiades, who wondered how he could endure the perpetual din of his wife's scolding: "Like those who are accustomed to the ordinary noise of wheels drawing water." I am quite the opposite. I have a mind that is sensitive and quick to take flight; when it is absorbed in itself, the least buzzing of a fly pesters it to death.

Seneca, in his youth, having bitten eagerly on Sextius' example of eating nothing that had been killed, did without it for a year with pleasure, as he says. And he left off only that he might not be suspected of borrowing this rule from certain new religions that were spreading it abroad. At the same time he took up one of Attalus' precepts, namely, not to sleep any more upon mattresses that yielded under his weight, and he continued even in old age to use those which do not yield to the body. What the practice of his time makes him consider austerity, ours makes us look upon as effeminacy.

Look at the difference between my laborer's way of living and mine. The Scythians and Indians are in no way more remote from my capacity and ways. I know I have lifted boys out of begging into my service, who soon after have left me, my kitchen, and their livery, merely to return to their former life. And I found one of them afterwards picking up mussels in the garbage heap for his dinner, whom neither by entreaties nor threats could I drag away from the savor and sweetness that he found in indigence. Beggars have their sumptuous ways and sensual delights as well as the rich, and, it is said, their political dignities and orders.

These are the results of habit. It can not only mould us into whatever form it pleases (therefore, say the sages, we must choose the best, which habit will quickly make easy for us), but also dispose us to change and variation, which is the noblest and most useful of its teachings. The best of my bodily attributes is that I am flexible and not very stubborn: I have some inclinations that are more personal and usual and more agreeable to me than others; but with very little effort I turn aside from them and easily slip into an opposite way of doing.

A young man ought to upset his own rules in order to arouse his vigor and keep it from growing mouldy and soft. And there is no way of life so stupid and feeble as that which is directed by rules and discipline.

> If she would drive out to the first milestone,
> The hour is chosen from a book; if chafed
> The corner of her eye itches, she scans
> Her horoscope before she gets the salve.[17]

---

[17] Juvenal

He will even plunge often into excess if he will take my advice; otherwise the slightest dissipation will ruin him, and he will become troublesome and disagreeable in company. The most unsuitable quality for a gentleman is over-fastidiousness and subjection to certain particular ways; and they are particular if they are not pliable and supple. It is shameful for a man to refrain from doing what he sees his companions do because he cannot or dare not. Let such men keep to their kitchens. In any other man it is unbecoming, but in a military man it is a grave fault and intolerable; this man, as Philopoemen said, ought to get accustomed to every change and vicissitude of life.

Though I was trained as much as possible for freedom and detachment, yet it is a fact that through carelessness, having dwelt more on certain ways as I grow old (my age now is past training and henceforth has nothing else to consider except holding its own), habit has already, without my thinking it, so imprinted its character on me in certain things that I call it excess to depart from it. And I cannot without an effort sleep by day, or eat between meals, or breakfast, or go to bed without a long interval of three hours or more after supper, or beget children except before sleeping, or beget them standing, or endure my own sweat, or quench my thirst with pure water or pure wine, or remain bareheaded for long, or have my hair cut after dinner; and I should be as uneasy without my gloves as without my shirt, or without washing when I rise from table or get up in the morning, or without a canopy and curtains for my bed, as I would be without really necessary things. I could dine without a tablecloth, but very uncomfortably without a clean napkin, in the German fashion; I soil them more than they or the Italians do and make but little use of either spoon or fork. I am sorry that they have not kept up a fashion that I saw begun, after the example of kings, of changing napkins with each service, as they do plates. We are told of that hardworking soldier Marius that in growing old he became fastidious in his drinking and drank only out of one particular cup of his. I too give way to an inclination for a glass of a certain shape and do not willingly drink from a common glass, any more than I like to be served by a common hand. I dislike all metal in comparison with a clear and transparent material. Let my eyes taste of it too according to their capacity.

I owe many such weaknesses to habit. Nature, on the other hand, has also brought me her share: such as no longer being able to stand two full meals a day without overloading my stomach, nor complete abstinence from one of those meals without filling myself with wind, drying up my mouth, and upsetting my appetite; and suffering from too long exposure to night air. For of late years, in military duties, when the whole night is spent in them, as commonly happens, after five or six hours my stomach begins to trouble me, together with a violent headache, and I do not last until daybreak without vomiting. When the others are going off to breakfast, I go to sleep, and when I rise, I am as gay as before.

I had always understood that the evening dew fell only at nightfall, associating these past years long and familiarly with a lord who was imbued with the belief that the dew is sharper and more dangerous as the sun is declining, an hour or two before it sets, when he carefully avoids it while despising the night dew, he has almost imprinted in me not so much his opinion as his feeling.

What shall we say of the fact that even doubt and inquiry strikes our imagination and changes us? Those who give way suddenly to these inclinations bring total ruin on themselves. And I am sorry for several gentlemen who, through the stupidity of their physicians, have made prisoners of themselves, though still young and in sound health. It would still be better to endure a cold than by disuse to lose forever the intercourse of social life by giving up so general a practice.[18] Vexatious science that decries the pleasantest hours of the day! Let us extend our possession to our utmost means—most often we

---

[18] of going out at night

harden ourselves by persisting and correct our constitution, as Caesar did his epilepsy, by dint of despising and combating it. We should apply ourselves to the best rules but not enslave ourselves to them; except to those, if there are any such, to which bondage and servitude is useful.

Both kings and philosophers defecate, and ladies too. Public lives must be devoted to ceremony; mine, obscure and private, enjoys every natural dispensation; soldier and Gascon are also qualities a little subject to indiscretion. Wherefore I shall say this of that action: that we should relegate it to certain prescribed nocturnal hours and force and subject ourselves to them by habit as I have done; but not subject ourselves, as I have done in my declining years, to any care about a particular comfort of place and seat for this function, and make it a nuisance by its duration and indolence. And yet in the dirtiest functions is it not in some measure excusable to require more care and cleanliness? *Man is by nature a clean and neat creature.*[19] Of all the natural functions that is the one in which I am most impatient of interruption. I have seen many soldiers inconvenienced by the irregularity of their bowels; mine and I never fail the moment of our assignation, which is on jumping out of bed, unless some violent occupation or sickness disturbs us.

I cannot think, as I was saying, where sick men can better place themselves in safety than in keeping quietly in the course of life in which they have been brought up and trained. Change of any kind is disturbing and harmful. Go ahead and believe that chestnuts will hurt a native of Périgord or Lucca, or milk and cheese the mountaineers. They keep prescribing for the sick a way of life not only new but contrary: a change that a healthy man could not endure. Prescribe water to a Breton of seventy, shut up a seaman in a steaming-hot room, and forbid a Basque footman to take walks: you deprive them of movement and, in the end, of air and light.

---

[19] Seneca, *Epistles*

To be alive is then worth so much?[20]

We are compelled to part our souls from cherished things,
And leave off living so that we may still exist.
Should I judge them to live to whom the air they breathe,
The very light of day is made a source of pain?[21]

If they do no other good, they do this at least, that they prepare their patients early for death, undermining little by little and cutting off their enjoyment of life.

Both in health and sickness I have readily yielded to the appetites that pressed upon me. I give great authority to my desires and inclinations. I do not like to cure one ill by another; I hate remedies that are more troublesome than the disease itself. To be subject to the stone and subject to abstain from the pleasure of eating oysters are two troubles for one. The disease torments us on one side, the rule on the other. Since there is a risk of making a mistake, let us run the risk rather in the pursuit of pleasure. The world does the contrary and thinks nothing beneficial that is not painful; it is suspicious of ease.

My appetite in many things has of its own accord happily enough accommodated and adapted itself to the health of my stomach. Tartness and pungency in sauces were pleasant to me when I was young; my stomach becoming troubled by them since, my taste immediately followed suit. Wine is hurtful to sick people; it is the first thing that my mouth finds distasteful, and with an invincible distaste. Whatever I take against my liking hurts me, and nothing hurts me that I do with hunger and liveliness; I have never received harm from any action that was very pleasant to me. And so I have made all medical conclusions very largely give way to my pleasure. And as a young man,

Around whom Cupid flitting to and fro
Resplendent gleamed in saffron-colored vest,[22]

---

[20] Anonymous [21] Maximianus [22] Catullus

I lent myself as licentiously and heedlessly as any other man
to the desire that held me in its grip,

> And served, not without glory, my campaigns,[23]

more, however, in continuation and endurance than in vigor of
attack:

> I scarce remember holding out for six.[24]

It is certainly distressing and extraordinary to confess at what
a tender age I first chanced to fall under its subjection. It was,
indeed, by chance, for it was long before the years of choice
and knowledge. I do not remember about myself so far back.
And my lot may be coupled with that of Quartilla, who had no
memory of her maidenhood.

> Hence goatish smells and early-growing hair,
> A beard to make my mother stare.[25]

Physicians adjust their rules, usually beneficially, to the violence of the sharp cravings that come upon the sick; this great
desire cannot be imagined in a form so strange and vicious that
Nature does not have a hand in it. And then how important a
thing it is to satisfy the imagination! In my opinion this faculty is all-important, at least more so than any other. The
most grievous and ordinary troubles are those that the imagination loads us with. This Spanish saying pleases me from several points of view: *God defend me from myself*. I am sorry
when I am sick that I do not have some longing that might
give me the pleasure of satisfying it; the rules of medicine
would hardly deter me from it. I do the same when I am well;
I see scarcely anything more to hope and wish for. It is pitiful
to be languid and enfeebled even in our desires.

The art of medicine is not so settled that we are without au-

---

[23] Horace, *Odes* [24] Ovid, *Amores* [25] Martial

thority, no matter what we do; it changes according to the climates and according to the moons, according to Fernel and according to L'Escale. If your physician does not think it good for you to sleep, to use wine or such and such food, don't worry: I will find you another that will not be of his opinion. The variety of medical arguments and opinions embraces all sorts of forms. I saw a wretched sick man fainting and dying with thirst in order to be cured and being laughed at afterwards by another physician who condemned that advice as harmful. Had he not tormented himself to good purpose? A man of that trade died recently of the stone, who had made use of extreme abstinence to combat his malady; his colleagues say that on the contrary this fasting from drink had dried him up and baked the gravel in his kidneys.

I have observed that, when I am wounded or sick, talking excites me and hurts me as much as any irregularity I may commit. It taxes and tires me to use my voice for it is loud and strained; so that when I have come to address the ears of the great about affairs of weight, I have often put them to the trouble of asking me to moderate my voice.

This story merits a digression. Someone in a certain Greek school was speaking loudly, as I do; the master of ceremonies sent word to him to speak lower. "Let him send me," he said, "the tone in which he wants me to speak." The other replied that he should take his tone from the ears of the person to whom he was speaking. That was well said provided that it was understood to mean: "Speak according to the business you have with your hearer." For if it means: "Let it be enough that he hears you," or, "Regulate yourself by him," I do not think it is right. The tone and movement of the voice have a certain expressiveness and signification for my meaning, it is for me to guide it to make myself understood. There is a voice for instructing, a voice for flattering, or for scolding. I want my voice not only to reach him, but, perhaps, to strike him and pierce him. When I take my footman to task in a sharp and bitter tone, it would be fine for him to say to me: "Master, speak lower, I can hear you very well." *There is a kind of voice adapted to the hearing, not by its volume, but by its quality.*[26] Speech is half his who speaks and half his who listens. The latter must prepare to receive it according to the speed that it takes. As among tennis players, he who receives shifts about and makes ready according to the movement of the man who is making the stroke and according to the nature of the stroke.

Experience has also taught me this, that we ruin ourselves by impatience. Evils have their life and their limits, their sicknesses and their health.

The constitution of maladies is patterned after the constitution of animals. Their destiny and their days are limited from their birth. He who attempts imperiously to cut them short by force in the midst of their course prolongs and multiplies them and stirs them up instead of appeasing them. I am of Crantor's opinion, that we must neither obstinately and heedlessly oppose evils nor limply succumb to them, but give way to them naturally according to their condition and our own. We ought to give free passage to diseases, and I find they stay a shorter time with me who give them a free hand; and I have thrown off some of those which are reputed most obstinate and tenacious by their own decay, without help and without the art of medicine, and against its rules. Let us leave it a little up to Nature; she knows her business better than we do. "But so-and-so died of it." So will you, if not of that disease, of some other. And how many have not failed to die of it who have had three physicians at their backsides? Example is an inconstant mirror, reflecting everything and in every way. If it is a pleasant medicine, take it; it is always so much present gain. I shall never balk at the name or the color if it is delicious and appetizing. Pleasure is one of the principal kinds of profit.

I have allowed colds, gouty discharges, looseness, palpitations of the heart, migraine, and other ailments to grow old and

----
[26] Quintilian

die a natural death in me; I lost them when I had half trained myself to be hospitable to them. They are conjured better by courtesy than by defiance. We must meekly suffer the laws of our condition. We are born to grow old, to grow weak, and to be sick, in spite of all medicine. It is the first lesson that the Mexicans teach their children, when, as soon as they come out of their mother's womb, they greet them thus: "Child, you have come into the world to endure; endure, suffer, and be quiet."

It is wrong to complain that what may happen to anyone has happened to someone, *be indignant if anything has been unjustly decreed against you alone.*[27] Look at an old man begging of God to keep him in full and vigorous health, that is to say, to restore him to youth.

> Why prayest thou, fool, such childish prayers in vain?[28]

Is it not madness? His condition does not admit of it. The gout, the stone, indigestion are symptoms of length of years, as heat, rains, and winds of long journeys. Plato does not believe that Aesculapius troubled himself to try by treatment to prolong life in a wasted and weak body, useless to its country, useless to its profession and for begetting healthy and robust children; and he does not think such concern consistent with divine justice and wisdom, which should direct all things to usefulness. My good man, it is all over. You cannot be put on your feet again; at the most they will plaster and prop you up a little and prolong your misery an hour or two:

> Like one who, eager to defer a while
> Impending ruin, props the tottering pile,
> Until one day the house, the props, and all
> Together with a dreadful havoc fall.[29]

We must learn to endure what we cannot avoid. Our life, like the harmony of the world, is composed of contrary things,

---

[27] Seneca, *Epistles*   [28] Ovid, *Tristia*   [29] Maximianus

also of different tones, sweet and harsh, sharp and flat, soft and loud. If a musician liked only one kind, what would he express? He must know how to use them together and blend them. And so must we the good and evil which are consubstantial with our life. Our being cannot subsist without this mixture, and one group is no less necessary to it than the other. To attempt to kick against natural necessity is to imitate the folly of Ctesiphon, who undertook a kicking match with his mule.

I seldom consult doctors about the changes I feel in my health for those fellows are highhanded when they have you at their mercy. They harass your ears with their prognostications. And once surprising me weakened by illness, they treated me insultingly with their dogmas and magisterial frowns, threatening me now with great pains, now with approaching death. I was not floored by them or dislodged from my position, but I was hit and jostled. If my judgment was neither changed nor upset, it was at least bothered. That is still agitation and conflict.

Now I treat my imagination as gently as I can and would relieve it, if I could, of all trouble and contest. We must assist it and flatter it and deceive it if we can. My mind is fitted for this service; it does not lack plausible reasons for everything. If it could persuade as well as it preaches, it would aid me very happily.

Would you like an example? It tells me that it is for my own good that I have the stone; that the buildings of my age must naturally suffer some leakage (it is time for them to begin to loosen up and give way. It is a common necessity; and if otherwise, would it not have been a new miracle that they had performed for me? I thereby pay the tribute due to old age, and I cannot expect a better bargain); that the company ought to console me, since I have fallen into the most common infirmity of men of my time of life (on all sides I see them afflicted with the same kind of disease, and their society is honorable for me, since by preference it attacks the great; its essence partakes of nobility and dignity); that of the men who are stricken by it few get off more cheaply; and even so they pay the penalty of a disagreeable diet and the daily annoyance of taking medicinal drugs, whereas I am indebted solely to my good fortune. For some ordinary broths of eryngo or rupture-wort that I have swallowed two or three times to please the ladies, who, more graciously than my pain is sharp, offered me half of theirs, seemed to me as easy to take as they were useless in their action. The others have to pay a thousand vows to Aesculapius and as many crowns to their physician for the easy and abundant voiding of gravel which I often get through the kindness of Nature. Even the correctness of my behavior in ordinary company is not disturbed by it, and I can hold my water ten hours and as long as anyone.

"Fear of this disease," says my mind, "used to terrify you when it was unknown to you; the cries and despair of those who make it worse by their impatience bred a horror of it in you. It is a malady that punishes those of your members by which you have most sinned. You are a man of conscience.

> 'Tis undeserved punishment that hurts.[30]

Εχρεrience of stone

✓ Consider this chastisement; it is very easy in comparison with others and inflicted with a paternal tenderness. Consider its slowness in coming; it only disturbs and occupies the season of your life which in any case is henceforth wasted and barren, having given way, as though by agreement, to the licentiousness and pleasures of your youth. The fear and pity that people feel for this malady is for you a subject of vainglory; a trait of which, even if you have purged your judgment and cured your reason of it, your friends still recognize, however, some tincture in your character. It is a pleasure to hear people say of you: 'There is real strength, there is real endurance!' They see you sweat in agony, turn pale, turn red, tremble, vomit

---

[30] Ovid, *Heroides*

to the point of blood, suffer strange contractions and convul-
sions, sometimes shed big tears from your eyes, pass thick,
black, and frightful urine, or have it stopped up by some
sharp, rough stone that cruelly pricks and scrapes the neck
of your penis, meanwhile maintaining conversation with the
bystanders with a normal countenance, jesting in the intervals
with your servants, holding up your end in an intense discussion, making excuses for your pain, and minimizing your
suffering.

"Do you call to mind those men of past times who so greedily
sought afflictions to keep their virtue in breath and exercise?
Put the case that Nature is bearing and forcing you into that
glorious school which you would never have entered of your
own free will. If you tell me that it is a dangerous and mortal
disease, what others are not? For it is a doctor's trick to except
some, which they say do not head in a straight line to death.
What does it matter if they go that way by accident, and if
they slip and sidle off easily towards the path that leads us
to it? But you do not die of being sick, you die of being alive.
Death kills you without the help of sickness. And sickness has
kept death off for some, who have lived longer because they
thought they were dying. Moreover there are sicknesses, as
there are wounds, that are medicinal and salutary.

"The stone is often no less attached to life than you. We see
men with whom it has continued from their childhood to their
extreme old age, and if they had not deserted it, it was ready
to accompany them still further. You kill it more often than
it kills you; and even if it put before you the image of approaching death, would it not be a kind service to a man of
such an age to bring him to meditate upon his end?

"And what is worse, you have no longer any reason for being
cured. In any case, the common fate will summon you any day.
Consider how artfully and gently she makes life distasteful
to you and detaches you from the world, not forcing you with
the tyranny of being chronically subject to it, like so many

other infirmities that you see in old people, which keep them continually hobbled and without relief from weakness and pain, but by warnings and instructions repeated at intervals, mingled with long pauses of rest, as if to give you the opportunity to meditate and repeat her lesson at your leisure. To give you the opportunity to form a sound judgment and to make up your mind like a man of courage, she puts before you in full the state of your condition, both in good and bad, and a life on one and the same day now very joyous, now unbearable. If you do not embrace death, at least you shake hands with it once a month. Whereby you have more reason to hope that it will some day catch you without threatening, and that, being so often led to the port, and trusting that you are still in the accustomed limits, you and your trust will one morning have crossed the water unexpectedly. We have no reason to complain of illnesses that divide the time fairly with health."

I am obliged to Fortune for assailing me so often with the same kind of weapons. She fashions and trains me to them by use, hardens and habituates me. Henceforth I know very nearly at what cost I shall be quit of them.

For want of a natural memory I make one of paper, and as some new symptom occurs in my disease, I write it down. Whence it happens that at the present moment, having passed through almost every sort of case, if some severe stroke threatens me, by thumbing through these little disconnected notes, like sibyl's leaves, I never fail to find grounds for comfort in some favorable prognostic in my past experience.

Familiarity also serves to give me better hope for the future. For this process of evacuation having continued so long, it is likely that Nature will not change this course, and that nothing worse will come of it than what I already feel. Besides the nature of this disease is not ill-suited to my eager and impetuous disposition. When it assails me mildly, it frightens me for it will be of long duration. But by nature it has vigorous and intense outbursts; it shakes me to pieces for a day or two.

My kidneys lasted an age without change for the worse; it will soon be another since they changed their state. Evil things as well as good have their period; perhaps this infirmity is drawing towards its end. Age weakens the heat of my stomach; its digestion being thereby less perfect, it sends this crude matter to my kidneys. Why cannot the heat of my kidneys be likewise weakened at a certain revolution so that they can no longer petrify my phlegm, and Nature set out to find some other way of purgation? Years have evidently made some of my rheums dry up. Why not these excrements which furnish matter for the gravel?

Furthermore is there anything comparably sweet to the sudden change when from extreme pain I come, by the voiding of a stone, to recover as in a flash of lightning the beautiful light of health, so free and so full, as happens in our sudden and sharpest attacks of colic? Is there anything in the pain suffered that can counterbalance the pleasure of such sudden improvement? How much more beautiful health seems to me after sickness when they are so near and contiguous that I can recognize them in each other's presence in their loftiest array, when they appear in rivalry, as if to square off against each other! Just as the Stoics say that vices are profitably introduced to give value to virtue and assist it, we can say with better reason and less temerity of conjecture that Nature has lent us pain for the honor and service of pleasure and painlessness. When Socrates, after his fetters were knocked off, felt the pleasant sensation of the itching which their weight had caused in his legs, he rejoiced to consider the close alliance between pain and pleasure, how they are associated by a necessary bond, so that they follow and beget one another by turns. And he called out to the good Aesop that he ought to have taken from this consideration subject matter suitable for a fine fable.

The worst thing that I see in other diseases is that they are not so serious in their immediate effect as they are in their after effects. A man is a whole year recovering, constantly full of weakness and fear. There is so much risk and so many steps in getting back to safety that there is no end to it. Before they have unmuffled you of a kerchief, and then a cap, before they have given you back the enjoyment of fresh air, and wine, and your wife, and melons, it is a great wonder if you have not relapsed into some new misery. The stone has this privilege, that it carries itself clean off, whereas the other maladies always leave some imprint and change for the worse that makes the body susceptible to a new disease, and they lend a hand to one another. Those maladies are excusable that content themselves with their own possession of us without extending it and without introducing their followers; but courteous and gracious are those whose passage brings us some profitable issue. Since I have had the stone, I have found myself rid of other ailments, more so, it seems to me, than I was before, and I have had no fever since. I argue that the extreme and frequent vomitings that I suffer purge me; and, on the other hand, my loss of appetite and the unusual fasts I keep digest my morbid humors, and Nature voids in these stones its superfluous and harmful matter.

Do not tell me that it is a medicine too dearly bought. For what about all the stinking potions, cauteries, incisions, sweatings, setons, diets, and so many other methods of cure which often bring us to death because we are not able to endure their violence and harassment? So when I have an attack, I take it as medicine; when I am exempt, I take it as sure and complete deliverance.

Here is another benefit of my disease, peculiar to it: that it almost plays its game by itself and lets me play mine unless I lack courage. In its greatest throes I have held out for ten hours on horseback. Just endure it, you need no other regimen. Play, dine, run, do this and that if you can; your dissipation will do you more good than harm. Say as much to a man who has the pox, the gout, or a hernia! Other maladies have more comprehensive bonds, cramp our actions far more, disturb our whole order, and involve the whole state of life in consideration of them. Mine only pinches the skin; it leaves your understanding and will at your disposal, and your tongue and your feet and your hands; it rather awakens than stupefies you. The soul is attacked by the burning of a fever, and laid low by an epileptic fit, and dislocated by a severe migraine, and, in short, stunned by all the maladies that hurt the whole body and the noblest parts. It is not attacked by my malady. If it fares badly, it is its own fault; it betrays, abandons, and unseats itself.

It is only fools who let themselves be persuaded that this hard and solid body which is baked in our kidneys can be dissolved by potions. Therefore when it is put in motion, there is nothing to do but give it passage; it will take it in any case.

I observe also this particular convenience, that it is a disease wherein we have little to guess at. We are relieved of the worry into which other diseases throw us by the uncertainty of their causes, conditions, and progress—an infinitely painful worry. We have no need of doctoral consultations and interpretations; the senses indicate to us what it is and where it is.

By such arguments, both strong and weak, I try to lull and beguile my imagination and salve its wounds as Cicero did his disease of old age. If they get worse tomorrow, tomorrow we shall provide other means of escape.

Here is proof of it. Recently it has happened again that the slightest movements force the pure blood out of my kidneys. What of it? I do not on that account fail to stir about as before and to prick after my hounds with a youthful and insolent ardor. And I believe that I fare well from such a serious accident when it costs me nothing but a dull heaviness and uneasiness in that region. It is some big stone that is crushing and consuming the substance of my kidneys and my life that I am draining off little by little, not without some natural pleasure, as an excrement that is henceforth superfluous and troublesome. Do I feel something stirring? Do not expect me to go and spend my time in examining my pulse and my urine in order to take some troublesome precaution; I shall be in time enough when I feel the pain, without prolonging it by the pain of fear. He who fears he will suffer already suffers from his fear.

Besides, the doubts and ignorance of those who take it upon them to explain the workings of Nature, and her inner movements, and all the false prognostications of their art should make us know that she has utterly unknown ways. There is great uncertainty, variety, and obscurity in her promises to us or threats. Except for old age, which is an indubitable sign of the approach of death, in all other ills I see few signs of the future on which to ground our divination. vs doctors

I judge myself only by actual sensation, not by reasoning. What would be the good since I intend to apply nothing but waiting and endurance? Do you want to know what I gain by this? Look at those who do otherwise and who depend upon so many different persuasions and counsels: how often imagination presses hard upon them, without the body at all. Many a time when I was safe and free from these dangerous attacks, I have taken pleasure in communicating their symptoms to the physicians as though they were just beginning in me. I suffered the doom of their dreadful conclusions quite at ease and remained that much more obliged to God for this grace and better informed about the vanity of this art.

There is nothing that ought so much to be recommended to youth as activity and vigilance. Our life is nothing but movement. I get underway with difficulty, and I am late in everything: in rising, going to bed, and at meals. Seven o'clock is early for me, and where I am master, I do not dine before eleven or sup till after six. In the past I attributed the fevers and sicknesses into which I have fallen to the sluggishness and drowsiness that that long sleep brought on me, and I have always repented going back to sleep in the morning. Plato is more opposed to excess in sleeping than excess in drinking.

I like to sleep hard and alone, even without a woman, in the royal fashion, fairly well covered up. My bed is never warmed, but since I have grown old, they give me, when I need them, cloths to warm my feet and stomach. They used to find fault with the great Scipio for being such a sleeper, in my opinion for no other reason than that men were annoyed that in him alone there was nothing to be found fault with. If I have particular concern about my way of living, it is rather about sleeping than anything else; but generally I give way and accommodate myself to necessity as much as anyone. Sleeping has taken up a great part of my life, and even at this age continues to do so eight or nine hours at a stretch. I am weaning myself profitably from this lazy propensity and am evidently the better for it. I find the change a little hard, but in three days it is over. And I hardly know anyone who can live with less sleep when necessary, or who can take exercise with more steadfastness, or to whom military duties are less troublesome.

My body is capable of steady but not of violent or sudden exertion. From now on I avoid violent exercise such as puts me into a sweat; my limbs grow weary before they grow warm. I can stay on my feet a whole day, and I do not weary of walking; but on pavement, from my early youth, I have not liked to go except on horseback. On foot I get covered with mud up to my buttocks, and in our streets small men are subject to be jostled and elbowed for want of presence. And I have always liked to rest, whether lying or sitting, with my legs as high, or higher, than my seat.

There is no occupation so pleasant as the military, an occupation both noble in its execution (for valor is the strongest, most magnanimous, and proudest of all virtues) and noble in its cause. There is no more just and universal service than the protection of the peace and greatness of one's country. You take pleasure in the company of so many noble, young, active men, in the regular sight of so many tragic spectacles, in the freedom of that artless relationship, in a manly and unceremonious way of living, in the variety of a thousand different actions, in that spirited harmony of martial music which sustains and warms your ears and your soul, in the honor of this exercise, even in its severity and hardship, which Plato esteems so lightly that in his Republic he makes women and children share them. A volunteer soldier, you invite yourself to particular tasks and hazards according to your judgment of their brilliance and importance, and you see when life itself is with good reason devoted to them,

> And I reflect how noble 'tis to die in arms.[31]

To fear the common dangers that affect so great a throng, not to dare what so many kinds of souls dare, that is for a heart weak and mean beyond measure. Company reassures even children. If others excel you in knowledge, in grace, in strength, in fortune, you have outside causes to blame for it; but if you yield to them in firmness of soul, you have only yourself to blame. Death is more abject, more lingering and painful in bed than in battle; fevers and catarrhs are as painful and fatal as a harquebus shot. Whoever is prepared to bear valiantly the accidents of everyday life would not need to swell his courage to become a soldier. *To live, my Lucilius, is to fight.*[32]

I do not remember that I ever had the itch; yet scratching is one of nature's sweetest gratifications and as handy as any. But repentance follows too annoyingly close upon its heels. I mostly scratch my ears, which are at times apt to itch on the inside.

I was born with all my senses sound almost to perfection. My stomach is tolerably good, as is my head and also my wind, and they generally hold up during my fevers. I have just past six years beyond the age of fifty, which some nations, not without reason, had prescribed as such a just term of life that they

---

[31] Virgil, *Aeneid*   [32] Seneca, *Epistles*

allowed no one to exceed it. Yet I still have moments of such clear recovery, though inconstant and brief, that they fall little short of the health and freedom from pain of my youth. I do not speak of vigor and sprightliness; it is not reasonable that they should follow me beyond their limits;

> My sides no longer can sustain
> The hardships of the wind and rain.[33]

My face betrays me immediately, and my eyes; all changes in me begin there, and they appear a little worse than they really are. I often arouse pity in my friends before I feel the reason for it. My looking glass does not startle me, for even in my youth it has happened to me more than once to wear a muddy complexion and an ill-omened appearance without any serious consequences; so that the doctors, finding no cause within to account for the outward change, attributed it to the spirit and to some secret passion that was gnawing me within. They were mistaken. If my body were as responsive to my control as my soul is, we should get along a little more comfortably. My soul was then not only free from trouble, but also full of satisfaction and gaiety, as it commonly is, half by nature, half by design:

> Nor do the ailments of my mind infect my limbs.[34]

I am of the opinion that this temperature of my soul has many a time raised up my body from its falls. My body is often depressed; while, if the other is not merry, it is at least tranquil and at rest. I had a quartan fever for four or five months which had quite disfigured me; my mind still went on not only peacefully but cheerfully. If the pain is outside of me, the weakness and languor do not afflict me much. I know several bodily infirmities that provoke horror just to name them which I

---

[33] Horace, *Odes*   [34] Ovid, *Tristia*

should fear less than a thousand passions and agitations of the spirit that I see commonly existing. I reconcile myself to not being able to run any more; it is enough that I crawl. Nor do I complain of the natural decay that has hold of me,

> Who marvels at a goiter in the Alps? [35]

any more than I regret that my span of life is not as long and sound as that of an oak.

I have no reason to complain of my imagination. I have had few thoughts in my life that have even interrupted the course of my sleep, unless they have been those of desire, which awakened me without afflicting me. I dream seldom, and then it is of fantastic things and chimeras usually produced by amusing thoughts, rather ridiculous than sad. And I believe it to be true that dreams are faithful interpreters of our inclinations, but there is an art in sorting and understanding them.

> The things engrossing men in life, their thoughts, and
> cares, and sights,
> The things that move them when awake, if these in
> dreams recur,
> It is by no means strange. [36]

Plato says, moreover, that it is the function of wisdom to draw from them instructions for divining the future. I see nothing in that, except for marvelous experiences that Socrates, Xenophon, and Aristotle, men of irreproachable authority, relate of it. Historians say that the Atlantes never dream and also that they eat nothing that has been killed; which I add because that is, perhaps, the reason why they do not dream. For Pythagoras prescribed a certain preparation of food to cause appropriate dreams. Mine are gentle and occasion no bodily agitation or vocal utterance. I have known many men of my time to be astonishingly disturbed by them. Theon the philosopher

[35] Juvenal [36] Accius, in Cicero, *De Divinatione*

walked in his sleep, and Pericles' servant did so on the very tiles and roof of the house.

I make little choice at table and take up the first and nearest thing, and I change reluctantly from one flavor to another. I dislike a crowd of dishes and of courses as much as any other crowd. I am easily satisfied with few dishes, and I hate Favorinus' idea that at a feast the food should be stolen from you just when you are getting an appetite for it, and a new dish always be substituted, and that it is a wretched supper if the guests have not been glutted with the rumps of various birds, and that the beccafico is the only bird that deserves to be eaten whole.

I often eat salt meats; yet I prefer bread that has no salt in it, and my baker at home serves no other at my table, contrary to the custom of the country. In my childhood they had to correct principally my refusal of things that are generally best liked at that age: sweetmeats, preserves, pastry. My tutor fought this aversion to dainty foods as being a kind of daintiness. And, indeed, it is nothing else but finical taste, whatever it applies to. Whoever cures a child of some particular and obstinate liking for brown bread, bacon, or garlic, cures him of fastidious taste. There are some who act like patient victims through lamenting the absence of beef and ham when they are in the midst of partridges. They have a good time; that is the daintiness of the dainty; it is the taste of a soft existence that is palled by the ordinary and accustomed things, *by which luxury beguiles the tedium of wealth.*[37] Not to make good cheer with what another does, to take finicky care about what you eat and drink is the essence of this vice:

And if you fear a meal of only greens upon a modest dish.[38]

There is, indeed, this difference, that it is better to enslave your desire to the things that are easiest to obtain; but it is al-

[37] Seneca, *Epistles*   [38] Horace, *Epistles*

ways a vice to enslave yourself. I once called a kinsman of mine fastidious, who in our galleys had lost the habit of using beds like ours and of taking off his clothes when he went to sleep.

If I had any sons, I should cordially wish them my own fortune. The good father that God gave me (who has no repayment from me except gratitude for his goodness, but certainly a very hearty gratitude) sent me from the cradle to be brought up in a poor village of his, and kept me there all the while I was at nurse, and even longer, training me to the humblest and commonest way of living: *A well-conditioned stomach is a great part of liberty.*[39] Never assume, and still less give to your wives, the charge of their upbringing. Let them be formed by Fortune under the laws of the common people and of Nature; leave it to custom to train them to frugality and austerity, that they may have rather to come down from hardship than climb towards it. His notion aimed at still another end, to ally me with the people and that class of men that needs our help; and he held that I was duty bound to look rather to the man who extends his arms to me than to the one who turns his back upon me. And this was the reason why he also had me held over the baptismal font by persons of the lowliest fortune, to bind and attach me to them.

His plan has succeeded not at all badly. By inclination I devote myself to the little people, whether because there is more vainglory in it, or out of natural compassion, which has infinite power over me. The faction which I condemn in our wars, I will condemn more severely when it is flourishing and prosperous; it will make me be somewhat reconciled to it when I see it miserable and crushed. How I enjoy reflecting upon the fine spirit of Chelonis, daughter and wife of kings of Sparta! While her husband Cleombrotus had the advantage over her father Leonidas in the strife within the city, she behaved like a good daughter, rallied to her father in his exile,

---

[39] Seneca, *Epistles*

in his misery, in opposition to the conqueror. Did Fortune happen to turn? There she is, her will changed with the turn of Fortune, courageously taking her husband's side, whom she followed everywhere that his ruin bore him, having, it seems, no other choice than to hasten to the side where she was most needed and where she could best manifest her compassion. I am more naturally inclined to follow the example of Flaminius, who lent himself to those who had need of him more than to those who could be of benefit to him, than that of Pyrrhus, who was disposed to truckle to the great and to domineer over the small.

Long sessions at table annoy me and disagree with me; for, perhaps because I took the habit as a child, through lack of better self-restraint, I eat as long as I am there. Therefore in my own house, though the meals there are of the short type, I like to sit down a little after the others, in the manner of Augustus; but I do not imitate him in also rising before the rest of the company. On the contrary, I like to rest a long time after and listen to the stories, provided I do not participate, for it tires me and disagrees with me to talk on a full stomach, whereas I find it a very wholesome and pleasant exercise to shout and argue before a meal. The ancient Greeks and Romans had more sense than we, assigning to eating, which is one of the principal actions of life, several hours and the best part of the night, if some other unusual business did not take them away, eating and drinking less hastily than we do, who perform all our actions posthaste, and in prolonging this natural pleasure with greater leisure and amenity, interspersing in it various agreeable and useful duties of society.

Those whose duty it is to take care of me could easily deprive me of what they think may be harmful to me; for in such matters I never desire nor miss what I do not see. But likewise they waste their time in preaching to me abstinence from those things that are brought before me. So that when I want to fast, I have to be set apart from the supper table and be served just so much as is necessary for a prescribed collation; for if I sit down to table, I forget my resolution. When I order a change in the preparation of some meat, my household know that it means that my appetite is flagging and that I will not touch it.

All meats that will stand it I like rare, and I like them very high, in some even to the point of smelling. Nothing but toughness generally offends me (about any other quality I am as indifferent and tolerant as any man I have known), so that, contrary to the common humor, even in fish I sometimes find some too fresh and too firm. It is not the fault of my teeth, which have always been good, even excellent, and which are only just now beginning to be threatened by age. I learned from childhood to rub them with my napkin every morning and before and after meals.

God is merciful to those whose life he withdraws bit by bit; that is the only benefit of old age. The last death will be so much the less complete and painful; by then it will kill only a half or quarter of a man. Here is a tooth that has just fallen out, without pain, without effort; that was the natural term of its duration. Both that part of my being and several others are already dead, others half dead, even among the most active, which held the highest rank in the prime of my life. Thus do I melt and steal away from myself. What folly it would be on the part of my understanding to feel the last plunge of this fall, already so far advanced, just as if it were the whole way! I hope I shall not.

In truth, I gain one principal consolation in meditating on my death, that it will be normal and natural, and that henceforth I cannot in this matter seek or hope for any but illegitimate favor from destiny. Men delude themselves into believing that in former times their lives, like their stature, had a bigger span. But Solon, who belongs to those old times, nevertheless limits the extreme duration of life to threescore and ten years. Shall I, who in every way have worshipped so much that *golden mean* of ancient times and have taken the moderate measure for the most perfect, aspire to an immoderate and prodigious old age? Whatever happens contrary to the course of Nature may be troublesome, but what happens according to her should always be pleasant. *All things that happen according to Nature should be accounted good.*[40] Thus, says Plato, the death which is occasioned by wounds or maladies may be called violent, but that which takes us by surprise while old age is leading us to it is the easiest of all and in a way delightful. *Young men have their lives taken away by violence, old men by ripeness.*[41]

Death mingles and blends with our life throughout. Decline anticipates death's hour and makes its way even into the course of our growth. I have portraits of myself at twenty-five and thirty-five years of age; I compare them with one of the present: how many times over it is no longer myself. How much more remote is my present picture from those than from that of my death! It is too much of an abuse of Nature to fret her so far that she is constrained to leave us and abandon our guidance—our eyes, our teeth, our legs, and the rest—to the mercy of foreign assistance begged by us, and to resign us to the hands of art, weary of following us.

I am not excessively fond of either salads or fruits, except melons. My father hated all sorts of sauces; I love them all. Eating too much troubles me, but I have as yet no really certain knowledge that any kind of food disagrees with me because of its nature; even as I do not distinguish a full or waning moon, or spring from autumn. There are changes going on in us, irregular and unknown. For radishes, for example, I first found agreed with me, then later disagreed, now they agree again. In several things I feel my stomach and appetite keep on varying that way: I have changed back from white wine to claret, and then from claret to white. I am a great lover of fish, and the lean days become my fat days, and the fast days my

---

[40] Cicero, *De Senectute*   [41] Cicero, *De Senectute*

feasts. I believe what some people say, that it is easier to digest than meat. As it is contrary to my conscience to eat meat on fish days, so it is contrary to my taste to mix fish and meat; the difference between them seems to me too great.

Ever since my youth I have at times omitted a meal, either to sharpen my appetite for the next day, for, as Epicurus used to fast and to make lean meals in order to accustom his appetite to do without abundance, I do it, on the contrary, to train my appetite to take better advantage and make more cheerful use of abundance; or I fasted to conserve my vigor for the benefit of some action of body or mind; for both of these become cruelly sluggish in me through repletion, and I hate above all things the stupid coupling of so healthy and sprightly a goddess with that little unruly, belching god, all bloated with the fumes of his liquor; or to cure my sick stomach; or for want of fit company, for I say, like that same Epicurus, that we should not so much consider what we eat as with whom we eat, and I commend Chilo because he would not promise to be at Periander's feast till he was informed who were the other guests. There is no preparation so sweet to me, nor sauce so appetizing as that which is derived from society.

I think it is healthier to eat more leisurely and less, and to eat oftener. But I want to make the most of appetite and hunger. I should take no pleasure in dragging out three or four wretched meals a day, restricted in the manner of a doctor's regimen. Who would assure me that I would find again at supper the gaping appetite that I had in the morning? Let us take—especially the old men—let us take the first opportune time that comes our way. Let us leave the daily schedules to almanac-makers and doctors.

The greatest benefit that I get from good health is sensual pleasure; let us take hold of the first that is present and known. I avoid consistency in these laws of fasting. He who wants a habit to be of use to him, let him avoid continuing it; we become hardened to it, our powers go to sleep in it; six months later you will have made your stomach toady so to it that your only profit will be to have lost the freedom of making different use of it except to your harm.

I do not keep my legs and thighs any more covered in winter than in summer; simply silk hose. For the relief of my colds I have allowed myself to keep my head warmer, and my belly, because of my stone; my ailments became accustomed to it in a few days and disdained my ordinary precautions. I had risen from a cap to a kerchief, and from a bonnet to a lined hat. The padding of my doublet serves now only for ornament; it is worth nothing unless I add a hare's skin or a vulture's, and a skullcap for my head. Follow these stages and you will go on at a fine pace. I shall do nothing of the sort and would gladly disown the beginning I have made if I dared. Are you falling into some new trouble? This reform is of no more use to you; you are accustomed to it; seek another. Thus men ruin themselves when they let themselves be entangled in restricting regimens and adhere to them superstitiously. They need more and more, and still more after that; it is never done.

For the purposes of our occupations and pleasure, it is much more convenient to omit dinner, as the ancients did, and to defer making good cheer till the hour of retirement and rest, without breaking up the day; this is what I used to do formerly. For our health, on the contrary, I have since found by experience that it is better to dine, and that digestion is carried on better when awake.

I am not much subject to thirst, either in health or in sickness. In the latter case my mouth is quite apt to be dry, but without thirst. Ordinarily I only drink from the desire for it that comes to me in eating, and far along in the meal. I drink pretty well for a man of ordinary build; in summer, and at an appetizing meal, I not only exceed the limits of Augustus, who drank only three times, but in order not to violate the rule of Democritus, who forbade stopping at four as an unlucky number, I run on, if need be, to five, about three half-pints. For the little glasses are my favorites, and I take pleasure in emptying them, a thing which others avoid as unbecoming. I mix my wine most often with half, sometimes with a third part of water. And when I am at home, by an ancient practice that my father's physician prescribed for him and for himself, they mix the wine that I need in the buttery two or three hours before it is served. It is said that Cranaus, King of the Athenians, was the inventor of this practice of mixing wine with water; whether to its advantage or not, I have heard it argued. I think it more proper and healthy for children not to use it until they are sixteen or eighteen years old. The most usual and common way of living is the best; all particularity seems to me a thing to be avoided, and I should hate as much to see a German putting water in his wine as a Frenchman drinking it pure. Public usage lays down the law in such things.

I fear a close atmosphere and mortally avoid smoke (the first repairs I hurried to make in my house were in the chimneys and the privies, a common and unbearable defect in old buildings), and among the hardships of war I reckon those dense clouds of dust in which we are kept buried in the hot weather for a whole day's journey. My breathing is free and easy, and my colds most often pass off without a cough and without injury to my lungs.

The rigor of summer is more hostile to me than that of winter; for, besides the discomfort of heat, less easily remedied than that of cold, and besides the beating of the sun's rays on my head, my eyes are hurt by any dazzling light. I could not at this moment dine seated opposite a bright, blazing fire. To dull the whiteness of paper, in the time when I was more in the habit of reading, I used to lay a piece of glass upon my book and found great relief in it. I am to this hour ignorant of the use of spectacles, and I see as far as I ever did, and as any other man. It is true that at the decline of day I begin to feel a little dimness and weakness in reading, an exercise that has always tired my eyes, but especially at night. Here is a step backward, just barely perceptible. I shall drop back another step, from the second to the third, and from the third to the fourth, so gently that I shall have to be an out-and-out blind man before I feel the decay and age of my sight. So artfully do the Fatal Sisters untwist the thread of our life! And so I doubt that my hearing is on the point of growing dull, and you will see that when I have half lost it, I shall still be blaming the voices of those who are speaking to me. A man must really strain his soul to make it feel how it ebbs away.

My step is quick and firm; and I know not which of the two, my mind or my body, I have had more difficulty in keeping in one place. That preacher is indeed my friend who holds my attention through a whole sermon. In ceremonial surroundings, where everyone bears such a starched expression, where I have seen the ladies keep even their eyes so steady, I have never succeeded in keeping some part of me from forever wandering; even though I may be seated there, I am by no means settled there. As the chambermaid of the philosopher Chrysippus said of her master that he was only drunk in his legs (for he had the habit of moving them about, whatever position he was in, and she used to say it when wine excited the others and he felt no effect from it), so it might have been said of me from my childhood that I had madness in my feet, or quicksilver, so fidgety and restless are they wherever I place them.

It is unmannerly; besides being harmful to health and even to pleasure, to eat greedily as I do. I often bite my tongue, and sometimes my fingers, in my haste. Diogenes, coming upon a boy who was eating that way, gave his tutor a box on the ear. There were men at Rome who taught people to chew, as well as to walk, gracefully. I lose thereby the leisure for talking which is such a sweet seasoning for the dinner table, provided the conversation is suitable, pleasant, and brief.

There is jealousy and envy between our pleasures; they clash, and they impede one another. Alcibiades, a man well versed in making good cheer, banished even music from the table, so that it should not disturb the pleasantness of the conversation, for the reason that Plato ascribes to him, that it is a practice of vulgar men to call in instrumentalists and singers to their feasts, for want of good remarks and agreeable conversation with which intelligent men know how to entertain one another. Varro asks this of a banquet: "A gathering of people of handsome presence and agreeable conversation, who are neither silent nor garrulous; cleanliness and delicacy in the food and the place; and fair weather." A well-managed dinner is an entertainment of no little art and of no little pleasure; neither the great military leaders nor the greatest philosophers have disdained the practice and science of it. My imagination has confided three banquets to the keeping of my memory, which Fortune rendered particularly pleasant to me at different times in my more flourishing years. For each of the guests contributes the principal charm according to the good temper of body and mind in which he happens to be. My present condition excludes me from this pleasure.

I, who always hug the ground, hate that inhuman wisdom that would make us disdainful and hostile to the cultivation of the body. I look upon it as an equal injustice to take an intense dislike to natural pleasures and to take too great a liking to them. Xerxes was a fool who, wrapped in all human pleasures, went and offered a prize to the man who would find him others. But he is hardly less of a fool who cuts off those that Nature has found for him. We should neither pursue nor flee them, we should accept them. I accept them a little more generously and graciously and more readily let myself follow natural inclination. We have no need to exaggerate their inanity; it makes itself felt enough and apparent enough. Thanks to our sickly, kill-joy mind, which disgusts us with them as well as with itself. It treats both itself and all that it receives, now better, now worse, according to its insatiable, erratic, and versatile nature.

Unless the jar is pure, whatever you pour in turns sour.[42]

I, who boast of embracing the enjoyments of life so carefully and so particularly, find in them, when I look at them very keenly, little more than wind. But what of it? We are all wind. And even the wind, more wisely than we, loves to bluster and toss about and is content with its own functions, without desiring stability and solidity, qualities that do not belong to it.

The pure pleasures of the imagination, as well as the pains, some say, are the greatest, as was expressed by the scales of Critolaus. It is no wonder; it composes them to its own liking and cuts them out of whole cloth. Every day I see notable, and, perhaps, desirable, examples of this. But I, who am of a mixed and coarse make-up, cannot bite so fully at this single and simple object, but that I let myself go quite grossly after the present pleasures of the general human law, intellectually sensible, and sensibly intellectual. The Cyrenaic philosophers hold that like bodily pains, so also bodily pleasures are more powerful, as being both double and more fit.

There are some who from savage stupidity, as Aristotle says, are disgusted with them; I know some who are so from ambition. Why do they not also give up breathing? Why do they not live on their own air and refuse light because it is free and costs them neither invention nor effort? Just to see, let Mars, or Pallas, or Mercury supply them with sustenance instead of Venus, Ceres, and Bacchus. Will they not try to square the circle while perched on their wives? I hate to have people tell us to keep our minds in the clouds while our bodies are at table. I would not have the mind nailed down to it nor wallowing at it, but paying attention to it; sitting at it, not lying down to it.

Aristippus defended the body alone, as if we had no soul; Zeno embraced only the soul, as if we had no body. In error, both of them. Pythagoras, they say, followed a philosophy that

---

[42] Horace, *Epistles*

was all contemplation; Socrates, one that was all conduct and action; Plato found the balance between the two. But they say this to tell a good story, and the true balance is found in Socrates, and Plato is much more Socratic than Pythagorean, and it becomes him better.

When I dance, I dance; when I sleep, I sleep; yes, and when I walk alone in a beautiful orchard, if my thoughts have been concerned with extraneous incidents for some part of the time, for some other part I lead them back again to the walk, to the orchard, to the sweetness of this solitude, and to myself. Nature has in motherly fashion observed this principle, that the actions she has enjoined on us for our need should also give us pleasure; and she invites us to them not only through reason, but also through appetite. It is wrong to infringe her laws.

When I see both Caesar and Alexander, in the very thick of their great undertakings, so fully enjoying natural and, therefore, necessary and just pleasures, I do not say that this is relaxing their minds, I say that it is making them firmer, subjecting these violent occupations and laborious thoughts, by the vigor of their spirit, to the usage of everyday life. Wise men, if they had believed that the latter was their ordinary occupation, and the former the extraordinary.

We are great fools. "He has passed his life in idleness," we say; "I have done nothing today." What! have you not lived? That is not only the fundamental but the most illustrious of your occupations. "Had I been put in a position to manage great affairs, I would have shown what I could do." Have you been able to think out and manage your life? You have performed the greatest work of all. In order to show and release her powers, Nature has no need of fortune; she shows herself equally on all levels, and behind a curtain as well as without one. To compose our character is our duty, not to compose books, and to win, not battles and provinces, but order and tranquillity in our conduct. Our great and glorious masterpiece is to live appropriately. All other things, to rule, to lay up treasure, to build, are at most but little appendices and props.

I take pleasure in seeing an army general, at the foot of a breach he intends to attack presently, giving himself up wholly and freely to his dinner and to conversation with his friends; and Brutus, with heaven and earth conspiring against him and the Roman liberty, stealing some hour of the night from his rounds to read and annotate Polybius with full composure. It is for little souls, buried under the weight of business, not to be able to disengage themselves cleanly from it, or to lay it aside and take it up again:

> Brave men, who oft with me have borne
> Worse plights, now banish care with wine. We'll ship
> Again tomorrow o'er the mighty sea.[43]

Whether it be in jest or in earnest that the theological and Sorbonical wine has become proverbial and their banquets too, I think that it is right that they should dine all the more comfortably and pleasantly for having employed the morning profitably and seriously in the duties of their schools. The consciousness of having spent the other hours well is a proper and savory sauce for the dinner table. Thus did the sages live. And that inimitable striving after virtue which astounds us in both of the Catos, that disposition, severe to the point of being troublesome, did thus submit gently and contentedly to the laws of human nature, and of Venus and Bacchus, in accordance with the precepts of their sect, which require the perfect sage to be an expert and versed in the use of natural pleasures as in any other duty of life. *In him whose heart is discerning the palate should be discerning.*[44]

Ease and affability does marvelous honor, it seems to me, and is most becoming to a strong and generous soul. Epaminondas did not think that to join in the dance of the boys of

---

[43] Horace, *Odes*   [44] Cicero, *De Finibus*

his city, to sing, to play an instrument, and to engage attentively in these things detracted at all from the honor of his glorious victories and the perfect purity of character that was his. And among so many admirable actions of Scipio, the grandfather, a person worthy to be reputed of a heavenly extraction, there is nothing that imparts more charm to him than to see him playing carelessly and childishly at picking up and selecting shells and running potato-races along the seashore with Laelius, and in bad weather amusing and tickling himself by writing comedies depicting the meanest and most vulgar actions of men; and, with his head full of that wounderful campaign against Hannibal and Africa, visiting the schools in Sicily, and attending lectures on philosophy to the point of arming to the teeth the blind envy of his enemies at Rome. Nor is there anything more remarkable in Socrates than that in his old age he finds time to take lessons in dancing and playing instruments, and thinks it time well spent.

This same man was once seen standing in a trance a whole day and night in the presence of all the Greek army, caught up and enraptured by some profound thought. He was seen, the first among so many valiant men of the army, to run to the relief of Alcibiades, who was overwhelmed by the enemy, to cover him with his body, and to free him from the press by sheer force of arms; and the first among all the people of Athens, outraged like him at so shameful a spectacle, to come forward to rescue Theramenes, whom the Thirty Tyrants were having led off to death by their satellites, and he desisted from this bold undertaking only at the remonstrance of Theramenes himself, though he was followed by only two men in all. He was seen, when courted by a beauty with whom he was in love, to maintain strict abstinence when necessary. He was seen, in the battle of Delium, to pick up and save Xenophon who had been thrown from his horse. He was constantly seen to march to war and walk on ice barefoot, to wear the same gown in winter and in summer, to surpass all his companions in the endurance of toil, and to eat no differently at a feast than at an ordinary meal. He was seen for twenty-seven years to endure with the same countenance hunger, poverty, the indocility of his children, the claws of his wife; and in the end calumny, tyranny, imprisonment, fetters, and poison. But if that man was invited to a drinking bout by the duty of civility, he was also the one in the army with whom the advantage remained. And he never refused to play at nuts with the children, or to ride a hobby-horse with them, and he did it gracefully, for all actions, says philosophy, are equally becoming and honorable in a wise man. We have material enough, and we ought never to weary of presenting the image of this great man as a pattern and model of all kinds of perfection. There are very few examples of life that are full and pure, and they harm our education in putting before us every day weak and defective models, scarcely good in a single trait, which rather pull us backward, corrupters rather than correctors.

People are wrong: it is much easier to go along the sides where the far edge serves as a limit and a guide, than by the middle way, which is broad and open, and to go by art, than by nature; but it is also much less noble and commendable. Greatness of soul is not so much mounting high and pressing forward, as knowing how to put oneself in order and circumscribe oneself. It regards as great all that is enough and shows its elevation by preferring moderate things to eminent ones. There is nothing so beautiful and just as to play the man well and fitly, nor any knowledge so arduous as to know how to live this life well and naturally; and of all our maladies the most barbarous is to despise our being.

He who wants to set his soul apart, let him do it boldly, if he can, when the body is ill, to free it from the contagion; otherwise, on the contrary, let the soul assist and favor the body and not refuse to participate in its natural pleasures and take conjugal enjoyment in them, bringing to them moderation, if it is the wiser of the two, lest through lack of discretion they be confounded with pain. Intemperance is the plague of sensual pleasure; and temperance is not its scourge, it is its seasoning. Eudoxus, who set up pleasure as the sovereign good, and his fellows, who raised it to such a high value, savored it in its most charming sweetness by means of temperance, which they had in singular and exemplary degree.

I order my soul to look upon pain and pleasure with a gaze equally disciplined—*for the expansiveness of the soul in joy is as much of a fault as its contraction in sorrow*[45]—and equally firm, but gaily at the one, and severely at the other, and according to its ability, as anxious to extinguish the one as to extend the other. Viewing good sanely involves viewing evil sanely. And pain has something not to be avoided in its gentle beginning, and pleasure something to be avoided in its excessive ending. Plato couples them together and holds that it is equally the duty of fortitude to fight against pain and against the immoderate and seductive blandishments of pleasure. They are two fountains from which whoever draws from the proper one, at the proper time, the proper amount, whether city, man, or beast, he is very fortunate. The first must be taken as medicine and through necessity more sparingly; the other through thirst, but not to drunkenness. Pain, pleasure, love, hatred, are the first things that a child feels; if, when Reason comes, they attach themselves to her, that is virtue.

I have a vocabulary all my own. I "pass the time" when it is lowery and disagreeable; when it is good, I do not want to pass it; I savor it, I cling to it. We must hasten over the bad and settle upon the good. This ordinary phrase "pastime" and "passing the time" represents the practice of those wise folk who think they cannot realize more from their life than to let it flow away and to escape from it, to pass it away, and to dodge it, and, as far as in them lies, to ignore it and to run away from it as something tiresome and contemptible. But I know it to be otherwise and find it both agreeable and worthy

---

[45] Cicero, *Tusculans*

to be prized, even in its last decline in which I now enjoy it; and Nature has placed it in our hands fitted out with such favorable conditions that we have only ourselves to blame if it burdens us and if it escapes from us unprofitably. *The life of a fool is without contentment, full of alarm, and wholly given to the future.*[46] Nevertheless I am composing myself to lose it without regret, but as something that by its nature has to be lost, not as something irksome and troublesome. Moreover not to dislike dying is properly becoming only to those who like living. It requires management to enjoy it. I enjoy it twice as much as others, for the measure of enjoyment depends on the greater or lesser degree of attention that we give it. Especially at this moment when I perceive mine to be so brief in time, I try to increase it in weight; I try to arrest the rapidity of its flight by the rapidity with which I seize upon it, and by vigor in using it to compensate for the haste of its ebb. The shorter my possession of life is, the deeper and fuller I must make it.

Others feel the sweetness of contentment and of prosperity; I feel it as well as they, but it is not in passing and slipping by. Rather we must study it, savor it, and ruminate it in order to give due thanks for it to Him who grants it to us. They enjoy the other pleasures as they do that of sleep, without being conscious of them. To the end that even sleep should not escape me thus stupidly, I once saw fit to have mine be disturbed so that I might catch a glimpse of it. I meditate upon a pleasure, I do not skim over it; I sound it and bend my reason, now grown peevish and hard to please, to welcome it. Do I find myself in some state of tranquillity? Is there some sensual pleasure that tickles me? I do not let my senses purloin it, I make my soul join in it, not to bind herself to it, but to take pleasure in it, not to lose but to find herself in it. And I set her on her part to viewing herself in this prosperous estate, to weighing and appreciating and amplifying the happiness of it. She makes due reckoning of how much she stands indebted to God for be-

---

[46] Seneca, *Epistles*

ing at peace with her conscience and free from other inner passions, for having her body in its natural state, enjoying regularly and adequately the gentle and pleasing functions by which He of His grace is pleased to compensate the sufferings wherewith His justice chastises us in its turn; of how much it is worth to her to be lodged at such a point that wherever she casts her glance the sky is calm about her: no desire, no fear or doubt that troubles the air for her, no difficulty past, present, or future over which her imagination may not pass without hurt. This consideration takes on great luster by being compared with conditions different from mine. Thus I place before myself in a thousand aspects those who are carried away and tossed about by fortune or their own error, and also those nearer my bent who accept their good fortune so listlessly and indifferently. These are the people who really "pass their time"; they pass over the present and what they possess to be the slaves of hope, and for shadows and vain images which fancy dangles before them,

> Like ghosts that, so they say, flit after death,
> Or dreams that mock our sleeping faculties,[47]

which hasten and prolong their flight the more they are pursued. The fruit and goal of their pursuit is to pursue, as Alexander said that the objective of his work was to work,

> Believing nothing done, while aught was left to do.[48]

For my part, then, I love life and cultivate it, such as it has pleased God to bestow it upon us. I do not go about wishing that it might be free from the necessity of eating and drinking, and I should think I erred no less excusably to wish that the necessity might be doubled (*The wise man is the keenest seeker of natural riches*[49]); nor that we should sustain ourselves by

---

[47] Virgil, *Aeneid*   [48] Lucan   [49] Seneca, *Epistles*

merely putting into our mouth a little of that drug by which Epimenides took away his appetite and kept himself alive; nor that we should beget children insensibly with our fingers or heels, but rather, speaking with due reverence, that we might beget them voluptuously with our fingers and heels; nor that the body should be without desire and without titillation. Those are ungrateful and unfair complaints. I accept heartily and gratefully what Nature has done for me, and I am pleased with myself and proud of myself for it. We do wrong to that great and omnipotent Giver by refusing His gift, nullifying and disfiguring it. Being all good, He made all things good. *All things that are according to nature are worthy of esteem.*[50]

Of philosophical opinions, I most readily embrace those that are most solid, that is to say, most human and most our own; my opinions, in keeping with my conduct, are low and humble. Philosophy plays the child, in my opinion, when she bristles up and preaches to us that it is a barbarous alliance to marry the divine with the earthly, the reasonable with the unreasonable, the severe with the indulgent, the honorable with the dishonorable; that sensual pleasure is a brutish thing unworthy of being enjoyed by a wise man; that the sole pleasure he derives from the enjoyment of a beautiful young wife is the pleasure of his consciousness of performing an action that is fitting, like putting on his boots for a useful ride. May her followers have no more right or sinews or sap in deflowering their wives than her lessons have.

This is not what Socrates, her teacher and ours, says. He prizes, as he ought, bodily pleasure, but he prefers that of the mind, as having more power, constancy, ease, variety, and dignity. The latter by no means goes alone according to him (he is not so fantastic), but only comes first. For him temperance is the moderator, not the adversary of pleasures.

Nature is a gentle guide, but no more gentle than wise and just. *We must penetrate into the nature of things and see thor-*

[50] Cicero, *De Finibus*

oughly what it demands.[51] I seek her footprints everywhere.
We have confused them with artificial tracks, and because of
that the sovereign good of the Academics and the Peripatetics,
which is "to live according to her," becomes hard to limit and
express; as does that of the Stoics, a neighbor to the other,
which is "to consent to Nature." Is it not an error to consider
some actions less worthy because they are necessary? So they
will not knock it out of my head that the marriage of pleasure
with necessity, with which, says an ancient, the gods always
conspire, is a very fitting one. To what end do we dismember
by divorce a structure composed of so close and brotherly a
correspondence? On the contrary, let us bind it together again
by mutual services. Let the mind rouse and quicken the heaviness of the body and the body check and fix the levity of the
soul. *He who lauds the nature of the soul as the sovereign good
and condemns the nature of the flesh as evil, assuredly both
carnally desires the soul and carnally shuns the flesh, for his
feelings come from human vanity and not from divine truth.*[52]
In this gift that God has made us there is no part unworthy of
our care; we stand accountable for it even to a single hair. And
it is not a perfunctory charge to man to direct man according
to his nature; it is express, plain, and of prime importance, and
the Creator has given it to us seriously and sternly. Authority
alone has power over common understandings, and it bears
more weight in a foreign language. Let us make the charge anew
here. *Who would not say that it is the characteristic of folly to
do sluggishly and recalcitrantly what has to be done, to drive
the body in one direction and the soul in another, and to be
torn between the most conflicting motions?* [53]

Come on now and see, have some man tell you some day the
engrossing ideas and fancies that he gets into his head and for
the sake of which he diverts his thoughts from a good meal and
complains of the time he spends in feeding himself. You will

---

[51] Cicero, *De Finibus*   [52] Saint Augustine, *City of God*
[53] Seneca, *Epistles*

find there is nothing so insipid in all the dishes on your table as this fine entertainment of his mind (for the most part we would be better off to go to sleep completely than to keep awake for what we do stay awake for), and you will find that his ideas and his aims are not worth your stew. Though they were the raptures of Archimedes himself, what of it? I am not here referring to or mixing up with the childish rabble of men that we are, or with the vanity of the desires and thoughts that distract us, those venerable souls exalted by the ardor of devotion and religion to a constant and conscientious meditation on divine things, who, anticipating by force of a lively and vehement hope the enjoyment of eternal nourishment, the final goal and last step of Christian desires, the sole constant and incorruptible pleasure, disdain to apply themselves to our beggarly, fleeting, and ambiguous comforts, and readily resign to the body the care and enjoyment of sensual and temporal fodder. That is a privileged study. Between ourselves, these are things that I have always seen to be in remarkable agreement: supercelestial thoughts and subterranean conduct.

Aesop, that great man, saw his master making water as he walked. "What," said he, "must we defecate as we run?" Let us manage our time, there will still remain a great deal that is idle and ill employed. Quite likely our mind has not enough other hours to do its business without dissociating itself ·from the body for that little space it must have for its needs. They want to get out of themselves and escape from the man. That is folly: instead of transforming themselves into angels, they transform themselves into beasts; instead of raising, they lower themselves. These transcendental humors frighten me, like lofty and inaccessible places; and nothing is so hard for me to digest in the life of Socrates as his ecstasies and possessions by his daemon, nothing is so human in Plato as that for which they say he is called divine. And of our sciences those seem to me the most terrestrial and low that have soared the highest. And I find nothing so humble and so mortal in the life of Alexander

as his fancies about his immortalization. Philotas gave him a
witty nip in his answer. He congratulated him by letter on the
oracle of Jupiter Ammon which had placed him among the
gods; "As far as you are concerned, I am very glad of it, but
the men may well be pitied who will have to live with and obey
a man who exceeds and is not contented with a man's measure:"

> Since you are reverent towards the gods, you rule.[54]

The nice inscription with which the Athenians honored the
entry of Pompey into their city is in agreement with my meaning:

> You are as much a deity
> As you admit yourself a man.[55]

It is an absolute perfection and, as it were, divine for a man
to know how to enjoy rightfully his being. We seek other conditions because we do not understand the use of our own, and
go out of ourselves because we do not know what it is like
within. So it is no use for us to mount on stilts, for on stilts we
must still walk with our own legs. And on the loftiest throne in
the world we are still sitting on our own behind.

The most beautiful lives, in my opinion, are those which conform to the common and human model, with order, but without miracle and without extravagant behavior. Now old age
needs to be treated a little more tenderly. Let us commend it
to that god who is the protector of health and wisdom, but a
gay and sociable wisdom:

> Grant me enjoyment, O Latona's son,
> Of health and of contentment, and I beg,
> With mind intact, to pass away old age
> With honor clear and with no lack of lyre.[56]

---

[54] Horace, *Odes*   [55] Amyot (from Plutarch)   [56] Horace, *Odes*

MODERN LIBRARY GIANTS

A series of full-sized library editions of books that formerly were available only in cumbersome and expensive sets.
THE MODERN LIBRARY GIANTS REPRESENT A
SELECTION OF THE WORLD'S GREATEST BOOKS

These volumes contain from 600 to 1,400 pages each
